BUGLES, BANNERS AND WAR BONNETS

The Custer statue was erected in Monroe, Michigan.

BUGLES, BANNERS AND WAR BONNETS

by

ERNEST LISLE REEDSTROM

THE CAXTON PRINTERS, LTD.
CALDWELL, IDAHO
1977

Library of Congress Cataloging in Publication Data

Reedstrom, Ernest Lisle.
　　Bugles, banners, and war bonnets.

　　Bibliography: p.
　　1. United States. Army. 7th Cavalry.
2. Custer, George Armstrong, 1839-1876. I. Title.
UA317th.R4　　　357'.1'0973　　　77-165608
ISBN 0-87004-230-0

Lithographed and bound in the United States of America by
The Caxton Printers, Ltd., Caldwell, Idaho
117447

TO MY WIFE,
SHIRLEY
who has seen little of a husband —
TO MY CHILDREN,
who have seen little of a father —
ALLOWING THIS BOOK
TO BE WRITTEN

A clean-shaven Custer after being wounded in Virginia during the War, he returned to Monroe in 1863 to court Elizabeth Bacon.

TABLE OF CONTENTS

Chapter   *Page*

LIST OF ILLUSTRATIONS ix

PREFACE xiii

ACKNOWLEDGMENTS xv

BUNKIES xvii

INTRODUCTION xix

1 FORT RILEY AND THE 7TH CAVALRY 1

2 AN ACT OF WAR 23

3 FROM FLAMING PLAINS TO A WINTER CAMPAIGN . 33

4 CAPTIVES, BUFFALO, AND THE YELLOWSTONE 63

5 THE LAND OF PROMISE 82

6 CUSTER'S MARCH TO VALHALLA 99

7 CIVIL WAR UNIFORMS 155

8 ARMY MORALE AND FRONTIER SERVICE 173

9 CAVALRY TACTICAL MANUALS 197

10 RHYMING RULES OF HORSEMANSHIP 209

11 ACCOUTERMENTS AND BASIC WEAPONS 237

12 A UNIFORM CHANGE-OVER 286

13 THE RED MAN 311

BIBLIOGRAPHY 349

INDEX 357

A Brady photo, taken in 1864, of General Custer and his bride.

LIST OF ILLUSTRATIONS

Custer statue Monroe, Michigan .... frontispiece

Page

A clean shaven Custer vi
General Custer and his bride viii
General Custer was a loyal Republican xvi
A classic example of a cavalryman 1
A trooper poses for a photograph 2
Cavalry officers 2
Custer. Photo taken shortly before journey to
    Fort Riley 3
Custer's "Autie," brother Tom and Elizabeth 3
Union Pacific work train 4
The "Seminole," woodburning locomotive 5
Construction crew and soldiers fighting off
    Indian attack 6
Poster — map.................................... 7
Indians tearing up railroad tracks 8
Indians making a buffalo surround 9
An attack on a hand car 10
Gaugers and spikers were constantly harassed
    by Indians 11
Trooper with full equipment 11
Fort Riley Hospital 12
Custer House. A modern photo 12
Fort Riley 12
Another view of Fort Riley 13
Sod houses peppered the Kansas Plains 13
A Mormon family 14
Emigrant train crossing Platte River.............. 16
A Sioux and Cheyenne Village — the calm
    before the storm 17
Fort Harker.................................... 19
Typical cavalryman 20
Major General Hancock 23
Custer in parley with Indians 24
One of the Cheyenne Chiefs 24
Osage Scout 25
Sergeant to horse 26
Custer in buckskins 27
Document ordered by General Hancock.......... 29
Custer's signature 30
Map — scene of General Hancock's operations 31
Indian revenge 33
Custer's tent near Fort Dodge 34
Custer carving a prairie chicken 35
Soldiers, officers and civilians on the Parade
    Grounds 36
General Custer at Fort Hayes.................... 37
John Baird in Scouts clothing 38
Hawken "Big .50" half stock rifle 39
"California Joe"................................ 40
A rare tintype of Moses E. Milner 40
Custer's four trusted scouts 41
Oil and lamp black helped 42
Nude Kiola girl 47

Page

Custer and his Osage Indian scouts 48
Custer's dress at the Washita 51
Kiowas and Cheyennes......................... 52
Cheyennes captured during the Battle of the
    Washita 58
Sly Fox.. 60
Kiowa Chief 61
Fatbear, Big Head and Dull Knife 61
Major Joel H. Elliott 64
Personal items of an officer 66
General Custer and the Grand Duke Alexis 68
A buffalo hunt 70
Scouts and packers 71
Custer and scouts 72
Trooper in early 1870's......................... 73
General Custer in 1872.......................... 75
Buffalo Bill Cody 76
Taking a water break 79
Fort Abraham Lincoln, D.T. 83
Another view of Fort Abraham Lincoln 84
General Custer's study 85
Bloddy Knife 86
Captain Smith 87
Custer's wagon train on the prairie 88
Custer's permanent camp....................... 90
Camp at French Creek 91
A champagne supper given by Colonel Tilford 92
Custer's camp in Castle Creek Valley 93
Sioux camp in Castle Creek Valley 94
First Black Hills Expedition 95
Custer claims his grizzly 96
Custer after the Black Hills Expedition 97
Ludlow's map 98
Officers of the 7th U.S. Cavalry at Fort
    Abraham Lincoln 101
Hunting party from Fort Abraham Lincoln 102
Rain in the Face 103
Sitting Bull 104
Custer in 1875 105
General Alfred Terry 106
One of Elizabeth Custer's favorite pictures 107
Custer's arrest in Chicago 107
Lieutenant General Philip H. Sheridan 108
Brigadier General Alfred H. Terry 108
The Steamer "Far West" 112
Major Marcus Reno 112
General John Gibbon 113
A .50 caliber Gatling gun...................... 113
General Ulysses S. Grant's hat.................. 114
Captain Thomas Ward Custer 114
Lieutenant W. W. Cooke 114
Boston "Bos" Custer 115
Captain Frederick W. Benteen 116
White Swan 117

Page

One of Custer's Crow scouts 118
Curley — one of Custer's Crow scouts 118
Curley 119
White Man Run Him 119
Hairy Moccasin 120
Harry Armstrong Reed 121
The Seventh's Regimental Standard of 1876 125
Cavalry guidons were swallow tailed 126
Indian beaded bag 126
The personal Headquarters Flag of
    General Custer 127
Gall 128
Rain-in-the-Face 128
Sitting Bull 129
Low Dog 129
Crow King 130
Little Big Man 130
Dull Knife 130
Sioux warriors 131
Sitting Bull 131
A desperate message for ammunition 132
Martini bringing Custer's last message 132
Trumpeter John Martini 133
Tom Custer and his brother George 134
Captain Myles W. Keogh 135
Mark Kellogg's shirt 136
Lieutenant James E. Porter 136
Brigadier General E. S. Godfrey (retired), and
    White Man Runs Him 136
Elizabeth Bacon Custer 137
Elizabeth Custer and the General's only sister
    Margaret Custer 137
The field scattered with bleaching bones 140
Socks, shirts, clothing — all were searched for 140
Bones, from every part of the field were piled
    in heaps 142
Shallow graves were dug 142
Captain Nowlan and another man pay their last
    respects 143
Captain C. K. Sanderson's camp at the Ford
    in 1879 143
The bodies of Custer's men were buried in
    shallow graves 144
The remains of three soldiers killed in the battle .. 144
Robert Bray, Archeologist; and Don Rickey, Jr.,
    Historian 144
The remains of a trooper at Reno Battlefield 145
Custer Battlefield relics 145
Mark Kellogg's monument 146
General George Crook 146
Map — Custer's Last Battle 146
Map — Custer divides the Seventh Cavalry into
    three Battalions 147
Map — "A three pronged march." 147
Officers killed at the Little Big Horn 148
Ulysses S. Grant 149
Battle map to scale of the Little Big Horn 150
Discharge of William E. Smith 151
The New-York Times 153
The Infantry was sad looking in appearance 155
Cape shown is minus the yellow flannel lining 156
The Cavalry "Shell" jacket 156
Two "pillows" or "belt supporters" at bottom
    of jacket 157
A regulation 1858 four button fatigue blouse 157

Page

Trousers showing stripe 158
Cavalry trousers were reinforced in the seat 158
Dark blue vest 159
Custer's uniform coat of a Major General 159
Forage cap or kepi 160
Black felt hat 160
Enlisted man's "Jeff Davis" hat 160
The Army campaign hat of 1872 160
U.S. Army bootee 162
Fifteen inch high Jefferson boot 162
Trooper in "Hardy Hat" 163
Typical Cavalry trooper 163
Cavalry musicians 165
Bucked and gagged 173
A soldier and his family 177
Fort Hays, Kansas in 1868 179
Two dead troopers from Fort Hays 183
Poncho, Civil War 185
Hardtack 189
School of the Trooper 198
Corporal Rod Paulsen 198
Trooper pulling at his canteen 199
The 2nd Reactivated Cavalry 200
Lisle Reedstrom and Sergeant Bob Craig 201
A cavalry charge 202
The Company's First Sergeant eyes his troopers ... 202
2nd U.S. Reactivated Cavalry 203
Regulation bugle 204
Horse holder 206
The horse 210
Model 1859 McClellan saddle 211
McClellan saddle after the rawhide split 212
Saddle after re-leathering 212
Cavalry bits 212
Link strap variations 213
Model 1858 saddle bags 213
Model 1872 pommel bags 213
Picket pins 216
Picket pins 217
Model 1872 McClellan saddle in "fair" or
    russett leather 219
Quartermaster wagon 222
Private John Burkman, "Dandy," and "Vic" 223
Comanche stands between blacksmith Gustav
    Korn and Captain Ilsley 224
Comanche followed where ever the 7th went 224
Blacksmith Gustav Korn holding the reins of
    Comanche 225
Comanche encased 225
1872 — McClellan saddle with skirts removed 226
Six-mule team complete 228
1861 Cavalryman's horse saddled 231
The McClellan saddle 232
Horse equipment 233
Custer's McClellan saddle 234
Custer's McClellan saddle 235
Close-up of the Cavalryman's equipment 238
Sergeant J. J. Narus 238
The Blakeslee cartridge box 239
Loading the Spencer 239
Ready to fire 240
Firing the Spencer 241
The small pistol cartridge pouch 242
Pouch shows loops for waist belt 242
Pouch developed late in the Civil War 243

Page

Dyers cartridge pouch fleeced-lined 243
Dyer pouches shown here in several variations 244
Model 1855 cap pouch 244
Model 1861 pistol cartridge box 244
Model 1855 Infantry box 245
1874 pattern Dyer pouch 245
Infantry cartridge box 246
1872 pattern Infantry box 246
Black leather waist belt with sliding saber slings .. 246
Custer's accouterments 247
Civil War saber belt and accoutrements 250
Civil War issue saber belt with shoulder strap 250
"Fair-Weather" belt or "Prairie Belt" 251
Civil War carbine sling with brass buckle 252
Custer's 7-shot Spencer 252
Custer's Spencer 253
Cartridge collection 254
Cartridge collection 255
Sharps carbine 255
Trooper J. J. Narus loads a Sharps carbine 256
Percussion caps were scattered everywhere 256
Springfield Carbine, model 1873 257
1872 officer's saber 258
1860 enlisted man's saber 258
Remington "New Model" .44 caliber percussion
    revolver 260
Colt model 1860, .44 caliber percussion revolver .. 260
Colt single action Army revolver 261
Gatling gun at Washington Arsenal 265
Gatling guns are posed on the banks of the
    Potomac 267
Gatling gun of the 1-inch caliber 268
20th Infantry men stand next to Caissons and
    1-inch Gatling guns 269
General Custer's Springfield 269
Custer's .44 caliber Remington percussion revolver 270
Captain Tom Custer's Galand and Somerville
    revolver 270
Cased set presented to General Custer 271
Custer's cased Smith and Wesson revolvers 271
Model 1865 Gatling gun 272
Gatlings 273
Fatigue hat 286
Cavalry enlisted man's helmet 287
Custer's model 1872 Cavalry dress helmet 287
Dress coat for enlisted men 287
Coat, showing shoulder straps 288
Coat, rear 288
Fatigue coat 289
Rear of fatigue coat 289
Sergeant's fatigue 289
Custer's 5 button blouse 290
Undress blouse for officers 290
Dress coat for officers 290
Buffalo coat 291
Buffalo soldier of the 25th Infantry 291
Leather gauntlets 292
Leather gauntlet owned by General George A.
    Custer 292
Shirt, drawers and stockings prior to 1872 292
Shirt, drawers and stockings subsequent to 1872 ... 293

Page

1st Sergeant John W. Comfort 294
Private Comfort, Troop "A," 4th U.S. Cavalry 294
Chapeau-De-Bras, pattern of 1872 294
Hat, pattern of 1872 295
1872 pattern campaign hat 295
Wide brim hats in light colors were favorites 295
Recent arrival from Jefferson Barracks 295
Full dress 296
Buckskin jackets were in style 296
Capt. Ludlow's jacket 296
Beaded designs on buckskin jacket 297
Trousers with beaded design 297
Rear view of Captain Ludlow's beaded buckskin .. 297
Custer had several buckskin outfits 298
Buckskins belonging to Custer 298
Plain fringed buckskin jacket 299
Scout in fringed buckskins 299
Troops in fringed jackets 300
"Buffalo" Bill Cody 300
U.S. Army bootee 301
Shoes, new and old patterns 301
General Custer's boots and trunk 302
Officer's saber and officer's shoulder straps 304
Cord with tassels for U.S. Helmet 305
Indian bows 312
Indian arrows 312
Indian tools of war 312
Northwest type flint lock trade muskets 313
Flint lock musket 313
Indian trade rifle 314
Carbines, Spencer and Winchester 315
Springfield trap door rifles 316
Carbines, Remington and Sharps 317
Cheyenne Warrior 318
Yankton Sioux 318
Gun stock war club 319
Pipe tomahawk 319
Plains type tomahawk 319
Plain haft tomahawk 319
Large plains type pipe tomahawk 319
Plains type tomahawk with intricate piercings 320
Pipe tomahawk with crude engravings 320
Spontoon pipe tomahawk 320
Cheyenne finger necklace 322
A Cheyenne finger necklace 322
Tintype of Good Buffalo 323
Commanche braves 323
Big Elk, Cheyenne chief 324
Big Horse — Cheyenne chief 324
Commanche brave and squaw 325
White Ghost 325
Cotton Man 326
Thunder Hawk 326
Kiowa chief 327
White Swan 327
Indian style blanket wrap-around 328
White Eagle and trooper Narus 328
Bows and quivers 330
Human scalp mounted 331
1866 Winchester rifles 332
Indian war shields and a lance 334

PREFACE

The cavalry of General Custer's day is no more. Like coal oil lamps, horse cavalry has been relegated to the past. With it went a certain glamour not evident in the army of today. There was a liveliness to a cavalry camp not evident in a motor pool, and an odor that was unforgettable. The pounding of hoofs, clank of sabers and rubbing of leather has gone. Roaring motors, screeching brakes, and an air polluted by a haze of burned petrol have taken its place.

On the Western plains of Custer's day the horse provided a companionship for the lonely trooper a Jeep couldn't provide. It was his fastest means of escape when retreat became a necessity.

The trooper and his horse were constant companions, each dependent upon the other. The mount was the cavalryman's first concern on arising each morning and his first and last concern when retiring at night. His life might be forfeited because of the improper care of his horse. There were instances where the attachment between a trooper and his horse grew so strong that when the latter was transferred to another regiment the trooper abandoned his own friends by requesting a transfer to accompany his horse.

A portion of this volume is devoted to the cavalryman and his horse. Equally interesting is that portion devoted to the cavalryman's adversary during the settlement of the West, the American Indian.

There is a tendency to view the military men and their engagements of Custer's day on the basis of present day standards. To properly and objectively evaluate the subject it is imperative that the reader or student of Western history be supplied with reliable background material of the people, the places, the problems and the accoutrements of that period.

Lisle Reedstrom has spent many years as an artist and illustrator of the Old West. Meticulous in his art and methodical in his research he has accumulated an amazing amount of background material not commonly known, all for the purpose of providing authenticity in his productions.

I recall his desire to obtain accurate and firsthand information of cavalry drills and charges. He was not content with the usual written descriptions. The retirement of the horses from the military service had erased all opportunity for him to view such drills. Learning of a reactivated cavalry unit in Indiana there was no rest for him until he could join them during their maneuvers. It was just a matter of time before he had sketched from life what he had been unable to obtain in any other way.

Since the formation of The Little Big Horn Associates in 1967, he has generously supplied its publications with the products of his pen. Now, just as generously, he supplies all of us with the products of his research.

LAWRENCE A. FROST
MONROE, MICHIGAN

General Custer was a loyal Republican, while his father Emanuel H. Custer was opposed to him in politics.

ACKNOWLEDGMENTS

I wish to acknowledge my gratitude for the never-failing help and encouragement from the many people who rallied to a distant call and helped compile the necessary ammunition to complete this book.

I respectfully mention the following names who graciously submitted a vast amount of photography from their private collections: Dr. Lawrence Frost, Dr. Elizabeth A. Lawrence, Randy Steffen, Gordon Corbett, Jr., Herb Peck, Jr., Arnold Marcus Chernoff, Thomas M. Heski, Grant Dinsmore, Fred Hackett, Robert J. McDonald, George A. Rummel, Jr., Gary Reusze, First Sergeant Robert M. Craig and Sergeant J. J. Narus from the Second U.S. Reactivated Cavalry.

From the various archives and museums around the country, my sincere thanks to the many people at West Point Museum, New York; The Library of Congress, Washington, D.C.; National Archives and Records Service, including the Old Military Branch Division, Washington, D.C.; Smithsonian Institution, Washington, D.C.; U.S. Army Quartermaster Museum, Fort Lee, Virginia; Custer Battlefield National Monument, Crow Agency, Montana; Chicago Historical Society, Chicago, Illinois; Union Pacific Railroad Company, Omaha, Nebraska; Nebraska State Historical Society, Lincoln, Nebraska; Kansas State Historical Society, Topeka, Kansas; State Historical Society of North Dakota, Bismarck, North Dakota; Arizona Historical Society, Tucson, Arizona; U.S. Cavalry Memorial Association, Inc., Midway City, California.

For additional help in supplying books and reference data, I am appreciative to William A. Graff, book dealer in Iowa City, Iowa; George A. Willhauck, Norm Flayderman & Company, Inc., The Westerners, Chicago Corral; and the Lake County Reference Library, Merrillville, Indiana, where the librarians worked endless hours compiling data and requisitioning books from out-of-state libraries.

I am especially indebted to the troopers of the Second U.S. Reactivated Cavalry, particularly Mitchell Swieca, who have all worked many hours in the field with me during weekends, helping to recreate conditions from original cavalry manuals, risking dangerous maneuvers to carry out some task. They are, by far, truly cavalrymen.

For documents loaned and permission to reproduce them, I am grateful to Paul Hoag, autographs and books; William A. Bond; Dr. Elizabeth A. Lawrence; and The Library of Congress, Washington, D.C.

Special thanks for photographs taken of Basil White Eagle in costume; J. J. Narus; Robert M. Craig; Victor Studios for their wonderful service in film developing; and many more, whose names were not submitted to me for acknowledgments.

My appreciation to David Harman for permission to reprint my painting of Custer's Last Campaign on the cover, Conrad Kleinman and Petley Studios, all from Phoenix, Arizona, assisting in photography. To Mike Koury, Old Army Press; and the Little Big Horn Associates, who graciously gave permission to reprint a number of my pen-and-ink drawings, especial acknowledgment is made to them.

Above all, to the individuals whose unselfish aid in typing, proofreading and editing made it possible to complete this book, I am indebted to Gib Crontz, Theada Davis, Kay Pleasha, and Joan Tutsie who served as secretarial assistant. To Don Russell who edited the book, my thanks and deepest gratitude.

BUNKIES

"I say, Billy, give us a smoke."
'Twas a rough, stalwart, generous fellow who spoke,
With heavy mustache, a sort of devil-may-care;
One of those sort of men who'd go anywhere —
Who'd share half his pay with a bunky or chum,
The first in a fight, the last on a bum.
"Go ahead, Jack" — handing the pipe — "I'm through."
There was a very great contrast in the build of the two.
Bill, quiet in manners, unused to rough ways;
In fact, one of the many who've seen better days,
With very fair hair, eyes decidedly blue —
Yes, a very marked contrast there was in the two.

A sort of attachment had sprung up 'tween the men,
I can't say exactly why it was, how or when.
To proceed with my yarn:
"Bill, have yer made down the bed!
'Cos I'm awfully tired, and very near dead."
(Impulsively striking the bunk with his fist).
"Bill, what a d—— fool I was to enlist."
"Well, it's no use your growling, it makes matters worse,"
Jack only replied with a forcible curse;
"You ain't fixed, Bill, as I am; I do more 'n my share;
You've got a soft thing, and of course you don't care.
I enlisted to soger, and I'm willing to fight —
Not to whack Government mules and stay out half the night.

I've soger'd for years, fit during the war,
But I never did see sich fatiguing before.
One day I'm on guard, the next cuttin' ice,
Then on kitchen police, which ain't over nice;
A fourth, layin' brick (I ain't used to the thing),
A fifth day on guard, with just three nights in;
Sometimes I'm detailed to drive a company team,
Which if yer aint keerful, or the mules rather green,
You're apt to upset, and the Lord only knows,
If yer don't get a tumble, ye're nearly half froze.
Then yer unhitch the mules, feed, and water 'em too,
And it's hard to say which eats the most of the two.
Yer dinner is cold, the soup's all played out,
And at fatigue call you've again to turn out.

"Then, Billy, yer see they've cut the stamps down
That's allowed for the clothin'; a new plan they've found.
It may be all very well, tho' it doesn't look nice
To cut down the stamps and keep up the price.
If a greeny enlists and draws a full rig of clothes,
It'll take near three months to pay it off, I suppose;
Then agin the old hands'll make quite a stake,
And you bet a good many'll soon make a break.
Because, don't yer see, it's the last chance they've got,
And those who don't go'll spend it for rot.
Sogerin's all very well; I'd bet my last picayune
We know more of fatigue than we do of platoon.
Now what d' yer . . ."

"No loud talking up there," roars out Sergeant Schnapps.
(The bugle is sounding the last note of "taps.")

February 14, 1871.   F.H.[1]

---

1. Army Navy Journal, March 4, 1871, page 463. The Army Navy
Journal will sometimes hereafter be cited as A.N.J.

INTRODUCTION

These pages are dominated by mentions of General Custer, the 7th Cavalry, and the last stand on the Little Big Horn, but its objective is neither to tell again nor to offer a new version of that highly publicized disaster. Custer's campaign culminating in the last stand has been subject of more than a thousand paintings, drawings and miscellaneous illustrations and its bibliography far exceeds that figure. No battle of so little importance or decisive result has attracted such continuing attention. No analysis can account conclusively for this unfading interest, but certainly one element is mystery: there was no survivor to tell what happened, opening the way for endless speculation. Another is tragedy: a spectacular and acclaimed hero cut down with his immediate following and members of his family in mid-career. Both mystery and tragedy require explanation: why and how could such things be? Endless efforts have been made to assign a cause and to assess blame. Adding immeasurably to the interest is the romantic appeal of the American West that has been our heritage through Buffalo Bill's Wild West, the dime novels of Edward S. Ellis and Prentiss Ingraham, the Western fiction of Owen Wister, Charles King, B. M. Bower and Zane Grey, and the unrealistic but ever-popular Westerns of movies, radio and television.

It is in the area of ultimate cause that Ernest Lisle Reedstrom contributes an unexploited angle to this ever-unsaturated interest in Custer and his regiment. His story is that of the cavalry — how it was trained, armed, equipped, fed, moved and supplied. "Cavalry to the rescue" has become a cliché of Western romance, but even here little attention has been given to the trumpets and guidons that marked the charge, or whether it was made with saber, revolver or carbine. A count shows that Indian fights were few, and between them were months, even years, of boredom in garrison or of fruitless and exhausting marches, accompanied by such hardships that one of them was dubbed the "horsemeat march."

These facts about cavalry are found in obscure books called *Cavalry Tactics* (in later years, *Cavalry Drill Regulations*), *Army Regulations, The Ordnance Manual;* in General Orders and Special Orders of the War Department, its departments, divisions and other commands; in the files of the *Army and Navy Journal;* and in the reports, journals and reminiscences of those who served in the cavalry of the Frontier. Little of this gets mention in the voluminous writing about Little Big Horn.

While the book centers on Custer and the 7th Cavalry, its story is that of the cavalry service in the period between 1866 and 1876, the era of the Indian wars. The drill, the uniform, the weapons, and the accoutrements, the saddles and spurs, are here resurrected from the specifications set forth in official manuals with a full appreciation that an army does not always live by its regulations. A new and improved drill manual was adopted, but not enough copies were printed to supply the instructors, so the old one was used a few years longer. Boards of officers met to consider a uniform more suitable for use in the field, but leftover Civil War clothing was issued to the troops as long as it lasted, while soldiers in the field improvised from anything available. Photographs show that the troops chasing Indians little resembled H. A. Ogden's color plates representing the officially adopted army uniforms. Even the weevil-infested hardtack and mouldy bacon left over from the Civil War were issued to garrisons in the late 1860's, but soldiers on hunting passes and scouts like Buffalo Bill supplied buffalo meat to supplement the ration while men in garrison spent more time raising vegetable gardens than in drilling according to the tactics devised by Philip St. George Cooke.

The United States Army is among the most conservative elements in our population. A recent experience has shown that it retains an old-time courtesy in sharp contrast with the ill manners so commonly seen on the younger side of the generation gap. Yet it does change, even progress, and too many writers, either in the army or with experience in one of our numerous recent wars, assume its institutions to be identical with those of the times of Sherman, Sheridan, Crook and Custer. An example is confusion over brevet commissions, conferred from the Revolution through the 19th century (and a few after that). Nearly all works of reference define brevet as a commission that gives an officer rank above his pay. Actually so many officers were being paid in brevet rank at one period that Congress cracked down on it, adding to the confusion. Prior to this action, officers on court-martial duty were paid in brevet rank. An officer could always be called to duty in his brevet rank "by order of the President," and customarily was, if he commanded a department, a division or anything else beyond his permanent regimental assignment. Most recent writers have insisted on demoting Custer to his lineal rank of lieutenant colonel, 7th Cavalry, although actually he exercised his brevet rank as major general on several occasions, as noted in these pages. At all times, he was entitled to the courtesy title of "General," except in General Terry's often quoted order for the march to Little Big Horn, in which he is meticulously addressed as "Lieutenant Colonel G. A. Custer" because President Grant had banned Custer's acting in his brevet rank. But it must be admitted that the problem of brevets was endlessly confusing, even in its own time, as evidenced by the dispute with General Sully, Sheridan's solution of which was worthy of King Solomon.

It is with minutiae of military technicology that we are concerned here, a study that is not in vain if we are to understand the ways of life of another age. Much that is said here about the horse would have been everyday experience for persons living in the 1870's, whereas now only a few hobbyists know how to saddle a horse, and fewer would be able to hitch a team to draw a wagon.

Ernest Lisle Reedstrom has peculiar qualifications for his task. He has actually participated in field exercises employing the tactics set forth in the Civil War manuals and the Cavalry Tactics of 1873, mounted on a horse with the 2nd U.S. Reactivated Cavalry. So, much like Frederic Remington, he has ridden with the cavalry, and, like Remington, he has collected artifacts as models for his art work. His illustrations are based both on what the regulations prescribe and what the actual weapons, horse equipments and accoutrements were like when issued. These findings are supplemented by many contemporary photographs, many of which have not previously been reproduced. He has consulted much documentary material, and of especial value are many quotations from the *Army and Navy Journal,* a little exploited source for information about the army for the period of its publication.

So here is the cavalry of the Western frontier and its opponents — with trumpets, banners, and war bonnets.

DON RUSSELL

BUGLES, BANNERS AND WAR BONNETS

FORT RILEY AND THE 7TH CAVALRY

On July 28th, 1866, under an act of Congress, four new regiments of cavalry were organized. The 7th through the 10th were to be stationed at various posts to restore order on the troubled frontiers. One of the regiments, the 7th U.S. Cavalry, was assigned to Fort Riley, Kansas; its future duty was to protect the building of the Kansas Pacific Railroad against already menacing warlike Indian tribes. During August and September, 1866, Fort Riley was already a concentration of recruits, frontiersmen, fugitives, adventurers from the east, former Union soldiers along with a few rebels in disguise. The men were a rough-looking lot,

Courtesy Bob McDonald
A classic example of a cavalryman, armed with saber and revolver, and wearing the regulation shell jacket and universal forage cap.

many of them Irishmen newly-immigrated from the "old country," all seeking a meal ticket and their fortune in the western expansion. Others, while awaiting only to be issued clothing, arms and a horse, would desert at the first available opportunity.

Soon the post became a crowded and dusty parade ground of confused men and horses . . . shuffling about unorganized and restless. By September 10th, Major John W. Davidson of the 2nd Cavalry, an old army regular, carried his orders out to the letter by forming the several hundred recruits into companies. At the end of September, twelve companies had been organized with a total strength of 882 men commanded by officers of the 2nd Cavalry.

All through November and December, 1866, a casual flow of officers assigned to the 7th Cavalry was organized into a headquarters staff. All had served in the Civil War and could produce papers showing their services and combat records. As the officers reported, they were assigned quarters in one of the stone buildings on post. Officers take their quarters according to rank, and it was not an uncommon happening that another officer, already established in quarters, would have to vacate his quarters and give up his place to another who outranked him. The ranking officer is entirely in his right, according to the army code, and generally he does not hesitate to use this authority, although he may be a single man and the man displaced be a family man. Among veteran officers this is so well understood and accepted that no hard feelings or resentment occurred.[1]

---

1. Tenting on the Plains, by Elizabeth B. Custer (New York: C. L. Webster & Co., 1887), pages 372-373.

Most of the officers who served in the volunteer service during the war knew nothing of a full dress uniform, having spent the duration of the war in field tents. And so some ridiculous errors in uniform dress and deportment were made while reporting to headquarters on their arrival. Some sought to alleviate their embarrassment and mortification over these harmless mistakes by laying pitfalls for the greenhorns that were constantly arriving. To quote an example from "Tenting on the Plains" . . . "He wore cavalry boots, the first singularity I noticed, for they had such expanse of top I could not help seeing them. They are of course out of order with a dress coat. The red sash, which was then *en regle* for all officers, was spread from up under his arms to as far below the waist line as its elastic silk could be stretched. The sword belt, with sabre attached, surrounded this; and, folded over the wide red front, were his large hands, encased in white cotton gloves. He never moved them; nor did he move an eyelash, so far as I could discover, though it seems he was full of internal tremors, for

Courtesy Bob McDonald
Cavalry officers — late 1860's.

the officers had told him on no account to remove his regulation hat. At this he demurred, and told them I would surely think he was no gentleman; but they assured him I placed military etiquette far above any ordinary rule for manners in the presence of ladies, while the truth was I was rather indifferent as to military rules of dress."[2] No excuses were ever made by these pranksters, and none were expected. However, in later years, every time the episode was recalled by 7th Cavalry officers, laughter exploded with tear-filled eyes.

On the evening of November 3rd, 1866, Lieutenant-Colonel George Armstrong Custer arrived at Fort Riley in a somewhat embarrassing commotion. While Custer was reporting his arrival to Major Alfred Gibbs, a dog fight broke out in the ambulance,[3] where Elizabeth Custer, her

Courtesy Grant Dinsmore
Packed and ready for field duty a trooper poses for a photograph to send home.

---

2. Tenting on the Plains, by Elizabeth B. Custer (New York: C. L. Webster & Co., 1887), pages 376-377.

3. An ambulance carried the women, dogs and luggage from Junction City to Ft. Riley, some 10 miles distance. Custer rode on horseback.

Custer, brevet major general[4] and permanent captain, was appointed lieutenant colonel of the 7th Cavalry, and second-in-command to Colonel and Brevet Major General Andrew Johnson Smith, a veteran of the Mexican and Civil wars. Custer's appointment as lieutenant colonel was actually a sudden leap in promotion from captain in the regular army, though a step-down

4. Brevet commissions were permanent honorary recognition of distinguished service and an officer could serve, and be paid, in his brevet rank under prescribed circumstances.

Courtesy Author's Collection
Photo taken in Detroit, Michigan the Fall of 1866. Custer seated center, Libbie on the right. Man and young girl in background, standing, unidentified. Woman seated at left is believed to have been an actress starring at one of the leading theaters in Detroit.
Photo taken shortly before journey to Fort Riley, Kansas.

schoolmate, Diana, and Eliza, the family cook, were waiting to be quartered. Hostilities between the two Custer dogs, Turk and Byron, brewed during the short trip from Junction City, and now within close quarters they leaped at one another snapping their muscular jaws in rage. When Custer returned, he found Elizabeth and Diana each at a corner of the ambulance, their tiny white fingers clutching the collars of both dogs and trembling with horror. A few stern words from Custer settled the immediate matter.

Courtesy U.S. Signal Corps photo (Brady Collection)
The Custer's "Autie," brother Tom and Elizabeth. The War had finally ended, and the three would return to Monroe.

from the rank of major general of volunteers he had held the previous year. His pay of $8,000 as major general had been reduced to $2,000 with additional allowances and living quarters. Other regular officers found themselves similarly cut back in rank and pay when the volunteers they led as generals, colonels, and majors were mustered out during the process of disbanding the Union Army. Custer was always addressed as "general," as it was army custom to recognize the brevet rank.

To a man full of life and exuberant health, the thought of hunting wildlife on the plains was most enjoyable. Strange birds and wild beasts that roamed the wide and endless sweep of prairie were sufficient to keep a person of his danger-loving temperament continually active. The many herds of deer and antelope, along with the temperamental buffalo, would furnish ample sport for his rifle. Squirrels and jack rabbits, ducks and prairie chickens, were so generous in supply that hardly a day passed that Custer and his greyhounds would return from a hunt empty-handed. But another hunt, that of the hostile Indian would not be so easy.

Custer enjoyed having friends and relatives about him. He helped them to get positions in the new regiment including his younger brother, Lt. Thomas Ward Custer,

Courtesy Union Pacific Railroad   *Photo by C. R. Savage*

Union Pacific work train in 1870 near Green River, Wyoming.

Courtesy Union Pacific Railroad

The "Seminole," woodburning locomotive built in April 1867 for the UP eastern district (Kansas). Overall length 50 ft., weight 115,000 lbs., fuel capacity two cords, tender capacity 2000 gallons water, tractive power 11,000 lbs. The cab of the old "Seminole" was of varnished walnut and the engineer's seat was made of ash, the pilot was made of wood. Rogers Loco. & Machine Co., Paterson N.J.

holder of two Medals of Honor for meritorius service during the Civil War.[5] The "Custer circle" formed a clique within the new regiment inviting favorites to dinners and evenings of high-stake poker games. Custer may have been a born gambler in real life; he was, however, the poorest poker player within the circle. Many times his I.O.U. notes went unpaid, and Elizabeth reminded him to practice economy with the reduced income from his army pay. While champagne and light wines were toasting future victories for the 7th Cavalry, Custer accompanied each toast with water or lemonade. Two years after leaving West Point, Custer voluntarily gave up drinking. The reason was he could not be a moderate drinker.[6]

Schooling the young recruits was difficult. Some did not understand English, but they seemed to get by . . . by following the movements of their comrades. First was the "schooling of the dismounted soldier." Then the manual of the sabre, sabre exercise, manual of the pistol, manual of the carbine, and next, the principles of target practice. As the schooling of the soldier continued, endless duties and work details that plagued military life continued to irritate the men.

As one soldier wrote from Fort Harker, some 90 miles southwest of Fort Riley: "There has been no drills here the past

5. Thomas Ward Custer joined his brother at Fort Riley with a first lieutenant's commission, November 16th, assigned to Troop "A", but detailed acting regimental quartermaster. Tom Custer was one of two persons in the army ever to have been awarded twice the Medal of Honor for meritorious service during the Civil War. Tom Custer distinguished himself at Namozine Church, April 2nd, and at Sailor's Creek, Va., April 6th, 1865, by capturing a Confederate battle flag at each position. It was at Sailor's Creek that Tom leaped his horse over the enemy's breastworks and fearlessly dashed up to the rebel colors. When he reached the color-bearer he was immediately fired upon. A musket ball smashed into his right cheek and passed out behind the ear. However, Tom succeeded in capturing the rebel flag and dashed back to his lines, blood streaking his face. General Custer, noticing his brother's severe wound, ordered him to the rear to have it dressed. Tom refused, his young blood up, prepared to spur his horse forward for another charge. General Custer, grabbing the reins of the horse, ordered his brother under arrest and to return to the rear.

6. E. B. Custer; microfilm — Reel 4; Custer Battlefield Museum.

Courtesy Union Pacific Railroad
Construction crew and soldiers fighting off Indian attack (painting). Constant danger of Indian attack kept construction crews on
their toes during UP's building. Army detachments helped protect the workers but the railroadmen themselves had to be equally
handy with spike maul or rifle.

winter, the soldiers being all occupied in
building quarters. Isn't it a mistake on the
part of the government to require enlisted
men to work as common laborers with no
opportunity to perfect themselves in drill?
An officer cannot have proper discipline in
his command under such circumstances.
The men, too, labor somehow under silent
protest; desertions are more than frequent
. . .," and in ending the soldier makes this
point, ". . . making dirt shovelers of soldiers
may make them a source of profit in time of
peace, but it is equally sure to make them
worthless in time of war."[7]

Many a young man has been attracted by
the pomp and circumstance of soldiering,
tempted by the cheering music of military
bands, the brilliance of a new uniform, and
the prospect of a future promotion . . . wil-
fully signing on the dotted line, selling his
soul unknowingly. Anxiously waiting to be
sent to his new company to begin his sol-

diering, he is somewhat shaken to find that
he has been sent off to some unknown post
amidst the frightful solitude of rocks and
sagebrush in the summer, or the Siberian-
like snows of the winter. From the moment
of his arrival at the post, he is taught to
cease imagining himself as a soldier. In his
military future he is to suffer all the hardships of a soldier's life to the maximum
point of endurance, without any of its
privileges. He is issued a musket with
hardly any basic training on how to use it;
he is posted on guard duty without being
instructed his duties, and is forced to work
when not on guard duty . . . to work, drudge,
shovel with spade or fork, as soon as uniform and belt are off.

Frontier posts were so poorly garrisoned
that the number of men at most stations
were not equal to the work necessary to be
done. After hours of strenuous labor, men
depended on the smallest of rations provided by the government, and flour, salt
meat, and hardtack were often of the
poorest quality. Vegetables and sugar seldom showed up in the soldiers' diet, only
now and then did potatoes and cabbage
make their appearance. The usual rations
of eight ounces of bread, three-quarter
pound fat pork or salt beef, or one-quarter
pound fresh beef, were daily issues expected while in garrison. Occasionally, one
pint of soup made of hominy accompanied
a serving, otherwise a pint of hot steaming
army coffee washed down the meal.[8]
Laughing, singing, and cheerful conversa-
tions were seldom heard among men so
wanting; and as the heavy hand of time
dragged on so did the sad monotony of frontier army life. The majority of the enlisted
men, as well as a few officers, considered
themselves failures in their object of enlist-
ing, and thoughts of deserting or getting
drunk at the first opportunity became critical.

7. Army Navy Journal — Feb. 16, 1867, page 414.

8. Army Navy Journal — Sept. 1, 1866.

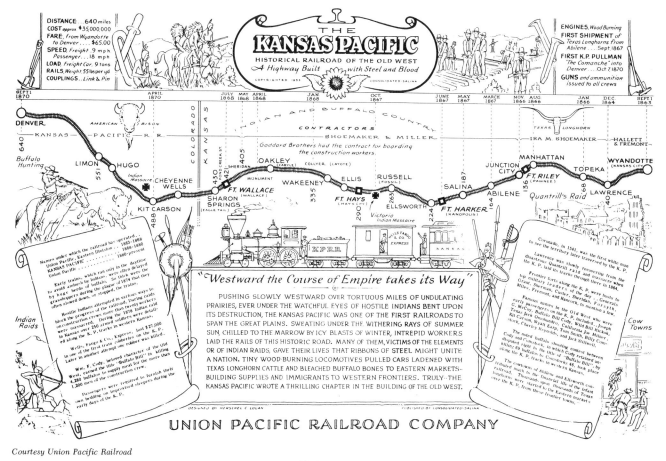

Courtesy Union Pacific Railroad

Poster — map

It was not uncommon to witness at a camp or garrison, some six or eight men walking what is known as "the ring," each carrying a log of wood on his shoulder for being dirty. If the offense were more serious, two logs were carried, one on each shoulder. Carrying a saddle for most of the day was a common punishment if the soldier was not present at an inspection at first call. These punishments often lasted 24 hours. For more serious misconduct, the prisoner was arraigned before a court martial, and if found guilty, was sentenced to confinement, and in many cases, with loss of a portion of his pay. Commanding officers called attention to the ever-rising tide of courts-martial. Too many trivial charges were filed, and many should have been brought before a Field Officer's or Garrison Court, and disposed of, instead of being referred to General Courts Martial, convened with great inconvenience and expense. Officers preferring charges seldom

examined the case thoroughly before resorting to courts-martial.

Discharging a soldier for desertion was no punishment at all. To the individual it meant a little humiliation and embarrassment, being drummed out of camp before his comrades, but with his dishonorable discharge he was finally free and rid of the army for good. Forfeiture of all pay and allowances then due, except the just dues of the laundress and sutler, were the only things that seemed to concern him. Having his head shaven, and his left hip branded with a two-inch letter "D", only hurt his pride. Punishments given by the courts did not seem to have the slightest effect in preventing desertions. The number of deserters was so high that it was almost impossible to make the soldiers look upon desertion as a serious crime.

Isolation to a soldier in a military fort on the plains was similar to that of a sailor on a ship at sea. Discipline was rigidly enforced

One of series of six paintings done by J. Gogolin, famous German artist in 1931 depicting events from life of Adolph Roenigk, member of a section crew working on the UPRR. This painting illustrates a band of Cheyenne Indians led by Tall Bull tearing up railroad tracks near Fossil Creek (now Russell) Kansas, about 1 p.m., May 28, 1869, following the attack upon the section crew.

by the supreme authority, the post commander. All forms of military etiquette were observed. The flag was hoisted at sunrise with the accompaniment of a long roll from the drum and was lowered at sunset with the added reverberations of the evening gun. The frontier soldier found much of his time occupied by many duties. Essentially, a good soldier was to be well drilled. The extent to which frontier garrisons were drilled depended largely on whether troops were veterans with past experience or recruits requiring further drilling. Special duties such as mending roofs, repairing fences, and building additions kept many recruits away from company and regimental drills. There were cases where soldiers served their entire enlistment without once drilling in regimental formation or even in battalion formation.

Another important function on post was

guard duty. Government property had to be protected day and night. Guards and pickets prevented Indians from entering the post or lurking near enough to shoot at its defenders, steal horses, or set fire to haystacks or storehouses. It was a very comfortable feeling to hear the hours called late at night, by those on guard duty with the announcement, "All's well." On hearing this the first sentinel repeated the message, and so on around the camp. When the last sentinel repeated the message, the sergeant of the guard called aloud, "Two o'clock and all's well all around." This was repeated at each hour during the night. In case of danger, an alarm to awaken the post was given by a continued beating of the drum — the long roll — without break, until the entire post was fully aroused.

To the soldiers whose lot it was to go on guard duty, hours were spent in cleaning

This painting illustrated a band of Cheyenne Indians led by Tall Bull making a buffalo surround near Fossil Creek about 4 p.m., May 28, 1869 after they had attacked the section crew. Later the same band began tearing up the railroad tracks and was instrumental in wrecking a train.

uniforms, polishing boots and brass buttons, and rubbing rifles down, before the time set for "guard mount."

From each guard detail the neatest and most soldierly-appearing trooper was chosen to be orderly to the commanding officer. He reported to post headquarters, where his main duty consisted of carrying messages and making himself useful. It was a high honor, but also he walked no post and slept in his bunk all night. "Bucking for orderly" resulted in rigid inspection of the man, his uniform, arms, and equipment. It was at guard mounting, dress reviews and inspections that the soldier presented his most soldier-like appearance.

Details sent out for escort duty often broke the monotony of "post boredom." It might be escorting the paymaster's wagon, scheduled for a visit every two months, or the monthly military train that supplied the post with mail or rations. Possibly an escort would be required for the inspector-general or the commanding general of the department or district. Soldiers at posts along well-traveled trails, often found escorting was a daily chore . . . and the only work for the cavalry. During Indian troubles, stages, mail wagons, generals, government trains, and paymasters, along with immigrant wagon trains bound for California, and freighters all required escorts; however, the size of the detachment depended upon the character and importance of the object escorted. Army details varied from three to four men to escort a mail carrier, to several companies as escort for a large supply train.[9]

Troops were often called upon to form scouting parties to locate the Indian and

9. My Life on the Plains, by G. A. Custer, pages 62, 68, 74, 78.

keep him in check. Generally, the marauding Indians were scattered in small bands far from their villages. It was a general policy to keep scouting parties out in summer to hold the hostiles in check, and give the impression the army was always ready for them. The soldiers were hardened by the experience of scouting in the field, and practically trained by experiences in maneuvers. For the soldier, it broke the monotony of garrison life with a change of scenery, and of diet. Shooting buffalo, antelope, or other game was encouraged. These expeditions were also welcomed by the men remaining at the post, as fresh meat was brought in to supplement their rations. The anticipation of being chosen to accompany the next scouting party was always the topic of the day. Many stories, somewhat blown out of proportion, of hair-raising experiences, were topics of garrison gossip.

Within a few months, a number of troops of the 7th Cavalry Regiment were organized and sent to more remote posts. Troops B and C were stationed at Fort Lyon, Colorado Territory; Troop E was sent to Fort Hays, Kansas; Troops F and G were assigned to Fort Harker, Kansas; Troop I was stationed at Fort Wallace, Kansas; Troop K at Fort Dodge, Kansas, and Troop L went to Fort Morgan, Colorado Territory. Only Troops A, D, H and M remained with the regimental headquarters at Fort Riley.[10]

10. Of Garryowen in Glory — by Lt. Col. M. C. Chandler.

Courtesy Union Pacific Railroad   *Painting by J. Gogolin*

This painting illustrates an attack on a hand car near Fossil Creek (now Russell) Kansas by Tall Bull's Cheyennes, about 10 a.m. May 28, 1869. Several men were killed and Mr. Roenigk was shot completely through the lung.

The deafening "ping" from steel hammers played the first grand chorus across the plains, as railroad crews of gaugers, spikers, and bolters, stretched the steel ribbons of rail westward. The Kansas Pacific had been completed as far as Junction City, and most of the grading had been done as far west as Fort Harker. The end of the Civil War produced an adequate labor force for the first time, particularly as financial depression in the East led many discharged soldiers to seek work on the railroads. The Indians were anything but pleased with the progress of the "iron horse," largely because of its push through their hunting grounds. Serious depredations developed. Engineers, surveyors, graders and bridge builders, plotting a course of construction toward the Rocky Mountains, always considerabley in advance of work gangs, faced the peril of being ambushed and killed. Armed with the best weapons the railroad could supply meant little or nothing against the swift attack from a band of hostiles. Even as the 7th Cavalry remained the watchful dog, the threat of these attacks always lingered and the building of the railroad appeared many times a small scale Indian war.

The overland stage lines to Denver and Santa Fe were protected by two lines of posts, one on the Smoky Hill River, the other on the Arkansas River. These posts, seven in number, were all of a temporary character, rudely constructed, usually of cottonwood logs and rough lumber. At some of them, particularly at Fort Dodge, many officers and men lived in dugouts, with dirt roofs and no floors. Temporary bunks with pole or board slats and a straw tick, empty boxes, cross sections of cottonwood logs, and barrels with the sides out and stuffed with hay, made up the furniture in the barrack room; tallow dips supplied illumination.

The uniformed cavalryman of the 1866-1867 period was bedecked in a maze

Courtesy Union Pacific Railroad
Gaugers and spikers were constantly harassed by Indians. Weapons, supplied by the railroad, were close at hand in case of another attack.

Courtesy Herb Peck, Jr.
Trooper of the late 1860's, with full equipment.

Courtesy The Kansas State Historical Society
Fort Riley Hospital 1867.

Courtesy The Kansas State Historical Society
Custer House, Fort Riley. A modern photo.

Courtesy The Kansas State Historical Society
Fort Riley, 1867.

of entangled leather straps, supporting-cartridge pouches, pistol and carbine. At his left trailed a three-pound, seven-ounce light cavalry sabre[11] totaling 42.35 inches in length and as useful as a club against hit-and-run tactics of the plains Indian. On his right, fastened to a wide leather shoulder belt[12] hung his most effective weapon, the Spencer, a seven-shot repeating carbine, caliber 56/50, model 1865. An average-trained marksman could fire the seven rounds in 12 to 18 seconds. It could throw a ball more than a mile and with a little accuracy, penetrate a foot of solid pine at 150 feet. Indeed, the Spencer was classified a potent short-range carbine. Loading was speeded up when Spencer incorporated the Blakeslee Quickloader. These leather boxes came with ten tin tubes,[13] each tube holding seven .52 caliber rim-fire cartridges. The arm was loaded through a trap in the butt plate, loaded singly one tube after another. This meant that the soldier had a fire power of 70 shots. The overall weapon was 38 inches in length, with a 22 inch barrel, and weighed approximately seven and a half pounds.

Snugly seated in a black holster with a large semi-circular flap, was the soldier's .44 caliber Remington or Colt percussion revolver. This heavy and unbalanced six-shooter could drop a man at 70 paces.[14] The trooper generally wore his holstered revolver on the right side and attached to the sword belt, with the butt of the weapon forward. Historians venture to guess that this

11. Ordnance Manual 1861, pg. 224.

12. This shoulder belt was a carryover from the Civil War and measured two and three-eighths inches in width.

13. In my article in Guns magazine, "Military Accoutrements, part 1, up to the Civil War," Oct., 1971, page 68, I mention seven tin tubes each holding seven cartridges. Scarcely anything has been written on the Blakeslee, so I referred to Bannerman's 1949 catalog, page 223, which advertises a seven-tube carbine cartridge box. Gun Digest, 1962, shows a photo of the Blakeslee as a ten-tube cartridge box, page 8. Collectors Guns, 1963, page 76, mentions that these boxes came in varying sizes, with the largest holding up to 13 tubes. At the West Point Museum, a box in their collection was found to have six tubes, for the 56/56 cartridge.

14. Cavalry Journal, Vol. 16, page 184, "The extreme useful range should be over 75 yards."

position of the revolver made it easier for the trooper to mount his horse. This is pure assumption. The primary weapon of the cavalryman was the sabre. The revolver was introduced much later.[15] Even during the Civil War it was labeled as an auxiliary weapon. Regulations specified that the holster must be worn on the right side, from which the left hand could draw it if necessary.[16]

The dark blue shell jacket with its two and one-half inch choke-collar, waist-length, were Civil War leftovers. Neither jacket nor blue woollen trousers seemed to fit any man without several visits to the company tailor. There appears to be no rule specifying whether trouser legs were to be

Courtesy The Kansas State Historical Society
Fort Riley, 1867.

worn tucked into the tops of boots or left hanging loosely about the boot when strolling about the post. An exception was made, of course, during an inspection or dress parade.

The floppy crowned "kepi"[17] or forage cap was habitual for casual headwear. From a current French pattern it gave a rather sloppy appearance. The crown was either

15. From a letter written by George B. McClellan, Capt. 1st Cavy., to the Honorable Jefferson Davis, Sec. of War, Oct. 3rd, 1856, Phila. "For my own regiment, armed with the revolvers, there need be no holster, (referring to the saddle holster) for the men should follow the Russian system and always carry the pistol on the waist belt." Cited from Cavalry Journal, Vol. 34, pg. 432.

16. The only possible place to hang the holster was on the right side. On the left is where the sabre hung with all its sabre belts sewn in place. Hypothetically, the right hand was meant for wielding the sabre and the left hand utilized the revolver. This, of course, would only be done at either close combat or dismounted close combat.

17. This cap was a poor imitation of the original French kepi, from a French word deriving from German origin to describe a military hat.

Courtesy Union Pacific Railroad
Sod houses peppered the Kansas Plains, most of them empty, the owners scared away by Indians or murdered in their bunks. It wasn't long before a new tennant, fresh from the East, would take up quarters, looking for a new life in the great Western expansion. Ox drawn covered wagon pulling up to empty sod house.

pushed back or sloped forward to suit the wearer, as there was no reinforcement to keep the hat in uniform shape. The kepi gave the soldier little protection from sun or rain. One use was recalled by an old cavalryman; filled with oats or corn, it served as feeding bag for his horse. For dress, the flat-topped, wide-brimmed "Hardee hat"[18] with brass embellishments counterbalanced with an occasional plume was seen in ranks. To distinguish cavalry from infantry, the wide brim was pinned up to the right side for cavalry, and to the left side for infantry.

The average weight of the cavalry soldier was approximately 140 pounds. With saddle, weapons, and accoutrements, the horse carried a little more than 240 pounds.

Sword, carbine, and tin utensils caused a continual din as horse and trooper crept along the trail at a rate of from three to four miles an hour. The trooper enlisted for five years and received $16 a month[19] in inflated greenbacks. This lasted him a short time, as gambling, whiskey, and the high-priced sutler exhausted his pockets quickly. There was nothing sensational or picturesque about these Indian-fighters and they accomplished more through threat than they achieved in actual battle.

State-side newspapers reported the renewal of hostilities by the Indians on the western plains. Easterners visualized Fort Riley as under constant siege with huge stone walls encompassing the small garrison. It would have been more realistic if

18. Sometimes called Jeff Davis hat, Hardee, or Kossuth. Secretary of War Jefferson Davis insisted upon the adoption of this hat.

19. Reduced to $13.00 in 1872, with small increases after 3 years and "bounties" for reenlistments on the frontier averaging $30.00 to $140.00, depending upon location of station.

Courtesy Union Pacific Railroad   *Photo by A. J. Russell*

Usually a shotgun or large caliber rifle hung over the door outside of the cabin. If a settler family laid claim to the land, built his sod house or log cabin, and planted his field, all within the year, he was then considered lucky he hadn't been payed a visit from "Mr. Lo." Pictured here is a Mormon family.

the newspapers had recorded continuation rather than renewal, for the sporadic warfare never altogether ceased. But at Fort Riley there were no huge stone walls. There were stables, five in number, a sutler's store, and billiard house for the officers, an express office and a post office. The quartermaster employees' houses were near the mess houses and sutler's residence. The chaplain's residence and chapel were surrounded by a white picket fence. The superintendent's house and ordnance building were situated in a group, away from the parade ground. Barracks included six large two-storied buildings, three were on each side of a hollow square, facing one another. Six double houses for officers' quarters were on the remaining two sides of the square. This square was the parade ground with a deep rich green lawn, in the center of which stood a cannon flanked by a flagpole. A carriage drive ran around the parade ground, and on windy days, clouds of Kansas dust never ceased to creep into the frontier-fashionable, neatly-kept quarters, irritating the officers' wives to extremity.[20]

This same Kansas wind played havoc with the ladies by upsetting their skirts, throwing hem after hem over their heads revealing white petticoats and dainty ankles beneath. The women soon learned that buckshot sewn into the skirts' lower hem-line would weigh down the outer skirts, hindering the wind from upsetting them. As soon as this problem was solved, curious soldiers had little more to hope for in the windswept future.

The establishment of Fort Riley was suggested by Colonel T. T. Fauntleroy, of the 1st Dragoons, in July, 1852. In a letter to General T. S. Jessup, then quartermaster general of the army, Fauntleroy urged that a post be located at a point where the Republican fork unites with the Kansas River. After careful deliberation, the secretary of war appointed a board of officers to locate a new post in the vicinity of the forks of the Kansas River. Escorted by Capt. Robert Hall Chilton of the 1st Dragoons, the board surveyed the area and approved the site. A report was submitted November 10th, 1852, and endorsed by Secretary of War Charles Magill Conrad, January 7th, 1853. A picket was established on the selected site, and because it was found to be very near the geographical center of the United States, it was called "Camp Center." In May, 1853, three companies of the 6th Infantry arrived at Camp Center with orders to erect temporary buildings. After construction had begun, an order changed the name of the camp to Fort Riley, honoring Brevet Major General Bennet Riley, who died at Buffalo, New York, June 9th, 1853.

Appropriations were made by Congress in March, 1855, to prepare Fort Riley for a cavalry training post by building new quarters, stables for five troops, storehouses and whatever was needed. Most of the buildings were built of stone taken from a nearby quarry, with all work done by hand. In the East, contracts were let for window sashes, doors, framework, ornamental woodwork for officers' quarters, glass and hardware. This was shipped by boat to Fort Leavenworth and then by wagon to Fort Riley.[21]

The vast undeveloped empire lying between Fort Riley, Denver, the Platte River, and Red River, was unoccupied except by bands of Kiowas, Cheyennes, Arapahoes, and Lipans, dependent for food and clothing on the vast herds of buffaloes that roamed the plains. Across these hunting grounds passed annually hundreds of wagons, battering hubs and scraping their sides in slashing newly-cut trails toward the mineral regions of the Rocky Mountains and the Pacific Coast. How many failed to reach their destination was manifested by numerous neglected graves of victims of

20. "The History of Fort Riley," by W. F. Pride.

21. "The History of Fort Riley," by W. F. Pride.

starvation, disease, and occasional Indian attacks.

Friendly Indians urged upon the government their need for arms and ammunition for hunting the buffalo on which they depended for subsistence. Indian traders could see their need for breech-loaders to increase their production of furs and hides, but these weapons could also be used in warfare. A report submitted by Major H. Douglas, 3rd Infantry, commanding Fort Dodge, sums up the difficulties.

Fort Dodge, Kansas
January 13, 1867

General: I consider it my duty to report what I have observed with reference to Indian affairs in this country, so that such representations may be made to the Department of the Interior by the commanding general of division as he may think proper, also other items of information which may be useful.

The issue and sale of arms and ammunition — such as breech-loading carbines and revolvers, powder and lead, (loose and in cartridges,) and percussion caps — continues without intermission. The issue of revolvers and ammunition is made by Indian agents, as being authorized by the Commis-

sioner of Indian Affairs, and the sale of them in the greatest abundance is made by traders. Butterfield, an Indian trader, formerly of the overland express, has the largest investment in Indian goods of all the traders. He has sold several cases of arms to Cheyennes and Arapahoes. Charley Rath, a trader, who lives at Zarah, has armed several bands of Kiowas with revolvers, and has completely overstocked them with powder.

Between the authorized issue agents and the sales of the traders, the Indians were never better armed than at the present time. Several hundred Indians have visited this post, all of whom had revolvers in their possession. A large majority had two revolvers, and many of them three.

The Indians openly boasted that they have plenty of arms and ammunition in case of trouble in the spring.

The Interior Department does not seem to appreciate the danger of thus arming those Indians. The evil of presenting a revolver to each of the chiefs of bands would hardly be appreciable, but when the whole rank and file are thus armed, it not only gives them greater courage to murder and plunder, but renders them formidable enemies.

The agents have no real control over the traders; in fact, they are accused by many, both Indians and white men, of being in league with them, and of drawing a large profit from the trade. Should such be the case, (and I think it highly probable,) it is a

Courtesy Union Pacific Railroad

Mormon emigrant train crossing the Platte River (painting).

A Sioux and Cheyenne Villege, "the calm before the storm."

natural consequence that the agent does not wish to control the trader.

The anxiety of Indians at the present time to obtain arms and ammunition is a great temptation to the trader. For a revolver an Indian will give ten, even twenty times its value, in horses and furs; powder and lead are sold to them at almost the same rate, and as the bulk is small, large quantities can be transported at comparatively little expense. This anxiety cannot be caused by a lack of such articles, because they have plenty to last for some time, but everything tends to show that the Indians are laying in large supplies, preparatory to an outbreak. When the outbreak occurs, we will see too late that we have provided our enemies with the means for our destruction.

A great deal of dissatisfaction seems to have been created among the Indians by the unequal distribution of presents.

The Kiowas complain bitterly of Colonel Leavenworth, their agent, stationed at Fort Zarah. Kicking Bird, a chief of the Kiowas, states that only a few small bands of Kiowas got any presents, the balance last year got nothing; that it had been represented to Colonel Leavenworth that most of the bands were bad in their hearts, and would not go in to get their presents; that he, Kicking Bird, sent runners to tell Colonel Leavenworth that his stock was poor and he could not move in there, but he would in the spring, if the agent would keep his share of the goods, but Colonel Leavenworth would not listen,

and either gave all the goods to the bands then in, or sold them to other Indians, and told them they would get no goods that year.

How much of this is true I know not, but from all I can learn there seems to be at least some foundation for the story. Bad management, bad faith, and injustice are sure to produce the worst results. Kicking Bird says that all bad feeling in his tribe is owing to the injustice of their agent; that it required all his influence to prevent an outbreak, and he is afraid that they will commence hostilities in the spring.

The Arapahoes, Cheyennes, and a large band of Sioux, under the leadership of Big Bear, are now en route for the purpose of crossing the Arkansas into the Kiowa country. They move ostensibly to graze and hunt buffalo. A portion of the Arapahoes, under the general leadership of Little Raven, crossed the river about four miles below this point.

The Sioux and Cheyennes are encamped about 100 miles north of this post on the Republican, and are said to be hostile. They are to cross about eleven miles below here. They are all well mounted and well armed with carbines and revolvers, and supplied with plenty of ammunition.

Kicking Bird says the Sioux and Cheyennes asked his permission to cross the river, and that he refused it for fear of trouble, but that his men wish them to cross, and he believes that they will all cross the river, and that in the spring, when the grass comes up, there will be war. He had been treated kindly at Fort Dodge, or he would not tell us so, but we must look out for our lives and for our stock in the spring. He says, as they talk now all the tribes north and south of the Arkansas will be in the outbreak, his own tribe among them.

He also states that Santante or "White Bear" a principal chief of the Kiowas, is always talking of war; that they have already had a counsel at the Kiowa camp, in which the Cheyennes, Sioux, Arapahoes, Kiowas, Comanches and Apaches were represented, and it was agreed that as soon as the grass was old enough they would commence war; that he (Kicking Bear) had been kindly treated at Fort Dodge, and he wished to put us on our guard; that before spring the Indians might change their minds, but at present their intention was war; he said he would be backwards and forwards frequently to give us the news.

The chief (Kicking Bear) is known to General Sherman who talked with him last fall, and is believed at this post to be the most reliable of all the Indians.

I would respectfully state that it is my purpose to keep the district and department informed of all movements of Indians in large bodies as far as it is possible.

I am, very respectfully, your obedient servant,

H. Douglas
Major Third Infantry
Commanding Post.[22]

With the increased number of officers and soldiers being sent west, there seemed to be a lamentable ignorance in the East of the vast extent of the country even among "army people," and of the wants and requirements of those whose professions sent them there for an undetermined tour of duty. It seems that when an officer was sent to the plains it was only necessary for him to pack a small trunk or valise with a few indispensable articles and immediately proceed to his station, much in the same manner as if he were joining his regiment in the field. Totally unprepared for the frontier life they were obliged to lead, they accepted various opinions from people with lesser experience than themselves, as to what should be taken and what should not. "Everyone told us that it was unnecessary to bring anything with us; that officers on

duty on the frontier have no need of anything save what they can get from the quartermaster," replied one young officer, somewhat disturbed with his predicament.[23]

Common ignorance brought one officer to the frontier with only two blankets for bedding, in the middle of December, with three inches of snow on the ground, and he was surprised that the surgeon could not furnish from hospital property everything he would require. In another instance a second lieutenant reported to his commanding officer without a uniform, and when asked what he proposed to do without a dress uniform, he explained that an older officer back east told him that officers never wore anything at a frontier garrison, except common soldiers' clothes. He was surprised that such was not the case. It was also supposed that while serving some distant garrison, or when on detached service, they would lose their quarters after being in the field for a number of weeks. Such false notions were often taken seriously because of the lack of information furnished from competent sources.

Quarters were furnished by the quartermaster with heating and cooking stoves; a plain table or two, a rough bunk or bedstead, and possibly a chair made of unfinished pine boards. Anything else that the officer should need, he must provide for himself. Surgeons are not in the habit of providing bedding or beds for the use of officers, and the quartermaster does not provide him with furnishings or blankets although he may purchase these items at government prices. Officers who have been on the frontier long enough to learn how to live, and who had any taste for living like gentlemen, usually furnished their quarters comfortably. Curtains and carpets were not altogether unknown, even in bachelor quarters. With the aid of a company carpenter, a few pine boards and empty hardtack boxes,

22. "Issue of Arms to Indians," Letter from the Secretary of War; (relative to the issue of a large number of arms to the Kiowas and other Indians) 39th Congress, 2nd Session; Mis. Doc. No. 41, 1867.

23. Army Navy Journal — January 11, 1868.

Courtesy The Kansas State Historical Society
Fort Harker, 1867. An army post established in 1866 to protect settlers and railroad construction parties.

chairs were built. Pictures and engravings hung in handsome gold frames along with stuffed birds and animals, adding a civilized appearance to these small quarters.

Officers in garrison generally wore the regulation uniform, even patronizing first-class tailors. It has been noted that officers on the plains were as well dressed as those who were on duty at Eastern stations. Officers prepared and well-advised as to what items were necessary for frontier duty were generally equipped with the following: A good mess chest, well-furnished for four or six persons, a good roll of bedding and a mattress, a few comfortable fold-up camp chairs, and a trunk filled with a good supply of clothing for at least one year. A wise officer will leave his measurements with a good tailor and bootmaker before leaving "the States," in order to replenish his wardrobe at any time by sending his order.

Books and weeklies offered relaxation during idle hours, and were often ex-

changed or passed on to someone else. Once the officer had established himself at a post, he found he was obliged to purchase what was available from the sutler at a cost of 100 or 200 percent more than he would have paid had he brought these items with him. Probably more than anything else, an officer would trade his most precious memento for a good mattress. A ticking filled with dry prairie hay was hard to get accustomed to. It constantly needed refilling, developed barbs and insects, and in a short time gave off a musty and offensive odor.

Even though these men lived in a frontier fashion, they always thought of themselves as gentlemen, and they lived as such. Their living habits may have been simple, but they were far from that of frontier ranchmen who ate fried bacon with their fingers and slept on the ground, a saddle for a pillow.

Women who accompanied their husbands to frontier posts generally complained of the great difficulty in getting food that was wholesome and nutritious. Laws passed by Congress allowed officers to purchase from the government such supplies as they could certify were needed for their own use; however, they criticized the limitations. A schedule of what items might be obtained was usually posted to keep everyone informed of their purchasing boundaries. An allowance for one month for each officer is as follows: Two cans peaches, one can oysters, one-half can jelly, one-half can jam, four cans of tomatoes, two cans corn, one can peas, two cans milk, three pounds soda crackers, two and a half pounds mackerel, one and a half pounds dried beef, two pounds Java coffee, two and a half pounds sperm candles, one-quarter pound officer's soap, one-quarter gallon syrup, one and one half pounds dried peaches, and two pounds lard.[24]

---

24. Army Navy Journal — August 24, 1867.

If the officer was lucky enough to have only a wife, he could get by replenishing his table with additional meat from a hunt. But for some, who had children and employed servants, the pitiful amount which they were allowed to consume each day was wholly inadequate. While many wives were willing to forego the privilege of delicious vegetables and sweet fruits and a comfortable home, to comfort and cheer husbands in their lonely and monotonous frontier life, other women returned to their eastern homes to wait for their husband's tour of duty to end.

Besides all this, what woman did not know was the frightfully exorbitant prices of the sutler and the great monopoly he exercised. Canned oysters, that they paid the government 29 cents for, were retailed by the sutler for one dollar, and nearly all canned vegetables sold for similar prices. Fruits in cans were higher still. There is no doubt that an officer's pay was inadequate if he were compelled to depend on the sutler, but if any major complaints were voiced by these frontier women it would probably be against the commissaries who told them that they could only have so much, and the rest of the time they lived on bacon, beans, beef, and flour.

Art by E. L. Reedstrom
Typical cavalryman standing to horse at Fort Riley.

ORGANIZATION OF CAVALRY, 1866-1876

July 28, 1866	*March 3, 1869*	*July 15, 1870*
1 colonel		
1 lieutenant colonel		
3 majors		
1 adjutant (extra lieutenant)		
1 quartermaster (extra lieutenant)		
1 regimental commissary (extra lieutenant)		no commissary
1 veterinary surgeon		
1 additional veterinary surgeon (not commissioned)		
1 sergeant major		
1 quartermaster sergeant		
1 commissary sergeant		
1 saddler sergeant		
1 chief trumpeter	1 chief musician added	chief musician continued
1 regimental hospital steward		no regimental hospital steward
12 companies each:		
1 captain		
1 first lieutenant		
1 second lieutenant		
1 first sergeant		
1 quartermaster sergeant		
5 sergeants		
8 corporals		
2 trumpeters		4 corporals
2 farriers and blacksmiths		
1 saddler		
1 wagoner		
78 privates	60 privates	60 privates

Acts of June 16 and 23, 1874; March 2 and 3, 1875; June 26, 1876:
  no commissary sergeant
  4 corporals in each company
  54 privates in each company

Chaplains: 1 in each colored regiment (9th and 10th Cavalry), not commissioned in 1866. By the act of 1869, there were 4 in the 4 colored regiments and 30 post chaplains, to rank as captains of infantry.

Indian scouts to the number of 1,000 may be employed as cavalry soldiers under all acts, 1866-1876. There were 474 in service in 1869.

Surgeons were Medical Department, not a part of regimental organization. Acts of 1866-1870 provided 1 brigadier general, 1 colonel, 5 lieutenant colonels, 60 majors, and 150 first lieutenants who were promoted to captain after three years, and 5 medical storekeepers who ranked as captains of cavalry. The only enlisted men were hospital stewards, 459 in 1866; 365 in 1869; 297 in 1870. Acts of 1874-1876 increased commissioned ranks: 6 colonels, 10 lieutenant colonels, 50 majors, 74 captains, and 51 first lieutenants.

OFFICERS, 7TH CAVALRY, 1866-1876

Colonels
    A. J. Smith   28 July 1866 — 6 May 1869
    S. D. Sturgis   6 May 1869 — 11 June 1886
Lieutenant Colonels
    G. A. Custer   28 July 1866 — 25 June 1876
    Elmer Otis   25 June 1876 — 2 April 1883
Majors
    Alfred Gibbs   28 July 1866 — 26 December 1868
    Wickliffe Cooper   28 July 1866 — 8 June 1867
    J. H. Elliott   7 March 1867 — 27 November 1868
    W. S. Abert   8 June — 25 August 1867
    J. A. Thompson   25 August — 14 November, 1867
    J. G. Tilford   14 November 1867 — 22 September 1883
    Lewis Merrill   27 November 1868 — 21 May 1886
    M. A. Reno   26 December 1868 — 1 April 1880
Adjutants
    W. W. Cooke   8 December 1866 — 21 February 1867 and
                             1 January 1871 — 25 June 1876
    Myles Moylan   21 February 1867 — 31 December 1870
    G. D. Wallace   25 June 1876 — 6 June 1877
Quartermasters
    T. W. Custer   3 December 1866 — 10 March 1867
    J. M. Bell   1 November 1867 — 31 March 1869 and
                            26 October 1869 — 31 December 1870
    A. E. Smith   31 March — 7 July 1869
    J. F. Weston   1 January 1871 — 29 February 1872
    H. J. Nowlan   1 March 1872 — 25 June 1876
    W. S. Edgerly   25 June — 14 November 1876
    C. A. Varnum   14 November 1876 — 31 October 1879
Commissaries
    T. B. Weir   24 February — 31 July 1867
    H. J. Nowlan   30 October 1867 — 15 July 1870
    No more until:
    S. R. H. Tompkins   1 July 1899

AN ACT OF WAR

Through the year 1866, the Kansas frontier was relatively quiet. Cheyennes in the North were helping Red Cloud's Sioux fight against traffic on the Bozeman Trail. They also took a leading part in the slaughter of Fetterman's command, and in 1867 they were back on the southern plains, restless and discontented. There were occasional encounters with overland travelers and settlers, but much talk of raids said to have been committed by Indians was reported to the military, with the threat of an uprising in the spring. The Government, seeking to do something to prevent this, sent an expedition to the plains under Major General Winfield S. Hancock, commanding the Department of the Missouri.

Prepared for war but intending to seek peace, Hancock left Fort Riley in April, 1867, with 1,400 men, cavalry, artillery, infantry, and a pontoon train. With a sometimes lagging supply train, the column presented a formidable appearance, and it is probable that the 'moral effect' served to awe the red man into good behavior for a time. General Hancock had reached Fort Riley, Kansas, from Fort Leavenworth by rail at the end of March; here four companies of the Seventh Cavalry and a company of the 37th Infantry joined Hancock's command. After leaving Fort Riley, the march continued to Fort Harker, some 90 miles. The command went into camp on the Smoky Bottom, just west of the post, drawing provisions and supplies for the expedition, and was reinforced by two more troops of cavalry. The troops then marched toward Fort Larned, near the Arkansas River, arriving there April 7. The command included eleven companies of the Seventh Cavalry, Lieutenant

Colonel Custer; seven companies of the 37th Infantry, Captain Parsons; a battery of the Fourth Artillery and an Engineer detachment commanded by Lieutenant Micah Ryder Brown. General J. W. Davidson accompanied the expedition as inspector general. Brevet Major General Andrew J. Smith, colonel 7th Cavalry, also accompanied the expedition as commander of the District of the Upper Arkansas.

James Butler Hickok, commonly known as "Wild Bill," was attached as a scout. Greatness had recently been thrust upon him by publication of an article in the February, 1867, issue of Harper's Magazine. A

Courtesy Author's Collection

Major General Hancock

number of Delaware Indians accompanied the command as scouts, guides, hunters and interpreters. They had no friendship for their wilder brethren, and moved with the command in full battle array with faces painted for war. Their services were very valuable to General Hancock, as they served as the command's eyes and ears.

A grand "pow-wow" was to be held near Fort Larned, and arrangements with the chiefs of a Cheyenne village nearby planned to effect greater security and safety for those whose business compelled them to travel through or reside in the valley of the Smoky Hill. Runners had been sent by the agent of the Cheyennes, Arapahoes, and Apaches, inviting their head chiefs to a council on April 10. A blinding snowstorm struck April 9, lasting the full day until late evening. Horses suffered from the severe cold and officers ordered double rations of oats to the horses, and guards were instructed to pass along the picket lines, whipping the horses to keep them moving constantly so they would not freeze. Eight to twelve inches of snow prevented travel,

and the council was postponed until the weather moderated.

One of the big attractions in the expedition's train was a six-year-old Cheyenne boy, survivor of Sand Creek, who was being carried back to his people, a recent treaty having stipulated the child's return. Colonel John M. Chivington's Colorado volunteers in 1864 attacked a camp of Cheyennes. While waving an American flag, and also a white flag of truce, Arapahoes and Cheyennes at Sand Creek were butchered brutally. Men, women and children tasted their own blood while pleading for their lives, trying to show the troopers that they were peaceful. The day after the battle, two soldiers found the boy concealed in a hole in the bank of a creek and rescued him. At the same time, two small Cheyenne girls were found, but only one girl returned with the boy.[1]

---

1. The Cheyenne boy and girl were exhibited in the Wilson and Graham Circus. After the Indians had demanded these children be returned, the government detailed an officer to trace them. Through some confusion, only the boy was secured. The girl disappeared with the showman, never to be heard of again. After the boy was returned to the Indians, it was said by some that the

Art by E. L. Reedstrom
Custer in parley with Indians.

Art by E. L. Reedstrom
One of the Cheyenne Chiefs.

The boy lived in the United States[2] for four years, showing an increasing amount of willingness to learn the white man's way. When troopers teased him, saying he would have to live with his savage uncle, the boy would draw a jack-knife of formidable dimensions and announce that if he didn't like his uncle, or if he was mistreated, he would kill him without notice. Civilization had little effect on the boy; through violent and ungovernable temper, signs of his savage ancestry became visible many times. The boy had lost whatever Cheyenne tongue he knew, which was probably very little when captured, but he could speak English far better than some white boys his age. Full realization of his immediate future with his new Cheyenne family and their barbaric way of outdoor living weighed heavily on the boy as the days grew closer. General Hancock manifested great interest in the youngster, keeping him at his quarters and treating him with favors and kindness.

In the late evening of April 12, a band of warlike Indians, mainly Cheyennes, appeared in Hancock's camp. Among them were two chiefs of the "Dog Soldiers" ready to parlay after a meal and the customary smoke. The Indians were magnificently dressed in gorgeous crimson blankets, their faces streaked with war paint, and buckskins embellished with fine designs of beads and porcupine quills. After the meal all were comfortably seated around a huge fire. General Hancock addressed the Indians:

I told your agent, some time ago, that I was coming here to see you, and that if any of you wished to speak to me, you could do so. Your agent is your friend. I don't find many chiefs here; what is the reason? I have a great deal to say to you, but I want to see all the chiefs together. I want to say it all at once. But I am glad to see those chiefs that are here. To-morrow I am going to your camp. I have a boy, said to be a Cheyenne, whom the Cheyennes claim. We have made a promise, in which we pledged ourselves, if possible to find this boy, and girl, who were somewhere in the United States. We have found the boy, and here he is, ready to be delivered to his nearest relatives, who may call for him. I will leave him at Fort Larned with the commander. He will deliver him up to them. The girl is in Denver. We have written for her, and she will no doubt be sent here, either to your agent, or to the commander at Fort Larned, for delivery to her relatives. You see, the boy has not been injured; the girl will be delivered by us, also uninjured. Look out that any captives in your hands be restored to us equally unharmed. I tell you these things, now, that you may keep your treaties. Now, I have a great many soldiers; more than all the tribes put together. The Great Father has heard that some Indians have taken white men and women captives. [These prisoners were taken by Kiowas in Texas. The Cheyennes had nothing to do with them.] He has heard, also, that a great many Indians are trying to get up war to try to hurt the

Courtesy Herb Peck, Jr.

Osage Scout for Custer.

---

boy was an Arapaho, son of Red Bull. The circus people named the boy Tom Graham, but army officers dubbed him Graham Wilson. "Life of George Bent," by Geo. E. Hyde, pg. 257.

2. East of the Mississippi was always referred to as "back in the states," or "state side."

white man; that is the cause of my coming here. I intend not only to visit you here, but my troops will remain among you so that the peace and safety of the plains is preserved. I am going also to visit you in your camps. The innocent and those who are truly our friends we shall treat as brothers. If we find hereafter that any of you have lied to us, we will strike you. In case of war we shall punish whosoever befriends our enemies. If there are any tribes among you who have captives, white or black, you must give them up safe and unharmed as they are now. I have collected the evidence of all outrages committed by you, so that your agents may examine into the matter, and tell me who are guilty and who are not. I have heard that a great many of Indians want to fight. If so, we are here and prepared for war. If you are for peace, you know the conditions. If you are for war, then look out for its consequences. Your agent is your friend, but he knows his friendship will not save you from the anger of your Great Father, if we go to war. If we find any good Indians, and they come to us with clean hands, we will treat them as brothers, and we will separate them from the malcontents, and provide for them if necessary. This we will do, that the innocent may escape the war which will be waged against the guilty. We are building railroads and military roads through the country; you must not let your young men stop them; you must keep your men off the road. These roads will benefit the Indian as well as the white man, in bringing their goods cheaply and promptly to them. The steam-car and the wagon-train must run, and it is of importance to the whites and Indians that the mails, goods and passengers carried on them shall be safe. You know very well, if you go to war with the whites, you will lose. The Great Father has plenty more warriors. It is true, you might kill some soldiers, and surprise some small detachments. But soldiers came here to be killed — that is what they are for; we have plenty more, and as soon as one is killed, we have another in his place. If you take a passenger train, and kill women and children, you will be exterminated. If there are any good Indians that don't want to go to war, I shall help them and protect them. If there are any bad chiefs, I will help the good chiefs to put their heels on them. I have a great many chiefs with me that have commanded more men than any of you ever saw, and they have fought more great battles than you have fought fights. My chiefs cannot derive any distinction from fighting with your small numbers. They are not anxious for wars against Indians, but they are ready to make a just war. Let the guilty then beware. Stick to your treaties and let the white man travel unmolested. Your Great Father is your friend, as well as the friend of the white man. If a white man behaves badly or does a wrong to you he shall be punished, if the evidence ascertained at the trial proves him guilty.

[With this, the Indians began to stir, look at one another, with a great sensation passing among them.]

We can redress your wrongs better than you can. [Grunts, groans of "wagh, ugh" rose above the crackling of embers from the council fire.][3]

Hancock noticed that the Indians were somewhat restless, and with a certain eagerness to hear their side, he shortened his speech.

I have no more to say. I will await the end of this Council, to see whether you want war or peace. You ought to be the white man's friend. Come to the white man, and he will take care of you. I would advise you to cultivate their friendship. That is all I have to say.

During Hancock's speech it was noticed that the Indians were entranced with the uniforms and sabers that flashed in the fire light, often fixing their eyes on the red horsehair plumes of the artillery officers swaying to and fro at each nod of the head. Some chiefs seemed puzzled in determin-

---

3. Army Navy Journal, "Hancock's Speech to Indians," Vol. IV, 1867, page 578.

Art by E. L. Reedstrom

Sergeant to horse.

ing whether they were confronted with "medicine men" or designated chieftains.

Tall Bull, pulling his blanket snugly around him, awaited his turn and said that his tribe was at peace and had no intentions of harming the whites. His brief response was noncommittal; chiefly he declared a pacific intent, but, "Your young men must not shoot us, whenever they see us they fire, and we fire on them . . . Whenever you want to go to the Smoky Hill, you can go. We are willing to be friends with the white man. If you go to the village tomorrow, I won't have any more to say to you than I have now. . . ." Hancock answered that he intended going to their village the next day, and hoped to see all the chiefs there.

The next day Hancock started for the village on the Pawnee Fork as planned. After traveling twenty-three miles from the fort, the command encamped for the night. At approximately 11 a.m. the next day the march was resumed. Only a few miles were covered before scouts raced back with hands held high, signaling a halt. It was obvious why the scouts returned so quickly. Before the troops, stretched across the prairie, was an Indian line of battle. An estimated 400 mounted warriors and chiefs bedecked with their brightest colors showed a number of breech-loading Sharps rifles in addition to sinew backed bows and quivers filled with arrows. Some rode double; others, scattered between ponies, were on foot. Far to the left of their line a white flag was seen, where some 30 or 40 chiefs assembled. Hancock lost no time in issuing orders to his aides. Commands echoed between the columns of the expedition and bugle after bugle sounded. Infantry moved out in advance of the reserve columns, and the forward line knelt loading their new transition Springfield breech loaders. Sabers, drawn, flashed in the morning sun. The artillery was somewhat slow in following up closely, but finally formed a line of battle, with the cavalry on their flanks. The only other sounds heard from both sides

were the nervous horses snorting the frigid air and pawing the ground.

As the warriors sat upon their ponies, black, white, spotted and bay, their chiefs were riding back and forth, gesturing and talking, trying to keep the hot-blooded braves in order. The bright colors of shields painted with sacred symbols blended with war bonnets flopping in the sharp wind. War paint streaked bronze faces and decorated ponies awaited the white man's first move.

Edmund Guerrier, scout and interpreter, with Wild Bill Hickok, rode boldly forward signaling peace, and invited the chiefs to

Courtesy National Archives
Custer began to adopt buckskins in the field, much like the frontiersmen he had seen lingering about the post.

meet them halfway, for the purpose of a council. Roman Nose accepted, and spurred his pony forward. He was accompanied by several other chieftains carrying a white flag of truce at the end of a pole. Guerrier signaled for Hancock and his officers to approach. Arriving in the circle of horses, Hancock was somewhat hesitant in shaking hands with Roman Nose and the other chiefs, but interpreter Guerrier lessened the tension by conversation in Cheyenne.

Hancock, through Guerrier, questioned the hostile attitude displayed. "If you desire war," said he, "I am ready here and now to gratify your wish." The chiefs answered that they did not desire war, but were peacefully disposed. They were told that the command would continue toward the village and camp with the promise that soldiers would not approach their village or disturb them. Roman Nose grew angry; he had told Bull Bear earlier that he intended to kill Hancock before all his troops, but Bull Bear argued that this would endanger the families in camp. Looks and behavior of the warriors, with bows strung, rifles and pistols ready to fire, seemed to indicate they were awaiting a signal to fire upon the troops. Hancock ended the talk by telling the chiefs it was too windy to hold council in the open, that he would receive them at camp that night. Roman Nose and the other chieftains promised they would be there, and started back to their village. Only Bull Bear remained with Hancock's officers, trying to convince them that a further march toward the village would alarm the women and children. The general did not agree with the idea. The troops, taking up the line of march behind Roman Nose and his warriors, traveled until mid-afternoon, continuing until the command came within three hundred yards east of the Indian encampment. In the village there were 300 lodges, generally averaging eleven persons per lodge, including warriors, women and children, or an estimated three thousand Indians. Situated on the banks of the Pawnee

Fork, with an abundance of wood, water, grass, it was an ideal encampment from which any approaching enemy could be spotted.

Shortly after tents were pitched, Hancock was told by prominent chiefs of the Cheyennes that many women and children had fled upon seeing the approaching column, fearing a second Chivington massacre. On hearing this, Hancock became angry and insisted they all return, promising good treatment to all.

The chiefs asked for two horses in order to pursue the fleeing women and children and try to bring them back. Guerrier was to be sent into the village to report every two hours whether any remaining Indians were leaving. The half-breed remained in the village only a few hours, reporting that the Indians were saddled up and moving out. At 11 p.m. Custer, who had just retired, was ordered to surround the village and prevent anyone from leaving. It was some time before all the troops in Custer's command were aroused and assembled. Verbal orders were to be administered and no bugle calls were to be sounded. Anything loose upon the saddles such as cups or sabers was tied down to prevent noise during their movement. Upon surrounding the village, Custer reported to Hancock that it appeared to be deserted but it was feared that the Indians were up to their old tricks by remaining silent, to decoy the troopers into a trap. There were only a few hundred cavalrymen surrounding three hundred lodges,[4] forming a human circle about the village with a radius of about a half mile. The unbroken silence was becoming unbearable. Finally, Custer organized a party of six, including an interpreter, to reconnoiter the village more closely. Nothing was seen indicating that any Indians were within the village. Examination of the lodges revealed that the Indians had departed swiftly, abandoning

---

4. My Life on the Plains, G. A. Custer; Sheldon and Company, N.Y., 1874, page 27.

nearly all household goods. There were enough trophies lying about to satisfy the intruding soldiers, almost forgetting the important mission they had set out upon. So great was the haste of the Indians in leaving that in some lodges kettles filled with meat still hung bubbling over the fire. Like the shadows of night, the Indians had stolen away, leaving their dogs asleep in the lodges, when the troopers peered in. Plundering committees were formed and the men ran from one lodge to another, picking up relics, carrying away as much as their arms and pockets could hold.

Hancock, upon learning of the deserted village, dispatched several companies of infantry to replace the cavalry and protect the village and its contents from any further looting, until its final disposition could be determined. Custer and his troops returned from the village after being relieved by the infantry, and reported the full particulars to General Hancock. Outraged by the Indians' movements, Hancock ordered Custer to take eight troops of cavalry and start in pursuit of the Indians at early dawn, April 15. There was no sleep for the command that night, as preparations for the march occupied the entire night and part of the morning.

About 2 a.m., April 16, General Hancock summoned his officers to his tent and informed them that he had decided to burn the village and everything within it the next morning; that he considered the Indians had acted treacherously towards him, and that they deserved punishment. Most of the officers and Edward W. Wynkoop, Indian agent, were against this, and urged the General to ponder well upon such a course. The village was not burned that day, but in the morning a courier from Custer arrived informing Hancock of the killing of two white men and the destruction of Lookout Station, on the Smoky Hill. Enraged by the dispatch, Hancock issued final orders that night for the burning of the Indian village,

to General A. J. Smith, to take place the morning of April 18.

Courtesy Dr. Elizabeth Lawrence
Document ordered by General Hancock may be classified as a Declaration of War against the Indians.

Headquarters Department of the Missouri, in the field, Camp No. 15, Pawnee Fork, Kansas, April 18th, 1867. Special Field Orders No. 13.

1 . . . As a punishment for the bad faith practiced by the Cheyenne and Sioux who occupied the Indian Village at this place, and as a chastisement for murders and depredations committed since the arrival on the command at this point by the people of these tribes, the Village recently occupied by them which is now in our hands will be entirely destroyed. All property within the village, such as tools, camp Equipage etc., will be preserved and taken up as captured property by Capt. G. W. Bradley, AQM, (Assistant Quartermaster) Chief Quartermaster of the Expedition.

Brevet Major General J. W. Davidson, Major, 2nd U.S. Cavalry, Acting Inspector General of the Department will take an accurate inventory of all species of property in the village, previous to its destruction.

Brevet Major General A. J. Smith, Colonel, 7th U.S. Cavalry, Commanding District of the Upper Arkansas, is charged with the execution of this order.

By Command of Major General Hancock
Signed: W. G. Mitchell
Captain and Assistant Adjutant General

Official Copy
W. G. Mitchell
Captain and Assistant General.[5]

The next day fire was set to the village and everything was burned excepting forty lodges, selected by General Hancock to be carried away as trophies. An old Sioux and a little girl, probably no more than ten years old, who had been atrociously outraged by Indian braves of the village, were found and taken to Fort Dodge. It has been charged that the girl was assaulted by troopers, but Custer reported that she was found badly injured. Within a few days after the troops left the fort, both captives died.

It was widely held then and now that Hancock was wrong in burning the Cheyenne village. The Cheyennes charged that the destruction of their lodges on the Pawnee Fork was the cause of the war that followed. In "My Life on the Plains," Custer quotes only the first paragraph of Hancock's field order, and comments, " . . .

This act of retribution on the part of General Hancock was the signal for an extensive pen-and-ink war, directed against him and his forces . . ." In the Philadelphia "Press," October 26, 1867, Colonel Wynkoop is quoted: "The Cheyennes had given me to understand recently that the destruction of the village by Hancock *was the cause of the war*. The Cheyennes have burned the plains all around us."

Conflict of opinion between the agents of the Indian Bureau and military officers continued. Wynkoop wrote to Washington that, ". . . Since the Indians of my agency have not yet retaliated for the wrongs heaped upon them, it may be possible, if proper action be taken by the Department of the Interior, to prevent the military from forcing trouble, that a general Indian war may be prevented." To make his case stronger against General Hancock, Wynkoop sent a list of articles destroyed in the Cheyenne village and the Sioux camps.

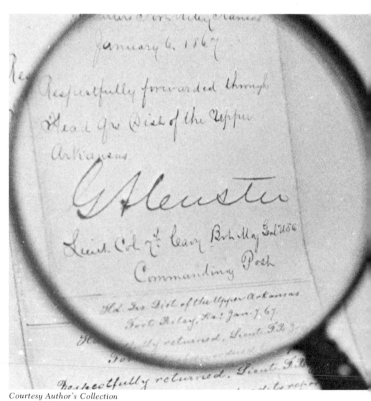

Courtesy Author's Collection

Custer's free scrawled signature was always predominant on written orders, autographed books, and letters to friends.

---

5. My Life on the Plains, G. A. Custer, Sheldon and Company, N.Y., 1874, page 42. (Original document in Dr. Elizabeth A. Lawrence collection.)

Map showing the scene of General Hancock's operations in the Indian Country, the Forts, Military Stations, Pacific Railroads, etc.

The Baltimore Gazette, Wednesday, June 5, 1867, published an item dated Washington, June 4:

The Commissioner of Indian Affairs has just received a dispatch from Superintendent Murphy, at Fort Leavenworth, Kansas, stating that the American Express Company have given the following instructions to their employees on the Smoky Hill route to Denver City: 'Every Indian that comes within shooting distance, shoot him. Show them no mercy. They will show none to you.' He also states that General Hancock has ordered his post commanders to shoot every Indian found north of the Arkansas and south of the Platte rivers. Superintendent Murphy calls the attention of the Commissioner to these orders, and says that the Cheyennes, Arapahoes and Sioux, by stipulations of treaties with the United States, have the privilege of roaming in this country until assigned to other reservations, and the consequences of these measures will be to inaugurate an interminable war with these tribes that will cost the Government hundreds of lives and millions of dollars to bring to a final adjustment.

Hancock's Kansas Expedition was estimated by the government at approximately $1,000,000.00 for active campaigning against Indians. With fourteen hundred men in the field for four months their accomplishments were: Burning of one empty Cheyenne village, and the killing of two Cheyenne Indians[6] at the Cimarron crossing. The absence of Custer's cavalry caused Hancock to give up any move across the Arkansas. The command marched by way of Fort Hays to Fort Hooper, the force was broken up and units sent to Forts Lyon, Dodge, Hays and Larned. A strong fort, well manned, would be built at Monument Station.

General Hancock planned a demonstration of military force in the spring of 1867. Actually his expedition had an effect which was opposite to the one that he intended. The Indians, further aroused and angered, fled the field to avoid another Sand Creek affair. In spite of the fact that Hancock engaged in no hostilities, his expedition left the plains in a fairly open state of war.

---

6. One Bear and Eagle's Nest — "Fighting Cheyennes," Grinnell, page 258.

CHAPTER THREE

FROM FLAMING PLAINS TO A
WINTER CAMPAIGN

After General Hancock retired from the field with his troops, Indian agents each asserted that his own tribe was innocent of any attacks on the overland stage routes, that it was others who burned the stations and killed the men in charge. All joined in denouncing Hancock for bringing on a general Indian war, and a pen and ink war developed between the two departments of the government that were dealing with Indians.

During the next three months, May, June and July, Custer led the Seventh Cavalry through Nebraska and Kansas, covering a thousand miles of scouting, purposes of which were to see what the Indians were doing; to hold parleys with chieftains in hope of a peaceful settlement; and to identify which bands were off raiding and who was leading them. Custer used much diplomacy with Indian councils, and the chieftains respected his methods. As time went on they also respected his bravery and the keeping of his word.

On the morning of June 26, 1867, Indians were reported running off stock from the

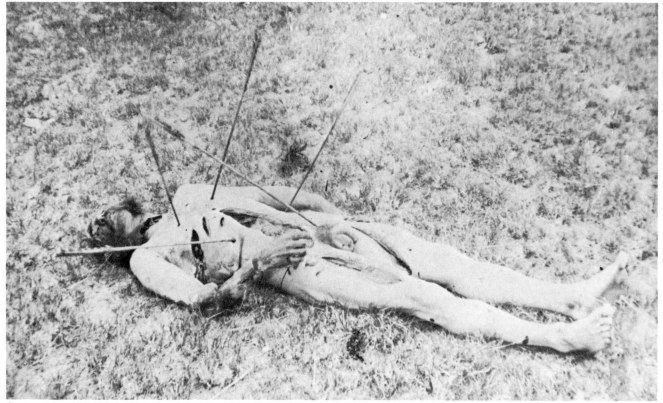

Courtesy Kansas State Historical Society

Typical example of Indian revenge. Sergeant Frederick Wyllyams, Company G, 7th U.S. Cavalry, was one of seven killed near Pond Creek Station, several miles from Fort Wallace, on June 26, 1867. Scalped twice, brained, throat cut, heart cut out, and body slashed. He was completely stripped of clothing.

Pond Creek Station, several miles from Fort Wallace. Troop G, 7th Cavalry, was sent to repulse the attack by Indians on the station and were soon caught up in a sharp fight. A description of the fight, from the Leavenworth Daily Conservative, July 10, follows:

GEN. WRIGHT'S EXPEDITION
THE ENGINEERS ON THE MARCH
They See "Lo" and "Lo" Shows His Hand
A Sharp Fight and the Indians Victorious
Out of 45 Men, 7 Killed and 5 Wounded
A Sergeant Scalped Twice, Brained, Throat Cut,
Heart Cut Out, and
Body Slashed to Pieces!

(From Our Special Correspondent.)
Camp No. 18, Ft. Wallace, Kansas
June 30, 1867

We arrived here on the 24th inst. . .
On the 26th they (the Indians) attacked Pond

Courtesy Custer Battlefield Museum
Greyhounds tied up outside Custer's tent near Fort Dodge in 1868. The sibley tent was adopted after the Indian tepee and used by Custer many times in the field, as compared to the wall tent. Note pet pelican at far right.

Creek Station, two miles from and in full view of the Fort (Wallace), and commenced running off the stage stock. Our cavalry escort went out in pursuit of them and soon got into a sharp little fight. Out of 45 men engaged we lost seven killed and five wounded. Our cavalry were driven back, the dead fell into the hands of the enemy, and the bodies were stripped entirely naked, and some of them horribly mutilated. Sergeant Wyllyams, Co. G, 7th Cavalry, was amongst the killed, he fought bravely, and out of revenge the savages cut him up terribly. He was scalped twice, and his brains knocked out, his throat cut from ear to ear, his heart cut out and carried away to be eaten, and his arms and legs slashed and gashed to the bone.[1]

Roman Nose and his band suffered heavy casualties, and early reports had Roman Nose killed, but this proved untrue. Soon after the fight, William A. Bell, a fellow countryman of Wyllyams, arrived and photographed the mutilated body. Only a few hours earlier, Sgt. Frederick Wyllyams had expressed a desire to help Bell print copies of photographs he had taken the day before. Bell had accompanied the expedition which was surveying a route west for the K.P. Railroad. The "greenhorns" who filled the ranks of the 7th Cavalry learned quickly that Indian warfare was serious business, and the sight of mutilated bodies would become a common experience.

During the hot summer of 1867, the Seventh Cavalry had another important fight with Indians, missed by Custer, to his regret. The command scouted the dusty plains for several weeks, subsisting on moldy hardtack, rancid bacon, beans and coffee, supplies drawn from Fort McPherson. When the rations became low, Custer sent a train of twelve wagons to Fort Wallace to draw supplies to sustain a lengthy scout. A mounted escort of forty-eight men, two officers, and a scout accompanied the wagons. On the way to Fort Wallace they encountered no Indians, but on the return trip with loaded wagons they were attacked by an Indian war party estimated at five

1. Leavenworth Daily Conservative, July 10, 1867, p. 1, c. 4; Kans. State Hist. Soc.

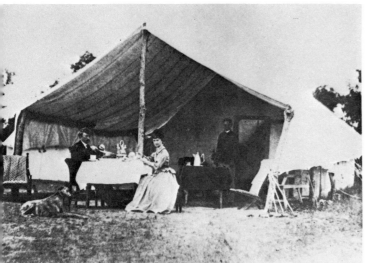

Courtesy Custer Battlefield Museum

There was plenty of game on the Kansas Prairie. Here on Big Creek, Custer is carving a prairie chicken. One of the greyhounds was constantly begging for scraps from the table.

hundred. Custer reported the attack by telegraph to Lieutenant General W. T. Sherman, Headquarters Army of the United States, as follows:

Headquarters Seventh U.S. Cavalry, Riverside Station, 40 miles west of Fort Sedgwick, July 6, 1867.

Lieutenant-General W. T. Sherman:

On the 24th inst., forty-five Sioux warriors attacked a detachment of this regiment under Captain S. M. Hamilton, near the forks of the Republican. Captain Hamilton's party, after a gallant fight, defeated and drove off the Indians, killing two warriors and wounding several others, his own party losing but one horse wounded. On the 26 inst., a war party of Sioux and Cheyenne combined, numbering between five and six hundred warriors, attacked and surrounded forty-eight men of this regiment, who, under Lieutenants S. M. Robbins and W. W. Cooke, Seventh Cavalry, were escorting my train of supplies from Fort Wallace. The Indians surrounded the train for three hours, making desperate efforts to effect its capture; but after a well-contested fight upon the part of Lieutenant Robbins, the Indians were repulsed with the loss of five warriors killed, several wounded, and one horse captured. Our injuries were but two men slightly hurt. The Indians were under the leadership of Roman Nose, whose horse was shot in one of the attempts to charge the train. At daylight on the morning of the 24th, a large band of Sioux warriors surrounded my camp, and endeavored to stampede my animals. My men

turned out promptly, and drove the Indians away without losing a single animal. One of my men was seriously wounded in the melee by a carbine shot.

To Captain Hamilton, Lieutenants Robbins and Cook, as well as their men, great praise is due for the pluck and determination exhibited by them in these their first engagements with hostile Indians.

G. A. CUSTER, Brevet Major-General[2]

Custer scouted in Kansas and Nebraska during the rest of the summer and longed to have his wife Libbie near him. Sherman granted approval of allowing Libbie Custer join her husband at a fort nearer to him. Custer had written to his wife suggesting she join a party going to Fort Wallace, and wait there till a wagon train could bring her the rest of the way but the letter miscarried. When Custer's supply train reached Fort Wallace, Lieutenant Cooke, who had been ordered to see that Libbie returned with him, found that she was not there but at Fort Hays. Cooke hurriedly rode to Fort Hays under escort, but General Hancock insisted that Mrs. Custer remain at Hays, fearing a possible attack on the wagons. His refusing Custer's young wife permission to leave the post possibly saved her life.

The wagon train, to Libbie's keen disappointment, left without her. Several months later Lieutenant Cooke told her that had she been with the train when the Indians attacked, it would have been his duty to shoot her, as directed by Lt. Col. Custer. Not believing Cooke at first, she asked whether she would have been given a chance for life. The tall slender Canadian explained that Custer had given all his officers instructions, should ever Mrs. Custer be under their escort when attacked by Indians, it was their duty to kill her immediately, taking no chances that she would fall into the hands of the Indians.

On June 29, 1867, Second Lieutenant Lyman S. Kidder, 2nd Cavalry, with a detail of 10 men from Company M, was given dispatches to deliver to Custer, believed

2. Army-Navy Journal, July 20, 1867; pg. 758.

camped at the forks of the Republican. Red Bead, a Sioux, was guide for the command. Kidder, inexperienced in Indian fighting, was twenty-five years of age, and a veteran of the Civil War. The 10 men under his command were mostly young boys, and about half of them foreign-born. Not knowing the fate in store for them, they set out on what was later termed as a "suicide mission."

Custer, meantime, had given chase to Pawnee-Killer, leading a band of several hundred warriors. An attempt to follow the Indians failed, as the Indian ponies outran and outdistanced the heavily burdened cavalry mounts. The command halted at the North Republican riverhead, near the South Platte in Colorado. Men dropped from their saddles under a hot July sun, and the animals groaned painfully for want of water. During the ordeal, many dogs, which accompanied the command as pets, died from thirst and exhaustion.

Custer telegraphed Fort Sedgwick for further instructions from General Sherman. He was told that Kidder had long since been sent by the Division Commander with letters of instruction. Custer reported that nothing had been seen of Kidder's detach-

ment, and requested telegraphic copies of the messages. General Sherman ordered Custer to march his command southward from the Platte to the Smoky Hill River, at Fort Wallace.

Temptations of mining towns and their saloons and the nearness of the overland route induced wholesale desertions from Custer's command, forty men leaving in one night. The deserters, knowing the country was infested with blood-thirsty hostiles, took their chances blinded by temptation of newly discovered gold fields. Their plot had been devised only the evening before, after orders had been issued to march at daylight. That morning, at 5 a.m., the column started out retracing their steps. There was no time to pursue the deserters and try to effect the capture of possibly a few. Chances were that Mr. Lo would have a few scalps before the day ended.

Custer's command marched southward until noon, having covered fifteen miles, then halted to rest and graze their horses. A group of men who plotted to desert with arms and horses had assumed that the halt was for the remainder of the day, and planned to slip away that night into the mountains. When orders were given to repack

Courtesy Custer Battlefield Museum
While the soldiers are preparing for another inspection, officers and civilians lounge on the Parade Grounds discussing the next field expedition. Near Big Creek, 1868.

Courtesy Custer Battlefield Museum
At either Fort Hayes, Kansas, or in camp near Big Creek, 1868.
General Custer, Elizabeth Custer and Captain Tom W. Custer.

and prepare to march in an hour, thirteen soldiers were seen leaving camp in the direction from which they had come. Six were dismounted and seven were riding off at a gallop. The boldness of this daylight desertion was a shock and a surprise to everyone. Desertion such as this, with their immediate officers watching, had never been heard of before.

Custer, seeing the fleeing men, shouted to Lieutenant Henry Jackson, Officer of the Day . . . "follow those men and shoot them and bring none in alive."[3] While Jackson was mounting his horse, Custer shouted orders to brother Tom, and Lieutenant W. W. Cooke, to follow suit. Major Joel Elliott swung into his saddle and took the lead, leaving Cooke and Tom some distance behind. Elliott was first to come within shouting distance of the men on foot, and ordered them to halt and lay down their weapons. Two of the deserters did so promptly and raised their arms. The third, Trooper Charles Johnson, swung about making a move with his carbine as if to fire. Elliott, a few yards off, thought the gesture to be threatening, spurred his horse to a gallop and rode into Johnson knocking him down, the weapon flying into the air. Cooke and Tom Custer arrived, jumped from their saddles and opened fire on the unarmed men. Johnson was hit twice, at least once while on the ground. Elliott galloped past, in pursuit of the mounted troopers. Shots from Cooke and Tom Custer found their marks on Bugler Barney Tolliver and Private Alburger. The bugler received one wound in the arm; Tolliver two wounds, one in the shoulder, the other in his side.[4] The fourth man flattened himself on the ground as the firing commenced and was not hit. Two other troopers moved out of the way of Elliott's horse as he raced by, but were later captured by a guard who accompanied the Officer of the Day.

Elliott and Jackson discontinued their pursuit of the mounted party of deserters, as they had gained too much ground to be captured. After returning, Elliott sent back for a wagon which arrived 45 minutes later and the wounded were loaded into it. When they returned to the column, men broke ranks and rushed to the wagon to see their wounded comrades. Custer ordered the gawking troopers to return to their places and form companies and prepare to move out. As the command resumed its march, the wagon with the wounded was ordered at the rear of the column in charge of Lieutenant Jackson. During the ten mile march, several men dropped from ranks to take their overcoats and blankets to the wounded men. Surgeon Coates testified at Custer's court-martial that he looked in on the wounded during the march and administered an

3. The Custer Court Martial, by Robert A. Murray (pg. 2) — Reprint, Wyoming State Historical Society.

4. Ibid.

opiate,[5] but Lieutenant Jackson, in charge of the wagon, insisted that he did not.

At night the command halted and tried to get water from a dried creek bed by digging deep into the sand. Coates said that he and Custer visited the injured men, and after examining their wounds, administered more opiates. He further states that Custer did not want anyone to know that he accompanied him. It was learned later that the wounds were not dressed until two days later, and Coates accepted full responsibility for this error.

Custer learned that more desertions were probable and he reacted swiftly by placing every available officer on guard duty with strict orders to shoot anyone who appeared outside the limits of his tent, after failing to answer a hail. The next morning, at roll call, everyone was present; in fact, from that moment on any thoughts of desertion were abandoned during the continuance of the expedition.[6]

Nothing had been learned of Lieutenant Kidder and his men, and no one could be sure which route he had taken. With concern growing day by day, Custer's officers consulted their scout, William Comstock. "Wild Bill" was frequently sought out by everyone, including Custer. With many years of experience in Indian fighting, he was the only one who might give some encouragement as to the possibilities of Kidder still being alive. Comstock gave his opinion to the concerned officers, "I'm told that the lootenint we're talkin' about is a new-comer, and that this is his first scout. Ef that be the case, it puts a mighty onsartin look on the whole thing, and twixt you and me, gentlemen, he'll be mighty lucky ef he gits through all right. To-morrow we'll

Courtesy Author's Collection

John Baird poses in Scouts costume, typical of the 1860 period. He cradles a Hawken .53 caliber rifle.

strike the Wallace trail, and I kin mighty soon tell ef he has gone that way."[7]

After Custer's column hit the Wallace trail, it was only a few miles before Comstock and the Delaware scouts discovered tracks by shod horses. "Well, what do you find, Comstock?" was Custer's inquiry. "They've gone toward Fort Wallace sure," Comstock reported. "The trail shows that twelve American horses, shod all around, have passed at a walk, goin' in the direction of the fort; and when they went by this p'int they were all right."[8]

5. Opiates; Medicines which procure sleep. (Sedatives) Reece's Med. Guide by Richard Reece, M.D.; Albert Colby & Sons, Baltimore, Md. (1873)

6. Life on the Plains, G. A. Custer; Sheldon & Company, N.Y., 1874, Page 73.

7. My Life on the Plains, G. A. Custer; Sheldon & Company, N.Y., 1874, Page 74.

8. Ibid., pg. 75.

As Custer's column rode on, something huge and strange looking appeared in their path, a mile ahead. A closer observation found it to be a dead horse. Further down the trail, another horse was found, also stripped of saddle and equipment. Continuing further, the scouts discovered shod tracks and pony tracks moving at a gallop. It was surmised that the Indians had gained no advantage over the small group and a running fight for life was most evident. The tracks led the scouts from the high plateau into a valley of tall grass and a shallow stream. Within a mile of the stream, the bodies of Lieutenant Kidder and his men were found.

Stripped of their clothing, mangled, brutally hacked and disfigured beyond recognition, lying in irregular order within a very limited circle were the remains of the men of Company M. Several bodies were lying in a bed of ashes, where the Indians had burned some of the troopers to death. Each was scalped, their heads bashed in, and the nose of each man was hacked off. All the bodies were pierced with many arrows (from twenty to fifty were counted). Empty cartridge shells were everywhere, and it was evident that Kidder and his little band of inexperienced Indian fighters had

fought to the end. Custer thought it fitting that the remains should be consigned to a common grave, and so a single trench was dug nearby and the grim task of burial proceeded in silence.

Arriving at Fort Wallace, Custer and his exhausted column found that the fort had been attacked several times, with casualties on both sides. All travel over the Smoky Hill route had ceased; stage stations were abandoned and stages were taken off the route. Mail and couriers had ceased to reach the fort, and communication seemed impossible. The fort and the immediate area was considered as undergoing a state of siege. As if the garrison did not have enough problems, cholera made its appearance, and death was a daily occurrence. Supplies were exhausted except for rancid bacon and hard-tack, left over from the Civil War. Fresh provisions were essential if the cholera epidemic was to be curbed. There were no supplies nearer than Fort Harker, two hundred miles away, to supply the garrison with the much needed fresh provisions.

At sunset, July 15, 1867, Custer left Fort Wallace with one hundred of the best mounted men to open the way to Fort Harker. Following the Smoky Hill stage route east, Custer planned to cover the 150

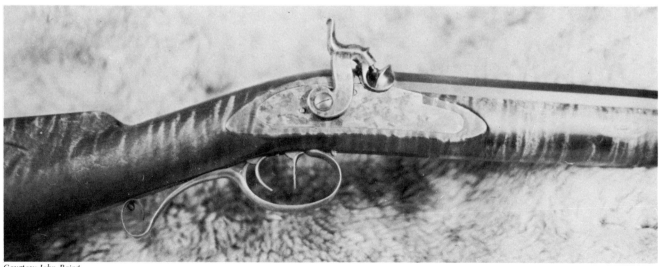

Courtesy John Baird

Close-up of Hawken "Big .50" half stock rifle.

miles to Fort Hays as rapidly as possible. After crossing this most dangerous route, he would continue to Fort Harker with a half dozen troopers, leaving Captain Hamilton to follow with the rest of the command. Because of the heavy marching of preceding weeks, the horses were generally in an unfit condition, yet serviceable. Custer hoped to have a train loaded with supplies at Fort Harker, and be ready to start back to Fort Wallace by the time Hamilton arrived with the rest of the column.

As cholera spread to Forts Larned, Harker and Riley, the death toll climbed rapidly. No one could pin-point the cause of this dreaded disease. Mass burials were many; coffins were make-shift and, toward the end, blankets were used to wrap the dead. The cholera epidemic was attributed to three causes: first, overcrowding; second, the accumulation of debris from recent great floods; and, third, bad whiskey. Along the Smoky Hill River and its tributaries were drifts, full of "rotten animals" and this, the Surgeons asserted, had affected the water which the men had to drink and use in their cooking. Modern medical science would agree that contaminated water would be a main cause.[9]

Cholera generally starts with noises in the head, vertigo, sickness, nervous agitation, colicky pains, discharge from the bowels, sickness of the stomach, slight cramps and decreased pulse. Sometimes these symptoms lasted for hours, at other times the patient would be struck down almost lifeless, without premonitory signs. When the disease is at its worst stage, there are cramps commencing at the fingers and toes, rapidly extending to the body. Eyes are sunken into their sockets, surrounded by a dark circle; there is vomiting and purging of a fluid resembling whey or rice-water; there is a wild and terrified expression on the face, which assumes a peculiar blue or

9. Army Navy Journal —, Aug. 10, 1867.

Courtesy U.S. Signal Corps photo (Brady Collection)
California Joe

Courtesy Nebraska State Historical Society
A rare tintype of Moses E. Milner, "California Joe," taken in Pioche City, Nevada in 1873. Pioche was a wide-open, roaring mining camp, shootings being so frequent "a man for breakfast" was a common expression.

leaden tint. Nails and fingers are the same color. The skin is cold, and the patient rolls about incessantly, as no position seems to relieve him. His voice has a peculiar sound and is almost gone, uttering a few words at a time. Breathing is sometimes short and wanting of air, but the mind is generally undisturbed. His only wish is to be left alone to die.[10]

Few garrisons had medical books or knowledgeable surgeons to cope with the situation. Folk remedies were at times administered, such as putting the patient's feet in hot ashes and water. Other remedies were taking ten grains of calomel and one of opium and covering up in bed with boiled ears of corn and hot bricks to induce sweating.[11]

The most effective way to check the epidemic was to catch it in its early stages. One belief has it that as nature has been aroused for its own protection, let no one interrupt or suppress this salutary process by administering such fluids as astringents, tonics, stimulants, and, above all, opium, brandy or wine. However, salt water fluids seemed best in most cases. With enough salt water (a pint of salt and water) swallowed, the patient will vomit the contents of his stomach; follow with 15 grains of calomel, and after four hours, an ounce of castor oil. By applying a hot bottle of water to the feet

10. Reece's Medical Guide, pg. 345 — Albert Colby & Sons — 1873.

11. Doctors of the American Frontier; Doubleday; pg. 189 (by R. Dunlop).

Courtesy Colonel Brice C. W. Custer

Custer's four trusted scouts, left to right: Will "Medicine Bill" Comstock, chief of scouts; Ed Guerrier, a half-blood Cheyenne; Thomas Adkins, a courier; "California Joe" (Moses E. Milner), chief of scouts, prospector, and Indian fighter.

and keeping the patient well covered with blankets, a gentle perspiration is started. With nothing in the stomach except cold water, the promonitory symptoms would pass, and all hazards of attacks are removed.[12]

When Custer became aware of the disease circulating among the forts, he became anxious to go to Fort Harker, where he assumed Libbie might be exposed to cholera. On July 19, 1867, at 2 A.M., Custer with his companions, brother Tom, Lieutenant Cooke and two troopers, reached Fort Harker, a ride of sixty miles in less than twelve hours. After telegraphing Fort Sedgwick, reporting the fate of Lieutenant Kidder and his group, Custer reported to Colonel A. J. Smith, telling him of the expected arrival of Captain Hamilton's column and the need for supplies for a return trip to Fort Wallace. There was no reason for Custer to await the train and escort, so he asked and received authority from Colonel Smith to visit Fort Riley, where he heard that Libbie had gone.

12. Reece's Medical Guide, Glossary of Medical Terms, Albert Colby & Sons, 1873, pg. 348.

Courtesy Author's Collection

McClellan saddle. Oil and lamp black helped to prevent rawhide from cracking but had to be constantly replenished.

Custer boarded the train for Fort Riley on the morning of July 19. Shortly after his arrival there, a telegram from Colonel Smith ordered him to rejoin his command immediately. Return by train was delayed for several days because of the Kansas Pacific Railroad's erratic schedule. Libbie Custer used what time they had together to enjoy every minute of her husband's stay. The torment of cholera and floods that had burdened their hearts were forgotten momentarily.

When Custer returned to Fort Harker, he reported to Colonel Smith as ordered, and found himself under arrest. The charges against him were: leaving Fort Wallace without permission, ordering his officers to shoot deserters, marching his men excessively, and abandoning two soldiers who were killed by Indians near Downer's Station. The charges made by Colonel Smith were instigated by General Hancock on the basis of complaints against Custer. Captain Robert M. West, 7th Cavalry, filed additional charges, based on the treatment of the deserters. Captain West had been ordered in arrest by Custer at Fort Wallace on charges of being drunk on duty and, for this, his actions may have been prompted. The most serious of the charges faced by Custer was that accusing him of ordering the shooting of deserters, one of whom, Private Charles Johnson, died of his wounds. Custer chose the religious Captain Charles Carroll Parsons, of the 4th Artillery, to assist in his defense. Custer felt justified in ordering his officers to shoot deserters, because of possible loss of many of his command while facing hostile Indians. Putting the fear of death into the men succeeded in stopping further desertions.

The court convened on Sunday, September 15, 1867, at Fort Leavenworth, Kansas. It was frequently interrupted by absences and illnesses. The active sessions totaled eleven days, and the findings were issued on October 11, 1867. Custer was found guilty on all charges but with exceptions to some of the specifications. He was sentenced to one year's suspension from duty with forfeiture of proper pay. It was considered that the lenient sentence was because of Custer's previous outstanding services.

Hancock was transferred in September, 1867, to General Sheridan's post in the South, and Sheridan became commander of the Department of the Missouri. When he arrived at Fort Leavenworth, he found Libbie and his old friend "Jack"[13] troubled as to their future. Sheridan turned over his quarters to the Custers in courtesy to his subordinate from the war days. Here the Custers spent the winter in idleness and quiet. Cold weather had put an end to hostilities, and the winter of 1867-68 was quiet.

Libbie and Autie entertained a circle of friends, some from war days, others within the command. Card games and piano playing accompanied with singing were evening entertainment. Tactics were often discussed by the men while the women impatiently looked on. Custer would select several atlases and with pencil outline the campaigns of Wellington and Napoleon, or discuss his own Civil War strategy. When talking of these matters, his thoughts and speech were so rapid that sometimes Libbie would be confused and interrupt, "General, is that an order or a request?"[14] While campaigning, Custer allowed himself the same rations as his men, adding nothing to the daily diet of hard-crackers, bacon and coffee. Autie's choice of food while in quarters was never a problem for Libbie and their black servant Eliza. His favorite was roast beef and horseradish, with a side order of stuffed apple dumplings. Even at "stateside" restaurants, he would never tire of the same dish.[15] When spring came,

they visited Libbie's home in Monroe, Michigan, renewing old acquaintances and visiting forgotten haunts.

While the Custers settled down to civilian life in Monroe, General Sheridan was already planning to beat the Indians at their own game. It was certain that the coming spring would bring a fresh campaign. "Little Phil" faced the threat of large scale outbreaks, even though the Medicine Lodge peace treaty had been signed the preceding fall. The treaty had set aside reservations south of the Arkansas River for the Cheyennes, Comanches, Kiowas, Arapaho and Lipan Apaches, clearing the way for railroad construction crews to lay track through the area bordered by the Arkansas and Platte rivers. Young blood was up, especially with the Cheyennes. They said the white man's treaties were worthless, that they had no right to take away their old lands. Perhaps a majority of the Cheyennes accepted the treaty, but chiefs did not have the right to speak for the minority group of the fraternity of Dogs who rejected any peace proposal. It was during this absence that many Cheyenne warriors fled north to join their Sioux allies harassing travelers on the Bozeman Road.

In the spring, when the grass was green and the ponies fat, the young warriors threatened to unleash a reign of terror against the whites for driving their families from their former hunting grounds. Telegraphs and dispatches were soon flashed from one command post to another. The warriors kept their word by striking the Saline and Solomon valleys, attacking wagon trains, burning homes, murdering men and ravishing women. The hostiles achieved what they set out to do, as scattered ranches and settlements were soon abandoned, and others fearful for their lives discontinued any travel in that immediate area.

General Sheridan held a series of command conferences at Fort Leavenworth in

---

13. The nickname "Jack" was given Custer by his close officers. It derived from his initialed luggage — "G.A.C."

14. E. B. Custer, Micro-film (Reed 4), Custer Battlefield, Mont.

15. Ibid.

early March. Companies and detachments of the 7th Cavalry, with enlisted replacements, were ready to go out to patrol stage routes, guard stations and scout areas around settlements. Winter rest and strict discipline brought the troopers into the field with new energy and anxiety for a long awaited patrol duty or scout. They all had a strong feeling of impending campaigning for the duration of the summer months.

Fort Larned, originally designed for the protection of the Santa Fe Trail, was located close to the Arkansas River. Here most of the peaceful Comanches and Kiowas assembled to receive the annuity goods promised them by the Medicine Lodge Treaty. Indian Agent E. W. Wynkoop, addressing the councilmen, told them that he could not issue the goods until the other tribesmen arrived. A large number of Cheyennes were still in the hills and not accounted for. The delay irritated the tribes and they became angry and restless. As Fort Larned housed only four companies of troops, the situation could become explosive. Agent Wynkoop was warned that if the annuities were not issued promptly, the so-called peaceful Indians would help themselves. Orders for a forced march reached the 7th Cavalry camp in mid-July. Leaving their tents standing, expecting a short absence, the command moved out for Fort Larned.

The 7th reached Fort Larned and went into a temporary camp near the post. Nearby the cavalrymen saw thousands of lodges, with Kiowas and Comanches shuffling about paying little attention to the arrival of the troops. Cheyennes and Arapahoes began to dribble in during the night, and Indian dogs kept a constant barking well into the morning. The arrival of a band of Cheyenne late-comers was heard from one end of the fort to the other, with their loud cries of lament for those of a war party who had not returned alive from a sortie against the Utes. That evening they held a scalp dance, honoring those who had shown valor against the enemy Utes. Dancing around a ritual fire council, the warriors enacted their battle as well as displaying captured relics adorned with fresh scalps.

Agent Wynkoop finally decided that his Indians were all in, and started to issue the eagerly awaited arms and ammunition to the supposedly peaceful plains dwellers. Food, tools, blankets, cooking gear, and hundreds of assorted items were distributed, much to the disapproval of army officers watching. It was seemingly senseless for one department of the government to give weapons to Indians who were potential enemies of another department. The Indian Bureau could explain that these people were hunters, and the weapons were needed to hunt buffalo and other game for food.

Army officers often asserted that the Indians were better armed that the soldiers. It is true that a few hostile Indians had standard weapons that the Army issued, but only after capturing them in skirmishes with the soldiers. Such captures were few, and ammunition for the newer models was hard to come by. What the Indians received from the Indian Bureau annuities were outmoded weapons, muzzle-loading rifles such as the Lancaster, manufactured in England in 1857; the Hawken percussion rifle, or the "St. Loui' Big .50"; early Springfield models; muskets with British proof marks, and a host of what is now known as "the Plains Rifle," a percussion gun either in a half or full stock. The flintlock was most useful to the Indian who might be far from trading posts. While percussion caps were not readily available, a flint could always be improvised for hunting or warfare.

The Indian gave little attention to the maintenance of his weapon. He left it neglected in the rain, dust, mud, and rarely cleaned it. When the stock was badly cracked or broken, he wrapped it with wet rawhide which when dried shrunk to a strong and usually satisfactory repair. Indians commonly used various sizes of brass tacks, making designs on both sides of the stock and forearm to induce good medicine. Mirrors were sometimes imbedded in the stock and might be used for sun signals.

After the big annuity issue, the Indians broke camp and disappeared, leaving the fort to its isolation. It was not long afterwards that the Cheyennes took to the warpath, raiding settlements on Walnut Creek and the Solomon River in Kansas. Indian chiefs and headmen protested they had no way to control the young headstrong warriors, and as the leaders disclaimed responsibility for the raids, they were charged by the Army with "practicing their well-developed act of cunning, deceit and deviltry."

Brevet Brigadier-General Alfred Sully moved out of Fort Dodge shortly after dusk on September 1, 1868, with an expedition including eleven companies of the 7th Cavalry, under the immediate command of Major Joel Elliott, three companies of the 3rd Infantry, several medical personnel and three citizen guides. Determined to punish the hostile Indians, he marched his punitive expedition south, deep into Indian territory. Marching the command out after dusk, Sully hoped to elude the eyes of any Indians who might be watching his movements from a distance. The General commanded his force while riding in an ambulance, a conveyance which everyone joked about after his defeat hastened him back to Fort Dodge.

With considerable success, Sully had fought plains Indians before, deep in the heart of Sioux country in Dakota, during 1863-64-65. Owing to this previous experience, the whole command looked forward to catching the perfidious warriors and whipping them soundly. Sully marched south and west with his cavalry and wagon-borne infantry, crossing the Arkansas River, into Indian territory toward the

Cimarron River, where they halted several hours before dawn. Pushing further on, in a southerly direction, with no Indians in sight, Sully believed he had succeeded in deceiving them. But when a small herd of buffalo was sighted, and several eager young officers went after the herd, they found themselves not alone in the hunt. A lone Indian, chasing the same herd, was equally surprised seeing the soldiers and sped away, dodging a few futile shots. The surprise the General had believed he had achieved by his stealthy approach had vanished as quickly as the fleeing warrior's pony.

Several days later, the command encamped at the confluence of Crooked Creek on the south side of the Cimarron River, unaware they had been surrounded by Indians. The next day, as the command was preparing to pull out, Captain Louis McLane Hamilton rode up to two soldiers who were some distance from the advancing column. Hamilton, who commanded the rear guard, reminded them of Sully's firm orders against stragglers. After leaving the two soldiers, Hamilton rejoined his own command for only a few moments, when screams from both stragglers were heard. Racing to the rear of the column, officers and a company of troopers saw both men scooped up by mounted Indians and carried off in the opposite direction. Gaining ground on the raiders, the company pressed forward, compelling the Indians to drop one of the wounded troopers. But before the pursuing soldiers could overtake the escaping foe, a mounted messenger caught up with the little troop with orders from General Sully to abandon the chase and return immediately to the forward command. The troopers halted in disbelief. To allow one of their men to be carried off by the enemy without any chance to rescue him was not soldier-like. From that day on, any regard for the General was expressed with salty comments, and the respect for all high ranking officers in general fell to a degrading level amongst the soldiers in the command. Later that day, after a halt, both men were allowed to be buried with full honors.

From September 11, and for five days afterward, Indians used hit-and-run tactics against the column, sniping from ambush during the day and showering the camp with arrows at night. During one of these engagements, Captain Keogh's horse was grazed by a bullet from a Comanche warrior. Keogh, impressed with the animal's steadiness under fire, decided to purchase the seven-year-old buckskin for himself, giving him the name of "Comanche."

The Indians that Sully faced were thought to be a mixed force of Kiowas, Comanches, Cheyenne Dog Soldiers and Arapahos, who were constantly aggravating the command with concentrated fire from behind one sand hill to another. Sully decided that it was useless and dangerous to pursue the warriors any longer. He would return to Fort Dodge and refit for another expedition. The wounded were cared for and the two men killed in the day's fighting were buried at the picket line, where the horses could trample down any signs of a grave being dug there. If found by Indians, the bodies would be dug up and scalped.

Sully's failure with the expedition, and the loss of respect by his men, had embittered General Sheridan, not only because of the abandoning of the two soldiers, but the overall supervision of the expedition. Sully's strategy lacked a great deal in planning, striking against the Indians when the grass was green and ponies able to outdistance the cavalry horse, demonstrated once more that any chance of combating the hostiles and bringing them to bay during the spring or summer campaigns was practically impossible. What Sheridan wanted was an experienced leader, with the energy and initiative to "bring the red fox in." After considering the records of several officers, Sheridan decided on Custer. He sent a telegram to Monroe, Michigan, which read:

General Sherman, Sully and myself and nearly all the officers of your regiment have asked for you and I hope the application will be successful. Can you come at once? Eleven companies of your regiment will move about the first of October against the hostile Indians, from Medicine Lodge Creek, toward the Wachita Mountains.
    P. H. Sheridan, Major General Commanding.

Custer did not wait for official orders from Washington, relieving him from the court-martial suspension. He immediately wired Sheridan that he would be on the next train to take command of the 7th. With a farewell kiss to Libbie, Custer boarded the train westbound with his luggage and his usual stag hounds. After ten months of forced vacation, Custer was eager to get back into action. Knowledgeable to the situation on the plains, Custer may have seemed puzzled with Sheridan's wire asking for him. Since winter was coming, either Sheridan was going to catch the Indians napping during the winter, or something else was in the breeze. Regardless what was before him, he was ready to accept anything just to be in the saddle again, chasing Indians.

On October 6, 1868, Custer rejoined his regiment as its field commander at camp on Bluff Creek near Fort Dodge. A freezing wind blew from the northwest, a forecast of coming wintry cold. Custer found the same low morale that he had to deal with a year before at Fort Wallace. Major Elliott, who had commanded the regiment since Custer's departure, was looked upon as a far less experienced leader. The men were poorly mounted and in shabby uniforms, and the failure of the summer campaign had left them disheartened.

Sheridan told Custer that he planned a winter campaign when heavy snows would slow down the warriors and their ponies would be too weak to travel. If the villages were hard hit and their supplies destroyed, the Indians would have to come into the reservations or starve. Sheridan's scouts deemed it impossible for the troops to survive such a winter expedition, but Custer approved the plan and was eager to march against the enemy.

Hostiles plagued the 7th's encampment by firing into tents and trying to scare off the horses. They were met with Spencer carbine fire, which sent the warriors off beyond carbine range. Late that night four columns left camp to scout the frozen upper streams, hoping to find the warriors' lodges. They turned up nothing, due mainly to the conduct of a whiskey-soaked scout called California Joe.

California Joe came into enduring fame through the writings of General Custer and his wife, Elizabeth. In "Life on the Plains," Custer described his first meeting with the scout near Fort Dodge in October, 1868, prior to the Washita Battle. A number of scouts were attached to the cavalry, each available separately to accompany detachments. One of their number, in this case California Joe, was designated Chief of Scouts.

In Custer's "Life on the Plains," he writes about the scout:

Being unacquainted personally with the merits or demerits of any them (referring to the scouts) the selection of a chief had necessarily to be made somewhat at random. There was one among their number whose appearance would have attracted the notice of any casual observer. He was a man about forty years of age, perhaps older, over six feet in height, and possessing a well-proportioned frame. His head was covered with a luxuriant crop of long, almost black hair, strongly inclined to curl, and so long as to fall carelessly over his shoulders. His face, at least so much of it as was not concealed by the long, waving brown beard and moustache was full of intelligence and pleasant to look upon. His eyes were undoubtedly handsome, black and lustrous, with an expression of kindness and mildness combined. On his head was generally to be seen, whether awake or asleep, a huge sombrero, or black slouch hat. A soldier's overcoat, with its large circular cape, a pair of trousers, with the legs tucked in the top of his long boots, usually constituted the make-up of the man whom I selected as Chief of Scouts. He was known by the euphonious title of "California Joe"; no other name seemed ever to have been given him, and no other name appeared to be necessary.

Custer seemed confident in California Joe on short acquaintance, but the mountain man was as much shocked by the appointment as the other scouts were in learning of his acceptance. Many were confident of their own appointment because of friendly association with officers close to Custer. After the official interview had opened, California Joe thought it proper to seek more intimate acquaintance. He frankly addressed Custer with a few questions of his own: "See hyar, Gineral, in order thet we hev no misunderstandin', I'd jist like ter ax ye, first, are ye an am'blance man or a hoss man?" Professing ignorance to the meaning of the question, Custer asked him to explain. "What I mean, do yer b'lieve in catchin' Injuns in am'blances or on hossback?"

"Well, Joe, I believe in catching Indians wherever we can find them, whether they are in ambulances or on horseback."

Courtesy U.S. Signal Corps photo (Brady Collection)
Nude Kiowa Girl

Changing position in his chair, California Joe inhaled deeply from his ash-caked briarwood pipe, which was in full eruption and belching smoke that seemed to bring tears to the General's eyes . . . "Thet ain't what I'm a-drivin' at. S'pose you're after Injuns and really want ter heve a tussel with 'em , would yer start after 'em on hossback, or would yer climb inter an am'blance and be hauled after 'em? Thet's ther pint I'm a headin' fer!"

Custer answered that he would prefer the first method, on horseback, providing he really desired to catch the Indians, but if he wished them to catch him, he would adopt the "ambulance system" of attack. "You've hit the nail squar' on the head!" said Joe, shaking a finger at the commander. "I've bin with 'em on the plains whar they started out after Injuns on wheels jist as ef they war goin' to a funeral in ther States, an' they stood 'bout as many chances uv catchin' In-

juns ez a six-mule team would uv catchin' a pack uv thievin' Ki-o-Tees, jes as much."[16]

California Joe's occupation as Chief of Scouts lasted about as long as a bottle of eastern whiskey would to a thirsty soldier.

Only weeks before the Battle of the Washita (November 27, 1868), four separate detachments were ordered to move on an all-night ride in search for indication of an Indian rendezvous. Each detachment numbered about one hundred cavalry, well mounted and well armed, with guides who knew the country well assigned to each. California Joe was assigned as Chief of Scouts. Ol' Joe, for the first few hours in the saddle, entertained his riding partner with tales of personal experiences with Indians, and episodes in mining life. Joe had a fondness for his canteen and was drawing upon it more than usual. Unknown to the officers riding with him, the canteen was filled with

16. Research Review; Vol. IV, Summer, 1970, No. 2, "Moses E. Milner or California Joe."

Courtesy Custer Battlefield Museum
Custer and his Osage Indian scouts camped near Fort Dodge in 1868. Pet pelican in front of guidon.

the worst brand of whiskey attainable on the frontier.

Perhaps Joe did not intend to indulge to that extent which might depose him from properly performing his duties, but he, like many other good men whose appetites for whiskey were stronger than their resolutions, failed in his reckoning. As the liquor took effect, Joe's independence increased until his mule, no longer restrained by his hand, slowly moved him away from the troops until the only part of the expedition which he recognized as important was himself and his mule. As the troops continued forward, none took notice of the disappearance of their Chief of Scouts. The troops had been marching constantly since leaving camp and some were almost sound asleep in their saddles when the column was halted shortly before daylight and the word was passed along that the advanced guard had discovered signs indicating Indians nearby. Every member of the command came alert, and any vestige of sleep disappeared. The advanced guard, consisting of a non-commissioned officer and a few privates, had reached a crest, and below them, in the heavy darkness, they could see several flashes of light. A party was chosen to crawl close to the enemies' camp and gather all information available. The Chief of Scouts was nowhere to be found. A search was made for him along both flanks of the column, but it was discovered he had not been seen for several hours. As the group of men was being selected to approach the supposed Indian village, a single rifle shot broke the stillness, followed by a most powerful howling and screaming, as if a terrible battle was taking place. Every carbine in the column was advanced and positioned for action. Charging wildly toward the column, now visible by the first rays of the sun, was California Joe. Shouting at the top of his voice, now almost hoarse in tone, he began striking wildly to the right and to the left as if beset by a whole tribe of warriors. It was good fortune alone that prevented him from receiving a volley before he was recognized. It took four men to pull California Joe from his mount and take from his hands a breech-loading Springfield[17] musket, from which he was inseparable. A Remington revolver and hunting knife were lifted from his waist belt. All efforts to quiet or suppress him proved unavailing until an officer ordered him bound hand and foot, and in this condition tied him to the back of his mule. In this sorry plight, the Chief of Scouts continued with the troops until their return to camp, where he was transferred to the guard house as a prisoner, for misconduct.

Sheridan was confident that his winter campaign would catch the Indians off guard. The cold weather would most certainly hold them in their villages. Their ponies would be thin and weak for lack of grass, and a surprise attack would have every chance of success. Sheridan's plan involved the operations of three columns: Colonel Andrew W. Evans with six troops of the 3rd Cavalry and two companies of the 37th Infantry were to march from Fort Bascom, New Mexico, and establish a supply depot at Monument Creek, then continue a scout along the Canadian and the North Fork of the Red River until they reached Red River, which was the boundary of the Department of the Missouri.

Seven troops of the 5th Cavalry under the command of Major Eugene A. Carr were to march southeast from Fort Lyon, Colorado, and make contact with Captain William H. Penrose and his column of five troops of cavalry, then scout toward Antelope Hills, along the North fork of the Canadian River.

The third column was to march from Fort Dodge under the command of General Sully, and move southward, establishing a cantonment at the fork of Beaver Creek and Wolf Creek. This column was made up of

---

17. This term was still being used — reference made to the 50/70 1866 Mdl. converted.

eleven troops of the 7th Cavalry and five companies of the 3rd Infantry. The 19th Kansas Volunteer Cavalry which was organized at Topeka, Kansas, was ordered to join the column at Camp Supply. The time set for all the columns to march was November 1; however, owing to many delays in getting supplies, the departure date was changed to November 12.

Several hundred recruits had recently joined the 7th, as well as a large number of green horses. This meant intensive training and drill to prepare the regiment for the winter campaign. Custer ordered target practice twice a day. He selected forty sharpshooters and placed them under Lieutenant Cooke.[18] Scouts, interpreters and couriers included a party of Osage Indians, led by their chiefs, Hard Rope and Little Beaver, many of whom had served with the cavalry on other expeditions. California Joe and Jack Corbin were employed as scouts, interpreters and couriers. Custer always referred to his scouts as the "eyes and ears" of the Seventh Cavalry.

Custer was anxious to catch the Indians napping. He called his scouts together and promised a bonus of one hundred dollars from his own pocket to the first man to lead the regiment to a hostile village. White scouts, hired by the government, were paid seventy-five dollars a month, and a bonus similar to the one Custer offered was not altogether an uncommon practice by officers.

In organizing his men for the winter campaign, Custer set about in assigning horses to companies by color, including gray horses for the band.[19] Winter clothing was issued and Custer equipped himself with special overshoes made of buffalo hide, heavy woolen underclothing, topped off with a buckskin shirt and trousers. A heavy buffalo overcoat and a beaver cap hid any

insignia of rank. With a rough scrappy beard beginning to show, Custer lost his usual dapper image. On November 12, 1868, General Sully's column of infantry, cavalry and four hundred wagons moved out, Custer's cavalry scouting ahead. On the sixth day Sully halted at a favorable camp site with an abundance of undisturbed pasture on Wolf Creek, at its confluence with the Beaver. A mile from this point, a site was staked out and named Camp Supply.

For the next few days the troops were busied in building stockades, construction of a blockhouse, and digging wells. Pits, four and one-half feet deep and walled with cottonwood logs, with a roof covering of logs, hay and earth, formed comfortable quarters for the men. The cavalry, working side by side with the infantry in construction of the camp, voiced no discontent. Their stay would be brief and their mission dangerous soon enough, without altercation amongst their own.

The expected arrival of the 19th Kansas Volunteer Cavalry to join the expedition provoked a dispute over rank between Custer and Sully. The Kansas regiment was raised by Governor Samuel J. Crawford, who took the field as its colonel. Both Sully and Custer were lieutenant colonels in lineal rank, but Army Regulations provided that brevet rank takes effect in commands or detachments "composed of different corps."[20] Sully, who had been serving in his brevet rank as brigadier general both as member of the Indian Peace Commission and as district commander, issued an order assuming command of the expedition. This order Custer disputed as he held the rank of brevet major general. When General Sheridan arrived at Camp Supply (escorted by

---

18. Expenditure for target practice did not come about for another 10 years or so, and was probably paid out of the officers' pockets.

19. Every man was furnished by Ordnance Dept. with a horse cover made from condemned canvas. — "Ten Years with Custer" by Capt. John Ryan, Newton Circuit, Mar. 19, 1909.

20. *Revised Regulations for the Army of the United States, 1861*, par 10, p. 10; Articles of War, Art. 61, p. 508. Sully had been commissioned major general of volunteers at the close of the Civil War but this rank became of no effect after discharge of Civil War volunteers. Custer had commissions both as brevet major general of volunteers and brevet major general. The second rank had permanent status in the Regular Army as had Sully's as brevet brigadier general.

two companies of the 19th Kansas), he settled the dispute by returning Sully to his district command at Fort Dodge (as brevet brigadier general) and appointing Brevet Major General George A. Custer to command the expedition. Ironically, the 7th Cavalry was almost immediately detached for the Washita expedition under command of Lieutenant Colonel Custer, and the expedition was not reassembled until the following spring.

From the diary of W. S. Harvey, blacksmith, Troop K, 7th Cavalry, the following:

We were grazing the horses in the sand hills on that day when, in the afternoon, orders came to return to camp at once and prepare for thirty days campaign. It is my recollection that three wagons were assigned to each troop, this for convenience for picket line — one for troop mess, etc., one for officers' mess, extra ammunition, etc., and one for forage. Baggage was limited to necessities.

November 23rd — Reveille at 3 o'clock. Snowed all night and still snowing very heavy. The darkness and heavy snowfall made the packing of the wagons very difficult, but at dawn the wagons were assembled in the train and daylight found us on the march, the band playing, "The Girl I Left Behind Me," but there was no woman there to interpet its significance. The snow was falling so heavily that vision was limited to a few rods. All land marks were invisible and the trails were lost. 'We didn't know where we were going, but we were on the way.' Then General Custer, with compass in hand, took the lead and became our guide.[21]

Courtesy Custer Battlefield Museum
Custer's dress at the Washita was buckskins, fur cap, and a full scrubby beard.

Much discomfort was felt by the men as large snowflakes fell lazily and melted almost immediately. All were wet to the skin. Luckily, there was no wind to drift the snow or freeze the wet clothing. The snow did create problems for the horses, however, as the snow balled on their feet, causing floundering and adding to the fatigue of travel. The column arrived at Wolf Creek about two o'clock with the wagon train far behind. Horses were unsaddled, and the men gathered fuel for fires. The valley was alive with rabbits, and soon all messes were supplied with rabbit stew. Everyone tried desperately to protect their rawhide McClellan saddles, partially soaked from the heavy snow. Unequal drying would warp the saddle trees, which would split at the seams, causing many sore backs on animals and raw buttocks on the troopers.

On the 24th, the skies cleared and the weather turned warmer. During the night the snow had ceased, but it had accumulated to a depth of eighteen inches, sagging many tent roofs, covering everything in sight. During the march of approximately eighteen miles, many of the men became snowblinded because of the reflection of bright sunshine glaring on the snow. Many deer were seen, but they were too swift to bag. A few buffalo were killed along with

21. "Some Reminiscences of the Battle of the Washita" —; Gen. E. S. Godfrey — Cav. Journal — Oct., 1928.

many rabbits. They camped that night on Wolf Creek.

November 25 found the column marching up Wolf Creek, then turning in a southerly direction toward the Canadian. The peaks of Antelope Hills loomed up before them and served as their marker for the rest of the day. Camp was made late that evening on a small stream about a mile from the Canadian. Tired men slid from their horses and bedded down almost immediately, some forgoing their warm meal. Others dried out socks and clothing before small camp fires. Wood was becoming scarce. Many soldiers

making a trip to the quartermaster sergeant's wagon for an armful of wood were turned away. The lookout for fuel on the march had been neglected and wood for tomorrow's camp would be even more scarce. A number of horses and mules were brought in late that night, totally exhausted from the day's march, and if they would not show any improvement by morning, they would be destroyed.

At daybreak, November 26, troops G, H and M, commanded by Major Elliott, found an Indian trail distinctly marked in the snow, estimated as made by a hundred war-

Courtesy Herb Peck, Jr.

Kiowas and Cheyennes. Left to right: Kiowa — Cheyenne and two Kiowa braves.

riors. Although some snow had fallen on the trail, it was calculated that the tracks were scarcely twenty-four hours old. A scout was sent to Custer, reporting the Indian tracks. Custer sent the scout back to Elliott with a hasty message, ordering Elliott to follow the trail until 9 P.M. and then wait until the rest of the command could catch up. In the meantime California Joe was given the task of finding a ford along the Canadian for the wagons to cross, as the river was rising rapidly with swift currents and floating ice. The cavalry crossed first, then the wagons rushed through without halting, to avoid bogging down in quicksand.

While the wagons made the cross over, Custer and a number of officers went to the top of the hills to view the surrounding countryside. Suddenly they were caught up in a cloud of frozen mist, and looking up in astonishment, they saw the sun surrounded by three ellipsoids with rainbow tints, the axis marked by sundogs, except for the third or outer ellipse, which seemed to hover below the horizon. This glorious sight was not visible to the troops below.

Soon after the courier's hasty departure to Elliott, Custer ordered Officer's call and reported the news. Eighty men were to be left with the wagons and the rest were to march at once. One wagon was assigned to each squadron (two troops); another to Troop G and the teamsters, and one to headquarters. To the quartermaster, Lieutenant James M. Bell, one ambulance was assigned. Every trooper was ordered to carry one hundred rounds of ammunition, coffee, hard bread, and overcoat, but no blankets. The men were to bivouac in the snow with just these bare necessities. The troopers were armed with Spencer metallic cartridge magazine carbines and the Colt revolver taking paper cartridges and caps. The men seemed to take on a different attitude as they prepared for the march. Old "Iron Ass" Custer had caught something in the wind. He was moving around camp faster than he did on any

normal day, and it was obvious with the additional rounds of ammunition assigned that a scrap wasn't too far off.

Weak horses were selected to pull the wagon train, commanded by the Officer of the Day, Captain Louis M. Hamilton, a grandson of Alexander Hamilton. Horses with more stamina would be able to stay with the attacking force. Hamilton was distressed because he would be left behind with the wagon train. He pleaded with Custer to change his assignment but was refused unless he could find an officer to exchange with him. Lieutenant E. G. Mathey, suffering from snowblindness, agreed to take Hamilton's place.

The weather turned warm as the regiment moved forward to intercept Elliott's trail. Horses slipped in mud and slush, almost toppling at times. Dogs accompanying the command strayed off the muddy trail, yapping and barking at fleeing rabbits. Custer was disturbed by the racket the dogs were making and sent orders to have it stopped. The noise would surely start up the Indian dogs and alarm the camp. According to the narrative of John Ryan (a trooper who accompanied the march), Custer had to destroy two of his own staghounds because of their persistent barking.

One dog in my company, of whom the men were very fond, was a little black dog called Bob, and as harmless as a kitten. We had to part with him, and one of our men drove a picket pin into Bob's head and he was left for dead. After that engagement was over and several days had elapsed, that dog joined us and the men cured him and brought him back to Kansas.[22]

The snow was now a foot deep on the plains. The horses were beginning to tire from breaking the hard upper crust of frozen snow. At 9 P.M., the regiment overtook Elliott who had halted near a stream in a timbered area. Horses were unsaddled, fed

22. The Newton Circuit; April 2, 1909; "Ten Years with Gen. Custer," by Capt. J. Ryan.

and rubbed down; fires were lighted but concealed as much as possible. Coffee was soon bubbling, and the men commenced breaking 'hardbread' with the butts of their pistols. After an hour's rest, orders were given to saddle horses with as little noise as possible. No matches were to be struck by smokers, and loud talking was forbidden. Little Beaver dismounted and with another tracker led out, followed by Indian and white scouts, with Custer riding near the advance. The cavalry trailed a half a mile behind, plagued with the crunching noise of frozen snow that could be heard a considerable distance away.

After several hours of tracking, the scouts hurried back to the command and a halt was ordered. Little Beaver had smelled smoke. Custer ordered the scouts to advance cautiously, carefully examining the area, while the cavalry slowly followed. A small camp fire was soon found still smouldering, and it was deduced by the Indian scouts that small boys had been trying to keep warm while herding and grazing the ponies. It was estimated that the Indian village was ahead two or three miles, and the scouts took up the trail once more. By now, the moon had risen, illuminating the surroundings, making it fairly easy to follow the trail. Above the steady crunching of ice and snow beneath shod hoofs an occasional cough from a trooper or a muffled sneeze broke the frigid air. Everyone tried to follow in the tracks of the one ahead, making the least noise possible. The wagons were still some distance behind.

Upon nearing a rise, an Osage tracker crawled to the crest to reconnoiter the area before him. On returning, he crouched close to the ground and rejoined the others to report what he had seen. On a return trip from one crest, Little Beaver reported to Custer, "Heaps Injuns down there."[23] Custer was soon peering over the same crest, taking the same precautions as his tracker.

Custer could only see what looked like a herd of animals off in the distance, and turning to Little Beaver asked him why he thought Indians were there. "Me heard dog bark,"[24] was the scout's reply. As both listened intently for several moments, they heard the distinct bark of a dog, followed by the tinkling of a bell, indicating a pony herd, and then the distant cry of an infant.

Custer was satisfied that the Indian camp lay before him, he was also satisfied that the troops were still undiscovered. It was past midnight when Custer assembled his officers. He asked each to remove his saber, so its rattling would not attract attention, and join him at the crest where the situation could be studied and action planned. Upon returning to the troops awaiting less than a mile from the crest, Custer explained his plan of attack and assigned squadron commanders their duties and positions.

Major Elliott was to take Troops G, H and M, and march around to the rear of the village, approaching from the northeast as determined by the lay of the land. Captain William Thompson with Troops B and F was to strike well to the right of the trail, approaching from the southeast, and connect with Elliott. Captain Edward Meyers, with E and I, was to approach from the southerly direction. Lieutenant Bell's wagons, along with Captain Frederick W. Benteen and his squadron, were to halt several miles down the trail to await the outcome. Soon Captain Benteen and his squadron were instructed to join the forward command and Lieutenant Bell was told to hold the wagons at that point until he heard the attack, which would commence around daybreak.

Custer and his four companies, A, C, D and K, moved silently into place, with Lieutenant Cooke's sharpshooters dismounted and close in advance. The four troops were divided into two squadrons, Captain Robert M. West on the right of the

---

23. "Life on the Plains" — Custer — pg. 158.

24. Ibid.

standard and guard, and Captain Hamilton on the left. Directly behind Custer and his staff was the regimental band, mounted on horseback and ready to sound off as the troops charged into battle. Many of the scouts, including California Joe, feared that the village was larger than estimated, and that the chances of a surprise attack were slim. There was no firm knowledge of the enemy's strength or the size of the village, as trees along the river bottom hid much of the encampment. How far along the frozen Washita[25] did the village spread? Custer did not know, but he had followed the trail of a war party to this village, and he had caught them napping.

The Osage scouts put on death paint, as was their custom before charging the enemy, using "fire paint" which is red. It was applied with the left hand all over the face. They chanted prayers, "As the fire has no mercy, so should we have none." Mud was then applied on the cheek, below the left eye, as wide as two or more fingers. Then each pony was painted with some of the same mud, on the left cheek, shoulder, and thigh. The war chant continued in low tones among the Osages as the white scouts looked on.[26]

Custer's strategy during the Civil War had been based on surprise attack, often regardless of numbers. Here, as well as at the Little Big Horn, eight years later, he divided his command to attack simultaneously from different directions. The village was partially surrounded, and no alarm had been given. As the dogs below continued their furious barking, it seemed possible that the village had been abandoned. The night was bitter cold, the men huddled in whatever shelter they could find, throwing the capes of their overcoats over their heads to shield them from the sharp winter breeze. Orders were issued for the men not to stamp their feet or swing their arms to step up circulation because of the possibility that the noise would be heard and attract the dogs. Some troopers kept active by checking their weapons, bridles and saddle girths several times to occupy the dragging hours till dawn. As the dawn broke through a wintery mist, orders were passed along to remove overcoats and haversacks, leaving one man in each company to load them into the wagons when Lieutenant Bell came up. At a little before sunrise, Custer ordered his men to mount and take their formation. Slowly the command marched over the crest of the ridge, hoofs breaking the snow crust at a walk, and advanced some distance toward a lower ridge. The dogs in the village continued their furious barking.

Suddenly an Indian emerged from one of the lodges, ran to the bank of the Washita, looked about and then fired his rifle into the air. It was later stated that the Indian had seen a trooper raise his rifle to take aim, beginning the Battle of the Washita. Upon hearing the rifle report, Custer turned to his bandmaster and shouted, "Give us Garry-Owen."[27] The first few notes of that rollicking march sounded across the valley and echoed back from opposite sides, but by the time the band had played one strain from GarryOwen, their spittle froze the instruments. Only the bugles sounding the charge and cheers from the entire command filled the air.

As the Indians ran from their lodges, terror stricken, some escaped toward the upward creek bank, others took refuge behind trees and logs. The Spencer carbines boomed, the pistols cracked, and the terrified pony herd thundered past lodges intermixing with warriors and racing past the bluecoats. It was hard to determine whether

25. In Cheyenne, Washita means "Lodge-pole" (O-Ke-a-a): Thirty-three Years Among Our Wild Indians, by Col. R. I. Dodge; Archer House, Inc., N. Y.

26. Annual Report of the Bureau of Ethnology; J. W. Powell, 1888-89, pg. 632. (Government Printing Office, 1893.)

27. "Life on the Plains" — G. A. Custer; Sheldon & Co., N. Y., 1874 — Pg. 163. Custer cites the title as "Garry Owen." See Boots & Saddles, E. B. Custer; N.Y., one word "Garryowen." "Of Garryowen in Glory," Lt. Col M. C. Chandler; 1960, we find "GarryOwen."

an Indian was knocked over by one of the ponies or had fallen from a wound received from the troopers' fire. Custer could hear his sharpshooters discharging their rifles with deliberate accuracy. The Indians began to return the fire with bullets and arrows from every direction. From sink holes and depressions warriors grouped to stand off the charging soldiers. Their raking fire was both deadly and accurate. Custer ordered his sharpshooters to clean them out, and, within a short time, seventeen warriors were killed in one depression. Those who sought only freedom raced toward the scattering pony herd trying to mount for a hasty exit. Only a few were successful. The screams of Indian women and children fell on the troopers' ears, and yelping hounds seemed everywhere and in everyone's way. The wild rush of charging troopers through the village was met by the defiant war cry of half-naked Cheyennes, as they leaped from their lodges, evidently awakened from a sound sleep. Those who fell wounded were at the mercy of steel shod hoofs spattering everything with mud, slush and human blood.

Lieutenant Bell, upon hearing the firing, rushed his teams forward to join the command. While loading the overcoats and haversacks into the wagons, he was attacked by a superior number of Indians and the greater part of the duffel was abandoned, but his arrival with the reserve ammunition was warmly welcomed. Custer noticed that Captain Hamilton had disappeared. Tom Custer was seen having his hand bandaged while holding a pistol in the other. While the fighting was still going on, Custer detailed men to round up the pony herd. A field hospital was established among the lodges with Captain Henry Lippincott, Assistant Surgeon, in charge. The surgeon had his own problems. He stumbled about with his hands over his eyes, suffering intense pain from snowblindness.

Major Elliott spotted a group of dismounted Indians escaping downstream and asked for volunteers to overtake them. Regimental Sergeant Major Kennedy and nineteen others responded,[28] and as the detachment swung into their saddles, Major Elliott turned and waved his hat to Lieutenant Owen Hale, standing nearby, and called, "Here goes for a brevet or a coffin." That was the last Hale saw of Elliott and his party.

Custer dismounted and entered the make-shift hospital to check on the wounded. Dr. Morris J. Asch was bending over and administering first aid to a trooper who was seriously wounded. Custer was soon advised of the death of Captain Hamilton, shot through the back. Custer was about to leave when he saw four troopers carrying another troop commander in a blanket into the hospital. It was Captain and Brevet Colonel Albert Barnitz, shot through the body near the heart with a rifle bullet, and in serious condition.

Custer's orders were to avoid killing of any but fighting men,[29] but the women were as dangerous an adversary as the warriors, and young boys between the ages of ten and fifteen were expert in the use of weapons and determined to count coup. Captain Benteen, after trying to take a youngster prisoner, was shot at by the lad several times, wounding the officer's horse in the neck. Benteen had no alternative but to kill the boy to save himself. An elderly woman bolted for a depression to hide with a captured white boy, but before any soldiers could snatch the boy from her, she drew a butcher knife and disemboweled the youngster. Before she dropped the gasping lad, several troopers shot at her, taking half her face away.

Lieutenant E. S. Godfrey, of Troop K, wrote in his reminiscences, "With Custer at the Battle of Washita":

---

28. There has been some doubt as to the number of men for this detail. See "Life of G. A. Custer" — by Jay Monaghan — footnote, Pg. 320, Chap. 23.

29. Life on the Plains, G. A. Custer; Pg. 164; Sheldon and Company, N. Y., 1874.

After passing through the village, I went in pursuit of pony herds and found them scattered in groups about a mile below the village. I deployed my platoon to make the roundup and took a position for observations. While the roundup was progressing, I observed a group of dismounted Indians escaping down the opposite side of the valley. Completing the roundup, and starting them toward the village, I turned the herd over to Lieutenant Law who had come with the second platoon of the troop and told him to take them to the village, saying that I would take my platoon and go in pursuit of the group I had seen escaping down the valley... I discovered a lone teepee, and soon after two Indians circling their ponies. A high promontory and ridge projected into the valley and shut off the view of the valley below the lone teepee. I knew the circling of the warriors meant an alarm and rally, but I wanted to see what was in the valley beyond them ... Arriving at and peering over the ridge, I was amazed to find that as far as I could see down the well wooded, tortuous valley there were teepees — teepees. Not only could I see teepees, but mounted warriors scurrying in our direction.[30]

Godfrey and his platoon were charged by the hostiles, but by deploying his men as skirmishers, he fought off the warriors. After the Indians left, Godfrey and his platoon raced back to the village where mop-up actions were diminishing, and reported to Custer. When the words "big village" were mentioned, Custer exclaimed ... "What's that?"[31] and put Godfrey through a series of questions. At the end, Godfrey indicated that he had heard firing in one of the valleys during his return to the village which continued long after he had arrived back with the remainder of his platoon. At first the shots seemed to indicate a constant battle, and then, after a short lull, the firing became heavier, lasting nearly all day.[32]

Godfrey was again questioned by Custer about the Indian village. At the end of the inquiry, Godfrey mentioned that he had heard that Major Elliott had not yet returned and suggested that the firing may have been an attack on Elliott's party. "I

hardly think so," Custer said slowly, as he thought for a moment . . . , "as Captain Meyers has been fighting down there all morning and probably would have reported it."[33]

Custer called Romeo, his scout, to question the women prisoners concerning the village reported by Godfrey. He ordered Troop K to destroy all Indian property with no carrying off of loot. Many soldiers had already gone through the lodges and come up with unusual items. Daguerreotypes of family groups and portraits were among the loot found, along with letters, clothing, mirrors, bits of flat metal, weapons and colorful cotton quilt bedspreads from farm settlements. Brims from the crowns of eastern felt hats and been cut away, and saved for making a war bonnet or other headpiece.

Custer was saddened by the report that his staghound 'Blucher' was found dead, shot through with an arrow, near the place where Lieutenant Bell was attacked and forced to leave some overcoats and haversacks captured by the hostiles.[34] Libbie would also be saddened and Autie would tell her of this brave dog chasing after the enemy while the command was attacking the village. He had been with Custer on many expeditions, and his loss was almost like that of one of the family.

Meanwhile Indians from the other camps down the river had begun to display a menacing front. Low in ammunition, the command must not be cut off from their main supply at the wagon train. Custer asked Romeo to assemble the captured women and children, some sixty in all, and place them in view of the gathering antagonists, with the hope that the hostiles would not fire endangering their own people. Custer realized that it would be but a matter of hours before the warriors from the farthermost villages would join the attack.

30. E. B. Custer microfilm, Reel 6 No. 6088; Custer Battlefield Hist. Museum. This account was written long after the battle by E. S. Godfrey for the Cavalry Journal.
31. "Some Reminiscences of the Battle of the Washita," by Gen. E. S. Godfrey, Cavalry Journal, October, 1928.
32. Ibid.
33. Ibid.
34. "Life on the Plains" — G. A. Custer — Pg. 173.

Custer abandoned the idea of saving all the ponies he had captured. He allowed the women to choose ponies to ride in retreat from the village. Each commissioned officer was allowed two ponies from the herd, and captured mules were hitched to the wagons to replace the ones played out. Lieutenant Godfrey was ordered to kill all ponies except those authorized for use and those given to the scouts. Godfrey and his troop tried to rope the animals and cut their throats, but the ponies were so frightened that this was almost impossible. Godfrey asked for help to shoot the ponies as his men tired of fighting the vicious animals. Four or five companies surrounded the herd to shoot them. During the killing of the eight hundred ponies, the hostiles, who had been watching from the furthest hill slopes, had disappeared. Apparently they realized that any shooting might endanger the women and children.[35]

John Ryan, of M Troop, noticed that his $14 overcoat which he had kept with him was covered with blood from an Indian scalp he had taken. He tore the scalp away from the saber hook it hung from and threw it to the ground. Ryan had taken the first Indian scalp for M Troop along with another trophy, a muzzle-loading buffalo gun made at Lancaster, Pennsylvania, of the style issued to Indians for hunting purposes. Lieutenant Owen Hale, company commander for M Troop, asked Ryan why he discarded the Indian scalp. Surely, after going through what he did to get it, it was considered an honor on that occasion. The trooper growled about his ruined overcoat, turned and marched away.[36]

Trumpeter John Murphy, while pursuing the Indian ponies with Troop M, saw a lone Indian fleeing and gave chase. Suddenly, the warrior stopped in his tracks, turned, and let fly an arrow at the trooper. Murphy threw himself to one side of the saddle to escape the arrow, but not being quick enough, it struck him in the right side, entering in an upward position and penetrating several inches. If Murphy had stayed erect in his saddle, the wound would have

35. Reminiscences of the Battle of the Washita, Godfrey, Cavalry Journal, October, 1928.

36. Ten Years with Gen. Custer Among the Indians; J. Ryan, Newton Circuit, April 2, 1909.

Courtesy Custer Battlefield Museum
Cheyennes, mostly women and children, captured during the Battle of the Washita, and concentrated at Fort Dodge, Kansas.

been fatal. The arrow was withdrawn quickly by a comrade, possibly saving the trumpeter's life. An arrow shot into the body must be withdrawn immediately, or the head will remain. Steel points were usually glued to the tips of war arrows by the warriors to prevent the extraction of these points. When the arrow enters the body, the glue, becoming softened with blood, readily detaches the head from the shaft.[37]

A detail from each company was assigned to destroy the Indian lodges. Lodge poles were hauled down and the hides fell to the ground. As most of the lodges had fires inside, the hides would start burning almost immediately. There were many explosions from stores of black powder inside the lodges. General Custer and several other officers selected trophies for personal collections, while the remaining stores were destroyed. Colorfully decorated bridles, saddles and beaded moccasins were among items taken by the officers. A dispatch case with orders from General Sheridan was found and given to Custer.[38]

Romeo assembled the prisoners so that Custer could speak to them with the scout acting as interpreter. The 'big chief,' as Indians referred to all officers, assured them of kind treatment, but they must accompany the command as prisoners. Custer gathered much valuable information from the women as to what chiefs were in command and which band of hostiles he had attacked. A middle-aged woman then told Romeo that she wished to speak to Custer on behalf of herself and her companions. Her name was Mah-wis-sa, and she was Black Kettle's sister. She told Custer that Black Kettle was one of the first to fall under the guns of 'the big chief.' On the preceding night war parties had returned from the settlements, and the entire village danced and sang of their achievements

until the late hours of the morning. It was because of this the soldiers had been able to steal as close to the lodges as they did without arousing the Indians. Then, as a petition for peace, she brought forth a young Indian girl no more than seventeen years of age, and began a marriage ceremony. Custer, who had no knowledge of what was happening, turned to his scout and asked him what she was preparing to do. Romeo grinned and explained, "Why, she's marryin' you to that young squaw!"[39] Custer interrupted Mah-wis-sa and told her that in all due consideration of her kindness, he could not accept the girl in accordance with the white man's laws, at the same time assuring them of his acknowledgment and gratitude. Finally, Romeo and the 'big chief' turned away and attended to more urgent business.

Custer, fearing an attack from the other villages, had already extended his position around the burning lodges. The Quartermaster at the wagon train had sent the ammunition wagon in, barely evading the encircling warriors. The guards, who were left with the haversacks and overcoats, also came in, leaving both clothing and food to the Indians. Search parties were sent to find the dead and wounded and bring them in to the hospital. The loss to the command was two officers and nineteen enlisted men killed or missing.[40] The wounded were three officers and twelve enlisted men. The enemy had one hundred and three warriors dead and an undetermined number wounded.[41]

Custer was later blamed by some officers for his lack of concern regarding the disappearance of Elliott's party, and some felt that he should have made more effort to locate the missing men rather than to abandon the field not knowing their fate. In

37. Report of Surgical Cases, Circular 3; from 1865 to 1871, War Dept., Surgeon General's Office.
38. Life of G. A. Custer; J. Monaghan, Pg. 318.
39. Life on the Plains, G. A. Custer; Pg. 172.
40. Hamilton, Elliott and his party.
41. Returns from the Regular Army (Cav. Ret.), Sept. 1866-Dec. 1873; Roll 71.

Godfrey's narrative,[42] he states that a scout had reported seeing Major Elliott and party, in pursuit of some escaping Indians, disappear down the right side of the valley. Captain Meyers rode down that valley for about two miles, but found nothing. Custer had experienced an extraordinary display of Indian force, a much greater opposition than he had anticipated. It is easy to understand Custer's anxiety to rejoin his wagons carrying subsistence stores and tents for the command, left miles away. The loss of overcoats and rations seized by the hostiles left the men without protection from the elements. The loss of the wagon train and the eighty men who guarded it could mean disaster in the icy wilderness. The safety of

42. Reminiscences of the Battle of the Washita, Godfrey; Cav. Journal, Oct. 1928.

Sly Fox, Kiowa — (1873)

the entire command was a first consideration rather than accounting for the loss of a small part of it. Elliott's long absence and the reports of lengthy firing left little doubt as to the fate they had met.

Immediately after dark, Custer ordered the command to form column of fours, throwing out a strong force of skirmishers. There was no attempt made to conceal the column or its direction of march. The prisoners were in rear, mounted on ponies, under sufficient guard. The chief trumpeter sounded the advance and the band began playing, "Ain't I Glad to Get Out of the Wilderness." Custer's first thought at observing mounted warriors on the ridges was that they would harass the column. The Indians seemed uncertain what to do at first, because of the direction the command was taking, directly toward their villages. Considerable confusion was apparent and chieftains raced their ponies from one end of the ridge to another as if in last minute consultation. The Indians did not fire into the column, probably fearing to endanger the women and children. Later most warriors disappeared, leaving only a few to observe the march. The column reached the deserted villages. Their occupants had swiftly departed during the battle at Black Kettle's village. After reaching this point, several miles below the site of Black Kettle's village, the command was ordered to face about and follow the earlier trail they had made in striking the village.

The command marched briskly until two o'clock in the morning, then halted and bivouacked until daylight. Most of the men had not eaten for twenty-four hours, and hard crackers and coffee were most welcome. Fires were kindled and wet clothing and equipment dried. Custer sent Colonel West's squadron forward to reinforce the wagon train. At daylight, the troopers were in their saddles again, rested after a somewhat hasty meal. At 10 o'clock, cheers rang out. The train was discovered safely in camp. Halting only to change teams, Custer pushed on to the point where they had at first struck the timbered valley, reaching there early in the afternoon. The men could now unsaddle, pitch tents, and cook up rabbit stew.

After dinner, Custer began writing his report to General Sheridan, to be carried by California Joe to Camp Supply that night. Officers were called to Custer's tent and each one questioned as to casualties and that of the enemy warriors, which totaled one hundred and three slain. Lieutenant Godfrey visited Captain Barnitz and told him California Joe would take mail. The wounded Captain asked Godfrey to write a note telling his wife of his injury, that he was improving from his serious wound, and not to worry as he was in good care.[43]

43. Captain Barnitz survived his injury from the Battle of the Washita and retired Dec. 15, 1870 — Heitman, Historical Register & Dictionary of the U.S. Army, 1789-1903.

Courtesy Herb Peck, Jr.

Kiowa Chief, one of the head tribesman with Black Kettle's Village.

Courtesy Custer Battlefield Museum

Cheyennes captured at the Washita, Fat Bear, Big Head and Dull Knife.

When California Joe reported at Custer's tent and found his commander busily penning a report to Sheridan, he was asked how many men he wanted to accompany him on the return trip to Camp Supply. California Joe replied, "I've just been talkin' the matter over with my partner, and him and me both concludes that as safe and sure a way as any is for him and me to take a few extra rounds of ammunition and strike out from here together the very minnit it's dark. As for any more men, we don't want 'em, because yer see in a case of this 'ere kind thar's more to be made by dodgin' an' runnin' than thar is by fightin', an' two spright men kin do better at that athan twenty; they can't be seen half as fur. Besides, two won't leave as much of a trail for the Injuns to find . . ."[44]

California Joe returned to his tarpaulin shelter and informed his partner, Jack Corbin, of their immediate trip. The two men prepared their mounts, stuffing food into their haversacks along with additional ammunition. By the time both scouts returned to Custer's tent the report to Sheridan was finished. Custer regretted the long hazardous journey, but stressed the importance of bringing the good news of Black Kettle's defeat to General Sheridan. As California Joe mounted his favorite mule, and Corbin his fine gray charger, Custer reached up and shook hands with both men, bidding them God-speed and a successful journey. Joe wiped his nose with torn piece of gunnysack and said in a loud tone, "Wal, I hope an' trust yer won't have any scrimmage while I'm gone, because I'd hate mightily now to miss anything of the sort, seein' I've stuck to yer this fur."[45] Spurring their horses, the two scouts melted into the darkness carrying Custer's detailed report of the Battle of the Washita.

44. Life on the Plains; G. A. Custer, Pg. 177.

45. Ibid., Pg. 178.

CAPTIVES, BUFFALO, AND
THE YELLOWSTONE

Early Saturday morning, November 29th, California Joe and Jack Corbin, half out of breath, jumped from their mounts in front of General Sheridan's tent at Camp Supply. They had been on the trail for 36 hours, hiding during daylight hours and traveling only by night. After Sheridan read the dispatch from Custer, the word spread throughout the post that the 7th Cavalry had destroyed Black Kettle's Cheyenne camp on the Washita River. Sheridan sent both scouts back to Custer with dispatches thanking him and all the men in his command for their heroism during the hard, cold campaign against the Indians on the Washita River.

Shortly after breakfast, on December 1st, word circulated through Camp Supply that the 7th Cavalry was not more than 10 miles from the post and would arrive early that morning. General Sheridan advised his staff officers to join him outside the stockade to review the heroes as they came in. Most of the garrison followed suit and stumbled outside straining their eyes toward the horizon for the column. A sudden lull passed over everyone, only the garrison colors were heard flapping in the wind. As the assembly waited silently, movement could be seen in the southwest hills. A rifle report sounded across the valley, followed by another. The chanting of war songs could be heard as the moving forms were recognized. Attired in their best costumes and streaked with war paint were the Osage scouts, riding their ponies in circles before the marching command and firing their rifles overhead. Following the Indian scouts were California Joe and Jack Corbin riding in front of Lieutenant Cooke's

sharpshooters. Directly behind them was the 7th Cavalry band playing the regimental song "GarryOwen." Between the band and the sharpshooters ambled Indian women and children riding their ponies and dressed colorfully for the occasion. Next came Custer, in fringed buckskin jacket with leggings to match, sitting erect on his spirited charger. Behind him followed his troopers, some displaying bandaged limbs and heads. And last, the wagon train, with its cargo of wounded and dead, creeping behind the command like a funeral procession.

News of the battle of the Washita flashed over the country while humanitarians with their sentimental feelings decried Custer's victory over the Indians. On December 2nd, the New York Herald headlined:

"DECISIVE BATTLE WITH THE INDIANS: ONE HUNDRED AND FIFTY CHEYENNES KILLED AND A VILLAGE DESTROYED: LOSSES IN GENERAL CUSTER'S COMMAND."

What Eastern readers did not know, they assumed. It was believed that the army had attacked friendly and peaceful Indians, not knowing to any limit or degree the dark side of the Indian question. Custer's prediction of this came true,[1] and the army's performance of duty was criticized as a vicious attack on a defenseless people. The blow Custer had struck was a hard one, and fell on the band that, without provocation, had massacred settlers on the Saline and Solomon, perpetrating cruelties too fiendish for recital.

December 7th found the 7th Cavalry back

---

1. Life on the Plains; G. A. Custer; (1874); page 183.

in the saddle, with the 19th Kansas Volunteer Cavalry reinforcing the column. The men were issued 30 days' rations and about one-quarter forage rations for the animals. General Sheridan accompanied the command this time, the destination being the site of the destroyed village on the Washita, where an effort would be made to learn the fate of Major Elliott and the 19 men who had disappeared on the morning of the battle just a week ago. In the early morning of December 10th, with the thermometer reading 18 degrees below zero, the expedition reached Black Kettle's village, now a charred battlefield. Half wild and spiritless Indian dogs cringed at the appearance of the column; crows flew, and wolves trotted away from grisly remains. Custer accompanied by Sheridan rode to a ridge where the movements of the battle could be reconstructed. Frozen bodies of Indians still lay where they had fallen during the battle, but those of Black Kettle, Little Rock and several other chiefs, had been removed before the hasty flight of the villagers.

Sheridan deployed a squadron to search the area that Elliott had covered when in pursuit of the escaping Indians. A little more than two miles from the village the bodies of Elliott and his men were found, stripped of all clothing and horribly mutilated, lying within a circle, not more than 20 yards in diameter. Empty cartridge shells scattered around each body were mute evidence of their resistance against overwhelming odds. The mutilations were sickening to those who handled the grim task of identifying the bodies, and among men who had never previously witnessed such scenes, there is no question as to the vomiting that occurred. Doctor Henry Lippincott, chief medical officer, examined each body, making a report on the character and number of wounds received by each, as well as the mutilations.

"Major Joel H. Elliott, two bullet holes in the head, one in left cheek, right hand cut off, left foot almost cut off . . . deep gash in right groin, deep gashes in calves of both legs, little finger of left hand cut off, and throat cut.

"Sergeant Major Walter Kennedy, bullet hole in right temple, head partly cut off, seventeen bullet holes in back and two in legs.

"Corporal Harry Mercer, Troop E, bullet hole in right axilla, one in region of heart, three in back, eight arrow wounds in back, right ear cut off, head scalped, and skull fractured, deep gashes in both legs, and throat cut.

"Private Thomas Christer, Troop E, bullet hole in head, right foot cut off, bullet hole in abdomen and throat cut.

"Corporal William Carrick, Troop H, bullet hole in right parietal bone, both feet cut off, throat cut, left arm broken.

Courtesy Custer Battlefield Museum

Major Joel H. Elliott, lead a handful of men at the Washita. They were ambushed and killed to the last man. Returning to the battleground a week later, the 7th Cavalry, accompanied by General Sheridan, located the bodies of Elliott and 19 men who disappeared on the morning of the battle.

"Private Eugene Clover, Troop H, head cut off, arrow wound in right side, both legs terribly mutilated.

"Private William Milligan, Troop H, bullet hole in left side of head, deep gashes in right leg . . . left arm deeply gashed, head scalped, and throat cut.

"Corporal James F. Williams, Troop I, bullet hole in back; head and both arms cut off; many and deep gashes in back . . .

"Private Thomas Dooney, Troop I, arrow hole in region of stomach, thorax cut open, head cut off, and right shoulder cut by tomahawk.

"Farrier Thomas Fitzpatrick, Troop M, bullet hole in back; head and both arms cut off; many deep gashes in back . . .

"Private John Myres, Troop M, several bullet holes in head, scalped, nineteen bullet holes in body . . . throat cut.

"Private Cal Sharpe, Troop M, two bullet holes in right side, throat cut, one bullet hole in left side of head, arrow hole in left side . . . left arm broken.

"Unknown, head cut off, body partially destroyed by wolves.

"Unknown, head and right hand cut off . . . three bullet and nine arrow holes in back.

"Unknown, scalped, skull fractured, six bullet and thirteen arrow holes in back, and three bullet holes in chest."[2]

An account of Elliott's fight was given later by Indians who had witnessed the fight and all agreed that the major could have escaped with all his men if he had turned back at the first sighting of the huge band of warriors approaching. Not realizing that these hostiles were afraid to follow him too closely because of the nearness of the main body of troops, Elliott waged his own battle.[3] It was estimated that the odds were one hundred to one[4] against the troopers, Elliott could have had no idea a force of this size was approaching, and of course, he had no knowledge of the other villages down the valley.

It was after dark when all the bodies were carried into camp and prepared for burial on a knoll close by. Under the dim light of torches, the bodies were consigned to a common grave, except the remains of Major Elliott, carried back by the column and interred at Fort Arbuckle.

There was some opinion that Custer's abandonment of Elliott and his party was deliberate. Captain Frederick W. Benteen, whose jealousy and hatred against his commander grew each day, determined in his own mind that Custer was responsible for the deaths of Elliott and his men. Benteen, in trying to discredit Custer, sought to get a statement from one of Custer's scouts, who had heard Elliott's call for volunteers and had seen him ride in pursuit of the fleeing Indians, to the effect that Custer had let Elliott ride to his doom without any effort on his own part to try to save the party or make any attempt to locate them later. The scout, Ben Clark, knowing the circumstances, declined, wanting nothing to do with it. Benteen was more determined than ever to lash out at his commanding officer regardless of consequences.

Several months after the Washita battle, an article appeared in the St. Louis Democrat, which was copied by the New York Times, February 14th, 1869, highly critical of the leadership during the battle. The writer was anonymous, but definitely a participant.

THE BATTLE OF THE WASHITA

Death and Barbarous Treatment of Maj. Elliott and His Band-Destruction of the Indian Camp and Property.

(New York Times, February 14, 1869)

2. Elizabeth B. Custer, microfilm, Reel 1, Item 0845; (Report submitted by G. A. Custer, Dec. 22, 1868) Custer Battlefield Museum. Also see *California Joe*, J. E. Milner and E. R. Forrest, pages 188-189; Caxton Printers, Ltd., Caldwell, Idaho, 1935.

3. Custer's Indian Battles; C. F. Bates, Bronxville, N. Y., 1936; page 15.

4. E. B. Custer, microfilm, Reel 1, Item 0844.

Personal items of an officer. Bible, ink bottle, mirror, folding knife and spoon, binoculars, folding cup (or telescope cup) matches, reading glasses, plug of tobacco, tin match container, razor, 10 inch blade hunting knife with bone handle. German imported playing cards.

Fort Cobb, I.T., Dec. 22, 1868

... On the 11th we camped within a few miles of our "battle of the Washita," and Gens. Sheridan and Custer, with a detail of one hundred men, mounted, as escort, went out with the view of searching for the bodies of our nineteen missing comrades, including Maj. Elliott.

The bodies were found in a small circle, stripped as naked as when born, and frozen stiff. Their heads had been battered in, and some of them had been entirely chopped off; some of them had had the Adam's apple cut out of their throats; some had their hands and feet cut off, and nearly all had been horribly mangled in a way delicacy forbids me to mention. They lay scarcely two miles from the scene of the fight, and all we know of the manner they were killed we have learned from Indian sources. It seems that Maj. Elliott's party were pursuing a well-mounted party of Cheyennes in the direction of the Grand Village, where nearly all the tribes were encamped, and were surrounded by the reinforcements coming to the rescue of the pursued, before the Major was aware of their position ... As soon as Maj. Elliott found that he was surrounded he caused his men to dismount, and did some execution among the Indians, which added to the mortification they must have felt at the loss of the village and herds of their friends and allies, and enraged them so that they determined upon the destruction of the entire little band.

Who can describe the feeling of that brave band, as with anxious beating hearts, they strained their yearning eyes in the direction whence help should come? What must have been the despair that, when all hopes of succor died out, nerved their stout arms to do and die? Round and round rush the red fiends, smaller and smaller shrinks the circle, but the aim of that devoted, gallant knot of heroes is steadier than ever, and the death howl of the murderous redskin is more frequent ... Soon every voice in that little band is still as death; but the hellish work of the savages is scarce begun, and their ingenuities are taxed to invent barbarities to practice on the bodies of the fallen brave, the relation of which is scarcely necessary to the completion of this tale.

And now, to learn why the anxiously-looked-for succor did not come, let us view the scene in the captured village, scarce two short miles away. Light skirmishing is going on all around. Savages on flying steeds, with shields and feathers gay, are circling everywhere, riding like devils incarnate. The troops are on all sides of the village, looking on and seizing every opportunity of picking off some of those daring riders with their carbines. But does no one think of the welfare of Maj. Elliott and party? It seems not. But yes! a squadron of cavalry is in motion. They trot; they gallop. Now they charge! The cowardly redskins flee the coming shock and scatter here and there among the hills scurry away. But it is the true line — will the cavalry keep it? No! No! They turn! Ah, 'tis only to intercept the wily foe. See! a gray troop goes on in the direction again. One more short mile and they will be saved. Oh, for a mother's prayers! Will not some good angel prompt them? ... There is no hope for that brave little band, the death doom is theirs, for the cavalry halt and rest their panting steeds ...

And now return with me to the village. Officers and soldiers are watching, resting, eating and sleeping. In an hour or so they will be refreshed, and then scour the hills and plains for their missing comrades. The commander occupies himself in taking an inventory of the captured property which he had promised the officers shall be distributed among the enlisted men of the command if they falter nor halt not in the charge.

... The work progresses! The plunder having been culled over, is hastily piled; the wigwams are pulled down and thrown on it, and soon the whole is one blazing mass... The huge fire dies out; our wounded and dead comrades — heroes of a bloody day — are carefully laid on ready ambulances, and as the brave band of the Seventh Cavalry strikes up the air, "Ain't I glad to get out of the Wilderness," we slowly pick our way across the creek over which we charged so gallantly in the early morn. Take care! do not trample on the dead bodies of that woman and child lying there! In a short time we shall be far from the scene of our daring dash, and night will have thrown her dark mantle over the scene. But surely some search will be made for our missing comrades. No, they are forgotten. Over them and the poor ponies the wolves will hold high carnival, and their howlings will be their only requiem ...

Two weeks elapse — a larger force returns that way. A search is made and the bodies are found strewn round that little circle, frozen stiff and hard. Who shall write their eulogy?[5]

Upon reading the article, Custer flew into a rage. He ordered officer's call and confronted his subordinates in his Sibley tent while slapping a leather rawhide whip against his cavalry boots. It was evident that some of the officers had read the article, but few knew who had written it. Custer had every reason to believe it was one of his own officers, someone who had participated in the battle. He "hoped that the officer in question would be gentlemanly enough to expose himself, as he deserves to be horsewhipped." Benteen pushed his way through the officers, at the same time shifting his holstered pistol to a handy position on his belt, "General Custer, while I cannot father all the blame you have asserted, still I guess I am the man you are after . . . , and I am ready for the whipping promised."[6] Custer was not only taken by surprise, but dumfounded at Benteen's bold movement. "Colonel Benteen," Custer barked, "I shall see you later, sir."[7] With that, Custer dismissed the officers, turned and left the tent.[8] Benteen later claimed that Custer, out of revenge, assigned him to Fort Dodge, during which period the Captain's child died and his wife lay seriously ill at Fort Harker.

The day after recovery of the bodies, the Sheridan-Custer column started down the Washita, following the Indian trail. The abandoned villages extended some 13 miles along the river, and from the appearance of cooking utensils, robes, provisions and other property lying everywhere, the Indians evidently had fled in great haste.

Marching through the ravines and canyons was toilsome and the troops moved out onto the divide only to encounter a blinding snowstorm. Fearing that segments of the command might get lost, they returned to the banks of the Washita. The next day the march continued down the river, still following the Indian trail, but slowed down considerably by crossing numerous ravines, some of which required digging out and bridging by pioneer parties. By the 16th, the column came upon a Kiowa village, and before the Indians knew of their presence, the soldiers were upon them. As they cautiously approached the village, a group of warriors came to greet them under a flag of truce with a letter from General W. B. Hazen, military superintendent of the southern Indians and acting agent at Fort Cobb.[9] The leading warriors were Lone Wolf, a Comanche, and Satanta, a Kiowa, both leaders of bands encamped near Black Kettle's village at the time of the battle. It was later learned that Mrs. Clara Blinn, a white woman, and her small son, Willie, had been held captives in Satanta's village, and were found murdered after the warriors abandoned the villages. The letter brought by courier from General Hazen stated that *all* the Indian camps near Fort Cobb were friendly and had not been on any war party for months. After the chiefs found that the column was not going to attack them, they proposed that the warriors join the column and march with it to Fort Cobb, while their villages moved to the same point on the opposite bank of the Washita. This was a deception, as toward night, most of the warriors slipped off, leaving about 20 chiefs and principal men with the column. Early the next morning these leaders escaped, with the exception of Lone Wolf and Satanta.

Sheridan saw that he had been deceived, and ordered Custer to arrest the two remaining chiefs. After reaching Fort Cobb that

5. Full contents of this letter is found in The Custer Myth; by Col. W. A. Graham Stackpole Co., page 212; New York Times, Feb. 14, 1869, on microfilm, author's collection.

6. Custer's Indian Battles; Bates, page 16. Also see E. B. Custer microfilm Item No. 3088, Reel 11, Custer Battlefield Museum.

7. Glory Hunter; Frederick F. Van De Water.

8. Custer's Indian Battles; Bates, page 16.

9. Hazen was assigned this duty by Sherman.

evening, Sheridan and Custer found that the Kiowas, instead of moving to Fort Cobb as they had promised to do, were headed down the main Red River, west of the Wichita Mountains, in the opposite direction, as fast as their ponies would carry them. The fabricated proposition that Satanta and Lone Wolf made to Custer and Sheridan was only a decoy to get the villagers out of harm's way. The villagers had probably put 100 miles between themselves and the column.

Sheridan ordered Lone Wolf and Satanta be hung by the neck unless the villagers returned within two days and delivered themselves at Fort Cobb. The message was most effective. The villagers soon began appearing at a gait as fast as that of their flight, taking only two days after the order was issued. In Sheridan's military report of operations for that year, he writes, "I shall always regret, however, that I did not hang these Indians; they had deserved it many times; and I shall also regret that I did not punish the whole tribe when I first met them. The graves along the Santa Fe road, and along the northern border of Texas, of murdered men and women, would give evidence of the justice of such a course; but where there are so many authorities a person sometimes gets confounded as what is his duty."[10] Perfectly convinced of the white man's power and that of his determined government, the lawless activities of the Kiowa declined and the tribe remained on their reservation with the exception of a few reckless young warriors, under the leadership of Satanta. Their raiding parties in Texas each summer were almost impossible to curb. These young bucks were headstrong and impatient, and slipping away from the villages at Fort Cobb was just as challenging as the plunder they anticipated.

The problem of the Kiowas seemed set-

tled, and Sheridan and Custer turned their attention to the hostile Arapaho and Cheyenne, and the possibility of rescuing two white women captives. Most of the Comanches and Apaches had hastened to the reservation at Fort Cobb, after the fight on the Washita and the destruction of Black Kettle's camp. Lieutenant Colonel A. W. Evans had also been operating against the hostiles from Fort Bascom down the main Canadian to Monument Creek, there establishing his depot. With commendable energy he struck off to the south, and at the headwaters of the Red River, surprised a group of Comanches who had refused to come in. Twenty-five warriors were killed and a large number wounded. The village was captured and burned to the ground de-

Courtesy Custer Battlefield Museum

General Custer and the Grand Duke Alexis of Russia, 1872. Custer is holding his 50/70 modified breech-loading Springfield rifle.

10. Report of the Secretary of war; Vol. I, 1869; Report written by P. H. Sheridan; pg. 49.

stroying a great amount of property. General Eugene A. Carr was scouting along the main Canadian, west of the Antelope Hills, forcing bands of Cheyennes into the eastern edge of the Staked Plains, where the Indians found game almost nonexistent. The supplies they had put up for the winter had mostly been lost at the Washita engagement. Little Raven, Little Robe and Yellow Bear along with the majority of the hostiles were forced to come in and surrender. The surrender was made by Little Robe for the Cheyennes, and Yellow Bear for the Arapahoes. They agreed to deliver their people at Fort Cobb as soon as possible, but because of the exhausted condition of their stock, it would take some time to get them in. The Arapahoes were faithful to Yellow Bear's promise, and came in under their head chief Little Raven. The Cheyennes, however, broke their promise and remained on the southern plains, challenging the army.

Sheridan left the Custer column February 13th, 1869 to return to Washington because of his promotion to lieutenant general. Marching off to Camp Supply, Sheridan found good company with Colonel Sam Crawford of the 19th Kansas who was succeeded in that command by Lieutenant Colonel Horace L. Moore. Custer was left to hunt the hostile Cheyennes, who were apparently moving north toward Camp Supply. On March 2nd, Custer and 1,500 men, the 7th mounted and the Kansas volunteers marching as infantry, struck out after the Cheyennes with limited rations. During the march, horses dropped in their tracks and died, leaving a third of the cavalry to continue on foot. Soon rations gave out and the men had to resort to mule meat, and with the loss of animals, many wagons had to be abandoned.

The soldiers, dog-tired and hungry, were ready to turn back but their tireless commander pushed them on. The Kansans, however, were determined to wreak revenge on the Cheyennes because of the white women captives, thus bolstering the stamina of the entire command.

Striking a trail, the command followed it to the north fork of the Red River, where in mid-March they came upon the Cheyenne camp. Custer rode ahead of the column with an orderly and reached the center of the valley within sight of the village. Riding his horse in a circle, which was a plainsman's signal for wanting a conference, Custer attracted the attention of the Indians. After a few moments, three pony riders galloped from the camp with others following at a distance. Custer extended his arm showing the sign of friendship, and the Cheyennes replied in sign talk. Having no knowledge of the Cheyenne tongue, Custer conversed in sign language, some knowledge of which he had picked up. This was the village of Stone Forehead,[11] the Arrow Keeper.

As the advancing troops reached the ridge, they halted while Custer's adjutant, Colonel Cooke, joined his commander and the orderly. Stone Forehead appeared, and invited Custer and his party to join him in his camp. Together they rode to the Medicine Arrow lodge, in the center of the Indian village. Dismounting, Custer entered the lodge with Stone Forehead. Among some of the 200 lodges that made up the village, the general noticed that a number were of the Dog Soldier fraternity, the most active of hostile bands. The Keeper of the Sacred Arrows lit a pipe and handed it to the white chief. Custer, not a smoker, puffed on it until the bowl was emptied. Self-educated in lodge procedures, he noticed that Medicine Arrow[12] did not share the smoking pipe, but continued to hold the pipe until Custer had finished it. Then it was filled again and passed among the council. Peace was the

11. Life of George Bent, G. E. Hyde; page 325, University of Oklahoma Press; the name Rock Forehead is mentioned, instead of Stone Forehead.
12. My Life on the Plains, G. A. Custer; page 238; he refers to the head chief of the Cheyennes as "Medicine Arrow."

topic of conversation, and yet Custer felt that if the subject of the two captive women was brought up and their release demanded, hostilities would erupt again between the forces, thereby endangering the women. The white chief proclaimed that his intentions were honorable and he desired a peaceful relationship with the tribe. Medicine Arrow claimed that Custer was a treacherous man and he had come there with a bad purpose, to do harm to the people. The Arrow Keeper then shook the ashes loose in the pipe bowl and scattered them on the toes of Custer's boots. This was, in their ceremonial custom, a malediction.[13] As they sat smoking, Custer was planning how to surround the village, attack and capture them.

Custer asked if a suitable campsite could be chosen for his command, and a bivouac area was selected by the Indians completely out of sight of the Cheyenne vil-

lage. This did not deceive the Indian fighter, as he presumed the entire camp would attempt to slip away during the night. After having settled down on the site picked by the Indian delegation, Custer posted pickets at prominent points, to observe the Indian village three-fourths of a mile away. This precautionary measure would insure immediately knowledge of any attempt to escape by the Indians, and at the same time observe any trickery they might possibly try while the soldier camp settled for the night.

Later that evening, 50 to 100 chiefs, warriors and young men arrived at camp and settled themselves around a campfire. Custer greeted Medicine Arrow and through an interpreter, found that the Cheyennes were desirous of manifesting their friendship. As evidence of their good faith, they were joined by a group of Indian entertainers who were dressed in a most fiendish and fantastic attire. As they commenced their program, Custer received reports from his lookouts of movements in the village that

13. Life of George Bent; G. E. Hyde; page 325.

Courtesy Custer Battlefield Museum

A Buffalo Hunt, Fort Hays, Kansas — Custer is just above Buffalo's head.

seemed to indicate they were getting ready to slip away. Now he understood the object of the entertainment; it was another attempt to occupy the soldiers' attention so the rest of the villagers could pack up and take flight. While pretending ignorance of the situation, Custer continued to converse with the chiefs, giving attention at the same time to the ceremonies. A plan was devised by Custer to seize the chiefs after the entertainers left and hold them as hostages for the surrender of the two white girls, along with a promise of future good behavior. How to do it without causing any bloodshed can only be told in the gallant leader's own words. "Quietly passing the word to a few of the officers who sat near me around the campfire, I directed them to leave the group one by one, and in such manner as not to attract the attention of the Indians, proceed to their companies and select quickly some of their most reliable men, instructing the latter to assemble around and near my campfire, well armed, as if merely attracted there by the Indian serenade. The men thus selected were to come singly, appear as un-

concerned as possible, and be in readiness to act promptly, but to do nothing without orders from me."[14]

Within a short time, 100 men appeared and intermingled with the Indians, laughing and pretending interest in the entertainment as they moved closer. The painted musicians apparently from exhaustion took their leave, informing Custer that they would return later that evening to repeat their performance. About 40 Indians were left, including a few chiefs that remained to continue their conversation with the commander. Custer indicated in a quiet manner the principal chiefs he wished to seize and hold hostage, but to do this without any loss of life was a problem.

He asked interpreter Romeo to say that the white chief wanted silence among the Indians as he was about to communicate something of great importance. Custer arose, unbuckled his revolver belt and threw his weapons upon the ground. He asked that they look about them and count

14. My Life on the Plains — G. A. Custer; (1874), page 242.

Courtesy U.S. Signal Corps photo (Brady Collection)
Scouts and Packers. A hundred and fifty pounds was more than an animal should pack. Sometimes a sturdier horse can haul up to two hundred pounds if evenly distributed. Army packers most generally loaded what they thought was enough and many times overloaded an animal. They were constantly trying to catch up to the command.

the armed soldiers that had cut off any avenue of escape. The Indians began to grow uneasy but Custer held their attention by talking. He demonstrated that he wanted no bloodshed by dropping his pistol belt but he stated that it was the Indians who came under false pretense to deceive the white chief while their camp was preparing to slip away.

An effort was made by the Indians to escape. Some of the younger men jumped to their horses, others pulled pistols and strung bows. For several moments it seemd as if Custer's strategy would fail. The older men counselled the young warriors not to provoke a fight. In the increased excitement the younger men made a rush for the village and although the armed soldiers could have easily picked the Indians off their mounts,

Custer ordered them not to fire. All but four broke through and escaped, those remaining being the prominent chiefs that Custer had planned to hold as hostages.

The four captives were told to choose one of their number to return to the village with a message. Custer demanded the unconditional surrender of the two white girls held captive and that the entire Cheyenne village return at once to the reservation near Camp Supply, reporting to the military commander at that station. In case they failed to comply, the command would at once pursue them. Stalling for time, several warriors came close to camp seeking proof that the chieftains were still alive. When challenged and asked to come into camp, they refused. Custer had the chiefs call in loud tones that they were safe. After being convinced that no harm would come to them, the warriors came into camp and were relieved to find their chiefs were still alive. Satisfied with their fair treatment, the warriors returned to the village. After several days passed, Custer, tired of transmitting messages without results, called for a delegation of chieftains to hear his ultimatum. They came not knowing what the white chief intended to do, but soon learned that if the white women were not released by sunset of the next day, the lives of the three chiefs would be forfeited.

Custer knew that the Indians would not act promptly to his reply, and they would practice every delay possible before complying with the white chief's demands. The hostages became despondent as the sun began its descent in the west, and asked for a talk with Custer. One of the chiefs offered to go to the village and hurry things up, promising to return immediately with the white women. He emphasized his influential standing, saying that the others would respond to his demands. Custer replied, as he recalled it in *My Life on the Plains:*

Courtesy Custer Battlefield Museum
Custer and scouts on the Yellowstone Expedition of 1873. Custer holds map, his scout, Bloody Knife (at left, kneeling), is pointing. Tent in rear was loaned by the N. P. Railroad.

"...if he was of such importance in his tribe as he claimed to be, he was the most proper person for me to retain possession of, as his people would be more likely to accede to my demands to save his life than that of a person of less consequence."[15]

Just before sunset, some 20 mounted figures appeared on the horizon to the west. Through a field glass Custer could not make out for certain their identity until he saw two figures dismount from a pony and advance toward camp. As they came closer they were seen to be the two white women he had been bargaining for. Daniel A. Brewster, brother to one of the women captives, who had accompanied Custer's column in hopes of finding his sister, now burst into tears and was the first to reach the girls as they feebly staggered toward camp. The story of their treatment, told by the captives, was of barbarous cruelties, and it was surprising any civilized persons could have endured it and survived.[16] Medicine Arrow now demanded the release of the three hostages, Big Head, Dull Knife and Fat Bear, but Custer refused until the tribe had completed the second part of the agreement by returning to the reservation. This Medicine Arrow agreed to do as soon as the grass was green for the ponies to travel.

Most of the tribe came to the vicinity of Camp Supply and communicated with the post commander. Only Tall Bull's band violated the promise made and rode north to the Republican, where they joined a party of Sioux. On May 13th, 1869, they were surprised and defeated with heavy losses, whereupon the tribe finally was assembled at Camp Supply.

Custer and the 7th Cavalry marched to Fort Hays with the 19th Kansas "foot-sore" volunteers. The cavalry would stay there most of the summer, but the Kansas volunteers, having found their captive women,

Courtesy Herb Peck, Jr.

Trooper (unknown) in early 1870's holding Sharp's carbine with homemade thimble "prairie belt."

were disbanded and returned home. The Indians who had plundered the Southern Plains were believed to be under control by the spring of 1869. The winter campaign was a total success. There had been a fulfillment of all the conditions that Sheridan had hoped for; namely, punishment of the hostiles, their property destroyed, and the Indians disabused of the idea that winter would bring them security from the army's long reach. Finally, the tribes south of the Platte were forced onto the reservations set apart for them by the government. There were a few wilder bands of Kiowas and Comanches remaining out on the Staked Plains who, feeling a strong lingering dis-

15. My Life on the Plains; Custer, page 249.
16. Captives were Mrs. Anna Belle Morgan and Brewster's sister, Miss Sara C. White, both women captured the year before on the Kansas frontier.

content toward the whites committed intermittent raids on a small scale. The Cheyenne Dog Soldiers were still hanging onto their hunting grounds and each summer raided Texas and below the Rio Grande. There were no real major outbreaks until 1874 when the Indians were driven to open hostilities again by unjust treatment on the part of agents of the Indian Bureau. It was believed by Custer that peace could have reigned much longer than it did, with the use of proper diplomacy and treatment.

While the Indian problem in the Southwest seemed settled for the time being, headquarters of the 7th withdrew from the field to its station at Fort Leavenworth, most of its companies being scattered in various posts from which patrols were sent on escort duty, and other scouts and expeditions. While in garrison during the winter of 1869-70 troopers entertained themselves with amateur theatrical shows, horse racing and card playing. Buffalo hunts were staged for visiting celebrities and lavish dinners followed by hops gave Custer and his wife Libbie a reputation for hospitality. All of this could not fill Autie's life in garrison, and he resumed his writings of plains experiences. The now-famous Indian Fighter[17] would relive his past by setting down on paper the free life of a cavalryman.

When there were rumors that the 7th might be transferred to the Department of the South, Custer, afraid of leaving his beloved plains, applied for a transfer to another regiment that would leave him on frontier duty. He was denied this and assigned to a two-company post at Elizabethtown, Kentucky, some 40 miles south of Louisville for two years of routine duty. In March, 1871, headquarters was established at Elizabethtown. The regiment, in small detachments, assisted United States marsh-

als in hunting illegal distilleries and in curbing activities of the Ku Klux Klan, hunting for moonshiners in Kentucky, Tennessee, and South Carolina.[18]

In January, 1872, the Grand Duke Alexis, third son of the Czar of Russia, arrived in the United States for an official visit. Because of the apparent friendship the Russian government had showed during the Civil War, he was received with governmental and public hospitality. Alexis, 22 years of age, was accompanied by Admiral Poisset, with whom he had been at sea since he was seven, and Vice Chancellor Machin. It was understood that the grand duke was to see everything possible, from manufacturing of goods, to schools, churches and prisons, but instead of being delighted with all this he seemed bored but acquiescent. Banquets were held in his honor with long speeches, salutes were fired, flags and banners raised, all in praise of the young Russian who responded with small dull speeches. Alexis spoke and understood English well, but did not enjoy American humor. He especially did not enjoy those who slapped his imperial back or dug an elbow into his royal ribs in emphasis. How could the public know that in Russia no one dared touch a person of royalty?

The banquet halls and torchlight ceremonies ended in Chicago, probably for the better, as the last hotel bill from the East came to $1,500 for one meal. General Sheridan had invited the grand duke to a buffalo hunt on the plains, his bored attitude changed to one of the greatest delight. Custer was summoned from his station in Kentucky to help conduct the hunt, and the special train, provided by the Pennsylvania Railroad, carried the party with General Sheridan and staff to their destination. All the way to Fort McPherson, Custer and Alexis acted like two small boys. They danced, sang, and wrestled in the aisles and

---

17. Although many will not agree to this statement of "Indian fighter," it was enough for hero-worshippers. Custer's rekindled fame after the Washita brought him back into public praise, and they watched him curiously.

18. See "Of GarryOwen in Glory," Lt. Col. M. C. Chandler; pages 35-38.

challenged each other to the Indian arm-wrestling game. At Fort McPherson, wagons awaited the party to take them 50 miles to Willow Creek, where their camp was laid out. Hospital tents, wall tents, and "A" tents had been erected. In an Indian village of 400 lodges, Spotted Tail, his braves and their wives, awaited the party's arrival. After eight hours of travel, escorted by two troops of cavalry, the party reached the camp where a band played at their entrance with the Russian national anthem. Dinner was served in flag-draped tents, and toasts from the officers wished the grand duke "a successful buffalo hunt."

At nine o'clock the next morning the first hunt began. Buffalo Bill Cody, who had tutored the grand duke the evening before, loaned him his trained horse, Buckskin Joe, and assured him that the animal was well trained for that purpose. At dawn, Spotted Tail's scouts had been out locating a herd, and upon finding the shaggy animals grazing, sent word back to Custer and Cody. Hasty preparations were made and the royal party, following the scout back to the location of the herd, formed in a gully and prepared for the charge. The grand duke was given the first shot. He fired six shots from his pistol while only 20 feet away from the buffalo, flinching each time, and failing to hit anything. Cody rode alongside the duke and handed him another loaded revolver, and six more shots were fired without dropping the animal. Cody, upon seeing that the buffaloes might dash off in the excitement, handed Alexis his .50 caliber Springfield rifle and slapped Buckskin Joe on the rump, whereupon the horse bolted to within 10 feet of the snorting bull. A cloud of smoke erupted as the recoil almost knocked the duke from his saddle, more surprised from the report of the rifle and its kick than the now-sprawling buffalo that dropped before him.[19]

Courtesy Dr. Elizabeth A. Lawrence Collections   *Art by E. L. Reedstrom*
General Custer in 1872 dressed in his usual field attire with fur cap, sporting a favorite 50/70 modified breech-loading Springfield rifle.

The grand duke reeled in his saddle, shouted and waved his hat to his comrades who were watching some distance back. They, too, cheered and applauded him, although the spectacle was more hilarious than rewarding. Later that day, the duke shot a buffalo cow with a revolver at the range of 30 yards, which surprised everyone, including the grand duke. All told, in that five-day hunt were eight buffaloes credited to the wild and inaccurate shooting of the Grand Duke Alexis. On the last day of the hunt, the Indians demonstrated their method of buffalo hunting, with bow and arrows and lance. The grand duke was thrilled by their expert horseman-

19. Newspapers back East reported Cody shooting the buffalo for the grand duke; in Lives and Legends of Buffalo Bill; Univ. of Okla., Don Russell, page 178, states that Cody may have

held the duke's hand, but the duke pulled the trigger. I am more inclined to believe Russell's account. Also see, L. B. Custer microfilm (Reel 4) No. 3267 (letters) page 69, Custer Battlefield, states Custer held buffalo while the duke shot. It is possible they mean — Custer held rifle, not buffalo.

ship, and stated that the Indians were better riders than the Cossacks of Russia.

After the hunt, Custer accompanied the duke East, and at Louisville, Mrs. Custer joined the party which continued on to New Orleans, where a Russian warship awaited the grand duke. Newspapers ran complete details of the buffalo hunt and of the grand ball given later at Louisville, and the event gave socialites and army officers something to wag their tongues about for some time to come.

Wedding bells rang for Margaret Emma Custer, the general's only sister. Her marriage to Lieutenant James Calhoun, newly-assigned to the 7th Cavalry at Custer's request, assembled the family in Monroe, Michigan, the first week of March, 1872. Boston Custer, Autie's youngest brother, expressed a desire to join the regiment in any capacity, and hoped that his influential brother could do something about it. Boston had been a consumptive for a number of years and believed that he would benefit from life in the open air of the plains.[20] Autie promised Boston that as soon as he and Libbie returned to Elizabethtown, an effort would be made to establish some sort of position for him in the 7th.

There were several vacancies in the regiment, and if he went through the proper channels, it might take some time to process, and again the chances of refusal were great. Custer decided to contact his political and influential friends and ask as a favor to him that his brother be appointed to the 7th as a second lieutenant. He would surely champion his young brother and help him in every way to become a credit to the cavalry corps. A letter to a close friend and superior officer is as follows:

Galt House
Louisville, Ky.
March 14, 1872.

My dear Genl.*
I want to ask a great favor of you. There are three or four vacancies in my regiment (7" Cavalry) in the grade of second lieutenant. These I presume will be filled by appointment. I am extremely anxious to obtain an appointment from the Secretary of War for my youngest brother Boston Custer as second Lieutenant in the 7" Cavalry. My brother is in every respect admirally adopted to perform the duties of a cavalry officer. He is nearly twenty four years of age, of excellent habits and character and I think would be a credit to the service. I would be under great obligations to you if you would interest yourself in my behalf with Genl. Belknap and endeavor to secure this appointment. If you can ascertain anything definitely regarding the prospect of obtaining it I would be glad if he received a note from you — I would write to Genl. Belknap, but to send through the regular channel would result in no benefit to my application considering delays, etc.[21]

21. Reproduced from the collections of the Manuscript Division, Library of Congress. (Record Group 11700). Copy in Author's collection.

Courtesy Dr. Elizabeth A. Lawrence
Buffalo Bill Cody served with Custer. He and the Grand Duke Alexis of Russia became favorite hunting companions.

20. E. B. Custer; microfilm. Reel 6, item 6295, Custer Battlefield Museum.
*General's name unknown. Possibly Lt. Gen. P. H. Sheridan.

Hoping you may find it consistant to grant me this favor,

I am Truly yours,
G. A. Custer

The letter is endorsed on first flap:

Genl. G. A. Custer
Louisville, Ky.
In relation to his brother's application for a Lieutenancy in the Army.
Answd. Mar. 27/1872
No appointments now being made.

The brief endorsements message in answer, "No appointments now being made,"[22] ended that effort. However, Boston was employed as a forage master from June 5th, 1875 to March 3rd, 1876, at a monthly compensation of $75. Later in 1876 Boston was employed as a civilian guide by the 7th Cavalry quartermaster, at $100 per month, His short career with the army ended when he followed his brothers to their doom at the Little Big Horn.[23]

Regulations observed in the examination of candidates for appointment to second lieutenant in the Army of the United States were published in the Army and Navy Journal, August 16th, 1873, as follows:

G.O. No. 81, Washington, Aug. 1, 1873:
1. No person shall be examined who has not a letter authorizing the same from the War Department.
2. No candidate will be examined who is under 20 or over 30 years of age; who, in the judgment of the Board, has not the physical ability to endure the exposure of service; who has any deformity of body, or mental infirmity, or whose moral habits are bad.
3. The Board being satisfied of these preliminary points, will proceed to examine each candidate separately:
First. In his knowledge of English grammer, and his ability to read and write with facility and correctness.
Second. In his knowledge of arithmetic, and his ability in the application of its rules to all practical questions.
Third. In his knowledge of geography, particularly in reference to the northern continent of America.

Fourth. In his knowledge of history, particularly in reference to his own country.
Fifth. In his knowledge of the Constitution of the United States, and of the organization of the Government under it, and of the general principles which regulate internation intercourse.
4. The Board will consider eight as the maximum of the first, fourth, and fifth heads, and ten as the maximum of the second and third heads; and no candidate will be passed by the Board who shall not have received at least half of the number of maximum marks on each head or subject of examination.
5. In addition of such Boards of Examination as may be appointed by the Secretary of War, a Military Division or Department commander, upon notification from the Adjutant-General of the Army that a candidate has been authorized to report to him, will convene, at division or department headquarters, a Board to consist of four commissioned officers, including a medical officer; the duties of the latter to be confined to the medical examination. The proceedings of the Boards will be forwarded to the Adjutant-General of the Army.
By order of the Secretary of War. (W. W. Belknap)
Thomas M. Vincent, A.A.-G.[24]

In the spring of 1873, the 7th Cavalry was reunited for the first time since the Washita campaign in 1868 when the restless and threatening mood of the Sioux made it necessary to send the regiment into the Dakota Territory. The Northern Pacific Railroad had asked the government to protect its survey west of the Missouri River from hostile Indian attacks. A considerable amount of Indian resistance was expected, so a large force of infantry, artillery, and cavalry, was sent to quell any attempted uprising.

After the regiment had assembled at Memphis, it was sent by steamboat to Cairo, Illinois, where horses, men, and luggage changed to railroad cars for another lengthy trip to Yankton, Dakota Territory. At Yankton the 7th went into camp on a low plain several miles from the city. Officers' wives stayed in a hotel in town except for Mrs. Custer and Maggie Calhoun (the General's sister) who took over a vacant house midway between town and camp. After several days, a typical Dakota blizzard struck,

22. Ibid.
23. Biographies of the 7th Cavalry; by Ken Hammer, Old Army Press, 1972, page 18-19. Also see Men with Custer; Hammer, Old Army Press. Also, in "The Custer Story" by M. Merington; shows "Bos" employed in the forage Dept. of the 7th Regiment in 1871; letter to Libbie from Autie; page 232.

24. A.N.J.; Aug. 16, 1873, page 4.

isolating everyone. Shelter was sought for the horses, as it was feared that they would be frozen if left out of doors. The snow was so blinding that it was impossible to see further than 20 feet. During the storm, which lasted four days, Custer was incapacitated by one of his brief illnesses,[25] but was nursed back to health in a short time by Libbie and Maggie. In the camp, tents had split from the heavy weight of snow and many cases of frozen fingers and frostbitten toes were reported. When the horses were brought back to camp, they were a sorry-looking lot, gaunt from hunger and thirst, and many were without their tails and manes. Crammed together in close quarters, they had nibbled at each other in efforts to obtain a little nourishment.

As the snow thawed, the camp seemed isolated in a vast lake. Movement to and from town was exhausting for both man and animal, as mud clinging to hoof and boot taxed muscle and energy. Custer was well enough to inspect the camp and make preparations for the last phase of their trip, a march of 350 miles up the Missouri to Fort Rice, where they would join the Yellowstone expedition of more than 1,500 officers and men under Colonel D. S. Stanley. On June 10th, 1873, Custer and his 10 companies arrived at Fort Rice. For the next 10 days the 7th practiced drill formation topped with a grand review and inspection by the department commander, Major General Alfred H. Terry.

Libbie and Maggie bade farewell to their husbands, and with an escort went on to Bismarck where they boarded a train to St. Paul, and then home to Monroe, Michigan.

The expedition, when completely gathered on the bank of the Missouri, at Fort Rice, was composed as follows:

Ten companies of the 7th Cavalry, Lieutenant Colonel G. A. Custer, commanding;[26]

Four companies of the 8th Infantry, and six companies of the 9th Infantry, Lieutenant Colonel L. P. Bradley, commanding;

Five companies of the 22nd Infantry, Senior Captain C. A. Dickey, commanding;

Three companies of the 17th Infantry, and one company of the 6th Infantry, Major Robert E. A. Croften, commanding;

Five scouts from Fort Totten and five from Fort Wadsworth;

Seventy-five Ree Indian scouts under Lieutenant Daniel Brush, 17th Infantry, and

Two Rodman guns, manned by Company E, 22nd Infantry, Lieutenant John McAdam Webster, commanding.

Major Henry Lazelle, 8th Infantry, an officer of fine scientific attainments, was in charge of the scientific party to accompany the expedition. The scientists were: Mr. Allen, zoologist, mineralogist, and paleontologist; Mr. Powell, photographer; Mr. Kempitski, artist; Dr. Retter, geologist, and Mr. Bennett,* general assistant. These men were all provided with the necessary instruments and equipage, all highly skilled in their professions and anticipating some important discoveries. As long as the government was footing the bill, it stands to reason that they should be the first to know what resources lay in the path of the expedition.

On July 20th, 1873, the column moved west to the Yellowstone River with Custer and two companies of cavalry at its head selecting the route of travel. A herd of 700 cattle trailed with the troops, furnishing fresh beef, slaughtered as the need arose, at a rate of five days' fresh meat to two days' salted bacon. The forage ration was five pounds of oats per day to each animal. To carry forage, rations and equipage, 300

---

25. Conversation with Dr. Laurence Frost, Monroe, Michigan; the doctor believes this illness was more than a touch of pneumonia (March 21, 1974).

26. Custer also arranged to have Mr. Baliran, sutler, accompany the column with two wagonloads of liquor and trade goods, much to the dislike of General Stanley.
*First names unknown.

mule-drawn wagons accompanied the expedition. A number of these mules were new to the harness, and it was believed that they would give a great deal of trouble before they were properly broken to drive. The steamer "Far West" would take supplies up the Missouri and Yellowstone rivers to a planned location, and junction with the column, taking a direct route across the plains.

The orders governing the expedition were somewhat rigid, and marching allowances for officers and men were reduced to the lowest possible amount. One overcoat per each enlisted man, one blanket, two pairs of drawers, four pairs of socks, and two pairs of shoes were allowed to be carried on the body and in the knapsack. In addition, one pair of shoes for each enlisted man was carried in the wagons. The allowances for officers were one "A" tent for each field officer or captain, and one for each subaltern; one field desk for each battalion commander and one ordinary mess chest of cooking utensils for every four officers. Before the expedition got under way, an inspection was made to see that officers complied with the order. One officer was fortunate enough to be overlooked, and managed to bring his small cooking stove with him. However, it wasn't long before the stove came to grief due to peculiar circumstances.

A card game at the cavalry camp had continued into early morning hours, contrary to a rule that all games cease at midnight. Reveille was at 3, breakfast at 4, and advance sounded at 5 in the morning. The poker players were late at breakfast, and when the column moved out, leaving them behind, an officer of the guard rode up to see what the delay was. The iron cook stove was too hot to load in the wagon, and until it cooled enough so it could be handled, they had to wait. As the column moved further away, the officers became more and more concerned, and eventually loaded the hot stove into the wagon regardless of several pairs of blistered hands.

The surveyors had driven their stakes into the banks of the Yellowstone, impatiently waiting the column that was to protect them. Rains and a heavy hailstorm slowed the column's movements to a snail's pace, and during the first six days it was able to travel only 45 miles. Bloody Knife, Custer's most knowledgeable scout, had predicted that they would come upon hostiles in the vicinity of the Tongue River. On August 4th, Custer, with Bloody Knife and a squadron of cavalry, was detailed by General Stanley to go in advance of the wagons and survey the road. When eight or nine miles ahead, they halted and picketed their mounts in a grove of trees near the river to wait for the train to come up. During this wait, six Indians were seen moving in the direction of the picketed horses. The alarm was sounded, and Custer formed a line of dismounted skirmishers, driving the Indians off. They proved to be the decoy of a larger party lying in wait in a grove of woods to ambush the cavalry. Seeing that their maneuver had failed, the Indians, numbering up to 300, rode boldly out and advanced on the grove occupied by the cavalry. Custer threw his dismounted skir-

Art by E. L. Reedstrom

Taking a water break on the trail.

mishers out again. His total strength was a squadron of 80 men, commanded by Captain Myles Moylan, with Lieutenant Charles A. Varnum leading one company.

The Indians dismounted and moved in a semi-circle around the soldiers who had the river at their backs. Rapid firing commenced at a distance of 400 yards. While the largest group engaged Custer in front, another party crawled along the river bank and tried to stampede the cavalry horses. When this failed, they set fire to the grass in several places. After three hours of continued fire, ammunition began to run low. Moylan and Varnum suggested a charge to scatter the Indians but Custer delayed, hoping that the main command would come up and assist in capturing the Indians. When ammunition for the .50 caliber Sharps was almost gone, Custer ordered a charge. The Indians precipitately fled, dropping much equipment, and headed toward the Bad Lands.

In this engagement one man was slightly wounded in the arm, and one horse was injured from a rifle ball. The Indians' loss was two killed and several wounded. At the beginning of the fight, a group of Indians had left the war party in search of stragglers. Coming upon Dr. John Honsinger, veterinary surgeon, and Augustus Baliran, the cavalry sutler, who were about a mile from the column, the Indians killed them, taking their valuables and horses. Private John Ball of the cavalry, while out hunting, strayed too far and met a similar fate.

Four days after the Tongue River engagement, the column came upon the site of an Indian village whose people had abandoned a considerable amount of property in hasty withdrawal. General Stanley ordered Custer and 450 troopers to follow their trail. Custer led his men out and marched all night and most of the next day. At sundown, on August 9th, after covering some 40 miles, he arrived at the Yellowstone River where Indians had crossed 24 hours earlier, taking their families in bull boats and rafts. The next day the troops attempted to cross at the same point, which was 450 yards wide, but the current was too swift and deep to swim horses and men. Late that evening, Custer's camp was discovered by a small party. The next morning at dawn, he was attacked by 800 Indians, who came down to the river and began firing on his camp. Skirmishers were deployed on the bluffs, their carbines answering the Indians' fire. After two or three hours of firing, it was seen that 300 Indians had crossed the river above and below the cavalry camp, and were endeavoring to gain the bluffs at the rear. Custer ordered a mounted charge and pursued the Indians for eight miles. About this time, the main column arrived dispersing the Indians with artillery fire. In this fight, within two miles of the Big Horn, Custer and Adjutant Ketchum had horses shot from under them; Lieutenant Charles Braden was seriously wounded in the upper left thigh;[27] Private Tuttle, Custer's orderly was killed, and 20 troopers were slightly wounded. Four cavalry horses were killed and three were wounded. The Indian loss was estimated by Custer at 40 killed and wounded. The Indians were armed with heavy rifles and had plenty of ammunition. The band was mainly Hunkpapa Sioux, said to be led by Sitting Bull, supplied from Fort Peck[28] on the Missouri, a trading post, and Camp Cooke.[29]

An appropriation was made by Congress the previous year for making the trading post at Fort Peck a military post. A large quantity of arms and ammunition was shipped to this post marked "hardware," as a report to the Department of the Missouri clearly states:

27. The bullet was from a Henry rifle, fired at a range of not over 50 yards, went clear through the leg, badly shattering the bone and splitting it down to the knee. The story of transporting the wounded lieutenant 62 days after the fight on an improvised four-wheel stretcher is found in the U.S. Cavalry Journal, October 1904.
28. Fort Peck, near mouth of the Poplar River, Montana.
29. Camp Cooke, at mouth of the Judith River, Montana.

"The commanding officer of a military post on the Missouri, 1,500 miles from St. Louis, officially reports that the steamer which passed up the river laden exclusively with Government annuity goods had on board a number of boxes marked hardware, an inspection of which showed them to contain 2,000 Sharp's rifles, with abundance of ammunition. General Sheridan in forwarding this report says that if it is the policy of the Government to furnish Indians with firearms the muzzle-loader will answer every purpose for hunting or the chase; but if it is to put them on an equality with the Army, and make them superior to the frontier settlers, the purpose of the latest approved patterns of weapons is probably the proper thing to do."[30]

It was seriously felt that these agencies

sadly needed investigation before the whole Indian question would once again erupt into a "total war" situation.

The Yellowstone Expedition arrived at Pompey's Pillar August 15th, and reached the Musselshell on the 19th, homeward bound. The geological survey and accompanying discoveries were important. The expedition had traveled 935 miles and completed the tour in 66 days. Custer was assigned to command Fort Abraham Lincoln for the winter, arriving there September 23rd with the 7th Cavalry. The health of the command was good, and Lieutenant Braden was getting on well.

---

30. A.N.J.; August 16th, 1873; page 4.

THE LAND OF PROMISE

For the next three years, Fort Abraham Lincoln was home for the Custers, and the 7th Cavalry had a post of its own with room for half of the command assigned to duty there. The garrison was an answer to a growing demand for mounted troops to restrain hostilities by the Indians while the Northern Pacific Railroad was pushing for completion. Indian hit-and-run tactics left foot soldiers powerless to pursue and punish them, and the cavalry was the only solution to this problem.

Fort Lincoln had been built with quarters for six companies, having three barracks, seven detached officers' quarters, a granary, office and dispensary, guardhouse, commissary storehouse, quartermaster storehouse, laundresses' quarters, quartermaster stables, six cavalry stables, accommodating 600 horses, and an ordnance depot. All buildings were of frame structure, except for a few built from logs. The exteriors of the buildings were painted a dull drab slate color, but colors might be varied according to the choice of the commanding officer who had the buildings painted differently every year or two. Some distance from the laundresses' quarters (dubbed "Suds Row") were the log huts of the Indian scouts and their families.[1] It was said that the scouts lived more outside the buildings than within, as huge kettles were constantly bubbling over a campfire, while hungry Indian dogs lay nearby awaiting their chance to snatch a portion.

Off by itself was the sutler's store, with a billiard room attached. This was patronized by officers who sought recreation in a few games of pool or cards. A citizen from Bismarck was permitted to establish a barber shop near the sutler, keeping beards and mustachioed soldiers in full fashion with stateside "dudes." Soon afterward a cabin built of cottonwood with a canvas roof made its appearance. Here a photographer took up quarters charging soldiers one dollar for tintypes and three dollars for a cabinet photo.

On the bluffs, 270 feet above Fort Abraham Lincoln, was a sister garrison first occupied by infantry during the summer of 1872. This post was called Fort McKeen, established June 14th, 1872, by the 6th Infantry, Companies "B" and "C", under the command of Lieutenant-Colonel Daniel Huston, Jr., in compliance with Special Order No. 77, Headquarters Department of Dakota.[2] Fort McKeen was soon renamed Fort Abraham Lincoln, and thereafter that name designated both the infantry post formerly Fort McKeen, and the cavalry post nearby which was authorized by act of congress of March 3rd, 1873, with construction nearly completed that year.[3] After arrival of the 7th Cavalry in the fall of 1873, Fort Abraham Lincoln was expanded into a nine-company post by 1874, with detachments from the 6th and 17th Infantry regiments added to its garrison. The total strength was 655.

Life was not without hardships, especially during the winter months. Snow sifted beneath doors, windows and wall corners, piling in drifts outside, making any

1. Boots and Saddles; E. B. Custer; Harper & Bros., N. Y., 1885; page 98-99.

2. The Historical Significance of Ft. Lincoln State Park, A. O. Goplen; reprint from N. Dakota History — Vol. 13, No. 4 — 1946; page 183.

3. Ibid.

form of travel impossible. Water barrels behind the barracks and officers' quarters, froze to a depth of several inches and it was necessary to hack through the ice with an ax to get water. Usually the water was unpleasant tasting during extremely cold weather and snow was often scooped up and melted. Unseasoned lumber warped the buildings and firewood usually had to be dried for several days before it could be used. Frostbitten hands were a constant danger, often the swelling of fingers beyond their proportions caused losing the nails. Everyone was plagued with hordes of mosquitoes that seemed to be able to penetrate blankets. Fort Lincoln was notorious as the best breeding spot in the United States for these pests. Soldiers and civilians gave battle to them daily and ate and slept with them as well. "If these little devils are hell-bent on sticking with the Army," complained one disgruntled sergeant, "they should be sent to chase Indians, where there is more of him exposed." Cattle and horses were sometimes driven mad by these pests, and dogs sought temporary relief in holes which they dug into the sides of hills.

Hunting antelope, deer, buffalo, and rabbit not only gave the garrison a change of menu from government beef, but also gave the men sport and recreation. Eggs, often packed in barrels filled with oats, were shipped from St. Louis and on one occasion were received by the Custer family with the greatest delight. Libbie thought how fortunate folks were back in the states where eggs were plentiful, whereas on the frontier an egg was considered a supreme luxury. Company gardens grew a variety of vegetables. Men with experience in farming were designated to work the gardens each day, while not letting their daily duties go unattended. Although not included in rations issued to soldiers, the officers realized that to avoid scurvy, a substantial amount of fresh vegetables must be contained in their diets. Soldiers were encouraged to raise vegetables in post gardens, and not always were they successful with this project. Even with the abundance of fertilizer at cavalry posts, some gardens sprouted weeds, while others flourished.

Many diversions broke the monotony of garrison life for the women. Visiting went on among cavalry wives and infantry wives, and many of the "social get-togethers" seemed like a sorority meeting. Included were sewing clubs, recitals of poetry, read-

Courtesy Custer Battlefield Museum
Fort Lincoln, D.T., in an evening winter panorama. Officers and their ladies took full advantage of winter sports, with sleigh rides almost an every day occurance.

ing sessions for the children, and book clubs. Planning a ball or hop at one of the company barracks was undertaken with enthusiasm by the women in making up decorations, arranging the menu, and choosing the entertainment for the evening. Theatricals were always favored, and considerable talent was sometimes displayed on an improvised stage with hand-painted canvas scenery. Occasionally, a professional would be found in the ranks, delighted with the opportunity to perform. Theatricals were attended by citizens from Bismarck, and in turn, a group from Lincoln would perform at Bismarck. The 7th Cavalry band was an added attraction at these social affairs, and commanded a large audience at each performance when it wasn't attending the numerous maneuvers and drills.

Baseball games were played between companies, and drew cheering crowds. Fort Rice sent teams to Lincoln,[4] contesting for supremacy. The presence of officers and their ladies cooled violent and abusive partisanship. Soldiers who had no sporting blood sought entertainment by frequenting saloons and gambling houses at the "Point" across the river from the post. Saloons were

numerous in Bismarck, and payday brought a rush of soldiers to bars and card tables. Games such as poker, Honest John, Keno, and Rush Rheuben took most of the pay from the soldiers' pockets.

The Black Hills Expedition was organized to explore the uncharted territory in the western and southwestern portion of Dakota and the eastern portion of Wyoming, with the intention of discovering practicable military routes between Fort Lincoln and Fort Laramie. It was said if more knowledge was learned of the resources in that particular area, military posts could be established with a better selection of suitable sites. Some believed that another purpose was to substantiate rumors that gold was to be found in the Black Hills. The government would, however, be pushing into this unexplored and sacred domain of the Sioux, violating the Treaty of 1868.

The original plan was to start the expedition off June 20th, 1874, but this was postponed to June 25th, because of awaiting the arrival of new arms. When these came, they were the latest improved pattern of Springfield carbines, calibrated for the 45/70 shell. Carrying these weapons in the field for experimentation and testing may have seemed a vital function to the government, but Custer would have rather kept the

---

4. Fort Rice's team was the "Athletes," and Lincoln had the "Actives." See *Custer's Gold*; Donald Jackson; page 84.

Courtesy Custer Battlefield Museum
Fort Abraham Lincoln, Dakota territory — The 7th Regimental Cavalry was the first to be garrisoned here.

Sharps improved .50 caliber carbine or retained the old reliable Spencer. Now, fully equipped with their new Colt. 45's and Springfield carbines, the command was ready to take to the field.[5]

The expedition left Fort Lincoln on July 2nd. It consisted of 10 companies of the 7th Cavalry,[6] Company I, 20th Infantry, and Company G, 17th Infantry. There was a battery of three Gatling guns, chambered for the .50 caliber and one-inch bore,[7] one three-inch Rodman gun, and a train of more than 100 wagons.[8] A detachment of 60 Indian scouts[9] were led by "Lonesome" Charley Reynolds and the Arikara-Sioux scout, Bloody Knife. Captain William Ludlow, chief engineer of the department, was assigned by the department commander as engineering officer. Unable to obtain funds for payment of salaries, Ludlow nevertheless secured the services of Professor N. H. Winchell of Minneapolis as geologist, and George Bird Grinnell, representing Professor Othniel N. Marsh of Yale College, who was to report on the paleontology and zoology of the region. Professor Winchell would also report on botany, assisted by Doctor J. W. Williams, assistant surgeon and chief medical officer. A photographer, W. H. Illingworth of St. Paul, went along to take pictures with the popular stereoscopic camera. Illingworth took along a wide variety of apparatus and chemicals in a spring wagon similar to one used on the Yellowstone Expedition in 1873. Ludlow had a

5. Black Hills Engineer; Nov. 1929; So. Dakota State School of Mines; page 230.

6. The 7th Cavalry left Fort Lincoln with six companies, picking up four more at Fort Rice.

7. The Gatlings could fire 250 rounds in one minute, and were good for 900 yards. In a two-column coverage of the Black Hills Expedition, the Army Navy Journal reported: "In case of a battle we shall also have the first opportunity yet presented, this side of the Atlantic, for testing the renowned Gatling gun in real action. In view of the contingency, Dr. Gatling hopes they will attack. For ourselves we are chiefly anxious for the scientific success of the expedition." (ANJ, Vol. XI, July 4th, 1874; page 745.)

8. This heavy train of supplies accompanied the troops with provisions for two months.

9. Rees, Santees, and a few Sioux.

Courtesy Custer Battlefield Museum   *Photo by National Park Service, Department of the Interior*

General Custer's study at Fort Abraham Lincoln. Newspapers and journals are stacked high in left hand corner. To the far right are seen (left to right) an English .44 caliber Galand & Somerville revolver; two Smith & Wesson .38 caliber spur trigger tip-up barrel revolvers; and a Colt .45, 7½ inch barrel revolver.

detachment of engineer soldiers, consisting of two sergeants and four privates who were to keep two sets of notes of the route measured by prismatic compasses and odometers, while Ludlow's assistant, Mr. W. H. Wood, attended to the general topography and the astronomical observations for latitude and longitude.[10]

The expedition also included two practical miners, Horatio Nelson Ross and William T. McKay to study mineral deposits found along the trail. Brevet Brigadier General G. A. Forsyth and Brevet Lieutenant Colonel Fred Grant, President U. S. Grant's oldest son, also accompanied the expedition; Colonel Grant served as acting aide to Custer.[11] There was nothing to indicate that young Grant performed any vital service toward the expedition, but it did give the anti-Grant newspapers back East some material for editorial comment.

Newspaper correspondents included William Eleroy Curtis of the *Chicago*

_____
10. A.N.J.; Ludlow's Report; Sept. 19th, 1874, page 91.

11. A.N.J.; Vol. XI; July 4th, 1874, pages 744-745.

Inter-Ocean, Samuel J. Barrows, of the *New York Tribune*, who had been on the Yellowstone Expedition, and Nathan H. Knappen, of the *Bismarck Tribune*, had all one thing in common, to report officially the first findings of gold in the Black Hills.

Ahead of the ambulances and the artillery were 16 musicians astride white horses, playing the regiment's favorite tunes, "The Girl I Left Behind Me," and "GarryOwen." It was Custer's whim from time to time to ask the bandmaster to play while marching to stimulate the soldiers and take their minds off the long dull ride. Game darted out from time to time, and Custer's hounds were constantly baying and flushing birds and rabbits from brush and coulees. Buckskin-clad Custer, on his bay Dandy, was seen many times taking off alone after his dogs in hot pursuit, sometimes returning with small game or an antelope stretched across his saddle.

For all purposes, the expedition had been well fitted with equipment to carry out its plan. General Terry explained that the reason for the size of the expedition was to prevent any trouble with the Indians, and made no mention of any attempt to initiate strategy against them. The route was southwesterly toward the bend of the Heart River, across the north and south forks of the Cannonball and from there over the Belle Pierre Hills, and westward to Hiddenwood Creek where they camped the evening of July 8th. Wood for campfires was scarce and only found in river valleys. Water was not always in sufficient quantity, and some of it was impregnated with salts, making it disagreeable and injurious to drink. There was a fair amount of grass for the horses and the 300 beeves that were to be butchered when needed. The country bordering on the Heart River was reported good and that on the Cannonball as fair. Grand River country was poor, as well as that near the headwaters of the Moreau or Owl River.

Art by E. L. Reedstrom

"Bloody Knife," Custer's scout.

The route brought the troops in view of Slim Buttes and Bear Butte, and as they approached the Black Hills, they could well understand the reason for the name. The hills looked very high and dark under their covering of pine timber. On July 20th, they crossed the Belle Fourche. The character of the country changed considerably; there was now an abundance of grass, timber, fruit trees and flowers, and most appreciated, ice-cold water. Journalist W. E. Curtis reported: "The guides so far have proven trustworthy and competent. They have without exception led us to excellent camping grounds, have shown us better roads than were anticipated.[12]

Private John Cunningham of Company H, decided to go on sick report because he had been feeling rather poorly.[13] The medical officer believed that his diarrhea was not really serious and returned him to duty. After several days, his condition grew worse. Again he turned himself in to the first sergeant and was sent to the examining officer. He was returned to duty once more. The following day when the column resumed the march, Trooper Cunningham collapsed and fell from his horse. The medical officer, now convinced of his illness, placed the soldier on sick report and assigned him to ride in one of the better ambulances. Custer, however, had put "the best ambulance" to use carrying natural history collections of the expedition, and there was no room for Cunningham. (These new vehicles provided much more comfort than the other broken-down contraptions.) The ailing trooper was obliged to ride in one of the older and less comfortable ambulances. On July 21st, after the column descended into the valley of the Red Water, a branch of the Belle Fourche, Cunningham died in camp around midnight. Much blame was cast on Captain J. W. Williams, medical officer of the right battalion,[14] who had examined Cunningham and had refused to administer any drugs. He was accused of being drunk the night the trooper died.

Cunningham was wrapped in canvas and laid in an ambulance the next morning. As the men were saddling their horses at the picket line, gunfire was heard. Troopers rushed from their companies to the scene of the shooting, and found Private George Turner, of Company M, lying on the ground with a bullet wound in the abdomen. Private William Roller stood over the wounded trooper, a revolver still in his hand. The pair had quarreled for years, finally drawing on each in a typical showdown.

Turner was also wrapped in canvas and placed alongside Cunningham, and as soon

14. The expedition had three medical officers: Dr. A. C. Bergen, assigned to the infantry battalion; Dr. S. J. Allen, Jr., assigned to the left cavalry battalion, and Capt. J. W. Williams handled the right battalion and was also chief medical officer of the command.

Courtesy South Dakota State Historical Society
Captain Smith, the Custer Expedition wagonmaster.

12. The Black Hills Engineer; Nov. 1929; published by The South Dakota State School of Mines; page 234
13. A.N.J.; Aug. 15, 1874; page 8.

as the command went into camp on Inyan Kara Creek on July 22nd, both were buried as the companies lined up for funeral services. After the graves were covered, fires were set to conceal any sign of the burial plots from the Indians.[15]

After this camp near Inyan Kara, the route led in an irregular easterly direction along a tributary of Spring Creek. The valley contained a variety of wild flowers in almost incredible numbers. As the command waded through the meadows knee-high, soldiers scooped up handsful of flowers, decorating bridles and festooning their hats. From an elevated rock ledge the band played popular tunes of the day: "The Blue Danube," "Artist's Life," "The Mocking Bird," and "GarryOwen." The valley echoed with music in a weird and fascinating mood, echoing each note in double harmony, while the soldiers, in full enjoyment, absorbed the fragrant sweet air from the meadows. Custer, revelled with delight, and because of the abundance of flowers

covering the valley floor, he named it Floral Valley.

Continuing up the valley, Custer wrote in one of his dispatches: "Favored as we had been in having Floral Valley for our roadway to the west of the Black Hills, we were scarcely less fortunate in the valley which seemed to me to meet us on the interior slope. The rippling stream of clear cold water, the counterpart of that we had ascended the day before, flowed at our feet and pointed out the way before us, while along its banks grew beautiful flowers, surpassed but little in beauty and profusion by their sisters who had greeted us the day before. After advancing down this valley about 14 miles, our course being almost southeast, we encamped in the midst of grazing, whose only fault, if any, was its great luxuriance. Having preceded the main column, as usual, with our escort of two companies of Cavalry, E and C, and Lieutenant Wallace's detachment of scouts, I came upon an Indian campfire still burning, and which with other indications showed that a small party of Indians had encamped there the previous night, and had evidently left that morning in ignorance of

---

15. It was common for Indians to dig up a grave and rob or mutilate the body.

Custer's wagon train on the prairies, four columns near the North Dakota and South Dakota line.

our close proximity. Believing that they would not move far, and that a collision might take place at any time unless a friendly understanding was arrived at, I sent my head scout, Bloody Knife, and 20 of his braves to advance a few miles and reconnoitre the valley. The party had been gone but a few minutes when two of Bloody Knife's young men came galloping back and informed me that they had discovered five Indian lodges a few miles down the valley, and that Bloody Knife, as directed, had concealed his party in a wooded ravine, where they awaited further orders. Taking E Company with me, which was afterwards reinforced by the remainder of the scouts and Colonel Hart's company, I proceeded to the ravine where Bloody Knife and his party lay concealed, and from the crest beyond obtained a full view of the five Indian lodges, about which a considerable number of ponies were grazing.[16]

Custer sent an interpreter with a flag of truce, along with two Sioux scouts to tell the occupants of the lodges that the troops were friendly and meant them no harm. After this was done, a signal was given and Custer and his company surrounded the lodges. Dismounting, and entering the village, Custer shook hands with its occupants and invited them to visit his camp, where he promised to present them with flour, sugar, and coffee. The invitation was accepted. To the head men it was suggested that the Sioux should encamp with the soldiers for a few days and give information of the surrounding country, in return for the rations. With this understanding, Custer left the lodges, whose occupants numbered 27. Later that afternoon, "One Stab," the chief, and four others visited Custer's camp and asked for the rations, saying they would join the camp the following morning. Custer writes in his report of the incident, ". . . I ordered presents of sugar, coffee, and bacon to be given them; and, to relieve their

pretended anxiety for the safety of their village during the night, I ordered a party of 15 of my command to return with them and protect them during the night. But from their great disinclination to wait a few minutes until our party could saddle up, and from the fact that two of the four had already slipped away, I was of the opinion that they were not acting in good faith. In this I was confirmed when the two remaining ones set off at a gallop in the direction of the village. I sent a party of our scouts to overtake them and request their return; not complying with this request, I sent a second party with orders to repeat the request, and if not complied with, to take hold of the bridles of their ponies and lead them back, but to offer no violence. When overtaken by our scouts one of the two Indians seized the musket of one of the scouts and endeavored to wrest it from him. Failing in this, he released his hold after the scout became dismounted in the struggle, and set off as fast as his pony could carry him, but not before the musket of the scout was discharged. From blood discovered afterwards, it was evident that either the Indian or his pony was wounded.[17]

One Stab was brought back to camp when it was found that the entire party had packed up and fled. The visit of the four Indians to obtain rations was a ruse to cover the flight of the rest. One Stab, who claimed to belong to both Red Cloud and Spotted Tail's agencies, protested, but remained with Custer for three days acting as guide. The chief said he had recently returned from the hostile camp on the Powder River, where a fight with the Bozeman exploring party had cost them 10 dead braves. One Stab was allowed to leave, as Custer had promised, and was reunited with his family.

After a further march of more than 10 miles, Custer went into camp early in the day, five miles from the western base of Harney's Peak. The following day, while

---

16. Army Navy Journal; Aug. 22nd, 1874.

17. A.N.J.; Aug. 22nd, 1874.

Courtesy South Dakota State Historical Society
Custer's permanent camp, French Creek (Golden Valley). Horses in foreground.

the command rested in camp, exploring parties set out in various directions. Horatio N. Ross and William McKay rode their wagon in and out of creek beds and up and over hills, prospecting for gold. Panning was the first step necessary to detect traces of gold in dry washes or creek beds but without water, little could be done. From dry washes, samples were brought to water and panned out there. In the dry washes, bedrock was reached by digging with a shovel, and a whisk broom, or a bristle brush was used to sweep around the imbedded rocks, collecting moist sand and placing it in a pan to be washed out. Gold generally runs with black iron granules in creek bottoms, imbedded between rocks and crevices. By working up the creek bed after color has been found, the prospector may find a larger deposit. The expedition did not stay longer than a day or two in any one area, so the findings were only traces of color here and there with an occasional showing of pinhead nuggets.

When a prospector was working a creek with an ample supply of water, his method of panning was as follows: After a scoopful of gravel or sand was dumped into the pan, it was covered with water and the pan was swirled around by hand, washing much of the mud away. The prospector then raised the pan from the water while continuing the circular motion accompanied by small jerks in and out of the water to wash away the lighter sand and cloudy water, leaving the gold-carrying residue. After the panner had eliminated rock and sand, leaving only the iron granules and the gold, the next step was to separate these two metals. A small magnet took out the iron, taking care not to carry off the few gold particles. This simple method is still used by prospectors searching for gold in the western mountains.[18]

Ross and McKay found likely looking

18. This author has spent six years prospecting in the West and has learned many tricks from older miners, using the same process the "forty-niners" were accustomed to use.

Custer's permanent camp, French Creek (Golden Valley). Dead tree branch in foreground.

gold-bearing quartz and to analyze this, another process was used to separate the gold from the rock. An iron mortar and pestle was used to crush the rock and pulverize it to dust. This process was long and tedious. While one person ground the rock into small pieces, the other took notes and marked the outcropping from which the specimen had been taken. By keeping records of each specimen, a general assessment could be established for the area. After the rock was pulverized, it was put in the gold pan and the same process of washing it out was used. One of the easiest things to forget is to burn out a gold pan after it had been commonly used to wash hands and faces in. Film from soap will cling to the metal pan after the wash water has been thrown out. If this residue is not burned out, the result of any further panning will be negative. This is brought up because when a little gold was found in Custer Gulch, soldiers in their excitement

tried to pan with tin plates and drinking cups, probably without success.[19] By observing Ross and McKay daily at their chore of panning the creeks, the soldiers had some acquaintance with the art.

Castle Valley was named for the castellated limestone ridges or precipices overhanging the route. The command camped there to examine the surrounding country during which time four surveying parties were sent out with shovels and pans to explore streams and tributaries. Beavers were seen in great numbers industriously making reservoirs of the streams with their dams. Springs were numerous and cold and pure. The soil was moist and fertile, and the vegetation fresh. Most of July 28th was spent in trying to find a way down Castle Creek. Custer had relied too heavily on an Indian

19. We are not assuming that this happened. Ross and McKay were experts in their field; however, the inexperience of a "greenhorn" panning some overlooked creek bed with a greasy pan or tin plate may have resulted in their total loss of interest.

guide, and an interpreter who misconstrued the guide's directions. The column wheeled about and made a second camp on Castle Creek, only a few miles below the previous one. The course on July 29th led southeasterly from Castle Creek up a small tributary, where was found heavy grass with wild oats and barley. A deeply worn Indian trail was followed up the creek, crossing a high prairie and passing boulders of red quartz. The wagon train in its slow and laborious fording of creeks and washes often dropped behind several miles but usually caught up in late evening.

July 30th, the command traveled most of the day through a pastoral scene of scattered woods and tall grass. Professor Winchell scribbled in his notebook, "The gold seekers who accompanied the expedition report the finding of gold in the gravel and sand along this valley."[20] The command went into camp on French Creek about three o'clock in the afternoon and remained there until the morning of August 1st. This allowed the animals to shed their burdens and rest their backs. Custer sent out surveying parties, and the gold hunters had the opportunity to prospect the area. While Custer and one company of cavalry attempted to climb Harney's Peak, the camp organized a baseball game which proved more exciting than the findings of a few glittering grains of gold. Up till now, the men were somewhat skeptical of any sizeable amounts of gold being found worth the taking in the Black Hills.

When the game was finished, the Actives scored 11 runs, the Athletes 6. Colonel Joseph G. Tilford, who had won a bet on the Actives, stretched a canvas between trees and gave a champagne supper for some of the officers. Illingworth, the photographer, was summoned with his equipment to photograph the posing officers sitting around the table filled with bottles. Colonel

20. Black Hills Engineer; page 245.

Fred Grant, notorious for his drinking parties, insisted on having his picture taken at the head of the table.

August 1st the expedition moved three miles down French Creek to give the animals fresh pasture. Custer announced that a courier would be sent to Fort Laramie within 36 hours, and mail would be taken.

Bloody Knife was summoned by Custer and asked for a scout to carry dispatches to Fort Laramie, 200 miles south of the command. Bloody Knife shook his head and replied, "My warriors are brave, but they are wise. They will carry a bag of letters to Fort Lincoln, but I cannot ask them to go through the Sioux country to Laramie." Bloody Knife knew that during this particular time of year, young Sioux braves were out hunting in parties so that the plains

Courtesy South Dakota State Historical Society   *Photo by Illingworth*
After a company baseball game a champagne supper was given by Colonel Tilford. Colonel Fred Grant insisted on having the head of the table. Fred Benteen (middle of picture, sitting) looks on (1874).

Courtesy South Dakota State Historical Society Photo by Illingworth

Custer's camp in Castle Creek Valley.

would be full of them. These scouts were Arikarees, hereditary enemies of the Sioux, and Bloody Knife was wise enough not to ask any one of them to undertake such a suicidal trip. Dispatches must be sent and Custer pondered the question of what to do. Charley Reynolds was sitting close by cleaning a revolver seemingly unattentive to the conversation. After a moment or two, Reynolds looked up and said, "I'll carry the mails to Laramie, General."

"I wouldn't ask you to go, Reynolds," said Custer.

"I have no fear," responded the scout quietly; "When will the mails be ready?"

"I was intending to send something tomorrow night," replied Custer.

"I'll go tomorrow night."

As Reynolds strode away, Custer remarked: "There goes a man who is a constant succession of surprises to me. I am getting so that I feel humble in his presence. Scarcely a day passes — and I have

known him three years — that does not develop some new and strong trait in his character. I would as soon have asked my brother Tom to carry mail to Laramie as Reynolds."[21]

The next day Reynolds was seen leading an old bony, dun-colored horse to the farrier. The horse's shoes were taken off, the hoofs pared, and a set of leather shoes were fitted to buckle around the fetlocks. When asked what they were for, Reynolds explained that it was a little dodge of his to fool the Indians as they would make no trail. Reynolds expected the trip to take three to four days, no more than five. He packed as many days' rations as he thought he might need, and an ample supply of ammunition. He distributed most of the shells in his prairie belt so as not to off-balance him, and the rest were carried in saddlebags. After eating dinner, he lay down under a wagon

21. The Daily Grafic; N. Y.; July 10th, 1876.

and took a nap. Late that afternoon, an engineering party started off in the direction Reynolds was to take, and saddling his horse and strapping on a canvas bag containing the letters, he accompanied them. The party rode till 10 o'clock, and went into camp in a cluster of brush and trees near a brook. After a fire was lit and a pot of coffee made, the men gathered around the campfire watching Reynolds as he checked his saddle girth. Finding his gear in satisfactory condition, he mounted and spurred his horse lightly. "Lonesome Charley" turned momentarily in his saddle in the direction of the engineers, touched the brim of his hat with a farewell salute, and rode off into the darkness.[22]

Ahead of Reynolds lay a trackless wilderness, not a foot of which had the scout ever seen before. Because of the danger of hostile Indians, he traveled at night, guiding himself with a compass and the stars. Reynolds had never been to Fort Laramie, but he knew the general direction. After four nights of riding and three days of sleeping in the brush, he reached his destination with the mail and dispatches from Custer.

There has been considerable discussion as to the exact date when gold was first discovered during Custer's Black Hills Expedition. From the first moment after entering the Black Hills, Ross and McKay found gold-bearing quartz of potential value. When camped at Harney's Peak, color began to show with pinpoints of gold after panning a small creek bed. A sand bar yielded five to seven cents a pan; but had more water been available, better samplings might have been possible. At Custer Gulch, color was found in loose soil along the creek bed, netting 10 cents a pan. Ross,

in his estimate of the area, doubted if gold would be found to yield more than $50 to $75 a day. It was thought that if the expedition had remained in one camp long enough to search further or follow up a potential "hot spot," a closer survey could have been conducted yielding better samples than that already found.

Dispatches from the three correspondents sent with Reynolds soon triggered newspaper reports with the finds of gold and silver, the "New El Dorado of America." The Bismarck Tribune, August 12th, was the first to publish news of the discovery, devoting the entire front page to the story. Meanwhile, in Custer's Gulch, soldiers waited for the general to return from his reconnaissance of the south fork of the Cheyenne. They had found what they were looking for and wanted to return to Fort Lincoln.

Base camp was broken on August 6th at 4:30 a.m. for the return trip to Fort Lincoln, 400 miles away. The trail was retraced for 30 miles, then turned eastward toward Bear Butte. After an advance party had located a

Courtesy Herb Peck, Jr.   Photo by Illingworth
Sioux camp in Castle Creek Valley.

22. Some historians have dubbed this story of Reynolds' trip to Laramie pure legend, but it is reported in The Daily Grafic; New York, July 10th, 1876. It was signed "C," possibly written by William E. Curtis, correspondent who accompanied the expedition. D. Jackson's "Custer's Gold" says Reynolds had been chosen to carry the mails out of the Black Hills at the beginning of the expedition. See page 86.

Courtesy South Dakota State Historical Society   Photo by Illingworth

First Black Hills Expedition, July 15th to late August, 1874. Custer's officer in camp. (Left to right), William Ludlow, Capt. of Engineers and Chief Engineer, Department of Dakota; Frederick D. Grant, Lt. Col. and Aide de Camp to Lt. Gen. Philip H. Sheridan; Lt. Tom W. Custer, 7th Cavalry; Lt. Donald McIntosh; Capt. Thomas H. French, 7th Cavalry, leaning on elbow; Lt. George D. Wallace, standing; Lt. James Calhoun (silhouetted), 7th Cavalry; Capt. George W. Yates, 7th Cavalry; unknown, sitting; unknown, sitting, unknown, standing; unknown, standing; Prof. George Bird Grinnell, with watch chain, standing; Maj. and Surgeon John W. Williams, sitting on ground; unknown, sitting in camp chair; Lt. Col. and Bvt. Major Gen. George A. Custer, 7th Cavalry, reclining. Prof. A. B. Donaldson, University of Minnesota, in shirt sleeves; Lt. Thomas M. McDougall, 7th Cavalry; Bloody Knife, Ree scout; Maj. J. G. Tilford, 7th Cavalry; Prof. N. H. Winchell, University of Minnesota (?), standing; Lt. E. G. Mathey, hands crossed on knee; Unknown sitting in chair; unknown, standing; unknown, sitting; Lt. Charles A. Varnum, 7th Cavalry, leaning on elbow; Capt. V. K. Hart, 7th Cavalry; Capt. Lloyd Wheaton, 20th Infantry; unknown, standing; Capt. Myles Moylan, 7th Cavalry; Lt. H. M. Harrington, in campaign hat, standing; Capt. Owen Hale, 7th Cavalry; unknown, standing (cap); Capt. F. W. Benteen, 7th Cavalry, campaign hat; Lt. Edward S. Godfrey, campaign hat; Lt. Francis M. Gibson, campaign hat.

campsite, Bloody Knife pointed out a large grizzly bear about 75 yards away, loping along the side of a hill. Custer reached for his Remington sporting rifle, .50 caliber,[23] and fired a shot that hit the animal in the thigh. The 800-pound grizzly wheeled around only to receive several more shots from Custer, Bloody Knife, and Ludlow, all firing at the same time. The bear dropped in his tracks, his huge form still quivering with life. Bloody Knife rushed upon the animal thrusting his hunting knife into the jugular vein dispatching him immediately. A close look showed the grizzly to be an old male, his teeth worn to stubs, his body riddled with scars. While the three hunters were trying to decide whose bullet had brought the animal down, Illingworth set up his equipment and took a photograph of the hunters and their prize. The subject of gold seemed to be forgotten for the moment, as the next day rifle fire echoed from hill to hill. The end results were 100 mainly white tailed deer shot by the soldiers.

On the afternoon of August 13th, Private James King of Company H died from a short and sudden illness.[24] It was ordered that King's body be sewn in a canvas and buried that evening. Colonel Tilford protested that no man in his battalion should be buried two hours after death and that a proper site for the burial should be picked and regular services held. Custer would not wait until morning, and said that if the left wing insisted on staying for the burial, they would be responsible for catching up with the rest of the command. The gray twilight of morning broke on August 14th, as Com-

23. Gun Report, Oct., 1968; Gen. Custer Favored a Remington, by L. A. Frost; page 13.

24. Custer's Gold; Don Jackson; page 96.

pany H prepared a final salute to their deceased comrade. Their faces wore the most solemn of expressions, as Colonel Benteen read the service, his gray hair tossing in a soft breeze. "We at death leave one place to go to another; he departs from a howling wilderness and goes to a heavenly paradise."[25]

The expedition passed a little to the east of Bear Butte on the morning of August 16th, the course lying nearly due north. After crossing the Belle Fourche River, Custer's scouts were met by four Indians en route to the Cheyenne Agency from their camp on Tongue River. Through sign language the scouts were told that Sitting Bull and 5,000 followers were lying in ambush to intercept the expedition at Short Pine Hills. The scouts reported to Custer what they had heard. Word was passed through the command, and everyone prepared for the expected ambush. The column marched northward passing between West Short Pine and East Short Pine Hills without seeing interceptors. It was decided that the report was a hoax, as no signs of pony tracks were seen. Custer later learned that the rumor was picked up by newspapers back East reporting that 4,000 Indians had jumped the column and a fight actually had occurred.[26] It was presumed that the Arikara mail carriers had passed the story on to the Fort Rice mail rider, who in turn reported the incident.

The draft horses and mules could scarcely keep pace with the rest of the column and they were constantly lagging behind. Camp was made the night of August 19th, near the northwestern base of Cave Hills where men and animals rested after the grueling

Courtesy National Archives   *Photo by Illingworth*
Custer claims his grizzly. Left to right: Bloody Knife, General Custer, Private Noonan, Captain William Ludlow.

march, averaging 30 miles a day. From this point, the route continued north and west, over a rolling prairie which the Indians had burned. The column avoided the charred prairie and sought the Little Missouri, where among the badlands, wood, water, and grass were found. Having had better traveling the last five days, they remained in camp August 21.

The hardships were accompanied by disciplinary problems. Colonel Tilford, who agreed to carry water kegs for companies K and H, had to turn his wagon over to the quartermaster for violation of an order by Custer, prohibiting carrying water for other companies. A teamster was spread-eagled to a wagon wheel for several hours because he had let two mules stray among the tents in camp. A long line of sick and fatigued soldiers stood outside the surgeon's tent seeking either medical attention or relief from duty. And finally, one, Sergeant Charles Sempker of Company L died of

25. Shallow graves were usually dug with haste on expeditions, and lime, often carried by the cavalry for their latrines, was scattered over the deceased as well as on the surface of the grave, as the lime helped to decompose the body, it also discouraged wild animals from digging up the remains. ("Along this line of forts, as the bodies were buried in the cemetery, the graves were covered with lime, and the ground looked as if there had been a slight snowstorm." E. B. Custer, Microfilm reel 6, No. 6402, Custer Battlefield Museum.)

26. Custer's Gold; Jackson; page 98.

chronic diarrhea and was buried August 26th by his company.

On the sixtieth day, August 30th, at 4:30 p.m., the column reached Fort Abraham Lincoln, at the end of a trail of 1,205 surveyed miles. Marching ahead were Lieutenant Wallace's scouts, behind them came mounted officers in single file with Custer. Next came the band, playing "GarryOwen," trumpeters leading the cavalry companies marching in columns of four; the wagon train, half-empty, but with some wagons filled with a natural history collection of snakes, owls, and various four-legged animals, rolled in behind exhausted rawboned mules. The infantry were the sorriest sight and last to reach the post. Clothing was spattered with mud and covered with dust. Some soldiers had wrapped their shoes with strips of gunny sack or canvas to keep them from falling off. From every

dwelling on the post came forth their occupants to welcome the regiment. Soldiers waved their hats, women and children waved hankies and miniature flags, their faces streaked with tears. The chanting of Indian women began, but was drowned out by the band. As some of the officers slipped from their saddles to embrace their wives, Elizabeth Custer stepped forward to greet her husband, only to faint momentarily in his arms.

Captain William Ludlow, in summarizing the information obtained on the expedition wrote, "Whatever may ultimately be determined as to the existence of large amounts of precious metal in the Black Hills, and the evidence gathered on the trip I conclude was on the whole discouraging to that supposition — the real wealth and value of the country are, beyond doubt, very great. Utterly dissimilar in character to the remaining portion of the territory in which it lies, its fertility and freshness, its variety of resource and delightful climate . . ."[27] Custer's brief summary, sent to the War Department on September 8th, touches on the Indian question and disparaged the finding of gold: "While I regard the gold discoveries as very important and of promising richness, I do not think they have been prosecuted to the extent, or that sufficient information has been obtained concerning them, to warrant an immense influx of gold hunters into that region in advance of a more thorough and deliberate examination . . ."[28]

News of the gold finds in the Black Hills brought an invasion of poverty-stricken whites. The panic of 1873 had plunged the nation into a six-year depression, and the rumors of new gold field discoveries gave the people and the economy a lift. But though the hopes of exhilarated prospectors had been aroused, they were to be disappointed. Four days after the official an-

Courtesy U.S. War Department
General Custer after the Black Hills Expedition in 1874. A rose in his lapel.

27. Black Hills Engineer, 1929; page 260.
28. Ibid.; page 261.

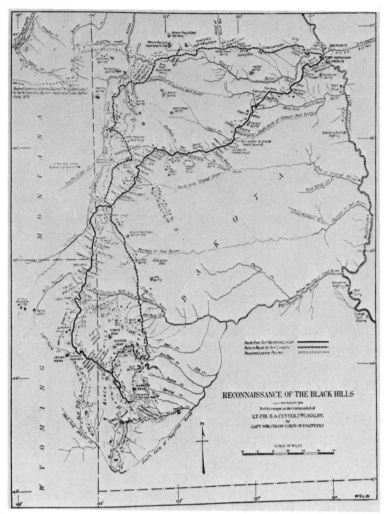

RECONNAISSANCE OF THE BLACK HILLS

Courtesy South Dakota State Historical Society
Ludlow's map showing Custer's route to and from the Black Hills.

nouncement of the discovery of gold, General Sheridan, from his Chicago headquarters, received information concerning the "grand rush" to the Black Hills by civilians. He immediately wired General Terry, in command of the Department of Dakota, to prohibit all white persons from entering the Black Hills; with further orders to move his forces along the Missouri River and the Platte, seizing wagons and outfits of all persons attempting to enter the Indians' domain, and destroy them. Violators were to be placed under arrest and held in the nearest military post. This order was carried out in the fall of 1874 and the spring of 1875. A number of parties did succeed in reaching the diggings, but stayed for a short time because of the weather; but they came out with exaggerated stories of the richness of the placers. Those who stayed on were removed by the soldiers but were speedily acquitted by local civil courts.

The Indians were displeased with the invasion of the Black Hills, but remained peaceful. The government assured them that the public would be kept out of the territory until a treaty could be negotiated for the purchase of the Black Hills. In June, 1875, the Secretary of Interior appointed a commission to secure from the Sioux, the right of mining along with other concessions. Reservation Indians offered to sell the Black Hills for $70,000,000, rejecting the government offer of $6,000,000.[29] The non-reservation Teton bands refused to sell under any conditions, warning all white men to keep out.

Under the Treaty of 1868, three-fourths of the adult male Indians would have to consent to any instrument of sale, relinquishing title to the Blacks Hills for any sum the government would be willing to pay. No matter how hard the commission tried, they were rejected. Frustrated, the commissioners returned to Washington, leaving the issue unsettled. The Indians now believed that the hills would be taken by force, regardless of existing treaty stipulations. The government withdrew military forces guarding entrances into the Black Hills, thus opening this area to the adventurous white man who poured in from every section of the country.[30] The wild Sioux bands retreated further into the wilderness, far from the agencies, their ranks now swelling with hot-tempered young warriors. War was inevitable. Sitting Bull and Crazy Horse would soon score their greatest triumph over the white intruder.

29. History of the Dakota or Sioux Indians; by D. Robinson; page 421.

30. Ibid.; page 421.

CUSTER'S MARCH TO VALHALLA

Winter and spring of 1875 found the troops performing their usual garrison duties along with endless hours of escort duty. Nefarious activity on post forced Custer to take action into his own hands and play the role of detective. He and Lieutenant Carland of the 6th Infantry, a former lawyer, had reason to believe that granary thefts on post were connected with certain characters in Bismarck. The difficulty they faced was tracing the stolen grain to the suspected parties, and what to do about it if they were successful. Custer could make no arrests outside the garrison, and any charges would have to be brought before civil authorities.

Playing the role of sleuths, the officers gathered evidence, until they uncovered a network of men implicated in the thefts. One day before the ice broke up on the river, Custer ordered the regiment to prepare to move out fully equipped and armed much to the surprise of many of his officers. Civilians in Bismarck were just as astonished when the column moved into the little town. Orders were issued to companies to search the various places pointed out by Custer, whereupon stolen grain was found bearing the government brand on each bag. Stolen grain was even found in the mayor's own warehouse, and being a prominent merchant as well as mayor, he showed a proper amount of surprise at the discovery. After a series of arrests (the mayor now collaborating with the military) the thieves were hustled back to Fort Lincoln and placed in the guardhouse. Their trial, in Fargo, Dakota Territory, continued for many months and ended with the convictions of the leading conspirators.

Early in December, 1874, Charley Reynolds had reported to Custer that an Indian at Standing Rock agency had boasted about the murders of Dr. Honsinger, the veterinarian and sutler Baliran, on the Yellowstone expedition. The Indian was named Rain-in-the-Face, a noted Sioux warrior, and he had come into the Standing, Rock agency to spend the winter, along with other Uncpapas. Custer immediately dispatched Captain George W. Yates and Lieutenant Tom Custer under sealed orders, along with a detachment of cavalry, to arrest the Indian and bring him back to Fort Lincoln. The troop left on December 12th and traveled 50 miles by night to the reservation, where Rain-in-the-Face was seized at the agency trader's store, returned to Fort Lincoln and placed in the guard house.

Kinsmen of the Sioux chief came to the garrison and pleaded for his release, but it was refused. After many hours of interrogation, Custer was successful in inducing Rain-in-the-Face to confess to the crime. The next day, a number of officers were present as witnesses, while the Sioux chief gave his account of the murders. He told of shooting Dr. Honsinger, and said the old man rode a little distance before falling from his horse. The sutler, Augustus Baliran, on seeing the Indians, had hidden in some heavy brush, but came out, signalling to them with his hands above his head. As they approached, Baliran gave them his hat as a peace offering, but they shot him, first with a gun, then pinned him to the ground with arrows. Honsinger was also shot with arrows and his brains bashed out with a stone mallet. Neither man was scalped because the doctor was bald and the sutler wore his hair short, otherwise they were badly mutilated.

Some believed that Rain-in-the-Face was nowhere near the incident, that he was far off hunting buffalo a hundred miles northeast, and that Custer had bullied him into confessing to the murders.[1] Others said that the interpreter whom Custer had selected took advantage of the opportunity to get rid of his personal enemies, and that Rain-in-the-Face did not understand what the interpreter was repeating to the white chief.

Custer could not decide what punishment would be justifiable for the crimes committed, and so he turned his attention to other matters. Rain-in-the-Face spent several months in the guardhouse until his chance came for escape. With the aid of two other prisoners, he cut a hole in the rear wall large enough to creep through and they quickly made their escape into the night.[2] There have been questions why the prisoners were not pursued by the army, and why no military action was taken against the sentry whose responsibility it was to keep a close guard on the prisoners, leading to an opinion that Rain-in-the-Face was allowed full opportunity to escape. After joining Sitting Bull's band of hostiles, the Sioux chief sent word to Fort Lincoln by way of agency Indians, that he was awaiting his revenge for his imprisonment. Legend has it that he blamed Tom Custer for his arrest and threatened to cut his heart out and eat it.

Graft and corruption were practiced by some dishonest agents of the government. On each reservation there was an Indian agent appointed by the Indian Bureau of the Department of the Interior, whose duty it was to furnish food and clothing to the Indians according to the terms stipulated in treaties. Indians in their ignorance, might sign for twenty bags of flour and receive only one. At times, a quarter portion of flour would be mixed with powdered clay, and often the flour was dark and of inferior quality. Pork rations were so poor that when the Indians received them, they threw them away in utter disgust. Cattle furnished them often were diseased, or undersized and underfed. Moth-eaten blankets and inferior clothing were issued and billed at the full value as first-class merchandise. As dishonest agents and traders grew rich with their money-making schemes, political influence in and out of the Indian Department kept investigators from finding legal evidence of fraud. Army officers, who knew the conditions, were powerless to act while they functioned under the War Department, since the Indian agents were under the Department of the Interior. The corruptive funds of this department were so great that it was impossible to abolish it even by appealing to Congress to do so through public opinion. Politicians of both parties needed election funds, and nothing other than graft money held the Indian Department together.

The summer of 1875 was without campaigns for the 7th Cavalry, dress parades and routine drills continued with the usual escort duty. The Custers spent their time reading newspapers, entertaining, and solving the daily problems of a post commander. Troopers complained of exorbitant prices charged by the sutler,[3] while in Bismarck the same item could be purchased at a cheaper price. Custer investigated and found the sutler's annual profit to be fifteen thousand dollars, three thousand of which he kept, with the remainder going to War Department grafters. When nothing seemed to induce the sutler to lower his prices, Custer instructed his officers to purchase supplies in Bismarck and resell the articles to the troopers at cost. Angered by this, the sutler wrote to Secretary of War

---

1. "Rain-in-the-Face and Curly, the Crow" by Thomas B. Marquis (1934)

2. A Life of Maj. Gen. G. A. Custer; Frederick Whittaker; page 536; Sheldon & Co., N.Y.

3. Robert C. Seip was civil sutler or post trader at Fort A. Lincoln.

Officers of the 7th U.S. Cavalry at Fort Abraham Lincoln shortly before the massacre. Front row from left to right: Second Lieutenant Bronson, 6th Infantry (sitting); Second Lieutenant G. D. Wallace, 7th Cavalry (standing); General George Armstrong Custer* (standing); Second Lieutenant B. H. Hodgson.* 7th Cavalry (standing); Elizabeth Bacon Custer, wife of General Custer (standing); Captain George W. Yates,* 7th Cavalry (sitting on step); Miss Annie Bates (sitting on step); Lieutenant Colonel W. P. Coclin, 17th Infantry (standing); Mrs. Donald McIntosh (standing; husband killed at Little Big Horn); Captain Myles Moylan, 7th Cavalry (sitting at end of row; with Reno at the Little Big Horn). Second row from left to right: Mrs. George W. Yates (first one in second row; sitting on steps; husband killed with Custer at Little Big Horn); Mrs. James Calhoun (sitting on steps; General Custer's sister; husband killed with Custer); First Lieutenant Charles A. Varnum, 7th Cavalry (sitting on steps; with Reno at the Little Big Horn; last survivor of the 7th Cavalry under Custer and as far as known he is the only one living who was in this photograph); Mrs. Myles Moylan, wife of Captain Moylan, 7th Cavalry (sitting on steps); First Lieutenant James Calhoun,* 7th Cavalry (standing); First Lieutenant Donald McIntosh.* 7th Cavalry (standing at end of row). Last row from left to right: Mrs. T. M. McDougel, wife of Captain McDougal (sitting); Captain T. M. McDougal, 7th Cavalry (with Reno at the Little Big Horn; sitting); First Lieutenant Badger, 6th Infantry; Charles Thompson (civilian; sitting; son of Captain Thompson; Colonel J. S. Poland, 17th Infantry (sitting); Captain Thomas W. Custer,* 7th Cavalry (sitting); Captain William Thompson, 7th Cavalry (in rear of Capt. Custer and standing).
*Killed with Custer at the Little Big Horn, June 25, 1876.

William W. Belknap who ordered the post commander to discontinue unauthorized purchases. Custer complied but lashed out and accused Belknap of favoritism and graft in the post-tradership racket. Col. William B. Hazen had made similar charges against the secretary of war, calling him a corrupt politician. Hazen, in reprisal for his charges, was ordered to the isolated post Fort Buford in the Northwest. Custer however, was somehow spared this embarrassment.

When Secretary Belknap stopped at Fort Abraham Lincoln in the late summer of 1875, he was snubbed by Custer. Military courtesy prescribed that Custer should have publicly welcomed Belknap; instead, the Indian fighter waited in his office for the secretary to call. When the sutler sent a basket of champagne for the reception, Custer returned it. After Belknap's visit to Fort Lincoln, the long awaited two month's leave was granted Custer. He departed with his wife and brother for a social fling in gay New York, where the theater and operatic music entranced them.

The summer of 1875 was followed by severe weather and heavy snows. Food was

Courtesy National Archives

Photograph of hunting party from Fort Abraham Lincoln, Dakota Territory 1875, at a camp on the Little Heart River. Left to right: *Lt. J. Calhoun*, 7th Cavalry; Mr. Sweet (standing), Capt. S. Baker, 6th Infantry; *Boston Custer* (in buckskin jacket); Lt. W. S. Edgerly, 7th Cavalry; Miss Watson (with fan); *Capt. M. W. Keogh*, 7th Cavalry (on Custer's right); Mrs. J. Calhoun; Mrs. George A. Custer (seated); Dr. H. O. Paulding (center, seated on ground); *George A. Custer*; Mrs. A. E. Smith; *Dr. G. E. Lord* (standing, on Custer's left); Capt. T. B. Weir (with whiskers), 7th Cavalry; *Lt. W. W. Cooke*, 7th Cavalry; Lt. R. E. Thompson, 6th Infantry, (standing on Lord's left); the Misses Wadsworth, seated; *Capt. T. W. Custer*, 7th Cavalry, *Lt. A. E. Smith*, 7th Cavalry, extreme right. Individuals that are italicized were killed during the massacre.

low at many reservations and Indian agents telegraphed for additional money to feed their charges. Congress was slow in passing the appropriations, and Indians began to starve.[4] The chiefs pleaded with the agents to let them go out and hunt buffalo in the Powder River country, as was their right under treaty. Permission was granted, and the Indians left before the heavy snows. On December 6th, 1875, the Indian Bureau issued orders that Indians not in the reservations by the end of January would be considered hostile. Runners were dispatched to locate the hunting parties and inform them that they must return immediately. In some cases the villagers answered that they could not return as they were engaged in hunting buffalo, and by the time the hides were prepared and a good supply of meat brought in to carry their families through the winter, they could hardly return within the deadline. The snows came and some of the runners themselves were not able to report back until February 11, 1876.

---

4. The appropriation was passed later in the spring.

When the deadline arrived, the War Department took steps to round up the non-reservation bands of Sitting Bull and Crazy Horse but it was so cold that frostbitten soldiers were unable to remain in the field, to carry out the winter campaign. General Sheridan's report stated, "General Terry also projected an expedition against Sitting Bull's band, which was then believed, from information he had received, to be located on the Little Missouri River, but afterward found to be on the Dry Fork of the Missouri, some two hundred miles further west. Before, however, the 7th Cavalry could be concentrated at Fort Abraham Lincoln, the season became so inclement — a great number of men being badly frostbitten endeavoring to reach the fort — and the snow so deep that it was thought advisable to abandon the expedition until later in the season."[5]

On February 10th, 1876, the New York Herald demanded a full investigation of possible corruption within the War Department, declaring Secretary of War W. W. Belknap to be farming out traderships in the Indian country, and these appointments in turn being passed on to others who sold them to the highest bidder. Belknap had invoked an 1870 law, giving the secretary of war sole power to appoint post traderships. Orvil Grant, the President's brother, was also implicated, according to the news release and it was suggested that President Grant ask his brother how much capital he had earned starving the Indian squaws and children.

Custer had voiced loud protests with regard to irregularities in post traderships along the Missouri River, and while in New York, joined in accusing the Indian Bureau and bureaucratic politicians. Whenever opportunity arose, he made statements of things he suspected, or thought he knew to be factual forgetting that as an officer in the United States Army, he should have proof before taking on his superiors. Among Custer's many friends was James Gordon Bennett, publisher of the New York Herald, who would make the most of any comments by the Indian fighter.

Libbie was enjoying New York too much to leave it for the frontier, so Custer asked for an extension of his leave which was granted. Another spree followed, but although money was running low, Autie requested another extension giving as his reason that the snow made it impossible to return to Fort Abraham Lincoln. There were parties, dinners and theatricals and visits with old friends. Politics was always a handy topic to argue over, and Grant's administration was drawing to a close. Custer, like many others who once supported the

Courtesy U.S. Signal Corps photo (Brady Collection)
Rain in the Face — Hunkpapa Sioux.

5. Army Navy Journal, Dec. 23rd, 1876, Gen. Sheridan's Report; page 309.

National Union Party, turned Democrat again, not to the surprise of his closest friends. He had reason to believe that Grant desired a third term, simply because "no other President had ever served a third term."[6] Custer also believed that General Sherman was fishing for a presidential nomination, but . . . "I think he is so unstable in his opinions that he would do like Grant did, accept from the first party that offered — with any chance of success. Sheridan would make a much stronger radical candidate than Sherman as far as controlling the soldier's vote goes, but he would be even more radical in his administration than Grant has ever been."[7] Who is to say that Custer himself had never professed ambitions toward political offices. It is believed that powerful and influential admirers saw Custer as presidential timber. A showy victory over the hostiles would make him a national hero overnight. With public acclaim and a powerful press to back him up, the Democratic convention would sit up and take notice.[8]

Autie's application for a third extension of leave was not because he and Libbie were enjoying the carefree way of New York's social life. On the contrary, their money had dwindled, but by moving across the street from the Hotel Brunswick, they were able to meet a more reasonable cost for room and board. The request for extension may have been prompted by a letter from his attorney asking him to prolong his stay in New York. It is evident that Custer was being considered to testify before a congressional committee in the Belknap scandal. The Democrats, who had won control of the House of Representatives in 1874, began rooting about, trying to dig up something to upset the Republican applecart.

6. From a letter loaned by William A. Bond; Vernon, Texas.

7. Ibid.

8. Also see "Custer, the Statesman"; by Georg Wenzel Schneider — Wettengel; Research Review, Little Big Horn Association; Vol. IV, Fall, 1970, No. 3, page 6; a good article on Custer's political ambitions.

Heister Clymer, chairman of the Committee on Expenditures of the War Department, found some evidence linking Secretary of War William Belknap in the dishonest sales of post tradership. It seems that Custer had volunteered earlier to contribute what he thought would be evidence against Belknap's operations.

Office of S. J. Storrs,
Attorney and Counsellor,
120 Broadway
New York, January 11th, 1876

Gen. G. A. Custer
   Dear Sir,
   In reply to your favor of a day or two ago. I have to inform you that the suit to which you are a party of has been placed upon the calender for trial and is likely to be called up for trial at any time as the state of the calender will permit.
   You are a necessary witness in the case and your absence at the trial will be necessarily fatal to your success therein.
   I hope that you will be able to prolong your stay in

Courtesy National Archives
Sitting Bull — spiritual leader — did not take part in battle.

Courtesy U. S. Signal Corps photo (Brady Collection)
Lieutenant Colonel George Armstrong Custer, taken in 1875. His close officers called him by the nickname "Jack" — as Custer's initials "G. A. C." were stenciled on his trunks.

New York till after the trial of this cause. Please inform me of your movements so that I may see you where it becomes necessary in this case.[9]
Yours Truly,
S. J. Storrs.

When Custer's third extension for leave was denied, he and Libbie packed their luggage and boarded a train for St. Paul, where a special coach would take them to Bismarck. The trip was long, but not uneventful. West of St. Paul, the train stalled in a snow drift making it impossible to continue. After six days of imprisonment, with food and fuel running low, desperate men found a way to cut into the telegraph wire and sent a message to Fort Lincoln for assistance.[10] After 40 miles of travel, Tom Custer arrived

at Crystal Springs, where the train was almost entirely buried in the snow. The Custers were rescued and hurried back to the garrison. The remainder of the crew and passengers had to wait another ten days for relief. Scarcely had they arrived at Fort Lincoln by a freezing sleigh ride, when Custer received an official dispatch ordering him to return to Washington immediately. He had anticipated such a communication, but not within such a short period of time. Custer sought council with General Terry, and acted upon his suggestion to seek another solution.

On March 16th, Custer wired Heister Clymer, leader of the congressional committee, asking if it was possible to answer questions by mail, as he was preparing to take to the field against hostile Indians early in April. A reply from Washington stated that he must appear in person to testify before the committee and any other arrangement was impossible. Custer now felt that he had brought disaster upon himself by becoming implicated in partisan political strife motivated by the Belknap scandal. His early offer to testify to the corrupt practices in the Indian agencies along with his exposé articles in the New York Herald regarding dishonest deals in army post traderships, were to be tapped by the Clymer investigating committee. Thirteen days later, Custer gave his first testimony before the Clymer committee, his statements being highly critical of Secretary of War Belknap. His allegations in the grain thefts, outrageous prices charged by post traders, and profit splitting with outsiders, were disclosed. Custer was then ordered to stand by for further questioning.

During the course of some four weeks of testimony, it seemed that Custer had little to offer the investigation committee other than hearsay. He did, however, show a hostile attitude toward the administration, and made several damaging statements implicating the President's brother, Orvil

_____
9. Custer file; National Archives, (Rec. file).
10. First Sgt. Hugh Hynds Reminiscenes; courtesy Custer Battlefield Museum.

Grant, as heading the Indian graft ring. Custer's testimony was a direct challenge to his Commander-in-Chief's integrity and honesty, but his charges had no proof to support them. While Custer's legal advisers were guiding him over the hot coals, the investigating committee was amazed at his over-confidence. Newspapers blared forth his statements as the champion of honest government and the Democratic press billed him as a star witness. Custer fretted. He had hoped he would be permitted to return to Fort Lincoln and lead the Dakota column in what he thought would be the greatest campaign against the Sioux. He feared the command would leave before he could return.

Custer, believing that the Clymer committee had completed its soul-searching questions, and was ready to release him, received a subpoena as a witness for the prosecution at the Belknap impeachment trial. Anticipating a longer stay in Washington, Custer appealed to Sherman, general of the army, to negotiate a release for his return to Fort Lincoln. Sherman contacted the new Secretary of War Alphonso Taft, and discussed the matter in full. Taft went directly to President Grant and relayed Custer's urgent plea to be released. Grant was determined to punish Custer, and saw no reason why the Dakota column could not march without him; and Sherman stated that the Indian fighter was not the only officer in the army capable of leading the expedition.

Determined now to see President Grant and to appeal his case, Custer made tracks to the White House. In the anteroom he waited for several hours without any word from the presidential chambers. Impatient and nervous, he stormed out of the White House and headed for the war department to see General Sherman. Unfortunately, the general was in New York and wouldn't be back until evening. That afternoon, Custer again sought an appointment with the Pres-

Courtesy U.S. Signal Corps photo (Brady Collection)
General Alfred Terry, Commander of the Department of the Dakota, left Fort Abraham Lincoln on May 17, 1876, with 925 men under his command. Terry was responsible for placing Custer in charge of his cavalry.

ident, and again was denied permission to see him. In a last effort of communication with his Commander-in-Chief, he hastily jotted the following note:

To His Exc'y the President,   May 1, 1876

Today, for the third time, I have sought an interview with the President, not to solicit a favor, except to be granted a brief hearing, but to remove from his mind certain unjust impressions concerning myself which I have reason to believe are entertained against me. I desire this opportunity simply as a matter of justice; and I regret that the President has declined to give me as opportunity to submit to him a brief statement which justice to him, as well as to me, demanded.

Resp'y submitted:

G. A. Custer
Lt. Col. 7th Cav.
Bvt. Maj. Gen. U.S.A.

Custer left Washington on May 4th, taking the night train to Chicago. When he arrived at that city and stepped from the train, he was met by one of Sheridan's staff members and informed of his arrest by order of General Sherman. Although Custer had been released from the Clymer committee, he had left Washington without seeking authorization from the war department. Grant now had the opportunity to even-up relationships with the arrogant young war hero, and he ordered him not to be allowed to engage or undertake in any part of the expedition against the Sioux. He was to remain in Chicago until he received further orders. The Chicago arrest was purposeful, the fear that Custer might escape his superiors is well-expressed in an article from the Army Navy Journal; ". . . General Custer did go in person and get temporarily excused from appearing as a witness, subject to call by telegraph, and start to join his command, when he could justly claim to go with the troops of his garrison, and therefore be out of reach of any summons, by telegraph or otherwise. In this there ap-

Art by E. L. Reedstrom

Custer's arrest in Chicago.

peared the spirit of insubordination, and the order to stop him at Chicago became imperative."[11]

General Sheridan gave Custer an Irish tongue-lashing, which didn't seem to do much good. However, feeling somewhat sorry for his lieutenant colonel, he permitted him to send several telegrams asking for a reversal of Sherman's decision. The replies never came.

Terry was headquartered in St. Paul and had picked Colonel Hazen to accompany the column in place of Custer, but Hazen was also summoned to Washington to testify before the Clymer committee. Fearing that his detainment in Chicago would interfere with his connecting with the Dakota column, Custer disobeyed General Forsyth's arresting order, and boarded a night train for St. Paul.

The Custer luck held out, and a telegram from Sherman permitted him to carry on to Fort Lincoln, but stipulated that the President had decided he was not to go on the expedition. Custer's last resort was General Alfred Terry, whose kindness of heart would possibly find a solution. If he was going to be detained under arrest, he might

Courtesy Herb Peck, Jr.

One of Elizabeth Custer's favorite pictures of "her" General, taken in New York, 1876. Probably one of his last photos in dress uniform.

11. A.N.J.; May 27, 1876.

Lieutenant General Philip H. Sheridan.

"I have seen your order transmitted through the General of the Army directing that I be not permitted to accompany the expedition to move against the hostile Indians. As my entire regiment forms a part of the expedition and I am the senior officer of the regiment on duty in this department I respectfully but most earnestly request that while not allowed to go in command of the expedition I may be permitted to serve with my regiment in the field. I appeal to you as a soldier to spare me the humiliation of seeing my regiment march to meet the enemy and I not share its dangers.

(Signed) G. A. Custer"

In forwarding the above I wish to say, expressly, that I have no desire whatever to question the orders of the President or my military superiors. Whether Lieutenant Colonel Custer shall be permitted to accompany the column or not I shall go in command of it. I do not know the reasons upon which the orders given rest; but if these reasons do not forbid it, Lieutenant Colonel Custer's services would be very valuable with his regiment.

(Signed) Alfred H. Terry,
Commanding Department.

Back East, editorials blazed away at what was termed "Grant's Revenge," asserting

as well be at Fort Lincoln with his family. Arriving in St. Paul on May 6th, Custer, desperate, disappointed, and hurt, went to Terry with tears in his eyes. Choked with emotion, he couldn't control himself and broke down and wept. Terry was deeply moved by the sight of his old comrade begging his help. How could he possibly refuse him?

With the aid of Terry, Custer penned a telegram with most humble words, forwarding it through military channels with an indorsement added by his department commander.

Headquarters Department of Dakota,
St. Paul, Minne., May 6, 1876.
The Adjutant General,
Division of the Missouri, Chicago.
    I forward the following:
"To His Excellency, The President:
(Through Military Channels.)

Brigadier General Alfred H. Terry was ordered by Sheridan to organize the Expedition to the Black Hills.

that Custer was persecuted for his decent opinions and honest testimony before the Clymer committee. Grant was branded as an irresponsible tyrant, for wreaking such vengeance against the Cavalier of the Plains. Angered Democrats threw up a shaking fist against Grant's continued abuse of his official power.

In Chicago, Sheridan received the dual dispatch, and forwarded it through the respective channels with an additional indorsement of his own.

Chicago, Ill., May 7, 1876
Brig. General E. D. Townsend,
  Washington, D. C.
  The following dispatch from General Terry is respectfully forwarded. I am sorry Lieut. Colonel Custer did not manifest as much interest in staying at his post to organize and get ready his regiment and the expedition as he now does to accompany it. On a previous occasion in eighteen sixty-eight I asked executive clemency for Colonel Custer to enable him to accompany his regiment against the Indians, and I sincerely hope that if granted this time it may have sufficient effect to prevent him from again attempting to throw discredit on his profession and his brother officers.
  (Signed) P. H. Sheridan, Lieutenant General.

Sherman's telegraphic message was received on the morning of the 8th, and passed on to Custer, who was anxiously awaiting the reply. He was overjoyed when he read the following communication;

Headquarters of the Army,
  Washington, May 8th, 1876.
To General A. H. Terry, St. Paul, Minn.:
  General Sheridan's enclosing yours of yesterday touching General Custer's urgent request to go under your command with his regiment has been submitted to the President, who sent me word that if you want General Custer along he withdraws his objections. Advise Custer to be prudent, not to take along any newspaper men, who always make mischief, and to abstain from personalities in the future . . .
  (Signed) W. T. Sherman, General.

After receiving the telegram, Custer dashed the few blocks to his hotel to pack his bags for a hasty journey to Fort Lincoln with Terry. On his way to the hotel,

he accidentally bumped into Captain William Ludlow of the Engineer Corps, presently on Terry's staff, but under orders to change stations. Both men greeted each other warmly and conversed for a time, Custer informing Ludlow that he had just recently been restored to duty and was making ready to join his command at Fort Lincoln once more. In Custer's excitement, he blurted out that once the command was underway, he would "cut loose and swing clear of Terry" making his operations independent of Terry's, as he alone saw fit to do. Ludlow did not take this favorably and he related Custer's remarks to several other officers on Terry's staff.[12] These officers thought that Terry should have full knowledge of Custer's intentions so that he would know how to deal with the situation. Terry did not get wind of Custer's remarks until he returned to St. Paul late in September of that year. Was this the appreciation one officer deserved from another? Had Terry been informed that same day of Custer's remarks, a whole chain of historical events might never have taken place. However, since it did not occur, the golden-haired Cavalier of the Plains continued to keep his date with destiny at the Little Big Horn.

Preparations having been completed for the summer's campaign against the growing force of Sitting Bull's hostiles and the continuous flow of reservation Indians joining them, the 7th Cavalry had been taken out of its barracks at Fort Abraham Lincoln to camp a short distance away from the garrison. Major Marcus Reno, commanding the 7th during Custer's absence, had divided the regiment into four battalions, captains commanding them. When Custer returned from Washington, he was sensitive to changes made without his concurrence and changed the order,

12. *Custer Tragedy*, by Fred Dustin; also *Custer's Luck*, by E. I. Stewart.

dividing the regiment into two wings, Reno commanding the right wing and Benteen the left.[13] This, of course, was resented by Reno. It would look as if he was incompetent of any major decisions without complying with other officers, and he resented Custer's actions.

While Custer was preparing the 7th for the expedition, other troops had been organized and placed under canvas, three miles below Fort Lincoln, on Cannon Ball Creek. When orders came through to be ready to move on the morning of May 17, the order of march was taken up outside the post, with the battery in advance, supported by the infantry and followed by the wagon train with the cavalry acting as advance guard and rear guard flankers.[14]

On the 17th of May, 1876, the expedition broke camp in an air of confidence, pomp, and regalia. "GaryOwen" the 7th Cavalry's battle tune broke the early morning silence as columns of platoons marched around the parade ground of Fort Lincoln. By their formidable appearance it seemed that they would be able to cope with any enemy which they might encounter. Despite this, only a few spectators and members of the officers' families came out to witness the pageantry, but many tear-filled eyes looked from the windows.

Custer promised Libbie and sister Margaret that they could accompany the column by horseback as far as the Little Heart River where a first campsite would be established. Libbie, in her quaint little riding habit simulating a tight form-fitting shell jacket with a row of brass sleeve buttons in front, rode next to her husband on Dandy.[15] After the regiment passed in review before their commanding officer, the

Custers galloped off to take their place before the column. From time to time, Autie would glance back to admire his men, and could not refrain from calling Libbie's attention to their grand appearance.

During the sunrise it was discovered a mist had enveloped everything. As the column marched off across the prairie, there occurred one of the rarest phenomena of the plains. The mist slowly began to lift and the sun shone through with its rays creating the colors of a rainbow. The column of troops moving over the ground, was mirrored as if in water in the sky above them.[16] A scene of wonder and beauty appeared as the mirage, taking up half the length of the cavalry, gave Libbie a premonition of disaster. This premonition was to stay with her, no matter how hard she tried to forget it, until the fatal news was brought to her.

At 2 p.m. the main body of the command reached the first crossing of the Little Heart River, having marched 13½ miles directly west from Fort Lincoln. The first camp being pitched at this point.[17] Libbie stayed that night with her husband, the last they were ever to know together. She could not help remembering his buoyant spirits over being in the field once again. The thought of departing in the morning to return to Fort Lincoln, again brought the premonition of disaster. That evening, the paymaster made his disbursements to the soldiers so that debts could be settled.

After reveille and breakfast the morning of May 18 Libbie and Margaret were to return to Fort Lincoln with the paymaster. As the troops were making ready for the day's march, Libbie said her goodbyes to Autie, showing no signs of apprehension. John Burkman, Custer's orderly, helped the women to their mounts, Libbie saying to him playfully, "Goodby, John. You'll look after the general, won't you?" Smiling at her

13. E. B. Custer, microfilm Reel 11, item 3089; Custer Battlefield Museum.

14. Narrative by Hugh Hynds, 1st Sgt. of Gatling Battery, Courtesy Custer Battlefield Museum.

15. Letter from Col. Brice C. W. Custer; Monterey, California; to author April 19, 1968.

16. E. B. Custer; Boots & Saddles.

17. Gen. Terry's Field Diary.

husband, she rode off. Burkman remembered that Custer hadn't returned her smile. Being a man of strong, simple emotions, apt to take himself seriously, and deeply devoted to his wife, Custer said to Burkman in a low tone, "A good soldier has two mistresses. While he's loyal to one, the other must suffer."[18]

The expedition consisted of the 7th Cavalry, commanded by Lt. Col. George A. Custer, 28 officers and 747 men; two companies of the 17th Infantry, and one company of the 6th Infantry, comprising eight officers and 135 men; one platoon of Gatling guns, two officers and 32 men in charge (from the 20th Infantry); and 45 enlisted Arikara or "Ree" Indian scouts. The wagon train had 114 six-mule teams, 37 two-horse teams, and 70 other vehicles, including ambulances, with 85 pack mules, employing 179 civilian drivers. Commanding the expeditionary forces was Brigadier-General Alfred H. Terry, department commander.

The marching formation of the 7th Cavalry was divided into two columns, designated right and left wings, commanded by Reno and Benteen. Each wing was subdivided into two battalions of three troops each. One battalion was advanced guard, one was rear-guard, and one marched on each flank of the train and the camping places at the end of the day's march. Two troops of the advance guard reported at headquarters for pioneer or fatigue duty to build bridges and creek crossings. The rear-guard remained behind everything. When it came to a wagon stalled in the mire, it helped to put the wagon forward. The battalions on the flanks were to keep within 500 yards of the trail and not to get more than a half-mile in advance or rear of the train. To avoid dismounting any more often than necessary, one troop marched until about a half-mile in advance of the train; it

then dismounted, the horses unbitted and allowed to graze until the train had passed and was about a half-mile in advance. At that time it took up the march again. Each of the two other troops would conduct their march in the same manner so that two troops would be alongside the train at all times. If the country was much broken, a half-dozen flankers were thrown out to guard against surprise. The flankers regulated their march to keep abreast of their troop. The pack animals and beef herd were driven alongside the train by the packers and herders.

The following day-by-day itinerary has been gathered from three sources, the Field Diary of Lieutenant Edward Settle Godfrey,[19] Mark Kellog's diary,[20] and General Alfred H. Terry's journal.[21] As most of the entries are brief, by weaving them together we can assimilate a better picture of daily events, with added notes on the column's progress.

The advance of the regiment left camp at 5 a.m., the train crossing the Little Heart River at 8:30 a.m. The main body of the command moved out at 9 a.m., a halt being made at 10:15, and a previously-selected campsite for the night was reached at 2 p.m., the first day's march covering 10.8 miles.[22]

May 19th, reveille sounded at 3 a.m. The men breakfasted and were on the march at 5 a.m. Three-quarters of a mile out, they came upon a ravine made impassable by high water. There was nothing else to do but return to camp and go around the ravine at a shallow ford. After this was done, a march of only three-quarters of a mile was made passing through a prairie dog village. At this point, a halt was ordered to close up

18. Old Neutriment; by Glendolin D. Wagner — Sol Lewis — N.Y. 1973 — (page 124).

19. Lt. E. S. Godfrey, Field Diary of; Publ. by Champoeg Press, 1957, 1000 copies.

20. Mark Kellogg's Diary, The Westerners Brand Book, 1945-46, Chicago Corral.

21. Gen. Alfred H. Terry, Publ. by Old Army Press, Ft. Collins, Colo., Intro by Mike Koury.

22. Gen. Terry's Field Diary.

the wagon train. Heavy rains the night before made travel heavy for forage and camp
teams. Guide Charlie Reynolds, with a
well-placed shot, bagged an antelope. Custer pioneered ahead with scouts and two
companies all day. The day had begun very
cloudy, clearing later in the morning, but at
noon a violent thunderstorm with hail
began and lasted into the afternoon. Scouts
reached the column with mail and news that
a Black Hills party had been massacred.
Wood scarce, grazing very light. The last
team came in at dark. A total of 13¾ miles
had been covered during the day.[23]

Because of the hard going of the previous day, the command was late getting
started May 20th. Reveille sounded at 5
a.m., and camp broke at 8 a.m. Artillery team
stampeded and ran a mile. Went into camp
on the west side of the Little Muddy about

23. Terry Diary and Mark Kellogg's journal.

Courtesy Custer Battlefield Museum
Major Marcus Reno was given orders to cross the Little Big Horn
with Companies A, G and M, of the 7th Cavalry.

noon. A bridge had to be built, which took
the rest of the day and wasn't finished by
dark. Slight showers through afternoon with
a westerly wind. Marched 9½ miles.[24]

May 21st, bridge completed at 6:30 a.m.,
the march being resumed with the customary halts. Weather misty, heavy dark clouds
overhead threatening rain, but passing by
noon. Indian scouts bring in seven antelope. Terry and Custer out in front most
of day. Roads better. One mule shot, diseased with glanders. Another, played out
and was left behind. Plenty water, no wood.
Three men invalids riding in ambulances,
one accidentally shot in heel. Unusual
names of various high buttes, Wolf's Den,
Rattlesnake Den, Cherry Ridge, Maiden's
Breasts. Camp reached at 3:30 p.m., distance covered 13½ miles. The command
tired from its bridge-building.[25]

Courtesy Custer Battlefield Museum
The Steamer "Far West". The 950 mile trip with wounded aboard
took Captain Grant Marsh 54 hours, a record breaking time, never
equaled since.

24. Ibid.
25. Ibid.

May 22nd, unlike the two previous days. Reveille at 3 a.m., camp broke up at 6 a.m. Weather cool and clear. Roads harder and drier. Little scouting done this day. Fourteen antelope brought in, Reynolds bags three. Struck Custer's Black Hills return trail in 1874. One wagon upset injuring driver seriously. The command covered 15⅓ miles before going into camp. Any traveling in this part of the country was no pleasure jaunt. But nothing seems to faze Custer; he thrives on hardship, and thinks everyone else should, too.[26]

May 23rd, camp broke at 5 a.m. Weather cool and clear with southerly winds. Plenty of wood was found for cook-fires, cold clear spring water for drinking, and good grass for

the animals. The Great American Desert did have its occasional oasis. Everyone made the most of it. While chasing elk ahead of advance, Custer came across a fresh camp fire left by hostiles. Marched eight miles and went into camp at Young Men's Buttes. The reason for such a short march was to give the column a chance to rest, as a longer march was expected the next day. Custer constantly visits with his Indian scouts, seems much at home with them. Indians were seen at dusk about three miles away, moving on top of Coteau.[27]

May 24th, broke camp at usual hour. Weather cool and clear. Good marching. Custer and brother Tom miles away on right flank hunting most of the day, killing a lynx and elk. Distance of this day's march was increased, 19 miles being covered. Unless in hot pursuit of an enemy or following a fresh trail, cavalry marches were made in easy stages both in length and duration. Reached Big Heart at 3 p.m. Plenty of wood and grass excellent. Stream clear and cold. Men fished and bathed. Rations were first issued all around.[28]

---

26. Terry and Kellogg's diary.

27. Ibid.
28. Ibid.

Courtesy U.S. Signal Corps photo (Brady Collection)
General John Gibbon led his cavalry from Fort Shaw, Montana, with a force of infantry, moving east down the Yellowstone River. His was one of the three pronged movements against the Indians.

Art by E. L. Reedstrom
A .50 caliber Gatling gun.

Courtesy Chicago Historical Society

General Ulysses Grant's hat. Straw hats, like the one displayed here, were permitted to be worn in the field. Navy straw hats were purchased from sutlers at 25 cents to 50 cents each.

Courtesy Custer Battlefield Museum

Captain Thomas Ward Custer was 31 years old when he met his fate at the Little Big Horn. His body was mutilated beyond recognition.

May 25th, column got under way at 5 a.m., marched over valley country with easy slopes for the most part. Weather beautiful, plenty grass, water, wood. Four men on sick report. Two government mules played out, had to be left behind. Millions of tiny locusts found in grass. Nineteen miles were again covered. Another bridge under construction.[29]

May 26th was uneventful. Camp broke at 5:30 a.m. Weather hot and dry, first day of real heat experienced. Good grass and water, but no wood. Three days without any signs of Indians. Went into camp at 2:30 p.m., marched 12 miles. Custer plans and picks all campsites. Mail arrives at 3 a.m. Considerable cactus found in the area, Custer's dogs having a hard time at it. Sometimes they ride in the ambulance to avoid cactus. Gentle rain this night.[30]

May 27th, column on march by 5 a.m. Weather warm and clear. After 10 miles of marching, the Bad Lands of the Little Missouri were sighted. Grass excellent, but water beginning to show signs of alkali. Total distance marched was 17¾ miles, going into camp at the head of Davis Creek. Everyone trying to spot General Stanley's old trail, going out of their way to locate it and wasting time. Band played while marching, and in the evening after supper. Custer familiar with the area from his '74 trip from the Black Hills.[31]

29. Terry and Kellogg's diary.
30. Ibid.
31. Ibid.

Courtesy Custer Battlefield Museum

Lieutenant W. W. Cooke, a Canadian, was with Custer to the end. On a scrap of paper he scribbled out his commanders last orders to bring up the ammunition packs.

May 28th, the first crossing of Davis Creek was reached at 5:45 a.m., this was one of those western streams with as many turns as a corkscrew, necessitating being crossed 10 times within eight miles. Sides were high and the bed miry. Marched 7¾ miles, pioneers ahead. Plenty wood, but water alkaline.[32]

May 29th, more bridge-building, rattlesnakes a hazard, one man bitten. No signs of Indians.[33]

May 30th, the main body of the command remained in camp. Only Custer turned out at 5 a.m. to scout for Indians or signs of them, finding neither after a scout of some 21 to 25 miles, returning to camp at 6 p.m. Men fished in the Little Missouri, catching a considerable amount. Hunting was not allowed. This evening it rained heavily, lightning lit up the night with lurid flashes.[34]

May 31st, broke camp at 8 a.m., skies dark, misty, threatening rain. Later heavy clouds lifted and weather turned more pleasant. Custer left the command early in the morning, without authority from General Terry. Apparently, Terry only complained about the matter in his field diary, but he also noted in a previous entry of this date that Custer had been "playing Wagon Master". It is evident from these notations the expedition's commander was becoming irritated with his chief subordinate. However, Custer wasn't being deliberately disobedient, he was simply used to having pretty much of a free hand. Terry should have told him in no uncertain terms this would not do. Custer always cheerfully obeyed a direct order. No order, or an ambiguous one was something else. Terry had chief command, but he simply did not exercise it with Custer or anyone of his subordinates. This was to be one of the fatal flaws in the whole campaign. Crossing of

Courtesy Custer Battlefield Museum
Boston "Bos" Custer the last man to join his General's doom. Only 25 years old he had served as a civilian forager with the 7th Cavalry.

the Little Missouri came off without difficulties. The trail over broken country, with one hill after another, was torture for mules and wagons. Marched 12⁹/₁₀ miles, camping at 2 p.m. in a valley. Wood and water available. Reynolds and Kellogg shot three Rocky Mountain sheep, and brought them back to camp dressed out. Rained heavy at 7 p.m.[35]

It commenced to snow on midnight of May 31st, continuing the next day, June 1st, until almost three inches had fallen. Since he felt under such conditions the command could not make more than 10 miles that day, Terry decided to remain in camp. Many played cards to pass the time, others rested, camp duties were endless. Still more snow the following day, June 2nd. Warning that marching in such bad weather might result

32. Terry and Kellogg Diary.
33. Ibid.
34. Ibid.

35. Terry and Kellogg Diary.

in much illness, such as diarrhea and colds, the expedition's chief medical officer, Dr. Williams, advised Terry to remain in camp. Terry agreed, delaying the march until next morning. Snowing heavy, the weather very cold. Wagons hauled over crossing and up hill in preparation for an early start in the morning.[36]

June 3rd, camp broke at 5 a.m., weather cold and clear with northwest wind. Met two white men and one Indian scout at head of column with dispatches from Gibbon's column on Rosebud, Gibbon on half rations. Same scouts were sent back to Gibbon with dispatches. Marched 25 miles and camped on Beaver Creek. Upon reaching Beaver Creek in the afternoon, it was found necessary to build another bridge, Stanley's old bridge being partly washed away.[37]

June 4th, column moved out at 5 a.m., weather clear and cool. Plenty of fresh water cool and clear, wood in abundance. Terry tired out and rode in an ambulance, four miles from camp. Passed through another prairie dog village, caution being taken so that horses would not step into any burrows. Most of day was spent in bridge-building. First discovery of Indian signs, three wickiups with the leaves still green. Two mules died during this night.[38]

June 5th, camp broke at the usual time. Descended into the Bad Lands. Another creek requiring another bridge. But the march was resumed "over very fine rolling country with luxuriant grass." Still, some road-making had to be done; More antelope were killed. First signs of buffalo. A distance of 20.5 miles had been covered. Grass and water fair, no wood. Sagebrush was used for fuel.[39]

June 6th, under way at 4:30 a.m. Weather cool, clear and breezy. The command's guides went astray, leading the column to

the South Fork of O'Fallon's Creek instead of to the main stream. This necessitated back tracking plus another bridge. First buffalo killed today. Pvt. McWilliams from Troop H, accidentally shot himself with his revolver, bullet entering calf of leg. He rides in an ambulance. Distance marched 16 miles.[40]

June 7th, column under way at 4:45 a.m., weather misty, clouds heavy and threatening rain. Pioneers spent most of the day in road cutting. Several mules and a few horses dropped out of teams, some wagons damaged. Camp pitched on a branch of Powder River, scouts being sent to its mouth at 10 p.m. Orders went out, no shooting or hunting. Excellent camp, good water, ample wood and sufficient grass. Men tired, stock completely so.[41]

40. Terry and Kellogg Diary.
41. Ibid.

36. Ibid.
37. Terry and Kellogg Diary.
38. Ibid.
39. Ibid.

Courtesy Custer Battlefield Museum
Captain Frederick W. Benteen, 7th U.S. Cavalry, received Custer's last message, "Benteen — come on — Big Village — be quick — bring packs. W. W. Cooke. P.S. Bring pacs." Benteen had command of Companies D, H, and K.

June 8th, Terry decided it was time to meet with General Gibbon's Montana column which had been marching eastward to join the Dakota column. The steamer *Far West*, which had been more or less accompanying the expedition where deep rivers made it possible, reached the mouth of the Powder. At noon, camp broke and Keogh's and Moylan's companies, along with Terry, went in advance on the march to the mouth of the Powder River. Much time was lost by the main command trying to find a ford practicable for the wagon train. Scouts sent by Terry the night before to the Powder's mouth, returned with mail from the steamer *Far West*. Gibbon's scouts, who met the forward column several days earlier, were driven back by hostiles while trying to make contact with that command. They finally had to retire to a stockade for protection. Hostiles were believed near the mouth of the Powder, or within the area of the Tongue River. Preparations are being made for an eight-day cavalry scout.[42]

June 9th, weather disagreeable and raining, laid over in camp. Scouts in from steamer brought news that Terry had gone up Yellowstone river 30 miles on *Far West* to meet Gibbon, marching down Yellowstone river valley. Terry returned late and preparations made for a scout, but nobody knows which companies or how many go out. Orders are for two days rations and forage on horses. One hundred rounds of carbine ammunition on person, six days ration and forage on pack mules.[43]

The next day, June 10th, Terry ordered Major Reno with six companies, B, C, E, F, I, and L, to scout up the Powder to its forks, thence to the head of Mizpah Creek, down to its mouth, then by Pumpkin Creek to the Tongue River. Reno left at 5 p.m. No doubt Custer enviously watched his departure, as he had hoped to be sent instead. In any case, Custer was sure, with good reason, Reno

Courtesy Custer Battlefield Museum
White Swan — one of Custer's scouts.

would botch it. The 7th's junior Major was a good officer only when there was someone else along to tell him what to do and how to do it. Both the officers and men of the command wondered at Terry's decision to send Reno instead of Custer, but Terry offered no explanation. Terry noted in his field diary at this time: "Also sent Gibson to find pass to plateau. Gibson did nothing."[44]

June 11th, Gibson having not returned, Terry decided to move out. Camp broke late because of the rain, canvases had to be dried out before storing. Sending Custer in advance with one company, Terry followed with the main body. There ensued much road-making until the plateau's pass was found. A march was then made on the plateau for three-quarters of a mile until the head of a ravine was reached where a halt

---

42. Terry and Kellogg Diary.
43. Ibid.

44. Terry's diary. In both diaries of Godfrey and Kellogg, it is mentioned that Reno had taken with him 12 days rations and forage.

Courtesy Tom Heski   *Photo by Barry*
One of Custer's Crow scouts. (Name unknown)

of infantry following on the *Far West*. Fifteen miles from the Powder the steamer's machinery broke down. It was repaired by the next day, June 16th, Terry joined Custer at the Custer camp.[46]

The next three days, June 17th to 19th were spent awaiting news from Reno's scout. The afternoon of the 19th, a courier brought Terry dispatches from Reno to the effect that he had been to the mouth of the Rosebud, where he had no business being, according to the expedition commander's orders. He had found a considerably large Indian trail about nine days old leading to the valley of the Little Big Horn, but forebore, however, to follow it up. Immediately upon receipt of this dispatch, Terry sent his brother-in-law Captain Hughes, who was

---

46. Terry's diary.

was made. Roads were heavy and hills difficult for pack mules to climb. Pack train lagged some three miles behind. Descending to the bottom lands of the Powder, another bridge had to be erected. Then back onto the plateau, more road-making, camp finally being made on the Yellowstone. Twenty-four miles traveled.[45]

The *Far West* having arrived at that point, June 12th, the day was spent in unloading her stores. She was then sent back down the river for more supplies and to carry the command's mail. June 13th was spent awaiting her return. June 14th Terry issued Custer orders to take six companies of the 7th the next morning for the Tongue River. June 15th, Custer moved out for the Tongue at 7 a.m., Terry with his staff and a company

---

45. Terry's diary and Godfrey's journal.

Courtesy Custer Battlefield Museum
Curley, one of Custer's Crow scouts — claimed he watched Custer's men massacred by the Sioux through field glasses.

Curley was told by Mitch Bouyer to leave the command and go to Terry. "That man (Custer) will stop at nothing . . . we have no chance at all."

called a conference of his principal officers aboard the *Far West*. Gibbon, Custer, Major Brisbin, commanding Gibbon's cavalry, together with some of Terry's staff attended. They knew General Crook was in the field against these same hostiles, but they did not know just where his command was operating. Obviously, his movements could not be coordinated with theirs; in fact, they could not even coordinate their own, except in the most general way. In sending three columns against large numbers of hostiles it was always hoped that the columns would converge on them, but at least prevent them from escaping. It was highly unlikely that Crook's Wyoming column would be able to assist the Montana and Dakota columns. It was not certain the latter two would be able to assist one another. There can be no question that Terry was very doubtful of this, regardless of what he was to say later. A few hours before the conference on the *Far West* took place, he ended a dispatch to

on his staff, to meet the major. The expedition commander plaintively noted in his field diary: "Reno gave him no reason for his disobedience of Orders."[47]

It was now known that there were no Indians on the Tongue or Powder rivers, and the net had narrowed to the Rosebud, Little Horn, and Big Horn rivers. June 20th, Terry ordered Custer to cross the Tongue and join Reno with the rest of the 7th. He was then to receive supplies from the *Far West* and march on to the Rosebud with the whole 7th. Terry, following Custer, reached Reno's camp at 12:30 p.m., then went on to Gibbon's the next day, June 21st.[48]

General Gibbon was found in camp at the mouth of the Rosebud, awaiting developments. The evening of June 21st, Terry

White Man Runs Him, scout with Custer.

47. Terry's diary.
48. Ibid.

Sheridan with the words: "I only hope that one of the two columns will find the Indians. I go personally with Gibbon."[49] The key words are: "I only hope . . ."

It was believed that the Indians were at the head of the Rosebud, or on the Little Big Horn, a divide of only 15 or 20 miles of ridges separating the two streams. Terry decided that Custer's column would strike the blow. Gibbon, upon hearing this, was disappointed, but not surprised. There was great rivalry between the columns, and each wanted desperately to be in at the death. General Gibbon's cavalry had been in the field since February 22nd, herding and watching these Indians, while the infantry had been in the field since early last March. They had come to regard the Yellowstone Indians as their peculiar property, and had worked and waited five months until the Indians could be corraled and concentrated, with Crook and Terry in position to prevent their escape.

However, Terry's reasons for according the honor of the attack to Custer were good ones. Custer had all cavalry and could pursue the Indians if they attempted to escape, while Gibbon's column was half infantry, and in rapid marching in approaching the village, as well as in pursuing the Indians after the fight, Gibbon's cavalry and infantry probably would become separated and the strength of the column weakened. Custer's column was numerically stronger than Gibbon's, and Terry decided that the strongest column would strike the Indians. A report from the commissioner of Indian Affairs in regard to the number of hostiles absent from the agencies, estimated a figure of not more than 1,500 warriors.[50] Custer had reason to believe that this figure was

Courtesy Custer Battlefield Museum
Hairy Moccasin — one of Custer's scouts.

not correct, and stated that they would probably face three times that number.

The conference on the *Far West* lasted from three in the afternoon till near sundown. Custer emerged apparently depressed, no one knew why, but it was noticed by some of his officers. Terry and Gibbon accompanied Custer to his tent, where a few moments were spent in conversation. Terry said he would give Custer written orders in the morning, being exhausted from the long hard ride he would also direct the campaign from the steamer *Far West*, which would ferry Gibbon's column to the south side of the Yellowstone and navigate as far as the Big Horn would allow.

Officer's call brought 7th Cavalry subordinates to Custer's tent. Orders were given

49. Edgar I. Stewart, Custer's Luck, page 239.

50. Legend Into History, Charles Kuhlman; Stackpole Company, 1951; page 32.
    Also see The New York Times, April 13, 1874; page 1, col. 4; "A show of counting the Indians has been made here — that is, the agent called in the head-men and took their word for the number they had . . ."

Courtesy Custer Battlefield Museum
Harry Armstrong Reed. Nicknamed "Autie" after his uncle, G. A. Custer, at the age of 18 followed his three uncles to their end.

to prepare the pack mules[51] in the morning with 15 days rations of hardtack, coffee, and sugar, and 12 days rations of bacon. Twelve strongest pack animals were to carry 24,000 rounds of reserve ammunition, and it was understood that no badly used-up animals were to be sent with the expedition. Each man was to be issued 100 rounds of carbine and 24 rounds of pistol ammunition, to be carried on his person or in his saddle bag. Sabers were ordered packed and stored on the steamer *Far West* until they returned. For every horse, 12 pounds of oats were to be carried by each trooper, with care to ration it after lengthy marches. Custer suggested that additional forage might come in handy, but troop commanders foresaw the difficulties of extra forage being packed,

and cautioned that it was certain the mules would break down sometime during the march if this was allowed. "Well, gentlemen," Custer replied in an excited manner, ". . . you may carry what supplies you please; you will be held responsible for your companies. The extra forage was only a suggestion, but this fact bear in mind: We will follow the trail for 15 days unless we catch them before that time expires, no matter how far it takes us from our base of supplies. We may not see the supply steamer again."[52] Custer continued, "You had better carry along an extra supply of salt; we may have to live on horse meat before we get through." As Custer retired to his tent, the wing and battalion commanders broke up and scattered in groups returning to their campsites.

After the officers informed their men that they were to move out the next day, letters home were hastily penciled, troop commanders made out their wills, and others gave verbal instructions for personal effects and mementos to be distributed to families back east. Many seemed to have an ominous presentment of disaster. While others fancied a night-long card game accompanied with a cup full of whiskey, which Terry gave permission to tap from the kegs. Custer returned to the *Far West* later that evening and was accosted by Major James S. Brisbin, Gibbon's second in command. Brisbin offered Custer four troops of the 2nd Cavalry to join the 7th, but Custer shook his head, "The 7th can handle anything it meets." An earlier plea made by Lieutenant Low to take all or part of his Gatling battery also was refused, on the ground that the cumbersome guns might impede the 7th's march.[53]

Gibbon's men grumbled about the favoritism the 7th was getting. Even Mitch Bouyer, the half-blood Sioux Indian interpreter, was assigned to Custer, leaving

51. There were 12 mules assigned to each troop. See *Glory Hunter*, Van De Water, page 317.

52. *Custer's Last Battle*; Gen. E. S. Godfrey, *Century Magazine*; Jan. 1892.

53. *Legend into History*; Charles Kuhlman; Stackpole Company, 1951, page 28.

Gibbon without a guide. The 7th seemed to be getting every assistance from Terry to make a successful pursuit.

The sutler, on board the steamer, had been kept busy selling last minute items to officers and troopers, including snuff, tobacco, sperm candles, small print flannel shirts, and straw hats* for the heat of the day. Little has been written about these straw hats and they are not described, but there is mention of soldiers purchasing straw hats from the sutler on board the *Far West* for 25 or 50 cents each.[54] It is probable that several types were sold by the sutler, a broad-brimmed civilian field hat and another with a small brim and low crown. The smaller straw hat was authorized for navy personnel for summer or tropical use and may have been purchased by the sutler from government surplus stores. The brim of the hat was three and one-half inches, and the body was six inches high, in shades of off-white or manila.[55] Photographs show that it was not uncommon to see a navy straw hat worn by a cavalryman.

All morning of June 22nd was spent preparing the 7th Cavalry for the 15-day planned expedition. Several hours before the regiment marched out, Custer received Terry's written orders. The instructions were implicit and fixed the location of the hostiles. It is quoted in its entirety:

CAMP AT MOUTH OF ROSEBUD RIVER, MONTANA TERRITORY, June 22d, 1876. LIEUTENANT-COLONEL CUSTER, 7TH CAVALRY. COLONEL: The Brigadier-General Commanding directs that, as soon as your regiment can be made ready for the march, you will proceed up the Rosebud in pursuit of the Indians whose trail was discovered by Major Reno a few days since. It is, of course, impossible to give you any definite instructions in regard to this movement, and were it not impossible to do so the Department Commander places too much confidence in your zeal, energy, and ability to wish to impose upon you precise orders which might hamper your action when nearly in contact with the enemy. He will, however, indicate to you his own views of what your action should be, and he desires that you should conform to them unless you shall see sufficient reason for departing from them. He thinks that you should proceed up the Rosebud until you ascertain definitely the direction in which the trail above spoken leads. Should it be found (as it appears almost certain that it will be found) to turn towards the Little Horn, he thinks that you should still proceed southward, perhaps as far as the headwaters of the Tongue, and then turn towards the Little Horn, feeling constantly, however, to your left, so as to preclude the possibility of the escape of the Indians to the south or southeast by passing around your left flank. The column of Colonel Gibbon is now in motion for the mouth of the Big Horn. As soon as it reaches that point it will cross the Yellowstone and move up at least as far as the forks of the Big and Little Horns. Of course its future movements must be controlled by circumstances as they arise, but it is hoped that the Indians, if upon the Little Horn, may be so nearly inclosed by the two columns that their escape will be impossible.

The Department Commander desires that on your way up the Rosebud you should thoroughly examine the upper part of Tullock's Creek, and that you should endeavor to send a scout through to Colonel Gibbon's column, with information of the result of your examination. The lower part of this creek will be examined by a detachment from Colonel Gibbon's command. The supply steamer will be pushed up the Big Horn as far as the forks if the river is found to be navigable for that distance, and

---

*Author's Note: Small and wide brim straw hats, many were from naval surplus with small brims. (Chicago Historical Society)

54. Reno Court of Inquiry; The Old Army Press — 1972 — page 411.

55. The Uniforms of the United States Navy; James C. Tily, Thomas Yoseloff, 1964.

the Department Commander who will accompany the column of Colonel Gibbon, desires you to report to him there not later than the expiration of the time for which your troops are rationed, unless in the mean time you receive further orders. Very respectfully, your obedient servant, E. W. SMITH, Captain 18th Infantry, Acting Assistant Adjutant-General.[56]

Terry's "Letter of Instructions," as some have termed it, prescribed what he expected Custer to find and what he should do in the most general way. Much ado about nothing has been made of it by Custer-phobes. The young Indian fighter certainly used his own judgment, which his commander had authorized in his order. Terry was not an experienced Indian fighter, Custer was.[57]

Confident of a successful expedition, Custer jotted a few lines in a letter to Libbie, emphasizing Terry's highly praised words, "the Department Commander places too much confidence in your zeal, energy and ability . . ." This letter was to be Custer's last to his wife, she would cherish it the rest of her life.

At noon, on the 22nd of June, 1876, "forward" was sounded and the regiment marched out of camp in column of fours, pack mules heavily burdened, following each troop. Generals Terry, Gibbon, and Custer reviewed the line of marching men and animals, returning salutes to each passing officer, Terry having a pleasant word for each of the troop commanders. The sky was gray, a raw northwest wind tormented the swallow-tailed banner, red and blue, with white crossed sabers, Custer's personal standard since the Civil War. As the column marched by, rank and file gave the appearance of veterans, although many had little battle experience. The sun had tanned their faces, and an outcrop of new beards evidenced a month's journey in the field.

Custer, in a fringed buckskin suit, sported two English self-cocking white-handled pistols with a ring in the butt for a lanyard, a hunting knife in a beaded, fringed scabbard, and a canvas cartridge belt supporting these tools of war. Snugly fitted into a Spencer carbine scabbard was a Remington sporting rifle, octagon barrel, and calibrated for the 50-70 center-fire cartridge. He wore a light gray hat, broad-brimmed and low-crowned to protect his sensitive face from the sun, but no matter how hard he tried to protect himself from the heat of the day, his boyish freckles would appear to his embarrassment. Captains Tom Custer, Calhoun, and Keogh, along with Adjutant Cooke and Bos Custer, dressed in fringed buckskin jackets, a fashion adopted by plainsmen since the opening of the west. When buckskins were not readily available, heavy cloth or canvas substituted, with added imitation fringe on sleeves and trouser legs. Like many other officers in the command, Major Reno wore an army blouse topped off with a rough-looking straw hat. Benteen also stayed away from buckskins, considering that they were too hot during the day, and when soaked by rain, they weighed heavily on a person.

As the end of the column neared, Terry and Gibbon passed compliments to Custer. Shaking hands with the two commanders, he spurred his horse and headed to the forward point. Gibbon called after him in jest, "Now, Custer! Don't be greedy! Wait for us!"[58] The buckskinned lieutenant colonel turns in his saddle and called back ambiguously, "No, . . . I won't."[59]

Lieutenant George D. Wallace, who kept the official itinerary of the 7th's march June 22nd through June 25th, wrote in his report to the chief engineer, department of

56. Custer's Luck; Edgar I. Stewart, page 239.
57. Report of the Chief of Engineers to the Secretary of War, 1876, Vol. II, Part III, Appendix 00; page 700.
58. Glory Hunter; Van De Water, page 324.
59. Ibid.

Dakota: "June 22 — At 12 noon the Regiment under Lieut. Col. George A. Custer, left camp on the Yellowstone and moved up that stream two miles to the mouth of the Rosebud, crossing the latter near its mouth. The Rosebud was there from thirty to forty feet wide and about three feet deep; clear running, slightly alkaline water and gravelly bottom. On account of delays to the pack train, the command marched only about twelve miles, camping at the base of a steep bluff on the left bank of the river; plenty of wood, grass and water."[60]

That evening, trumpeter John Martini, was sent by Custer to notify all officers of the regiment that he wished to see them at his headquarters upstream. After all the officers had gathered together, Custer revealed his plans and also warned them that the Indians would escape if they knew the presence of the command. Caution must be maintained. All commands would be given vocally and not by trumpet, there must be no shooting, and no other unnecessary noise. Then Custer asked for any suggestions from his officers. He also made it quite clear that strictest compliance with any orders from anyone senior to him would be faithfully carried out without discontent. Benteen covers the incident, in an unfinished, undated manuscript:

"... after arrival of the last officer, General Custer commenced his talk; which was to the effect, that it had come to his knowledge that his official actions had been criticised by some of the officers of the regiment at headquarters of the Department, and, that while he was willing to accept recommendations from the junior second lieutenant of the regiment, he wished the same to come in a proper manner; calling our attention to the paragraph of Army Regulations referring to the criticism of actions of commanding officers; and said he

would take the necessary steps to punish, should there be reoccurence of the offense.

I said to General Custer, it seems to me you are lashing the shoulders of *all*, to get at some; now, as we are all present, would it not do to specify the officers whom you accuse? He said, Colonel Benteen, I am not here to be catechised by you, but for your own information, will state that none of my remarks have been directed towards you; then, after giving a few excellent general orders as to what should be done by each troop of the regiment in case of an attack on our bivouac at any time, the meeting of the officers was over, and each adjourned to his palatial 'pup tent.'[61]

"June 23rd — Orders given last night to discontinue trumpet signals, stable guards to wake their respective companies at 3 a.m. and the command would move at 5. General Custer stated that for the first few days short marches would be made, and then increased. All were ready at the appointed time; moving out, we crossed to the right bank of the Rosebud.

"A very broken bluff obliged us to follow the valley for some distance, crossing the stream five times in three miles, thence up the right side for about 10 miles, where we halted to allow the pack train to close up. Soon after starting, we recrossed to the left bank; and, following that for 15 miles, camped on the right bank at 4:30 p.m., making over 30 miles. The last of the pack train did not arrive until near sunset.

"About five miles out today we came to the trail made by Major Reno several days ago, and a few miles farther on saw the first traces of Indians. All the signs were old, but everything indicated large numbers ..."[62]

Several Indian camping places were found at this time and the command was halted at each one so the scouts could de-

60. Annual Report of the Chief of Engineers (1876) — Report of the Secretary of War — 1877.

61. From the collection of manuscript division, Library of Congress; W. J. Ghent collection, Box 2, correspondent file.

62. Annual Report of the Chief of Engineers (1876) to the Secretary of War (printed 1877).

The Seventh's Regimental Standard of 1876. This flag was carried by the regiment to the Little Big Horn, but was encased and placed with the pack train. It was not unfurled during the battle. From the Revised U.S. Army Regulations, 1863 Standards and Guidons of Mounted Regiments; Paragraph 1468: Each regiment will have a silken standard, and each company a silken guidon. The standard to bear the arms of the United States, embroidered in silk, on a blue ground, with the number and name of the regiment, in a scroll underneath the eagle. The flag of the standard to be two feet five inches wide, and two feet three inches on the lance, and to be edged with yellow silk fringe.

termine how long before the Indians had camped there and roughly how many the 7th might encounter. The scout's estimates were high, much higher than Custer's and those of most of his officers. The officers, of course, still based their estimates on the numbers the agents had given on how many

of their charges had jumped the reservations. There is no question that the agents' figures were too low, whether through ignorance or deceit. But, it has always been debated just how many warriors there were at Little Big Horn.

Continuing the Wallace report: "June

24th — Started 5 a.m.; in about an hour the Crow scouts came in and reported fresh signs of Indians, but not in great numbers. After a short consultation, Gen. Custer with an escort of two companies moved out in advance, and the remainder of the command at a distance of about ½ mile. We followed the right bank of the Rosebud, crossing the first two running tributaries seen.

"At 1 p.m. the column was halted, scouts sent ahead and coffee made; about 4 the scouts returned with reports of a fresh camp at the forks of the Rosebud. It was now generally believed that the Indians were not more than 30 miles away. At 5 p.m. the command moved out, crossed to the left bank of the Rosebud and passed through what had been several large camps; the trail was then fresh, and the whole valley scratched up by trailing lodge poles.

"Camped, 7:45 p.m. on the right bank of the Rosebud, after a day's march of about 28 miles; weather clear and warm . . . Scouts sent ahead to ascertain which branch of the stream the Indians had followed, returned about 9 p.m., reporting that they had crossed the divide to the Little Big Horn River. General Custer then decided to continue on that night to conceal the movement, locate the Indian village the next day and attack at daylight the following morning. Orders were accordingly given to resume the march at midnight."

It should be clear by now from this official report of Wallace, (who was no great admirer of his commander), that Custer had not been pushing the 7th to exhaustion, all Custerphobes to the contrary notwithstanding. His plan was a good one and might well have fully succeeded. Unfortunately, as we shall see, he was unable to carry it out.

His intention to wait until June 26th before attacking had nothing whatsoever to do with Terry and Gibbon. He had no reason to expect their arrival in the valley of the Little Big Horn on June 26th or any other specific date. (In fact, they did not arrive

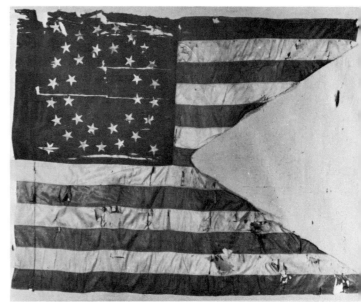

Courtesy Custer Battlefield Museum

In 1861, cavalry guidons were swallow tailed, dividing at the fork the top was red, below white. The letter of the company in red on the white field, on the red was U.S. in white. Later in 1863, regulations gave both cavalry and artillery the swallow-tail guidon in the Stars and Stripes. This provision was withdrawn in 1865, however, some regiments continued to use them regardless of regulations. Custer's famed Seventh carried at least one of these guidons to the Little Big Horn, pictured here is the Stars and Stripes guidon captured some two and a half months later from Indians in the Slim Buttes fight. Size: From lance to end of swallow-tail, 3′5″; from lance to middle of fork, 15″; height of flag, 2′3″. Blue field, 14″ x 14″; width of bars, 2¼″. 35 stars, each star 1⅓″ diameter from point to point.

Courtesy U.S. Signal Corps photo (Brady Collection)

In this Indian beaded bag was found Custer's Stars and Bars swallow tail guidon. The pouch and guidon were taken from Indians at Slim Buttes.

there until June 27th). Indeed, if Custer had followed Terry's suggestion as to the course he should take, the 7th would have been nowhere near the valley of the Little Big Horn on June 27th.[63] There then could have been not a CUSTER'S LAST STAND but a TERRY-GIBBON LAST STAND!

To return to Wallace again: "June 25th — Unable to start until near 1 a.m., and owing to delays with the pack train, had gone only about eight miles by early daylight, when the column was halted and the men prepared coffee. While waiting there a scout came from Lieutenant Charles A. Varnum, who had been sent ahead the night before; in a note, Varnum stated to Custer that he could see the smoke of a village on the Little Big Horn about 20 miles away. The

63. Dr. Charles Kuhlman, "Did Custer Disobey Orders at the Battle of the Little Big Horn?" Stackpole Co., 1957.

returning scout pointed out the butte, then about eight miles distant, from which it was visible.

"Nearing the butte on our march, Lieutenant Varnum joined us, reporting that the Indians had discovered the command, and couriers had been seen going in the direction of their village. General Custer then assembled the officers, told them what he had learned, and said that he would go ahead to attack as soon as possible. The route led through a section of low hills, poor soil and short grass, up the left branch of the Rosebud, then to and up a dry ravine to the crest of the divide between the Rosebud and the Little Big Horn.

"At noon we recrossed the divide from which the valley of the Little Big Horn could be seen; and from 15 to 20 miles to the northwest, a light blue cloud — showing to practised eyes that the Indian village was

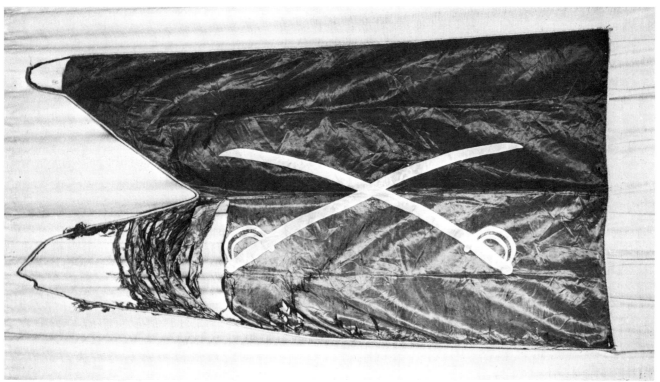

Courtesy Dr. Lawrence Frost

The personal Headquarters Flag of General Custer is 36 inches high, 5½ feet long, the center of the swallow tail cutting back about 22 inches. The crossed white sabers with points up are the length of an issue saber of the Civil War period and are on both sides (stitched on). The top half of the flag is red silk and the bottom is blue. The whole is bound in a ¼ inch woven silk cord. There are two ties each at the top and bottom corners. This flag was carried during the Civil War but is the same as the one Custer carried to the Little Big Horn. As a general officer (brevet), Custer retained the right to carry a personal flag. (See "The Custer Story". by Marguerite Merington.) pg. 147

Courtesy U.S. Signal Corps photo (Brady Collection)
Gall, a Sioux-Hunkpapa chief, led the main attack against Custer, after hitting Reno's line first.

Courtesy Tom Heski   *photo by Barry*
Rain-in-the-Face, Hunkpapa Sioux chieftan, who boasted of cutting the heart out of Tom Custer and eating a portion of it.

near. A small stream which started from a point near where we had passed over the crest flowed in the direction of the smoke. From there to the Little Big Horn the country is broken and the valley narrow, with some timber along the little stream we followed down.

"After assigning the battalions, General Custer continued down the right bank of this creek and Major Reno the left; when within three miles of the Little Big Horn, Reno was ordered to cross to the right bank, and the two columns marched for some distance together. Following orders to go ahead, Reno then recrossed the stream, moved down it and across the Little Big Horn; halting his column, he formed line and continued down the valley of the Little Big Horn, beginning the battle of June 25th, 1876."

The scout's report that the hostiles knew of the command's presence had been erroneous, however honestly believed. (Some of the Indians had seen the command, but they failed to warn the village.) So Custer was forced to attack prematurely, playing wholly by ear, not by sight or any preconcerted plan. Naturally, Wallace's official report is a condensed version of events, his main duty being to retell the 7th's actions.

On the morning of June 25th, Custer didn't know where in the valley of the Little Big Horn the hostiles were encamped or even if there really was such an encampment. True, his scouts had said they had seen the smoke from its campfires and even a vast pony herd. Custer himself had seen nothing, even after he had joined them on the height called the Crows Nest, which gave a good view of the Little Big Horn's valley, straining his eyes through his field-glasses. He knew his scouts to be competent, but they could be mistaken.

After returning to his command from the Crows Nest, Custer decided to send Captain Benteen with three companies on a scout to the left of the 7th's line of march to find the Little Big Horn's valley, and to see if there actually were any hostiles in it; this was about noon. The rest of the command he kept with himself until it was reported to him that Indians had been seen "running like devils" in the Little Big Horn's valley. Custer then detached Major Reno with three companies to chase them, telling the major he would "be supported by the whole outfit," or words to that effect.

He still had not seen anything himself. "The Fog of War" was thick about him. In any case, while Reno said later he expected his commander to support him from the rear, Custer decided to march his five companies along the bluffs of the Little Big Horn, find a practicable ford and attack the hostile encampment, wherever it might be, from the flank, which had been his usual tactic throughout the Civil War. Reno should have known this was Custer's favorite maneuver, since he "had known him throughout the war."

In any case, Reno, inexperienced in Indian fighting, incompetent as he was unless directly overseen by a superior officer, and seeing more hostiles than he had ever seen in his life, all apparently hankering after his scalp, and not seeing Custer coming up behind him in support, disobeyed orders, stopped his charge, made an abortive stand in some timber, finally fleeing *sauve qui peut** to the top of the bluffs. Here he was shortly joined by Benteen, who also disobeyed orders, having received a written communication from Custer through the regimental adjutant to join him at once with the ammunition packs. The pack train, of course, guarded by one company, was several miles back on the regiment's main trail. Benteen did nothing to join Custer with the ammunition packs even after the pack train finally came up, until Captain Weir forced Benteen's and Reno's hand by moving out in the direction Custer had gone without

_____
*From the French meaning — "Save himself who can."

Courtesy U.S. Signal Corps photo (Brady Collection)
Sitting Bull was the great spiritual leader of the Sioux Indians. At the sun dance, early in June 1876, he saw a vision of many soldiers coming up-side down into camp. In camp beside the Little Big Horn River, Sitting Bull again made medicine for strength and victory on the eve of Custer's Battle. Warriors believed his medicine was strong.

Courtesy Custer Battlefield Museum   Photo by Barry
Low Dog — Ogallala Sioux Chief.

Courtesy U.S. Signal Corps photo (Brady Collection)
Crow King — Sioux warrior Hunkpapa. Counted many coup that day.

Courtesy U.S. Signal Corps photo (Brady Collection)
Dull Knife — Cheyenne; it was a good day to die.

Courtesy U.S. Signal Corps photo (Brady Collection)
Little Big Man — Sioux — Ogalalas.

orders to do so. Firing from that direction had been heard more or less plainly by everyone in the command with Benteen and Reno, except themselves. Eventually, Custer and his five companies were wiped out to the last man, Reno and Benteen being effectively corralled by the hostiles on the bluffs until the final arrival of Terry and Gibbon on June 27th.

So, Libbie Custer's premonition of disaster had come true. Still, disaster though it was, it immortalized George Armstrong Custer and his 7th Cavalry as nothing else could have done. Yet, just as the rose has its

Courtesy of Herb Peck, Jr.
Sioux warriors, young and old.

Courtesy Herb Peck, Jr.
Sitting Bull. His autograph generally followed these prints.

thorn, the Little Big Horn has its sting. Custer's brilliant Civil War record is largely forgotten along with his almost equally brilliant nine years of service on the Great Plains prior to the Little Big Horn. The 7th Cavalry's splendid service to its country did not end on the banks of the Little Big Horn. It continued to gather laurels in nearly all of America's wars since. But it is chiefly remembered for the one battle it lost. *Sic transit gloria mundi!*

Instead of speculation concerning the annihilation of Custer's five companies of the 7th Cavalry, C, E, F, I, and L, and the rescue of the remaining seven companies by the timely arrival of General Terry, this author includes several communications and reports by the principal surviving officers of the Little Big Horn engagement. From these reports we can reconstruct a closer picture of the events. In many volumes on the battle, it has been found that official documents are quoted by extracts, leaving out the important context sought after by researchers. With these eyewitness reports there is no possible way we can stray from the truth, unless the particular officer had personal reasons to distort his story. Historians have questioned the credibility of some officers, as to the events leading up to the battle, but nothing officially is known concerning the actions of Custer's five companies and their staggering death toll. There has been a good deal of controversy over the years about this engagement, relying heavily on what the Indians have related, and the credibility of their testimony. And so some writers have pictured Custer as a blundering idiot who led his men down the path of death, while others envisioned him as doing no wrong, placed the blame on the shoulders of the regiment's second in command, Major Marcus A. Reno.

Following is General Alfred H. Terry's

first report of the battle, which was carried
to Fort Ellis, Montana, by the civilian scout
"Muggins" Taylor, and telegraphed there
to the adjutant general in Chicago, Illinois:

Headquarters Department of
Dakota
Camp on Little Big Horn River,
Montana
June 27, 1876

To the Adjutant General of the
Military Division of the Missouri,
Chicago, Illinois, via Fort Ellis.

It is my painful duty to report that day before
yesterday, the 25th instant, a great disaster overtook
General Custer and the troops under his command.
At 12 o'clock of the 22nd instant he started with his
whole regiment and a strong detachment of scouts
and guides from the mouth of the Rosebud.
Proceeding up that river about twenty miles he

Art by E. L. Reedstrom

Martini bringing Custer's last message. Benteen receives it and
hears from the trumpeter that the Indians are "skedadelling."

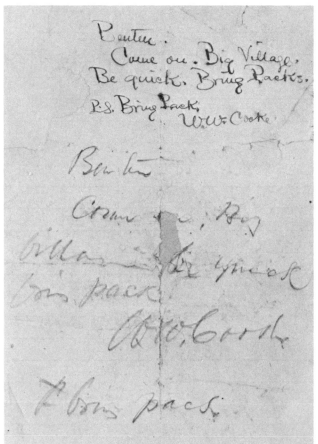

Courtesy West Point Museum Collections

A desperate message for ammunition, hurriedly scribbled by
Custer's adjutant W. W. Cooke to Captain F. W. Benteen. The
message was carried back to the pack train by trumpeter John
Martini who was the last trooper to see General Custer alive.
*Benteen: Come on. Big Village. Be quick. Bring packs. W. W.
Cooke. P.S. Bring packs.*

struck a very heavy Indian trail, which had previously been discovered, and pursuing it, found that it
led, as it was supposed it would lead, to the Little Big
Horn River. Here he found a village of almost unlimited extent, and at once attacked it with that portion
of his command which was immediately at hand.
Major Reno, with three companies (A, G, and M) of
the regiment, was sent into the valley of the stream
at the point where the trail struck it. General Custer,
with five companies, (C, E, F, I, and L,) attempted to
enter about three miles lower down. Reno forded the
river, charged down its left bank, and fought on foot
until finally, completely overwhelmed by numbers,
he was compelled to mount and recross the river, and
seek a refuge on the high bluffs which overlook its
right bank. Just as he recrossed, Captain Benteen,
who, with three companies, (D, H, and K,) was some
two miles to the left of Reno when the action commenced, but who had been ordered by General Custer to return, came to the river, and rightly concluding that it was useless for his force to renew the fight
in the valley, he joined Reno on the bluffs. Captain
McDougall, with his company, (B,) was, at first, some
distance in the rear with a train of pack-mules; he
also came up to Reno. Soon this united force was
nearly surrounded by Indians, many of whom,
armed with rifles, occupied positions which commanded the ground held by the cavalry — ground

from which there was no escape. Rifle-pits were dug, and the fight was maintained, though with heavy loss, from about half past 2 o'clock of the 25th till 6 o'clock of the 26th, when the Indians withdrew from the valley, taking with them their village. Of the movements of General Custer and the five companies under his immediate command, scarcely anything is known from those who witnessed them, for no officer or soldier who accompanied him has yet been found alive. His trail from the point where Reno crossed the stream passes along and in the rear of the crest of the bluffs on the right bank for nearly or quite three miles; then it comes down to the bank of the river, but at once diverges from it as if he had unsuccessfully attempted to cross; then turns upon itself, almost completing a circle, and closes. It is marked by the remains of his officers and men, and the bodies of his horses, some of them strewn along the path; others heaped where halts appear to have been made. There is abundant evidence that a gallant resistance was offered by the troops, but they were beset on all sides by overpowering numbers.

The officers known to be killed are General Custer, Captains Keogh, Yates, and Custer, Lieutenants Cooke, Smith, McIntosh, Calhoun, Porter, Hodgson, Sturgis, and Reilly of the cavalry; Lieutenant Crittenden, of the Twentieth Infantry, and Acting Assistant Surgeon De Wolf, Lieutenant Harrington,

of the cavalry, and Assistant Surgeon Lord are missing. Captain Benteen and Lieutenant Varnum, of the cavalry, are slightly wounded. Mr. B. Custer, a brother, and Mr. Reed, a nephew of General Custer, were with him and were killed. No other officers than those whom I have named are among the killed, wounded, and missing. It is impossible yet to obtain a reliable list of the enlisted men who were killed and wounded, but the number of killed, including officers, must reach two hundred and fifty; the number of wounded is fifty-one.

At the mouth of the Rosebud I informed General Custer that I should take the supply-steamer Far West up the Yellowstone, to ferry General Gibbon's column over the river; that I should personally accompany that column, and that it would in all probability reach the mouth of the Little Big Horn on the 26th Instant. The steamer reached General Gibbon's troops, near the mouth of the Big Horn, early in the morning of the 24th, and at 4 o'clock in the afternoon all his men and animals were across the Yellowstone. At 5 o'clock the column, consisting of five companies of the Seventh Infantry, four companies Second Cavalry, and a battery of Gatling guns, marched out to and across Tullock's Creek. Starting soon after 5 o'clock in the morning of the 25th, the infantry made a march of twenty-two miles over the most difficult country which I have ever seen. In order that scouts might be sent into the valley of the Little Big Horn, the cavalry, with the battery, were then pushed on thirteen or fourteen miles further, reaching camp at midnight. The scouts were sent out at 4:30 on the morning of the 26th. They discovered three Indians, who were at first supposed to be Sioux, but, when overtaken, proved to be Crows, who had been with General Custer. They brought the first intelligence of the battle. Their story was not credited. It was supposed that some fighting, perhaps severe fighting, had taken place, but it was not believed that disaster could have overtaken so large a force as twelve companies of cavalry. The infantry which had broken camp very early, soon came up, and the whole column entered and moved up the valley of the Little Big Horn. During the afternoon efforts were made to send scouts through to what was supposed to be General Custer's position, and to obtain information of the condition of affairs, but those who were sent out were driven back by parties of Indians, who, in increasing numbers, were seen hovering in General Gibbon's front. At 8.40 in the evening the infantry had marched twenty-nine or thirty miles. The men were very weary. Daylight was failing. The column was therefore halted for the night at a point about eleven miles in a straight line above the mouth of the stream. In the morning the march was resumed, and after marching nine miles Major Reno's intrenched position was reached. The withdrawal of the Indians from around Reno's command and from the valley was undoubtedly caused by the appearance of General Gibbon's troops. Major Reno and Captain Ben-

Courtesy Custer Battlefield Museum
Trumpeter John Martini was the last to see Custer alive. He carried the famous "last message" to Captain Benteen, written by Lieutenant W. W. Cooke.

teen, both of whom are officers of great experience, accustomed to see large masses of mounted men, estimate the number of Indians engaged at not less than twenty-five hundred; other officers think the number was greater than this. The village in the valley was about three miles in length, and about a mile in width. Besides the lodges proper, a great number of temporary brushwood shelter was found in it, indicating that more men besides its proper inhabitants had gathered together there. Major Reno is very confident that there were a number of white men fighting with the Indians. It is believed that the loss of the Indians was larger. I have as yet received no official reports in regard to the battle, but what is stated here is gathered from the officers who were on the ground there and from those who have been over it since.[64]

Alfred H. Terry
Brigadier General

On July 5th, Major Marcus Reno, senior surviving officer of the 7th Cavalry, sent his report addressed to Terry's adjutant general:

---

64. The report of the Secretary of War for 1876; Volume I.

Headquarters 7th U. S. Cavalry
Camp on the Yellowstone River
July 5th, 1876
Captain E. W. Smith
A. D. C. and A. A. A. G.

The command of the regiment having devolved upon me, as the senior surviving officer, from the battles of June 25 and 26, between the 7th Cavalry and Sitting Bull's band of hostile Sioux, on the Little Big Horn River, I have the honor to submit the following report of its operations from the time of leaving the main column until the command was united in the vicinity of the Indian village:

The regiment left the camp at the mouth of Rosebud River, after passing in review before the department commander, under command of Brevet Major-General G. A. Custer, Lieutenant-Colonel, on the afternoon of the 22nd of June, and marched up the Rosebud twelve miles and encamped; 23d, marched up the Rosebud, passing many old Indian camps, and following a very large lodge-pole trail, but not fresh, making thirty-three miles; 24th, the march was continued up the Rosebud, the trail and signs freshening with every mile, until we had made twenty-eight miles, and we then encamped and waited for information from the scouts. At 9.25 p.m., Custer called the officers together and informed us that, beyond a doubt, the village was in the valley of the Little Big Horn, and that to reach it, it was neces-

Art by E. L. Reedstrom

"Tom Custer and his brother George — at the final hour."

sary to cross the divide between Rosebud and Little Big Horn, and it would be impossible to do so in the day-time without discovering our march to the Indians; that we would prepare to move at 11 p.m. This was done, the line of march turning from the Rosebud to the right, up one of its branches, which headed near the summit of the divide. About 2 a.m. of the 25th the scouts told him that he could not cross the divide before daylight. We then made coffee and rested for three hours, at the expiration of which time the march was resumed, the divide crossed, and about 8 a.m. the command was in the valley of one of the branches of the Little Big Horn. By this time Indians had been seen, and it was certain that we could not surprise them, and it was determined to move at once to the attack. Previous to this no division of the regiment had been made since the order was issued, in the Yellowstone, annulling wing and battalion organization, but Custer informed me he would assign commands on the march.

I was ordered by Lieutenant W. W. Cooke, adjutant, to assume command of Companies M, A, and G; Captain Benteen of Companies H, D, and K; Custer retaining C, E, F, I, and L under his immediate command, and Company B, Captain McDougall, in rear of the pack-train. I assumed command of the companies assigned to me, and without any definite orders moved forward with the rest of the column, and well to its left. I saw Benteen moving further to the left, and as they passed he told me he had orders to move well to the left, and sweep everything before him. I did not see him again until about 2.30 p.m. The command moved down the creek toward the Little Big Horn Valley; Custer, with five companies, on the right bank; myself and three companies on the left bank, and Benteen further to the left and out of sight.

As we approached a deserted village, and in which was standing one tepee, about 11 a.m. Custer motioned me to cross to him, which I did, and moved nearer to his column, until about 12.30 a.m., when Lieutenant Cooke, adjutant, came to me, and said the village was only two miles ahead, and running away, "to move forward at as rapid gait as I thought prudent, and to charge afterward, and that the whole outfit would support me." I think those were his exact words. I at once took a fast trot and moved down about two miles, when I came to a ford of the river. I crossed immediately and halted about ten minutes, or less, to gather the battalion, sending word to Custer that I had everything in front of me, and that they were strong. I deployed, and with the Ree scouts on my left charged down the valley, driving the Indians with great ease for about two and a half miles. I, however, soon saw that I was being drawn into some trap, as they certainly would fight harder, and especially as we were nearing their village, which was still standing; besides, I could not see Custer or any other support, and at the same time the very earth seemed to grow Indians, and they

Courtesy Custer Battlefield Museum
Captain Myles W. Keogh and Company I, perished on the eastern slope of the Battle Ridge. He was identified by a crucifix about his neck. His horse "Comanche" was the only living thing that survived the battle.

were running toward me in swarms, and from all directions.

I saw I must defend myself and give up the attack, mounted. This I did; taking possession of a point of woods, and which furnished, near its edge, a shelter for the horses, I dismounted and fought them on foot, making headway through the wood. I soon found myself in the near vicinity of the village; saw that I was fighting odds of at least five to one, and that my only hope was to get out of the wood, where I would soon have been surrounded, and gain some high ground. I accomplished this by mounting and charging the Indians between me and the bluffs on the opposite side of the river. In this charge, First Lieut. Donald McIntosh, Second Lieut. Benjamin H. Hodgson, Seventh Cavalry, and Acting Assistant Surgeon J. M. DeWolf were killed. I succeeded in reaching the top of the bluffs, with a loss of the three officers and twenty-nine enlisted men killed and seven wounded. Almost at the same time I reached the top, mounted men were seen to be coming toward us, and it proved to be Colonel Benteen's battalion, Companies H, D, and K. We joined forces, and in a short time the pack-train came up. As senior, my command was then Companies A, B, D, G. H, K, and

Lieutenant James E. Porter, Company I, was reported missing with the Custer Battalion, but presumed killed. His remains were never identified.

(Right) — Brigadier General E. S. Godfrey, (retired) and White Man Runs Him pose in 1926 at the battlesite to propose a monument to the 7th Regimental Cavalry. Indians who were old enough to help dedicate the monument participated. In the ceremonies Godfrey wiped tears from his eyes, as he was emotionally moved. Godfrey, while commanding Company "K" held the rank of 1st Lieutenant.

M, about 380 men, and the following officers: Captains Benteen, Weir, French, and McDougall; First Lieutenants Godfrey, Mathey and Gibson; Second Lieutenants Edgerly, Wallace, Varnum, and Hare, and Acting Assistant Surgeon Porter.

First Lieutenant De Rudio was in the dismounted fight in the woods, but, having some trouble with his horse, did not join the command in the charge out, and, hiding himself in the woods, joined the command after nightfall of the 26th.

Still hearing nothing from Custer, and with this re-enforcement, I moved down the river in the direction of the village, keeping on the bluffs. We had heard firing in that direction and knew it could only be Custer. I moved to the summit of the highest bluff, but seeing and hearing nothing, sent Captain Weir, with his company, to open communication with the other command. He soon sent back word by Lieutenant Hare that he could go no further, and that the Indians were getting around him. At this time he was keeping up a heavy fire from the skirmish-line. I at once turned everything back to the first position I had taken on the bluffs, and which seemed to me the best. I dismounted the men, had the horses and the mules of the pack-train driven together in a depression, put the men on the crests of the hills making the depression, and had hardly done so when I was furiously attacked. This was about 6 p.m. We held our ground, with the loss of eighteen enlisted men killed and forty-six wounded, until the attack ceased, about 9 p.m. As I knew by this time their overwhelming numbers, and had given up any hope of support from the portion of the regiment with Custer, I had the men dig rifle-pits, barricaded with dead horses and mules and boxes of hard bread the opening of the depression toward the Indians in which the ani-

Mark Kellogg's shirt, found at the battlefield, 1876, along with several other items belonging to him. (Housed at the North Dakota State Historical Society.)

mals were herded, and made every exertion to be ready for what I saw would be a terrific assault the next day. All this night the men were busy, and the Indians holding a scalp-dance underneath us, in the bottom, and in our hearing. On the morning of the 26th, I felt confident that I could hold my own, and was ready as far as I could be, when at daylight, about 2.30 a.m., I heard the crack of two rifles. This was the signal for the beginning of a fire that I have never seen equaled. Every rifle was handled by an expert and skilled marksman, and with a range that exceeded our carbine, and it was simply impossible to show any part of the body before it was struck.

We could see, as the daylight brightened, countless hordes of them passing up the valley, from out the village, and scampering over the high points toward the places designated for them by their chiefs, and which entirely surrounded our position. They had sufficient numbers to completely encircle us, and men were struck on opposite sides of the lines from where the shots were fired. I think we were fighting all the Sioux Nation, and also all the desperadoes, renegades, half-breeds, and squaw-men between the Missouri and the Arkansas east of the Rocky Mountains, and they must have numbered at least 2,500 warriors. The fire did not slacken until about 9.30 a.m., and then we discovered that they were making a last desperate attempt, and which was directed against the lines held by Companies H and M. In this attack they charged close enough to use their bows and arrows, and one man lying dead within our lines was touched by the "coup-stick" of one of the foremost Indians. When I say the stick was only about ten or twelve feet long, some idea of the desperate and reckless fighting of these people may be understood. This charge of theirs was gallantly repulsed by the men on that line led, by Colonel Benteen. They also came close enough to send their arrows into the line held by Companies D and K, but were driven away by a like charge of the line, which I accompanied.

We now had many wounded, and the question of water was vital, as from 6 p.m. of the previous evening until now, 10 a.m., about 16 hours, we had been without any. A skirmish-line was formed under Colonel Benteen to protect the descent of volunteers down the hill in front of his position to reach the water. We succeeded in getting some canteens, although many of the men were hit in doing so. The fury of the attack was now over, and, to my astonishment, the Indians were seen going in parties toward the village. But two solutions occurred to us for the movement — that they were going for something to eat and more ammunition, (as they had been throwing arrows,) or that Custer was coming. We took advantage of this lull to fill all vessels with water, and soon had it by the camp-kettleful; but they continued to withdraw, and all firing ceased, save occasional shots from sharpshooters, sent to annoy us about the water.

Courtesy National Archives

"The Northern Pacific, to protect whose right of way my husband and his men had died, provided us with transport, not the government. Nothing beyond the cold official report came from the War Department. President Grant took no official notice of the tragedy." Elizabeth Bacon Custer, under her black crepe bonnet smiles weakly for a photographer. *Circa 1877*

Courtesy Library of Congress

Elizabeth Custer and the General's only sister, Margaret Custer. Photo taken 1879.

About 2 p.m. the grass in the bottom was set on fire and followed up by Indians who encouraged its burning, and it was evident to me that it was done for a purpose, and which purpose I discovered later on to be the creation of a dense cloud of smoke, behind which they were packing and preparing to move their tepees. It was between 6 and 7 p.m. that the village came out from behind the clouds of smoke and dust. We had a close and good view of them as they filed away in the direction of Big Horn Mountains, moving in almost perfect military order. The length of the column was fully equal to that of a large division of the cavalry corps of the Army of the Potomac, as I have seen it on its march.

We now thought of Custer, of whom nothing had been seen and nothing heard since the firing in his direction about 6 p.m. on the eve of the 25th, and we concluded that the Indians had gotten between him and us and driven him toward the boat at the mouth of Little Big Horn River; the awful fate that did befall him never occurring to any of us as within the limits of possibilities. During the night I changed my position in order to secure an unlimited supply of water, and was prepared for their return, feeling sure they would do so, as they were in such numbers; but early on the morning of the 27th, and while we were on the qui vive for Indians, I saw with my glass a dust some distance down the valley. There was no certainty for some time what they were, but finally I satisfied myself they were cavalry, and, if so, could only be Custer, as it was ahead of the time that I understood that General Terry could be expected. Before this time, however, I had written a communication to General Terry, and three volunteers were to try to reach him. (I had no confidence in the Indians with me, and could not get them to do anything.) If this dust were Indians, it was possible they would not expect any one to leave. The men started and were told to go as near as was safe to determine if the approaching column was of white men, and to return at once in case they found it so, but if they were Indians to push on to General Terry. In a short time we saw them returning over the high bluff already alluded to. They were attended by a scout, who had a note from Terry to Custer saying: "Crow scout had come to camp saying he had been whipped, but that it was not believed." I think it was about 10.30 a.m. that General Terry rode into my lines, and the fate of Custer and his brave men was soon determined by Captain Benteen proceeding with his company to his battle-ground, and where were recognized the following officers, who were surrounded by the dead bodies of many of their men: General G. A. Custer; Col. W. W. Cooke, adjutant: Capts. M. W. Keogh, G. W. Yates, and T. W. Custer; First Lieuts. A. E. Smith, James Calhoun; Second Lieuts. W. V. Reilly, of the Seventh Cavalry, and J. J. Crittenden, Twentieth Infantry, temporarily attached to this regiment. The bodies of First Lieut. J. E. Porter and Second Lieuts. H. M. Harrington and

J. G. Sturgis, Seventh Cavalry, and Asst. Surg. G. W. Lord, U.S.A., were not recognized, but there is every reasonable probability they were killed.

The wounded in my lines were, during the afternoon and evening of the 27th, moved to the camp of General Terry, and at 5 a.m. of the 28th I proceeded with the regiment to the battle-ground of Custer and buried 204 bodies, including the following-named citizens: Mr. Boston Custer, Mr. Reed, (a young nephew of General Custer,) and Mr. Kellogg, a correspondent for the New York Herald.

The following-named citizens and Indians who were with my command were also killed: Charles Reynolds, guide and hunter; Isiah, (Isaiah Dorman, colored interpreter); "Bloodly Knife," (who fell immediately by my side,) "Bob-tailed Bull," and "Stab," of the Indian scouts.

After following over his trail it was evident to me that Custer intended to support me by moving farther down the stream and attacking the village in flank; that he found the distance greater to the ford than he anticipated; that he did charge, but his march had taken so long, although his trail shows he moved rapidly, that they were ready for him; that Companies C and I, and perhaps part of Company E, crossed to the village, or attempted it at the charge, and were met by a staggering fire, and that they fell back to secure a position from which to defend themselves, but were followed too closely by the Indians to permit him to form any kind of a line. I think had the regiment gone in as a body, and from the woods in which I fought advanced on the village, that its direction was certain, but General Custer was fully confident they were running or he would not have turned from me.

I think (after the great number of Indians there were in the village) that the following reasons obtain for the misfortune: His rapid marching for two days and one night before the fight; attacking in the daytime at 12 m., and when they were on the qui vive, instead of early in the morning; and lastly, his unfortunate division of the regiment into three commands.

During my fight with the Indians I had the heartiest support from officers and men; but the conspicuous services of Brevet Colonel F. W. Benteen I desire to call attention to especially, for if ever a soldier deserved recognition by his Government for distinguished services he certainly does. I inclose herewith his report of the operations of his battalion from the time of leaving the regiment until we joined commands on the hill. I also inclose an accurate list of casualties as far as it can be made at the present time, separating them into two lists — A, those killed in General Custer's command; B, those killed and wounded in the command I had.

The number of Indians killed can only be approximated until we hear through the agencies. I saw the bodies of eighteen, and Captain Ball, Second Cavalry, who made a scout of thirteen miles over their trail, says that their graves were many along their line of march. It is simply impossible that numbers of them should not be hit in the several charges they made so close to my lines. They made their approach through the deep gulches that led from the hill-top to the river, and when the jealous care with which the Indian guards the bodies of killed and wounded is considered, it is not astonishing that their bodies were not found. It is probable that the stores left by them and destroyed the next two days was to make room for many of them on their trains.

The harrowing sight of the dead bodies crowning the height on which Custer fell, and which will remain vividly in my memory until death, is too recent for me not to ask the good people of this country whether a policy that sets opposing parties in the field, armed, clothed, equipped by one and the same Government, should not be abolished. All of which is respectfully submitted.[65]

M. A. Reno
Major 7th Cavalry
Com'd'g Regiment

For almost a hundred years now speculation has been rife as to what actually happened to Custer and the five companies under his immediate command. Dead men tell no tales. While most of the hostiles engaged survived the battle, little credence could be placed in what they had to relate about it. An Indian's sense of time was altogether different from a white man's. When engaged in battle he often ran together or juxtaposed the time sequence of its different events afterward. His vision of a battle was very limited. He saw only that part of it which related to him personally or to those nearest to him. The Indian warrior's ego was very well developed. His personal participation in a battle was the be-all and end-all of it to him. It was absolutely essential for him to boast about his own prowess in it afterward. In any case, after he had been thoroughly subjugated and was, in a sense, a prisoner, he told his white interrogators what he thought they wanted to hear. Too, his white interrogators usually didn't know his language or mode of thought, his questions being put through an interpreter, who was usually grossly incompetent. Consequently most Indian testimony is wildly at variance not only with

most of the known facts, but contradictory. In all fairness it must be admitted much of the testimony of the 7th's survivors under Reno and Benteen together with that of their commanders is equally untrustworthy.

Benteen said he thought what had happened on Custer Field had been "a panic-rout". Naturally, Benteen, while inspecting its bloody debris, saw only what he wanted to see, his psychopathic hatred of his commanding officer somewhat distorted his vision. Most of the officers with Custer were brave and experienced soldiers. Even if Custer himself had been killed at the beginning of the battle, (as some writers have alleged), his brother, Captain Tom Custer or Lieutenant Cooke or Captain Keogh, to name only a few, would have taken command and prevented "a panic rout." It is therefore inconceivable anything of that nature occurred.

Many of the surviving hostile chiefs and warriors alleged it took only a half hour or hour at the most to wipe out Custer and his battalion. Naturally, again, Benteen and the other Custer haters in the regiment agreed. Tying in very neatly as it did with the "panic-rout" theory. Too, it absolved them from any charges of having dragged their boots in going to Custer's aid. Yet, Benteen confessed he counted "only two" dead Indian ponies on Custer Field. It is evident, then, the hostiles did not over-run Custer and his battalion in a charge en masse. If they had done so there would certainly have been more than two dead Indian ponies. It is also evident the Indians fought almost entirely on foot, which again precludes "a panic-rout." In any case, Indians never charged head-long en masse into even a small body of well-armed troops. It formed no part of their way of fighting. They had far too much sense. This in no way implies the average Indian warrior was any whit inferior to the average white trooper in courage. His tactics were simply different. He preferred fighting from cover or making circling attacks. Undoubtedly the former

---

65. The Report of the Secretary of War for 1876; Volume I.

was used for the most part against Custer and his battalion. Such tactics naturally suppose a more or less lengthy engagement, certainly one lasting more than half an hour or an hour. In any case, most of the testimony of Reno's and Benteen's men clearly indicated the action on Custer Field was of several hours duration.

Probably, it was Custer's original intention after sending Reno across the Little Big Horn to march along its bluffs until he found a practicable ford for attacking the hostile's encampment from the flank. It wasn't until he actually sighted the vast aggregation of tipis that he realized what he was up against. True, he knew from experience a large village was just as apt to disperse as a small one. But, for once in his life, at least, Custer had decided to play it safe. He had sent a message back to Benteen ordering him to bring up the regiment's reserve ammunition packs. "BENTEEN: COME ON. BIG VILLAGE. BE QUICK. BRING PACKS. W. W. COOKE. P.S. BRING PACKS." He would wait for them before attacking, fighting a holding action in the meantime. The 7th's senior Captain would be along shortly.*

Granted, all of this may be considered conjectural. But, it is based upon known facts. With this in mind, we may legitimately conjecture Custer and his battalion did fight a holding action until near the end of the battle, expecting Benteen to appear any minute with the regiment's reserve ammunition. It may well be this was a fatal mistake. But how could Custer have known Benteen would not be along — ever?

But what if Custer had not elected to play it safe? What if he had charged across the river into the hostile encampment? There were then few warriors to contest his crossing. This is one piece of Indian testimony

we can safely rely on. Wouldn't there have been confusion compounded among the warriors still in it? The troopers would have been shooting, yelling, blowing bugles, setting fire to every tipi within reach, while women, children and old people would have been running helter-skelter, screaming at the top of their voices, getting in each others way and that of the few warriors present, dogs barking and howling, ponies rearing and neighing. The warriors streaming back from Reno would only have added to the confusion, dust and smoke obscuring everything. In short, it would have been one helluva donnybrook, a la GarryOwen! Even if Custer and his battalion had still died with their boots on, to a man.

Let us try to re-construct the actions at the Little Big Horn, from recent material gathered, basing facts originating from various authentic sources presented.

Custer turned his battalion away from the river to the prominence now known as Custer Hill, on which the monument stands. Here he dismounted his men, every fourth trooper being a horse-holder. There was little cover, but they wouldn't have to fight a holding action for very long. Benteen would soon be along with the regiment's reserve ammunition. A long range sniping contest then ensued. The hostiles, now gathering in full force, were also dismounted, their cover much better than that of the troopers. Armed mostly with bows and arrows they kept up a continual arcing shower of barbed shafts upon the pony soldiers, causing considerable casualties. Galling though it was, the troopers stood it manfully. Benteen would be along soon.

As the minutes slowly ticked by Custer was continually scanning with his field glasses, the direction in which he expected Benteen to appear. He hadn't sent him that far on the scout to the left of the 7th's line of march! He was only to find the valley of the Little Big Horn, "which was supposed to be nearby and to pitch into anything" he

---

* Trumpeter John Martini, who rode back to Benteen, carrying Custer's famous "last message," evidently failed to inform Benteen of Custer's last known position. Instead of moving cross country in his direction, Benteen kept on line of Reno's advance.

Courtesy U.S. Signal Corps (Brady Collection)

When the Army returned a year later, they found the field scattered with bleaching bones. Now and then a shoe or half a boot dotted the ground. Lonely wooden stakes, half tilted, towered above the bones, other markers were washed away. The grim task of identification and re-burial began.

pected momentarily. At his command post Custer anxiously scanned Weir Point for movement toward him. There was none! It looked like the troops on Weir Point were retreating instead of coming forward.

Tom Custer and Smith from their positions below Custer Hill could see nothing of this. They only knew there was no indication of Benteen's coming. They were under a galling fire, men were falling right and left, they couldn't hold their ground any longer. Trying to beat a hasty retreat back to the command post, most of the two companies were lost, a host of warriors under Lame White Man, seeing their chance, engulfing them in a red wave. Tom Custer and Smith and a handful of their men made it back to the comparative safety of the command post. They would live a little while longer.

might find. It was evident he hadn't found anything "to pitch into". Custer had!

Custer focused his field glasses on what afterward came to be known as Weir Point. Movement could be seen on it even through the dust and smoke of Custer Hill, flashes of blue, of sunlight striking metal. By God! There was one of the 7th's guidons! Benteen at last!

Swiftly Custer decided he must open a corridor for Benteen. Calling his officers around him, he ordered his brother Captain Tom Custer and Lieutenant A. E. Smith to take their companies down Custer Hill to the southeast. Then he ordered Captain Myles Keogh and his brother-in-law Lieutenant James Calhoun to take three companies along what is now known as Battle Ridge to the east of his command post, Calhoun diverging onto a ridge to the southeast.

Some men, we do not know how many, Custer kept with him at his command post. Taking up their assigned positions, Tom Custer, Smith, Keogh and Calhoun prepared to facilitate Benteen's arrival, ex-

Courtesy U.S. Signal Corps (Brady Collection)

Troopers usually marked their clothing. Socks, shirts, clothing — all were searched for markings hoping to establish some identification at that location. Many boot tops were cut-off by the Indians and used as moccasin soles, throwing the lower portion away. Note upper right corner.

Keogh and Calhoun found themselves in the same predicament. Both had dismounted their men upon taking their assigned positions, every fourth man a horse-holder. They, too, had come under a fierce fire with no sign of Benteen. It is evident from the positions of Calhoun and his men, as their bodies were found afterward, they had held a skirmish line to the end, the only such line to be found on Custer Field. Calhoun had once written his brother-in-law if ever the latter had need of him he would not be found wanting. Calhoun certainly kept this promise! Possibly, seeing Benteen wasn't coming he had determined to give Custer every chance, no matter how slim, to save what was left of the battalion. We do not know whether he advised Keogh of what we presume to have been his decision, or whether he would have been able to do so. In any case, it is evident from hostile testimony and the positions of the bodies of Keogh and his men, the fighting Irishman tried to lead a retreat

Courtesy U.S. Signal Corps (Brady Collection)

Shallow graves were dug. Only a few shovels were in the command. Hunting knives cut sections of sod to place over the victims. Boards from empty ammunition and hardtack boxes were used to identify officers who had fallen. Wooden stakes marked the troopers. Empty cartridges with rolled up paper inside for identification were driven into the stakes.

Courtesy U.S. Signal Corps (Brady Collection)

Bones, from every part of the field were piled in heaps. Human remains were mixed in and hard to identify. Wolves dug up what they could find of soldiers and scattered their remains.

back to the command post, but they were wiped out en route. Calhoun and his command had probably fallen to the last man before this.

Custer now had only about 40 officers and men left at the command post, most of them perhaps wounded. Probably, he had seen the slaughter of Keogh's and Calhoun's commands through his field-glasses. For whatever reason, Benteen had not come. It was all too apparent "Custer's Luck" had run out! He now realized he and the remanent of his battalion were doomed. All that was left for them was to sell their lives as dearly as possible.

For their part, the hostiles could see this last portion of pony soldiers could also be wiped out to a man with small loss to themselves. All they had to do was to worm their way closer and closer from cover to cover, picking off these enemies by ones, twos and threes, until a mounted charge could over-run the very few left. This they proceeded to do. According to hostile testimony, only seven troopers managed to evade the final onslaught, making a futile break for the Little Big Horn. They were swiftly ridden down, being tomahawked, lanced or shot in their tracks. It was all over. "We have killed them all!"

Again all of this may be considered as conjecture. But it is logical, being based upon the few new facts we admittedly possess. We know the terrain of Custer Field, which hasn't changed much since 1876. We know a person using field glasses can easily descry Weir Point from Custer Hill and anything appearing upon it. We know the Indian method of fighting. Some Indian testimony, after the wheat has been separated from the chaff, rings true. The same may be said for much of the 7th's survivors testimony at the Reno Court Of Inquiry in 1879.

There are certain things that are evident of themselves. It is evident from Custer's last order to Benteen, the famous "Bring packs," he had decided to fight a holding action until the 7th's senior captain joined him with the ammunition packs. It is evident he knew Benteen could join him in a short time. It must have been evident to Custer most if not all of the hostiles had concentrated against him. Therefore, either Reno had been wiped out or his own appearance across the Little Big Horn from their encampment had diverted their attention from the Major to himself. Probably Custer thought the last assumption to be the correct one. Benteen, then, could pick up Reno's battalion and hurry with it and his own and the ammunition packs to join him.

As we have pointed out, Custer must have seen the appearance of the rest of the 7th through his field glasses on Weir Point. It is evident Benteen must have thought so, since he testified at the Reno Court he had had one of the 7th's guidons planted there so Custer would know where the rest of the regiment was. He could then fight his way through to it. Still, it must also have been evident to Benteen from the "Bring packs" order Custer expected him to do just the

Courtesy U.S. Signal Corps (Brady Collection)

Captain Nowlan and another man (unidentified) pay their respects to old comrades. A wreath of tall grass was made up and placed on Keogh's marker. Others in the background continue with their gruesome chores.

Courtesy Library of Congress

Captain C. K. Sanderson's camp at the Ford in 1879 while gathering bones and building the monument. (See Graham's "The Custer Myth", pages 369-371). Photo from a stereo.

After the battle of the Little Big Horn, the bodies of Custer's men were buried in shallow graves where they had fallen. Rifle butts, cups and knives were used to dig the graves. A year later, the Army returned and re-buried the bodies properly and with honors. Soldier putting finishing touches on wooden monument.

The remains of three soldiers killed in the battle of the Little Big Horn were unearthed in an archeological research in June 1958. The National Park Service reported the finds on the eve of the 82nd Anniversary of Custer's famous last stand.

Just below the Reno-Benteen Monument are (left to right) Robert Bray, Archeologist; and Don Rickey, Jr., Historian (in trench coat). The other two men (behind Rickey and Bray, also far right) are not identified. Findings were a lime formation about the bones of one soldier. Several buttons, blue cloth, and a roll of bandages. The author was privileged to be there at that time.

opposite. Therefore, Benteen was to join Custer, not the other way 'round.

In the event, what would have been more logical for Custer than to have ordered the troop dispositions we have conjectured he did in order to facilitate Benteen's arrival. In this we agree with the late Dr. Kuhlman.* In any case, the positions where the bodies of Tom Custer's, Smith's, Keogh's and Calhoun's men were found bears this out. Unless we accept Benteen's wholly untenable theory it was all "a panic-rout."

Despite the faulty cartridge ejection of most of the 7th's weapons, the troopers were far better armed than the hostiles. Consequently the 7th's firepower was much greater. We may be sure the hostiles were well aware of this fact, acting accordingly, utilizing every bit of cover available to them, exposing themselves very little. As an inspection of the whole terrain of Custer Field shows, the Custer battalion was far more exposed. But, Custer didn't expect his holding action to last very long. Therefore he expected his casualties to be light.

It is only logical to assume if he had not seen the rest of the 7th on Weirpoint, deducing therefrom the swift arrival of Benteen, he would have sought a better defensive position he could hold for any length of time necessary, or as long as his ammunition held out. It does seem to us this may have been the crux of the matter. From Indian testimony it is evident the hostiles were successful in stampeding most of the 7th's mounts, their saddle-bags carrying most of the trooper's ammunition. This happened after Custer had made the troop dispositions we have recounted. Did Tom Custer's, Smith's, Keogh's and Calhoun's men run out of ammunition after their horses were stampeded? How long the Custer battalion's ammunition would have lasted if he had sought a better defensive

_____

*Custer and the Gall Saga; Billings Mont., 1940. Legend into History; The Custer Mystery; Harrisburg, Pa., Stackpole Co., (1951).

Courtesy Custer Battlefield Museum

The remains of a trooper at Reno Battlefield, excavated June 1958. The three unknown soldiers were buried in the National Cemetery. Note the single row of brass buttons indicating a shell jacket worn.

position and had simply sat tight with his whole battalion it is impossible to say. The hostiles would still have tried to stampede the pony soldier's mounts. But it is doubtful if they would then have been as successful, for Custer would have done his utmost to safeguard the precious ammunition reserve he had with him.

Whether Custer could have held out as long as Reno and Benteen is a good question. However, until he had made the troop dispositions we have recounted, the battle, if it could be so termed, had been a long-drawn-out sniping contest, as was most of the Reno-Benteen engagement on Reno Hill. This did not use up much ammunition. It is possible Custer might have held out until the arrival of Terry and Gibbon. We know Reno and Benteen did.

We also know the hostiles made no all-out effort to overrun the Reno-Benteen positions. In fact, they didn't even try to wipe out Reno when he made his *sauve qui peut* to the bluffs from his position in the timber. This they could easily have done, incurring very few casualties themselves. They

merely seemed content to have driven Reno away from proximity to their encampment. Of course, at the same time Custer was making his appearance opposite their encampment, which probably drew the hostiles' attention away from Reno and to him. This, together with the arrival of Benteen at about the same time, probably saved Reno.

While the defensive position Reno and Benteen selected on Reno Hill was better than any Custer would have been able to find where he was, it wasn't all that good. That is, if the hostiles had been as determined as white troops in a similar situation, they would have launched a head-long charge en masse on Reno Hill. And that would have been a Reno-Benteen Last Stand. But, this would have meant heavy casualties for them, so they were quite content to keep these pony soldiers effectively corraled away from their encampment. Isn't it possible they would have treated Custer's battalion in the same fashion if he had not made the final troop dispositions he did? Even though he was much closer to their encampment?

Actually, it is evident the hostiles acted almost throughout as defensively as the commanders of the 7th. Most hostile testimony states unequivocally their intention of not fighting at all. If forced to do so to

Courtesy Author's Collection

Custer Battlefield relics. 1. Remington new model Army cal. revolver. (Notice hammer screw replacement), probably Indian. 2. Sharp's hammer and lock plate. 3. .44 Henry pointed 4. Spencer .52 cal. 5. Spencer .52 cal. 6. Spencer .52 cal. 7. 50/70 8. 45/70 9. 50/70 10. Spencer .52 cal. 11. .50 caliber slug 12. .69 caliber ball 13. .44 caliber ball.

Mark Kellogg's last entry in his daily log, written June 24, 1876 reads, "I go with Custer and will be at the death."

fight defensively, buying time for their women, children and old people to escape the pony soldiers. While this may be taken with a grain of salt, the evidence strongly suggests it is true.

In short, the whole Battle of the Little Big Horn was partly a comedy of errors and could have resulted in a draw instead of only that portion of it fought by Reno and Benteen. There simply wouldn't have been a "Custer's Last Stand" and "Custer's Luck" would not have completely run out. Still, the key to the disaster it did become, was due to the actions, or rather, the lack thereof of Captain Frederick William Benteen; for whatever reason.

It may truthfully be said battles are seldom fought logically, regardless of how

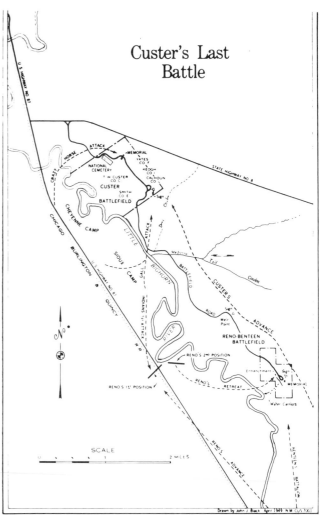

Map — Custer's Last Battle

General George Crook in a Civil War uniform. Crook, who had brought the Apaches on reservations, was transferred to the Department of the Platte in March, 1875. He was going to teach the Northern Indians to 'walk the white man's road.'

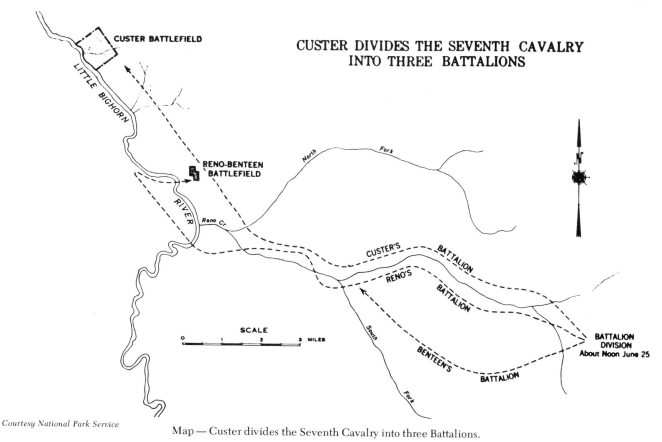

CUSTER DIVIDES THE SEVENTH CAVALRY
INTO THREE BATTALIONS

Courtesy National Park Service

Map — Custer divides the Seventh Cavalry into three Battalions.

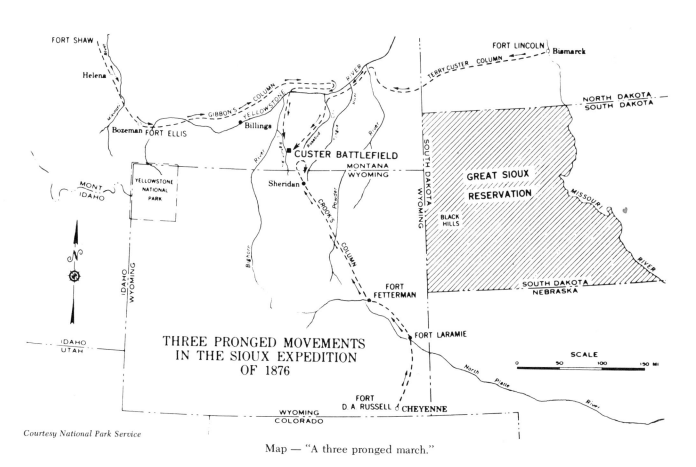

THREE PRONGED MOVEMENTS
IN THE SIOUX EXPEDITION
OF 1876

Courtesy National Park Service

Map — "A three pronged march."

LIEUTENANT W. W. COOK, ADJUTANT.

LIEUTENANT W. VAN W. REILY.

LIEUTENANT J. J. CRITTENDEN.

LIEUTENANT JAMES CALHOUN,
COMMANDING TROOP "L."

LIEUTENANT A. E. SMITH,
COMMANDING TROOP "E."

LIEUTENANT H. M. HARRINGTON.

LIEUTENANT J. E. PORTER.

LIEUTENANT J. G. STURGIS.

Officers killed at the Little Big Horn.

logically their commanders planned them. Far too much of the human element enters into them. However, once a battle has been fought and is brought into the light of the study lamp, a certain logic emerges, consisting of cause and effect, the sequence of events, the known facts, a knowledge of human nature. So it is with the Battle of the Little Big Horn, even though there were no survivors of a portion of one side engaged and much of the testimony of those who did survive on both sides is worthless. We believe we have elucidated this logic insofar as it can be. For those who may disagree, we can only say let them light their own study lamp and ponder far into the night.

EYEWITNESS OR LIAR?

By early afternoon on June 25, 1876, elements of the U.S. Army's Seventh Cavalry, under the command of General George Armstrong Custer, had been annihilated by a vastly superior force of Indian warriors, led by Sitting Bull. No survivors remained to tell details of the battle tactics. Even news of the event was weeks in reaching the civilized world; much of it was sketchy, imcomplete — and frustrating. What happened on the Little Big Horn?

It is fair to say that no other single event in

American history has captured the imagination of the public more completely than "Custer's Last Stand." Although most Americans are aware that the Indians gained a victory at the Little Big Horn, few are familiar with the details of the events of that day. In considering the reasons for this, it is well to note the time during which this event took place. In 1876, accurate reporting of historical events was slow and uncertain. A newspaper reporter accompanied the Seventh Cavalry detachment under the command of General Custer. He was killed during the battle of the Little Big Horn. Had he survived and written about the campaign, it is entirely possible that a great deal of time would have passed before his reports reached public attention.

A scant 10 years prior to Custer's defeat, this vast, untamed wilderness of south-central Montana had been known as a part of the Great American Desert. Many contemporary historians referred to Custer's last stand as a "massacre," although that term implies the slaughter of those who can make little or no resistance. In Custer's case, it was a bloody battle between armed antagonists, after the aggressor had attacked the Indians.

The lack of eyewitness reports from the battlefield has done much to confuse the situation. This frustrating condition has caused the event to remain shrouded in mystery. Yet there may be a clue to the events of that fateful day. Some months after the battle, a newspaper article appeared in the Minneapolis Tribune of September 8, 1876, and headlined, "Custer's Butcher." The Minneapolis Tribune and the St. Paul Pioneer Press had published an interview with a trapper by the name of D. H. Ridgeley, who had been in the Yellowstone country of Wyoming for many months. Ridgeley was aware of great Indian activity in the area in which he was trapping, and consequently took steps to avoid marauding Indian war parties. In late March 1876, he was captured by the Sioux and taken to the

Ulysses S. Grant

camp of Sitting Bull, where he was kept prisoner until the battle of the Little Big Horn. He was stripped of all his possessions and great mockery was made of him because of his thin build and facial whiskers. Forced to perform any tasks given him by the Indians, Ridgeley was subjected to daily degradation; other than that, his meals were regular and animal skins provided him warmth. The newspaper account continued, with Ridgeley supplying details of the Indians preparing for a great battle.

By the 25th day of June, 1876, the Indian nations under the leadership of Sitting Bull stood ready for an attack. This was the day of the battle against the long-knives of the U.S. Cavalry. A great number of Indians climbed the side of the hills overlooking the site of Custer's march down the valley along the Rosebud River. Examining the site where the Indian nation was encamped, we note that it was divided by a large bluff or ridge, the front of which ran well down toward the Rosebud and in the direction of the available fords along the river. It was as though Sitting Bull realized that this would be the site of a great battle for his people. He had divided his nation into two separate encampments. Some 25 teepees formed a village which could be visible to troops moving up the Rosebud River toward the bluff. However, another 75 teepees in a much larger village were located on the other side of the bluff, not visible to anyone moving up the river. The Indians had crossed the Rosebud to camp by this bluff along the available ford at the lower end of the bluff; Custer had followed their trail down to the water's edge. He noted the smaller village from across the river, and it was this village which he attacked first. He was immediately met by a strong force of 1,500 to 2,000 Indians in a regular order of battle, every movement by the Indians being made in a form of military precision. The trapper Ridgeley had been moved to the side of the hill, where he had a broad overview of the action taking place below him. He was still being kept prisoner, but he was not more than one and a half miles from the actual site of the fighting.

According to the Ridgeley report published in the Minneapolis newspaper, General Custer began his fight in a ravine near the ford where he crossed the river, fully one-half of the command immediately engaged and unhorsed by the first fire from the Indians. The cavalrymen immediately retreated toward a hill in the rear, and they were cut down on the way to that hill with astonishing rapidity. Ridgeley reported the commanding officer falling from his horse in the middle of this engagement, an astonishing admission and a notable discovery, if true. The battle continued to rage for

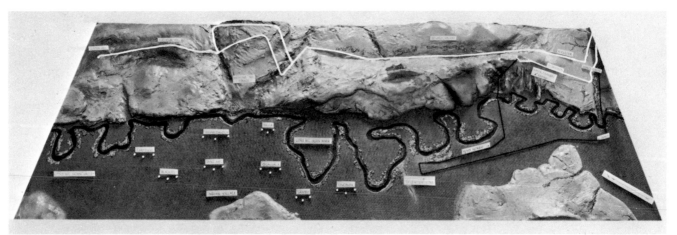

Courtesy Dr. L. A. Frost

Battle map to scale of the Little Big Horn, showing Custer's route (in white).

Discharge of William E. Smith, Company D (Private). Company D was one of the four companies under the command of Major Reno. Thomas B. Weir was Captain.

another half to three-quarters of an hour until the last soldier had been killed. At the conclusion of the battle, the Indians returned to their camp with 6 soldiers as prisoners. They were delirious with joy over their successes. The soldiers having been taken prisoner were tied to stakes at a large wood pile in the village around the point of the hill, whereupon the wood was set afire and all soldiers burned to death, the bodies dropping to the earth a blackened, roasted and hideous mass. Apparently not content to allow them death in this fashion, Indian boys were allowed to fire red-hot arrows into the flesh of these soldiers. This incredible "amusement" was allowed to continue until each of the unfortunate victims had fallen a corpse. Ridgeley stated that the sight was so horrible that it could never be erased from his memory.

This grisly scene concluded, the Indian women, with their children, armed themselves with knives, whereupon they proceeded to the field of battle to rob the dead of clothing, valuables, trinkets and such else as they could find. They further mutilated the bodies of the soldiers in a manner too shocking and sickening for description.

During the time when the six soldiers were being burned to death in the village, another force attacked the Indian village, and the Indians turned their attention to meeting this attack. Undoubtedly, this attack was led by the forces of Major Reno. All during this second attack, the soldiers were kept burning and subjected to every imaginable torture. Ridgeley estimated that the time which elapsed was 45 minutes to an hour and a half; he was not permitted to speak to the soldiers before their horrible death. He could not, therefore, give any indication of their identities. Possibly important is his description of one of the soldiers as being of small stature, with grey hair and whiskers. These physical attributes may lead to the identification of one of the unfortunate prisoners.

It was evening by the time all of the Indians returned from the field of battle. Many returned to their camps to drink whiskey, captured during the battle, and admire new weapons and clothing taken from the fallen soldiers. During the revelry, squaws performed the duty of guarding Ridgeley and two companions. Names of the other two men with Ridgeley were not mentioned, nor did Ridgeley state whether or not they were cavalrymen. Much pandemonium reigned during the night after the battle, and the guards became drowsy. At the first opportunity, Ridgeley and his companions slipped away from the main group. Groping through the darkness, they came across several Indian ponies and mounted them to make tracks toward civilization, only to find the countryside literally crawling with Indian war parties. There seemed to be no alternative but seclusion, so they came to a halt and hid in a section of woods for 4 days, concealed from all searching eyes. Discovering, after 4 days, that it was apparently safe to travel again, they moved on slowly and steadily, encountering numerous straggling Indians along their journey, and studiously avoiding contact with them. On the fifth night away from Sitting Bull's camp, Ridgeley's pony stumbled, throwing him to the ground and causing him to break his arm in two places. The men traveled generally eastward, north of Fort Abraham Lincoln, as they were fearful that small war parties moving west to join Chief Sitting Bull might stumble across them. They strove for Fort Abercrombie, and, after reaching that destination safely, one of the two men traveling with Ridgeley was afflicted with erysipelas and died a few days later. The other man joined his own friends and family at home in northern Minnesota, nevermore to be heard from.

Unquestionably shaken by the events which had taken place, Ridgeley himself reached his hometown of Minneapolis shaken by the Indian massacre and his broken arm. When he came among his friends, one of whom was Mr. Hall McCleave of the firm of Warner and McCleave, undertakers and furniture dealers, Ridgeley recounted the story of his events. Mr. McCleave insisted that the trapper tell his story to a local newspaper editor and allow it to be printed, leaving out none of the reported atrocities he had witnessed.

Reviewing the newspaper article, we note that Ridgeley described Chief Sitting Bull as a large man, a half-breed, and very intelligent. He reported that, owing to some sort of injury, Sitting Bull's right foot turned outward and the deformity affected his walk noticeably. Sitting Bull claimed that every white man would be driven from the Black Hills, and he would stand and fight if soldiers came. Noting that Red River carts had been in the camp of Sitting Bull 5 weeks or so before the Custer fight, Ridgeley concluded that regular supplies of powder and lead from Canadian traders was flowing to the Indian nation. He further mentioned that there were apparently two chiefs in Sitting Bull's camp who were believed to be white men; they could speak English quite well. Of further interest is Ridgeley's report that the Indians were maneuvered like soldiers, displaying a surprising knowledge of military tactics.

Ridgeley's integrity and his truthfulness was not in question at the time that his report to the newspaper was made; therefore, little reason to doubt the substantial accuracy of his narrative was voiced. Although Ridgeley's story surpasses anything of the imagination, his credentials were sufficient to lend credence to his report. The story was published in Minneapolis on September 8, 1876. The effect of its publishing was really no surprise to anyone. Over night, Ridgeley became a celebrity. The New York papers picked up the story immediately, reprinting it almost word-for-word. The New York Grafic published the following: "There ought to be a purse raised as a testimonial to the bravery and mendacity of that alleged white man who escaped from Sitting Bull

The New-York Times.

VOL. XXV____NO. 7742.　　　　　　　　NEW-YORK, FRIDAY, JULY 7, 1876.　　　　　　　　PRICE FOUR CENTS.

THE LITTLE HORN MASSACRE.

LATEST ACCOUNTS OF THE CHARGE.

FORCE OF FOUR THOUSAND INDIANS IN POSITION ATTACKED BY LESS THAN TEN THOUSAND MEN—OPINIONS OF LEADING ARMY OFFICERS ON THE DEED AND ITS CONSEQUENCES—FEELING IN THE COMMUNITY OVER THE DISASTER.

Special Dispatch to the New-York Times.

The dispatches giving an account of the slaughter of Gen. Custer's command, published in THE TIMES of yesterday, are confirmed and supplemented by official reports from Gen. A. H. Terry, commanding the expedition. On June 25 Gen. Custer's command came upon the main camp of Sitting Bull, and at once attacked it, charging the thickest part of it with five companies, Major Reno, with seven companies attacking on the other side. The soldiers were repulsed and a wholesale slaughter ensued. Gen. Custer, his brother, his nephew, and his brother-in-law were killed, and not one of his detachment escaped. The Indians surrounded Major Reno's command and held them in the hills during a whole day, but Gibbon's command came up and the Indians left. The number of killed is stated at 300 and the wounded at 31. Two hundred and seven men are said to have been buried in one place. The list of killed includes seventeen commissioned officers.

It is the opinion of Army officers in Chicago, Washington, and Philadelphia, including Gens. Sherman and Sheridan, that Gen. Custer was rashly imprudent to attack such a large number of Indians, Sitting Bull's force being 4,000 strong. Gen. Sherman thinks that the accounts of the disaster are exaggerated. The wounded soldiers are being conveyed to Fort Lincoln. Additional details are anxiously awaited throughout the country.

CONFIRMATION OF THE DISASTER.

DISPATCHES FROM GEN. TERRY RECEIVED AT SHERIDAN'S HEAD-QUARTERS—THEORIES OF THE BATTLE—PROBABLY TEN THOUSAND SIOUX IN POSITION—THE ATTACK CONSIDERED AS RASH BY OFFICERS OF EXPERIENCE—DISPOSITION OF THE WOUNDED.

CHICAGO, July 6.—At the head-quarters of Lieut. Gen. Sheridan this morning, all was bustle and confusion over the terrible massacre of Custer's command. Telegrams were being constantly received, but most of them were of a confidential nature and withheld from publication.

DISPATCHES FROM GEN. TERRY.

PARTICULARS OF THE PLAN OF THE MOVEMENT UNDER CUSTER AS AGREED ON BEFORE THE MARCH.

Special Dispatch to the New-York Times.

PHILADELPHIA, July 6.—This afternoon Gen. Sheridan received two dispatches from Gen. Terry relative to the Indian battle in which Gen. Custer was killed, and this evening the telegrams were handed to your correspondent.

DETAILS OF THE BATTLE.

GRAPHIC DESCRIPTION OF THE FIGHTING—MAJOR RENO'S COMMAND UNDER FIRE FOR TWO DAYS—EVERY MAN OF CUSTER'S DETACHMENT KILLED EXCEPT ONE SCOUT—AFFECTING SCENES WHEN RELIEF ARRIVED.

Special Dispatch to the New-York Times.

CHICAGO, July 6.—A special to the *Times* to-night from Bismarck, recounts most graphically the late encounter with the Indians on the Little Big Horn.

THE SCENE OF THE MASSACRE.

DESCRIPTION OF THE REGION BY MAJOR GRIMES, WHO REMOVED THE FORTS IN 1868, UNDER THE TREATY.

Special Dispatch to the New-York Times.

ST. LOUIS, July 6.—The news of the massacre of Gen. Custer with seventeen commissioned officers and 315 men, near the Little Big Horn River, has created an extraordinary sensation here.

THE CAUSES AND CONSEQUENCES.

FRUITS OF THE ILL-ADVISED BLACK HILLS EXPEDITION—TWO YEARS AGO—ABILITY OF THE ARMY TO RENEW OPERATIONS EFFECTIVELY DISCUSSED—THE PERSONNEL OF THE CHARGING PARTY STILL UNDEFINED.

WASHINGTON, July 6.—The news of the fatal charge of Gen. Custer and his command causes great excitement in Washington, particularly among Army people and about the Capitol.

VIEWS AT THE WAR DEPARTMENT.

THE CONFIRMATORY DISPATCHES FROM SHERIDAN'S HEAD-QUARTERS IN CHICAGO—FEELING AMONG CUSTER'S FRIENDS.

WASHINGTON, July 6.—Not until late this afternoon did the War Department receive confirmatory reports of the news published this morning of the terrible disaster in the Indian country.

MISCELLANEOUS DISPATCHES.

A LIST OF OFFICERS KILLED—FEELING OVER THE DISASTER—A REGIMENT OF FRONTIERSMEN OFFERED FROM UTAH.

ST. LOUIS, July 6.—A telegram from Gen. Ruggles at St. Paul to Capt. Green Hale, commanding the cavalry at the arsenal here, gives the following as the names of the officers killed in the fight between the Sioux and Gen. Custer's command:

Gen. Custer,	Lieut. Reily.
Col. Custer,	Lieut. Porter,
Capt. Custer,	Lieut. Calhoun,
Col. Yates,	Lieut. Harrington,
Col. Keogh,	Lieut. Sturgis,
Col. Cook,	Lieut. Riely.
Lieut. Smith,	
Lieut. Hodgson,	

SKETCH OF GEN. CUSTER.

Major Gen. George A. Custer, who was killed with his whole command while attacking an encampment of Sioux Indians, was born in New-Rumley, Harrison County, Ohio, on the 5th of December, 1839.

RECORD OF THE REGIMENT.

THE OFFICERS, AND WHAT THEY HAVE DONE—THE DATES OF THEIR PROMOTIONS.

The Seventh Regiment of United States Cavalry was organized by act of Congress July 28, 1866.

A TILDEN ELECTIONEERING TRICK.

STATE ENGINEER VAN BUREN'S REPORT TO THE CANAL BOARD—WHAT IT REALLY IS AND WHAT IT PURPORTS TO BE.

ALBANY, July 6.—State Engineer Van Buren's report to the Canal Board on pending contracts for extraordinary repairs on the canals was taken up at the meeting to-day.

MR. BLAINE'S ILLNESS.

NO CHANGE IN HIS CONDITION—A EUROPEAN TRIP RECOMMENDED.

AUGUSTA, Me., July 6.—Mr. Blaine has now been some eight days. So far there has been no special change in his case.

THE DEMOCRATS IN WASHINGTON.

A WEAK RATIFICATION OF TILDEN—A FOUR MINUTE TORCH-LIGHT PROCESSION.

Special Dispatch to the New-York Times.

WASHINGTON, July 6.—The Democracy held their ratification meeting to-night.

FRENCH POLITICS.

DIFFERENCES AMONG THE REPUBLICAN DEPUTIES ON MUNICIPAL MATTERS—REFUSAL OF PARLIAMENT TO SHOOT THE DUC DE CHARTRES

PARIS, July 6.—Differences have arisen among the Republican Deputies over the Municipal Bill.

and now gives a history of the fight through a Minneapolis paper. We will keep all money sent to us for that purpose." In the tumult over celebrating Ridgeley's reports, many would forget Custer and his brave men who lay dead on the hillsides of the Little Big Horn.

For 17 days, Ridgeley basked in the reflected glory of his reports. On the evening of September 25, 1876, a small column appeared in the Pioneer Press and Tribune in Minneapolis, puncturing a hole in Ridgeley's story, and bringing his period of exuberance to an end:

To the Editors of the Pioneer Press and Tribune:

I saw in your paper the other day, a statement of the trapper Ridgeley about the Custer fight on the Little Big Horn. Now, as I know this man Ridgeley well, and also knew his whereabouts since the first of July, 1875, I thought that a few words from me might be of interest to you and your many readers. Ridgeley claims he had been absent for two years on a trapping expedition. Now, Mr. Editor, he worked for me all through haying and harvesting in the summer of 1875; he left my place about the 25th of September of last year, but I saw him several times in October. He says he, with others, was captured by Indians in March last, and was still a prisoner in Sitting Bull's camp at the time of Custer's annihilation on the 25th of June. Now, I saw Ridgeley and conversed with him about the middle of April last, on the Platte River, in Morrison county, in this state; he was then at work for Hill Bros., in their logging camp on Platte River. More over I received the following letter from him early in July:

Sauk Rapids, Minn., July 3, A.D. 1876. 'Mr. Ward, Der Sir I wish that you Wold let me Know What the chance is Down there for Work in haying this yer, if there is a good chance and Wages I will come Down thare to Work this yer again plese let Me Know as soon as you git this good By From Your friend D. H. Ridgeley.'

Now, Mr. Editor, I am prepared to prove every statement made by me should our friend Ridgeley desire it. Why Ridgeley should invent such a story, of course is beyond my comprehension. He is of an imaginative mind, and is continually telling something to stir up a confusion.

Yours Respectfully, T. A. WARD, Anoka, Minn.

How could anyone now believe the account which Ridgeley had given? It appeared foolish to do so, as T. A. Ward seemed so certain of Ridgeley's whereabouts. Yet no published reports are made of any response Ridgeley might have made to the accusation by Ward. Did he have an answer on his whereabouts? Did he truly write the letter of July 3, 1876? How did he explain his report of the Custer massacre in such a short period of time?

History is ready to welcome another hero to its ranks. Had he not been pitching hay at the time of Custer's last stand, perhaps D. H. Ridgeley would have joined the ranks of national heroes. Yet who can say today whether or not things happened as Ridgeley reported? It is a nagging question which troubles historians and which, some day, may have an answer. Our "17-day hero" is lost to history.

CIVIL WAR UNIFORMS

The Army and Navy Journal[1] from its beginning in 1863 had large circulation among regular and volunteer forces. Its weekly pages carried first-hand accounts of victories and defeats with detailed descriptions. Medical and casualty reports were scanned by relatives, friends and comrades. Foreign military matters, including naval service, were covered weekly. Dishonorably discharged officers who sought to restore their commissions were exposed. The Journal often served as a whipping post and wailing wall for officers and enlisted men, in letters to the editor. Complaints as well as inventive ideas were aired, repeated and summed up over and over again. Uniforms, weapons and accoutrements were frequent topics. The standard uniform drew heavy criticism from soldiers who had to deal with the Quartermaster's issue. Letters to the editor pointed out the unfitness of the uniform.

One reader wrote to the editor: "Taking a stroll down Broadway some days ago with a friend who, during his travels since, has seen most of the troops in the old world, we came across a party of about half-a-dozen of Uncle Sam's infantry, as good looking men as you can find anywhere; but oh! how shabbily got up; three of them were above the average height, and consequently their pantaloons, though roomy enough otherwise to accommodate two instead of one, were not turned up at the bottom, but they had over-reached their tunics by some inches in the sleeves, which appeared to be dreadfully tight about the elbows, and gen-

erally giving one the impression of a straight jacket. As to the cap, I can only say that it never did, and never will, look well on any man; so the less said of it the better. The others of the party were about the average height — rather under-enveloped in pantaloons of the standard width, with a large, thick roll at the bottom; coat sufficiently roomy for an extra occupant, sleeves rolled up, and collars that if allowed to stand erect would completely extinguish all profile. The bugles were visible on their head gear, as well as letter of company; but

Courtesy Bob McDonald Collection

The Infantry was sad-looking in appearance. A soldier who loses faith in his uniform . . . loses faith in himself and the branch, yet everyone wondered why there were so many desertions. This was one of the reasons.

---

1. First publication in August, 1863, it was a weekly national military trade newspaper, published in New York City.

I defy any to tell what regiment they belonged to, from any distinctive mark on their uniforms."[2]

The writer, who signed himself as "American," continued with additional criticism of the shabbily dressed soldiers, concluding: "With the many reasons given for the distaste for the service, and numerous desertions, might be classed that of having to wear the plainest, poorest, and most unbecoming uniform in use in any nation on either continent, and which gives the wearer the appearance of a man who has sold himself cheaply, and who assumes in consequence a most woe-begone air of res-

2. Army and Navy Journal, June 1, 1867, pg. 650.

Courtesy Gordon Corbett, Jr.
Cape shown here is minus the yellow flannel lining (color for Cavalry). Cape provided additional protection for shoulders and chest. When thrown over head it acted as a hood. The Infantry coat had a shorter cape and was single breasted. By the early seventies, the Cavalry coat was prescribed for all troops.

Courtesy Author's Collection
The Cavalry "Shell" jacket was in use since 1833, served with little criticism through the Civil War and into the middle 1870s. Troopers modified this jacket to their taste at frontier posts by either removing the trim or altering the collar.

ignation, and reckless slovenliness in many cases."

Frontier duty on the plains during midsummer saw the horse soldier perspire to such a degree that salt crystals accumulated on his shoulders, oozing from his dark blue tunic. After a time, the hand stitched seams,[3] especially beneath the arm pits, would rot away, leaving the trooper faced with spending his small pocket money on repairs, or doing away with the tunic and reporting it as stolen. At the end of the year, his clothing allowance would have to cover the loss.

Early in 1861 a Board of Officers con-

3. Quartermaster Support of the Army, 1775-1939. Risch.

Two pillows or belt supporters at bottom of jacket were usually the first to be cut off and dispensed with by the trooper while making alterations.

Royal Artillery. The French shako and the Austrian tunic (same color) could be given to "foot troops." Two uniforms should be given all arms of the service, one for dress parades, and the other for fatigue duty.[5]

Most of the uniforms issued at Fort Riley during the infancy of the 7th Cavalry came from stock piles often suffering from mildew at Quartermaster depots. From these, only slight alterations were made for the individual by company tailors, at his request. The soldier was obliged to pay the tailor at least once in three months. Charges included $6 for altering a dress coat, $1 for alterations on the blouse, and $3 for letting

5. Army and Navy Journal, August 4, 1866.

vened to adopt a new code of uniform dress, but in the press of war demands the results of their labors went down the drain, as many other constructive ideas had done in the past. No one can deny that a new uniform would not only improve the appearance of the men, but the "esprit de corps" of our army.[4]

Of the many letters that poured onto the editor's desk at the Army and Navy Journal, some were constructive, others somewhat a few years ahead of themselves. One writer asked whether the government could acquire samples of the different uniforms, from European armies, from examination of which minor improvements might be suggested as: Give the Cavalry a neatly braided jacket with facings, jack boots and a helmet for dress occasions. For the Artillery, a coatee similar to that worn by the

4. Army and Navy Journal, Vol. 3, 1865-66, p. 794.

A regulation 1858 four button fatigue blouse was used well into the 1870s by both Infantry and Cavalry.

out or taking in the seams of his pants. Ten dollars for alterations was a high price out of $16 a month pay, and some soldiers suggested that, without additional expense, the government could purchase the cloth and issue it to the soldier and pay the company tailor for making it up, saving the soldier the expense he had to incur in having it altered. A typical complaint voiced by the soldiers was that they could not understand why their pockets should be depleted by the company tailor for work that the contractor had been already paid for performing.[6]

Overcoats, tunics, blouses and pants were of inferior quality. "We would like to see the four deformed women upon whose measurements the contractors made clothing from," was a typical over-the-shoulder remark after receiving a too tightly fitted uniform. Surely the pants were not made from the measurements of a man, or the coats from the measurements of a person not deformed. The underclothing caused little grumbling. Strings of the drawers were much too short to tie comfortably about the leg. Socks issued could have been more durable. "All men with small feet are vain of them, yet on marches we find music boys and men with small feet breaking down from the weight of shoes three or four sizes too large for them, and foot-sore from slipping about in large shoes."[7] Blankets in better shape and form could be purchased from citizens at one-third less than the government's price.

A soldier wrote, September 28, 1867, from a far western post, his ideas of what the American soldier should look like. The letter refers to an article printed earlier in the Army and Navy Journal, titled, "A Uniform Needed."

"Now I think we need a showy uniform for places where they do soldiering. But here we work, and have no time to spend in pipeclaying belts or any fancy work. Then in addition let us have a field uniform that will stand wear and look neat. I propose that we adopt cadet grey for cavalry, artillery and infantry. Coats all double breasted, with collars and cuffs of a different color. Hat . . . same shape as officers' hat now prescribed, only gray felt, and say three and a half inches high in crown, for both officers and enlisted men. Abolish the cap and flannel sack-coat. Have the uniform made so as to suit the climate — light for Summer and heavy for Winter . . . We need some regulations as to swords. That now prescribed for infantry officers looks well for a short time, but soon wears out the scabbard. Let us wear the sword now prescribed for staff officers. It is light, and heavy enough for all we need of it."[8]

One soldier who signed himself as "Far West" had many suggestions to improve uniforms and equipment. In a letter dated

8. Signed "Infantry" Far West, Oct. 17, 1867 (Army and Navy Journal, Nov. 9, 1867, p. 186.)

6. Army and Navy Journal, August 10, 1867, pg. 809.

7. Army and Navy Journal, Aug. 10, 1867, p. 809.

Courtesy Gordon Corbett, Jr.
During the Civil War, yellow stripes ran down the outer seam; 1⅛″ wide for officers; 1½″ wide for Corporals. In 1872 the stripes were changed to 1½″ wide for officers; 1″ wide for Sergeants; ½″ wide for Corporals.

Courtesy Gordon Corbett, Jr.
Cavalry trousers were reinforced in the seat and down the inner leg.

December, 1867, he writes: "Blankets are issued at seven dollars each. I can buy them here at four. They are dear at that price. The blanket for a soldier should be close, thick and of a good size. For cold countries an additional blanket should be issued, thick and with longer wool than those we get. A very fine blanket is made upon the Pacific coast. Those who have used them prefer them to the blankets generally found in the East. Then I would prefer a slit in the center, so the blanket can be worn Mexican fashion in case of rain. Have this fastened with hooks and eyes. Do away with the rubber blanket. The socks issued to us are worse than the blankets in quality but not so bad in price. They will not stand washing more than twice. Indeed I think it will take about ten pairs to last a year."[9]

In the hot southwest, it would be cheaper and more comfortable had the soldier worn only a straw hat, shirt, drawers, socks and slippers. None would deny that a neat and well-fitted uniform would influence pride,

9. Army and Navy Journal, December, 1867, p. 299.

Courtesy Author's Collection

Officers were permitted to wear the dark blue vest with nine small buttons of their corps, regiment or department. The vest was usually worn when not serving with troops in dress uniform. However, undress, it is always seen in photo's when the blouse was open. Despite General Orders, the vest was worn by Sergeants as well, displaying fancy watch chains with ornaments attached.

Courtesy Smithsonian Institute

Custer's uniform coat of a Major General. (Civil War)

Courtesy Author's Collection

Forage cap or kepi. A design influenced by a French pattern. Made of dark blue wool flannel with an adjustable chin strap and sliding brass buckle. First issued in 1859, it saw service well into the 1870s where it was replaced by the 1872 regulation fatigue hat, a slightly modified version issued to the troops in 1875.

Courtesy Gordon Corbett, Jr.

Enlisted man's "Jeff Davis" hat. Brim of hat pinned to right side for Cavalry, left for Infantry.

manners and discipline. The soldier who was issued a uniform combining elegance and comfort would take proper care of it. If dressed as a day laborer, he would be apt to neglect the uniform entirely. Why appeal to force when pride could be made to accomplish the result much better? Many veterans regarded "cadet gray" as the most satisfactory color for all conditions. A Surgeon General's report held that gray was six degrees cooler than darker colors. It did not show as much dust and dirt. The gray dye did not rot or injure the cloth as much as had some darker dyes. However, strong opposition to the use of gray arose because the color was adopted by the Rebels in the Civil War, while the blue became endeared to the Union by song and sentiment. But gray had been used by the Army long before there was any thought of rebellion, and the soldier who trudged in it under a burning sun would, if he had ever worn dark blue under similar circumstances, thanked God if sentiment was displaced for comfort.

On April 15, 1868, Surgeon General J. K. Barnes issued a pamphlet entitled, "A Medical Report upon the Uniform and Clothing of the Soldiers of the United States Army," demanding a new uniform. The pamphlet was a digest of reports from experienced medical officers expressing their opinions

Courtesy West Point Museum Collection

The Army campaign hat of 1872. The crown of the hat is made lens-shaped so as to fold with crease in center length-ways of the hat. The brim turns up at each side and is hooked at the outer edges in front and rear of body of hat thus giving the outline of a sweep nearly semi-circular from extreme point of front to extreme point of rear. Brim is flat and is 4½ inches wide — the outer edges slightly concave where the hooks and eyes are sewed.

Courtesy Author's Collection

Civilian contractors manufactured a variety of designs in black felt hats. These hats were condemned by the troops . . . as they lacked quality and durability. The trooper was allowed one hat a year as issue.

based on research concerning the hygienic fitness of the present uniform and the sufficiency of clothing allowance for the soldiers. Opinions of 160 medical officers were gathered from stations from Maine to the Pacific. They all agreed in condemning the present hat and uniform of clothing. A few reported on the quality of the goods, rather than the fitness or the "shoddy" appearance of the uniform.

The recommendations were gathered, compiled and presented by Brevet Lieutenant Alfred A. Woodhull, assistant surgeon U.S.A. The report indicated a radical change in uniforms was necessary in the immediate future. The hat,[10] which had originally been issued to the 2nd Dragoons in Texas in 1853, suggested by General William S. Harney, was considered as most appropriate. It could be manufactured for as little as $2.50 each. The coat was approved with change of color to light gray, or light blue. Leather gaitors were suggested for the infantry and jack-boots for the cavalry. More frequent issues of blankets were urged, as well as sheep-skin coats for guards and exposed stations, and extra issues of uniforms for men stationed where they were required to do severe labor that would wear out their clothing rapidly.

But when the next year rolled around with officers and men expecting a new uniform as a result of the reports, no change occurred probably because of the great quantities of Civil War goods stockpiled in warehouses. This surplus of uniforms and accoutrements ended the possibility of passing the "new clothing act" which had given the soldiers the impression that the "Woodhull" report would be accepted.

Both hand-sewn and pegged bootees[11] were disliked by soldiers. The general complaint was the clumsy shape of the heel, the ill-fit of the shoe itself, the softness of the afterpart and the worthlessness of the sole. The heel of the shoe was criticized because of its flat and awkward positioning. The broad heel was not half high enough to keep the shortest breeches out of mud in wet weather, and trouser leg bottoms weighed heavy during a march if soaked in water and clotted with mud. When a soldier was issued a pair of bootees, he usually went to the shoemaker to have the heels torn off, replacing them with smaller and higher heels. This cost the soldier about 75 cents. After two weeks of marching, the soles usually were worn through and the shoes had to be thrown away. A soldier who wore a pair of bootees for more than six weeks was exceptional. He was allowed four pairs a year, but usually wore out eight pairs. The quality of these shoes varied. It was because of frequent fraudulent production and inspection. A so-called leather composition, that looked like and smelled like leather, went to pieces when it became wet.

These bootees were of the "Jefferson pattern," rights and lefts,[12] made of heavy leather, rough side out, containing no grommets in the lace holes, and with heavy rawhide laces. This ankle-high shoe, with a square toe, would last the soldier a long while if properly made. It was not uncommon for men to draw two pairs of bootees in one month, wear them out, and find themselves short half their pay at the pay table because of "clothing overdrawn." It was no wonder that nine-tenths of the men wore citizens' boots while in service, rather than those issued. There was nothing so ridiculous as to see a chunky fellow with a pair of number nine or number ten bootees on, his heels lower than his toes, endeavoring to put his full weight on the ball of his feet, which was impossible unless he raised his

---

10. This hat is called the "Andrew's Hat," or "Harney's Hat," see "The Army Campaign Hat of 1872" by James Hutchins, Military Collector and Historian, Fall, 1964.
11. To avoid confusion between "boot" and "bootee" (ankle high shoes) when requisitioned.

---

12. Because the bootees looked alike, Quartermaster sometimes stamped "R" for right and "L" for left. Stamping did not last long, but size markings were more permanent.

heels from the ground. But regulations were strict in most companies and, if you were issued bootees, there had better be a reason why you weren't wearing them.[13]

"Gun-boats" or "mudscows" as these shoes were sometimes called, were either hand-sewn or machine stitched. The leather was either oak-tanned or the less expensive hemlock-tanned.

The Quartermaster Department insisted on purchasing handsewn bootees instead of pegged shoes, even though the sewn bootees were more expensive. The poor quality of the pegged shoes initially procured by the quartermasters had served to confirm its belief that almost all pegged work was unserviceable. It was called the "Jefferson" bootee because it was introduced during the term in office of President Thomas Jefferson who popularized it.

Jack-boots were worn by most officers during the Civil War. The leather tops reached above the knees in a bell shape and were usually turned down when the wearer

13. Army and Navy Journal, July 4, 1868, p. 730.

was not seating a horse. They were hot, bulky and heavy. Toward the end of the war, jack-boots were less popular for officers and in the cavalry, but were worn by frontier scouts when acquired as surplus or as a gift. Many photographs of Buffalo Bill show him in buckskin and jack-boots. These very expensive boots were in many cases bequeathed to a son or near relative, and undoubtedly tucked away in the family attic and forgotten. A reduced version of the army boot was used by the Infantry, Artillery and the Cavalry, each arm having the boot altered according to specifications by the Quartermaster Department and the Surgeon General's office. The cavalry boot ended just under the bend of the knee and behind the leg, arching higher in front so the leather covered the knee cap. The back of the boot measured 15½ inches, rising to 19½ at the front. Stamped under the heels was the marking, "U.S." A double row of stitching ran up both sides, starting from the inset of the heel. A 14- or 15-inch boot with a straight cut across the top was issued to the infantry, with "mule-ears" tucked on the insides. The heel was a 1½-inch cuban, with a heavy arched insole. Square toes were found on all bootees and boots. Most boots throughout the service were wider at the top to accommodate the tucking in of trouser legs. The tops were usually of calf's skin or grain leather, the bottoms of much heavier leather. Black was the predominant color, with low flat leather heels or small

Courtesy Author's Collection

Fifteen inch high Jefferson boot (Civil War) with square toes and a cuban heel. Brass spurs are regulation.

Courtesy Smithsonian Institution

U.S. Army Bootee of type used during Civil War.

Courtesy Herb Peck, Jr.

Trooper in "Hardy Hat" or "Jeff Davis" with a brace of 1861 Navy colt revolvers. This glassy-eyed Cavalryman sports his hat with what was called a "50-mission crush," generations later.

In most cases, it was the man's incompetence that subjected his feet to swelling blisters. If an officer humored such soldiers, he might find himself with a cart-load of men unfit for duty. If the men ignored a fold in a sock, causing swelling and blistering, they suffered for the mistake. Not too many men in the infantry or cavalry were informed of the causes of crippling sores, although it was learned by experience during many foot-weary miles of marching.

A simple prescription passed on by older regulars seemed to alleviate one problem. "If by accident, the feet should be blistered, pass a darning needle with a woolen thread through the blister and leave the latter in it for some time. It will absorb the moisture and the sore will dry, while, when you cut the blister, the wound will be exposed to pressure, rubbing and dirt, which

cuban heels, with a heavy leather sole, and the front of the boot boasting a prominent square toe.

Reasons for complaints of foot-soreness because of over-sized bootees or boots were many. Uncleanliness was responsible for some ailments although this was not commonly recognized. Troop commanders took the soldiers' complaints as an excuse to avoid extra duty. The men were apt to neglect parts of the body that were not exposed to view, such as their feet. Some sanitary measures were prescribed. Paring the toe nails was to be as frequent as that of the nails of the hands. If boots were worn, they were not to be taken off immediately after a march. The feet would be heated and a sudden exposure to the air would cause them to swell. The soldiers would become painfully aware of this when they donned their boots the next morning.

Courtesy Herb Peck, Jr.

Typical Cavalry trooper bedecked in a maze of accouterments and weapons. *Circa* 1866

will lay up the strongest man for some time. Socks should be knitted of woolen yarn, which absorbs perspiration and remains soft; they are superior to cotton ones. Socks not properly darned will hurt the feet."[14]

14. Army and Navy Journal, Sept. 5, 1863, p. 26.

Bootees were more easily thrown off after a march than boots. It generally took two men to assist in relieving a man of his boots or "mud plows." If bootees were damp they were stuffed with hay, greased on the outsides and allowed to dry out slowly. If left wet, the bootees would dry out hard and cut the soldier's feet.

QUARTERMASTER'S DEPARTMENT — ALLOWANCE OF CLOTHING

Clothing	1st	2nd	3rd	4th	5th	Total in the Five Years
Cap, complete	2	1	2	1	1	7
Hat with trimmings complete	1	1	1	1	1	5
Fatigue forage caps, of pattern in the Quartermaster-General's Office, will be issued, in addition to hats	1	1	1	1	1	5
Pompon	1	—	1	—	—	2
Eagle and Ring	1	—	1	—	—	2
Cover	1	1	1	1	1	5
Coat	2	1	2	1	2	8
Trowsers	3	2	3	2	3	13
Flannel shirt	3	3	3	3	3	15
Flannel drawers	3	2	2	2	2	11
Bootees,* pair	4	4	4	4	4	20
Stockings, pair	4	4	4	4	4	20
Leather stock	1	—	1	—	—	2
Great-coat	1	—	—	—	—	1
Stable-frock (for mounted men)	1	—	1	—	—	2
Fatigue overalls (for engineers and ordnance)	1	1	1	1	1	5
Blanket	1	—	1	—	—	2

*Mounted men may receive *one* pair of "boots" and *two* pairs of "bootees" instead of *four* pairs of bootees.[15]

15. Revised U.S. Army Regulations, 1861, changes and laws affecting Army Regulations and Articles of War to June 25, 1863, p. 170.

REVISED REGULATIONS
for the
ARMY OF THE UNITED STATES
1861.

ARTICLE LI.
UNIFORM, DRESS, AND HORSE EQUIP-
MENTS.
COAT.
For Commissioned Officers.
1442. All officers shall wear a frock-coat of dark blue cloth, the skirt to extend from two-thirds to three-fourths of the distance from the top of the hip to the bend of the knee; single-breasted for Captains and Lieutenants; double-breasted for all other grades.

1443. *For a Major-General* — two rows of buttons on the breast, nine in each row, placed by threes; the distance between each row, five and one-half inches at top, and three and one-half inches at bottom; stand-up collar, to rise no higher than to permit the chin to turn freely over it, to hook in front at the bottom, and slope thence up and backward at an angle of thirty degrees on each side; cuffs two and one-half inches deep to go around the sleeves parallel with the lower edge, and to button with three small buttons at the under seam; pockets in the folds of the skirts, with one button at the hip, and one at the end of each pocket, making four buttons on the back and skirt of the coat, the hip button to range with the lowest buttons on the breast; collar and

Courtesy Herb Peck, Jr.

Cavalry musicians (1866)

cuffs to be of dark blue velvet; lining of the coat black.

1444. *For a Brigadier-General* — the same as for a Major-General, except that there will be only eight buttons in each row on the breast, placed in pairs.

1445. *For a Colonel* — the same as for a Major-General, except that there will be only seven buttons in each row on the breast, placed at equal distances; collar and cuffs of the same color and material as the coat.

1446. *For a Lieutenant-Colonel* — the same as for a Colonel.

1447. *For a Major* — the same as for a Colonel.

1448. *For a Captain* — the same as for a Colonel, except that there will be only one row of nine buttons on the breast, placed at equal distances.

1449. *For a First Lieutenant* — the same as for a Captain.

1450. *For a Second Lieutenant* — the same as for a Captain.

1451. *For a Brevet Second Lieutenant* — the same as for a Captain.

1452. *For a Medical Cadet* — the same as for a Brevet Second Lieutenant.

1453. A round jacket, according to pattern, of dark blue cloth, trimmed with scarlet, with the Russian

shoulder-knot, the prescribed insignia of rank to be worked in silver in the centre of the knot, may be worn on undress duty by officers of Light Artillery.

UNIFORM FOR ENLISTED MEN.

For Enlisted Men.

1454. The uniform for all enlisted *foot* men, shall be a single-breasted frock of dark blue cloth, made without plaits, with a skirt extending one-half the distance from the top of the hip to the bend of the knee; one row of nine buttons on the breast, placed at equal distances; stand-up collar to rise no higher than to permit the chin to turn freely over it, to hook in front at the bottom and then to slope up and backward at an angle of thirty degrees on each side; cuffs pointed according to pattern, and to button with two small buttons at the under seam; collar and cuffs edged with a cord or welt of cloth as follows, to wit: Scarlet *for Artillery;* sky-blue *for Infantry;* yellow *for Engineers;* crimson *for Ordnance* and *Hospital stewards.* On each shoulder a metallic scale according to pattern; narrow lining for skirt of the coat of the same color and material as the coat; pockets in the folds of the skirts with one button at each hip to range with the lowest buttons on the breast; no buttons at the ends of the pockets.

1455. *All Enlisted Men of the Cavalry and Light Artillery* shall wear a uniform jacket of dark blue cloth, with one row of twelve small buttons on the breast placed at equal distances; stand-up collar to rise no higher than to permit the chin to turn freely over it, to hook in front at the bottom, and to slope the same as the coat-collar; on the collar, on each side, two blind button-holes of lace, three-eighths of an inch wide, one small button on the button-hole, lower button-hole extending back four inches, upper button-hole three and a half inches; top button and front ends of collar bound with lace three-eighths of an inch wide, and a strip of the same extending down the front and around the whole lower edge of the jacket; the back seam laced with the same, and on the cuff a point of the same shape as that on the coat, but formed of the lace; jacket to extend to the waist, and to be lined with white flannel; two small buttons at the under seam of the cuff, as on the coat cuff; one hook and eye at the bottom of the collar; color of lace (worsted), yellow for *Cavalry,* and scarlet for *Light Artillery.*

1456. *For all Musicians* — the same as for other enlisted men of their respective corps, with the addition of a facing of lace three-eighths of an inch wide on the front of the *coat or jacket,* made in the following manner: bars of three-eighths of an inch worsted lace placed on a line with each button six and one-half inches wide at the bottom, and *thence* gradually expanding upward to the last button, counting from the waist up, and contracting from

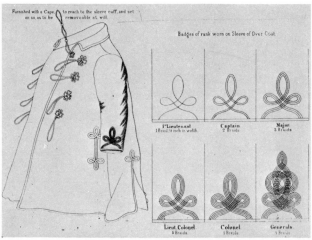

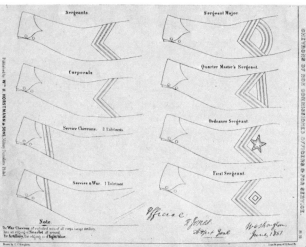

thence to the bottom of the collar, where it will be six and one-half inches wide, with a strip of the same lace following the bars at their outer extremity — the whole presenting something of what is called the herring-bone form; the color of the lace facing to correspond with the color of the trimming of the corps.

1457. *For Fatigue Purposes* — a sack coat of dark blue flannel extending half-way down the thigh, and made loose, without sleeve or body lining, falling collar, inside pocket on the left side, four coat buttons down the front.

UNIFORM. — BUTTONS.

1458. *For Recruits* — the sack coat will be made with sleeve and body lining, the latter of flannel.

1459. On all occasions of duty, except fatigue, and when out of quarters, the coat or jacket shall be buttoned and hooked at the collar.

BUTTONS.

1460. *For General Officers and Officers of the General Staff* — gilt, convex, with spread eagle and stars, and plain border; large size, seven-eighths of an inch in exterior diameter; small size, one-half inch.

1461. *For Officers of the Corps of Engineers* — gilt, nine-tenths of an inch in exterior diameter, slightly convex; a raised bright rim, one-thirtieth of an inch wide; device, an eagle holding in his beak a scroll, with the word *"Essayons,"* a bastion with embrasures in the distance surrounded by water, with a rising sun — the figures to be of dead gold upon a bright field. Small buttons of the same form and device, and fifty-five hundredths of an inch in exterior diameter.

1462. *For Officers of the Corps of Topographical Engineers* — gilt, seven-eighths of an inch exterior diameter, convex and solid; device, the shield of the United States, occupying one-half of the diameter, and the letters T. E. in old English characters the other half; small buttons, one-half inch diameter, device and form the same.

1463. *For Officers of the Ordnance Department* — gilt, convex, plain border, cross cannon and bombshell, with a circular scroll over and across the cannon, containing the words "Ordnance Corps;" large size, seven-eighths of an inch in exterior diameter; small size, one-half inch.

1464. *For Officers of Artillery, Infantry, and Cavalry* — gilt, convex; device, a spread eagle with the letter A Q, FOR Artillery — I, for Infantry — C, for Cavalry, on the shield; large size, seven-eighths of an inch in exterior diameter; small size, one-half inch.

1465. *Aides-de-camp* may wear the button of the General Staff, or of their regiment or corps, at their option.

1466. *For Medical Cadets* — same as for Officers of the General Staff.

1467. *For all Enlisted Men* — yellow, the same as is used by the Artillery, &c., omitting the letter in the shield.

TROWSERS.

1468. *For General Officers and Officers of the Ordnance Department* — of dark blue cloth, plain, without stripe, welt, or cord down the outer seam.

1469. *For Officers of the General Staff and Staff Corps*, except the Ordnance — dark blue cloth, with a gold cord, one-eighth of an inch in diameter, along the outer seam.

1470. *For all Regimental Officers* — dark blue cloth, with a welt let into the outer seam, one-eighth of an inch in diameter, of colors corresponding to the facings of the respective regiments, viz.: *Cavalry,* yellow; *Artillery,* scarlet; *Infantry,* sky-blue.

1471. *For Medical Cadets* — same as for Officers of the General Staff, except a welt of buff cloth, instead of a gold cord.

UNIFORM. — HAT.

1472. *For Enlisted Men,* except companies of Light Artillery — dark blue cloth; *sergeants* with a stripe one anene-half inch wide; *corporals* with a stripe one-half inch wide, of worsted lace, down and over the outer seam, of the color of the facings of the respective corps.

1473. *Ordnance Sergeants and Hospital Stewards* — stripe of crimson lace one and one-half inch wide.

1474. *Privates* — plain, without stripe or welt.

1475. *For Companies of Artillery equipped as Light Artillery* — sky-blue cloth.

All trowsers to be made loose, without plaits, and to spread well over the boot; to be re-enforced for all enlisted mounted men.

HAT.

1476. *For Officers* — of best black felt. The dimensions of medium size to be as follows:
Width of brim, 3¼ inches.
Height of crown, 6¼ inches.
Oval of tip, ½ inch.
Taper of crown, ¾ inch.
Curve of head, ⅜ inch.
The binding to be ½ inch deep, of best black ribbed silk.

1477. *For Enlisted Man* — of black felt, same shape and size as for officers, with double row of stitching, instead of binding, around the edge. To agree in quality with the pattern deposited in the clothing arsenal.

UNIFORM. — HAT. — TRIMMINGS.

1478. *Medical Cadets* will wear a forage cap according to pattern.

Trimmings.

1479. *For General Officers* — gold cord, with acorn-shaped ends. The brim of the hat looped up on the right side, and fastened with an eagle attached to the side of the hat; three black ostrich-feathers on the left side; a gold-embroidered wreath in front, on black velvet ground, encircling the letters U.S. in silver, old English characters.

1480. *For Officers of the Adjutant-General's, Inspector-General's, Quartermaster's, Subsistence, Medical and Pay Departments, and the Judge Advocate, above the rank of Captain* — the same as for General Officers, except the cord, which will be of black silk and gold.

1481. *For the same Departments, below the rank of Field Officers* — the same as for Field Officers, except that there will be but two feathers.

1482. *For Officers of the Corps of Engineers* — the same as for the General Staff, except the ornament in front, which will be a gold-embroidered wreath of laurel and palm, encircling a silver turreted castle on black velvet ground.

1483. *For Officers of the Topographical Engineers* — the same as for the General Staff, except the ornament in front, which will be a gold-embroidered wreath of oak leaves, encircling a gold-embroidered shield, on black velvet ground.

UNIFORM. — TRIMMINGS.

1484. *For Officers of the Ordnance Department* — the same as for the General Staff, except the ornament in front, which will be a gold-embroidered shell and flame, on black velvet ground.

1485. *For Officers of Cavalry* — the same as for the General Staff, except the ornament in front, which will be two gold-embroidered sabres crossed, edges upward, on black velvet ground, with the number of the regiment in silver in the upper angle.

1486. *For Officers of Artillery* — the same as for the General Staff, except the ornament in front, which will be gold-embroidered cross-cannon, on black velvet ground, with the number of the regiment in silver at the intersection of the cross-cannon.

1487. *For Officers of Infantry* — the same as for Artillery, except the ornament in front, which will be a gold-embroidered bugle, on black velvet ground, with the number of the regiment in silver within the bend.

1488. *For Enlisted Men,* except companies of Light Artillery — the same as for officers of the respective corps, except that there will be but one feather, the cord will be of worsted, of the same color as that of the facing of the corps, three-sixteenths of an inch in diameter, running three times through a slide of the same material, and terminating with two tassels, not less than two inches long, on the side of the hat opposite the feather. The insignia of corps, in brass, in front of the hat, corresponding with those prescribed for officers, with the number of regiment, five-eighths of an inch long, in brass, and letter of company, one inch, in brass, arranged over insignia.

UNIFORM. — CAPS.

1489. *For Hospital Stewards* the cord will be of buff and green mixed. The wreath in front of brass, with the letters U.S. in Roman, of white metal. Brim to be looped up to side of hat with a brass eagle, having a hook attached to the bottom to secure the brim — on the right side for mounted men and left side for foot men. The feather to be worn on the side opposite the loop.

1490. All the trimmings of the hat are to be made so that they can be detached; but the eagle, badge of corps, and letter of company, are to be always worn.

1491. For companies of Artillery equipped as Light Artillery, the old pattern uniform cap, with red horsehair plume, cord and tassel.

1492. Officers of the General Staff, and Staff Corps, may wear, at their option, a light French chapeau, either stiff crown or flat, according to the pattern deposited in the Adjutant-General's office. Officers below the rank of field officers to wear but two feathers.

FORAGE CAPS.

1493. For fatigue purposes, forage caps, of pattern in the Quartermaster-General's office: dark blue cloth, with a welt of the same around the crown, and yellow metal letters in front to designate companies.

1494. Commissioned officers may wear forage caps of the same pattern, with the distinctive ornament of the corps and regiment in front.

UNIFORM. — CRAVAT. — BOOTS. — CRAVAT OR STOCK.

1495. *For all Officers* — black; when a cravat is worn, the tie not to be visible at the opening of the collar.

1496. *For all Enlisted Men* — black leather, according to pattern.

BOOTS.

1497. *For all Officers* — ankle or Jefferson.

1498. *For Enlisted Men of Cavalry and Light Artillery* — ankle and Jefferson, rights and lefts, according to pattern.

1499. *For Enlisted Men of Artillery, Infantry, Engineers, and Ordnance* — Jefferson, rights and lefts, according to pattern.

SPURS.

1500. *For all Mounted Officers* — yellow metal, or gilt.

1501. *For all Enlisted Mounted Men* — yellow metal, according to pattern. (See par. 1620.)

GLOVES.

1502. *For General Officers and Officers of the General Staff and Staff Corps* — buff or white.

1503. *For Officers of Artillery, Infantry, Cavalry, Dragoons, and Riflemen* — white.

SASH.

1504. *For General Officers* — buff, silk net, with silk bullion fringe ends; sash to go twice around the waist, and to tie behind the left hip, pendent part not to extend more than eighteen inches below the tie.

UNIFORM. — SWORD-BELT.

1505. *For Officers of the Adjutant-General's, Inspector-General's, Quartermaster's, and Subsistence Departments, Corps of Engineers, Topographical Engineers, Ordnance, Artillery, Infantry, Cavalry, and the Judge Advocate of the Army* — crimson silk net; *for Officers of the Medical Department* — medium or emerald green silk net, with silk bullion fringe ends; to go around the waist and tie as for General Officers.

1506. *For all Sergeant Majors, Quartermaster Sergeants, Ordnance Sergeants, Hospital Stewards, First Sergeants, Principal or Chief Musicians and Chief Buglers* — red worsted sash, with worsted bullion fringe ends; to go twice around the waist, and to tie behind the left hip, pendent part not to extend more than eighteen inches below the tie.

1507. The sash will be worn (over the coat) on all occasions of duty of every description, except stable and fatigue.

1508. The sash will be worn by "Officers of the Day" across the body, scarf fashion, from the right shoulder to the left side, instead of around the waist, tying behind the left hip as prescribed.

SWORD-BELT.

1509. *For all Officers* — a waist-belt not less than one and one-half inch nor more than two inches wide to be worn over the sash; the sword to be suspended from it by slings of the same material as the belt, with a hook attached to the belt upon which the sword may be hung.

UNIFORM. — SWORD-BELT PLATE. — SWORD AND SCABBARD.

1510. *For General Officers* — Russia leather, with three stripes of gold embroidery; the slings embroidered on both sides.

1511. *For all other Officers* — black leather, plain.

1512. *For all Non-commissioned Officers* — black leather, plain.

SWORD-BELT PLATE.

1513. *For all Officers and Enlisted Men* — gilt, rectangular, two inches wide, with a raised bright rim; a silver wreath of laurel encircling the "Arms of the United States;" eagle, shield, scroll, edge of cloud and rays bright. The motto, "E PLURIBUS UNUM," in silver letters, upon the scroll; stars also of silver; according to pattern.

SWORD AND SCABBARD.

1514. *For General Officers* — straight sword, gilt hilt, silver grip, brass or steel scabbard.

1515. *For Officers of the Adjutant-General's, Inspector-General's, Quartermaster's, and Subsistence Departments, Corps of Engineers, Topographical Engineers, Ordnance, the Judge Advocate of the Army, Aides-de-Camp, Field Officers of Artillery, Infantry, and Foot Riflemen, and for the Light Artillery* — the sword of the pattern adopted by the War Department, April 9, 1850; or the one described in General Orders No. 21, of August 28, 1860, for officers therein designated.

1516. *For the Medical and Pay Departments* — small sword and scabbard, according to pattern in the Surgeon-General's office.

1517. *For Medical Cadets,* the sword and belt and plate will be the same as for non-commissioned officers.

UNIFORM. — SWORD-KNOT.

1518. *For Officers of Cavalry* — sabre and scabbard now in use, according to pattern in the Ordnance Department.

1519. *For the Artillery, Infantry, and Foot Riflemen,* except the field officers — the sword of the pattern adopted by the War Department, April 9, 1850.

1520. The sword and sword-belt will be worn upon all occasions of duty, without exception.

1521. When on foot, the sabre will be suspended from the hook attached to the belt.

1522. When not on military duty, officers may wear swords of honor, or the prescribed sword, with a scabbard, gilt, or of leather with gilt mountings.

SWORD-KNOT.

1523. *For General Officers* — gold cord with acorn end.

1524. *For all other officers* — gold lace strap with gold bullion tassel.

BADGES TO DISTINGUISH RANK.
Epaulettes.

1525. *For the Major-General Commanding the Army* — gold, with solid crescent; device, three silver-embroidered stars, one, one and a half inches in diameter, one, one and one-fourth inches in diameter, and one, one and one-eighth inches in diameter, placed on the strap in a row, longitudinally, and equidistant, the largest star in the centre of the crescent, the smallest at the top; dead and bright gold bullion, one-half inch in diameter and three and one-half inches long.

1526. *For all other Major-Generals* — the same as for the Major-General Commanding the Army, ex-

cept that there will be two stars on the strap instead of three, omitting the smallest.

1527. *For a Brigadier-General* — the same as for a Major-General, except that, instead of two, there shall be one star (omitting the smallest) placed upon the strap, and not within the crescent.

1528. *For a Colonel* — the same as for a Brigadier-General, substituting a silver-embroidered spread eagle for the star upon the strap; and within the crescent for the *Medical Department* — a laurel wreath embroidered in gold, and the letters M.S., in old English characters, in silver, within the wreath; *Pay Department* — same as the Medical Department, with the letters P.O., in old English characters; *Corps of Engineers* — a turreted castle of silver; *Corps of Topographical Engineers* — a shield embroidered in gold, and below it the letters T.E., in old English characters, in silver; *Ordnance Department* — shell and flame in silver embroidery; *Regimental Officers* — the number of the regiment embroidered in gold, within a circlet of embroidered silver, one and three-fourths inches in diameter, upon cloth of the following colors: *for Artillery* — scarlet; *Infantry* — light or sky blue; *Cavalry* — yellow.

1529. *For a Lieutenant-Colonel* — the same as for a Colonel, according to corps, but substituting for the eagle a silver-embroidered leaf.

1530. *For a Major* — the same as for a Colonel, according to corps, omitting the eagle.

1531. *For a Captain* — the same as for a Colonel, according to corps, except that the bullion will be only one-fourth of an inch in diameter, and two and one half inches long, and substituting for the eagle two silver-embroidered bars.

1532. *For a First Lieutenant* — the same as for a Colonel, according to corps, except that the bullion will be only one-eighth of an inch in diameter, and two and one-half inches long, and substituting for the eagle one silver-embroidered bar.

1533. *For a Second Lieutenant* — the same as for a First Lieutenant, omitting the bar.

1534. *For a Brevet Second Lieutenant* — the same as for a Second Lieutenant.

1535. All officers having military rank will wear an epaulette on each shoulder.

1536. The epaulette may be dispensed with when not on duty, and on certain duties off parade, to wit: at drills, at inspections of barracks and hospitals, on Courts of Inquiry and Boards, at inspections of articles and necessaries, on working parties and fatigue duties, and upon the march, except when, in war, there is immediate expectation of meeting the enemy, and also when the overcoat is worn.

Shoulder-Straps.

1537. *For the Major-General Commanding the Army* — dark blue cloth, one and three-eighths inches wide by four inches long; bordered with an embroidery of gold one-fourth of an inch wide;

three silver-embroidered stars of five rays, one star on the centre of the strap, and one on each side equidistant between the centre and the outer edge of the strap; the centre star to be the largest.

1538. *For all other Major-Generals* — the same as for the Major-General Commanding the Army, except that there will be two stars instead of three; the centre of each star to be one inch from the outer edge of the gold embroidery on the ends of the strap; both stars of the same size.

1539. *For a Bridgadier-General* — the same as for a Major-General, except that there will be one star instead of two; the centre of the star to be equidistant from the outer edge of the embroidery on the ends of the strap.

1540. *For a Colonel* — the same size as for a Major-General, and bordered in like manner with an embroidery of gold; a silver-embroidered spread eagle on the centre of the strap, two inches between the tips of the wings, having in the right talon an olive-branch, and in the left a bundle of arrows; an escutcheon on the breast, as represented in the arms of the United States; cloth of the strap as follows: for the *General Staff and Staff Corps* — dark blue; *Artillery* — scarlet; *Infantry* — light or sky blue; *Cavalry* — yellow.

1541. *For a Lieutenant-Colonel* — the same as for a Colonel, according to corps, omitting the eagle, and introducing a silver-embroidered leaf at each end, each leaf extending seven-eighths of an inch from the end border of the strap.

1542. *For a Major* — the same as for a Colonel, according to corps, omitting the eagle, and introducing a gold-embroidered leaf at each end, each leaf extending seven-eighths of an inch from the end border of the strap.

1543. *For a Captain* — the same as for a Colonel, according to corps, omitting the eagle, and introducing at each end two gold-embroidered bars of the same width as the border, placed parallel to the ends of the strap; the distance between them and from the border equal to the width of the border.

1544. *For a First Lieutenant* — the same as for a Colonel, according to corps, omitting the eagle, and introducing at each end one gold-embroidered bar of the same width as the border, placed parallel to the ends of the strap, at a distance from the border equal to its width.

1545. *For a Second Lieutenant* — the same as for a Colonel, according to corps, omitting the eagle.

1546. *For a Brevet Second Lieutenant* — the same as for a Second Lieutenant.

1547. *For a Medical Cadet* — a strip of gold lace three inches long, half an inch wide, placed in the middle of a strap of green cloth three and three-quarter inches long by one and one-quarter inches wide.

1548. The shoulder-strap will be worn whenever the epaulette is not.

Chevrons.

1549. The rank of non-commissioned officers will be marked by chevrons upon both sleeves of the uniform coat and overcoat, above the elbow, of silk or worsted binding one-half an inch wide, same color as the edging on the coat, points down, as follows:

1550. *For a Sergeant Major* — three bars and an arc, in silk.

1551. *For a Quartermaster Sergeant* — three bars and a tie, in silk.

1552. *For an Ordnance Sergeant* — three bars and a star, in silk.

1553. *For a Hospital Steward* — a half chevron of the following description, — viz.: of emerald green cloth, one and three-fourths inches wide, running olbliquely downward from the outer to the inner seam of the sleeve, and at an angle of about thirty degrees with a horizontal, parallel to, and one-eighth of an inch distant from, both the upper and lower edge, an embroidery of yellow silk one-eighth of an inch wide, and in the centre a "caduceus" two inches long, embroidered also with yellow silk, the head toward the outer seam of the sleeve.

1554. *For a First Sergeant* – three bars and a lozenge, in worsted.

OVERCOAT.

1555. *For a Sergeant* — three bars, in worsted.

1556. *For a Corporal* — two bars, in worsted.

1557. *For a Pioneer* — two crossed hatchets of cloth, same color and material as the edging of the collar, to be sewed on each arm above the elbow in the place indicated for a chevron (those of a corporal to be just above and resting on the chevron), the head of the hatchet upward, its edge outward, of the following dimensions, viz.: *Handle* — four and one-half inches long, one-fourth to one-third of an inch wide. *Hatchet* — two inches long, one inch wide at the edge.

1558. *To indicate service* — all non-commissioned officers, musicians, and privates who have served faithfully for the term of five years, will wear, as a mark of distinction, upon both sleeves of the uniform coat, below the elbow, a diagonal half chevron, one-half an inch wide, extending from seam to seam, the front end nearest the cuff, and one-half an inch above the point of the cuff, to be of the same color as the edging on the coat. In like manner, an additional half chevron, above and parallel to the first for every subsequent five years of faithful service; distance between each chevron one-fourth of an inch. Service in war will be indicated by a light or sky blue stripe on each side of the chevron for Artillery, and a red stripe for all other crops, the stripe to be one-eighth of an inch wide.

OVERCOAT.
For Commissioned Officers.

1559. A *"cloak coat"* of dark blue cloth, closing by

means of four frog buttons of black silk and loops of black silk cord down the breast, and at the throat by a long loop *à échelle*, without tassel or plate, on the left side, and a black silk frog button on the right; cord for the loops fifteen-hundredths of an inch in diameter; back, a single piece, slit up from the bottom, from fifteen to seventeen inches, according to the height of the wearer, and closing at will, by buttons, and button-holes cut in a concealed flap; collar of the same color and material as the coat, rounded at the edges, and to stand or fall; when standing, to be about five inches high; sleeves loose, of a single piece, and round at the bottom, without cuff or slit; lining, woolen; around the front and lower border, the edges of the pockets, the edges of the sleeves, collar, and slit in the back, a flat braid of black silk one-half an inch wide; and around each frog button on the breast, a knot two and one-quarter inches in diameter of black silk cord, seven-hundredths of an inch in diameter, arranged according to drawing; cape of the same color and material as the coat, removable at the pleasure of the wearer, and reaching to the cuff of the coat-sleeve when the arm is extended; coat to extend down the leg from six to eight inches below the knee, according to height. *To indicate rank*, there will be on both sleeves, near the lower edge, a knot of flat black silk braid not exceeding one-eighth of an inch in width, arranged according to drawing, and composed as follows:

1560. *For a General* — of five braids, double knot.
1561. *For a Colonel* — of five braids, single knot.
1562. *For a Lieutenant-Colonel* — of four braids, single knot.
1563. *For a Major* — of three braids, single knot.

SHIRTS, BLANKETS

1564. *For a Captain* — of two braids, single knot.
1565. *For a First Lieutenant* — of one braid, single knot.
1566. *For a Second Lieutenant and Brevet Second Lieutenant* — a plain sleeve, without knot or ornament.

For Enlisted Men.

1567. *Of all Mounted Corps* — of sky-blue cloth; stand-and-fall collar; double-breasted; cape to reach down to the cuff of the coat when the arm is extended, and to button all the way up; buttons (1467).
1568. *All other Enlisted Men* — of sky-blue cloth; stand-up collar; single-breasted; cape to reach down to the elbows when the arm is extended, and to button all the way up; buttons (1467).
1569. *For Cavalry* — a gutta percha talma, or cloak extending to the knee, with long sleeves.

OTHER ARTICLES OF CLOTHING AND EQUIPMENT.

1570. *Flannel shirt, drawers, stockings, and stable-frock* — the same as now furnished.
1571. *Blanket* — woolen, gray, with letters U.S. in black, four inches long, in the centre; to be seven feet long, and five and a half feet wide, and to weigh five pounds.

1572. *Canvas overalls for Engineer Soldiers* — of white cotton; one garment to cover the whole of the body below the waist, the breast, the shoulders, and the arms; sleeves loose, to allow a free play of the arms, with narrow wristband buttoning with one button; overalls to fasten at the neck behind with two buttons, and at the waist behind with buckle and tongue.

UNIFORM. — MISCELLANEOUS.

1573. *Belts of all Enlisted Men* — black leather.
1574. *Cartridge-box* — according to pattern in the Ordnance Department.
1575. *Drum-sling* — white webbing; to be provided with a brass drum-stick carriage, according to pattern.
1576. *Knapsack* — of painted canvas, according to pattern now issued by the Quartermaster's Department; the great-coat, when carried, to be neatly folded, not rolled, and covered by the outer flap of the knapsack.
1577. *Haversack* — of painted canvas, with an inside sack unpainted, according to the pattern now issued by the Quartermaster's Department.
1578. *Canteen* — of tin, covered with woolen cloth, of the pattern now issued by the Quartermaster's Department.

*   *   *

MILITARY STORE-KEEPERS.

1627. A citizen's frock-coat of blue cloth, with buttons of the department to which they are attached; round black hat; pantaloons and vest, plain, white or dark blue; cravat or stock, black.

MISCELLANEOUS.

1628. General Officers, and Colonels having the brevet rank of General Officers, may, on occasions of ceremony, and when not serving with troops wear the "dress" and "undress" prescribed by existing regulations.
1629. Officers below the grade of Colonel having brevet rank will wear the epaulettes and shoulder-straps distinctive of their army rank. In all other respects, their uniform and dress will be that of their respective regiments, corps, or departments, and according to their commissions in the same. Officers above the grade of Lieutenant-Colonel by ordinary commission, having brevet rank, may wear the uniform of their respective regiments or corps, or that of General Officers, according to their brevet rank.
1630. The uniform and dress of the Signal Officer will be that of Major of the General Staff.
1631. Officers are permitted to wear a plain dark blue bodycoat, with the button designating their respective corps, regiments, or departments, without any other mark or ornament upon it. Such a coat,

however, is not to be considered as a dress for any military purpose.

1632. In like manner, officers are permitted to wear a buff, white, or blue vest, with the small button of their corps, regiment, or department.

1633. Officers serving with mounted troops are allowed to wear, for stable duty, a plain dark blue cloth jacket, with one or two rows of buttons down the front, according to rank; stand-up collar, sloped in front as that of the uniform coat; shoulder-straps according to rank, but no other ornament.

1634. The hair to be short; the beard to be worn at the pleasure of the individual; but, when worn, to be kept short and neatly trimmed.

1635. *A Band* will wear the uniform of the regiment or corps to which it belongs. The commanding officer may, at the expense of the corps, sanctioned by the Council of Administration, make such *additions* in ornaments as he may judge proper.

ARMY MORALE AND FRONTIER LIFE

Army punishment was severe even for minor offenses, and some officers believed that every violation committed deserved some infliction of bodily pain. It was also believed by hardcore veteran officers of the Civil War that brutality would instill fear into the men, and by this fear they would be controllable. However, this was not always the case. As severe punishments continued, a higher rate of desertions followed. Gambling, insubordination, absence from garrison without pass, being unruly after taps, drunkenness, theft and tardiness at roll call were considered serious violations of military discipline. There were many ways to punish a man for stealing, and Custer's method of degrading a man for this offense was sometimes successful. One-half of the offender's hair, mustache and beard was shaved off, he was stripped to his waist under a tormenting Kansas sun, and with a wide board tied to his back marked in large letters, "I AM A THIEF,"[1] he would be paraded around the garrison for a day without food and drink. At the end of the day he was sent to his company officer for a lecture and then back to his quarters to face his comrades, some of whom had been waiting for his return to give him a good thrashing.

If a trooper were caught selling or destroying government property, or was insubordinate to an officer, he was certain to be bucked and gagged. The man was forcibly seated on the ground, feet flat and knees up. His wrists were bound in front, somewhat hugging his legs. A short pole or stick was then thrust across the bend of his arms and beneath the knees, thus rendering him helpless. Finally he was gagged with a piece of soap or scrap wood and left for a period of from four to six hours.[2]

A man might be condemned to stand on the edge of a barrel for half a day, requiring something like a circus acrobat's balance and form. One false move and the soldier might find himself sprawling on the ground with damage to leg or knee, or heaped within the barrel wedged like a sardine. This form of torture was called "on the chimes." Close by, a guard would be stationed to make certain the condemned soldier would fully serve out his sentence.

Wearing a "wooden overcoat" was another method of punishment. The bot-

2. Hardtack & Coffee — John D. Billings — Chap. VIII; Offences & Punishments. Also see The Troopers, by S. E. Whitman; Chap. 6.

Art by E. L. Reedstrom

Bucked and gagged.

1. E. B. Custer/micro-film No. 6431; Custer Battlefield Museum.

tom of the barrel was knocked out and a hole cut out at the top end, large enough to slip over a man's head. The victim would be paraded around post in this manner for the duration of the day.

Other punishments were "knapsack-drill" wherein the soldier carried heavy stones in his backpack, marching to the beat of a guardsman for several hours; some underwent "isolation on a platform," or were spread-eagled and tied to a wagon wheel. This punishment was more common in the artillery. Carrying a twenty-five or thirty pound log on one's shoulder for half a day would almost make anyone believe the log grew in size and weight after the first few hours. Careless saddling of horses, causing galls on the animal's back, was punishable by carrying the fully packed saddle about the parade grounds for several hours. Being strung up by the thumbs to a beam overhead for four hours left a man completely helpless against gnats and flies that swarmed about his sweat-beaded forehead. The offender was not totally suspended off the ground, however, but either stood with both feet flat on the ground or on his toes for a more severe punishment. A six-foot plank, passed across the man's back with his arms outstretched and tied to it, was a similar torment for a few hours. These punishments were carried out regardless of heavy rains, scorching sun, or subfreezing weather.

For leaving a post without proper authorization, failure to salute an officer, being seated while on duty, or reporting without proper equipment, a man might be committed to double guard duty. Instead of the customary two hours on guard and four hours off, it was reversed to four hours guard and two hours off.

Policing the camp, cleaning about the picket lines where the horses were tied, or digging new latrines was punishment assessed for the least offenses. If a man could keep off the black-list in his company, he might be exempt from these less agreeable jobs because of a lengthy list of sentenced offenders.

Company punishment for being drunk and disorderly generally meant being bucked and gagged or spread-eagled on a wagon wheel, but this only gave the soldier a bad taste or sore arms and legs. Digging a hole approximately ten feet square by ten feet deep under the watchful eye of a guard restored him to sobriety by the time the hole was filled in. If a trooper was found with a bottle in his possession he was ordered to dig such a hole and bury it.

It was generally accepted that if an officer drank, his men would drink also. If he gambled, his men would do likewise. Many officers thought their commissions were secure after being posted to a frontier garrison and, once established there, they would have no further concern but to go through the routine of duty, draw their pay, and spend it for liquor and gambling. But there were few forms of relaxation a man could find while confined to a garrison with little to do except follow the boring duties of military frontier life. Through heavy drinking and games of chance, too often officers found themselves faced with heavy debts. What made matters worse were the families back "state-side" awaiting the small support their officer-husbands sent them.

To some soldiers, gambling was a source of extra income. At times, non-commissioned officers played a hand of cards with any private who seemed to have additional money, in violation of army rules and custom. A court-martial for either might result. Stealing an overcoat from someone in the company and selling it to finance a card game was common practice. Overdrawing a blanket or any other article expressly to sell it, knowing the final allotted settlement was months in advance, was another way to get extra money.

Once a man was caught and branded a thief, the shame was endured by the whole company. In many cases the accused victim would desert within a few months, mainly because of humiliation heaped on him by his officers or the severity of the punishment for a small offense. Seasoned veterans who had seen severe punishments handed out for incidental offenses urged formation of a "Company Q," where a deserter or thief might serve in a corps and by a period of good conduct reinstate himself.[3] Although many punishments imposed were in direct violation of existing orders, only in a few cases were any steps taken to cause their discontinuance.[4]

Although flogging was abolished in 1861 by the Army,[5] this punishment was still ordered by some veteran officers who believed in severity. At Fort Sedgwick, Colorado, an epidemic of flogging affairs was investigated. Within four days the following punishments were alleged to have been inflicted: June 12, 1867, a soldier from the Thirtieth Infantry received twenty-five lashes with a plaited thong for stealing a gun. The next day, a man was bucked and gagged for an hour. Next was laying a soldier "spread-eagle" on the ground for two hours under a hot sun, buffalo gnats covering his face and hands, putting him in horrible torment. Finally, on the 15th, a citizen received one hundred lashes for giving a bottle of whiskey to several soldiers. The man was bound, naked except for a short shirt, to a rude cross and two muscular soldiers, one on each side, applied their hissing leather thongs to his back, as two hundred soldiers and citizens watched.

"Gradually the deep red wheals assumed a blackish color, and in a short time crimson drops of blood rolled down the naked legs, filling his shoes, some splashing over the clothes of the spectators. At about the seventy-fifth stroke, the flesh around the hips hung in shreds, as if torn by an animal's claws. From the middle of the back to within six inches of the knees, the body was raw and black with congealing blood. At last a citizen named Seward, of New Julesburg, entreated Lieutenant Lautz, 'to stop, for God's sake.' The man's screams were terrible; he impelled himself from side to side, spasmodically jerking upward, and finally hung as if lifeless on the cross. His lacerated body was frightful. After 108 lashes had been administered, Lautz gave the signal to desist. The orderly sergeant said he counted 82, but two or three bystanders stated they had counted 108."[6] The unenviable fame acquired by Colonel Dodge was shared by Lieutenant Lautz, who supervised the flogging. Correspondents of the New York Times, New York Tribune, and Cincinnati Gazette agreed in their descriptions of the scene.

Discipline in the Seventh Cavalry was much the same as in other units. Lacking a building to serve as a guard house, Custer had offenders thrown into a hole, deeply dug in the Kansas prairie. Here a man could sit and ponder his fate while serving out his sentence. A wide variety of insects and snakes might crawl into the hole with the prisoner, giving him much opportunity to keep busy twenty-four hours of a day. No one was allowed near the hole, and the soldier was completely out of touch with his comrades until the term of his sentence expired.

As late as December, 1868, a private who deserted was tried before a General Court Martial, found guilty and sentenced to a dishonorable discharge. He was obliged to forfeit all pay and allowances due him, except the just dues owed the laundress and sutler. He was to have his head shaved and his left hip branded with a hot iron bearing the letter "D" for deserter, two inches in length, and drummed out of camp. Later on an indelible ink that took many washings to erase was substituted for the branding iron.

---

3. Army, Navy Journal; May 11, 1867 — Pg. 603.

4. Ibid., May 4, 1867; Pg. 585.

5. Ibid., July 6, 1867, Pg. 725; 3rd Section, 84th Chap., Act of Congress, Aug. 5, 1861: "Flogging as a punishment in the Army is hereby abolished."

---

6. Army, Navy Journal — July 6, 1867 (Title Page).

With this change the letter "D" was reduced to one and a half inches in length.[7]

There were always a few individuals in each company who would feign illness and ask permission to visit the surgeon's tent for treatment. Their object was to escape guard or fatigue duty by showing signs of unfitness, hoping the surgeon would accept their counterfeit ailment and prescribe medication and rest on a cot for the day. The large number of these fakers deserved no better treatment than they received from some incompetent physicians, and even charlatans, by some means or other, would receive appointments as contract surgeons.

A healthy looking set of soldiers stand in a long line outside the surgeon's tent awaiting the surgeon's arrival. As soon as he approaches, the men snap to attention, some holding their stomachs and coughing, others seemingly doubled with pain, but all able to salute as he passes into the tent. The steward inside shows the officer the sick list and clears his throat as he points to several names on the chart. The physician seems to take his time in going over the names and then shuffles behind the dispensary counter, pours a glass of water and seats himself. Picking up a scalpel, he begins to clean his fingernails. Without looking up, he asks the steward, "Any new cases this morning, steward?"

"Yes, sir; two," replies the steward, running his eye over the company books.

"Well, have them in first, and then I'll take the old standbys.

"Schweitzer!" calls the steward, and Schweitzer shuffles in, one hand on the pit of his stomach, the other on the back of his neck, looking the picture of misery, with a face as long as the morale law of Connecticut.

"Well, Schweitzer, what's the matter with you?" says the doctor.

"Der matter ish, ich habe pains in mein pelly und der copn und der brust und back so ever ash I eat anytings, und ich can eat notings und nicht schlafen deese dree nachts, und bin so krank ich nicht bin fit fur dooty, und der sarchint he say gottam ven I tells him so."

"Bad case," says the doctor who has heard of this particular Dutchman before. "I haven't got the medicine I need to cure your disease, but come again in a week if you don't get better. Next man, steward." Schweitzer turns and exits with utter disgust; as he walks past the long awaiting line he notices a smile or two on several of the men who had heard the conversation and diagnosis.

"Jenks!" and at the word, a rather good-looking fellow steps in, briskly enough, but with a decidedly seedy appearance.

"You sick, Jenks! I thought you never got sick; what's the matter now?"

"So I don't very often doctor; but the truth is, I've been drinking pretty heavy for a week, and got so I can't eat now. Drank about a gallon of water last night, and kept throwing it up every time. I'm for duty today, and don't feel able, I'm sort of a tremble and light-headed . . ." says Jenks, who has heard the old saw about honesty.

"Yes, I see, you want something to set you up; I'll give you a good dose, and then you go lie down in your bunk and stay there. You're excused. Try to eat some dinner; you must eat, or you will be having the the jim-jims."

Jenks gets his ammonia cocktail,[8] and leaves, feeling better.

"What diagnosis, doctor," says the steward, entering Jenks in the register.

"Inebriation, of course."

"You forget, doctor," reminds the young steward, "there's no such disease in the new Army Nosology."

"Hum! That's a fact! Well, it's got to be

---

7. Army, Navy Journal — Jan. 12, 1867, Pg. 326.

8. The subcarbonate of ammonia, in the dose of 15 grains dissolved in water, and the spirit of Hartshorn, in the dose of 2 teaspoonsful in a glass of water. The Medical Guide, Richard Reece, M.D., Albert Colby & Sons, 1873, Pg. 213.

Courtesy Custer Battlefield Museum

A soldier and his family in front of their tent home at Fort Hays, Kansas (about 1868).

something. How many acute diarrheas have we had this month, steward?"

"Eleven, sir."

"Too many already; that won't do; any skin disease yet?"

"No, sir."

"Put him down acne rosacea then; he'll have it sometime, if he hasn't got it now; now rattle 'em off. Call Mooney."

Mooney is at the door and steps in, limping as usual. This soldier has been nursing a blue-ball for a month or more, and feeding on iodine of potassium till he had got to like the latter, and to have a real affection for the former; besides, being on sick report suits him. The doctor had long ago played out all his variations on his method of talking to Mooney, and Mooney has gone over his usual gamut of replies several times. In fact, they would have grinned at each other, if Mooney dared, and the doctor hadn't to preserve his dignity, in addition to having

been so heartily sick of the sight of that particular blue-ball, colored Indian red with iodine. The steward grins on the side of his face away from the doctor. The only recourse is for the doctor at periodical times to propose surgery, then Mooney invariably, with an affectionate rub of the place, knows he is getting much better, and gets out of the way as fast as he can. On this particular occasion the doctor, who hasn't quite recovered from Schweitzer, makes such a determined gesture with his scalpel that Mooney starts for the door, and declares he is fit for duty.

"All right," says the doctor, "I thought it was about time. Work him off, steward." And Mooney is worked off accordingly.[9]

As the remaining dreary batch file in and out, one by one, the steward looks on blandly, thinking to himself that he would

9. Army, Navy Journal — July 31, 1869 — Pages 790-791.

rather be a steward than a doctor after all, if it wasn't for the difference in pay. Just then the doctor slips out the rear entrance of the tent, eluding several prisoners who marched down in charge of a guard to get a dose of salts, ostensibly "to clean out their blood," but actually only to get the chance for a good walk from the guard house to the surgeon's tent. The steward apologizes for the doctor's hasty departure and quickly excusing himself, hurries off to the adjutant's office with the sick book, barely in time to catch the officers before they relax for breakfast.

Stealing away from camp and making tracks to a nearby frontier settlement for whiskey and "soiled doves" was common among cavalrymen after tramping over hill and stream with nothing but coffee and alkaline water to cut the dust. Knowing from experience that he placed himself in peril by entering the town alone, the trooper often made arrangements with several comrades, with at least one pugilist in the party, to accompany him to assure a safe evening at trouble spots. With some luck and if the money held out, their return trip to camp with several saddle bags full of bottled whiskey would have proved lucrative, and the trip worth the effort. If the event passed unnoticed, you can be certain anyone who condoned their short leave was due a canteen filled with spirits.

Throughout the Kansas frontier, lusty and brawling little communities sprang up near garrisons, expecting to reap a harvest from the soldiers' pockets by filling their bellies with bad tasting whiskey and cheating them at card tables and faro games. If you weren't a drinking man, you might loll about the cribs where the town's Jezebels would sell what was left of their charms. These gaily dressed women tried desperately to hide the lines of age by applying heavy make-up to their faces and colorful ribbons to their hair. But the grim artist of time and bitterness could not be erased easily with pow-

der, paint and perfume. These fallen women had greater success by lamplight and evening darkness.

Hays City was indeed an "ungodly place," located on the line of the Kansas Pacific Railroad, which eventually ran from Kansas City, Missouri to Denver, Colorado. The main street was wide and dusty, running parallel with the railroad track. Fronting the street was an array of saloons, dance halls and a few photograph parlors. It was a melting pot for scouts, soldiers, desperados and drivers of many passing bull teams, principally Mexicans. According to the laws of the town, each businessman was to construct a sidewalk in front of his place, but there was no uniform building code. One sidewalk would be at ground level, while another would be four or five steps higher. The walkways were built according to the construction of the building's ground floor. Most were a step or two below the door. Whiskey sold for 25 cents a glass and was usually cut and bitter tasting, whereas the gambling tables were always open to anyone who felt lucky.

Hays City boasted one hotel in its early days, known as the Bailey House. The building was put together with one thickness of boards, with the rough side out. Partitions between the rooms were pasteboard that gave no protection from any stray bullet from the street. It was the custom to sleep between two ticks or generally feather beds, with constant fear of a bullet penetrating the walls from the streets or from below.[10]

James Butler Hickok, better known as Wild Bill, scouted for Custer's command on occasion. In Hays City, Bill lounged at Drum's saloon when he wasn't hunting buffalo or scouting for the Seventh Cavalry. One of Bill's pastimes was sitting on the railroad track and shooting at an old-

10. The Newton Circuit Newspaper, Newton Centre, Mass., July 16, 1909. Also see E. B. Custer micro-film; roll 6, no. 6427; Custer Battlefield Museum.

fashioned bucket windlass used for drawing water. The windlass stood in front of John Bitters' saloon, and quite frequently one of Bill's bullets would cut the rope dropping the bucket into the dark waters below. Bill would then pay Bitters to recover the bucket, which the German saloon keeper could do in a short time.[11]

Shootings were common in Hays City, and every night seemed like a Fourth of July celebration.[12] On one such day, a party of men were sitting around a table gambling while several others drinking at the bar were watching. Hickok walked in, paused for a moment, then cautiously walked directly to the table. Without the slightest suspicion of motive, he drew a pistol from his sash, reached over one man's shoulder and shot another, who instantly fell dead. Wild Bill flashed another pistol and asked if anyone else demanded satisfaction. Except for a few grunts, nobody seemed in great haste to answer, and the game continued. The next morning a vigilance committee, formed at the same saloon, pronounced the shooting justifiable. A colored man was paid $1.50 to take the dead man away and bury him in the new cemetery which was laid out about half a mile north of the city.[13]

Wild Bill had another dispute in the temporary post office with a man named Strawhorn[14] only a month after the saloon incident. Strawhorn, a wiry and calloused teamster, was another victim who played out a slow hand against Hickok's swift and deadly shooting. Colored troops stationed at the fort made a few visits to Hays in groups; the outcome on one occasion was that three of them were found suspended from a trestle over a creek above the town. Investigators could find no one who had anything to do with the incident.[15]

A Frenchman named Tefault ventured alone to Hays City for a one-night racket. On his way back to the fort he was jumped by a number of Mexicans, relieved of his money and other personal effects, dragged into the timber and stripped of his clothing. At first Tefault thought they were going to hang him, but they tied him up and left him. Somehow, he worked the ropes loose and

11. Newton Circuit — July 9, 1909 — E. B. Custer, roll 6, No. 6426.
12. E. B. Custer, Following the Guidon, Harper & Brothers, N. Y., Pg. 154.

13. Newton Circuit; July 9, 1909; E. B. Custer, roll 6, No. 6426.
14. Newton Circuit; July 9, 1909; E. B. Custer, roll 6, No. 6426.
15. Newton Circuit; July 9, 1909.

Courtesy Custer Battlefield Museum

Fort Hays, Kansas in 1868. Evening parade and inspection.

returned to camp. After he reported his experience, two officers and one hundred troopers rode to where Mexicans were encamped. In a search for the men who committed the outrage upon Tefault, no identification could be made.[16]

Hays City attracted riffraff from the plains who acted as bouncers and strongarm men for the floating games. If the sucker was allowed to win the pot, his chances of ever keeping it were slim. He was drugged, robbed, stripped of this clothing and thrown into a gutter. If he escaped with his life he was fortunate.

Troops F, I, L and M of Custer's command left Fort Leavenworth for Camp Sturgis south of Fort Hays, on the Big Creek (Big Timber), arriving there May 18, 1870. A permanent camp was established there for the summer and, being the only available portion of the Seventh in that section of the country at that time, they were appointed to protect settlers from Indian depredations. The cost was much less in keeping a regiment encamped on the prairie than when garrisoned. In the fort the horses were generally cut down to two-thirds forage, depending upon the grass for the other third. When troops were encamped in the field, they had everything in readiness and would be able to strike out on a moment's notice. When the weather turned colder and the grazing around camp was well used up, the command would be broken into companies and distributed to different forts in the department for permanent winter quarters.

After tattoo roll call one night, Privates John Kile (alias Kelly) and Jeremiah Lanigan of Troops I and M slipped from camp unnoticed to visit Hays City, some two miles west of Camp Sturgis. Their destination was the popular Thomas Drum saloon. Lanigan, a powerful man, had been in the company for only a short time, but was considered one of the top pugilists of M Troop.

The two soldiers stepped into Drumm's saloon hardly noticed by anyone. Lanigan spotted Wild Bill standing at the bar chatting sociably with the bartender. He walked casually up behind Bill, and suddenly threw both arms around Hickok's neck with a choking grip and pulled him over backwards onto the floor, holding his arms out in a spread-eagle fashion. Somehow, Hickok freed his right hand and slipped his pistol out of his sash. Meanwhile, Kelly saw the opportunity to finish the gunfighter off and drew his pistol, ramming the muzzle into Hickok's ear, and pulled the trigger. Fate endeavored to keep her appointment with Wild Bill in Deadwood City some years later, and Kelly's pistol misfired. Lanigan grabbed Hickok's right hand again, preventing a scoring shot, but Bill turned his hand far enough to one side to enable him to fire his pistol. The bullet tore through the right wrist of Kelly. He jerked back. The second shot from Bill's pistol ripped through Kelly's side, dropping the soldier like a sack of oats. Lanigan, his face smeared with sweat and black powder, tried to hold Hickok's right wrist to prevent him from getting another shot off. But the gunfighter's luck was in his favor. Another shot went off, shattering Lanigan's knee cap. This caused Lanigan to release his hold and double up with pain. Wild Bill saw his chance, jumped up and made tracks for the rear of the saloon, jumping through a window, taking glass and sash with him. Kelly lasted only a few hours after the fight.[17]

When the news reached Camp Sturgis, a number of troopers seized their guns and started for Hays City, hell bent on revenge. The soldiers forced their way through every saloon and dive in town but could not find Wild Bill. If he had been found, it would be left to anyone's imagination what would have happened to the famous scout and gunfighter. Kelly's body was taken back to

16. Ibid.

17. Newton Circuit — Sept. 3, 1909 — E. B. Custer Micro-file, roll 6, No. 6434.

camp and Lanigan was sent to the post hospital at Fort Hays.[18]

What happened to Wild Bill Hickok? Many stories have it that he fled the city swinging aboard an outbound train at the railroad station. But, in reality, Bill raced to his room close by, took up his rifle and a hundred rounds of ammunition and proceeded to the cemetery west of town. There he laid in waiting until the next morning, as he expected the soldiers to find his hiding place. Bill declared that he would never be taken alive, and many more soldiers would pass into the other world before he would give an inch.[19] At daybreak he left the cemetery and started for Big Creek station, on the line of the Kansas Pacific Railroad, eight miles east of Hays City, and boarded a train.

Kelly was buried at the Fort Hays cemetery with full honors, and Lanigan recoverd from his wound, rejoining his company. He was a good trooper until he decided to desert, taking horse and provisions with him. Some time later, members of his old company heard that a man named Kelly, belonging to an infantry regiment, shot and killed Lanigan in some distant Kansas town.

Traveling on the raw edge of the wilderness rarely led to meeting romantic characters, despite adventures described in Eastern pictorial magazines. We often read of people who could work all day skinning buffaloes and tanning hides, and then read Tennyson aloud around the campfire at eventide, but they were an uncommon exception. "The only real romance in the west is chasing Indians, but fighting them is another story," explained a veteran Indian campaigner. He might even further explain the many hardships endured during frontier service. "Fort Harker, where we at present dwell, is twenty miles from the centre of the United States; if it were twenty miles from the centre of the earth it would be quite as

useful. It has been an established post for two years, but those two years have failed to rear a single comfortable habitation for man, to say nothing about the hundreds of horses and mules that have stood all winter shelterless. Our own dwelling, twelve feet square, is made of rough logs, set upright and plastered with mud; the roof is a heterogeneous mass of mud, sticks, straw, and boughs. The former owing to its profound respect for the law of gravitation, would persist, at first, in falling in clods at all hours. It dropped upon our plates at dinner and into our mouths in dreams, till finally, a bright idea striking us, we stretched a piece of tent cloth above our bed and defied the mud. It snowed the night of our experiment, and a bushel or so of snow sifted into the tent cloth. Toward morning came a thaw. We were dreaming ourselves a victim of the Spanish Inquisition, and they were trying on us the torture of the shaven head and ice-cold drops of water. Just as we were about to renounce Protestantism in toto, we were awakened to a sense of the reality. The water was dripping from our cotton roof in quarts, and, as we wrung ourselves out, a few clods of mud fell with a loud thump, in the opposite corner, as if to remind us that in an uncivilized country man can never war successfully with the elements."[20]

In stationary camps and barracks, soldiers were constantly plagued with chronic dysentery. Especially was this so with green troops who had left their comfortable homes in the East for frontier duty in the West. This malady raged with violence, striking down the hardiest of men, many of those being raw recruits. In this matter, the doctor was usually powerless. All efforts of medical science failed to cure chronic dysentery when it had once taken hold among new troops. Where medicines were basically useless, campaigning generally cured it, if not already in advanced stages. A

18. Ibid.
19. Ibid.

20. . . . Author's collection, Letter to Editor of the A.N.J. (date blurred, but definitely 1868).

change of scenery and diet had effectively cured many cases within a week, but no doctor could help the sufferers. As one soldier wrote of this complaint, "I may be able, however, to throw some light on this subject from my own experience. On two occasions before going into active service I was attacked with this distressing and prostrating malady. The first time it was owing simply to constant wet feet, mounting guard in wet weather, and doing all sorts of open-air duty with dilapidated boots. A new pair, purchased, for at the time we could draw none, cured this. The second time I suffered . . . on account of bad water. The spread of the disease was marvellous. On this occasion it was a matter of observation to me, quite unfailing, that there was but one class of men in camp unaffected by dysentery, namely, the 'old bumpers', or men addicted to strong drink, openly and secretly. Whatever else ailed them, dysentery or diarrhoea never did. Acting on this hint, I determined to test it by experiment on my own person. When the regiment turned in, I slipped out of camp, running the guard, and deliberately went to work to get drunk, with some others. The effect was magical. Three days' pretty free drinking seemed to effect a complete change in my constitution, and I never suffered from dysentery afterwards. This is the only case in which I can conscientiously recommend the use of spirits in the Army. On every other occasion, without exception, I never saw it do anything but unmitigated harm. It transforms many a good man at other times into a fiend; and as for officers, I feel no hesitation in saying that nine-tenths of the disasters in our civil war were owing to drunkenness among officers."[21]

The winter was bitter cold and much of the time the men huddled about small fires, warming frost-bitten hands and drying out clothing. "Isn't it a mistake on the part of the Government to require enlisted men to work as common laborers, with no oppor-

tunity to perfect themselves in drill?" questioned one soldier. "It's bad enough working out there in below zero weather, let alone drilling," another soldier might answer. However, the men did labor somewhat under silent protest, and even though the work was slow in progress, it was finally completed, much to the satisfaction of the officers. Another question kept arising in the minds of the enlisted men. If they were to be driven into slave labor, how could they show proper respect toward their officers, when the officers showed no mercy toward the men. Discipline under these circumstances began to crumble. Forty men of the Third Cavalry left from Fort Morgan, taking with them their horses, carbines, pistols and ammunition. Intending to throw off their trackers, the group headed southwest toward New Mexico and then scattered up through California. Making "dirt-shovellers" of soldiers only caused the desertion rate to climb higher, with the loss of government equipment and the time spent in training the men. It was the deserters who found a source of profit in time of peace, and it was equally certain that Rank and File would become worthless in time of war, if it continued.

Newspapers, books and any other kind of reading material were scarce and in demand by both troopers and officers. A few kept journals and diaries and many more wrote letters to families back home. An Indian attempt to steal the horses or cattle might merit a lengthy letter or at least several pages in a diary, adding a few remarks of their own in magnification. The postal delivery was uncertain away from the railroad. One traveler told troopers that he had seen two hundred bushels of papers deliberately burned at one time in Atchinson, the upper stage route terminus. A German officer, from the southwest corner of New Mexico, said he received his German papers regularly, but never any others, which would seem to indicate that more widely readable

---

21. Army and Navy Journal, Mar. 18, 1871.

papers were confiscated by stage drivers and their friends. If someone wanted to assure himself of getting a newspaper or magazine, he would have to send to Denver or some other remote spot, although letters averaged about ten days from Boston to Fort Harker.

There were about eight hundred Omaha and Kaw Indians encamped near Fort Harker, with the Cheyennes and Arapahoes not far away. Kaws came into the garrison daily with fresh hides from smaller animals, to barter with the soldiers. Their knowledge of tanning skins was amateurish, and it wasn't long after a trade that a soldier began to notice a peculiar scent coming from his newly bartered Indian memento. To amuse themselves from time to time, and break the monotony of daily routine, the Kaws were sometimes asked to join the troopers around a fire. Their body odor was hard to overcome, but one could be amused enough to tolerate their presence at a fireside. Few could speak English but their sign language, used to communicate among Plains tribes speaking different languages, was readily understood. If asked, "Have you seen any soldiers pass this point?" their hands went up to give the number by tens, accompanied by the words "Walk a heaps! Walk a heaps!", meaning infantry. They placed two fingers astride a third to designate cavalry. (See Indian chapter — sign language.)

In earlier times a buffalo robe or a wolf skin was bartered for glass beads or brass jewelry, but with changing times Indians would ask Boston prices in greenbacks for their commodities, and might drive a sharp bargain with motioning hands, a head shake and a few grunts. The Government built a stone lodging at Council Grove and presented it to the Indians, with suitable ceremony. When the Indian agent next visited them, he found mules and ponies tied in the rooms, while their owners had gone back to their tent lodges located in the front of the

Two dead troopers from Fort Hays share a mud spattered board walk after whooping-it-up in Hays City the night before. Shootings were common and could be heard as far as Fort Hays. "It sounded like a Fourth of July celebration" Mrs. Custer noted in her memoirs.

building. All the woodwork had been torn out of the building by the Indians and used for firewood.

It was often suggested that the Seventh Cavalry was entertaining a menagerie of prairie animals. Relatives and visitors would bring back to Eastern cities fantastic stories of soldiers harboring wild animals in their quarters and living with them. And quite true were these stories essentially however, blown out of proportion. Almost every soldier and officer owned a prized treasure boasting his was superior over the rest. Prairie dogs, porcupines, wildcats, raccoons, badgers, buffalo calves, young antelopes, and a curious number of mongrel dogs of every size were quartered with the men. At night lonely cries from captive animals answered distant wolf calls, but did not seem to bother the soldiers' rest. When arising in the morning, first duty for the men seemed to be to care for the animals.

At Fort Abraham Lincoln it was always a delight for Libbie Custer and the General to watch their hounds frolic, as if to show off or attract attention. The hounds, Liberty and Mischief, and their pups ran through the Custer quarters nipping and biting at each other's heels and were always creating some kind of disturbance. When the bugler sounded the daily calls of guard mount, stables or retreat, several hounds would sound off with their own peculiar bugling and strike a similar key-note, after which the remainder of the pack would join in.

Frontier life was boring but only if one made it so. The Custers regularly gave socials and entertained at the piano. Much of the social life of dinners, dances, and the whisper of pasteboards shuffling to high stakes were meant for only a handful of officers and their ladies. The Custer circle, or "closed clique" within the outfit grew with the General's reputation. Many officers such as Captain Frederick W. Benteen had little to do with this inner circle outside the line of duty, and only then by mutual necessity. While the Seventh waited for active duty, the Custers were busy preparing for hunts with Eastern visitors or occasional foreign dignitaries, and dogs were ever present. At one time the General and Libbie reached a peak of forty dogs. The best was not considered good enough for these animals . . . and no one ever thought of repressing them. The stag-hounds running by sight, or the fox hounds hot on a trail with noses close to the ground formed picturesque scenes with the General in their midst. During winter the fox-hounds were used for hunting in underbrush and low timber. On hunting sorties the General would ride either Vic or Dandy, his thoroughbreds. Horses and dogs seemed to share in the excitement. Custer's favorite dog, Blucher, would often leap up with him in the saddle, and, after licking his master's face, return to the ground. Following the dogs' baying voices, the hunting party would then gallop off down the valley, hoping for a sight of game.

The stag-hounds would sometimes run off together for some length of time to return with the leader proudly holding a rabbit in his mouth. At times during the winter wolves would frequent the bluffs, exciting the stag-hounds within their kennels. On one occasion when let out by their keeper for exercise, the hounds made a mad dash for the bluffs with the half-grown pups following behind. The soldier who cared for the dogs followed and, after a long and cold hike, found the pack wagging their tails at the sight of him and standing over a dead coyote. Dragging it back to the post, the soldier urged Custer to come see what his hounds had done. After seeing the carcass, the General knelt and began petting the dogs, feeling just as proud as they must have felt with their kill. In one of Custer's letters to a friend, he mentions with deep pride an event that took the hounds off by themselves: "My dogs hunt up and down the creek every day. Last night a man living eight miles below here came to camp and told me that four of my dogs, Lufra, Juno, Blucher, and Maida, had driven a large buffalo near his ranch, and that he had gone to them when he found the buffalo about used up and unable to get away, and that they would have killed it alone but he finished it with his rifle. They had probably been running it for several miles. I call that pretty good work for green dogs. I took them with me the other day, and it was a sport. Juno sprang right at the nose the first time she saw a buffalo. Lufra took the ear, and Blucher got hold of the side. Juno is as savage as a tiger, and so is Lufra." It wasn't unusual for the Custers to see their dogs drag themselves into camp after a two-day chase. They would generally sneak off one by one when tired of waiting to be taken out and go on a hunt by themselves.

A veteran teamster who had accompanied Custer on many hunts recorded: "During the summer campaign into the Black Hills in 1874, I saw antelope run away from General Custer's pack of wire-haired Scotch stag-hounds or greyhounds. They chased the antelope on many occasions but never caught up to one, though the General said they caught quite a few. The antelope

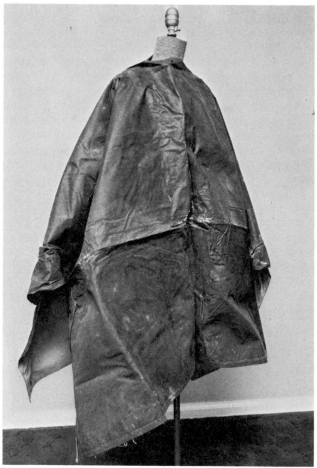

Poncho, Civil War, used extensively by Infantry and Cavalry. Made of muslin and rubber coated on the outside. Has brass grommets along edge, six feet long and four feet wide, generally known as a "gum blanket," it slipped over the head and acted as a rain-coat.

would get so far ahead of them at the end of a mile that he'd stop a moment or two and look back at the dogs. Besides . . . the hounds had a good start after that big buck. In the fall of the year, when the antelope were in huge bands, similar to sheep flocking together, the odds were in favor of the dogs bagging one or two. Crowding themselves tightly together, the antelope would run against one another, making it difficult to gain any speed. It is hard to believe that any dog of Custer's could catch a buck antelope that was in favorable condition."

The joy in hunting often led to sorrow. Custer describes losing the faithful friend, Maida: "I took with me from camp about half a dozen fine stag-hounds. Foremost among all these was Maida, my favorite dog, the companion of all my long and terrible marches of last winter; she who by day trotted by my side, and at night shared my camp-couch. In the first run after buffaloes the dogs, contrary to their usual custom, became separated from me and accompanied others of the party. They soon singled out a buffalo, and readily brought it to bay. With little forethought or prudence, several of the hunters opened fire upon the buffalo while the latter was contending with the dogs. Maida had seized hold of the buffalo, and while clinging to its throat was instantly killed by a carbine-ball fired by someone of the awkward soldiers who accompanied the party. Words fail to express the grief occasioned by the untimely death of so faithful a companion." Jack (as Custer was accustomed to being called at times by his intimates because of the initials G.A.C.) could never bring himself to eat mule or horse meat, no matter how short the rations. The idea occurred to him that to save himself from starvation, he might make his mind up to eat his dogs' ears, but the thought of mutilating his devoted friends was soon dismissed.

Tom Custer kept well within the shadow of his more famous brother, but was equally as colorful and dashing but more mischievous than the General. Tom was proud of mementos hung on the walls of his quarters. Necklaces, war-bonnets, and buffalo hide shields were arranged in no special order among ghastly scalp-locks. Tom was expert in catching rattlesnakes but would never take one alive unless it had seven or more rattles. Many a visitor was startled by seeing these live trophies in patched-up hardtack boxes. Tom's bull-dog, a four-legged ruffian, when loosed from confinement, would head straight for the general's hounds with frenetic growls. It usually took both brothers to separate their dogs with much difficulty. Tom's bull-dog would not have lasted long against such odds, so was swiftly whisked away and safely penned. Although stag-hounds showed gentleness to human beings, they can be terrible fighters. Standing on hind legs and facing each other, they would claw and tear until one or the other would fall.

Knowing Custer's love for pets, the soldiers brought him everything they could capture. Despite her reluctance to accept another mouth to feed, Libbie always thanked the donor with a soft smile. When the Seventh packed up for a lengthy journey, it was almost certain that several wagons would contain a scattering of "prairie dandies."

To fight Indians it was necessary for the cavalry to pursue and overtake them. If the Indians allowed themselves to be overtaken, it was understood that they were ready for a fight, usually in a defensible position. The troopers were at a disadvantage as both men and horses would be exhausted from the long chase and lack of sufficient food and rest.

The Indians generally had two or three fresh ponies close at hand on which they could fight or flee. Changing horses during the pursuit enabled the red man to keep well away from the troopers' carbines. The Indian traveled light, without a saddle or other equipment, making it easier for the Indian pony to cover more ground. The cavalry horse, grain fed and much heavier in weight, became short winded too early in the chase, with saddle, light camp equipment, and trooper, the load totaled approximately 240 pounds, and nothing could be discarded to help lighten it. Only upon dismounting could the trooper relieve his horse of 150 pounds of his own weight. At different time intervals a fifteen minute walk was necessary. The troopers' Cavalry Tactics, 1874, section 1193, titled "Marches," prescribes:

The average march for cavalry is from fifteen to twenty miles per day. The walk is the habitual gait, but, when the ground is good, the trot may be used occasionally for short distances ... A halt of from five to ten minutes is made at the end of every hour for the purpose of adjusting equipments, tightening girths, etc. .... On long marches, officers and men, except the sick, are required to dismount and lead from twenty to forty minutes every second or third hour; to save their backs, horses will always be led over steep ground, and particularly down hill.

If any horse became jaded or back weary, disabled or killed, leaving the trooper horseless, he must either double up with his "bunky" or walk the rest of the way. It was easier to catch hold of the tail of an animal or something securely attached to the saddle, and the resulting pulling effect would make the journey by foot easier. Under no circumstances must the horseless trooper become separated from the command. If he did, the alternatives were to blow out his brains, or take his chances by hiding during the day and traveling back to the nearest post at night. It was generally understood by every seasoned trooper that he must never allow himself to be captured alive by the Indians.

One soldier wrote a letter to a girlfriend that contained this cheerful passage: "I would ... send you a lock of my hair, but I fear it would be a fraud upon the savages of this vicinity. There is a fair prospect that one of these noble red men will be my barber before Spring."[22]

With tin utensils and bobbing carbine, there was a continual din as horse and trooper crept along a trail at a rate of from three to four miles per hour. There was nothing picturesque about the field cavalryman. Wearied and weather-beaten by exposure, uniform torn and spattered with mud, salt crystals covering his shoulders and back from constant sweating, his bronze face half hidden by hat and beard, he had the appearance of a slouchy soldier, unbecoming to his duty and profession. At first glance anyone might think he accom-

22. ... ANJ — March, 1867.

plished more through his threatening appearance than he achieved in actual battle.

The gaits of horses are walk, trot and gallop. The walk is at the rate of about three and three-quarter miles per hour; the trot, at the rate of seven to eight miles per hour; and the gallop, at the rate of nine to eleven miles per hour. The gallop very soon breaks down horses and is the exceptional gait used mostly at drill and in campaign; on all other occasions it is strictly prohibited.[23] Usually, the trot would come just before the rest, and at this point the trooper would dismount and loosen the cinch a little so the horse could graze. Just before remounting, the cinch was tightened before proceeding. Some horses had the habit of taking in a deep breath as the cinch was tightened, enlarging the chest. As soon as he was ridden for a short distance, he released this air and the cinch had to be tightened again. If he lets the air out too soon, the saddle slips when the trooper tries to mount. (Note: The cinching system that was in use in 1876 used buckles instead of the cinch straps that most saddles have today.) It was common practice on lengthy marches for officers and sergeants to ride up and down the command watching to see that men did not slouch in their saddles, as this caused sore backs for the horses. Some troopers found it difficult to maintain the "sitting up straight" attitude. This is not riding at "attention" but it is a way of keeping the rider more comfortable. With this posture the body rolls with the horse's gait and a day's march would pass without saddle-sores.[24]

Any campaign without water can threaten disaster. A regulation canteen holds a quart and a half of water and weighs approximately four pounds. This canteen could keep a man going for a good day's march. If hot weather did not persist, rationed water could be extended for two days. On the plains, where horses could march without water for the entire day, they would be watered after being fed, just before leaving camp in the morning. While on the march, the oftener horses were watered the better, as it was not usually known when another watering place would be reached. If a mounted command had to march a considerable distance without water, making it necessary to camp en route, the animals would be well fed but denied water until just before starting, when they were permitted to drink freely. The command continued the march in the afternoon, and did not encamp until it had accomplished at least half of the distance, then moved early the next morning to reach water. During hot months, horses were watered thrice daily; in the morning, at noon, and just before grooming in the afternoon. At other times, two waterings were sufficient; after morning and at evening stable-duty. During cold weather, a noon watering was enough. A trooper had always to remember that a horse will rarely drink enough early in the morning.[24] If he was to travel a considerable distance, a route would be planned on a map, showing water holes or streams. Torrential rains and severe weather often caused muddy streams where neither cooking, drinking nor washing clothing could be attempted. While troopers strained, boiled, and let the mud settle, commonly all efforts failed to clear the water. Vinegar helped to settle the mud, but the bitter taste of the vinegar had to be tolerated.

When a detachment of cavalry went on a scouting expedition, the troopers were reduced to light marching order. Officers, troopers and scouts carried little baggage. If the scout were to be an extensive one, an extra shirt and toilet articles were approved. A trooper's bed consisted of a "Gum Blanket" or poncho and saddle blanket. The poncho was an article carried over from Civil War stock-piles. It was a sheet of rub-

23. Drill Manual, 1874, Section 1180.
24. Sgt. Bob Craig, 2nd Re-activated Cavalry, a 20-mile experiment with horses and saddles, at Oklahoma's 1st Cavalry meet, April, 1972, letters and tape.

berized cloth, six feet long by four feet wide, with an eighteen-inch slit running crosswise in the center. It was worn by slipping the head through the slit with the gum coating on the outside. This acted as a raincoat, saddle roll, and ground sheet for bedding — and a dry area for a fast hand of cards. The edges were hemmed and had eyelets reinforced with double thickness of cloth. This enabled the trooper to double-up with his "bunky" and couple two ponchos into an "A" tent for protection against the sun or rain. Ponchos were generally black, had a most unusual smell, and stuck to almost anything in the hot weather.

Troopers were exasperated by the neglect of the government to furnish suitable clothing to those stationed in different latitudes. Troopers serving in Southern states in an almost tropical climate wore the same uniform in quality and quantity as were issued to troops stationed in the cold northern plains.

An enlisted man wrote to the Army-Navy Journal with a few suggestions he thought would benefit the troops serving in the Southern states, Texas in particular. "The present blue uniform (woollen clothing) is too heavy and oppressive for the summer season. The sack-coat will do well, but the trousers are too heavy, particularly when the men are on guard or on post. The dress coat is much too heavy, and when closely buttoned up, gives a man no chance of feeling the cooling breeze of the Gulf. My suggestion is, that for fatigue purposes, the present blouse or sack coat, and linen or cotton trousers of the unbleached kind be used; and for guard mount or parades, the present style of coat, but of lighter material, and white trousers of either linen or cotton. I would also suggest that after guard mount, the blouse and white trousers be permitted to be worn by the guard, not the uniform coat. The Armies of the European continent are always clothed in light material during the summer." It is evident that this soldier

was personally conversant with different Armies of the European and American continents.[25]

Soldiers at frontier posts depended on rations provided by the government, and frequently flour, salt meat and hardtack were of the poorest quality. Not until after 1861 was "hardtack" referred to by name. It was called hard bread or hard crackers by the Army. Hardtack was a plain flour-and-water biscuit measuring three and one-eight inches by two and seven-eighths inches, its thickness varying around one-half inch. Biting into this cracker was impossible. Only a hard blow with an instrument would break it. Soaking hardtack or frying it in bacon grease was a substitute for a meal in bivouac. Indian-fighting troopers found many boxes of hardtack stamped 1864 that were infested with maggots and weevils which, after having riddled the crackers with tiny holes, spun webs to incubate their eggs. If a soldier was issued one of these riddled crackers, he was congratulated by a seasoned trooper of his fortunate luck in getting meat with his meal.

What soldier in field or garrison has not felt his heart lighten and the blood quicken in his veins as the sound of "GarryOwen"[26] from the 7th Cavalry Regimental Band beat out the rhythmical motion for horse and man. To the soldier of the 7th it gave an *esprit de corps* and life to the command that would never have been felt without it. Even when the band was not present, the haunting tune was whistled or sung in the marching column as the words seemed to bid defiance to the enemy. This jaunty tune was an inspiration to soldiers long before General George Armstrong Custer caught wind of it. It was written between 1770 and 1780, in commemorating young hooligans who ran riot in Limerick.[27] In 1811, when the

25. Army-Navy Journal, Aug. 3, 1867.

26. GarryOwen, the Gaelic word meaning "Owen's Garden"; Of Garryowen in Glory, Lt. Col. M. C. Chandler, p. 412.

27. Songs and Music of the Red Coats, 1642-1902, Lewis Winstock; Stackpole, 1970.

French stormed the beach at Tarifa, Spain, the 87th Royal Irish Fusiliers fought off and reversed the counterattack with their band in the immediate rear playing "Garry-Owen."[28] The same tune was played fifty-seven years later in Indian territory, on the banks of the Washita River. On November 27, 1868, Custer arrived at Washita with eleven companies of the 7th Cavalry. Before them lay Black Kettle's Cheyenne village completely unaware that troops were nearby. Before the charge, Custer had the band members assemble on a nearby slope with their instruments. When the command "charge" was sounded, Custer turned to his half-frozen band and shouted: "PLAY." First Lieutenant Edward S. Godfrey recalled what happened: "While playing GarryOwen, before the first strain, the instruments froze up." As the mouthpieces were placed to the lips and after blowing the first few bars, saliva froze to lips, causing an inseparable situation. One cannot imagine what wild thought raced through Custer's busy mind as he glanced back at his half-frozen band standing in complete bewilderment, listening to the dying strains of music that squealed and varoomed from their instruments as if in rudeness to a great battle.

Captain Myles Walter Keogh, who had earned Civil War distinction in some thirty engagements, ended his career as a dashing cavalier at the Battle of the Little Big Horn, June 25, 1876. Keogh has been credited with the introduction and adoption of "GarryOwen" to the 7th Cavalry. Since a general acceptance has been made over the years as to Keogh's adopted Irish tune, it is with some great pleasure to reveal a favorable piece of accepted material recently researched in the files at the Custer Battlefield.

Elizabeth B. Custer, during the years of her widowhood, received thousands of letters from friends she had known while on

Courtesy Smithsonian Institution

Hardtack or hard bread, usually 3⅛″ by 2⅞″ and nearly half an inch thick. It was a plain flour and water biscuit. Typical mess gear sold commercially or by sutlers. Hard bread and utensils of Civil War vintage.

the plains, and during the Civil War, many of whom had sent pages of forgotten experiences. On May 8, 1887, Mrs. Custer received a lengthy note from Alcatraz Island, signed by Elias Van Arsdale Andruss,[29] who said he had been a member of the same cadet company at West Point with Custer mentioned as a second classman while he was a 'plebe'.

"On entering West Point," Andruss writes, "every plebe is supposed to be gifted with some accomplishment. Mine was to hum and drum by ear on the guitar and I was always sure of an attentive listener in General Custer which was very flattering to me as a 'plebe'. I remember his asking me if I played "GarryOwen" or "The Girl I Left Behind Me." They seemed to be his favorite airs. I could not gratify his wish as the tunes did not belong to my repertoire! If my memory serves me correctly, he afterwards had Mr. Appeles, the leader of the

28. Ibid., p. 101.

29. Letter to the author from West Point, Aug. 1, 1972: "After checking the classes for several years after Custer's graduation, I finally found an Elias Van Arsdale Andruss who graduated in 1864; admitted to the Academy in 1860. I could find no other possible cadet. Andruss was stationed at Alcatraz Island in 1866. He died in Brooklyn in 1910. Michael J. McAfee, Museum Curator, West Point."

band, to arrange the airs to different instruments and they were performed on appropriate occasions." He continues, "During the General's service in the field against hostile Indians, in reading newspaper accounts of the same, I have in several instances read of his directing the band to play GarryOwen before the charge. It called to my mind his fondness for the air while at the Academy."[30]

GarryOwen

1. Let Bacchus's sons be not dismayed,
   But join with me each jovial blade;
   Come booze and sing, and lend your aid
   To help me with the chorus:—

   Instead of Spa[31] we'll drink brown ale,
   And pay the reckoning on the nail,[32]
   No man for debt shall go to jail
   From GarryOwen in Glory!
   No man for debt shall go to jail
   From GarryOwen in Glory!

2. We are the boys that take delight in
   Smashing the Limerick lamps when
      lighting,
   Through the streets like sporters fighting,
   And tearing all before us.

3. We'll break windows, break the doors
   The watch knock down by threes and fours;
   Then let the doctors work their cures,
   And tinker up our bruises.

4. We'll beat the bailiffs, out of fun,
   We'll make the mayor and sheriffs run;
   We are the boys no man dares dun,[33]
   If he regards a whole skin.

5. Our hearts, so stout, have got us fame,
   For soon 'tis known from whence we came;
   Where'er we go they dread the name
   Of GarryOwen in glory.

6. Johnny Connell's tall and straight,
   And in his limbs he is complete;
   He'll pitch a bar of any weight,
   From GarryOwen to Thomond Gate.[34]

7. GarryOwen[35] is gone to rack
   Since Johnny Connell went to Cork,
   Though Darby O'Brien[36] leapt over the
   dock
   In spite of judge and jury.

GarryOwen was perhaps the most famous regimental march and fighting song in the U. S. Army. Inseparably identified with the Seventh Cavalry, this jaunty Irish tune had many variants. It began as an Irish drinking song, a lively dance and jig, and much later it was adopted by the soldiers during the Civil War. At last, it finally came to be adopted by the fighting Seventh Cavalry as a marching song, for horse and man. Its words and music gave each cavalryman an inspiration for battle with much of the expectant glory sought by officers.

HINTS FOR FRONTIER SERVICE

The following instructions and suggestions for troops that served in the Indian country were prepared by an old Army officer as the result of actual experiences of thirty years of frontier service. They were published by General Reynolds, in General Orders No. 77, headquarters Department of Texas, with reference to the fact that "so many of the officers now serving in the Indian country have not had handed down to them the usages of the old Army in Indian matters and in travelling over the great plains. We publish them now, when most of our Army are serving in the Indian country and are likely to have abundant occasion to make use of all their Indian lore."

Marching and Encamping

• No soldier will leave a military post or station, on field service, without first having been carefully in-

30. From E. B. Custer Micro-film, Custer Battlefield, item No. 4868 (letter).

31. The general term "Spa" referred to the mineral waters of Castle Connell, near Limerick, a fashionable haunt of the time.

32. "On the nail" means knocking a person on the head, instead of paying spot cash.

33. "Dun" refers to a lawsuit and imprisonment for debts.

34. "Thomond Gate" is a suburb on the opposite side of Limerick from GarryOwen. The suburbs maintained a permanent feud.

35. "GarryOwen" (Owen's Garden) is a suburb of Limerick. In the 18th Century, up to about 1780, it was notorious for riots and melees of soldiers.

36. Darby O'Brien and Johnny Connell, mentioned in the last two stanzas, were notorious for their exploits around 1770-80.

spected by the commanding officer, or by some suitable person by him designated. The inspector will see that such soldier is provided with arms and equipments, serviceable in every particular; that he has the prescribed amount of ammunition; good shoes; a change of underclothing; blanket, haversack, canteen, knife, fork, spoon, tin cup, tin plate, towel, comb, and a piece of soap. The inspector will see that the horse of a cavalry soldier is in apparent good health and well shod; that the horse equipments are in good repair and well oiled; that there is a lariat at least twenty-four feet long, an iron picket pin, or, in lieu thereof, a side line; also a curry-comb and horse-brush. If an officer, whether of the line or staff, is to have charge of soldiers leaving a post or station for field service, or as escort, such officer must be present at this inspection, personally to know the condition of his men and animals before he starts. Means of transportation leaving a post or station with or without troops, to be absent in the field or on ordinary roads, should in like manner be critically inspected.

• If the journey lies through a country infested with thieves or hostile Indians, each teamster and employee must be armed and supplied with ammunition. Each teamster must have a curry-comb, horse-brush, bucket, axe and extra helve, hand-axe or hatchet, and spade. In a train of three or more wagons there should be a pick-axe and two spades to every three wagons, with which to repair roads. With each of such trains there should be two or three scythes, complete, and scythe-stones; a hand-saw; two augers of suitable sizes; a monkey-wrench; one or two mortising chisels; a coil or less of lariat rope; one or two lanterns; a band and shoeing hammer, wrought nails, mule shoes and nails; extra linchpins, tongues, bounds and coupling poles; the timbers to be tied on the outside of wagon-beds. Also extra hames, collars, halters, single and double trees, and trace chains; some open links; saddler's awls; and a few buckskins. A teamster with an awl and a strip of buckskin can soon repair broken harness. There should be for service in a country infested with hostile Indians, a six-gallon water keg in good order and tight, hung under each wagon. Larger kegs cannot well be carried from where filled to the wagon by one man. If troops are to travel with a train, or with wagons, there should be enough more of these kegs to afford at least two quarts of water to each man, including teamsters and employees.

• In ordinary marches the cavalry soldier should march on foot, leading his horse, every third hour. Of course all mounted officers marching with cavalry organizations will set the example of travelling on foot, when the cavalry soldier is required so to travel.

• There should be a halt of ten minutes after the first fifty minutes of a day's journey, and of at least five minutes at the end of every subsequent hour.

• When animals receive grain forage and are in good order, a day's journey can be made without unsaddling cavalry horses or taking draught animals out of harness. When animals depend entirely on grazing, it will keep them up longer, especially if not in good flesh, to make, say, two-thirds of the journey or thereabout, and then turn out and graze, and rest until the heat of the day is past; then saddle, harness, and move on so as to arrive at camp by or before sunset. It is always better to have daylight to see the surroundings of the camping place, collect fuel, get water, etc. When grass is scarce or lacks nutriment, and horses and mules are thin in flesh and travel-worn, two halts a day should be made to enable them to graze, or they will give out and break down entirely.

• If a party is small and liable to be attacked at night, it should do all its cooking in the daytime. Supper should be eaten before dark, water kegs filled, and bundles of fuel with which to cook breakfast tied under the wagons. The party should then move away from the water-hole or spring, and, after nightfall, move off the road, and camp in some valley or depression in the ground where the men, animals, and wagons will not be seen relieved by the sky, and where an enemy, if he come, will be thus made visible. Each depression in the ground camped upon will doubtless have some run or ravine by which it is drained. In this, a gunshot distance from camp, three sentinels, if the size of the command will admit of it, should be posted — one to stand post, the others in turn to sleep near him. Indians creep up such hollows when they would surprise a camp; they might shoot one sentinel with arrows; they could rarely shoot three before alarm would be given. Under such circumstances a good sentinel will sit down near his comrades so that he can awaken them by a touch in case of need; will keep in the shadow, and depend in his vigilance at night as much upon his ears as his eyes. Of course there will be other sentinels posted if the command can afford them; and these in like manner should be posted by threes within the depression so as just to look over its rim, being in shadow and bringing against the sky any one who approaches. In a camp thus set for the night, there must be no loud talking, no fire, no light, no striking of flint and steel, no burning of matches. When it is determined upon before night that such a camp is to be made, the men with their knives (if there be no scythes along) should cut grass enough for the horses and mules for the night. This they bring in their blankets and stow it away in bundles in the wagons. By doing this, when danger of attack is impending, all the horses and mules can be tied to the wagons or to a line and be securely fed, while the men, not being embarrassed by loose or scattered animals, have nothing to do but fight any one who menaces the camp. It often occurs when horses and mules are picketed out that a single Indian will crawl among them, cut a lariat, and gradually crawl away, leading a horse or mule until out of range. He will then mount and ride slowly away until beyon earshot, and afterward double by circles of miles to catch views of the ground passed over by his own trail, that he may watch and count his pursuers as they slowly follow his tracks, step by step, himself unseen.

• In the Indian country a small escort should always precede the person escorted. On such occasions creeks or ravines to be crossed, or canons or other dangerous places to be gone through, should be first carefully reconnoitred. After these are passed the escort will never move on without having the person escorted well up to it. If danger be imminent, two or more men will travel as an advance guard — some fifty or one hundred yards in front, and a like number in rear as rear guard. In broken ground, one man, at least, should march a hundred yards or more on each flank abreast of the advance guard, but always in sight of it.

• Arms should be carefully inspected by the officer in charge every night just before the men lie down to sleep. The carbine or musket of each soldier should be carefully loaded, the piece left at half cock and laid beside its owner on his blanket, muzzle toward his feet to prevent danger from accidental discharge, and also to be in position to be readily seized and aimed. If the man have a revolver, the inspector will see that it is not only loaded and capped, and that the cylinder revolves easily, but that the hammer is on the stop. When danger of an attack during the night is apprehended, the man will not be permitted to remove his pistol from his person, or his shoes from his feet. In the morning, without fail, the men, teamsters and all, will fall in quickly and completely armed, when called by signal or otherwise. This practice will accustom the men to seize their arms ready to fight the moment they spring from bed — even when awakened at any hour. When everything has been prepared for the march, the officer in charge, before a man leaves the ground, will have another careful inspection of the arms and the outfit generally, personally to know that each man is ready to fight at a moment's notice. He will see that the canteens and kegs are filled, if he be still near water; if not near water, this will be done under his own supervision at the next water on the route. Under no circumstances will teamsters' arms be stowed in wagons or feed boxes, or in ambulances under other things, but be kept strapped to the bows of the wagon, or stanchions of the ambulance, breech toward the owner, at half cock, ready for use in a moment. Let this be remembered. Many a life has been lost by forgetting it.

• The person in charge of an escort, detachment, or train should, by previous inquiries, have learned as far as possible all about the road or country he is to pass over from day to day, to the end that if no fuel is to be found at his next camp or halting place, he may have a few fagots or "buffalo chips" (bois de vache) put on his wagons for cooking. Fires made of green wood make much smoke, which at nightfall settles along valleys and low places, and can be seen a long way off. Fires made of dry hard wood make but little smoke, which seldom settles or becomes visible, even when a norther or other sudden cold change in the weather is about to take place. The burning brands of wood left after cooking is done should at once be scattered and extinguished by shoveling dirt upon them, especially so at night when fire is no longer required, even though the camp is to remain for the night; first, that the fire may not be seen; second, that sudden gusts or gales of wind may not blow sparks into wagons, tents, or beds, or set the neighboring grass on fire; third, that the remaining unburned wood may be used next morning, or by yourself on your return trip, or by some needy traveller. Soldiers and teamsters have the bad habit, when about to leave a camp or halting place, of piling all remaining wood on the fires. Fires should be extinguished and the remaining brands and logs should be scattered. It takes but very little fuel, if carefully husbanded, to boil a kettle of water for coffee, bake bread, or fry a pan of meat. If possible, bread should be baked in the daytime at points where fuel is plenty. If properly made, it will last and be good for two or three days, especially in cold weather.

• In Texas especially, and on the plains generally, all rivers, streams, and dry beds of creeks are subject to very sudden and dangerous floods, sometimes from distant rains, when overhead the sky is clear and not a drop of rain has fallen. Therefore troops and trains should always cross one of these and then move on to ground certain to be above the reach of any freshet, before they encamp. This rule should never be forgotten.[1]

Care of Animals on the March

• When grain (corn, wheat barley, or oats) is to be fed at camp or stopping places on long marches, or *jornadas*, where no water for the animals is to be had, such grain should be kept in water the night before starting. If no barrels or tubs can be had in which to soak it, put the sacks, each half filled with grain, into the creek, spring, or water hole. As the grain swells it will not then burst the sack. Wet, well-soaked grain is refreshing to animals exhausted by fatigue and thirst, and can easily be digested though the animal which consumes it have no water where it is fed. Seldom do animals have the colic, even when fed upon wheat, if the grain has been well soaked, although the weather be warm and the grain already grown hot from fermentation.

• A tablespoonful of chloride of lime in a pint of water is a good remedy for ordinary colic in a mule or horse. The dose can be repeated without danger.

• In an Indian country, on going into camp, wagons should always be formed in corral; that is, arranged in an elliptical or circular form, with the main open-

1. Army and Navy Journal, July 29, 1871.

ing and spaces between the wagons closed by bearing chains, or by ropes; at night all the animals should be tied on the inside, and if danger be imminent fed with grass, cut and brought in blankets as before stated. Teamsters should be practised in forming a corral rapidly, at least once after starting every day, and when halts to graze are made. The teams should be numbered from front to rear each morning, as they should alternate in leading day after day. At a signal all odd numbers should move to the right and even numbers to the left. When the two columns thus formed are, say, twenty or more yards apart, according to the ground and the size of the train, the leading wagons halt and the others close up. They can then move on in parallel columns until another signal is given to form the corral. Then the two leading wagons turn and approach each other, passing only until their teams lap, when they halt; the next wagon in each column is directed so as to bring its team inside and just lapping the wagon in front. In this way the teamsters soon learn how large the corral should be, and to form it promptly. The opening is between the rear ends of the last two wagons. Ambulances and carriages are driven between the two columns, and to the centre as the corral is forming. A corral thus formed, with not a mule unhitched, makes a very good defence, the mules of each team being more or less protected by the wagon in front. It often happens that Indians menace a train when on the march. To have the teamsters practised, so as to know precisely what to do in such an emergency, prevents the confusion which, without such practice, would be sure to ensue, especially under fire, when no plan had been agreed upon beforehand. The moment each team comes to a halt in forming a corral, the lead mules are hitched to the wagon in front, and its teamster, rifle in hand, posts himself outside of the corral opposite his own team, unless otherwise directed, and at once commences to fight if the enemy be within range on his side. Indians have a wholesome respect for determined men, and, unless in overwhelming force, will not long stay under an effective fire. If the attacking force is large and holds the train in corral for a day or days, and if the firing be heavy, some of the men should dig the earth from under the wheels of the wagons, on the most exposed side first, and so let the wagons down, axles to the ground. The men and animals then get better protection. If Indians make signs for a talk, only two or three should be permitted to come within rifle shot — none inside of the corral. In the night, men can dig rifle-pits outside of the corral, or take shelter behind any neighboring obstacle. A bold front will cause Indians to be wary of you; the least sign of timidity emboldens them; turn to run from them, and you are lost. Always form your wagons in corral, especially where camp for the night is to be made. You may be attacked. At all events you have the practice; and besides, a corral is a convenient enclosure for loose stock.

• If you think yourself pursued when on the march, leave, if you can spare them, two or three well-mounted men just on the hither side of some elevated ground to watch the country passed over for distant pursuers; if possible, to count them if seen, and then to gallop up and give timely notice. Indians themselves nearly always leave some one on or near their back track, to look out for an enemy who may chance to follow. Scouts thus left by them generally come up at night if no hostile followers have been seen.

• During the day, when you halt to graze, a trusty sentinel or two should be posted if possible on some neighboring elevation, so as to command a good view of the camp and of the animals while grazing. This should be done by the commander himself, and before a horse or mule is picketed, or turned out with side lines to graze. If the command is large, of course sentinels will be well outside in other directions, and some will be posted near the herd. Any person on the watch will give notice of a sudden dash or close proximity of an enemy by discharging his piece. A distant or stealthy approach can be indicated in some other agreed-upon method, such as the sentinel putting his cap or jacket on his piece and waving it about, or running around in a circle, etc. In either case every horse and mule will at once be brought in, the cavalry saddle their horses, and all have their arms in hand, ready to fight.

Treatment of Wounds and Diseases

• Small detachments of troops, escorts, and trains, about to march without a doctor through a country infested with hostile Indians, should be furnished with such medicines and appliances as will meet ordinary casualties and emergencies, and suffice temporarily, until assistance can be rendered by a medical officer. For example: a few dozen pills of opium and of quinine; some cathartic pills; an ounce or two of tincture of opium; a few doses of salts; a bottle of volatile liniment; a pocket case; a set of splints; a few roller bandages; a fine sponge; some patent lint; a few square inches of oiled silk; a yard of adhesive plaster; a package of tow; and a few bottles of whiskey or brandy. In the event of a gun-shot wound the proper dressing is two layers of lint, say an inch and a half square, saturated with cold water and placed on each orifice of the wound. A piece of oiled silk, twice as large, is laid on that; and all retained in place, say, by a pocket handkerchief. This dressing should be kept on until the parts become stiff and painful — two to six days, according to the season — when the dressing should be removed, and either a similar dressing or warm water, or a bread-and-water poultice, should be applied and renewed once or twice daily. The less a wounded man eats the first five or six days, the better. After that he requires nourishment. If the wound is a simple punctured wound, and if at any time it becomes severely painful, the pledget of lint wetted with the tincture of opium instead of water will be applied, and water should be instituted at the next dressing if the pain has been relieved. If a bone has been fractured by the ball in transit, the first mentioned dressing must be used as directed; then a roller bandage will be applied to the limb, commencing at the fingers or the toes according to the limb wounded; a splint is then applied to two or four sides of the limb to steady the bone, and is retained by another roller bandage. Care should be taken not to apply the bandage too tight at first, lest the swelling of limb should occasion much pain. An incised wound — that is, a wound made by a sharp cutting instrument — should be drawn together closely, the surface of the skin about the wound should be wiped dry, and strips of adhesive plaster, half an inch wide and several inches long, should be applied across it so as to keep the parts in contact, and cold water, lint, oiled silk, and handkerchief employed as directed above.

• Should the blood be jetting from an incised wound, the wound must be pressed open, the mouth of the vessel at the point where the blood jets out must be seized by a pair of tweezers or forceps, and turned around once or twice, and the wound be then closed and dressed as above directed. A simple contused wound does best without any application. A limb bitten by a snake should be tied by a band above the place bitten, volatile liniment kept upon the wound and constantly applied to the whole limb, the patient at the same time sustained by draughts of whiskey or brandy sufficient to stimulate but not intoxicate. Scouts that visit the settlements of Mexicans along the Rio Grande should learn from that people how to employ in snake bites the *golondrineria* or swallowwort. It is said to be a prompt specific for the rattlesnake bite. It may be bruised, leaves, stem, and root, the juice expressed and drunk by the spoonful, and also be applied to the wound. Wounds made by Indian arrows may be treated as incised or punctured wounds. If suspected of being poisoned, they should be treated as snake bites. Stretchers, if necessary, may be extemporized by poles and pieces cut in the woods, or by using tent poles, and a blanket lashed to them. In the event of sunstroke, if the patient have a pale face and feeble pulse, apply the cold douche by pailfuls of cold water dashed over his head and body, and whiskey or brandy toddy constantly given until he revives or his pulse becomes natural.

• If, when marching or in camp, by day or night, the Indians set fire to the grass to the windward, to burn your train or camp you must at once set the grass on fire to the leeward, and keep it from burning up toward your train or camp, by the men beating it out with their blankets. Then move on to the burnt place far enough to the leeward to be out of danger of the approaching flames.

• It will be well for soldiers always to remember this simple rule when travelling in a country infested with hostile Indians: If you think there are no Indians near, then is the time to be especially on your guard. The Indians are wily and very patient. They will hover about and watch you sometimes for days and days, to find you relaxing your vigilance and at length off your guard. They see and know full well when you think they are not near. That is just the time when, as a panther which has patiently watched its prey, they make their spring. It is better to be prudent all the time — and even more than cautious — than to be left on foot, or to lose life.[2]

The following was published for the information and guidance of commanders of Indian scouts:

The general impression that Indians cannot be caught is erroneous, and the methods usually employed are faulty. Indians committing depredations, which is the vocation of all hostile ones, usually move in parties of from four to eight, and after a depredation move night and day with rapidity for the first seventy or eighty miles, when their animals become foot-sore and weary and themselves careless, believing they are safely beyond pursuit, as they usually are. To attempt overtaking them at once is folly and ruin of the command; but by moving on steadily, never, under any circumstances, giving up the trail, keeping the animals well shod, for if not they are eventually lost, using all of daylight in the pursuit, the Indians, nine cases out of ten, will be overtaken before the eighth day, and since you travel at about equal rates, only gaining on him by moving more hours, he will almost invariably be found halting without lookouts and his animals grazing. By charging at the instant without waiting for any charge formation, his animals are captured and some Indians killed. For this, the men should at all times be kept well in hand, and as you approach the Indians, which a vigilant officer can always know by the appearance of the trail, they should be cautioned to mount their animals, and put their arms in readiness for instant use.

A trail of two footman or a single horseman need never be lost unless washed out by rains, and then should not be difficult to find again by a practised guide who knows the country. The guide should be used as a trailer, and to give information of water and grass, and should never be permitted, in any other manner, to influence the scout. When reaching crests, or debouching from ravines or woods the officer should go forward singly and scan closely ahead of him, and by having his entire mind and attention in his work, he will almost invariably discover the Indians before his party is seen. The trails always pass water, and, although suffering must be expected from want of it, one seldom travels twenty-four

2. Army and Navy Journal, August 5, 1871.

hours without finding it. Riding animals are indispensable at the moment of the charge, but are not useful at any other time, as men can march further in fifteen days than horses without forage. Great care must be taken in packing the mules, and they must not be burdened by blankets and trash, which will always be done if not prevented.

To send out expeditions under officers who will not literally attend to all of the foregoing instructions, and much besides; who will not, without regard to hunger, thirst, and suffering, continue on their course, and who do not possess the faculty of creating expedients to overcome all the many obstacles liable to present themselves each day, is a waste of time and material.

The foregoing is drawn from an unusual experience and invariable success in Indian service.

Fresh trails are to be the first sought, and when found should be equivalent to finding the Indians who made them.[3]

ARMY SLANG

Whiskey soak — Typical drunk; extremely heavy drinker.

Jerked Beef and Pinole — Chasing Indians on jerked beef and pinole. Pinole is a Mexican flour (southwestern).

Accoutrements — Soldiers' equipment (such as belt, buckles, leather, etc.), other than clothes or weapons.

Nooning — Midday rest of troopers on march, or midday lunch while on campaign.

Forage — Food other than straight rations for men or animals. The 1863 daily forage, according to regulations, permitted 10 pounds of hay and 14 pounds of grain for each horse working, campaigning or training.

Shavetail — A new lieutenant. Green mules had their tails cut off, trimmed or "shaved," so that the packers could recognize them. "Shave-tails" for the inexperienced young officer, and "bell-sharp" for the experienced officer.

Charioteers — Cavalrymen called "wagon riding doughboys."

Wind-suckers — Horses.

Walks-a-Heap — Indian name for Infantry.

Brunettes, to the white soldiers; Buffalo Soldiers, to the Indians — Colored soldiers.

Bob-Tail — A discharge without honorable character, because the part of the discharge paper describing his character was simply cut off.

The Grand Bounce — To desert. (From Neb. History, Mar. 1954, p. 31).

Wrangle — a hot fight or argument. (Sgt. Stall & Pvt. Smith had a wrangle, E. B. Custer Microfilm, Roll 6, No. 6403.)

Breechers Scouts or Beecher Scouts (given both ways) — a company of frontiersmen and scouts. (E. B. Custer Microfilm, Roll 6, No. 6410)

"Telegraph" Smith (or "John" or some other name)— designation for being a liar. (E. B. Custer Microfilm, Roll 6, No. 6416)

Blown the Horse — Fatigued. (E. B. Custer Microfilm, Roll 6, No. 5621)

Taking "French Leave" — deserting; same as "Grand Bounce." ("Bloody Knife," Ben Innis, p. 53.)

Jenny Lind Steak — choice cut from upper lip of a mule.

Walking Draft — man with a price on his head.

Whiskey — Coffin varnish — Sheepherder's delight.

Saloon — a guilded slaughterhouse of morality.

A "Little Drop of the Creature" — drinking or referring to whiskey. (E. B. Custer Microfilm, Roll 6, No. 6423)

Uncle Sam's Watch & Chain — convict's ball and chain. (Ibid., No. 6425)

I.C. Brand — Inspected and Condemned (on a horse). (Ibid., No. 6427)

"Old Bummers" — men addicted to strong drink. (Army and Navy Journal, Mar. 18, 1871)

Knitting Bag — wool-lined cartridge box carried by the cavalry. (Army and Navy Journal, Oct. 16, 1869, p. 130)

Cartridge belt — 3rd loop — as seen in '66 and '68 by frontiersmen. (Army and Navy Journal, Oct. 30, 1869, p. 162; Ibid, Nov. 6, 1869, p. 178)

"Heavies" — story or "Heavy" — "Our friend heavy" — "All ye young heavies" — similar to a man in dismounted service, and not capable of riding well or keeping on a horse. (Army and Navy Journal, Nov. 6, 1869, p. 179)

A Hard Crowd — group of Company drinkers; a Company whose men drink to excess. (Army and Navy Journal, Sept. 24, 1879, p. 90)

G.C.M. — General Court Martial, as, "He'll get a G.C.M. for sure!" (Army and Navy Journal, Sept. 24, 1876, p. 90)

"Show the White Feather" — cowardice. (Reno Court of Inquiry, p. 196)

Hardtack — better known as "Uncle Sam's seed cakes." (E. B. Custer Microfilm, Roll 6, No. 6408)

Mr. Bogy — Ex-Commissioner Bogy (Indian Bureau?).

Top-Knot — top of a man's head, or referred to as a man's scalp ("Keep yer top-knot").

Skylarked — smoked and gossiped.

A cup of skalljaw — coffee (S. D. Williams Diary, Second Cavalry, p. 47).

Cavy — Cavalry.

Coffee — "Today I parched some coffee, old java." (S. D. Williams Diary, Second Cavalry, p. 47).

Hawgo full — when the infantry had a kind of a blow-out, most everybody was "Hawgo full." (Ibid.)

---

3. Army and Navy Journal, Aug. 29, 1868, p. 18.

"Coffee cooler" — skulker, loafer, escaping duties. (Ibid.)

Clothing sacks — to carry clothing.

"Dron out" — a bad wetting; a heavy rain.

Goose wine — "Our First Sergeant forgot the coffee and we had to drink goose wine for breakfast." Similar to a tea; anything added to hot water, to conjur a brew.

Dog robber — striker; officer's soldier servant; one who takes extra duty for extra pay.

Wind jammer — Bugler.

Slum Burner — Cook.

Hop (or Hops) — any type of dance.

Old file — long-term service for an officer.

Snow-bird — a man who enlisted in the army during winter and deserted come spring.

"Mr. Lo" — (Indian) "Lo, the poor Indian! whose untutored mind . . . (etc.)," from Alexander Pope's, "Essay on Man" (No. 1); 1733-1734.

Note: Most "Army Slang" titles were drawn upon from the army, navy journals (from 1864 to 1890).

CAVALRY TACTICAL MANUALS

Most of the Union Cavalry fought the Civil War in double rank deployment, under the 1841 *Cavalry Tactics* or "Poinsett Tactics." The double rank system was derived from "Scotts 1834 Tactics" wherein a regiment of eight troops, each of 4 officers and 76 men, was organized into four squadrons of two troops each. Squadrons formed up mounted in two ranks, two feet from head to croup. The *Cavalry Tactics* adopted February 10, 1841, by order of Secretary of War J. R. Poinsett, modified the organization somewhat, the main change being that a regiment now consisted of five squadrons or 10 companies. The "Poinsett Tactics" were used by the Eastern armies all through the Civil War, and by the Western cavalry until 1864. French influence dominated both "Scotts 1834 Tactics" and "Poinsett's Tactics," both drill regulations being mainly translations from French sources.[1]

[It was not until 1854, during the Crimean War, that the War Department selected young professional officers to observe and study first-hand foreign military systems to incorporate their best features and revise our Army's tactical manuals. Captain George B. McClellan was among those chosen, and one result of his report was introduction of the Russian system of carrying a pistol on the waist belt.]

The "Poinsett Tactics" used by the cavalry during the Civil War was designated "The system of Cavalry Tactics, adapted to the organization of Dragoon regiments." When adopted in 1841, the cavalry consisted of the First and Second Regiments of Dragoons only, but these tactics prescribed in detail the training of Dragoons, Chasseurs, Hussars, and Lancers.[2]

Both Dragoon regiments were armed with sabers, muzzle-loading pistols and a Hall's muzzle-loading carbine. DOUBLE RANK WAS PRESCRIBED. The Hussar saddle was recommended by the Scott Board of 1824, and the soldier was taught to sit down in the saddle at a trot. The recruit was given a period of two months' instruction on foot before being advanced to the next phase; instruction on horseback. The School of the Trooper included 120 lessons, two each drill day. After 60 further lessons in the School of the Platoon, the soldier proceeded to the School of the Squadron.

During field duty, the horse was equipped with curb and snaffle bits, a blanket folded into 12 or 16 thicknesses, the Hussar saddle with a buckled girth, breast strap and crupper. Slung from the soldier's waist was a heavy saber. Strapped on the left side of the pommel was the holster housing a percussion pistol. The carbine was at times attached to a shoulder carbine sling, its muzzle nosed into a small leather boot attached to the off side of the saddle just behind the trooper's thigh.

There were no march regulations prescribed in the 1841 manual, even though this publication came in three volumes: Part 1, Dismounted; Part 2, Mounted; Part 3, Evolutions of a Regiment. Volume 3 contained the manual of the Colt's Revolver. In 1864, a one-volume edition was printed by order of the War Department.

In 1864, the cavalry in the West began to

---

1. They Fought for the Union; F. A. Lord, Page 50.

2. Cavalry Journal, Vol. 34, Page 482.

use the Cooke Tactics system, which had been officialy adopted on November 1, 1861 by order of Secretary of War Simon Cameron. It was directed for publication and use as "The System of Tactics and Regulations for the Cavalry of the United States, by Col. Phillip St. George Cooke, 2nd Cavalry." Cooke's tactics were based on the single rank formation; however, this was not adopted until 1874.[3]

The War Department did not receive Cooke's Tactics until January, 1860, and it was not issued until almost two years later, after the war between the states had been going on for several months. The Cavalry continued their battles in double rank, under the Poinsett Tactics.

Cooke, an 1827 graduate from West Point, served with infantry until 1833, when he

_____
3. Cavalry Journal, Vol. 34, Page 429.

was transferred to the First Dragoons. Twenty-seven years of fighting, marching and camp life qualified him to write tactics for the cavalryman.

Rules and regulations for service of cavalry in the field, as set forth in Cooke's manual, were quite complete. One chapter in particular is worthy of study; its title, "Special Service of Cavalry in the West." Basic principles governing cavalry marching and camp sites were formulated.

Cooke writes:

It is very certain that bodies of cavalry, performing the same amount of marches and duties — one, under a commander ignorant, or injudicious and careless in this respect, will have broken down horses, whilst the other may maintain them in good condition.

A commander in the west is subject commonly to the great difficulty and risk of necessarily grazing his animals at night, whilst they must be protected from an enemy. The camp should be formed early; sometimes it is protected in rear by a wide river, and the squadrons disposed on three sides of a parallelogram; sufficient space is included for night grazing.

Courtesy Author's Collection
Corporal Rod Paulsen, color bearer, catches up to the forward scout with a message from the troop commander. "Compliments from Lieutenant Swisher, we are to take noon camp at the next tributary." (Ft. Benjamin Harrison, Indiana — 1971) Field exercise.

SCHOOL OF THE TROOPER DISMOUNTED.

Plate 12.

2nd Lesson _ 2nd Part.

Fig. A   Fig. B   Fig. C

Support Arms.   *Sling Carbine.*

Courtesy Author's Collection
From the 1841 "Poinsett" Cavalry tactics (in three parts).

To encamp regularly, the squadrons are formed in line with squadron intervals; they are dismounted; without forming ranks, the troopers unsaddle and unbridle; they deposit the saddles in line in front of all the horses, and place upon them their sabres; the horse blankets are retained surcingled to the horses; if to be picketed, under charge of an officer they are let out as far as is safe in order to preserve the nearer grass for the night.

The author proceeds with a set of march regulations that have been rated as the best ever published in any cavalry manual:

The march should generally be in column of fours, the squadrons[4] with 40 or 50 paces interval, in order that a check in one squadron should not extend its disturbing influence by causing the next to stop; it also tends to the avoidance of dust. From 40 minutes to an hour after the march, a halt of five minutes should be made, the squadrons to be dismounted, informally in column, at the command 'dismount' from their Captains. If there be grass, the squadrons should oblique from the road before dismounting. The horses should be encouraged to feed at the shortest halts; at those for 10 minutes or more, as when watering, the commander should give the command 'unbit.'

_____
4. In this manual, the word 'Squadron' means Companies.

Courtesy Author's Collection

Trooper pulling at his canteen during a 10 minute break from field maneuvers in Southern Indiana. Author and troops from the 2nd U.S. Reactivated Cavalry studied the 1873 field manual with actual uniforms and equipment for 3 days.

Every hour, a halt of from two to five minutes should be made.

Troopers are prohibited to leave the ranks for any purpose on the march, unless on foot, leaving the horse led.

About noon, or about the middle of the march, when circumstances allow a choice of time, the "watering call" should be sounded; the troopers should generally dismount and unbit. The watering is superintended by the officers. Often the horse would fail to be watered from the impatience or want of perseverance of the trooper. This halt is from 20 to 45 minutes. Videttes or sentinels from the advance guard are posted.

After one of the halts the troopers should lead, about 45 minutes; or twice for 30 minutes.

There are several advantages in trotting a part of the march; By it the horses are sooner relieved of the saddle burden, and have longer time for feed and rest. Horse and man are relieved from the constant motion and fatigue of the same muscles and parts. It avoids a bad carriage of the person of the troopers, sometimes injurious to the horse; it awakes and relieves him. It is found, from experience, to lessen the liability to sore backs.

Long marches or expeditions should be commenced very moderately. The horses, if untrained, must be gradually inured to their labors; in other words, the march must be a training. Fifteen miles a day at first; — afterwards they will be equal to twenty-five.[5]

Secretary of War William W. Belknap approved, July 17, 1873, a revised set of tactics for Artillery and Cavalry known as "Upton's Tactics." At this time the cavalry was organized as ten regiments of three battalions each; with four companies to a battalion. Each company had one captain, one first lieutenant, one second lieutenant and 77 enlisted men.

Upton's "Cavalry Tactics, assimilated to the Tactics of Infantry and Artillery" was revised from the "New System of Infantry Tactics, Double and Single Rank," of 1868. The McClellan saddle, single (curb) bit bridle, and six-fold blanket were now regulation. The mounted trooper carried a light cavalry saber suspended from the waist belt. A pistol was carried on the right side, but forward, in a large flapped holster (Civil

_____
5. The walk was estimated at 3¾ miles an hour; the trot, at 7½; the gallop, at 10.

Photo by Sgt. Bob M. Craig

The 2nd U.S. Reactivated Cavalry — awaiting orders to begin a 2 day exercise on the trail in Southern Wisconsin with equipment specified in 1874 manual.

War vintage), and a single-shot, breech-loading .45 caliber carbine, hung from a carbine sling and was tucked into a leather socket affixed to the saddle behind the trooper's thigh. Dismounted, companies now formed in double rank, and mounted in single rank.

Lieutenant-Colonel Emory Upton, 1st Artillery, was the instructor of tactics at the U.S. Military Academy. Upton was graduated from West Point in 1856, and was assigned to the 4th Artillery. He commanded the 121st New York Infantry from October, 1862, until he was promoted to brigadier general of volunteers in May, 1864. His distinguished Civil War record included brevet promotions to major general.

The march and camp instructions are covered in his revised tactical manual much the same as in Cooke's Tactics:

Commanding officers must bear in mind that the efficiency of cavalry depends almost entirely upon the 'condition of the horses,' which alone makes them able to get over long distances in short spaces of time. The horses must, therefore, be nursed with great care, in order that they may endure the utmost fatigue when emergencies demand it.

Reveille, ordinarily, should not be sounded on the march before daylight, as horses rest better from midnight until dawn than at other times.

The average march for cavalry is from fifteen to twenty miles per day. The walk is the habitual gait, when the ground is good, the trot may be used occasionally for short distances.

Long marches or expeditions should be begun moderately, particularly with horses new to the service. Ten or fifteen miles a day is enough for the first marches, which may be increased to twenty-five miles when necessary, after the horses are inured to their work.

In campaign, the usual precautions against surprise are taken, and an advanced guard and flankers are thrown out.

The march is usually in column of fours; when practicable, it may be in double column of fours; in small commands it is often in column of twos.

In small commands, not in campaign, distances of forty to fifty yards may be taken between the companies, so that checks will not extend from one to another and cause unnecessary halts. A halt of from five to ten minutes is made at the end of every hour, for the purpose of adjusting equipment, tightening girths, etc. The companies are dismounted in column at the command of their captains; if there be grass, each captain first obliques his company a short distance from the road to let the horses feed, as horses must always be encouraged to graze as much as possible on the march. When troops march for the greater part of the day, a halt of from twenty to forty-five minutes is usually made about noon. In campaign, videttes are posted during the halts.

On long marches, officers and men, except the sick, are required to dismount and lead from twenty to forty minutes every second or third hour; to save their backs, horses will be led over steep ground, and particularly down hill.

In passing obstacles, each company commander halts at a sufficient distance beyond the obstacle, and requires his men to close up at a walk. When necessary, the column is halted by the commanding officer for the companies to close up.

When water call is sounded, the Captains cause their companies to dismount, and usually to unbit. The watering is superintended by the officers, who see that all the animals are watered without confusion. No horse of a cavalry command on the march should be watered unless all are watered.

In each company, the chiefs of platoon, and particularly those in rear, are held responsible that the troopers do not lounge in their saddles, so as to chafe their horses' backs. Any man who fails to sit up squarely on his horse, must be made to dismount and lead.

No enlisted man will be permitted to leave the ranks for any purpose, except on foot, leading his horse.[6]

The chapter on 'Camping' goes into detail on sanitation, and specific instructions were given governing precautionary measures to be taken while in "hostile Indian country."

Upton's Tactics was by far the perfect tactical manual for the Cavalry, and it was used until October, 1891, when Secretary of War Redfield Proctor authorized the "Cavalry Drill Regulations" prepared by a Board of Officers from all three branches of the service. It may be noted that the word "regulations" was used, and "tactics" removed.

On the Frontier, Upton's Tactics were received by officers with mixed comments. Letters to the Editor of the *Army and Navy Journal* support this, along with the Journal's own views:

Brigade movements mounted are not prescribed to be made by general commands, but by despatched orders and bugle calls. So far as all these movements,

and those of divisions and corps, are concerned, the changes are in the right direction, and the Cavalry Tactics are amply sufficient to meet all the necessities occurring in maneuvring either large or small bodies of horse, in the simplest and most rapid manner . . . As the tactics stand now, it would save the Government a good many dollars, and our so-called "cavalry" much needless trouble, to have every sabre used by an enlisted man turned into the arsenals.

Saber (or Sabre) Exercises, with all its useless flourishes and cuts at the empty air, were retained in Upton's "new" tactics because of tradition. Exercises were still practiced in the cavalry although sabers were only used in "pomp and ceremony." If saber drill was only an exercise, what confidence could the men put in their swords? In some regiments, by disregarding Tactics, the men were made into fair swordsmen, and would charge with the saber. When the tactics were followed, charges became almost a nullity, and firing carbines was the only recourse of the so-called "cavalry." If the cavalry officers on the Board of Revi-

Courtesy Author's Collection

Lisle Reedstrom and Sergeant Bob Craig, 2nd U.S. Reactivated Cavalry, in the field on exercise. Troopers trained from the 1874 Cavalry manual in order to help author with his book project. Problems studied were tactics and horse furniture. Photo taken in Greencastle, Indiana.

---

6. Upton's Cavalry Tactics, under "Marches," Page 478.

sion decided to use the saber as a weapon, it should have been given a fair chance, but if they distrusted its efficiency, it should have been abolished.

Astonishing as it may seem, during the first three years of the Civil War, reports of 105 saber cuts were recorded. From Sheridan's campaign in the Shenandoah Valley, only 25 saber wounds were reported. Late in the war, use of the saber was diminishing.[7] The saber was mostly used to club the enemy when close up.[8]

Charging Indians with a saber may seem preposterous, but it did happen. An Oregon paper gave details of the running off of a pack train by the Indians near Camp Watson, and their pursuit by Brevet Lieutenant-Colonel John P. Baker's First U. S. Cavalry command. When about twenty miles from the post, the troops came up with the Indians and charged on their camp. The

Courtesy Author's Collection

"Field Exercise." The Company's first Sergeant eyes his troopers as they form a line of skirmish with regimental standards in full view. Awaiting his order . . . "Prepare to mount . . . Mount." (Posed) 2nd U.S. Reactivated Cavalry — 1971, at Ft. Benjamin Harrison, Indiana.

Indians stood their ground, but during a preceding snow storm their rifles had become damp and failed to fire. The soldiers, observing the state of affairs, drew their sabers and cut the hostiles down, killing 14 men and capturing 5 women and all the stolen mules, together with 10 horses. A great amount of supplies was destroyed and it was considered one of the most complete victories ever gained over the Snake Indians.[9]

English and German soldiers were seen fencing most of the time, with a certain love for it. Confidence in this weapon was entirely lacking in our cavalry, mainly because American troopers never used it except to cut at the air in exercise. Not knowing how to guard against cut or point in actual battle, except as laid down in manuals, why was it that our cavalry clung to the saber that rattled and rusted and was in need of repairs most of the time?

Generally little complaint was expressed by army officers concerning the wisdom

7. Army Navy Journal, Nov. 16, 1867, Page 199.

8. Journal of the U. S. Cavalry, 1905, pages 183-185, "The service pistol and its caliber."

Courtesy Author's Collection

A cavalry charge lead by Sgt. Doyle Swisher . . . at Greencastle, Indiana. Full field equipment as specified in manual was tied down to saddle, exhausting horses at the end of the day. Troopers found it awkward while mounting, as equipment and rolls were constantly in the way.

9. Army Navy Journal, January 12, 1867, page 326, Col. 3.

Courtesy Author's Collection

2nd U.S. Reactivated Cavalry, a non-profit organization, hope to uphold the old Cavalry standards of by-gone days. Amongst their ranks are policemen, doctors, lawyers, bricklayers and one old Cavalry regular. Sgt. Bob Craig heads the group.

and judgment shown in the cavalry's tactical manuals. These manuals were written by veteran cavalrymen in the "day of the horse" when traveling anywhere was done by or on the horse. They expounded a system with organization and theory and exhibited practical common sense. Despite changes in equipment, training and tactical use of the mounted trooper, the principles involving mounted men and wagons traveling over ground changed but little. The greatest value of the cavalry was in its mobility, which enabled it to arrive in time and place for effective action.

Four great elements of a successful campaign advocated in the manuals were: equipment, horse rations, footing and timing. The fifth tactical principle added by seasoned troopers was "surprise" in battle. Detail on the subjects of training young horses, gaits, seating and equitation aids was necessary, as many recruits knew nothing about equitation and horse management and cared less until their lives depended on it.

The Infantry Tactics are now ready, the Cavalry Tactics will be ready March 14. By the terms of an agreement with the War Department, the publishers Messers. D. Appleton and Company, will sell the new Tactics to officers of the Army for $1.33 per volume, while they will charge all others $2.00 per volume. The War Department has subscribed for 500 volumes of the Tactics for each arm of the service, and will supply them to companies and posts; but cannot supply each officer. The volume is bound with a flexible cover, and clasp, and is of a size to be carried readily in the pocket. The Infantry will be bound in light-blue, the Artillery in red, and the Cavalry in orange— so that the color of binding will indicate the arm of service of each volume.[10]

10. Army and Navy Journal, March 7, 1874, p. 472.

"ARTICLE 7"
MANUAL OF INSTRUCTION FOR THE VOLUNTEERS AND MILITIA OF THE UNITED STATES
BY MAJ. WM. GILHAM
(Philadelphia 1861 — Published by Chas. Desilver)

SABRE EXERCISE.

439. For instruction in the use of the sabre the men of the squad are on foot, and in one rank about nine feet apart.

The right side of the gripe is the side opposite the guard.

The left side of the gripe is the side next the guard.

Tierce is the position in which the edge of the blade is turned towards the right, the nails downwards.

Quarte is the position in which the edge of the blade is turned to the left, the nails upwards.

440. The squad being in position, the instructor commands:

Draw — SABRE.
Two times and two motions.

First motion. At the first part of the command, which is *draw*, turn the head slightly to the left, without changing the position of the body; unhook the sabre with the left hand, and bring the hilt to the front; run the right wrist through the sword-knot; seize the gripe, draw the blade six inches out of the scabbard, pressing the scabbard against the thigh with the left hand, which secures it at the upper ring, and turn the head to the front.

Second motion. At the last part of the command, which is *sabre*, draw the sabre quickly, raising the arm to the full extent; make a slight pause, carry the blade to the right shoulder, the back of it against the hollow of the shoulder, the wrist resting against the hip, the little finger on the outside of the gripe. This position is the same when mounted, except that the wrist then naturally falls upon the thigh.

Present — SABRE.
One time and one motion.

441. At the last part of the command, which is *sabre*, carry the sabre to the front, the arm half extended, the thumb opposite to, and six inches from the neck, the blade perpendicular, the edge to the left, the thumb extended on the right side of the gripe, the little finger by the side of the others.

Carry — SABRE.

442. At the command *sabre*, carry the back of the blade against the hollow of the shoulder, the wrist resting against the hip, the little finger on the outside of the gripe.

Return — SABRE.
Two times and two motions.

443. *First motion.* At the command *return*, execute the first motion of *return sabre.*

Second motion. At the command *sabre*, carry the wrist opposite to, and six inches from, the left shoulder; lower the blade and pass it across and along the left arm, the point to the rear; turn the head slightly to the left, fixing the eyes on the opening of the scabbard; return the blade, free the wrist from the sword-knot, turn the head to the front, drop the right hand to the side, and hook up the sabre with the hilt to the rear.

GUARD.
One time and one motion.

444. At the command *guard*, carry the right foot two feet from the left, the heels on the same line; place the left hand, closed, six inches from the body, and as high as the elbow, the fingers towards the body, the little finger nearer than the thumb (*position of the bridle-hand*); at the same time, place the right hand in *tierce* at the height of, and three inches from the left hand, the thumb extended on the back of the gripe, the little finger by the side of the others, the point of the sabre inclined to the left, and two feet higher than the hand.

In tierce — POINT.
One time and three motions.

445. *First motion.* At the command *point*, raise the hand in tierce as high as the eyes, throw back the

Courtesy Author's Collection
Regulation bugle with tactical manuals to the right on the left the "Revised U.S. Army Regulations" for 1863.

right shoulder, carrying the elbow to the rear, the point of the sabre to the front, the edge upwards.

Second motion. Thrust to the front, extending the arm to the full length.

Third motion. Return to the position of guard.

In quarte — POINT.
One time and three motions.

446. *First motion.* At the command *point*, lower the hand in quarte near the right hip, the thumb extended on the right side of the gripe, the point a little higher than the wrist.

Second motion. Thrust to the front, extending the arm the full length.

Third motion. Return to the position of guard.

Left — POINT.
One time and three motions.

447. *First motion.* At the command *point*, turn the head to the left, draw back the hand in tierce towards the right, at the height of the neck, the edge upwards, the point directed to the left.

Second motion. Thrust to the left, extending the arm to its full length.

Third motion. Return to the position of guard.

Right — POINT.
One time and three motions.

448. *First motion.* At the command *point*, turn the head to the right, carry the hand in quarte near the left breast, the edge upwards, the point directed to the right.

Second motion. Thrust to the right, extending the arm to its full length.

Third motion. Return to the position of guard.

Rear — POINT.
One time and three motions.

449. *First motion.* At the command *point*, turn the head to the right and rear, bring the hand in quarte opposite to the right shoulder, the arm half extended, the blade horizontal, the point to the rear, the edge upwards.

Second motion. Thrust to the rear, extending the arm to its full length.

Third motion. Return to the position of guard.

Against infantry, left — POINT.
One time and three motions.

450. *First motion.* At the command *point*, turn the head to the left, raise the hand in tierce near the neck, the point of the sabre directed to the height of the breast of a man on foot.

Second motion. Thrust down in tierce.

Third motion. Return to the position of guard.

Against infantry, right — POINT.
One time and three motions.

451. *First motion.* At the command *point*, turn the head to the right, carry the hand in quarte near the right hip, the point of the sabre directed at the height of the breast of a man on foot.

Second motion. Thrust in quarte.

Third motion. Return to the position of guard.

Front — CUT.
One time and three motions.

452. *First motion.* At the command *cut*, raise the sabre, the arm half extended, the hand a little above the head, the edge upwards, the point to the rear, and higher than the hand.

Second motion. Cut, extending the arm to its full length, and give a back-handed cut, horizontally to the rear.

Third motion. Return to the position of guard.

Right in tierce and carte — CUT.
One time and four motions

453. *First motion.* At the command *cut*, execute the first motion of *right cut.*

Second motion. Execute the second motion of *right cut.*

Third motion. Turn the hand in quarte, and cut horizontally.

Fourth motion. Return to the position of guard.

Left in quarte and tierce — CUT
One time and four motions

454. *First motion.* At the command *cut*, execute the first motion of *left cut.*

Second motion. Execute the second motion of *left cut.*

Third motion. Turn the hand in tierce, and cut horizontally.

Fourth motion. Return to the position of guard.

In tierce — PARRY.
One time and two motions.

455. *First motion.* At the command PARRY, carry the hand quickly a little to the front and right, the nails downwards, without moving the elbow; the point inclined to the front, as high as the eyes, and in the direction of the right shoulder; the thumb extended on the back of the gripe, and pressing against the guard.

Second motion. Return to the position of guard.

In quarte — PARRY.
One time and two motions.

456. *First motion.* At the command *parry*, turn the hand and carry it quickly to the front and left, the nails upwards, the edge to the left, the point inclined to the front, as high as the eyes, and in the direction of the left shoulder; the thumb extended on the back of the gripe, and resting against the guard.

Second motion. Return to the position of guard.

For the head — PARRY.
One time and two motions.

457. *First motion.* At the command *parry*, raise the sabre quickly above the head, the arm nearly

extended, the edge upwards, the point to the left, and about six inches higher than the head. The hand is carried more or less to the right, left, or rear, according to the position of the adversary.

Second motion. Return to the position of guard.

Against infantry right — PARRY.
One time and three motions.

458. *First motion.* At the command *parry,* turn the head to the right, throwing back the right shoulder, raise the sabre, the arm extended to the right, and rear, the point upwards, the hand in tierce, the thumb extended on the back of the gripe, the edge to the left.

Second motion. Describe a circle quickly on the right, from rear to front, the arm extended; turn aside the bayonet with the back of the blade, bringing the hand as high as the head, the point upwards.

Third motion. Return to the position of guard.

Against infantry left — PARRY.
One time and three motions.

459. *First motion.* At the command *parry,* turn the head to the left, raise the sabre, the arm extended to the front and right, the point upwards, the hand in tierce, the thumb extended on the back of the gripe, the back of the blade to the front.

Second motion. Describe a circle quickly on the left, from front to rear along the horse's neck, the arm extended; turn aside the bayonet with the back of the blade, bringing the hand, still in tierce, above the left shoulder.

Third motion. Return to the position of guard.

460. When the troopers begin to execute the above cuts, thrusts, and parries, correctly, the instructor requires them to make the application of them by combined motions, as follows:

In tierce — POINT AND FRONT CUT.
In quarte — POINT AND FRONT CUT.
Left — POINT AND CUT.
Right — POINT AND CUT.
Rear — POINT AND CUT.
Against infantry right — POINT AND CUT.
Against infantry left — POINT AND CUT.

Inspection of SABRE.
One time and seven motions.

461. *First motion.* At the word *sabre,* execute the first time of *draw sabre.*

Second motion. Execute the second time of *draw sabre.*

Third motion. Present sabre.

Fourth motion. Turn the wrist inwards to show the other side of the blade.

Fifth motion. Carry the sabre to the shoulder, as is prescribed in *carry sabre.*

Sixth motion. Execute the first time of *return sabre.*

Courtesy Author's Collection
Every fourth man in ranks is tagged "horse holder." When engaged in battle, this fourth man takes hold of all four horses and links them together with a link strap attached to headstalls. This still does not guarantee the horses from stampeding under heavy fire. Above all, it calls for plenty of muscle and stubbornness.

Seventh motion. Execute the second time of *return sabre.*

MANUAL FOR A BREECH-LOADING CARBINE, OR RIFLE, THE TROOPERS MOUNTED.

462. Whenever the troopers are not exercising with the carbine, or rifle, it is slung by a belt, which passes from the left shoulder to the right side, the muzzle down, and in such a position that it may be seized by the right hand at any moment, and at the same time be entirely out of the way when the trooper is exercising with the sabre or pistol.

The trooper, in conducting his horse to the ground before mounting, has the carbine passed over the right shoulder, the muzzle in the air.

After mounting let the carbine fall by the side.

At the first command to dismount, seize the carbine with the right hand a little above the band, and pass it over the right shoulder, the muzzle in the air.

463. The trooper being mounted, with the carbine hanging by his right side, the instructor commands:

Advance — CARBINE (or RIFLE).
Two times.

At the command *advance,* seize the carbine at the small of the stock with the right hand. At the command *carbine* (or *rifle*), elevate it, and place the butt upon the thigh, the muzzle at the height of the eye and opposite to the right shoulder, the lock to the front.

To load.

464. The squad being in the position of *advance carbine* (or *rifle*), the instructor commands: *Load in four times.*

1. LOAD.
One time and two motions.

First motion. At this command, place the carbine (or rifle) in the left hand, which seizes it a little below the band, the thumb along the stock, the muzzle elevated, at the height of, and opposite to, the left shoulder, with the right hand move back the catch, and seize the lever with the thumb and first two fingers.

Second motion. Spring open the chamber, and carry the hand to the cartridge-box and open it.

2. *Charge —* CARTRIDGE.
One time and two motions.

First motion. At the command *cartridge,* draw a cartridge, and insert it in the barrel, and seize the lever with the thumb and first two fingers.

Second motion. Draw back the lever to its place, half cock, remove the old cap, and carry the hand to the cap box, and open it.

3. PRIME.
One time and one motion.

At the command *prime,* place a cap on the nipple, press it down with the thumb, let down the cock, and seize the piece by the small of the stock with the right hand.

4. *Advance —* CARBINE.
One time.

As prescribed above.

To fire.

465. The squad being in the position of *advance carbine,* the instructor commands:

READY.
One time.

At this command let fall the carbine in the left hand as in the first motion of load, cock it, and return to the position of *advance carbine.*

AIM.
One time.

At this command, carry the butt to the shoulder with the right hand, support the piece with the thumb and first finger of the left hand, a little below the barrel, the others closed in order to hold the reins without slackening them; place the face against the stock, shut the left eye, direct the right along the barrel to aim, and place the forefinger of the right hand on the trigger.

FIRE.

At the command *fire,* pass the forefinger against the trigger and fire, without lowering the head or turning it, and remain in this position.

If, after firing, the instructor wishes to load, he commands:

LOAD.

At the command *load,* bring down the carbine to the first motion of *load;* load at will, and take the position of *advance carbine.*

If, after firing, the instructor does not wish to load, he commands:

Advance — CARBINE.

Which is done as already prescribed.

To drop the carbine, the instructor commands:

Drop — CARBINE.
One time.

At the command *carbine,* lower the muzzle of the carbine, and cast the butt to the rear.

Inspection of arms.

466. The instructor commands:

Inspection — CARBINE.
One time and two motions.

First motion. At the command *carbine,* take the position of *advance carbine.*

Second motion. Drop the carbine.

MANUAL FOR COLT'S REVOLVERS.[1]

467. The troopers being mounted, the pistol either in the holster or pistol-case, the instructor commands:

---

1. With very little modification this manual will serve for Carbine and Rifle.

Draw — PISTOL.[2]
Two times and two motions.
First motion. At the first command, unbuckle the holster or pistol case, seize the pistol by the handle with the right hand, holding it between the palm of the hand and the three last fingers, the fore-finger resting on the guard, the thumb on the handle.

Second motion. At the second command, draw out the pistol and elevate it, the guard to the front; the wrist at the height of, and six inches from, the right shoulder.

Load in six times.
1. LOAD.
One time and one motion.
Place the pistol in the bridle hand, holding it by the handle in front of the body, the hammer between the thumb and forefinger, and turned to the left, the muzzle pointing upwards. Carry the right hand to the cartridge-box, and open it.

2. *Handle* — CARTRIDGE.
One time and one motion.
Seize the cartridge with the thumb and the first two fingers, and carry it to the mouth.

3. *Tear* — CARTRIDGE.
One time and one motion.
Bite off the end and carry the cartridge opposite the chamber nearest the lever, or, if the cartridge is furnished from the manufactory with the pistol, seize the end of the cord, which projects from one end of the cartridge, between the teeth, tear open the outer case, and take out the cartridge.

4. *Charge* — CARTRIDGE.
One time and two motions.
First motion. Empty the powder into the chamber, and insert the ball, pressing it down as far as possible with the thumb and fore-finger; or, if it be a cartridge furnished from the manufactory, simply insert it in the chamber, pressing the ball down as before.

Second motion. Turn the pistol with the left hand, bringing the hammer towards the body, and cock it with the thumb of the right hand.

5. *Ram* — CARTRIDGE.
One time and two motions.
First motion. Seize the lever with the catch, with the thumb and fore-finger of the right hand, ram down the ball, and replace the lever.

Second motion. Let down the hammer with the right hand, and carry the hand to the cartridge-box.

Repeat as above directed until all the chambers are loaded.

6. PRIME.
One time and two motions.
First motion. Lower the muzzle towards the right

side by turning the wrist of the bridle-hand, the muzzle pointing downwards, the hammer to the front, the left wrist resting against the stomach; half-cock the pistol with the left thumb; turn the cylinder with the thumb and forefinger of the right hand until it clicks. Take a cap and press it on the cone. Turn the cylinder again until it clicks, and so on until all the cones are capped, the hammer resting on the safety notch.

Second motion. Seize the pistol at the handle with the right hand, and bring it to the position of *draw pistol*.

468. The instructor wishing to fire, will command:

READY.
One time and two motions.
First motion. Place the pistol in the left hand, the little finger touching the key, the barrel nearly vertical, the muzzle a little inclined to the left and front, the guard to the front, the thumb on the head of the hammer, the forefinger along the guard.

Second motion. Cock the pistol, and bring it to the position of *draw pistol*.

AIM.
One time.
Lower the pistol, the arm half extended, and place the forefinger lightly on the trigger, the muzzle directed to the height of a man's waist.

FIRE.
One time.
Press the forefinger steadily on the trigger, fire, and retake the position of *draw pistol*.

The men being at a ready, and the instructor wishing to fire all the barrels in quick succession, will give intimation to that effect, and command:
1. AIM. 2. FIRE.
The men will aim and fire, come to the first position of ready, cock, aim, fire again, and so continue until the pistol is discharged; then take the position of *draw pistol*.

469. The instructor wishing to reload, commands:
Load at will.
LOAD.
One time.
Load the six chambers as heretofore directed, and take the position of *draw pistol*.

Return — PISTOL.
One time.
Lower the muzzle of the pistol, and return it to the muzzle, or pistol-case.

---

2. If it is a carbine or rifle, the command will be, *advance — carbine* (or *rifle*).

RHYMING RULES OF HORSEMANSHIP

The following "rules" have grown up with the English love of horsemanship:

1. Judging rule:
   One white leg buy a horse
   Two white legs try a horse
   Three white legs look about a horse
   Four white legs do without a horse.

2. Rule of the road:
   The rule of the road is contrary quite
   In riding or driving along.
   If you turn to the left you are sure to be right
   If you turn to the right you'll be wrong.

3. Drinking rule:
   Cider on beer—no fear.
   Beer on cider—no rider.

4. Riding rule:
   Your head and your heart keep boldly up
   Your hands and your heels keep down
   Your knees keep close to your horse's sides
   And your elbows close to your own.

5. The Golden Rule:
   Up the hill gallop me not
   Down the hill trot me not
   On the plain spare me not
   In the stable forget me not.

WAR HORSES — THEIR EQUIPMENT & TRAINING

On the eastern branch of the Potomac, just opposite the Capitol, the army established a principal depot for supplying horses to the artillery and cavalry during the Civil War. The depot at Giesboro, D.C. occupied a farm of about 625 acres with provision for 15,000 animals. Within six months its capacity was enlarged to 30,000; the largest number at any one time was 21,000. From its construction in 1863 to June, 1866, records show 208,659 horses received, issued, sold or died. Of horses returning from the field, broken and disabled, 25,958 died. Other depots supplied the army with mules as well as horses. These were established at Wilmington, Del.; Harrisburg, Pa.; Nashville, Tenn.; Greenville, La.; and St. Louis, Mo.[1]

It was recommended by the Quartermaster General in 1868 that a stock farm be established at some healthy location in Texas, and that there be kept a year's supply of horses for that district. An appropriation of $50,000 would be asked for the purchase of land in Texas for breeding animals. The Quartermaster General, in 1868, suggested:

"Officers on duty in Texas, in which district a large portion of the cavalry of the army must for some years continue to be employed, report that horses of the native stock, though hardy and wiry, are not stout enough to last under the severe duty to which our cavalry horses in pursuit of Indians are subjected.

"The Northern horse, bred in Missouri, Kentucky, or Virginia, or the States still further north, requires a year's residence in Texas before he becomes acclimated. If put to severe work at once on arriving in the State, he breaks down. After a year he seems to become acclimated, and then will outwear in this service several of the native horses.

"It is recommended that a stock farm be established at some healthy position, and that there be kept there a year's supply of horses for the district. It is stated that many of the Northern horses taken to

---

1. From the Annual Report of the Quartermaster General, Brevet Maj. Gen. M. C. Meigs, 1866.

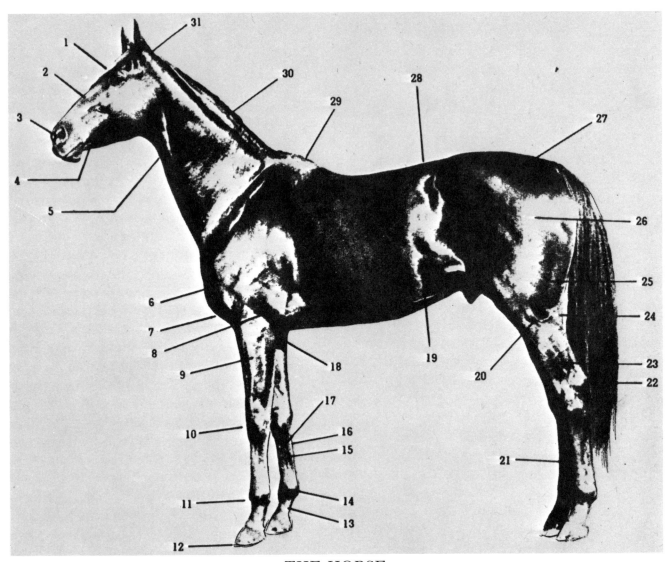

THE HORSE

1 .... FOREHEAD	12 .... HOOF	22 .... HOCK
2 .... FACE	13 .... PASTERN	23 .... SECOND THIGH, GASKIN
3 .... MUZZLE	14 .... FETLOCK	24 .... QUARTER
4 .... JAW	15 .... CANNON BONE	25 .... THIGH
5 .... WINDPIPE	16 .... TENDON	26 .... HIP JOINT
6 .... POINT OF SHOULDER	17 .... CHESTNUT	27 .... CROUP
7 ...... BREAST, BRISKET, CHEST	18 .... ELBOW	28 .... LOINS
8 .... ARM	19 .... FLANK	29 .... WITHERS
9 .... FOREARM	20 .... STIFLE	30 .... CREST
10 .... KNEE	21 .... CANNON	31 .... POLL
11 .... FETLOCK JOINT, ANKLE		

Texas by the volunteer cavalry regiments, at the termination of the war, are still sound and serviceable, while two or three sets of native horses, bought in Texas, have worn out alongside of them."

The recommendation undoubtedly was buried, as no action seems to have been taken.

Purchasing and inspection of remounts continued as before. Purchases were made by boards of officers assembled by department commanders, each board consisting of a quartermaster and one or two officers of the regiment for which the horses were intended. The boards moved through the various districts assigned for their operations, printed posters of their wants, and purchased from stockraisers direct, without intrusion of a middleman. The end result was satisfactory, and the army obtained good horses at fairly reasonable prices.[2] The average cost of cavalry horses was $142, whereas artillery horses were $155.

Before any horse was accepted for a regiment, a board of two or three officers of that regiment examined the animals to see that they conformed to standards. The horse must be in fair condition, of a hardy color, not less than 14 nor more than 16 hands high; weight not less than 750 nor more than 1100 pounds; age not less than 5 nor more than 8 years; head and ears small, forehead broad, eyes large and prominent, shoulders long and sloping well back, fore-legs straight and standing well under, chest broad and deep, barrel large, and increasing from girth to flank; withers elevated, back short and straight, loins and haunches broad and muscular, hocks well bent and under the horse, pasterns slanting, and feet small and sound. Special care was taken that the withers were not too sharp, and that the horse was neither sway-backed nor roach-backed. In time of war, horses should not be accepted under 6 nor over 10 years of age; young animals, as a rule, were not able to stand the exposure of a campaign.[3]

One of the inspectors should mount and ride each horse to see whether he had an easy and free action at the walk, trot and gallop. The board, after study of a few horses, selected a suitable horse, and kept him as a model during subsequent inspections. In the presence of the board, every horse was branded on the left shoulder with the letters "U.S.", on the same day the horse was received. Branding the company letter or regimental number varied; sometimes both were seen on the left thigh, one over the other. An officer prepared a descriptive list of each horse at the time of purchase.

2. From an extract; Annual Report of the Quartermaster General, June 30, 1873.
3. Cavalry Tactics, U.S. Army, 1874, p. 458 (No. 1165).

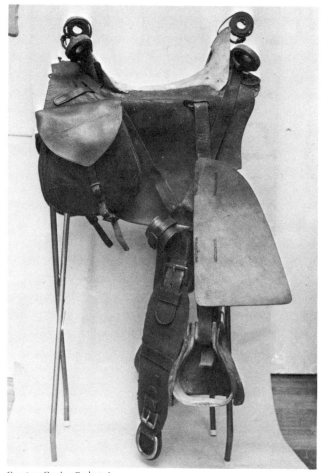

Courtesy Gordon Corbett, Jr.
Model 1859 McClellan saddle with saddle bags and girth. The seat is rawhide, the skirts are black leather and screwed to the side bars. (off-side)

This information accompanied the horse wherever he went, listing wounds, height, weight, and general description and markings.

The Army divided cavalry horses into four classes: condemned; presently unfit; unfit or nearly so; and serviceable. Inspections were made of these horses at the end of every month and reports were sent to the head of the Cavalry Bureau in Washington. With these reports, the Bureau could examine the service condition of the animals as well as determining the state of the entire cavalry service. As the horse was the mobile power for the cavalry these monthly reports were of major importance. The four classes of animals were determined by the

Courtesy Author's Collection

Riding a McClellan saddle after the rawhide split gave some troopers awfully sore bottoms. The sharp edges would cut into a man's flesh as quickly as the edge of a knife. Canvas and calf skins helped re-inforce the seats of their trousers. This wasn't the only reason for adopting this idea — trouser seats usually wore out in time.

War Department, Adjutant General's Office, Washington, July 28, 1863, General Orders No. 237:

(1) Those which are to be condemned as unfit for any use whatever in any branch of the service. With regard to this class, proceedings are to be had as required by existing regulations.

(2) Those now unfit for cavalry service, and not likely to be efficient again for such service, which may be used for team or draught horses, or for herding purposes. Horses of this class are to be turned in to the Quartermaster's Department.

(3) Those which are now unfit for service, or nearly so, but which, by timely care and treatment in depots, will regain condition. Such horses are to be sent to such depots as may be established for the army, to be replaced by an equal number of good animals from the depots. As soon as serviceable, the horses turned in will be eligible for reissue.

(4) Serviceable horses.

With the enormous expenses in the maintenance of stables, blacksmith tools, forage for animals, the animals themselves, the government stressed the necessity of greater care and more judicious management on the part of cavalry officers. Neglect of duty could be charged to cavalry officers where animals and horse furniture were not kept up to the standards of efficient service. The War Department dismissed from service any officer whose inefficiency and inat-

Courtesy Gordon Corbett, Jr.

The skirts were replaced after re-leathering the saddle probably at the owner's wishes. Many skirts were discarded to lighten the saddle. (near-side)

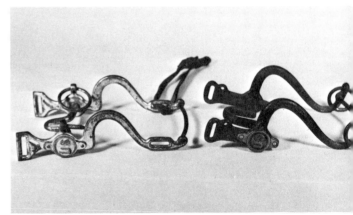

Bit on the left is a U.S. Artillery bit model 1863. Some Cavalry officers preferred this model with spirited horses. (This is a four rein bit). The bit on the right is the model 1859, curb bit used by both officers and enlisted men. Regulation bit generally came in four sizes. Both bits pictured here were used well into the late 1870's, until the shoemaker curb bit (adopted 1874) was issued in the early 1880's.

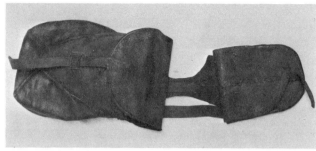

Courtesy Gordon Corbett, Jr.

Model 1872 pommel bags. As specified in Ordnance Memo No. 13. These were not issued during the Civil War — only model 1858 saddle bags were.

Courtesy Gordon Corbett, Jr.

Model 1858 saddle bags. Used through the Civil War and carried with Custer's troops in 1876.

Courtesy Gordon Corbett, Jr.

Link strap variations. (Left to Right) (A) Civil War and earlier (B) Civil War (C) Lariat straps (D) Late model (1915 on) link strap.

tention resulted in the deterioration and loss of public animals under his charge.

The main function of the remount section of the cavalry was to supply at the cheapest price the best horses and mules, both for mounted men and as draught animals. This, of course, ruled out the blooded horse from Virginia and Kentucky, which could be purchased by officers as their personal mounts.[4] An officer might have from two to three animals; one would be considered a charger, another a trotter, and possibly the third used as an all-around rider.* Horses accepted by the remount service were generally sturdy, hard riding, half-wild western strains. The mustang was a highly durable animal. In 300 years of migration over the Great Plains, wild horses became accustomed to rugged conditions. Short rations, brackish water, and frequent running from predatory animals and Indians reduced their size considerably over the generations. When caught comparatively young and trained in the cavalry's gentling school, they were found to become spirited mounts and most affectionate to their owners. The average size ranged from 15 to 16 hands high, weighing between 850 and 1000 pounds. This breed was tougher, smaller, lighter and faster than most animals from the East or Midwest.

The term "veterinarian" made its appearance in 1835 Army Regulations, requiring inspectors to see that veterinarians perform their duties. This is the first known use of this term in official records of the army.[5] There were no veterinarians authorized in the army up to this period, and it is probable that the term refers to farriers, a term at one time including blacksmith and vet-

4. In 1866, regulations required a cavalry officer to provide his own horses and equipments, and there was no means of recovery for the loss of a horse except when "killed in action." Army and Navy Journal, February 16, 1867, p. 410.

*Note: An officer could choose his horse from animals supplied by the remount service, by paying the cost of the animal to the government.

5. Cavalry Journal, Historical Sketch of the Veterinary Service, p. 45, Vol. XX, July 1909.

erinarian. As the mounted forces increased in 1861 to six regiments, changing mounted riflemen and dragoons into cavalry, the Act of July 29, 1861 provided for a veterinary sergeant for each battalion of cavalry, and two farriers for each company. There was no provision for a separate blacksmith. The year following, the office of veterinary sergeant was abolished and each company was provided with "two farriers or black-smiths." The Act of March 3, 1863 provided: "Each regiment shall have one veterinary surgeon with the rank of regimental sergeant-major, whose compensation shall be seventy-five dollars per month.[6] President Lincoln, hearing of the enormous rate of sick and injured horses, offered a lieutenant's commission to several qualified veterinarians, but all refused unless offered the rank of captain. At that time there were only six veterinarians in the army, stationed at remount depots.

The Act of July 28, 1866 provided that the four new, additional cavalry regiments, the 7th, 8th, 9th and 10th, should have one veterinary surgeon, whose compensation should be $100 a month. The first six regiments were left with one veterinary surgeon which previous laws provided, at $75 a month. However, one additional veterinary surgeon had been authorized for the newer regiments under the 1863 bill, but as a civilian employee. This civilian-employed surgeon was allowed the same quarters and fuel as a sergeant-major, but was not entitled to a clothing issue or rations, although he was allowed to purchase supplies from the commissary. For a number of years, most veterinarians were men that came either from the ranks of former farriers of the army or were appointed from civil life with no qualifications other than those they professed to possess. Because of the inefficiency of many early

veterinarians, troop commanders relied upon themselves or experienced troopers for veterinary work. From this, a number of self-practiced veterinarians soon developed an interest in the subject in every regiment of cavalry.

A cavalryman often retained the same horse through his enlistment. Working together daily brought the trooper and animal closer together, and commonly an intimate friendship was formed. A gentle pat, a soft word or two, an extra portion of grain were the simplest signs of affection a soldier could provide for his companion. It would be sad to imagine the suffering the horse must have faced in exhaustion from a lengthy campaign or starvation. Worst for the trooper was to stand over his fallen mount, knowing he must end his horse's misery with a bullet in the brain. Eyes that followed the soldier in wondering affection would haunt him forever. Few could stand to shatter the brain of an affectionate companion, and the pistol was usually passed to someone else who ended the matter quickly.

Eating horse meat was the last thing a cavalryman would think of doing. It would take a foot soldier's teasing tongue to make any mention of it, or a hard-pressed ranking officer to decide on cutting rations in half or running out of rations to do it. Such was the necessity with Crook's command in September, 1876, with two and a half days' rations left for a seven-day march to the Black Hills. "If necessary," a soldier remarked, "we can eat our horses." An aging lieutenant of many field campaigns stammered, "As for eating a horse, I'd as soon think of eating my brother." After a few days of hunger pains, the noble lieutenant feasted on horse steaks with no further complaints.[7] General Custer could not think of dining on horse meat when reduced to desperate straits. He did, however, confess to consid-

---

6. Ibid., p. 50 — This proposal was assailed by Congressmen who were not favorably inclined toward employing veterinarians because of the cost. Although the need for this service was apparent.

---

7. War-Path and Bivouac, Finerty, pp. 276-277.

ering saving himself from starvation by eating his dogs' ears; but, as he looked at his devoted friends, the thought of mutilating them was rejected.[8]

One who tried horse meat on Crook's starvation march attempted to describe it:

Horse meat generally has an ominous odor about it, when hungry this is surpassed. Fried and without salt, it is stringy, leathery and nauseating. Looking back at this sore-backed, played out bag of bones, one could hardly wonder what kept the poor animal on his feet so long . . . after a hard campaign. Take a younger horse, not as lean and rawboned as the latter, its taste resembles very bad beef. That of the adult Indian pony, its description of taste is in similarity to elk, and a young Indian pony tastes much like young mountain sheep or antelope. Mule meat, on the other hand, has all the above tastes and flavors mixed into one. It is offensive in smell and taste, with a considerable amount of fatty portions.[9]

The cavalry horse was groomed twice a day, at morning and at evening stable-calls. A commissioned officer in each company was present to see that the task was done properly. The grooming was always done at the picket-line, except in wet weather. The men were marched to the horses, and as soon as the command, "Commence grooming," was given by the first-sergeant, all hands prepared to groom in a military manner. The implements necessary were the curry-comb, brush, wisp, sponge, and rubber. The sponge and rubber were not furnished by the Government, and their use depended on company rules. Towels made from grain sacks were found to be good substitutes for the linen rubber. The trooper took the brush in his right hand and worked away at the head and face until he had thoroughly cleansed those parts, carefully cleaning out the dust and dirt from the roots of the ears, and continually cleansing the brush with the curry-comb held in the other hand. Proceeding to the neck, he worked at that part in the same way, throwing the

mane over to the other side, then going to the shoulders, breast, belly, flank, loins, back and legs, finishing off with a wisp of hay,[10] slightly damped, instead of the brush. He then would go to the near side[11] of the horse, taking the brush in the left hand and the curry-comb in the right, dressing the animal in the same manner. In the Spring or Autumn, when the coat was being shed, the curry-comb was little used, but was used freely when the hair was long. The curry-comb was not used on the head or tender parts. When the brush and wisp satisfactorily cleaned the horse, the finishing touch was given with the linen rubber grooming cloth, passed over the surface in the direction of the hair. A sponge was squeezed out and used to clean the eyes, nostrils and anus. The mane was dampened and brushed smoothly down on its right side. The tail was carefully combed out, beginning at the lower end, not touching the top until the bottom was smoothly arranged. Lastly, the legs and feet were attended to, the hoofs picked out, the legs washed if stained with mud, and then carefully rubbed dry.

When grooming was done within the stables, the horses were turned around in their stalls, and the forequarters dressed first. The horse was then turned around again, and the hindquarters dressed. When the horses were to be taken out for parade or drill, the whole body was smoothed over with the linen rubber or towel, the hoofs picked, and the mane and tail dampened and brushed smooth.[12]

The horses' feet required almost constant care by the trooper. If neglected they became hard or brittle, or, if constantly wet, the soft covering of the frog became decomposed and thrush ensued. Insanitary

8. Following the Guidon, E. B. Custer, N.Y., Harper & Brothers, 1890, pp. 62-63.

9. War Path & Bivouac, John F. Finerty, pp. 307-308.

10. A wisp of hay is used for wet places; it is gently rubbed over the hair until the area is dry. From "Cavalry Tactics," 1894, pp. 473-474.

11. "Near side" is the left side of horse; "off side" is the right.

12. Cavalry Tactics, 1874, pp. 473-474.

places caused severe hoof damage, and troopers constantly tried to provide matting of dried litter on the stall floor. It was necessary to remove the shoes from the horses' feet every four weeks, and cut away a portion of the sole and crust before the shoes were replaced, even if the shoes were little worn. Each shoe was inspected every day, making certain that they were securely nailed, and that the clenches had not started. Nothing was more annoying to the cavalry officer than to find horses casting their shoes during a march. This was usually chargeable to the carelessness of the trooper, who should have examined his horse before the march to see that the shoes were tight and the clenches not raised. Every trooper was furnished with a set of shoes and nails fitted to his horse. It was up to the trooper to have these handy items with him in such cases, in camp and on all marches.

A good trooper knew from experience that, if the saddle and blanket are removed when the skin beneath is hot and wet from perspiration, inflammation would surely follow. This could be prevented by loosening the girths, leaving the saddle in place for a short period. If the saddle was immediately taken off, the folded blanket remained on the horse's back until the bridles were removed and hung up, and arrangements made for dressing down the animal prepared. The blanket was then dried and the dust beaten out with a stick. The girths were washed with soap and water, and leather articles on the saddle were brushed and wiped clean with a damp cloth. After cleaning the saddle leather, neatsfoot oil was gently rubbed in, if the condition of the leather required it. If any spots showed a reddish hue, a little lamp-black was mixed with the oil.[13]

Cavalry scheduled for a long campaign were ready as early as the season of the year

13. Army and Navy Journal, September 24, 1864, p. 68.

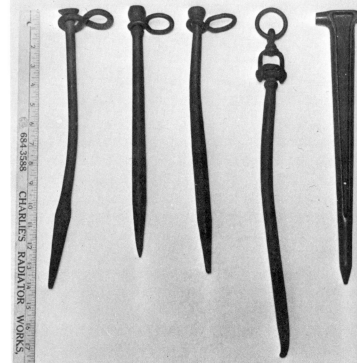

Picket Pins, left to right: (A) Pre-Civil War type. (B) Standard Civil War type. (C) Variation Civil war type. (D) Model 1874 — Lyons. (E) Model 1912 picket pin. The object of the iron picket pin was to thrust it deep into the ground, snap a 25 foot linen plaited rope (⅜″ dia.) on to it, the other end affixed to the horse's halter. If a horse was staked out for any period of time while grazing he generally wrapped the rope around the iron pin, thus, shortening his movements. Swivels were adopted later on top of the pin so the rope couldn't become entangled. The next step was to keep the horse from pulling up the picket pin.

permitted. First call for reveille sounded at the crack of dawn; the men turned out promptly, struck their tents and packed their saddles. Fifteen minutes later, reveille was sounded and the men fell in for roll-call. After roll-call, the troops were marched to the stables by their first sergeants and horses were watered, groomed and fed. The men were dismissed for breakfast. In the field, the rations were hardtack, bacon and coffee. Half an hour before departing time, "boots and saddles" was sounded, followed 15 minutes later by "to horse," when the roll was again called. First sergeants reported results of the roll-call to troop commanders, who in turn reported to the adjutant. Troop commanders then ordered "prepare to mount" and moved out when the "advance" sounded.

After 30 minutes of marching, the troops

were halted, the men dismounting to check packs and tighten girths. Such short halts were usually made at the end of each hour and, if the march should be lengthy and the terrain rough, a halt of an hour was made around mid-day. The horses were generally watered once during the day's march.

If the trail or road was clear of obstacles, a trot was ordered, giving horse and man a different pace. No gait faster than a trot was ordered, except in emergency. There was no reason for using up all the strength of the horses. When a campsite was chosen, the troopers unbridled, tied up the horses, and wiped saddles and bridles. If water was available, they would sponge the eyes and

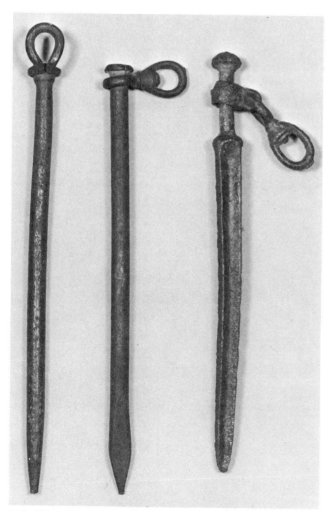

Picket Pins, left to right, Civil War variation: (A) Late type (used from 1865 on). (B) Found at Fort Missoula, Montana (post established June 25, 1877). (C) Pre-Lyons patent (1874-1880's).

nostrils, wisp around the horses' heads, pick the hoofs, and feed the animals a little hay. After this, there was a short interval for the men to refresh themselves before "stable-call" was sounded. Saddles were removed, and the horses were watered, groomed and fed. After removing the saddles, the troopers inspected the backs of their mounts, and any signs of galling were reported to the sergeant. The least flinching on the part of the animal would warn the trooper to cease working his horse or put anything on his back. Hot poultices were applied to infected areas to prevent inflammation. Retreat sounded at sundown, and the men were allowed to go to bed if they wished. The signal to "extinguish lights" was sounded at 8:30 p.m., after which no loud talking or unusual noises were permitted.

Cavalry horses were liable to many ailments. Two ailments were frequently reported in the Returns of Regular Army Regiments, Reports and Records of Events,[14] submitted each month by the Regimental Commander. The principal ailment occurred in summer under conditions of extreme heat and was commonly known as sore back, or saddle gall. The other most common disease was known to cavalrymen as "the thumps."[15] The thumps was a heart ailment, caused by lengthy marches in hot weather. The animal's sides seemed to palpitate suddenly at intervals, and often, without other symptoms, he would drop dead. A splendid horse, seemingly in perfect condition, might become afflicted by this disease, sometimes causing injury to the mounted trooper in an unexpected fall. For the "thumps," there was no satisfactory treatment during that period. Rest and recuperation might aid the animal to normal health.

If an observing officer noticed the disorder, he might save the animal's life by ordering the rider to dismount and lead his

14. Army and Navy Journal, February 26, 1871, p. 446.
15. Idem.

horse for a day. Bleeding from the mouth was a common symptom. A horse's blood runs much more rapidly than does a human being's, and many disorders arose from overheating the blood.

Epizootic, having appeared among public horses in the States, was a constant threat to cavalry mounts on the frontier. Contact with public horses affected with this disease caused many deaths. No absolute cure was found; some tonics were effective, others failed. The symptoms of epizootic were recognized as early as 1868, at Fort Mason, Texas. An extract of that report is as follows:

"Fort Mason, Texas, Feb. 15, 1868

"I respectfully report for the information of the regimental commander that the disease prevailing among the horses of the detachment Fourth Cavalry, at this post, and which rages through Mason County, is from evidence adduced and my personal knowledge by diagnosis, diphtheria (tracheities exsudatoria). Owing to the fact that this sickness very seldom prevails among horses, it is not recognized by persons unacquainted with it, being often taken for glanders (ozoena) on account of the running of matter from the mouth and nostrils.

"Its symptoms are as follows:

"1st. Costiveness, or hard and dry dung. 2nd. Small ulcers in the throat. 3rd. The ulcerations grow bigger, and exude an offensive matter, having its passage through the mouth and nostrils. 4th. Swelling ensues in the throat. 5th. Symptoms of choking, want of breath, and last death. All these symptoms appeared here, and, as before said, owing to this disease being unknown to men, they could not do anything to prevent or cure it.

"The treatment of it is as follows.

"Purging, gargle of vinegar and alum, cataplasm round the throat, steaming the animal under any circumstances, in very well closed stables. For food and drink, bran mashes and flour gruel, with nitre potassis until the swelling disappears, and the animal shows signs of better appetite, breathing more freely, and is in a more healthy condition. If found out too late, unfortunately every effort will be useless.

"The reasons for the appearance of this disease are climatic causes, and a liability of the animal, and only through uncleanness is it contagious. Climatic causes are, for instance, very severe northwest winds, and generally produce, if the animal is not in perfect health, throat and bronchial diseases; too dry and heating food, as corn and hay alone, with no change of diet, and little exercise, will also increase the liability of the animals to the disease. Sometimes the disease is epidemic to a certain part of the country (epizootie), the proof of which is that the disease prevails at not this post alone, but around the entire vicinity, and I suppose that in this case the climatic and telluric influences are more the cause of the prevailing disease than the liability of the horse.

"The above treatment I would improve upon according to circumstances, if present, but if followed as a general rule, will be found to answer in most cases.

"The disease which prevailed in January and February, 1868, in the vicinity of and at Fort Mason, Texas, seems to me to be the same as that now prevailing in the States, called epizootic, and in comparing the treatment as per my report, with that recommended in the Army and Navy Journal of date November 2, 1872, I find they generally agree, as in steaming, cleanliness, exercise, cataplasm around the throat, change of diet, as bran mashes and nitre, and in using vinegar. Also in stating that if the case be taken in time the treatment will be successful.

"Owing to the limited variety of medicines furnished by the United States Government, I was compelled to practice as above, though other remedies are known to me.

"I hope that you will be able to find room to insert this article in your valuable paper, as it may invite attention, and maybe cause a discussion through the columns of your paper for general information.

"Respectfully, your obedient servant,
PAUL NITSCHKE
Veterinary Surgeon Fourth Cavalry
FORT RICHARDSON, TEXAS, Dec. 13, 1872."[16]

If requisite care was taken of the McClellan saddle, in training and marches, it can be called one of the best military saddles in the world.[17] If the blanket was kept smooth and the load equally distributed, sore backs would not have occurred, even on long marches. Once a sore back was noticed by the trooper, a piece of coarse gunny-sack bagging was laid beneath the blanket and this usually relieved the soreness and effected a cure. This remedy was known to old cavalrymen and was passed on from them to recruits. The gunny-sack bagging kept the harsh woolen fibres of the issue blanket from aggravating the sore, allowing it to heal. Another remedy was bathing the sore spot with castile soap and warm water.

---

16. Army and Navy Journal, January 4, 1873, p. 331.
17. Idem.

Courtesy Randy Steffen
Model 1872 McClellan saddle in "fair" or russett leather. Quarter straps, stirrup leathers and stirrup hoods are black. A square leather safe should be fastened to the rigging, where the quarter straps were stitched to the "D" ring. (near side)

This was quite helpful when practiced continuously, but was not always practicable on a lengthy march.

It was almost impossible to treat scratches or grease-heel[18] during a fast march on wet, muddy roads. But if time were available, the use of castile soap and warm water to bathe the animal's legs was often effective. If the animal was lucky enough to be standing in a dry area, it was well to bandage an injured pastern, between the times of washing, with a rag greased on the inside. This

kept out dust and dirt, preserving a healing scab soft and pliable, allowing new skin to form beneath. If the march continued for a number of days with animals plodding in mud and water, it was likely that infection would render the animal useless.

After a long day's march, it was customary to picket the horses nearby, leaving them all night, despite heavy rains, falling snow or cold winds. Whether their legs were spattered with mud or were clean, they would get cold during the night. A long continuance of cold, wet feet and legs induced "scratches." Torn strips from an old blanket were used to wrap around the horse's legs, beginning with the pastern, thus guarding the animal's heels from "scratches." If the strips were warmed at a campfire before being applied to the legs, the added comfort would prevent the horse from becoming restless during the night. If these strips were not properly wrapped and watched by an alert trooper, the horse might trip on them or get caught somehow, possibly disabling him and throwing the rider.

Horse shoes were inspected frequently, in spite of every care, shoes were sometimes left on too long, and sometimes they were knocked off, and the horse became lame on rocky roads. Indians, however, never shod their horses, the hoofs of their animals became nearly as hard as flint. They traveled over the rockiest roads with the cavalry chasing them, and as the shoes of the cavalry horses were torn off by the rocks, they became disabled and the Indians laughed at the cavalry's efforts to overtake them.[19]

Most troopers were constantly moving about, checking shoes for tightness and rubbing the heels and pasterns with their fingers. If grease or oil was available, it would be rubbed into heels, pasterns and fetlock. Back-sores and hoof diseases caused the loss of many animals. Company

18. Scratches and grease-heel are common hoof disorders. "Scratches" usually sets in with swelling, heat and tenderness of the hollow of the heel. Soon slight cracks appear transversely, gaining in depth and width. "Grease-heel" is an abscessed heel, giving off a greasy discharge. "Diseases of the Horse," Department of Agriculture, 1907, pp. 444-445.

19. Army and Navy Journal, Sept. 9, 1865.

and regimental commanders were constantly calling for more horses to fill vacancies. Yet such simple attention as smoothing a blanket beneath a saddle, or checking a horse's lame foot, would have saved much of this loss. If an officer quartered his men for the night in mud holes, he had only himself to blame for his horses falling lame.

Stable duty was perhaps the most necessary chore for the trooper and the most disagreeable part of a cavalry officer's duty. If horses were not looked after carefully by officers, the men would neglect them.

In 1847, a board of officers adopted the Grimsley saddle, which served the dragoons with considerable satisfaction. Until 1855, there appeared a number of new designs for saddles which were offered to the War Department for use in the mounted services. Among these were the Hope saddle, which found favor in Texas; the Jones saddle, adjustable by the use of hinges; and the Campbell saddle, which was somewhat adjustable by springs. The rival claimants persuaded the War Department to purchase several hundred varieties of saddles for experimental purposes. Upon hearing this, Thornton Grimsley, pioneer merchant and manufacturer, who had been furnishing the adopted saddles, reminded the War Department that they should not abandon his saddle for these untried models. In the midst of this saddle competition, Captain George B. McClellan, First Cavalry, offered his model saddle with other suggestions. McClellan, as one of a commission of officers, had observed the war in the Crimea and had made extensive studies of horse furniture and other equipment used by the armies of Europe.

In order to select the best saddle out of the many varieties on hand, Ordnance Department conducted extensive tests, as indicated in a report from the Chief of Ordnance, October 25, 1855, Ordnance Notes No. 2, as follows:

"The duty of furnishing horse equipment having been transferred from the Quartermasters to the Ordnance Department (G.O. 5, W.D., 1855), these articles now come under the designation of ordnance stores . . . For the purpose of testing practically the merits of different patterns of horse equipments, the cavalry regiments have been supplied with those known as Grimsleys, and also with those prepared after the pattern of Campbell — the latter having been examined and recommended by a board of cavalry officers."

Unfortunately, four years passed with no decision on a prescribed pattern for cavalry or dragoon horse equipment. The Grimsley, McClellan, Jones, Campbell and Hope patterns were all in experimental stages. As a result of the experiments, a board of officers convened in January, 1859, to decide on a service saddle and other equipment. The board, after considering the reports of officers covering experiences on marches of 1,000 and 2,000 miles, accepted the McClellan saddle, the War Department approving the recommendation.

The McClellan saddle has been vaguely characterized as "European," but no specific features support this claim. McClellan's statement placed him on record as saying, "I shall always claim it as my own invention." McClellan stated in a letter of December 25, 1856: "I cannot pretend to say that this equipment is by any means perfect, but I feel safe in asserting that it is an important step in the right direction; that it is not a copy of any European model and that it is superior to any equipment I saw in Europe. I am content to allow it to rest on its own merits, and I believe that it will, in its most important points, meet the approval of our cavalry officers."[20]

The McClellan saddle may not be a reproduction of any one European model, but it does have characteristics derived from the French. Captain McClellan's Report in a Senate Document of 1857, in addition to a review of the Crimean operations, includes

---

20. Cavalry Journal, Vol. 22, Sept. 1911, p. 237, "History of the McClellan Saddle," by Capt. Edward Davis, 13th Cavalry.

observations on the armed forces of Great Britain, France, Austria, Russia, Sardinia and Prussia, as well as opinions for recommendations regarding the army of the United States. On page 283, McClellan reports: "I would recommend that the tent be adopted as part of our system. A specimen, slightly altered from the French, will be submitted with the saddle shortly to be forwarded." And on page 246, in discussing French horse equipment, McClellan notes: "The new saddle [i.e., new in contrast with a different French model] is the invention of Captain Cogent, director of the saddle factory at Saumur. [21] The tree is cut out of a single piece of white wood, the cantle only being glued on; a piece of walnut, the grain running across the tree, is let into the pommel . . . The whole is covered with wet raw-hide, glued on and sewed at the edges; no iron bolts or fastenings are needed."

In the Ordnance Manual of 1861, what is believed to be the earliest official description of the McClellan saddle reads: "Saddle-Tree.—Wood, (bleach) — 1 pommel, made of two pieces framed together at top and glued; 1 cantle, formed of 2 pieces, like the pommel; 2 side bars, (poplar) each made of 3 pieces glued together . . . It is covered with raw hide, put on wet and sewed with thongs of the same, and held in place by stitches through the wood along the junction of the pommel and cantle with the side bars, where they will not chafe the horse nor rider."[22]

Captain Cogent's saddle may have been suggestive to Captain McClellan, as a comparison of sketches and other data in his report reveal vague similarities between the McClellan saddle and the French equipment. McClellan's close observations of European armies may naturally have influenced his thoughts and ideas toward saddle construction when he developed his own model. And with an admirable and modest brand of patriotism which flourished in that eventful era, all things American were, per se, considered to be superior to anything European.

The McClellan tree also bears a remarkable resemblance to the western tree of the 1850's, with the exception of the horn at the pommel of the western tree. The McClellan saddle is similar to the Campbell tree, but only in construction. In a letter to Jefferson Davis, Secretary of War, October 3, 1856, Captain McClellan wrote: "I have shown to several officers . . . the Prussian Cavalry Equipment, all agree that with certain quite essential modifications, it would be better equipment than any we have yet had in our service. From the tree that is known as the Hungarian; I would remove all the unnecessary iron with which the Prussians have encumbered it, reduce the height of the cantle, and adopt very nearly Nolan's tree."[23]

When Captain McClellan approached Lacey & Philipps[24] of Philadelphia in 1856 with his new sample model tree, supposedly resembling the Hungarian saddle, the result bore little likeness to any European models. In a letter to the War Department, accompanying his newly completed saddle, McClellan said that the new saddle was not a copy of any European model, and was better than any he had seen in Europe. What happened to his Hungarian tree idea proposed in that letter to Secretary Davis? Lacey and Phillips went out of business and all traces of their sample product disappeared in the obliterating growth of a great city. If the original model of the McClellan saddle could be inspected, possibly some new evidence might be brought forth as to its origin.

There was far too much toggery strapped to the McClellan saddle. The flaps, sweat-

---

21. Saumur, a town in Western France. The famous cavalry school of Saumur was founded in 1768.
22. Also see Ordnance Manual, 1862, pp. 156-157.
23. Nolan's tree was designed by a British officer, Captain Lewis E. Nolan, 15th Hussars.
24. Saddle manufacturer.

leathers and saddle-bags were useless and dead weights. Too small to hold anything, the saddle-bags were discarded along the trail by many a trooper, to help lighten the load. The prime trouble with the McClellan saddle was the want of room for provisions and forage, primary essentials. On summer campaigns, a soldier had little use for an overcoat, too often he threw it away at the risk of needing it later. The weight a trooper carried besides rations and forage included himself and arms, one blanket, half a section of a shelter tent or poncho, a shirt, drawers and socks, a towel, comb and piece of soap. The blanket and poncho were often placed beneath the saddle as added cushioning, also eliminating another roll tied to the saddle. Older campaigners advocated this as helping to alleviate sore backs. It was up to the trooper to carry for-

age and rations the best way he knew how. The one haversack issued to the soldier by the government was soon filled with extra ammunition or a couple of spare horse-shoes and nails.

The Model 1859 McClellan saddle was covered with rawhide and had black leather skirts screwed to the side boards.[25] Rain and snow soaked into the rawhide, and as the sun dried it out the rawhide became taut and split and cracked at the seams. A saddle in this condition was uncomfortable for the trooper and soon an improvised schabraque[26] was cinched down over the McClellan seat, with an additional blanket

---

25. Revised U.S. Army Regulations of 1861, Washington 1863, pp. 477-479.
26. From the German word "Schabraken," overhousings gener-ally covering the entire saddle. Mostly used by officers during the Civil War.

Courtesy U.S. Signal Corps photo (Brady Collection)

Quartermaster wagon.

for padding. For those who lacked an extra blanket, skins or gunny-sack bagging was used. The McClellan, though almost indestructable, began to deteriorate at the edge of the cantle and, once the rawhide was gone, the saddle soon racked to pieces.

One bad feature about the McClellan saddle, aired by many veterans, was that it had no breast strap. Many saddles were issued with "cruppers," which consisted of a dock, a padded ring which fitted around the horse's tail, plus attached straps which were to fasten to the crupper rings on the rear of the saddle. This was supposed to keep the saddle in place, but during a hard and lengthy march the horse was often found to have a sore tail. In active service, the crupper usually was discarded by the trooper. Many soldiers found that if their horse was "slim bellied," a breast-strap was needed.[27] Ordinarily, breastplates and martingales were dress trappings for officers that were seldom seen on the frontier. This rig could be fabricated by the trooper himself or the company saddler.

Many used surcingles for the same pur-

27. Breast-straps or breast-plates were used during the Civil War to keep saddle and equipment from moving backward. See Army and Navy Journal, March 4, 1871, p. 462.

Courtesy Custer Battlefield Museum
Private John Burkman stands between "Dandy" (left), Custer's favorite hunting mount, and "Vic" (right) the charger that Custer rode in his last battle. Stag hounds lounging in background.

pose, but soon gave it up. A breast-strap to a cavalry horse was almost indispensable. In ascending hills, his load inclined to pitch backward, causing the horse to be off balance. With a breast-strap, the girth could be loosened and the horse was much more at ease. More than once did a blanket slip slowly under a carelessly put on saddle, until it dropped over the croup, the trooper being not conscious of his loss until informed by others.

The stirrups on the McClellan saddle had good and bad points, but over all they sadly needed improvement. The hooded stirrup was meant to keep the foot from slipping through the opening. It also prevented chilling the foot in cold winds and protected it from heavy brush. During training, however, it was found that in many instances a man would get his foot stuck between the stirrup and the hood, finding it worse than the open one for that reason. A second objection was that the stirrup wood had a tendency to rot as the bolts rusted, making the platform of the stirrup unsafe, and, in some cases, troopers dismounting would crash through a stirrup.[28]

It was said by both officers and enlisted men that the McClellan saddle had a poor endurance record. Two years knocked all the glory out of it. Small items attached to the saddle were constantly getting lost or coming undone.[29]

Basic horsemanship was the first stage in the soldier's training, preceding any experience with the three basic cavalry weapons, the saber, the pistol and the carbine.[30]

Basic horsemanship began with the ability to maintain a proper military seat along with the knowledge of how his animal moved and reacted. When a trooper was in

28. Army and Navy Journal, March 4, 1871, p. 462.
29. Idem.
30. From a researched paper written by Mitchell Swieca, (Cpl.) 1st Squad, Company E, Second Re-Activated Cavalry. Established 1966, at Greencastle, Indiana (Headquarters); with minor changes and additions by the author.

Comanche, Captain Myles Keogh's horse, stands between blacksmith Gustav Korn and Captain Ilsley.

the military seat, his head was held erect,
square to the front and without constraint,
the buttocks bearing equally upon the
horse's back, and as far forward as possible.
The thighs were turned upon their flat side
without effort, embracing the horse equally,
and stretched only by their own weight and
that of the legs. The knees were bent without stiffness. The soldier's feet were parallel to the horse with his toes pointed inward
so that his spurs did not make unwanted
contact with his animal. Legs and feet fell
naturally and the trooper's right arm hung
straight down. His left arm was slightly bent
outward so that his hand was directly over
the pommel of the saddle holding the reins.
His shoulders were equally thrown back. If
thrown forward, the back would have
curved or arched and the breast contracted;
if not thrown back equally, the position of
the body would have been distorted.[31] The
reins ran from the bit through the third and
fourth fingers of the left hand. They passed
over the index finger and were held in place
with the thumb. The slack then hung in
front of the hand. There was little slack
between the bit and the left hand; darting
forward unexpectedly, the horse could have
been under control with only a slight

movement from the trooper's hand. If there
was too much slack in the rein between the
bit and the hand when the animal moved
forward, the trooper had to lean back in the
saddle to make contact with the bit. This put
the soldier off balance and could possibly
have caused a fall.[32]

A trooper countered unwanted movements by his horse by reverse actions. If the
horse moved forward, the trooper slightly
shifted his weight to the rear, pulling his
rein hand straight back until the horse
stopped. If the horse moved backward, the
trooper moved his weight forward, making
contact with both spurs, increasing the
spurring only with short taps until the animal moved forward. If the horse moved to
the right, the trooper moved his rein hand to
the left, making contact with the spur, until
the horse straightened out. If the horse

---

31. Cavalry Tactics, 1874; School of the Soldier Mounted pp.
139-140.

32. On many occasions in a field test exercise, Corporal Mitchell
Swieca, 2nd Re-Activated Cavalry, found it better to move the left
hand forward rather than slacken the reins. Also, the left hand
should be moved forward during mounted weapons training. This
allows the horse to see the weapons by turning his head. It also
relieves tension on the bit to prevent pain when a weapon is fired.
Such an incident would cause the horse to associate pain with the
use of the weapon. Other members with the 2nd Re-Activated
Cavalry have also tested various exercises from original cavalry
manuals provided by the author, to determine their usefulness,
prior to the period. (Report of Cpl. Swieca — in author's collection).

Where ever the 7th went, Comanche followed. During any engagements with Indians, Comanche was led to the rear.

Blacksmith Gustav Korn holding the reins of Comanche. Probably taken late in 1878, with the model 1863 curb bits, model 1859 saddle bags. The felt padding beneath the McClellan saddle was after 1876.

The saber (the 1862 Ordnance Manual used the French spelling, "sabre") is the first weapon which was used mounted, because, for the most part, the horse only had to cope with the sight of it. As in all mounted training, the left hand was moved forward to take pressure off the bit. Before the weapon was drawn, the trooper moved his right hand back and forth around the animal's head to see how he reacted to objects in motion. If the horse passed this test, he was ready for the next. The trooper then moved his right hand to the saber grip and drew the saber about six inches from the scabbard. With a quick motion, he slammed the saber back into the scabbard. This was done to determine the animal's reaction to sound. This action was continued until the horse was well acquainted with it and no longer affected by the sound. The trooper then put his right hand through the saber knot and drew the saber completely from the scabbard, bringing it to the position of carry saber. The saber was then brought to the position of guard. During the saber exercise, the saber was always returned to the

moved to the left, the trooper moved the rein hand to the right, making contact with the left spur. If the horse reared up, the trooper stood up with his hands pushing on the animal's neck, and brought all of his weight forward. This forced the horse back down. If the animal tried to sit down, the trooper quickly gave him both spurs, pulling up on the reins at the same time.

The soldier was first thoroughly trained with the weapons dismounted, where his knowledge of the saber, pistol and carbine was fully understood. The manual termed this "School of the Soldier Dismounted." After graduating from this level of basics, he entered "School of the Company Dismounted," "School of the Battalion Dismounted," "School of the Regiment Dismounted," and finally "School of the Soldier Mounted." The last title was not by any means the last phase of his schooling, but, up to that point, his basic training was fairly well covered. Quiet and well-trained horses were generally chosen for the first lessons, each recruit being required to change his horse from day to day. All mounted exercises began and ended at a walk, as a general rule, and troopers were required to talk to their animals to calm any nervousness during drills.

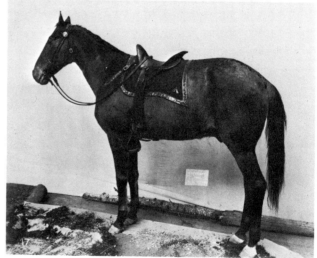

Comanche — Captain Myles Keogh's mount — was one of several wounded 7th Cavalry horses found on the battlefield on June 27. Although badly wounded by arrows and bullets, because he was known and recognized, he alone was saved and nursed back to health. He became the living symbol of the spirit of the men of the 7th Cavalry and became famous as the "only survivor" of the Battle of the Little Big Horn. Comanche was retired from all duties at Fort Riley, Kansas, and died there in 1891.

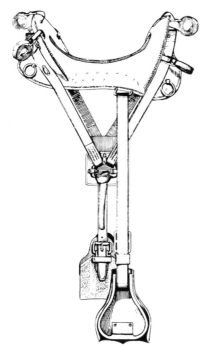

1872 — McClellan saddle with skirts removed. "D" rings on quarter straps (safe added), 7½" width girth, fair leather mixed with black leather.

position of guard after a movement was completed. The saber was then moved up and down the sides of the horse's head and over the top of it. The speed of these movements was increased until they became swift saber cuts. This was followed by the entire saber manual.[33]

The manner in which the trooper accustomed his horse to firing and other noises seemed simple enough, after reading the basis of instruction set forth in the training manual. And on a few occasions it was the soldier who sometimes took the longest to accustom himself to the firing, while his horse grew more and more gentle during loud reports.

A few trained horses, accustomed to pistol reports, were sent into a corral and mounted by trained soldiers and a sergeant. They mingled with recruits mounted on the younger horses to acquaint them with pistol fire. The horse was kept in motion by walk-

ing him about the corral; his walking gave him something to think about instead of merely standing there, waiting for something to happen to him. The forward movement also limited his direction in case he became nervous and afraid. As the pistol firing came closer to the younger horses, the troopers took care to quiet and caress those that were excited or frightened. This training was continued for several days, firing pistols closer to the animals, at first at the rear of the column, then near the center, and at last at the head of the column, and facing it at a distance of a few paces. At first the shots were fired at long intervals, then they were stepped up as the horses became more calm. After the younger horses became somewhat accustomed to the firing, the troopers who rode the younger horses began to fire their pistols, one after another, at a signal from their instructor. Carbines were used last in weapons training.[34]

The "Manual of the Pistol" is first performed dismounted. At the command, "Draw," the trooper unbuttoned the flap of of the holster with the right hand, grasping the stock, the back of the hand to the body. At the command, "Pistol," the trooper drew and raised the pistol, the hand holding the stock with the thumb and last three fingers, the forefinger over the guard, guard to the front, barrel vertical, elbow near the body, the wrist as high as the right shoulder and six inches in front of it. This was the position of raise pistol.[35]

Before the pistol could be loaded while the trooper was mounted, the reins in the left hand were readjusted. This was done by moving the index finger of the left hand out from beneath the overlapping reins and placing it over the reins, which would lie over the second finger. The index finger

---

33. The saber is always returned to the scabbard before dismounting. Cavalry Manual 1874, p. 166, par. 44.

34. Cavalry Tactics, Dismounted, 1862, vol. 1. Other military noises were manual of arms, drums, cannons, bugles and waving of standards; any of these could provoke an animal to skittish behavior.

35. Cavalry Tactics, 1874, D. Appleton & Co., N.Y., Manual of the Pistol, p. 44, par. 123.

was then free to hold the pistol. This readjustment of the reins prevented the pistol from being tugged from the trooper's hand, should the horse have pulled out the reins. The right hand then set the pistol down on the left hand. The pistol was then held in place by the thumb and index finger of the left hand. The barrel of the pistol was pointed to the left of the horse's neck and slightly downward. The thumb of the right hand then flipped open the cylinder gate and pulled the hammer back to half cock; the cylinder then rotated freely. The right hand then moved back to the cartridge-box, which was attached to the waist belt. Six cartridges were taken from the box and loaded into the pistol. As each chamber was loaded, the thumb of the left hand rotated the cylinder to the next chamber. After the pistol was loaded, the thumb of the right hand closed the chamber gate and brought the pistol to the position of "raised pistol." The thumb and index finger of the right hand worked the pistol's action down to the first click, or safety cock. The pistol was then raised upward and slightly to the right, with the butt pointing to the right. It was then fully cocked, with one round squeezed off. The pistol was then brought back to the position of "raise pistol." When the pistol had exploded a single round, the horse may have flinched, but the bit and spurs were not used until a second or two after the pistol had been discharged. If the horse felt pain when he heard the report, he would associate the two. The pistol was repeatedly fired in various directions, the last of which was over his head. Firing continued until the animal had little or no reaction to it. The pistol was emptied of its spent cartridges in the following manner: The pistol was placed in the left hand with the barrels pointed upward, the hammer facing the trooper. As in the loading process, the thumb and the index finger of the left hand held the pistol in place. The thumb of the right hand pulled the hammer back to half

cock and opened the cylinder gate. The index finger of the right hand then brought down the ejecting rod, thus driving out the spent shells. The thumb of the left hand rotated the cylinder until all shells had been ejected. The pistol was then taken by the right hand and returned to the holster. The pistol was the primary weapon of the mounted man. Like the saber, only one hand was required to use it in combat. Unlike the carbine, the pistol fired more than one shot without reloading.

Mounted carbine training was preceded by the "Dismounted Manual of Arms." When the trooper had the knowledge of his weapons, he was ready to be instructed to mount his horse with his equipment in an orderly fashion. One of the most awkward positions, cursed by the troopers, was mounting a horse with a carbine attached to the shoulder sling. On command of the instructor, "Prepare to mount," the recruit threw the carbine over his right shoulder, letting it rest on the back, muzzle downward. While the instructor was watching that the others were properly obeying, the heavy 2⅜" leather carbine sling was pushing against the soldier's adam's apple with a 7½ pound carbine dangling at the other end. At the command, "Mount," he positioned himself in the saddle as quickly as he could, reaching back with his right hand, and grasped the carbine, bringing it to his side, inserting the muzzle into the carbine socket. Many soldiers felt that this choking position when mounting could be done away with and a more suitable method introduced.

At the command, "Prepare to dismount," the trooper took the carbine from the socket with the right hand and threw it over his right shoulder, in the same manner as at the command, "Prepare to mount." As soon as the trooper had dismounted, he let the carbine fall back to his right side, letting it hang free.[36] There was no deviation in the "Manual of the Carbine, Mounted" from that prescribed in Civil War and earlier manuals; although many changes were made in the manuals between 1841 and 1874, the mounted drill with carbine remained much the same.

The carbine rested in a socket attached to a girth strap on the right side of the saddle, or was strapped to the "D" ring attached to both girth straps. Either way had been used. In the socket, the carbine sat with the barrel down and the butt up. The carbine was as vertical as possible, so that the barrel would not get in the way of the trooper's right spur when he needed to make contact with the horse. The left hand was moved forward, the right hand reached back and grasped the stock of the carbine directly behind the hammer. The fingers wrapped around the stock just behind the trigger guard. The right hand drew the carbine from the socket by first tossing it up and catching it with the right hand, just behind the rear sight. The right hand then fully drew the carbine from the socket. The right hand spun the carbine barrel up and set the butt of the carbine on the trooper's right thigh. The left hand readjusted the reins as during pistol training. The right hand set the carbine in the left hand. It was held in place by the thumb and

index finger of the left hand. The thumb of the right hand pulled the hammer to half cock, and opened the breech. The right hand then moved back to the cartridge box which was suspended on the trooper's waist belt directly behind him. The right hand took one cartridge and loaded the carbine, then closed the breech. The thumb and the index finger of the right hand worked the carbine's action down to the first cock, or safety cock. The right hand then brought the carbine back, resting on the trooper's thigh. There were two ways of firing the carbine mounted. One way was to slacken the section of the rein between the bit and the left hand, so that the left hand could be raised to support the front of the carbine without making contact with the bit. The left hand held the carbine at the front ring. The right hand held the carbine at the grip. The thumb of the right hand pulled the hammer back to full cock, and the index finger of the right hand pulled the trigger. This method was dangerous because, if the animal were to take off, the trooper would have had to use both hands to tighten the reins. This was difficult because both hands would be on the carbine. If by some accident the trooper were to fall with his carbine clipped to the shoulder sling and hooked up in the carbine socket, he would have been dragged and could do little about it. The second way of firing the carbine, mounted, kept the reins short, the left hand and the elbow up. The barrel of the carbine was

36. Cavalry Tactics, 1874, p. 169, par. 450. Also see Cavalry Tactics (in three parts), J. R. Poinsett, 1864; Trooper Mounted, p. 148, par. 266. Describes same position of carbine over the shoulder when mounting. The Hall carbine is mentioned here (p. 88).

Six-mule team complete, harnessed and hitched to U.S. Army wagon.

placed across the elbow to support it for firing. In this method, if the horse happened to take off, he could be brought under control without any trouble. The carbine was too long to be used mounted. It took two hands to fire it, yet it had about one-third the target range as the pistol. The carbine was a single-shot weapon and took too long to load. The trooper was given the carbine for the purpose of increasing his effective fighting distance. The use of the carbine, mounted, defeated this purpose. Accuracy depended on the trooper's ability to aim and fire the carbine with as little movement as possible. The horse was nearly always in motion; even when he was standing, he was either stretching or shifting his weight. For these reasons, the carbine was mainly used when dismounted.

Just as the army cherished legends of their fighting men, so did they honor their "war horses." One of the most famous and beloved of all cavalry chargers was Comanche, the only survivor of the Custer battle.

While General Sully was organizing his command at Fort Dodge, in southwestern Kansas, for the expedition against southern Indians, Captain Myles W. Keogh was in need of a second horse. It was not unusual for officers to purchase "second" mounts from issue stock. Keogh was inspector-general on Sully's staff in early September, 1868, when he purchased Comanche as a field mount. "Paddy," Keogh's other horse, was ridden during the marches, reserving Comanche for battle action. Comanche was almost five years old, weighing under 925 pounds and standing 15 hands high. (One hand equals four inches.)[37] Terminology used today would probably classify Comanche as a bay, as he was a mixture of yellow and red coloration with a predominance of red, with a black mane and tail. Although "claybank" has been used in de-

scribing Comanche's color in some books, that term is now obsolete. Anthony A. Amaral's "Comanche" dates Keogh's purchase as June, 1868. General Godfrey reported that Comanche was selected in September, but Keogh's use of the horse that month in action makes that date impossible.

During a fight against Comanches, near the Cimarron River, September 13, 1868, Keogh's mount was hit in the right quarter by an arrow. Somehow, during the conflict, the shaft of the arrow was broken off and was first noticed by a farrier in camp much later. The wounded horse no doubt was given his name because of the Comanche arrow.

Comanche received a second wound in June, 1870, in another fight against Indians. This wound in his right leg was superficial and kept him lame for about a month. Comanche was shot in the right shoulder in an encounter with moonshiners in Kentucky, January 28, 1873, but the injury was slight and recovery was rapid.

Comanche, the nearest approach to the distinction of lone survivor of the Custer fight, was the only living possession of the 7th Cavalry to be led away from the battlefield by troops who found the Custer dead early on the morning of June 27, 1876, two days after the battle.

While Gibbon's command was engaged in identifying the dead on Custer Hill, Comanche appeared, grazing, some distance from the hill, neighing softly.[38] The poor animal was limping toward the burial detail, with saddle beneath his belly, the bit dangling from a broken cheek strap and throat-latch keeping the headstall from slipping off. Almost too weak to walk further, and near exhaustion, he was approached by officers and examined. Three wounds he had sustained in the Custer battle were severe, in the neck, groin and lung.

---

37. Comanche, by Anthony A. Amaral, Westernlore Press, Calif., 1961, p. 79.

38. Cavalry Journal, July, 1926, Vol. XXXV, p. 433.

It seemed almost conclusive that Keogh went down with Comanche. A wound was found in the right shoulder of the horse and emerging from the left, where Keogh's knee would have been. When Captain Keogh's body was found, his left leg and knee were badly shattered by a bullet.[39] Captain Keogh had changed from Paddy, his first field mount, to Comanche just before the battle.

Testifying at the Reno Court of Inquiry, Benteen and Girard told of finding another horse, wounded, lying on its side in a pool of mud and water on the bank of a stream where it was supposed Custer and his men had attempted to cross in his attack on the Indian village. Benteen stated he shot the horse to put him out of his misery.[40] Thus, Comanche was possibly one of several horses found on the battlefield that day, as it is not certain what happened to the others; they were presumably shot. Why Comanche was spared remains a mystery. Yet during the eight years since Captain Keogh purchased Comanche, many troopers learned to recognize the horse, and may have spared his life out of friendship for Keogh.

After the dead were buried, Comanche was led along with the wounded, toward the steamer *Far West*, anchored at the junction of the Little and Big Horn Rivers. Several times Comanche was unable to move during this 15-mile march, and a conveyance was used to move the veteran horse down to the river. It is not recorded what kind of conveyance was used, but Comanche could have been dragged with a tarpaulin or large canvas.

Aboard the steamer *Far West*, a stall was prepared near the rear paddle wheel, where a soft bedding of fresh cut grass was prepared, and Comanche was attended by veterinarian Stein during the trip to Bismarck.

The 950-mile trip was made in record time of 54 hours.

For almost a year, Comanche recuperated from his wounds, suspended in a sling with only a little space between the floor and his hoofs. After the "sole survivor" had regained his strength, he had the free-run of the post and roamed at will. Favorite hangouts were the officers' mess and the enlisted men's club, where he occasionally obtained a bucket of beer from a casual admirer. At parades and ceremonies, Comanche led his old Troop "I," draped in mourning with a black net and an empty saddle with the symbolic empty boots reversed in the saddle stirrups.[41]

Comanche was in demand by the ladies of the post for riding parties outside the garrison. Some officers expressed disapproval, and suggested that a retired mascot should not be subject to special privileges for anyone, much less the women on post. The officers' objections were passed on to Brevet Major General Samuel D. Sturgis, post commander and Colonel of the 7th Cavalry. Sturgis, who had lost a son in the Custer battle, may have been personally irritated with the problem of the women wanting to ride Comanche. He issued the following order:

"Head Quarters Seventh U.S. Cavalry
"Fort Abraham Lincoln, Dakota Territory, April 10, 1878.
"General Orders No. 7
"1. The horse known as "Comanche" being the only survivor or living representative of the bloody tragedy of the Little Big Horn, June 25, 1876, his kind treatment and comfort should be a matter of pride and solicitude on the part of every member of the 7th Cavalry, to the end that his life may be prolonged to the utmost limit. Wounded and scarred as he is, his very existance speaks in terms more eloquent than words of the desperate struggle against overwhelming numbers of the hopeless conflict, and of the heroic manner in which all went down on that fatal day.
"2. The Commanding Officer of Troop "I" will see that a special and comfortable stall is fitted up for him, and he will not be ridden by any person what-

---

39. Comanche, by Anthony A. Amaral, Westernlore Press, Calif., 1961, p. 75.
40. Reno Court of Inquiry.

41. Winners of the West, April, 1934.

ever, under any circumstances, nor will he be put to any kind of work.

"3. Hereafter, upon all occasions of ceremony (of mounted regimental formation) Comanche, saddled, bridled, draped in mourning, and led by a mounted trooper of Troop "I," will be paraded with the regiment.

"By command of Colonel Sturgis.

"(Signed)   Ernest A. Garlington,

"First Lieutenant and Adjutant 7th U.S. Cavalry.

Comanche may have officially been relieved of duty, but he continued with Troop "I" on many marches and skirmishes. If a fight seemed probable, Comanche was picketed with the other horses in a rear area.[42]

Comanche accompanied the regiment on its moves from Fort Abraham Lincoln to Fort Totten, and Fort Meade, and then to his final pasture at Fort Riley. His reputation grew, and many stories of the old war horse, or "Second Commanding Officer," as he was sometimes called, spread from post to post.

A fourteen-year association with Farrier Gustav Korn, who was designated as Comanche's caretaker, came to an end when Korn was killed in action at Wounded Knee, South Dakota, on December 29,

---

42. Comanche, by Anthony A. Amaral; Westernlore Press, Calif., 1961, p. 47.

1861 Cavalryman's horse saddled.

1890, while still a member of Troop "I." From that time on, Comanche seemed to have little interest in life. His concern for living seemed hopeless. After long continued decline and weakness, on November 6, 1891, an attack of colic ended the life of the "Second Commanding Officer." Comanche was close to 29 years old.

Officers at Fort Riley decided that Comanche should be preserved and mounted as a last tribute to the old "war horse." A telegram was sent to Professor Lewis Dyche, naturalist in Lawrence, Kansas, requesting him to come to Fort Riley. The professor agreed to mount and preserve the skin of Comanche for $450. The officers did not have this sum available and agreed that the professor would mount the horse and have the privilege of exhibiting it for two years, including the 1893 World's Fair in Chicago. When the $450 bill was paid, the horse would be returned to Fort Riley. No attempt was made to pay the bill, and the University of Kansas Museum of Natural History became the permanent home for Comanche. While the hide was being mounted, the remains of the old "war horse" received burial, with military honors, at Fort Riley, but the place of burial is not known there.

Comanche still carries on the spirit of the old 7th Cavalry, as he stands in the Dyche museum of the University of Kansas. Here he remains a silent memorial to the 7th Cavalry's most bitter defeat at the Little Big Horn.

"HORSE EQUIPMENTS FOR THE CAVALRY SERVICE"
From Ordnance Manual
1862

A complete set of horse equipments for cavalry troops consists of 1 *bridle*, 1 *watering-bridle*, 1 *halter*, 1 *saddle*, 1 *pair of saddle-bags*, 1 *saddle-blanket*, 1 *surcingle*, 1 *pair of spurs*, 1 *curry-comb*, 1 *horse-brush*, 1 *picket-pin*, and 1 *lariat*; (1 *link* and 1 *nose-bag*, when specially required.)

HEAD-GEAR.

All the leather is black bridle-leather, not less than 0.1 inch thick, and the buckles are malleable iron flat bar-buckles, blued.

BRIDLE.

It is composed of 1 *headstall*, 1 *bit*, 1 *pair of reins*.

HEADSTALL. — 1 *crown-piece*, the ends split, forming 1 *cheek-strap* and 1 *throat-lash billet* on one side, and on the other 1 *cheek-strap* and 1 *throat-lash*, with 1 *buckle* No. 11A; 2 *chapes*, and 2 *buckles* No. 10A, sewed to the ends of cheek-pieces to attach the bit; 1 *brow-band:* the ends, doubled and sewed, form 2 loops on each end, through which the cheek-straps, throat-lash, and throat-lash billet pass.

BIT, (shear steel, blued.) — 2 *branches*, S-shaped, pierced at top with an *eye* for the cheek-strap billet, and with a small hole near the eye for the curb-chain, terminated at the bottom by 2 *buttons*, into which are welded 2 *rings* No. 5 for the reins. The lower curve of the branch is tangent to the line through the axis of the mouth-piece and the centre of the eye. 1 *mouth-piece*, curved in the middle; its ends pass through the branches, and are riveted to them; 1 *cross-bar*, riveted to the branches near the lower ends; 2 *bosses*, (cast brass,) bearing the number and letter of the regiment and the letter of the company, riveted to the branches with 4 *rivets;* 1 *curb-chain*, hook, steel wire No. 10, fastened to the *near* branch; 1 *curb-chain*, steel wire No. 11, curb-chain links 0.7 inch wide, with 1 *loose ring* in the middle, fastened to the *off* branch by an S-hook, cold-shut; 1 *curb-strap*, (leather,) fastened to the curb-chain by 2 *standing-loops*.

1 *curb-ring* for bit No. 1 replaces the curb-chain and curb-strap. They are of 2 sizes: No. 1, interior diameter 4 inches; No. 2, 3.75 inches, — the number marked on the outside of the swell. Three-fourths of the bits of this kind to have the large ring, one-fourth the small ring.

There are *four* varieties of bits; they are all alike below the mouth-piece.

	No. 1	No. 2	No. 3	No. 4
Height of arch	2.25	2.	1.5	0.5
Opening of arch	0.8	1.1		
Distance of eye from axis of mouth-piece	1.5	2.25	2.25	2.25
Diameter of mouth-piece at shoulder	0.5	0.5	0.5	0.65

Distance from axis of mouth-piece to axis of cross-bar, 5 inches.

Distance from centre of button to the axis of cross-bar, 0.5 inch.

Length of mouth-piece in all bits, 4.5 inches; square tenon of mouth-piece, .35 inch.

At centre of arch, .325 inch vertical thickness, 0.45 inch horizontal. Thickness of branch at mouth-piece, 0.225 inch.

REINS.—2 *reins*, sewed together at one end, — the other ends sewed to the rings of the bit.

WATERING-BRIDLE.

The watering-bridle is composed of 1 *bit* and 1 *pair of reins*.

BIT, (wrought iron, blued.) — 2 *mouth-piece sides*, united in the middle by a loop-hinge: their ends are pierced with 2 holes to receive 2 *rings* No. 1 for the reins; 2 *chains* and *toggles*, 3 links, each 1 inch X .55 inch, welded into the rein-rings.

REINS. — 2 *reins*, sewed together at one end, — the other sewed to the rings of the bit.

HALTER.

2 *cheek-pieces*, sewed, one end to 2 *square loops* No. 2A, and the other to 2 *cheek-rings* No. 1A; 2 *standing-loops* for the toggles of the watering-bridle, sewed to the cheek-pieces near to the square loops; 1 *crown-piece*, sewed to the *off* cheek-rings; 1 *buckle* No. 7A and *chape*, sewed to the *near* cheek-ring; 1 *nose-band*, the ends sewed to the square loops; 1 *chin-strap*, the ends sewed to the square loops, and passing loose through the hitching-strap ring; 1 *throat-strap*, folded on itself, making two thicknesses, and forming at top a loop for the throat-band to pass through, and embracing in the fold at the other end 1 *bolt*, which holds 1 *hitching-strap ring*; 1 *throat-band* passes loose through the loop in the throat-strap, and sewed to the cheek-rings; 1 *hitching-strap*, 6½ feet long; 1 *buckle* No. 6A, and 1 *standing-loop*; 1 *billet*, sewed to the buckle end by the same seam which holds the buckle.

SADDLE

All the leather is black bridle or harness leather, and the buckles are malleable iron blued.

The SADDLE is composed of 1 *tree*, 2

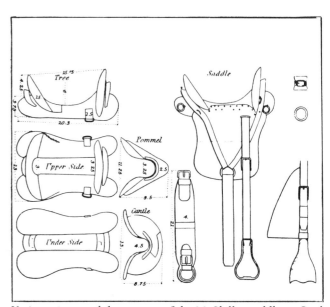

Various views and dimensions of the McClellan saddle — Civil War period.

saddle-skirts, 2 *stirrups*, 2 *stirrup-leathers*, 1 *girth* and *girth-strap*, 1 *surcingle*, 1 *crupper*.

SADDLE-TREE. — Wood, (beech.) — 1 *pommel*, made of 2 pieces framed together at top and glued; 1 *cantle*, formed of 2 pieces, like the pommel; 2 *side bars*, (poplar,) each made of 3 pieces glued together: they are glued to the pommel and cantle, and fastened by 2 *rivets* No. 1, 2 *burrs*, and 4 *nails*, — the burrs let in on the under side; 1 *strap-mortise* in the pommel; 3 *strap-mortises* in the cantle.

There are three sizes of trees, varying in the length of the seat:

No. 1, 11 inches length of seat, 15 per cent.,   to be marked
No. 2, 11½ inches length of seat, 15 per cents.,   } on the pommel-
No. 3, 12 inches length of seat, 35 per cent.   ornament.

IRON. — 1 *pommel-arc*, .1 inch thick, with 3 small holes on top, fastened to the side bars by 4 *rivets* No. 1; 1 *pommel-plate*, .1 inch thick, semi-circular, fastened to the front of the pommel by 4 *rivets* No. 1; 1 *cantle-arc*, .1 inch thick, with 3 small holes on top, fastened to the side bars by 4 *rivets* No. 1; 1 *cantle-plate*, .1 inch thick, fastened to the rear of the cantle by 4 *rivets* No. 1; 2 *stirrup-loops*, hinged in 2 *iron straps*, which are fastened to the side bars by 6 *rivets* No. 1.

The tree is painted with one coat of white lead. It is covered with raw hide, put on wet and sewed with thongs of the same, and held in place by stitches through the wood along the junction of the pommel and cantle with the side bars. The seams are made on the edges of the side bars, where they will not chafe the horse nor rider.

2 *rings*, held by staples driven into the front ends of side bars; 2 *foot-staples* for coat-straps, fastened to the front of the pommel by 4 *brass screws* No. 6, ¾ inch; 2 *crupper-rings*, (japanned black,) fastened by staples driven into the rear ends of side bars; 2 *foot-staples*, fastened to the rear of cantle by 4 *brass*

screws No. 6, ¾ inch; 1 *guard-plate*; 1 *pommel-ornament*, shield-shaped, (sheet brass,) fastened to the pommel, each by 3 *brass screw-pins*; 6 *guard-plates*, fastened to the cantle by 12 *screw-pins*; 2 *foot-staples*, fastened on the back strap by 4 *brass screws* No. 6, ¾ inch; 1 *saddle-bag stud*, fastened on the back strap to the cantle-arc by 2 *copper rivets* No. ½C.

2 SADDLE-SKIRTS, (thick harness-leather,) fastened to the side bars by 38 *brass screws* No. 6, ¾ inch; 2 *stay-loops* for the saddle-bag straps, sewed to the rear edge of the skirts.

2 STIRRUPS, (hickory or oak,) made of one piece bent, the ends separated by 1 *transom* and fastened by 2 *iron rivets* No. 2B, 4 *burrs* each; 2 *leather hoods*, (thick harness-leather,) fastened to the stirrups by 12 *copper rivets* No. ½ and *burrs*, — distance of hood from rear of stirrup, 6 inches; 2 *stirrup-straps* — 2 *buckles* No. 5A; 2 *sliding-loops* — pass through the stirrup-loops and through a hole cut in the skirt; 2 *stirrup-leathers*, (thick harness-leather;) 2 *standing-loops*.

GIRTH. — 2 *girth-straps* pass over the pommel and cantle-arcs, to which they are fastened by 4 *copper rivets* No. ½C and 4 *burrs*: they are fastened to the side bars by 4 *brass screws* No. 6, ¾ inch: the ends are sewed into 2 *D-rings* No. 1A; 2 *girth-billets*, sewed to the straight side of the D-rings; 1 *girth*, 4.5 inches, (blue woollen webbing;) 1 *chape*, 1 *buckle* No. 2A, 1 *standing-loop*, and 1 *safe* on the off end, and 1 *chape*, 1 *buckle* No. 4A, 1 *D-ring* No. 1A, 1 *standing-loop*, and 1 *safe* on the near end; 1 *standing-loop* on the middle.

6 COAT-STRAPS, 6 *buckles* No. 11A, 6 *stops*: they pass through the mortises in the pommel and cantle and the foot-staples.

CARBINE-THIMBLE. — 1 *strap*; 1 *buckle* No. 10A sewed to the socket: the thimble is buckled to the D-ring on the off side of the saddle.

SURCINGLE, 3.25 inches, (blue woollen webbing.) — 1 *chape*, 1 *buckle* No. 4A, and 1 *standing-loop* on one end, and 1 *billet* on the other; 1 *billet-lining*, sewed over the end of webbing to the billet; 2 *standing-loops* near the buckle end.

CRUPPER. — 1 *dock*, made of a single piece and stuffed with hair, the ends sewed to the body of the crupper; 1 *body*, split at one end, has sewed to it 1 *chape* and 1 *ring* No. 3A; 2 *back-straps*: each has 1 *buckle* No. 10A and 2 *sliding-loops*: they pass through the rings of the side bars and the ring on the body of the crupper.

SADDLE-BAGS.

The saddle-bags are composed of 2 *pouches* and 1 *seat*, the ends of the seat sewed to the pouches. Each pouch has 1 *back*, sewed to the gusset and upper part of inner front with a *welt*; 1 *gusset*, sewed to the back and to 1 *outer* and 1 *inner front* with a *welt*; 1 *flap*, sewed to the top of the back and to the seat by 2 *seams*; 1 *flap-billet*, sewed to the point of the flap; 1

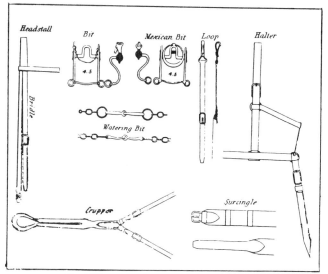

Civil War period — Horse equipment.

chape and 1 *buckle* No. 11A, sewed to the outer front; 1 *billet* and 1 *buckle* No. 11A, sewed to the chape. The seat is sewed to the pouch by the same seams which join the flap to the back of the pouch. It has 2 *holes* for the foot-staples, and 1 *hole* for the saddle-bag stud; 2 *keystraps*, sewed to the seat near its ends; 4 *lacing-thongs* for the pouches.

SADDLE-BLANKET.

To be of pure wool, close woven, of stout yarns of an indigo-blue color, with an orange border 3 inches wide, 3 inches from the edge. The letters U.S., 6 inches high, of orange color, in the centre of the blanket. Dimensions, 75 inches long, 67 inches wide. Weight, 3.1875 lbs.; allowance in weight, 0.1875 lb.

SPURS, (brass.) — 2 *spurs*; 2 *rowels*; 2 *rivets*; 2 *spur-straps*, 19 inches long; 2 *roller-buckles* No. 11B; 2 *standing-loops*.

Length of heel — for No. 1, 3½ inches; for No. 2, 3¼ inches } inside
Width of heel — for No. 1, 3¼ inches; for No. 2, 3 inches } measure

Length of shank to centre of rowel, 1 inch.
Diameter of rowel, 0.85 inch.

Weight of pair of spurs and straps, .57 lb.

HORSE-BRUSH.—1 *Body*, (maple;) Russia bristles; 1 *cover*, glued and fastened to the body by 8

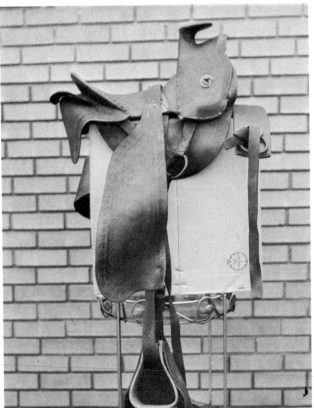

McClellan saddle, probably designed by Custer, as were many others, and used in the southwest.

screws No. 3; 1 *hand-strap*, (fair leather,) fastened to the sides of the body by 6 *screws* No. 5; 2 *leather washers* under the heads of screws.

Dimensions. — Body, 9.25 inches long, 4 inches wide, .5 inch thick; cover 0.1 in. thick; bristles project .9 in.; hand-strap, 2 in. wide. Weight, .57 lb.

CURRYCOMB, (iron, japanned black.) — 1 *body*, (sheet iron, 0.4,) the top and bottom edges turned at right angles, forming 2 rows of teeth riveted to the body by 6 *rivets*; 1 *cross-bar*, riveted across the top by 2 *rivets*; 1 *handle-shank*, riveted to the body by 3 rivets; 1 *handle*, (wood,) turned and painted, passes over the shank, and is held by the riveted end of the shank; 1 *ferrule*, sheet iron.

Dimensions. — Length 4 inches, width 4.75 inches, thickness .75 inch; length of handle, 4 inches. Weight .75 lb.

PICKET-PIN, (iron, painted black.) — The parts are, *the body, the neck, the head, the swell, the point*, 1 *lariat-ring* around the neck, 8-shaped, the larger opening for the lariat.

Dimensions.—Length, 14 in.; diameter at swell, 4 in. from point, .75 in.; at neck, .5 in.; at head, 1 in. Lariat-ring, .2-in. wire, welded. Int. diameter, 1 inch. Weight of pin, 1.25 lbs.

LARIAT. — Best hemp 1¼-in. rope, 30 ft. long, of 4 strands, an eye spliced in one end, the other end whipped with small twine. Weight, 2.38 lbs.

LINK. — 1 *strap*, embracing in the fold at one end 1 *spring-hook*, and at the other 1 *buckle* No. 10A and 1 *billet*. Weight, .2 lb.

NOSE-BAG. — 1 *body*, (strong linen or cotton duck,) 1 *bottom*, (harness-leather,) 6 inches diameter, 4 inches deep, pressed in a mould, sewed to the body; 1 *head-strap* with 1 *buckle* No. 8 and 1 *standing-loop*, sewed to the top of the bottom, and fastened by 2 *copper rivets* No. 1; sewed to the top of the body and to an inside leather washer by the same seam, and fastened by 1 *copper rivet* No. 1; 1 *head-strap billet*, sewed to the top of the bottom, and fastened by 2 *copper rivets* No. 1; sewed to the top of the body and to an inside leather washer by the same seam, and fastened by 1 *copper rivet* No. 1. Width of bag at top, 15 inches; whole height, 15 inches.

"ORDNANCE MEMORANDUM NO. 13"
1872
"CAVALRY EQUIPMENTS"

MODIFICATIONS OF THE PRESENT EQUIPMENTS.

The Bit. — The present bits, Nos. 1, 2, and 3, as described in the Ordnance Manual, are deemed unnecessarily severe and injurious to the horses.

The Board therefore recommend that No. 1 be abolished as unalterable, and Nos. 2 and 3 be altered in the mouth-pieces as follows: one-half of the numbers to be 5″ between branches; opening of arch, 1″.5; height of arch, 0″.5; the diameter of all mouth-pieces 0″.7, and cylindrical from branch to spring of arch; at center of arch vertical thickness 0″.325; horizontal thickness, 0″.450.

The present No. 4 should be used until new ones are required to be made, when it will be advisable to introduce the same mouth-pieces as above, and make one-half 5″ between the branches, and one-half 4″.75, thus giving for future issues two degrees of severity only, and two widths of mouth-pieces, to be designated as follows:

No. 1. 5″ between branches; 1″ height of arch.
No. 2. 4″.75 between branches; 1″ height of arch.
No. 3. 5″ between branches; 0″.5 height of arch.
No. 4. 4″.75 between branches; 0″.5 height of arch.

Curb-strap Loops. — To be welded in the present chain-hook holes to receive a strap 0″.625 wide, and the

Curb-chain — To be abolished.

Saddle-tree. — The saddle-tree to be covered with black collar leather, without skirts, as at present being made at Watervliet Arsenal, with safes under the D rings, 4″.5 by 4″.75.

Girth. — As woolen web is rapidly injured, both by moth and the perspiration from the horse, and hair girths (if suitable and durable) are too expensive for general use, the Board recommend the trial of linen

web for cavalry girths and surcingles. To prevent chafing from the selvedge, it is suggested the material be woven of double width, and the edges joined at the center. Girth of linen web, of dark-blue color, 6″ wide, made as at present. The safes should be 6″ wide where sewed to web, and 3″ wide at the other end.

Stirrups. — The Board recommend that the sole of the wood stirrup be made 4″ wide (when new ones are required); that the present hood be retained, and that it be stamped "U.S." on the center of front, like the present cartridge-box flaps.

Surcingle. — Of blue linen web 4″ wide, made as at present.

Saddle-bags. — The present pattern of leather saddle-bags to be abolished, and replaced by saddle-bags composed of two pouches of No. 3 linen duck, sewed to a leather seat.

The pouches to be made 10″ by 12″ in clear, sewed to a gusset 3″ wide at bottom, and 2″.5 at mouth. The off-side pouch is intended to carry the soldier's clothing, and has an inside pocket for brush, towel, soap, etc., of planter's linen, of same size as front, and sewed with it to the gusset. The near-side pouch is for the rations. A flap 12″ by 14″ for each pouch is secured to the top of the back and to the seat by two seams, and by two No. 12 rivets. A pocket 7″ by 5″, and 1″.5 wide in the clear with its flap, is sewed on the outside of each pouch-front: the one on the off side to carry two packages of cartridges; the one on the near side a tin can with handle and cover, to carry the meat ration on the march. This can has a bent handle of tin, riveted at top and detached at bottom, so that it projects outside and in rear of pocket. The can is intended to be used also to cook coffee, while the cover, fitting within the can, forms a drinking cup 1″.5 deep, with a handle folding upon the top.

The seat of the bags, 20″ long between pouches, is cut to fit smoothly over the cantle; it has one hole for saddle-bag stud, and two holes for foot staples, with key-straps sewed to each.

The pouch flaps have each two 0″.75 billets sewed on inside near lower edge, 6″ apart, to enter brass buckles secured by chapes sewed to under side of gusset.

The pocket flaps have each one billet, fastening to a brass button riveted to the bottom of gusset. All the flaps are bound with thin leather 0″.5 wide on the face, and the large pouches are re-enforced around the mouth by a strap 0″.75 wide, secured by two seams to gusset and front, and by two brass rivets (No. 12) passing through flap, back and seat. A leather loop of 0″.75 wide is sewed to back of each pouch, 3″ from bottom and 1″ from front edge, by means of which they may be tied to the D rings, if desired.

The seat straps and bindings will all be of fair leather.

Brush and Shoe Pouch. — Composed of two pockets sewed to a strap 4″ long between pockets, and 3″

Courtesy Colonel Brice Custer   *Photo by E. L. Reedstrom*
One of the many McClellan saddles Custer had reconstructed through the company saddler.

wide at seams, narrowed at center to 1".5, having at center a loop, with 1" opening, riveted on top by two rivets. A second strap, 1" wide and 12" long, is fastened by one rivet to each pocket, at 5" from the top.

The off pocket is 7" deep by 5" wide, and 1" in clear, and carries two shoes and fifteen shoe nails.

The near pocket, 10".5 deep by 6" wide, and 2".5 in clear, is to receive the brush and curry-comb; one loop, with opening 1" wide, is riveted on the underside of each pocket. This pouch is carried over the pommel under the cloak; the wide strap in front, and second strap on the seat. The cloak straps pass through the loops before receiving the cloak.

Forage Sack. — To be made of planter's linen, 24" long, and bottom 7" diameter; to be tied with a choke string; to hold fifteen pounds of oats; is to be secured over cantle by the cantle straps.

Overcoat and Lariat. — The overcoat rolled 30" long, and the lariat rolled around its pin, and on top of coat, are secured by the pommel straps.

Nose Bag. — The Board recommend that the nose bag be dispensed with, as it does not offer the best means of feeding horses, and the new saddle-bags will carry all that has heretofore been carried in it on the march.

Saddle Cloth. — They recommend that a piece of cotton duck, No. 6, 28" by 30" (the size of the folded blanket), be issued to each soldier, to be carried over the blanket and under the saddle when on the march. This can be spread to receive the ration of grain, when feeding, and also be used to cover the saddle and its trappings when at rest or in the stable. This cover will weigh not more than one pound, and both on campaign and in garrison will be of constant value. Two edges should be hemmed, and the selvedge left on the other two. The letter of the company and the number of the regiment may be painted on the corners, when used as a saddle cloth.

Spurs. — The Board recommend that the spurs be smooth finished before issue, as they can be thus kept in better order.

ACCOUTERMENTS AND BASIC WEAPONS

In order to cover fully the various changes in designs of Infantry and Cavalry cartridge boxes, this chapter will begin from the Civil war, partly through the Indian Wars, up to Custer's battle on the Little Big Horn, touching lightly on the ordnance-accepted boxes and a few experimental accouterments. It would be almost impossible to elaborate on all military boxes without spending a high degree of research to cover the experimental designs as well as the accepted boxes.

During military campaigns in this country, our soldiers contributed much toward changes in their accouterments because of necessity. Cumbersome bullet pouches, heavy with lead balls, unevenly distributed on shoulder or waist belts, slowed down the soldier on the field of battle. During this period, the Ordnance Department was bombarded with suggestions for changes and alterations, from officers returning from the field. However, appropriations were meager and serviceable equipment was on hand. Not until supplies were exhausted could a Board of Officers consider drastic changes. Only with a complete changeover in weapons and a standardized cartridge would there be modifications in leather equipment and accouterments.[1]

The Infantry cartridge pouch of the Civil War was much the same in appearance as that of the Model 1855 box, with only a few modifications. This box was almost universally used by both Northern and Southern armies throughout the Civil War. Because of the wartime shortage of brass, the newly

manufactured boxes were altered slightly by dropping the oval brass U.S. plate and substituting an embossed oval and U.S. on the flap. This box could be used with the shoulder sling or suspended from the belt. Two separate tin inserts, each one with a lower division, open in front to contain one bundle of 10 cartridges, and two upper divisions, one to contain 6 and the other 4 cartridges, a total of 40 rounds. The box was double flapped with an implement pocket sewn to the front of the box. The complete box was made of black bridle leather, and to the accompanying shoulder sling was affixed a round brass plate with an eagle.

The cap pouch, made of black bridle leather and lined with sheepskin, was styled after the 1855 model. A steel-wire cone pick with a ring handle was carried in a loop in the inner left-hand corner of the cap pouch. The sheepskin lining kept the percussion caps from falling out during an engagement while the flap was open. Included with his equipment, the infantryman carried a combination tool, open-end nipple wrench, and 2 screwdrivers.

While the Seventh Cavalry was organizing in the fall of 1866, various methods for carrying ammunition were tested. Although issued the Spencer .50-caliber rim-fire repeating carbine equipped with the Stabler cut-off, the only available cartridge boxes on hand were the common Civil War cavalry-belt cartridge box, housing a 20-hole wooden block.[2] According to the Chief of Ordnance, summary statements of the Ordnance and Ordnance stores in the

---

1. "Accouterment," also spelled "accoutrement," means trappings, equipment, a soldier's outfit other than clothing and weapons.

2. Early boxes had tin cases inside, totally unsuited for metallic cartridges. The ammunition would rattle loudly, whether afoot or mounted. Anson Mills, My Story, p. 111, Washington, 1918.

hands of troops for the second quarter, June 1867, shows the Seventh Cavalry was issued "Spencer Cartridge Boxes"[3] practically through the regiment. It is believed that a few Blakeslee carbine boxes were scattered in various companies, for a short period, as it was too heavy, cumbersome, and troops armed with it expended their rounds very quickly.[4] An early version of the wool-lined Dyer carbine cartridge pouch was recorded in March, 1871 as being issued to several companies, and a few companies retained these.

---

3. The Civil War cavalry belt cartridge box with the 20-hole wooden block has been referred to as the Spencer cartridge box. When the Sharps carbine was introduced, this box was also called the Sharps carbine cartridge box.
4. A soldier would also insert a 7-round tube, leave it in the butt of the Spencer, turn the Stabler cut-off to single-shot and fire individually, loading each time, leaving the 7-round tube as a reserve. (Correspondence with George Rummel, Jr., June, 1973; President of the U.S. Cavalry Collectors, "The Guidon.")

Photo by E. L. Reedstrom

Sergeant J. J. Narus, 2nd U.S. Reactivated Cavalry, demonstates the use of the Blakeslee cartridge box. This photo represents a Cavalryman in the late 1860's, adorned with a series of leather accouterments, the Spencer carbine and the Colt percussion revolver.

"CAVALRY ACCOUTERMENTS"
From Ordnance Manual
1862

Cavalry Accouterments

CARTRIDGE-BOX FOR CARBINE. — Like the infantry cartridge-box, except in dimensions. Two loops are placed upright on the back of the box, to receive a 2-inch waist-belt. Special boxes are made for the carbines now on trial in the hands of troops.

CAP POUCH (black bridle-leather). — The same as for the infantry. Length and depth, 3 inches; width, 1.25 inch; *inner cover*, with end pieces; *flap*, made of the same piece as the back, with a button-hole strap at the bottom; *brass button*, riveted under the bottom of the pouch; 2 *loops*, sewed to the back, 2.25 inches long, to admit a waist-belt of 2 inches; *lining*, a strip of sheep-skin, with the wool on, 1.5 inch wide, glued with fish-glue, and sewed to the back at the mouth of the pouch.

CONE-PICK (steel wire No. 18). — The same as for the infantry. 1.5 inch long, with a ring handle 0.5 inch diameter; it is carried in a loop in the inner left-hand corner of the cap-pouch.

SABRE-BELT (buff-leather). — *Waist-belt,*

Photo by E. L. Reedstrom

Close-up of the Cavalryman's equipment in 1867. McClellan saddle, spurs, Blakeslee cartridge box (10 tube), and Spencer carbine.

Photo by E. L. Reedstrom

A single tin tube is extracted from the Blakeslee cartridge box.

sheepskin protects the cartridges from injury, and keeps them from falling out without interfering with their ready extraction by hand. The small pocket is for revolver cartridges. The pouch is supported by a shoulder belt, which also serves as a carbine sling.[5]

This pouch was developed late in the Civil War but of an earlier pattern. It was a little larger than the Dyer pouch of the middle 1870's, on some specimens the front cover carried the U.S. stamped in an oval, a brass button and clasp to hold the flap down, with 2 belt loops on the back. This pouch was usually attached to a shoulder sling and was carried in this manner either in garrison or mounted. However, the only record of shoulder slings is found in the summary reports of the second quarter June 30, 1871, only listing these as "on hand." It

5. The Ordnance Department, U.S. Army, at the International Exhibition, 1876, First Lieutenant Henry Metcalfe, Ordnance Department, Washington; Government Printing Office, 1884.

length 36 to 40 inches, width 1.9 inch; 1 *square loop* No. 46, 2 *D rings* No. 2B, (brass), for attaching the slings and the shoulder-strap; 1 *hook* (brass), riveted on one end by 3 brass wire rivets No. 15; 1 *loop* (cast brass), sewed on the other end to connect with the plate; 1 *shoulder-strap*, 41 inches long, 1.125 inch wide, with 2 *hooks* (brass); 2 *sabre-slings*, 1.125 inch wide; front sling 17 inches long, rear sling 34 inches; 4 *studs* (brass) for slings; 1 *sabre-hook* (brass wire No. 7).

SABRE-BELT PLATE (cast brass). — Rectangular, 3.5 inches long, 2.2 inches wide, with an *eagle* surrounded by a wreath (German silver); 1 *slot* at one end, to receive the belt.

SWORD-KNOT (buff-leather). — *Strap* 1 inch wide, 36 inches long; one end of the strap is fastened to a *tassel* 3 inches long; the other end is passed through the tassel after going round the guard of the sabre, and is fastened by one of the tags of the tassel; 1 *sliding-loop*.

CARBINE-SLING (buff-leather). — Leather 56 inches, width 2.5 inches; 1 *buckle* and 1 *tip* (brass), *swivel* and *D* with *roller*, bright iron, 2.62 inches wide; *link* and *hook*, iron; *guard-spring*, steel.

General A. B. Dyer's Cartridge-Box

A pouch lined with sheepskin, designed to carry about 60 cartridges, caliber .50, when full. The

Photo by E. L. Reedstrom

Suspended from the carbine sling, the Spencer is swung from side to front, inserting the tube (holding 7 cartridges).

is likely that these pouches were worn on the waist belt.

In 1866, the trooper wore the Cavalry Sabre Belt and Shoulder Sling, a carryover from the war, and described in the 1862 Ordnance Manual under "Cavalry Accouterments." Made of buff leather, the waist belt measured 36 to 40 inches with a 1.9-inch width. Two brass "D" rings were attached to accept a 1.125-inch width shoulder strap, 41 inches long; the second ring supported the short sabre belt. To the left and at the rear was sewn a brass rectangular ring, connected to it was the shoulder strap and the rear sabre sling, measuring 34 inches in length. Attached to the belt was the rectangular cast-brass belt plate, 3.5 inches long, 2.2 inches wide; on the face was an eagle surrounded by a wreath of German silver. On the waist belt was carried the pistol, cartridge box, and a small percussion-cap pouch of Civil War vintage housing pistol cartridges. The shoulder

Photo by E. L. Reedstrom

The piece is now ready to fire. The Stabler cut-off system can either be set for "single shot" or "repeater". Dropping the block moves a cartridge forward into the chamber, when set for "repeater".

straps did not last long. They were either misplaced, lost or thrown away. Sabre belts, being fixed with stationary straps, could not be adjusted to please the trooper. The plain, standard Civil War belt was preferred over the buff leather waist belt and shoulder strap, because nothing sewn or riveted to it would be in the way of any adjustments of cartridge boxes or holster. The earlier buff sabre belt pattern soon faded out. Under an excess of perspiration, it cracked, split and seemed to absorb faster and harden more than other belts.

By March 31, 1871, the summary statements for Ordnance and Ordnance stores show the Seventh Cavalry armed with the Sharps carbine, altered for the .50-caliber metallic cartridge. Here again, the Civil War belt cartridge box with the 20-hole wooden block was utilized, with no transitions. This particular box was adapted for many other carbines during the War; the outer dimensions of the wooden blocks were the same and the holes were drilled in different sizes for various calibers. These blocks could easily be replaced with the correct-diameter hole and depth to accommodate the caliber used. If a .50-caliber Sharps cartridge could be dropped easily into one of the openings in the block, it could very well be classified as a Sharps cartridge box. Similarly the block could be adapted to Spencer carbine ammunition.

By the end of 1871, various patterns of carbine cartridge boxes and other leather goods had been distributed among some of the companies of the 7th on an experimental basis. The Ordnance Department was concerned with using up vast stores of surplus equipment already on hand from the War, proposing changes in obsolete leather goods to suit the new metallic ammunition. Company G, stationed at Spartanburg, South Carolina, received 45 infantry boxes (type not known); Company K, 60 Dyer's; and Troop M, 67 Dyer's, both companies serving in South Carolina. The Stewart's

Photo by E. L. Reedstrom

Battle range was up to 300 yards, with a 6-inch grouping at 100 yards.

Attachment for Pistols and Sabres, issued to Companies B, D and G, found favor with troopers.

The infantry was furnished with 2 leather cartridge boxes, pattern 1872, Type 1, holding 24 metallic .50-caliber cartridges and carrying a tool in a side compartment, and Type 2, pattern 1872, holding the same number of shells but a smaller box.[6] These boxes were suspended from the belt by a "Brace Yoke," but only if both boxes were worn with a total of 48 rounds of ammunition. A single cartridge box (No. 1) could be worn alone for drills or garrison duty, supported by the waist belt and placed either in front or behind. On the front flap of both 1872 patterns was embossed the U.S. oval. The loops for holding the cartridges were cloth strips shellacked to some degree of stiffness and sewn to the inside of the box in 3 rows (8 loops to a row).[7]

Between 1866 and 1880, hundreds of car-

tridge boxes were submitted for trial by the army. Many were issued on an experimental basis and then discarded. Most boxes that were used by the army were made at the arsenals; however, during the Civil War, it was necessary to have many made by contract. The "Half Moon" Dwyer pattern cartridge pouch shows up again, issued in 1874, holding 40 cartridges, wool lined,[8] and carried on the waist belt. It was modified from an original pattern of the early 1870's, when it was carried on the shoulder sling by mounted companies and, although several other types of pouches were used, the Dwyer pattern seemed to be a favorite. On the front flap was the usual embossed U.S. oval. This later pouch, being a little smaller, lacked the inside pocket for revolver cartridges.

Cavalrymen during the Civil War carried their percussion revolvers holstered, butt forward and on the right side. This holster was designed with a belt loop to accommodate the regulation belt, 1.9 inches wide. A larger loop on the back of the same pattern holster was designed for looped cartridge belts, of the Mills patent, and was not accepted by the army until 1878. The huge flap on the holster was designed to protect the cylinder and its percussion caps from rain and snow. With the introduction of the metallic cartridge, the wide flap was no longer needed and, in 1874, a narrow flap was recommended. Although the new pattern holster seemed more practical, the army continued using the older pattern well after the 1880's, because of the tremendous stockpile of goods left over from the Civil War.

Most popular of cartridge boxes to come out of the experimental period of the 1870's was the McKeever pattern. This box was in continuous service for 36 years in the regular army, and can still be found in use by guards at Arlington National Cemetery as

---

6. Mentioned in General Orders 60, 1872, as "patterns now being prepared for trial."

7. There is no doubt that these boxes were issued to the Seventh Cavalry.

8. The wool lining held the cartridges together so they would not bounce around, much like the Civil War percussion cap box.

Courtesy George A. Rummel, Jr.

The small pistol cartridge pouch is shown sewn to front of pouch, both flaps connect to same brass stud.

The cartridge box had become almost obsolete after the introduction of metallic cartridges, although it was still furnished to the troops. A newspaper correspondent who had been on the summer's campaign wrote in the Army and Navy Journal, December 9, 1876, "... The soldiers wear their cartridges in a belt around their body, in a manner that equalizes the weight, and makes it possible to load and fire rapidly." The cartridge boxes issued by the Ordnance Department were found utterly impracticable by the soldiers, and they would not wear them. Instead, they constructed cartridge belts at their own expense, which seemed to serve the purpose in a more convenient fashion. An ordnance officer, doing staff duty, accompanied a command on an expedition, and it was said that he looked through the entire command for the cartridge box that had been recently issued. He finally found an old Irish sergeant who had kept his car-

standard dress equipment. With the Springfield breech-loading rifles, the combination tool, Model 1879 was issued. It has a screwdriver, pin punch, mainspring wrench, and a secondary screwdriver riveted to the tool. This combination tool was made only at the Springfield Armory.

As early as 1866, the importance of the cartridge belt was realized. Getting shells for the new breech-loading rifles from the black leather cartridge boxes was slow, so the soldier remedied this by copying the ammunition belts used by civilian scouts. Scouts, hunters and frontiersmen put their cartridges within easy reach by fabricating homemade leather and canvas belts with loops to hold revolver and rifle ammunition.[9]

---

9. Army and Navy Journal, Nov. 6, 1869, p. 178. (Shortly after the metallic cartridge was adopted, these belts began to show up on the frontier.)

Courtesy George A. Rummel, Jr.

Rear side shows loops for waist belt, if not worn with shoulder sling.

Courtesy George A. Rummel, Jr.

This pouch (name unknown) was developed late in the Civil War. It is larger than the Dyer pouch adopted late in the 1870's. It carried 60 cartridges. The shoulder belt was 2½ inches wide with a brass buckle. The Dyer's pouch superseded this earlier pouch in the 1870's — however, it is possible these were used for several years after.

tridge box according to regulations. The officer, inquisitive, asked the veteran why he carried it, when others did not. "Lunch, sur," was the reply. The sergeant was recommended for court martial by the ordnance officer, but his superior officer appreciated the humor of the situation and saved his stripes.

General Anson Mills devised a woven-web ammunition carrier. In 1878, after years of rejections, Mills succeeded in getting the Army to accept his woven belt, which carried 50 .45-70 cartridges.[10] The government arsenals did not produce these belts; instead, they were purchased from contractors. Leather equipment was to be replaced by web ammunition carriers and its accompanying web equipment throughout the world. In later years, General Anson

_____
10. My Story, Anson Mills, published by the author, 1918, p. 317.

Mills stated, "I only regret that they (meaning his equipment) were not designed for construction but . . . rather for destruction."

From "Ordnance Memorandum No. 13, 1872 — Cavalry Equipments" with Modifications of the Present Equipments:

Remarks

In connection with the subjects particularly submitted to the Board, it became necessary to try the complete equipments of the horse and man, with rations, arms, and accouterments. In doing this, the Board tested the various parts of the new sets of cavalry accouterments recently ordered to be made at this arsenal, as well as those now in service. It was soon seen that the brace system of belts, found advantageous for the infantry soldier in relieving the pressure from the chest, is not of like value to the mounted man, as the chief weight of his arms is not borne by the man, but comes directly upon the horse; hence the shoulder-braces, while necessarily incommoding the trooper more than the foot soldier, do not give him like compensatory advantages.

The experience of our cavalry, as far as known to the Board, proves that the present system requires very slight alteration to be fully satisfactory, and no change in the carbine sling.

In order to test the full equipment for horse and man, the changes deemed necessary were made in a trial set, which proved to be very satisfactory, and it is respectfully submitted with this report.

With the mounted soldier, the weight of the carbine, to a great degree, is sustained by the socket fixed to the saddle, being merely steadied by the sling; when he is dismounted, the carbine is carried "at will," either on the shoulder, behind the back

Courtesy George A. Rummel, Jr.

Dyers cartridge pouch fleeced-lined, of the late 1870's period — with brass studs.

Dyer pouches shown here in several variations. Left pouch is the earlier standard model (right) of a later period.

thrown over the shoulder while held by the sling, or in the hand; without pressure, in either mode, upon the chest.

The extra ammunition, blanket, ration, and clothing, all bearing directly upon the person of the foot soldier, are arranged to be carried on the saddle or in the pouches of the saddle-bags now proposed by this Board; hence, there remains to be worn on the waist-belt only, the pistol, its cartridge pouch, and the carbine cartridge pouch, and sometimes the saber. The weight of these, either with or without the saber, is not sufficient to make the brace system necessary to relieve the chest, nor can the weight be so distributed as to keep the bearing steady, and prevent the straps slipping from the shoulders.

MODIFICATIONS IN CAVALRY ACCOUTERMENTS

The Board respectfully suggests the following changes in the cavalry accouterments described on page 229, Ordance Manual, ed. 1861:

Carbine Cartridge-Box or Pouch. — To be worn on waist-belt of the patterns now being made for trial; to carry 24 carbine cartridges, and one screw-driver in special pocket.

Pistol Cartridge-Box. — For the present, the infantry cap pouch, to carry 12 pistol cartridges.

Pistol Hoster. — Same as present belt holster, with a pocket riveted to the barrel by three rivets, to carry wiping rod; the holster-body to be attached to the belt-loop by a brass swivel and stud.

Waist Belt. — Of black bridle leather (without the shoulder straps), having 2 brass squares to receive sabersling hooks attached by leather loops and rivets horizontally upon the belt about the center of its width. In the front square the saber-hook (same as at present, of brass wire No. 7), is also fastened by cold shut bend;[11] a brass hook is riveted (to shorten belt) on one end of the belt, by 3 brass rivets; a loop of cast brass, sewed and riveted on the other end to connect with the plate.

Saber Slings and Sling-Hooks. — Two saber slings, 1″ wide (front sling 15″ long, rear sling 28″ long) are buttoned to the scabbard rings by one brass stud each, and have a hook of No. 11 sheet brass, 0″.5 wide, and 2″.25 long, at upper end of each sling, riveted by 3 brass rivets. These hooks hook into the waist-belt squares, when the saber is attached to the person, or into the saddle rings, if it is carried on the saddle.

Waist-Belt Plate. — Cast brass; rectangular, 3″.5 long, 2″.2 wide; with the letters "U. S." in raised type, surrounded by an oval raised ring; one slot at

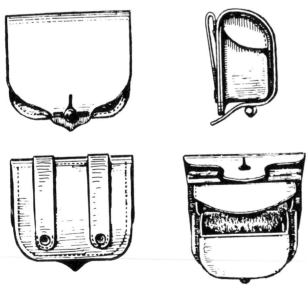
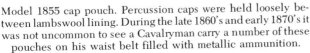

Model 1855 cap pouch. Percussion caps were held loosely between lambswool lining. During the late 1860's and early 1870's it was not uncommon to see a Cavalryman carry a number of these pouches on his waist belt filled with metallic ammunition.

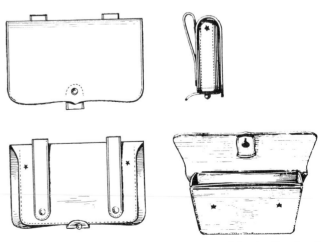

Model 1861 pistol cartridge box was designed for the Cavalry. It held six packets of cartridges.

one end to receive belt, and one hook of cast metal, 0″.55 wide, to enter the plate loop on belt.

Saber Knot. — Black bridle leather (thin); strap 0″.625 wide, 30″ long; one end fastened to a braided knot, without tassel, 1″.5 long, and the other passed through the knot after going round the guard of the saber; one sliding loop.

Carbine Sling. — Black bridle leather, same length, width, and finish, as at present.

WEIGHTS OF HORSE EQUIPMENT AND CAVALRY ACCOUTERMENTS

We attach hereto a table showing names of the parts, and weight of each part, of the cavalry equipments and accouterments, together with the total weight borne by a horse, with rider of average weight, at the commencement of a march of 5 days:

	Pounds	Ounces
Halter	2	1
Watering bridle	1	1½
Bridle	2	13
Saddle	14	13½
Saddle-bags	2	2
Filling of near-side pouch of saddle-bags — 10 pounds rations, with meat in the can	11	2
Filling of off-side pouch of saddle-bags — 1 pair socks, 1 pair drawers, 2 shirts, 40 rounds ammunition, small articles	7	8
Forage sack	0	6
15 pounds of oats	15	0
Lariat and pin	3	1½
Overcoat	4	6½
Brush and shoe pouch	1	0
Curry-comb and brush in near-side pocket	1	8
2 shoes and 15 shoe nails in off-side pocket	2	0
2 blankets (one for soldier's use)	6	14
Saddle cover	1	0
Surcingle	0	11½
Saber and slings	4	12
Waist-belt and plate	1	0
Pistol and holster	3	2
Carbine sling and swivel	10	4
Carbine cartridge box	1	0
24 rounds of ammunition in box	2	0
Pistol cartridge pouch	0	4
12 rounds of ammunition in box	0	14
Man	140	
Total carried by a horse at the commence of a march of 5 days	240	12½

CARBINES

Officers from various cavalry stations complained that many weapons issued by the government did not meet standards demanded for frontier service. Many of these complaints were directed against the Sharps carbine with which, on the average, three companies in every regiment, or approximately one-fourth of the entire cavalry corps, were armed. The Remington revolver, adopted as the standard arm of the service, had also its share of criticism, directed mainly against imperfect earlier issues. The inferior quality of these arms was attributed to unwise and short-sighted

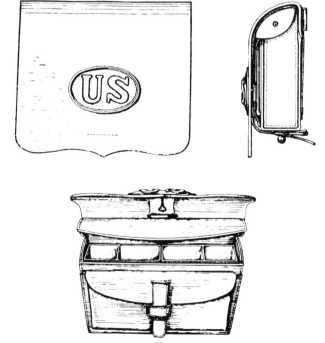

Model 1855 Infantry box with removable tinned liners to hold .58 caliber paper cartridges.

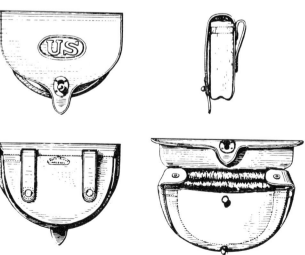

1874 pattern Dyer pouch, sometimes called "Dwyer." Metallic cartridges held loosely between lambswool.

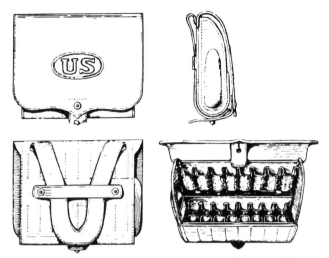

Infantry cartridge box, pattern 1872, type 1. Contained 24 cartridges. A small tool was carried in side compartment.

economy rather than to neglect or oversight on the part of the government. After the Civil War, a huge stock of used and new pistols, carbines and sabers remained in warehouses at government arsenals. Despite adoption of modern and improved arms, this stockpile of weapons was issued and distibuted to new cavalry regiments and also was used to fill past requisitions from some of the older regiments. While some companies of the regiments were armed with the Spencer and Henry carbines along with the improved Remington revolver, others were consequently compelled to use the old Sharps carbine and the unimproved Remington.[12]

The Spencer

The Spencer carbine first made its appearance on the field in 1862, but was used in limited numbers until 1863. Its production and popularity increased during the

12. Collier's, The National Weekly, Jan. 29, 1927, "A Soldiers Widow" by J. B. Kennedy: "The arms of our garrison were old Civil War models . . . in firing practice the rifles fouled, Indians were better armed."

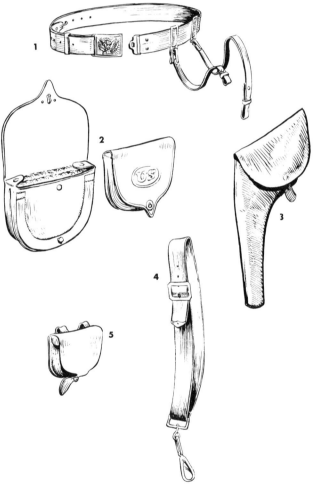

Art by E. L. Reedstrom

1. Black leather waist belt with sliding saber slings (used in the 1870's). The brass rectangular buckle, with silver wreath beneath spread eagle was prescribed for all officers and enlisted men in the 1851 uniform regulations, G.O. No. 31; however, prior to 1861, officers wore this plate. During the Civil War, and well into the 1870's, mounted men replaced the oval "U.S." buckle with this plate. 2. Wool-lined Dyer carbine cartridge pouch. 3. Black leather Civil War holster, with large oval flap. 4. Civil War carbine sling, with a width of 2⅜". Brass buckle and roller loop steel snap. 5. Civil War percussion cap box was also used for carrying pistol cartridges.

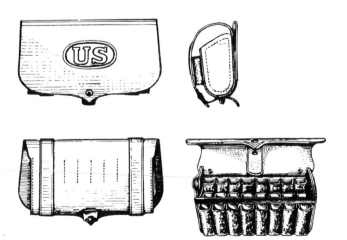

1872 pattern Infantry box, type 2, holding 24 cartridges.

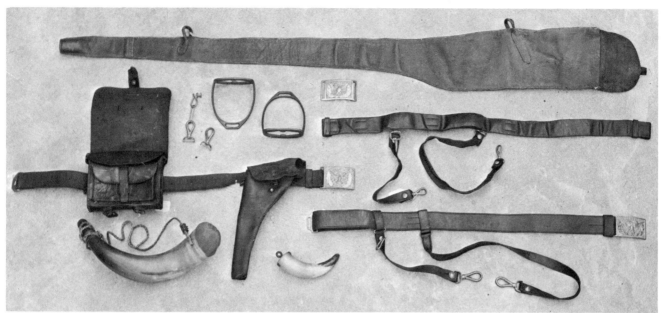

Courtesy Dr. L. A. Frost Collection

Custer's accouterments: (Top) Rifle case for his Springfield & Remington sporting rifles. Civil War stirrups, belt buckle with German silver wreath. (Left) Cartridge box, belt, and holster, Custer's field equipment. (Right) Dress saber belts. Two hunting powder horns (Bottom).

last two years of the war, and it became the Army's principal carbine for the cavalry. The Spencer was used effectively by Custer's Michigan Cavalry Brigade and by other Brigades at Gettysburg. Armed with these repeaters, in 1868, the Seventh Cavalry also demonstrated its devastating fire power at the Washita. The 56-56 was the cartridge used in the Civil War Spencers. The "ideal" cartridge produced at Springfield was the 50-50, but was adopted too late to be useful during the War. Spencer, in 1866-67, improved the 56-50 by removing the excess crimp and giving the cartridge a slight bottleneck. This was the 56-52, interchangeable in the 56-52 and the 56-50 rifles and carbines, both having a .50″ bore diameter.[13]

The 56-52 was strictly a sporting cartridge, also usable in the 56-50 weapons. Spencer never promoted the 56-50 commercially or to any great length. The Model 1865 Spencers in the 56-50 caliber saw service at the end of the Civil War and continued in use through the post-war years.[14]

Cartridge Data

Drawn copper cases, rimfire ignition, using a Smith & Wesson patent for the cases.

Bullet weights run between 350 and 400 grains, flat base lead. The 56-50 features inside lubrication of the bullets compared to the 56-56 which had the lube grooves exposed. Usual bullet configuration was that of a tapered round nose, though some have a slightly flattened tip.

Ballistic data is not available from those days, but a target report shows the Spencer cartridge having a horizontal deviation of 1.084 feet at 300 yards and 1.397 feet at 500 yards. Penetration of pine at 500 yards was 5.91 inches.

13. The Cavalry had been supplied with Spencer Carbines altered to use the musket metallic ammunition; Secretary of War Report, 1869, Army and Navy Journal, Dec. 11, 1869.

14. An offshoot of the original 56-56, the 56-50 was designed at the Springfield Armory in the fall of 1864, during attempts to standardize the military to a single size of ammunition. At this time, the military was using several different shoulder weapons firing paper, linen and some rimfire ammunition. The 56-56 was one of several rimfire cartridges in production at that time.

Powder charge was 43 to 45 grains. (Grain sizing not specified.)

The wide variation in data figures result mostly from the fact that specimens examined nowadays are from many different manufacturers; there wasn't a standard product as there is now. Case and bullet dimensions vary quite a bit on the 56-50 and were even worse in the 56-56. Ballistics must have varied greatly too.

Thumbnail differences from the original 56-56 down to the 56-50 are as follows:

56-56 short case, exposed bullet lube grooves, original cartridge.

56-52 bottleneck-appearing case due to lower, heavier crimp on bullet. Lube grooves still exposed.

56-50 longer case covering the lube grooves. This case has a slight taper into the mouth. Every bit as efficient as a modern rimfire cartridge.

All three cartridges are essentially .52 caliber; as the cartridge progressed through its development, the only change made was to alter the chamber length. The "56" part of the cartridge designation refers to the diameter of the case head. All will measure between .556″ and .565.″

The Spencer carbine had a large musket hammer and weighed about seven and a half pounds. It had a seven-shot tubular magazine that slid into the butt end of the weapon, upward into the stock. The rimfire copper-case cartridge was fed forward to the breech by a coiled spring. The downward action of the trigger guard lever dropped the breechblock, extracted the empty case, and moved a cartridge out of the magazine, into the chamber. Rifling consisted of six grooves on some specimens and three on others, both types were produced during the Civil War. The length overall measured 39 inches with a 22-inch round barrel.

The approximate rate of fire for this carbine was 10 rounds per minute. Without the tubular magazine, it could also be fired as a single-shot carbine. The single-leaf rear sight, with a sliding "V" notch elevating bar, was graduated to 800 yards. Ordnance states that this arm was sighted for 1000 yards, with an effective range of 400 yards. Battle range was from 200 to 300 yards, with a 6-inch group at 100 yards. Reloading rate using preloaded tubes was 10 to 12 seconds.

The elimination of caps, cap boxes, and other priming devices that accompanied percussion weapons was a relief to the cavalryman. Also, cartridges supplied for the Spencer were water-proof, a great improvement over the paper- or linen-wrapped cartridges. With the adoption of the Spencer carbine, toward the end of the war years, the Blakeslee patent cartridge box was issued. Containing 10 removeable tinned tubes, each holding 7 copper-cased cartridges, a 70-round total, it was the quickest loading device ever seen. The box was made of light wood, covered with leather, with 7 or 10 holes in the wood block, which contained the 7 or 10 tin tubes, each holding 7 cartridges. Francis Bannerman's 1931 catalog, page 304, shows a cavalry trooper loading his Spencer. The trooper is wearing the box in front, almost beneath his left arm; however, regulations prescribed the box should be worn on the back. A leather loop on the bottom rear part of the box was for attaching to the waist belt; an adjustable sling or strap was to suspend the box from the shoulder.

The only drawback to the Spencer noted by Ordnance officers was the dangerous way the cartridges nested in the magazine, nose to tail. If a trooper should drop the carbine butt first to the ground, the shock could unexpectedly discharge one or more shells with disastrous effects. Ordnance finally gave up on what was called a "fool killer" and began to look for a substitute. "Isn't it a pity," some Custer buffs might remark, "Custer could have saved his command at the Little Big Horn had he had the Spencer seven-shot carbine."

At Gettysburg, 3,500 Spencers were in the hands of federal cavalrymen. Jeb Stuart's cavalry, 10,000 strong, met with 4 regiments of the Michigan Brigade led by Major General Judson Kilpatrick, on June 30, 1863, at Hanover, 14 miles southeast of Gettysburg. Custer, recently promoted brigadier general, led his Spencer-armed 5th and 6th Michigan regiments, flanked by the 1st West Virginia Cavalry, against Stuart's gray-clad soldiers. The volume of fire power poured into the rebels from Custer's Spencers sent Stuart's men reeling back, to swing wide of Lee's main army toward Carlisle, 35 miles to the north. The hard-riding Stuart and his troopers did not reach Gettysburg until late evening of July 2, too late to attempt to turn the tide for Lee and the Confederacy.

Custer may have fallen at the Little Big Horn as an indirect casualty of the Army's discontinuance of the Spencer carbine. Many officers who served the Union and were familiar with the Spencer's firepower were reluctant to accept the excuses given by Ordnance for exchanging the new single-shot 45-70's for the repeating Spencers. Incredible as it may seem, the Spencers were used in the west by Indian scouts, packers and Army game hunters as late as the 1880's.

Metallic Cartridges

The *Scientific American* gives the following description of the manner of manufacturing metallic cartridges:

They are made of sheet copper. The copper is cut by a punch into a circular disk, which at the same time, by means of a punch and die, is formed into a cup shape, the punch forcing the centre of the copper disc down through a die. This operation is repeated, by means of constantly-diminishing punches and dies, until the requisite diameter and length are obtained; annealing and washing being occasionally resorted to for softening the metal and removing the oxydized scales.

When brought to the proper size and shape, the shells are placed upon a revolving spindle and cut to the required length, the upper edges being, of course, irregular in outline when the shell comes from the last die. The shell must then receive a head, or rather the head or bottom, which is now of no larger diameter than the bottom, (must be "upset") to make a receptacle for the fulminating compound, which is distributed around its circumference. To

secure this result, the shell is slipped on a spindle, having a shoulder at the proper distance as a "header" strikes a blow against the bottom, which bulges out equally all around, forming a narrow rim at the base of the shell, of larger diameter than the body of the shell itself, and hollow.

The fulminate, precisely like the explosive preparation used in percussion caps, is spread over copper plates, perforated with holes about $3/16''$ in diameter. The material lodges in the perforations, which, by a suitable device, are brought over the shells so that the fulminate may be dropped into them. As this substance is to be confined to the rim of the head, it must be distributed. For this purpose each shell is held under a vertical spindle which is made to revolve very rapidly. The end of this spindle is cut into radial teeth, similar to the congeries of radii on the face of the millstone, by which the fulminate is forced centrifugally into the rim of the shell head. This is the only process in the manufacture of these cartridges attended with danger, as the compound is of a highly explosive character. The shell is then filled with powder, the base of the projectile inserted, and the copper crimped around its base. These cartridges stand the test of rough handling, dampness, climbing, and time, better than any others yet invented. They are fast superseding all other cartridges.[15]

Sharps

The M70 carbines were altered percussion weapons that first used the .52 linen cartridge. This was the first of the Civil War alterations where the entire barrel was replaced instead of relining it to a smaller caliber as had been done with the M69 weapons.[16] The cartridge that the M69 was altered to use, was the 50-45-400.[17] This is the shorter cased, lower-power loading as used in the Springfield carbines. These alterations were issued to the cavalry for trial in May, 1871, as recommended by the St. Louis Board of 1870.[18]

The M70 rifles were also altered percussion weapons, formerly in the linen .52 caliber. These had the barrels replaced with M68 Springfield barrels in 50-70-450 caliber. These were issued for regular in-

15. Army and Navy Journal, Oct. 13, 1866, p. 120.
16. The Sharps Rifle, Sharpe-Morrow Co., p. 193.
17. Cartridges for the Collector, Datig, Vol. 1, p. 164.
18. The Sharps Rifle, Sharpe-Morrow Co., p. 193.

fantry trials in 1870 as recommended by the St. Louis Board of 1870.[19]

The caliber .50 government in centerfire versions was made in two styles, one with a .45 grain charge and a 400-grain bullet for the carbines and a 70-grain, charge 450 grain bullet for the rifles. This cartridge is an offshoot of the 50-70 rimfire.[20] The centerfire priming was of the Martin bar-anvil type, replaced by the Benét cup primers in the later issues. It was during the 1866 to 1872 era that much experimentation was done on case priming systems and, although the Benét priming was the "issue" item, in the 1870's possibly some trial ammunition also saw service.*

Occasionally troops in fighting Indians found themselves at a great disadvantage, armed with a weapon that had to be loaded each time it was fired, as was the case with the Sharps carbine, as compared with the

---

19. Ibid.

20. The American Cartridge, Suydam, p. 134.

*The government also ordered some .52 Sharps & Hankins ammunition along with some 52-70 Sharps cartridges just prior to the 1870 period, which quite probably saw service in the west in unaltered weapons.

Spencer carbine which could be fired ten times in a minute, or the Henry which held 16 cartridges. However, some veterans of the Civil War would uphold the Sharps, saying, "an experienced marksman can discharge a Sharps carbine with accuracy, not less than four times a minute, and with the use of paper cartridges, not less than three times a minute."

The Sharps single-shot, breech-loading percussion carbine was popular with the Cavalry during the Civil War and, with minor modifications, served on the western frontier. It was a .52 caliber and fired a linen cartridge by either a disc primer or percussion cap. The New Model 1859 incorporated the pellet cut-off feature, enabling a standard percussion cap to be used instead of the pellet primers. This carbine was rifled with 6 grooves, had an over-all length of 39⅛ inches, and weighed 7 pounds, 12 ounces. The breech block dropped down to open the chamber by lowering the trigger guard lever. After loading the chamber with a skin cartridge, the lever was returned to a closed position. Cocking the hammer and

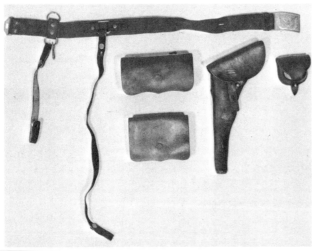

Courtesy Gordon Corbett, Jr.

Civil War saber belt and accoutrements. Top: Saber belt (buff leather). Top left: Carbine box for Spencer or Sharps. Has wooden block for metallic cartridges. Bottom left: Pistol cartridge box held 4 packets of 6 skin cartridges for model 1860 Colt. Center: Army holster for Colt. Right: Cap box for pistol percussion caps, lined with wool.

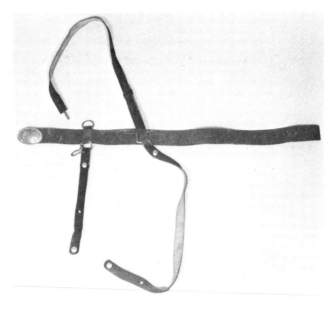

Courtesy Gordon Corbett, Jr.

Civil War issue saber belt with shoulder strap. This model was soon dropped by the Cavalry around the late 1860's. Buff leather with a U.S. brass oval dragoon buckle.

seating a percussion cap readied the arm for firing.

The front sight is a brass blade pinned to an iron lug, and the rear site, graduated to 800 yards, was the spring-base type with a single folding leaf and sliding "V" notch bar. Effective range (according to Ordnance reports) was 500 yards; battle range, 300 yards.

One of the danger points with the Sharps was the flash-back. On closing the breech, the sharp front end of the breech block cut through the paper of the inserted cartridge, exposing the powder for ignition from the percussion cap. This powder became loose and was generally ground between the block and breech, causing an additional burn when fired. Percussion caps and black powder soon fouled this carbine to such a degree that the lever could not be forced into place, making the weapon useless until cleaned. Moreover, while the Spencer and Henry carbines retained a full load for an indefinite period, the Sharps had to be loaded almost at the moment of firing. The Sharps carbine seemed completely unsuited for the demands of the Cavalry which, because of emergency situations, required effective and reliable weapons.

Springfield 45/70

The army was dissatisfied with the Model 1870 Springfield "trap-door" carbine and

the performance of the .50-70 cartridge as it lacked power and range.[21] Already, carbines with the Allin conversion[22] were issued to the cavalry for field trial, with the intention of replacing the miscellaneous assortment of arms inherited by the mounted troops as a result of the Civil War. June 30, 1871 shows the Springfield Model 1870, .50-caliber experimental, in the hands of Company K, Yorkville, South Carolina, where 28 carbines were distributed.[23] From March 1872 until March 1873, only 3 companies were issued from 14 to 21 Springfield .50 calibers on a trial basis.[24]

Under Brigadier General Alfred Terry, an Ordnance Board convened in 1872 to select a breech-loading system for rifles and carbines. Over 108 different arms were examined, including some developed in European countries. In reviewing the reports after testing these arms, 12 to 1 were in favor of the Springfield, and on May 5, 1873, specified the Springfield to be retained in the service. An Ordnance Memorandum, Number 15, was printed by the Government Printing Office in 1873, entitled, "The Proper Caliber for Small Arms," and distributed as an officers' report from the Bureau of Ordnance. One officer, who is not on record as being mentioned, wrote to the Army and Navy Journal expressing his views with deep criticism:

To the Editor of the Army and Navy Journal

Sir:

We are just in receipt of "Ordnance Memorandum Number 15 — Small Arms" . . .

The Terry Springfield Board appears to give a considerable weight to the army report in its "conclusion"-selection, page 12. After an examination of the army report most people will agree with

"Fair-Weather" belt or "Prairie Belt." As early as 1866 troops sewed leather thimbles loops to Civil War belts to evenly distribute their metallic carbine ammunition. (*Circa 1875*)

---

21. 50-70 Government center fire. A .50-caliber bullet with 70 grains of black powder.
22. The Allin (Erskine S. Allin) action had been definitely approved for retention in the service by the Board of Officers in 1868.
23. Chief of Ordnance Record Group 156, for the Seventh Cavalry, Summary Statements of Ordnance and Ordnance Stores in the hands of the troops. National Archives, Old Army Branch, Washington, D.C.
24. Ibid.

Civil War carbine sling with brass buckle.

General Townsend, as per letter to General Terry, April 29, 1872, in which he shows that the report is as perfect a muddle of opinions as a report can be . . .

Another singular fact is that not an army man finds any fault whatever with the Springfield gun, or hints at any change required in it. To read the army report it is perfection itself, and the captains of companies are only called on to pick out the defects of other systems, and to select other systems only when they have no defects, when they exceed the Springfield and the Springfield's virtues. They evidently feel that the Springfield comes to them with *authority*. No one refers to the uncouth breech block of 3¼ inches, adding that much to the length and leverage of the gun. No one refers to the cam frequently choking in firing, so as to require a kit to open the block. No one refers to the change of tactics required by the necessity of loading the piece muzzle down. No one refers to its greater number of pieces, nor to its wood-binding in the lock. No one refers to its

annoyance to the elbows of the front rank when the rear rank are coming up to an aim. This latter very important and telling defect was fully demonstrated at St.Louis Arsenal to reduce materially the percentage of hits in all firings in double ranks.

We even find some in the army to say that the Springfield is preferred for its quicker loading. This is odd. At least it differs from all official trials. Until Colonel Benton's improvement on Gun Number 99 (we are not told what that improvement of Diary, April 29, Ordnance Memorandum, was), all experiments both with Schofield and Terry Board are very decidedly in favor of the Remington. Terry Board (old soldiers firing), R. 13.02, S. 11.59 per minute. Recruits firing, R. 10.80, S. 8.51 per minute. Then comes in the Springfield Number 99, doctored by Colonel Benton, and *Mirabile!* (sic) of April 29 Standards 19.86 shots per minute. On May 3, Private Henck could only get 15.6 out of it, and on the same day five (new) soldiers only got 8.6 out of it. That is .09. more than 5 recruits got out of the undoctored gun of April 24, but still far less than any or all soldiers got out of the Remington. For *show*, on April 14, Remington No. 86 gave 19.78 per minute.

Some officers of the army report weakness of the breech in the Remington system. The artillery broke few breeches — one or two, I believe; the infantry more; the cavalry freely. This was to have been expected, from the difference of service, but was the same care used with the weapons of the different systems? The Terry Board established no test to determine the relevant strength of the breech in the different systems. We know of none tried by the army except in breaking the breeches, which all will admit is rather a crude way of getting at the thing. In adopting the Martini-Henry the British did experiment, and decided just the other way, namely, that the divided stock and the metal waist was the stronger system.

It appears that though the recoil of the Remington was one of the faults found by the army, and that of the Martini-Henry by the Caliber Board, yet no trial, after the adoption of the .45 inch caliber, was made by the Terry Board, to show recoil. We are forced to assume that it was not considered, and that the S. and

Custer's 7-shot Spencer, caliber 56/50. Next to his Remington and Springfield sporting arms this was his favorite fighting weapon.

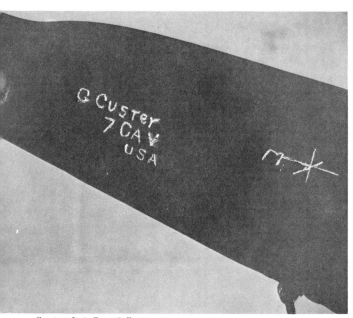

Courtesy L. A. Frost Collection

On the left side of Custer's Spencer is carved his name and regiment.

R. will kick in reverse proportion to their weight, caliber and charge being the same. Judging by the army reports, the Springfield "Rekiles Furrads."

The writer has been told that accidents have occurred in loading the Remington caused by the non-retraction of the firing pin and the consequent impact on the subsequent oversensitive cartridge in closing the breech block. No reports of this kind come from the army, none from the Terry Board, none from the Caliber Board, none from the Schofield Board. No experiments were done by the Terry or Schofield Boards to show the relevant injuries that would result from such an accident in the different systems subject to it, as the R. and S. systems. In either the shock in closing the breech block would be about the same; reliability of non-retraction of the firing-pin about the same in both systems. Though the possibility of such an accident cannot be denied, I strongly suspect they have never happened out of the Springfield Armory.

Upon the whole, we sympathize with the Board. When they have to determine among so many things that are good — the Russian-Berdan; the Spanish and our own Navy Remington; the beloved of the British, their Martini-Henry, with its flat trajectory; the Springfield, with its receptacle service proof and the whole American Ordnance Corps to back it; the Chassepot, that put France at the head of the world arms; the Zundnadeigewehr, that beat the French; the Elliott, the Peabody, etc., etc. But what is a little singular is to find army answers differing so much as to what should constitute a good or the best weapons. Some will reject a whole system for what is evidently but the accident of imperfect workman-

ship or of a non-adaptation of some of the parts (not vital to the system), to some service. Some will reject all bolt guns, *vide* the Schofield Board. Some will recommend the quickest loader, and some will recommend (when in doubt), *vide* the Terry Board played a trump, that which is in use . . .

To show how men will like what they are accustomed to, we would relate that one day during the war we remarked to a private of a regiment armed with Enfield rifles, that it was to be regretted that the country could not arm its soldiers with our own neat, light (muzzle-loading) Springfield. He put on a knowing look, rolled his quid into the other cheek, and patting his cumberous shooting-iron, said, "Yer can't make our boys think so" . . .

Ronervog[25]

The Ordnance Summary, first quarter, March 1874, statements show that the Seventh Cavalry was already anticipating the new trap-door Springfields, caliber 45-70; however, the record does not show issuance of this carbine until June 1874, when Companies B, G and L, stationed at Fort Abraham Lincoln, received 83 carbines each. By the third quarter, September 30, 1874, all companies of the Seventh Cavalry had in their possession the 45-70 Springfields.[26]

Year	Carbines Issues	Officers' Rifles	Serial Numbers
1873	1,942		1-1,949
1874	10,874		35,224
1875	7,211	10	60,327
1876	2	115	74,215

A description of the Carbine Model 1873:

Caliber . . . . 45-70 Government, center fire .45-caliber bullet, 70 grains of black powder with a .405-grain lead bullet.

Barrel . . . . 21¾ inch, round mild steel barrel with 3 grooves for riflings, with one turn every 22 inches.

Metal . . . . All metal dark blue.

Weight . . . . 7 pounds, 9 ounces.

25. Army and Navy Journal, January 17, 1874, p. 362.

26. Under provisions of Act of Congress, June 6, 1872, a board of officers of which Brigadier General Alfred H. Terry was president, was convened in New York City, September 3, 1872, for tests of breech-loading systems with view to adoption of a modern breech-loading arm in military service. The board was in session until May 5, 1873, and after "exhaustive" examination and trial of over 100 arms, including those adopted by the first military powers of Europe, the board recommended the retention of the Springfield breech-loading system for the military service of the U.S. The proceedings of the board were approved May 20, 1873.

Lock-plate . . . .   Unbeveled and flush with stock.
                                           Eagle, "U.S. Springfield" and
                                           "1873" in 3 horizontal lines.
Hammer . . . .   More rounded than the Model 1870.
                                           Strengthened.
Ejector Stud . . . .   Most screw heads were rounded off.
Screws . . . .   Enlarged and moved forward.
Rear Sight . . . .   Marked "Model 1873."
Breech-Block . . . .   Stacking swivel attached to under-
Stacking Swivel . . . .   side of barrel band.

The Seventh Cavalry had already begun to find fault with the Model 73 Springfield. One of the main drawbacks was the breech block. When the loaded piece dangled at the side of the mounted man, the block was liable to be thrown open and the cartridge lost. Thus the soldier would be uncertain if his piece was loaded while galloping into action. It was also difficult for a mounted man to load the Springfield when his horse was in motion, because of its peculiar mechanism. The ejector spring often failed to eject the cartridge shell, leaving it partially pulled out. Should the ejector spring cut through the head of the cartridge, or the head become detached from the shell after the piece was fired, the soldier was left powerless until he picked the empty shell out with the point of a knife, if he was lucky enough to have one on hand.[27] During cavalry operations in the field, the men did not have much time to clean their carbines therefore, the piece fouled frequently.

Another contributing factor with the failure of extracting shells was in the shells themselves. During rapid fire, the breech became foul and greasy, cartridges often swelling in the bore and jamming. The basic cause was in the poor and soft quality of brass making up the cartridle.[28] With government cutbacks in expenditures for the army, it is no wonder that other problems could have developed.

After the Custer battle, there was much controversy over the performance of the 45-70 Springfield. Its functioning and durability had not previously been questioned, but it had run its full field test against superior odds of Indians, much more conclusive than Ordnance tests made in the spring of 1873, when an "exhaustive examination" of this arm was conducted. In his report after the battle, Major Marcus A. Reno expresses his views on the carbine:

27. Army and Navy Journal, November 4, 1876, p. 203.
28. Ibid.

Courtesy Author's Collection
(Reading left to right) .45 caliber pistol cartridges (2), .45 caliber Schofield cartridges (2), .44 caliber "Henry" flat nose (2) (long case and short case), .52 caliber Sharps linen cartridge (1), Spencer 56/60 copper case cartridge, Spencer shot-wood "Sabot", Spencer shot, full length case, 50/70 Benet inside primed (1) Carbine, 50/70 Benet inside primed (1) Rifle, 45/70 Inside primed blank cartridge (1), 45/70 Rifle and carbine inside primed (2).

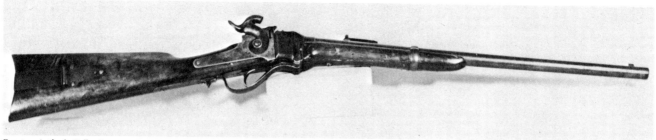

Courtesy Author's Collection

Sharps carbine taking the .52 linen cartridge.

Headquarters Seventh Cavalry
Camp on the Yellowstone River
July 11, 1876

General S. V. Benét
Chief of Ordnance, U.S.A.

I have the honor to report that in the engagement of the 25 and 26 of June 1876 between the 7th Cav & the hostile Sioux that out of 380 carbines in my command, six were rendered unserviceable in the following manner, (there were more rendered unserviceable by being struck with bullets) failure of the breech block to close, leaving a space between the head of the cartridge & and end of the block, & when the piece was discharged, & the block thrown open, the head of the cartridge was pulled off & the cylinder remained in the chamber, where with the means at hand it was impossible to extract it. I believe this is a radical defect, & in the hands of hastily organized troops would lead to the most disastrous results. The defect results, in my opinion in two ways — in the manufacture of the gun the breech block is in many instances so made that it does not fit snug up to the head of the cartridge, after the cartridge is sent home, & it has always been a question

in my mind whether the manner in which it revolves into its place does not render a close contact almost impossible to be made. Another reason is that the dust, always an element to be considered on the battlefield, prevents the proper closing of the breech block, & the same result is produced. There may be a want of uniformity in the flange of the head of the cartridge which would also render the action of the extractor null, altho' when the shell was left in the chamber the head would not be torn off.

I also observed another bad fault of the system altho' it did not render the guns unservicable, viz, the weight of the breech block is such that the hinges on which it revolves is very soon loosened, giving to the block a lateral motion, that prevents its closing.

I can also state that the blowing up of the breech block was a contingency that was patent to members of the Board which adopted the system & induced strong opposition to it, in the part of a minority. I send you these observations made during a most terrific battle, under circumstances which would induce men to fire with recklessness, as one's capture was certain death & torture, & the men fully ap-

(Left) 45/70 blank cartridges. (Right) Revolver ball cartridges, caliber .45.

preciated the result of falling into the hands of the indians, & were not as cool perhaps as they would have been fighting a civilized foe. An indian scout who was with that portion of the Regt. which Custer took into battle, in relating what he saw in that part of the battle, says that from his hiding place he could see the men sitting down under fire & working at their guns, a story that finds confirmation in the fact that officers, who afterwards examined the battlefield, as they were burying the dead, found knives with broken blades lying near the dead bodies.

I also desire to call attention to the fact, that my loss would have been less had I been provided with some instrument similar to the "Trowel bayonet," & I am sure had an opponent of that arm been present with my command on the night of June 25th, he would have given his right hand for 50 bayonets, I had but 3 spades & 3 axes & with them loosened ground which the men threw into piles in front of them with tin cups & such other articles as could in any way serve this same purpose.[29]

Very Resp'y
M. A. Reno
Maj. 7th Cav'y.
Cmdg. Regt.

---

29. Army and Navy Journal, August 19, 1876, p. 26.

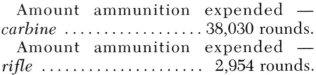

Amount ammunition expended — *carbine* . . . . 38,030 rounds.
Amount ammunition expended — *rifle* . . . . 2,954 rounds.

The 45-70 rifle-carbine round was first made in quantity in January, 1874, and underwent many changes between then and 1880.

Cartridge Data

Drawn copper case, center fire-inside primed using a cup anvil in a reinforced head. Bullet weight was 405 grain, lead with a flat-base-round-nose configuration. The bullet was 3 grooved (lube grooves) and was inside lubricated. In the late 1870's, many experiments were conducted in search of an easily reloaded case. In 1879, cases with Berdan priming (1- and 3-hole) and Boxer priming were tested. The inside-primed case was replaced by the Boxer-primed case in 1882. In addition to the Frankfort Arsenal ammunition 3 com-

Photo by E. L. Reedstrom

Trooper J. J. Narus, in the field with the 2nd Reactivated Cavalry, loads a Sharps carbine with a skin cartridge.

Photo by E. L. Reedstrom

Trooper Narus forgets to close patch box (box is open) and stored percussion caps were scattered everywhere.

Springfield Carbine, model 1873 ("Trap-Door") caliber 45/70. Original front-sight has been replaced. Fore-arm band has the stacking swivel, however, it was little used in the Cavalry, and later dropped altogether on carbines. Total length 41.313 inches, weighing approx. 6½ pounds.

mercial versions of the 45-70-405 were made, by Winchester, Union Metallic Cartridge Company and the United States Cartridge Company. The commercial cartridges used both Berdan and Boxer priming depending on the company and the priming systems they preferred. Standard bullet makeup was 16 parts lead to 1 part tin, compressed.

Ballistics

M. V. for the 405-grain bullet was listed at an average 1315 FPS for the original round. The 1882 separate-primed rounds showed a M. V. of 1364 FPS, 1330 FPS at 50 feet from the muzzle.

Comparison between the 56-50 Spencer weapon-cartridge combination and the 45-70 weapon and ammunition:

	Spencer	*Springfield*
caliber bullet	.50	.45
bullet weight	350 to 400 grain	405 grain
ignition weight	rimfire	centrefire (inside prime)
powder weight	43 to 45 grain	70 grain
muzzle velocity	unknown	1315 FPS
muzzle energy	unknown	unknown
weapon	repeater, magazine fed	single shot-breech load*

(While both of the above are unknown, they could be figured out. A glance will show that the 45-70 had a substantial advantage in raw hitting power, based on bullet weight and powder charge. The Spencer had little going for it besides a larger cross-sectional density (weight-caliber combination).

---

*Author's Note: Based solely on what I have seen of the 2 weapons, the Springfield would have an advantage over the Spencer in long-range, selective-fire. However, the Spencer, with its repeating action and shorter construction, would certainly have been more useful at the Battle of the Little Big Horn.

The following official reports with reference to the complaints made by cavalry officers on the Springfield carbine, were published in the Journal, Aug. 19:

Ordnance Notes — LVI Washington, August 17, 1876
Headquarters Military Division of the Missouri
Office of Chief Ordnance Officer
Chicago, Ill., August 2, 1876
Chief of Ordnance, Washington, D. C.:
SIR: As telegraphed to you to-day, Colonel Mackenzie requested Winchester rifles for the Fourth Cavalry. I informed the Lieutenant-General that we did not furnish these arms, but that by using the rifle cartridge in the carbine some causes of complaint would be removed; or, if this was not sufficient, the calibre .45 rifle could be issued to replace the carbine, thus making the regiment mounted infantry... I quote this as an illustration of the dissatisfaction with the carbine; and while it is impossible to gratify all the caprices of officers, yet the very general complaints at the inefficiency of the carbine must be based on some real grounds. Its defects are inaccuracy and short range. It may be said that it is not expected to be as complete as the rifle in these respects, but the nature of our cavalry service demands equal capabilities in both arms, and I think this can be obtained by adopting, instead of the carbine, a longer arm, of the dimensions of the officers' model of Springfield (sporting) rifle and using the 70 grain cartridge in it. I would suggest setting the front and rear sights as far apart as possible, the rear sight being on top of the small of the stock. In general, I would suggest getting out of the gun everything possible, running the arm to its extreme limits of range and accuracy. This model should also be provided with a ramrod, to remove cartridge shells which the extractor fails to eject, and to clean the arm.

Very respectfully,
your obedient servant,
J. W. Reilly, Captain of Ordnance
Chief Ordnance Officer.

(First Indorsement.)
Ordnance Office, Washington, August 4, 1876.
Respectfully referred to the Commanding Officer of National Armory for report.
  S. V. Benét, Brigadier-General,
  Chief of Ordnance.

(Second Indorsement.)
National Armory, August 8, 1876.
Respectfully returned to the Chief of Ordnance.

For Captain Reilly's information I would state that the most powerful Winchester rifle for frontier service carries a cartridge of 40 grains of powder and 200 grains of lead; the extreme range for which this arm is sighted is 300 yards. The cartridge of the Springfield carbine contains 55 grains of powder and 400 grains of lead, and is sighted for an extreme range of 1,300 yards. The penetration of the Winchester rifle in pine, at a distance of 100 yards, is less than one half of that of the Springfield carbine at the same distance, and not so much as the penetration of the latter arm at the distance of one-half mile. I hope in the course of to-day or to-morrow to forward a report of a very careful test of the Winchester rifle now used on the frontier.

As regards a ramrod for the carbine, I can only say that it had always been customary to issue wooden rods with carbine in the ratio of one to ten. It would appear from late experience that every carbine should be provided with rod. I would recommend for this purpose a rod made in sections, screwed or hinged together after the manner of the one submitted from this Armory March 13, 1875, and referred to in my letter of that date. Such a rod could easily be carried in the soldier's pocket, or in some part of his equipment . . . Knowing the Springfield rifle and carbine to be more powerful and accurate than any arms of their kind ever before issued to our troops, I am at a loss to understand the "general complaints of their inefficiency" to which Captain Reilly refers. I have carefully examined many of the bi-monthly reports, where commanders of companies are required not only to report their opinions of the arms in their charge, but to specify in detail each and every defect of arms and ammunition that comes under their observation. So far as I know the complaint of inefficient range has not been made in a single instance in the nine years that the Springfield system has been in use. On the contrary, a reduction of the charge has been asked for on the ground of severe recoil. I hope that Ordnance officers serving with troops will make personal investigations into all complaints of defects of arms and ammunition, and that speciments of defective arms and ammunition will be forwarded to this Armory for further examination. It is important to know whether the trouble is in the arm or in the ammunition, or in both. I would also call attention to the importance of officers reporting, in their bi-monthly reports, the date of the fabrication of the ammunition. This point seems to have been omitted, in some instances, when it had a very important bearing in investigating causes of the defects complained of.
  J. G. Benton
  Lieutenant-Colonel, Commanding.[30]

THE SABRE

Pomp and ceremony kept the sabre in the ranks of the cavalry for many years. In the Civil War there were numerous sabre charges,[31] but on the frontier it saw little action except for dress parades and fancy balls. It was designed to hang on the left side of the cavalryman during conflict so that the right hand could draw either the sabre or pistol, leaving the left hand controlling the reins. The light cavalry sabre weighed 3 pounds, 7 ounces, totaling 42.35 inches in over-all length.

During the war, many officers contracted a prejudice against use of the sabre and in some regiments, mostly Confederate, it was entirely laid aside, charges being done with the pistol. The soldiers also had little or no confidence in the sabre, mainly because they were never taught to use it properly. The system of sabre exercise, as laid down in the tactics, was radically bad, and the men never learned to fence properly. The opinions of a colonel generally regulated the matter for his regiment. If he were an enthusiastic swordsman, he would infuse the same spirit into his men, and such regiments depended on their sabres with confidence. But few colonels on either side were swordsmen. The sabre required constant practice to keep one's hand in, and most cavalry officers were entirely deficient in that practice.

Many officers advocated the pistol as a charging weapon, in preference to the

---

30. Army and Navy Journal, Aug. 26, 1876, p. 43.

31. The Surgeon-General's Report shows that, out of an aggregate of 253,142 cases of wounds analyzed and recorded in that office, only 906 sabre cuts or bayonet stabs were reported during the Civil War; of these, only 52 resulted in deaths. This gives a percentage of wounds at one wound in every 279 and one death in every 4,868. And, of the sabre and bayonet wounds, only one in every 17 resulted in death.

Drawing by E. L. Reedstrom
Model 1872 Cavalry Officers Saber. Not an issued item.

Drawing by E. L. Reestrom
U.S. Regulation Light Cavalry Saber, Model 1860, issued to the enlisted men.

sabre. They insisted that a pistol shot kills, while a sabre cut only wounds. Some officers held the sabre to be useless. In one regiment, it was boasted that they never had drawn a sabre in a charge and never would charge with anything but pistols.

But, in all instances during the war in which the sabre proved ineffective, it may safely be asserted that it was because of want of fencing practice and blunt sabres. The latter cause, as much as the former, conduced to this want of confidence in the sabre. The men shrank from using a weapon with which they never had encountered a foe, and they also knew that the weapons would not cut.

It was strange that, after all that was said and written about sharp sabres by everyone who has written on the subject of cavalry, the sabres remained as blunt as ever. Sabres were issued blunt enough that they could not cut a slab of bacon. The steel was hard, but grindstones were not to be found. The soldiers soon lost all confidence in the weapon, and much preferred the revolver.

If the War Department had required in all contracts that sabres should be sharp enough to cut a sheet of paper by striking it on the sword lightly, the American cavalry would have been revolutionized.

If whetstones were furnished to the men, a sabre issued sharp would have been kept sharp. But, as it was, the men could not get them sharp. Soldiers and officers stood at grindstones turned by steam and tried to grind an Ames sabre, for over an hour of the hardest kind of work. Authorities held that, if sharpened while in soft temper, at the factory, the hardening temper subsequently received would have left the sabres sharp, and easily kept so.

There is little doubt that the men would have kept them sharp. Soldiers were fond and proud of good weapons and generally took good care of them. All men are apt to be vain of bodily strength and skill. It gave a man a braver feeling to cut down an adversary than to shoot him and, by just so much as he trusted his sword, his morale was raised.

If the men had sabres half as sharp as ordinary cutting knives, which they might have had without added expense, there would not be so many complaints of "useless sabres." A sabre should have been kept as sharp as a razor. It could have been done; it should have been enforced. Fancy our men, armed with razors three feet long. What ghastly wounds they could have inflicted on an enemy, when every forceful slash would have opened a gash a foot long; and how reluctant an enemy would be to fight such men, however well armed. But the greatest superiority of the sabre would have been its moral effect.

THE PISTOL

During the Civil War, the revolver became a necessity for every cavalryman, along with the saber and carbine. While in mounted motion, the trooper had to choose which weapon to rely upon. Although the saber cannot reach beyond the horse's nose, the soldier could put himself on equal terms with his enemy with the pistol. The pistol was used with much accuracy in many Civil War conflicts. The heavy pistol had an additional function besides firepower; when empty, it was used as a club. In many cases where the saber was used, the damage was slight, for it was exceptional to "run through" an opponent.

Courtesy Author's Collection
Remington New Model .44 caliber percussion revolver, six shot, single action. Total length 13¾ inches, weight 2 pounds 14 ounces. New Model design prevented the cylinder pin from being entirely withdrawn from the frame.

Had the pistol more often been used as a club instead of the saber, it would have dealt a more deadly blow.[32]

It was only during the Civil War that the pistol proved its necessity and efficiency. Between 1873 and 1894, the Army's experi-

ence in Indian warfare showed the pistol playing a minor part.[33] The reason is this: the cavalry relied heavily on mobility. During running fights with Indians, the distance between cavalry and hostiles was usually far beyond range of pistol or car-

32. U.S. Cavalry Journal, Oct., 1905; Vol. XVI, p. 183.

33. Ibid., p. 185.

Courtesy Author's Collection
Colt model 1860, .44 caliber percussion revolver, 6 shot, single action. Total length is 14 inches, weight is 2 pounds 11 ounces. Colt Manufacturing Company produced 200,000 of these revolvers, including the civilian model, from 1860 into 1873.

bine. In many cases, the trooper would have traded both weapons for one long-ranged rifle.

The single action, percussion-type pistols were magnificent weapons. The fine performance during the Civil War won for the revolver a high rating in American military development but, in spite of their reputation and excellence, they became outdated with the advent of the metallic cartridge.

Custer's arrival at Fort Riley in November, 1866 found the soldiers armed with various models and calibers. Among these were the Colt and Remington percussion pistols, but in .44 caliber. The Army Starr was also a favorite, but was in less supply than the Colt and Remington. Most pistols had a barrel length of approximately 8 inches and weighed up to 3 pounds. All were single action, employed paper cartridges and were six-shot.

Colt's first successful conversion employed a patent granted to Charles B. Richards on July 25, 1871. This patent converted the 1860 Army percussion to the .44-caliber metallic cartridge, and its design led the way to the .44-caliber, open-top Model 1872, finally resulting in the .45-caliber Army Model of 1873. The Colt

Model 1872 sold widely in Mexico and Southern states because of an abundance of rimfire ammunition available there. In 1872, Colt won approval for the .45-caliber solid-frame Model 1873 from the Ordnance Testing Board. Immediately after this, Colt began disposing of the obsolete 1872 Model.

Early in 1874, Custer's soldiers were issued the new Colt Model 1873, caliber .45.[34] Colt and Remington percussion models were turned in and exchanged for the newer model. For many years after the Army's adoption of the Colt .45, the percussion pistol was commonly a second weapon in the private possession of officers. A report, "Summary of Ordnance and Ordnance Stores in the Hands of the Troops," during the first quarter ending March 31, 1875, showed 64 Remington percussion, caliber-.44, still remaining on hand in Company D, Seventh Cavalry, at Fort Totten, D. T.[35]

When the percussions were becoming

---

34. Summary of Ordnance and Ordinance Stores in the Hands of Troops in Service of the U.S., 2nd Quarter, June, 1874; Colt .45 issued to all units except Company D in the field and Company I in the field.
35. Records of the Office of the Chief of Ordnance, Record Group Number 156.

Courtesy Author's Collection
Colt single action Army revolver, caliber .45, model 1872, with a 7.5 inch round barrel, its total length is 12.5 inches, weight 2 pounds 5 oz.

obsolete, they were sold at a much reduced price. The old "horse pistol" was not always happily exchanged for a cartridge revolver. One question was, "How long a service life can these new cartridge revolvers withstand, in comparison to the old reliable percussion, especially in the Cavalry Corps?" Company Returns indicated the average service life of a cavalry percussion pistol was from 4 to 5 years. This was calculated for times of active service in war and with ordinary repairs.[36] The new Colt Army revolver, caliber .45, had yet to prove itself.

An initial order for 8,000 Colt pistols for Cavalry use was placed by the government in 1873. The cartridge was a 250 lead grain bullet backed by 30 grains of FFg powder instead of the factory 40, and made at government arsenals.[37] A report to the Chief of Ordnance for 1873 discloses:

"The general and constant demand from the field for revolvers using metallic ammunition, together with the urgent necessity for some improved weapon to replace the revolvers previously used in service using the paper or linen cartridge, caused early efforts to be made to reach a solution to this very difficult problem. After trials in the field of two kinds, and experimental trials of improved models, this Bureau recommended for approval the purchase of a sufficient number of the Colts to supply the cavalry arm of the service. They are now being made, and it is hoped that the whole number will be in the hands of troops before the next spring."[38]

Throughout many publications, photographs in many instances have been mislabeled and incorrectly dated. This makes it difficult for the researcher to accurately associate subject matter in the photograph to a specific time period especially when the photograph is the only piece of evidence on hand. Such is the case with one photograph showing General Custer in a sitting position with a map on his knee, a white man and several Indian scouts surrounding him. Headquarters tent is in the background with dogs lying casually about in the foreground and the Indian scouts are each holding what appears to be nickel-plated Colt revolvers. In many instances, this photo has been labeled, "Black Hills Expedition, 1874." According to a reliable authority this photo should read, "Yellowstone Expedition, 1873."[39] Much discussion has been brought up about the nickel-plated Colt revolver as being issued to scouts prior to that period, and it does seem that the scouts have these weapons. An article published in the *American Rifleman*, May, 1970, states: "Of the 37,000 Colt Single Action revolvers purchased by the U.S. Government, the least-known and rarest variation is the Indian Scout and Police Issue. Its only basic difference from the Cavalry Model, which made up 31,800 of the total, was that it was nickel plated. One authority claims this was done as a rust deterrent because the Indians generally neglected to take care of their arms. . . . The three issues, Cavalry, Artillery and Indian Scout Police, were bought by the Government between 1873 and 1891. The *first acquired* under these transactions *actually reached Federal hands in 1874*, not 1873. Only 6,000 Government arms are believed to have been among the first 30,000 Single Actions manufactured. Of the *200 made in 1973*, none were bought by the Government. . . . We know that only about one-fourth of the 114,000 single actions produced between 1873 and 1891 went to the Government."

In John E. Parsons' and John S. du Mont's "Firearms in the Custer Battle," page 23-24, the same interpretation shows up, identifying the "Yellowstone" photograph of Cus-

---

36. Army and Navy Journal, Jan. 19, 1867, p. 343.

37. Cartridges of the World, F. C. Barnes, Gun Digest, Chicago, 1965, p. 172. The Book of Pistols and Revolvers, W. H. B. Smith, Stackpole, p. 483. History of the Colt Revolver, C. T. Haven and F. A. Belden, Bonanza Books, N.Y., p. 145.

38. Reports of Chief of Ordnance, 1873, p. 10, Serial 1599.

39. Lawrence A. Frost's "The Custer Album," page 119 (Superior Publ. Co.)

ter and his scouts as being taken on the Black Hills Expedition, 1874. If the American Rifleman article can be taken as 100% correct, and the Indian Scouts in the photo are indeed armed with the nickel-plated, Indian Scout and Police Issue Colt Revolver, then the photo in the "Custer Album" by Dr. Frost is captioned incorrectly as to date and place, because the plated Colts in question were not issued until 1874. If, on the other hand the Colts are not plated, then Dr. Frosts' photo labeled "Yellowstone Expedition, 1873" can possibly be correct.

With due respect to all authors, their grounds for labeling this photograph with different dates may stem from some unknown authoritative material. It is quite possible that the scouts do have plated Colts, as it certainly appears that way in the photograph; however, factory records of Government purchases below the serial numbers of 30,000 were destroyed by fire many years ago, and further research on the subject will have to be undertaken before a total acceptance of the above captions.

Colt's only rival was the Schofield modification of the Smith and Wesson .44 (American Model).[40] The War Department's Small Arms and Accouterments Board met in St. Louis, June 10, 1870. Submitted to this board were a variety of long arms, percussion pistols and pistols altered to cartridge, bayonets, cartridge boxes, infantry equipment, and other incidentals. Not one example of a Colt model, altered or otherwise, was among the pistols submitted. The Board selected, in order of relative merit, the Remington single shot, the Smith and Wesson, and one of the Remington pistol alterations.[41] The Chief of Ordnance, Brevet Major General A. B. Dyer, whose findings were approved by the Secretary of War, recommended 1,000 of each pistol mentioned to be issued for comparative trials in frontier service.

The 1874 Ordnance Testing Board was assembled by the new Chief of Ordnance, Brigadier General Stephen Vincent Benét, to examine further samples of pistols on their individual merits. Both Smith and Wesson and Colt were in competition and rigid tests were made of both pistols in firing, sanding and rust trials. In a comparison test with Colt, the Smith and Wesson Schofield was loaded on horseback. At a hard gallop, an expert horseman was able to eject from his pistol 6 empty shells in 26 seconds, whereas the Colt took 60 seconds. This was noted by the Board in reporting tests of both pistols on June 30, 1874. Colt won over the Schofield model whose only superiority noted was its speed in ejecting empty cartridges. Colt was found to have fewer, simpler and stronger parts, and was much easier to dismantle for cleaning.[42] However, the Board recommended the Schofield model for further trials in the hands of troops, and that a limited number of these pistols be purchased. This recommendation was approved by the Secretary of War on July 3, 1874, and 3,000 were chambered for the .45-caliber center-fire cartridge with 28 grains of black powder and a bullet of 230 grains.[43]

Colt was recognized "king of pistols" in all parts of the world, and now, under the new regime of fixed ammunition, "Colt's New Model 1873 Army Metallic Cartridge Revolving Pistol" had beaten all competitors, and stood at the head of all cartridge pistols as the Army's weapon, *par excellence.* During the Civil War, it was the old model of Colt pistols that had virtually superseded all others for army use in all parts of the world, the only objection being its high price.

40. Army and Navy Journal, Mar. 18, 1876, p. 514.
41. Army and Navy Journal, Jul. 23, 1870, p. 768.

42. The Peacemaker and Its Rivals, John E. Parsons, William Morrow & Co., 1950, p. 31. Also, "Research Review," Little Big Horn Associates, Winter 1969, Vol. 3, No. 4, p. 6 (Par. B).
43. Ibid., pp. 31-32.

Shortly after the Army's adoption of the new service revolver, the .45 Colt began to acquire odd and expressive names. To the soldier, it was a "Thumb-buster" or an "Army .45." To the lawman, it was a "Peacemaker" and "Equalizer." When it got around to the civilian, it was tagged a "Hog-leg" or a "Plow-handle." Regardless of the name, the .45 Colt was accepted gladly by those who had use for its block-busting effect.

This new weapon soon won the approval of most cavalrymen compared to his old percussion pistol. The revolution effected by the introduction of metallic ammunition caused the old "Colt" to disappear at last. It shot as well as ever and, for frontier use, where powder and lead were more easily procurable than fixed ammunition, it retained favor. In the pistol trade, the percussion was being pushed out of the general market by its younger competitors, only to regain ground by a change of model suiting it to metallic cartridges.[44] Those in the habit of using the old model Colt knew the reason for its preference by practical men over all others. This was its accuracy. It was a weapon a man could stake his life upon in a fight. It shot wherever it was pointed and hit its target. The great pistol shots of the frontier and in the Army could put 6 shots into a telegraph post when passing it at a full gallop. These old-time marksmen all used "Colt's Navy" or the "Colt's Army," and had a prejudice against later pistols.

The trooper was repeatedly reminded that proper care of his Colt metallic cartridge pistol was important; with constant care, it would last the soldier almost indefinitely. The pistol served the trooper in every type of climate, and was certain to rust and foul when subjected to rain and snow. Generally, the trooper took care in oiling his weapon and keeping it in top shape. This was one of the general attitudes some men took in garrison. But it was a different story for the men while on bivouac in some remote area; there, many resented the time spent cleaning the pistol and felt that it was up to the manufacturer to produce a pistol to cope with all conditions.

The greatest fault with any rifle or pistol is the owner. Most gunsmithing problems are traced to the individual who tinkered with the mechanism or otherwise mistreated the weapon. Lead and black powder act as a fouling agent and can build up in the intricate mechanism. The Colt was a strong weapon, and at times might function despite deliberate abuse. To guard against such abuse, sergeants and officers held frequent pistol inspections, reporting on any malfunctions found in the companies.

Screws in the Colt were seldom tightened, and only after lengthy firings was this necessary. The chief objection to the pistol was its ejector, which often blew off after firing for some time, and was slow in ejecting spent cartridges.[45] The chief objection to the ejector-tube housing was that it frequently loosened. The housing was held to the barrel with one small screw (ejector-tube screw), which often came loose after a series of firings. To correct this, the trooper had to keep a screwdriver on hand or use the point of his knife to tighten the screw.

Other major problems would include: One, a broken sear and bolt spring, which the soldier could replace. Two, a broken arm from the bolt, which locks the cylinder in place and must be replaced by a gunsmith. Three, breaking the mainspring, which drives the hammer forward. The cylinder bolt, during the pistol's constant revolving action, wears down, leaving the cylinder shaky or loose. If the cylinder does not align with the barrel after the hammer is pulled back for firing, the pistol may burst; if out of alignment slightly, lead slivers will eject, possibly injuring the hand of the

44. The Peacemaker and Its Rivals, John E. Parsons, Wm. Morrow & Co., N.Y., 1950, p. 158 (see ad).

45. Cavalry Journal, Vol. 15, p. 680, The Colt Revolver by Captain A. Gray.

trooper.[46] One might add that if the trooper ever took note of these items mentioned, his pistol may have very well lasted him the duration of his enlistment.

The Army adopted this pistol for its reliable action, and continued it in service until 1894, when the double-action Colt was introduced and adopted. The Peacemaker was also used by many famed frontier fighters as the court of last resort. It was a vital stabilizing factor for the pioneers in settlements along the new Western horizons.

The new Colt pistol was designed for the .45-caliber metallic cartridge ball. This cartridge was made at Frankford Arsenal as early as 1873 and had progressed by 1874 from the Colt length-case (approximately 1.26 inches) to the shorter Smith and Wesson Schofield model length (approximately 1.10 inches), which would chamber in both

revolvers, Colt and the Smith and Wesson. The first order for Schofield-length caliber .45 ammunition was issued to Frankford Arsenal on August 20, 1874. This was a copper casing, generally referred to as gilding metal or Bloomfield Gilding Metal, inside primed, straight case, rimmed, and frequently referred to as a "cup anvil" with a reinforced head. This successful invention of the self-primed metallic-case cartridge greatly simplified the construction of breech-loading small arms.[47]

Colt .45, inside primed (Colt length)			
(Long)	Rim	.404″	For Colt Army Revolver,
	Head	.475″	Model 1872. Some refer-
	Neck	.480″	ences say it was issued in
	Bullet	.450″	1873 and had a 250-grain bul-
	Case	1.285″	let. Casing "copper", inside
	Overall	1.608″	primed, with no headstamp;
			bullet flat nosed.

---

46. The author has had much experience with early model Colt's caliber .45; his knowledge of gunsmithing has helped in this chapter.

47. History of Modern U.S. Military Small Arms Ammunition, F. W. Hackley, W. H. Woodin, E. L. Scranton; Vol. 1, 1880-1939, Macmillan Co., N.Y., p. 10.

Courtesy National Archives

Gatling Gun at Washington Arsenal viewed from the rear, May 26, 1866.

Colt .45, inside primed (S & W Schofield length)

(Short)			
Rim	.524″		Introduced in 1874 to chamber both the Colt and the Schofield chamber (Smith & Wesson). First order was issued to Frankford Arsenal on August 20, 1874. Initially it was made with a 230-grain bullet. Casing "copper," inside primed with no headstamp; bullet flat nosed.
Head	.481″		
Neck	.477″		
Bullet	.450″		
Case	1.110″		
Overall	1.420″		

THE GATLING GUN

Military historians and armchair Indian War buffs have never quite forgiven Custer for refusing the 3 Gatling guns offered by General Alfred Terry, commander of the Department of Dakota, or the additional force of the Second Cavalry battalion prior to the march to the Little Big Horn. Custer refused the Gatling guns, it is said, because they were drawn by condemned horses, and would slow and impede his march.[48] More likely, Custer's refusal was not because the Gatling guns were hauled by condemned horses, but because of the terrain which he confronted. Second Lieutenant W. H. Low, 20th Infantry, had problems with the Gatlings upsetting several times on the march. Custer sought and obtained permission to have the battery of Gatling guns detached from his regiment and the battery was accordingly ordered to join General Gibbon on the north bank of the Yellowstone.[49]

The Gatling gun had proved itself and played a decisive part in a fight against Comanches and Kiowas on August 30, 1874 at Mulberry Creek in El Llano Estacado, the "Staked Plains" of West Texas. From ambush, some 200 Indians charged Brevet Major General Nelson A. Miles' Indian Territory Expedition, almost destroying an advanced party of scouts in the first assault. Lieutenant James W. Pope, commanding a Gatling gun battery, moved into action swiftly, scattering the attacking warriors. On other occasions, the Gatlings were reported to "have done splendidly" in brief encounters with Indians.

The Little Big Horn terrain was quite different. Much of the area shown on maps studied by Custer was unsuited for wagons, or for wheeled Gatlings pulled by condemned cavalry horses and their ammunition limbers. The ground was hilly and the trail was undetermined. Like wagons, the Gatlings might straggle behind, placing the command in a dangerous position. Every seasoned officer knew that mobility was the key to Indian warfare. In order to fight Indians, you had to find them. One of the main reasons Custer ordered pack trains instead of wagons to carry food and ammunition was because of the fast pace needed. He proved his point by arriving at the Little Big Horn on June 25 instead of the proposed June 26.

General Terry's confidential telegram to General Sheridan, July 2, 1876, reads in part:

"The plan adopted was the only one that promised to bring the infantry into action and I desired to make sure of things by getting up every available man. I offered Custer the battery of Gatling guns but he declined it saying that it might embarrass him; that he was strong enough without it."[50]

Custer's attitude toward Gatlings was different in 1874, when he commanded the expedition into the Black Hills. In a letter to a friend, Custer wrote:

Fort Lincoln Dakota, May 19th, 1874.
My Dear Laurence . . .
. . . I will have ten full companies of the best Cavalry in Uncle Sam's service, a detachment of Indian scouts taken from (sic) friendly to the whites and

---

48. Custer would have known these horses were condemned because of their brands "I.C.," which means "Inspected and Condemned," E. B. Custer microfilm, Roll 6, No. 6427, Custer Battlefield.

49. Narrative of First Sergeant Hugh A. Hynds, Sergeant of the Gatling gun battery which General Terry offered Custer and he declined. Hynds mentions four Gatlings, two .50 calibers or ½-inch guns and two .100 or one-inch guns. On file at the Custer Battlefield Museum Library. Also see Research Review, Little Big Horn Associates, Vol. VI, Winter, Number 4.

50. For full text see: The Custer Tragedy, by Fred Dustin, privately printed by Edwards Bros. Inc., Ann Arbor, Mich., 1936, p. 197.

hostile to the Sioux, and a section of Gatling guns, the latter capable of being fired fifty times a minute.[51] I will tell you candidly that we will have contests with the noble red man but my friend Laurence need feel no anxiety on that score as he can remain an impartial witness of the battle and be exposed to no danger whatever.[52]

Many officers had objections to the Gatling gun, even though its fire-power was that of two companies of infantry while it took the services of only four infantrymen to operate it. However, training of gun crews was often inadequate. During the late 1860's and early 1870's, target practice was infrequent because of objections to extra

expenditures for ammunition. It was said that the weapon was clumsy and hard to conceal. The operators were exposed to enemy fire,[53] in a stationary position, and the weapon would soon lose its effectiveness with several men wounded.[54] Officers cautioned the operators to keep their heads down when firing, but, towering above the men was the Gatling's gravity-fed ammunition case. A stray bullet might slam into the feed case, rendering it useless or exploding several cartridges within it.[55]

In swinging the gun about to change firing positions, two men were exposed, one at each wheel; one man would push one wheel forward, the other pull back on the opposite wheel. This lateral roll gave the Gatling a wider field of fire power, but exposed the men operating it.

It has commonly been assumed that the Gatling guns of the Little Big Horn expedi-

51. The Gatling Gun, by Paul Wahl & D. R. Toppel, p. 30, includes a report by T. G. Baylor, Captain of Ordnance, Ft. Monroe Arsenal, Virginia, July 14, 1866, "I had the oil rubbed off this gun, drenched it with water, and then exposed it for two nights and a day to rain and weather, but though it was quite rusty, it was fired 97 times in a minute and a half, one man turning at the crank."

A short time after the Gatlings were delivered to the Army, it was noted that, when cranking at top speed to attempt the firing power of two hundred shots in one minute, shots occasionally struck the front cross bar of the frame, throwing lead and parts of metal back into the crew. This could very well be the reason for Custer's mention of 50 shots per minute. See "The Gatling Gun," p. 32.

52. From the collections of the Manuscript Division, Library of Congress (AC. 11700), Ghent Collection.

53. Infantry Uniforms, Book No. 2, 1855-1939, p. 210, Robert and Christopher Wilkinson-Latham; MacMillan Co.

54. See this chapter for "The Gatling Gun Battery Manual" for duties of each man.

55. Army and Navy Journal, Feb. 21, 1874, p. 443.

Courtesy National Archives Records Group – Washington, D.C.
At the Washington trials, May 8, 1866, three Gatling guns are posed on the banks of the Potomac; the .50 caliber and the 1 inch guns have all passed severe tests.

tion were of 45-70 caliber, the standard carbine and rifle ammunition of 1876. Unim-
portant as this might seem, it has confused
the subject. Dr. Gatling had made various
improvements and a new patent was
awarded in 1865. After a number of tests
and inspections, the battery was approved
and 100 guns were distributed to various
commands.[56] Gatlings were shipped by rail
to Fort Sully, Fort Rice and Fort Randall.[57]
These weapons were of the modified
model of 1866, and in both .50- , and 1-inch
calibers. The report of the War Department, 1876 (Vol. 2, Part 3, p. 700) refers to
"A battery of three half inch Gatling guns,
(.50 caliber)[58] commanded by Second
Lieutenant W. H. Low, Twentieth Infan-

try," substantiating that the .50-caliber was
in use instead of the 45-70 caliber.

Dr. Richard Jordan Gatling did not have
an opportunity to see his "battery gun" in
action during the Civil War. It was introduced too late to be used in many campaigns. However, it had been put to many
practical tests by officers of the Ordnance
Corps, who spoke of its performance in
high terms. At the beginning, Gatling's gun
was called a "novel engine of war" that
would prove useful in guarding bridges,
fords and roadways. There was little recoil
to affect the accuracy of its aim, and, once
sighted on a target, it can be fired day or
night from an aimed position. Lieutenant
Maclay, U.S. Ordnance, reported: "The advantages claimed for this gun are: 1st. There
is no escape of gas at the breech. 2d. There
is no recoil, which can destroy its accuracy.
3rd. It performs the operations of loading,
firing, and extracting the case, by simply
revolving the crank. 4th. Accuracy. 5th.

56. Army and Navy Journal, Aug. 20, 1870, p. 6.
57. Ibid., Aug. 3, 1872, p. 813.
58. Author's note. See reference No. 49 in this chapter: Narrative of First Sergeant H. A. Hynds who states two Gatlings were
.50 calibers, and two were one-inch. I am more inclined to take the
War Department's word of three Gatlings in the .50-caliber; the
fourth in the one-inch caliber.

Courtesy National Archives
Custer refused to take these weapons along because the necessary teams of horses might impede his march. The Gatling gun shown here is
of the 1-inch caliber.

Courtesy Custer Battlefield Museum

At Fort McKean, North Dakota, in 1877, members of the 20th Infantry stand at ease next to Caissons and 1-inch Gatling guns. (Note bore of Gatling in foreground — compared to soldier's 45/70 ammunition in "Prairie Belt.")

Rapidity of fire." The report concludes, "All parts of the gun work well."[59]

Army plans placed the Gatling in the artillery arm. It was contemplated that in campaigns against the Indians the gun could be used to advantage as a "flank defense gun."

Two sizes of Gatlings were manufactured by the Colt's Arms Company, Hartford, Connecticut, one of 1-inch caliber, capable of being fired 100 times a minute, and one of .50 caliber, which could be fired 200 times a minute. Copper-case primed cartridges were used in both guns. Each gun had 6 steel rotating barrels. The reason the

Gatling had little recoil is that gun and carriage were of sufficient weight to overcome the recoil of each discharge without movement and therefore no time was lost in sighting after each fire. If an operator other than the one who was cranking moved a wheel forward or backward, the gun was given a lateral movement while firing, to sweep a sector of any circle within its range.

An order for 100 Gatling guns was issued to Talbot, Jones & Company of Indianapolis, Indiana, August 24, 1866. Fifty .50-caliber, or half-inch guns, and 50 1-inch caliber guns were ordered by General A. B. Dyer. Each weapon had 6 steel barrels, all rifled. The wooden field gun carriages were to be of seasoned white oak, with all iron or steel parts blued, with the exception of the gun barrels which were to be browned, a blue-black rusting process.

The weapons that Custer declined were of the 1866 improved models, chambered for the 50-70-450 centerfire infantry cartridge, interchangeable for rifle. The weight of the machine, not including the carriage and limber, was 224 pounds. Total weight of carriage, omitting the gun, was 202 pounds. The limber (empty) weighed 200 pounds. The smaller sized gun had a range up to one mile, while the larger gun had a range up to two miles. Of course, the extreme ranges would seldom produce accurate hits.[60] Open sights were located cen-

59. Army and Navy Journal, July 13, 1867, p. 741.

60. Author's Note: A good example of this particular model can be found in Francis Bannerman Sons, Military Goods Catalog, Illustrated and Descriptive, 1931, "Cannons...p. 134..." Gatling Rapid-Fire Guns, Cal. 50; the breech mechanism was encased in a bronzed jacket with four-foot wheels.

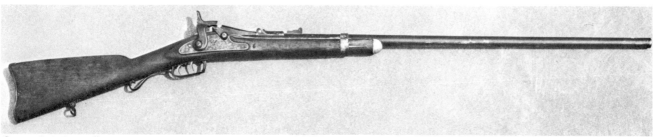

Courtesy L. A. Frost Collection

General Custer's Springfield 50/70 modified breech-loading sporting rifle.

General Custer's .44 caliber Remington percussion revolver. The cased set, with a portrait of Custer on the grips, was presented by E. Remington & Sons. The powder flask is missing from the set.

A close-up of Captain Tom Custer's Galand and Somerville revolver. Stamped T.W.C. on leather carrying case.

trally upon the breech housing; when the sights were not used, they could be retracted into the case. Elevation was attained by use of a jackscrew in the trail.

The mobility of the Gatling gun had not been criticized by other commands. The gun and its carriage, compared to other artillery, was light in weight and could be drawn by two horses.[61] Four horses or six were required for field guns. The lives of three or four men at the most need only be exposed; and the results attained can only be measured by the exposure of as many as a hundred men armed with ordinary rifles.

The men of the Seventh U.S. Cavalry had already found uses for the Gatling gun. One company, returning from the Hancock Expedition in 1867, ran into a large herd of buffalo while escorting a wagon train on the Smoky Hill route. When the buffalo threatened to stampede the wagon train, two companies of cavalry dismounted, knelt and fired volleys into the oncoming herd. This only frightened the animals and they headed straight for the train. Two Gatling guns then came into position and began

firing. After a number of buffalo were killed, the rest of the herd broke around the wagon train. A detailed group of soldiers went forward to cut the hind quarters of the dead buffalo, loading them into the wagons for garrison consumption.[62]

The Gatling gun manual and firing tactics in battery formation are as follows:

The New Battery Manual of the Gatling Gun

Positions of the Cannoneers in Battery Figure One

Nos. 1 and 2 on the right flank of the piece, No. 1 opposite the cascabel, No. 2 opposite the rear end of the hand spike, and both facing towards the piece, 18 inches outside of the face of the nave of the wheel, Nos. 3 and 4 on the left flank piece, No. 3 opposite the cascabel, No. 4 opposite the rear end of the hand spike, both facing toward the piece, 18 inches outside of the face of the nave of the wheel.

A feed-drum has been placed on the piece, the crank and traversing apparatus has been placed in action, and the hand spike has been placed at the end of trail.

At the command PREPARE TO FIRE, No. 1 places himself in position to turn the crank with his right hand, No. 2 directs the piece and seats himself on the trail seat, prepared to elevate or depress the piece. No. 3 goes to the feed-drum, and attends it, No. 4 goes to the limber, and gets a second feed-drum all ready to relieve No. 3. At the command FIRE, No. 1 turns the crank, No. 3 attends the feed-drum, seeing that the cartridges are fed regularly, No. 2 sees that the piece is properly aimed. When the

61. General E. S. Godfrey had four Gatlings hauled by two mules during the fall of 1867. Guns were receipted to Godfrey from Ft. Harker. Winners of the West, March 30, 1930.

62. Elizabeth Custer microfilm, Roll 6, No. 6402, Custer Battlefield.

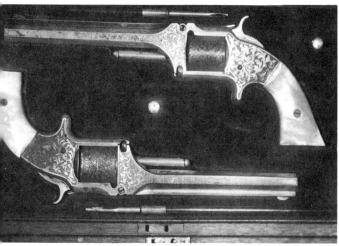

Courtesy L. A. Frost Collection

General Custer's cased Smith and Wesson revolvers, .38 caliber rim fire, presented to him by Major General J. B. Sutherland, October, 1869.

Courtesy Monroe County Historical Museum Collection

Cased set presented to General Custer from Lord Berkley Paget, as a token of appreciation while buffalo hunting in Kansas in September, 1869. Made in Birmingham, England, under the Galand & Sommerville patent and sold by J. D. Dougall of London and Glasgow. It fired a .44 Webley cartridge. Captain Tom Custer received a similar set.

feed-drum is nearly exhausted, No. 3 warns No. 4 by calling out, "Drum," when No. 4 brings up a loaded feed-drum, and when the first drum is exhausted, No. 3 lifts it off, takes it to the limber chest, and gets another loaded feed-drum ready. No. 4 at the same time takes his feed-drum on the piece, and takes the duties previously performed by No. 3. He is in turn relieved by No. 3, and so on. At the command CEASE FIRING, No. 3 or No. 4, as the case may be, keeps the feed-drum stationary. No. 1 turns the crank until the loose cartridges are fired. All then take the positions "in battery."

When feed-cases are used instead of feed-drums, the duties of the cannoneers No. 1 and No. 2 are not changed. The duties of the cannoneers No. 3 and 4 are to supply the piece with the feed-cases. At the command PREPARE TO FIRE, No. 3 inserts the lower end of the feed-case in the hopper, and No. 4 stands by ready to insert a filled case when the first is exhausted. At the command FIRE, No. 3 sees that the cartridges feed regularly, withdraws the case when it is empty, and No. 4 inserts at once a filled case, and is in turn relieved by No. 3, and they too keep up a constant supply of cartridges. At the command CEASE FIRING, Nos. 3 and 4 remove the feed-cases to the limber, and place them in the chest. At the command LIMBER TO THE FRONT, No. 1 fastens the crank, ungears the traversing apparatus, and goes to the end of the trail. No. 3 and No. 4, as the case may be, takes off the feed-drum and places it in the limber chest, where the other feed-drums, ready for use, are also placed. No. 2 unships the hand spike, keys it in its place on the trail, and places himself at the end of the trail opposite No. 1.

The limber is brought to the front of the piece, passing it on the right, and No. 1 and No. 2 bring the piece to the right about, limber up and key the pintle. All then take the positions "in battery," except that Nos. 1 and 3 are opposite the naves of the wheels of the piece, and Nos. 2 and 4 opposite the naves of the limber wheels. At the command LIMBER TO THE REAR, the actions of the cannoneers are the same as in the last command, except that the limber is brought to the rear of the piece and is brought to the left about, and the piece is limbered and keyed, but not brought to the right about. On the march, the cannoneers march in the places indicated in the last two commands. At the command CANNONEERS MOUNT, Nos. 1 and 3 mount on the rear side of the limber, Nos. 2 and 4 on the front side. The piece being limbered, and on the march, at the command IN BATTERY, the piece halts, the cannoneers, if mounted, dismount. Nos. 1 and 2 unlimber the piece and bring it to the right about. The limber is brought to the left about, is taken 20 paces to the rear, and is again brought to the left about. No. 1 frees the crank and gears in the traversing apparatus. No. 2 detaches the hand spike, places it on the trail, and gives the general direction to the piece, and notes whether the traversing apparatus works properly. Nos. 3 and 4 go to the limber and get out two loaded feed-drums. No.

3 takes one to the piece, places it on the pintle, and gets it ready for feeding. Then all take the positions of the cannoneers "in battery". The foregoing instructions apply to pieces of ordinary musket caliber, and mounted as small field-pieces.

For the large calibers, the feed-drums are so heavy that two men will be required to handle them. An additional man must therefore belong to each piece, who may be called No. 5, and whose position "in battery" will be in the rear of the limber box, and on the march midway between Nos. 3 and 4. His duty will be to assist Nos. 3 and 4 in getting the feed-drums in readiness, and in carrying them to and fro between the limber and the piece, and in packing them in the limber chest. He must be mounted with the other cannoneers on the front of the limber chest or on a caisson if there be one.

With the guns of musket caliber disposed for transportation on animals' backs (camel guns), the number of cannoneers will be the same as that given above for small field-pieces. Any intelligent officer can make the modifications that the case requires, thus No. 2 should arrange the tripod for field-carriage and keep the gun accurately pointed. No. 1 should adjust the crank and traversing apparatus, and Nos. 3 and 4 should see that the supply of cartridges is kept up. Nos. 1 and 2 will remove the gun from the back of the animal and adjust it on the carriage. With guns of caliber larger than that of the musket, it will be advisable to have a sixth cannoneer, whose duty it shall be to relieve No. 1 at the crank.

In drilling at the school of the cannoneer in garrison or camp, it will be well to remove the locks, to prevent the unnecessary snapping of the springs, and the cartridges can then be run through the hopper at will, familiarizing the men with the use of the

Model 1865 Gatling Gun, caliber 1-inch.

gun without waste of ammunition or injury to the locks.[63]

Second Lieutenant William Hale Low and Second Lieutenant Frank X. Kinzie arrived at Bismarck, Dakota Territory, March 20, 1876 with 32 half-frozen men from the 20th Infantry[64] with orders to report to the commanding officer of Fort Abraham Lincoln and organize a Gatling battery for an expedition against hostile Indians. Some of the men remembered seeing General Custer driven in an ambulance to a railway terminal at Bismarck, en route to Washington, D.C., to give evidence in the Belknap case.[65] The snow had drifted into huge banks, swept by the winds, making travel difficult by foot or wagon. After reaching the fort, Low began to train his men with the Gatling guns awaiting them. Within 6 weeks they would be ready to march. May 10, the command moved to Cannon Ball Creek, 3 miles south of the fort on the west bank of the Missouri River. Here organization of the expedition was completed and troops were put under canvas until the march began on May 17.[66]

Orders to Lieutenant Low were:

Headquarters, Fort Abraham Lincoln, D. T., March 18, 1876.
Special Orders No. 48[67]
Article 8. Upon the arrival at this post of the detachment of the 20th Infantry under command of Second Lieutenant Low of that regiment the officers and men of the Detachment will be provided with quarters at Infantry Barracks and under the direction of Lieutenant Low will be organized and drilled for service in the field with a Gatling gun battery consisting of four pieces.

As soon as the weather will permit horses to be kept on the picket line at night the Post Quartermaster will turn over to Lieutenant Low for services with the Gatling gun battery such numbers of horses as may be suitable and may be required to supply the battery, not including mounts for the cannoneers. Two horses will be supplied for use of officers serving with the Battery. The officers and men composing the Gatling gun detachment will not be required to perform any duty at this post which will conflict or interfere with their organization and preparation for the field.

Lieutenant Low will fully instruct his men in the duties pertaining to the Gatling Gun service in the

63. Army and Navy Journal, June 15, 1872.
64. Narrative of First Sergeant Hugh A. Hynds, on file at Custer Battlefield Museum.
65. Ibid.
66. Ibid.
67. Records of U.S. Army Continental Commands, 1821-1920, Fort Abraham Lincoln, Special Orders, Vol. 83; Special Orders 48, 1876, Record Group No. 393.

field and render them as familiar as practicable in the proper care and management of horses.

By order of
Brevet Major General Custer
(Signature) W. W. Cooke
1st Lt. & Adjt. 7 Cavy.
Post Adjutant.

The lighter 45-70 Gatling guns could have been available for the Little Big Horn campaign, had not it been for a delay in communications among department headquarters in Chicago and Washington Ordnance offices, which held up requisitions for the distribution of the weapons for 5 months. We would have to wade through a tide of letters, telegrams and second- and third- endorsements to pin down the responsibility.

On November 17, 1875, Brigadier General S. V. Benét, Chief of Ordnance, Washington, D. C., announced that 45-70 Gatling guns at various arsenals were available, and asked what disposition the Lieutenant General wished to make of the guns. The weapons could be requisitioned by commanding officers of posts needing them most. There were 10 Gatlings at the San Antonio Arsenal to be issued to posts in the Department of Texas, 5 guns at Fort Union Arsenal for the Department of the Missouri, and 17 guns at Rock Island Arsenal, of which 8 were to be allotted to posts in the Department of Dakota and 9 to the Department of the Platte. With each weapon, a sufficient supply of ammunition would be furnished with harness for 2 horses. It was noted that these guns were much lighter than the 1-inch caliber and ½ inch, or .50 caliber, already serving garrisons in many departments.[68]

Five months dragged by before communications from officers reached General Benét's desk in Washington; meanwhile, Benét sent a second communication:[69]

Ordnance Office
War Department
Washington, May 5th, 1876

Captain J. W. Reilly, Chief Ordnance Officer
Military Division of the Missouri, Chicago, Illinois

Sir:

Referring to my letter of November 17, 1875 (copy enclosed) directing you to advise to this office, what distribution the Lieutenant General of the Army desired to make of the 17 Gatling guns Cal. 45, on hand at the Rock Island Arsenal, I infer that as this information has not yet been furnished, it may have been overlooked.

Respectfully
Your obedient servant,
(Signed) S. V. Benét
Chief of Ordnance

Captain Reilly had reported:

Headquarters Military Division of the Missouri,
Office of Chief Ordnance Officer
Chicago, Illinois,
April 6th, 1876

Chief of Ordnance U.S.A.
Washington, D. C.

Sir,

I have the honor to inform you that your communication of November 17th, 1875, relative to the distribution to Troops in this Division of certain Gatling Guns in the possession of the Ordnance Department, was referred by me with an Endorsement to the Lieutenant General November 20, 1875. I recommended that the 10 at San Antonio Arsenal be issued to Posts and Troops in Department of Texas.

Although Custer favored the early Gatlings on a previous expedition he refused to have the battery accompany him to the Little Big Horn.

---

68. Record Group No. 156, Records of the Office of the Chief of Ordnance, Letters Received, 1875.

69. Records of the Office of the Chief of Ordnance, Letters Received No. 2520, 1876, Record Group No. 156.

Five at Fort Union Arsenal be issued to Posts and Troops in Department of Missouri. Nine at Rock Island Arsenal to Posts and Troops in Department of the Platte. Eight at Rock Island Arsenal to Posts and Troops in Department of Dakota. The Commanding Generals of the Departments were instructed by the Lieutenant General, if they desired these Guns to designate, their disposition in the proportion I recommended. Reports have been received from Generals Terry and Crook; and Generals Pope and Ord have today been directed to forward reports at once.

The delay in returning the complete papers to your office, has been caused by the failure of the latter named officers to answer the communication. The matter will now however be pushed to a conclusion . . .

> Very respectfully
> Your obedient Servant
> (Signed) J. W. Reilly
> Captain of Ordnance
> Chief Ord. Off. Mil. Div. Mo.

Eventually, all department commanders replied. General Terry designated the companies to receive the 8 guns allotted to his department. General Crook stated that he did not wish the guns. General Pope designated posts to receive the 5 guns at Fort Union Arsenal and requested 3 additional guns. They were allotted from those apportioned to the Department of the Platte. General Ord designed the disposition of 8 guns at San Antonio Arsenal, but asked that 2 remain there for emergencies. The 6 guns remaining at Rock Island Arsenal were retained there for possible use in the Department of the Platte.[70]

Abbreviations used in Summary statements of Ord. and Ord. stores in the hands of troops:

Ft. — Fort
Lt. & Adj. — Lieutenant and Adjutant
Cal. — Caliber
Rem. — Remington
Cav. — Cavalry
D.T. — Dakota Territory
Reg. Q.M. — Regimental Quarter Master
Car. — Cartridge
Rev. — Revolvers
Spring. — Springfield
Ser. — Serviceable
Met. Cart. — Metallic cartridge
Breech Load. — Breech Loading
Lt. — Light
Mdl. — Model
Ammo. — Ammunition
Spen. — Spencer
Per. — Percussion
Sngl. — Single
Brl. — Barrel
S/W — Smith and Wesson
Equip. — Equipment

70. Record Group No. 156, Records of the Office of the Chief of Ordnance, Letters Received, No. 2520, 1876.

Chief of Ordnance
Record Group 156 — 7th Cavalry
SUMMARY STATEMENTS OF ORD. AND ORD. STORES IN THE HANDS OF TROOPS

2nd Quarter – June, 1867

		Spencer Rifled Cal. 52	Spencer Rifled Cal. 50	Total Breech Loading Carbines Serviceable	Rem. Army Cal. 44	Total Revolvers Serviceable	Light Cav. Sabres	Spencer Cartridge Boxes
A	Ft. Dodge, Kansas	44		44	15	15	55	4
B	Ft. Dodge, Kansas	75		79	3	3	97	82
C	Ft. Lyon, Cal. Terr.		60	60			81	76
D	enroute to Ft. Sedwick, C.T.		67	67	7	7	88	63
E								
F	Monument Sta., Kansas		75	75	3	3	64	77
G								
H	Ft. Hays, Kansas		46	46	4	4	57	46
I	Ft. Wallace, Kansas		82	82	5	5	87	99
K								
L	Ft. Reynolds, C.T.		39	39			61	
M								
Sin. C., Lt. & Adj. Ft. Wallace, Kansas		1	1	2	2	6	1
Sin. C., Lt. & Adj. Reg. Q.M. Ft. Hays, Kansas		4	4	29	29		

NOTE: 6 companies carrying better than 50% of Spencer carbines.

Chief of Ordnance
Record Group 156 — 7th Cavalry
SUMMARY STATEMENTS OF ORD. AND ORD. STORES IN THE HANDS OF TROOPS

1st Quarter – March 31, 1871

		Altered for Met. Cart. Sharps Cal. 52	Total Breech Loading Carbines Unserviceable	Breech Loading Spencer 50 Cal.	Colt Army .44 Cal. Old & New Mdl.	Rem. Army Cal. 44	Light Cav. Sabres
A	Elizabethtown, Ky.	88			12		85
B	Camp near Unionville, S.C.	94			78		78
C	Chester, S.C.	79			79		83
D	Mount Vernon, Ky.	78		4	13		72
E	Spartanburg, S.C.	50			11		30
F	Louisville, Ky.	87			70		95
G	Ft. Lyon, C.T.	59	7		6	13	70
H	Ft. Hays, Kans.	56			6	58	91
I	Post Bagdad, Ky.	69			71		56
K	Yorkville, S.C.	77			53	11	80
L	Ft. Wallace, Kans.	78			65		51
M	Ft. Hays, Kans.	61			6	6	68
Sin. C. Adjt. — Taylor Bks., Louisville, Ky.				3		5

Chief of Ordnance
Record Group 156 — 7th Cavalry
SUMMARY STATEMENTS OF ORD. AND ORD. STORES IN THE HANDS OF TROOPS

2nd Quarter – June 30, 1871

		Breech Loading Carbines				Revolvers				
		Spring. Mdl. 1870 .50 Cal. Exper.	Rem. Mdl. 1870 .50 Cal. Exper.	Sharp's Mdl. 1870 .50 Cal. Exper.	Sharp's Rifled Cal. 50	Spencer Rifled Cal. 50	Colt Army .44 Cal. Old & New	Rem. Army Cal. 44	Lt. Cav. Sabres	Car. Cart. Pouches Butler's Pattern	Cartridges for Breech Loading Carb.
A	Elizabethtown, Ky.				86		12		78		Spencer
B	Unionville, S.C.				94		89		92		& Rem.
C	Camp Rutherford-town, N.C.				85		69		83		cartridges rim-primed
D	Mount Vernon, Ky.				72	4	10	63	67	3	metallic
E	Spartanburg, S.C.				52		10		60		.50 cal.
F	Louisville, Ky.				87		70		95		————
G	Post Sumter, S.C.				56		3	59	54		Sharps &
H	Post Nashville, Tenn.				56		5	54	45		Spring.
I	Post Bagdad, Ky.				66		67		56		Cart.
K	Yorkville, S.C.	28	28	28			59	4	80		Center-primed
L	Winnsboro, N.C. .				78		65		51		primed
M	Darlington, S.C.				61		5	6	68		metallic
Sin. C. (adjt.), Louisville, Ky.							3		5		cal. 50

NOTE: Co. "I", located in Shelbyville, Ky., had received 20 nickeled plated Smith & Wesson's and 59 non-plated. As shown in 3rd quarter, Sept. 30, 1871.

Co. "M" shows 6 unserviceable Colts.

Chief of Ordnance
Record Group 156 — 7th Cavalry
SUMMARY STATEMENTS OF ORD. AND ORD. STORES IN THE HANDS OF TROOPS

3rd Quarter – September 30, 1871

		Spencer Rifled 50 Cal.	Sharp's Rifled .50 Cal.	Smith & Wesson	Rem. Army Cal. 44	Colt Army .44 Cal. Old & New	Rem. Army Cal. 44	Unservice-able Colts .44	Lt. Cav. Sabres	Cart. Pouches
A	Elizabethtown, Ky.		86			11			78	
B	Unionville, S.C.		82			85			84	3 Dyer's
C	Rutherfordtown, N.C.		86			69			83	
D	Columbia, S.C.	4	72		61	9	61		66	
E	Spartanburg, S.C.		52			10			60	
F	Meridian, Miss.		87			70			95	
G	Spartanburg, S.C.		62			76			59	71
H	Nashville, Tenn.		76			4	54		65	
I	Shelbyville, Ky.	20 nickeled 59 plain	66			3			56	
K	Yorkville, S.C.					59	4		80	
L	Winnsboro, S.C.		72			59			76	
M	Darlington, S.C.		69			9	1	6	81	71 Dyer's*
Sin. C. (adjt.) — Taylor Bks., Ky.						3			5	3

*67 Dyer's carbine slings
72 (no) carbine slings

NOTE: Most companies wore various patterns of cartridge boxes for carbines.
Stuart's attachments for pistol and sabres were found in Company "B" (81) amount, "D" (65), and "G" (72) amount.

Chief of Ordnance
Record Group 156 — 7th Cavalry
SUMMARY STATEMENTS OF ORD. AND ORD. STORES IN THE HANDS OF TROOPS

4th Quarter – December 31, 1871

| | Breech Loading | | | | | | | | | | | | |
	Spring. M-70 Carb. Cal. 50	Rem. Car. M-1870 Cal. 50	Sharp's Car. M-1870 Cal. 50	Sharp's Rifled Improv. Cal. 52	Colt Army Old & New Models Cal. 44	Rem. Army Cal. 44	S/W Nickel Cal. 44	S/W Non-Plated Cal. 44	Lt. Cav. Sabres	Inf. Cart. Boxes	Carb. Cart. Pouches Var. Pat.	Car. Cart. Boxes Var. Pat.	Stewart's Attachment for Pistol & Sabres
A Elizabethtown, Ky.				86	9				78			62	
B Spartanburg, S.C.				82	80				84		3	68	74
C Rutherfordtown, N.C.				86	69				83			74	
D Chester, S.C.				72	5	56			64			115	61
E Unionville CH, S.C.				39	10				60			49	
F Louisville, Ky.	28	28	28	2	70				95			83	
G Spartanburg, S.C.				62		75			59	45	59		72
H Nashville, Tenn.				76	4	54			65			96	
I Shelbyville, Ky.				66			20	58	53		Dyer's	84	
K Yorkville, S.C.	24	28	28		56	4			80		60	46	
L Yorkville, S.C.				72	51				76		Dyer's	55	
M Unionville, S.C.				68	11				80		67		
Sin. C. (adjt.), Louisville, Ky.					3				5		3		

Chief of Ordnance
Record Group 156 — 7th Cavalry
SUMMARY STATEMENTS OF ORD. AND ORD. STORES IN THE HANDS OF TROOPS

1st Quarter – March, 1872

| | | | | | Using Per. Caps | | | | | Ammo—44 Cal. | |
	Spencer Cal. 50	Spring. Cal. 50	Rem. Cal. 50	Sharps Cal. 50	Sharps Cal. 50 Mdl. 70	Colt Cal. 44	Rem. Cal. 44	S/W Cal. 44	Lt. Cav. Sabres	Met. for Colt	S/W
A Elizabethtown, Ky.				86		9			78		
B Post of Spartanburg, S.C.				82		84			84		
C Lincolnton, N.C.				84		69			83		
D Opelika, Ala.	4			72		4	52		64		
E Unionville CH, S.C.				68		9			60		
F Louisville, Ky		28	28		28	70			94		
G Spartanburg, S.C.				59		72			58		
H Nashville, Tenn.				73		3	53		65		
I Shelbyville, Ky.				66				77	53		4000 rnds.
K Post of Yorkville, S.C.			24	28	1	28	56	4		81	
L Yorkville, S.C.				78		53	19		84		
M Unionville, S.C.				75		11			80		
Sin. C. (adjt.) Taylor Bks. Louisville, Ky.						3			11		

9th U.S. Cav. Co. "D"
(May 14, 1892) Stationed
at Ft. Stockton, Texas   40

Chief of Ordnance
Record Group 156 — 7th Cavalry
SUMMARY STATEMENTS OF ORD. AND ORD. STORES IN THE HANDS OF TROOPS

2nd Quarter – June, 1872

		Breech-loading Carbines						Pistols				Ammo
		Spencer .50 Cal.	Spring. .50 Cal.	Rem. .50 Cal.	Sharp's 50 Cal.	Sharp's Cal. 50 1870 Mdl.	Ward Burton .50 Cal.	Colt. Per. .44 Cal.	Rem. Per. .44 Cal.	S/W .44 Cal.	Lt. Cav. Sabres	S/W .44
A	Elizabethtown, Ky.				83			8			78	
B	Post of Spartanburg, S.C.				72			78			79	
C	Lincolnton, N.C.				85			65			83	
D	Opelika, Ala.	4			107			4	66		94	
E	Unionville, S.C.				68			9			60	
F	Louisville, Ky.		21	21		21	21	69			94	
G	Post of Spartanburg, S.C.				80				78		81	
H	Nashville, Tenn.				72			3	53		65	
I	Shelbyville, Ky.				53					65	53	2170
K	Yorkville, S.C.		17	21	1	21	21	55	4		73	
L	Yorkville, S.C.		14	14	78	14	14	46	19		84	
M	Unionville, S.C.				68			1			73	
	Sin. C. (adjt.) Taylor Bks. Louisville, Ky.							3			11	

Sin. C. (adjt.) — Taylor Bks. (R.Q.M.) Louisville, Ky. (obsolete)

Chief of Ordnance
Record Group 156 — 7th Cavalry
SUMMARY STATEMENTS OF ORD. AND ORD. STORES IN THE HANDS OF TROOPS

3rd Quarter – September, 1872

		Breech-loading Carbines						Pistols				Ammo
		Spencer .50 Cal.	Spring. .50 Cal.	Rem. .50 Cal.	Sharp's 50 Cal.	Sharp's .50 Cal. M. 70	Ward Burton .50 Cal.	Colt. Per. .44 Cal.	Rem. Per. .44 Cal.	S/W .44 Cal.	Lt. Cav. Sabres	S/W .44
A	Elizabethtown, Ky.				83			8			78	
B	Post of Spartanburg, S.C.				72			78			79	
C	Lincolnton, N.C.				85			65			83	
D	Opelika, Ala.	4			107			4	63		94	
E	Unionville, S.C.				59			9			58	
F	Louisville, Ky.		21	21		21	21	69			94	
G	Post of Spartanburg, S.C.				62				77		70	
H	Nashville, Tenn.				70			3	53		56	
I	Shelbyville, Ky.				51					59	57	7214
K	Yorkville, S.C.		17	17	1	21	21	52	4		63	rnds.
L	Yorkville, S.C.		14	14	22	14	14	44	19		84	
M	Unionville, S.C.				65						63	
	Sin. C. (adjt.) Taylor Bks. Louisville, Ky.							4			11	

No (RQM)

Chief of Ordnance
Record Group 156 — 7th Cavalry
SUMMARY STATEMENTS OF ORD. AND ORD. STORES IN THE HANDS OF TROOPS
4th Quarter – December, 1872

		Breech-loading Carbines					Pistols				Ammo
	Spencer .50 Cal.	Spring. .50 Cal.	Rem. .50 Cal.	Sharp's 50 Cal.	Sharp's .50 Cal. M. 70	Ward Burton .50 Cal.	Colt. Per. .44 Cal.	Rem. Per. .44 Cal.	S/W .44 Cal.	Lt. Cav. Sabres	S/W .44
A Elizabethtown, Ky.				86					8	78	
B Post of Spartanburg, S.C.				72			78			79	
C Charlotte, N.C.				69			64			83	
D Opelika, Ala.	4			84			3	64		76	
E Unionville, S.C.				59			9			58	
F Louisville, Ky.		21	21	6	21	21	69			94	
G Post of Laurensville, S.C.				64				75		70	
H Nashville, Tenn.				71			3	51		56	
I Lebanon, Ky.				53					59	51	7214
K Yorkville, S.C.		15	11		18	17	51	4		48	
L Jackson Barracks, La.		14	14	22	14	14	13	17		84	
M Oxford, Miss.				67						63	
Sin. C. (adjt.)			2			4			11		

Chief of Ordnance
Record Group 156 — 7th Cavalry
SUMMARY STATEMENTS OF ORD. AND ORD. STORES IN THE HANDS OF TROOPS
1st Quarter – March, 1873

		Breech-loading Carbines					Pistols					Ammo
	Spencer .50 Cal.	Spring. .50 Cal.	Rem. .50 Cal.	Sharp's 50 Cal.	Sharp's .50 Cal. M. 70	Ward Burton .50 Cal.	Colt. Per. .44 Cal.	Rem. Per. .44 Cal.	S/W .44 Cal.	Lt. Cav. Sabres	Cav. Equip. Sets Of	S/W .44
A Louisville, Ky.				77			3			76		
B Camp Sturgis, D.T.				73			78			79		
C Memphis, Tenn.				41			64			82		
D Ft. Snelling, Minn.	4			80			3	54		76		
E Memphis, Tenn.				59			9			58		
F Louisville, Ky.		19	20	6	20	21	67			94		
G Memphis, Tenn.				64				75		70		
H Louisville, Ky.				82			3	51		83	84	
I Ft. Snelling, Minn.				51					57	51	84	7214
K Camp Sturgis, D.T.		15	11		18	17	49	4		48	83	
L New Orleans, La.		14	13	16	14	14	50	14		83		
M Memphis, Tenn.				54						63		
Sin. C. (adjt.) Louisville, Ky.							4			11		

Chief of Ordnance
Record Group 156 — 7th Cavalry
SUMMARY STATEMENTS OF ORD. AND ORD. STORES IN THE HANDS OF TROOPS

2nd Quarter – June 30, 1873

		Breech-loading Carbines					Pistols						Ammo	
		Spencer .50 Cal.	Spring. .50 Cal.	Rem. .50 Cal.	Sharp's 50 Cal.	Sharp's .50 Cal. M. 70	Ward Burton .50 Cal.	Colt. Per. .44 Cal.	Rem. Per. .44 Cal.	S/W .44 Cal.	Lt. Cav. Sabres	Cav. Equip. Sets Of	S/W .44	Rem. Met. Cal. 50
A	Ft. A. Lincoln, D.T.				77			3			76			
B	Camp in Field, M.T.				85			85			89	80		
C	Yellowstone Exped., D.T.				81			60	12		82	78		
D	Ft. Penbrina, D.T.	4			77			3	78		61			
E	In the Field, D.T.				72			9			58			
F	Camp Muddy Creek, D.T.*		18	19	6	15	19	65			87	78		18,000
G	Ft. A. Lincoln, D.T.				74				69		80			
H	Camp near Harts Butte, D.T.				73			3	74		78	78		
I	Ft. Pambrina, D.T.				75					42	51	62	5580	
K	In the Field, D.T.		14	9		24	11	40	1		75	83		
L	Little Hart River, D.T.				42			46	21		45			
M	In the Field, D.T.				30						60			
	Sin. C. (Adjt.), St. Paul, Minn.							4			2			

*Also — 84 Single Barrell Rem.

Chief of Ordnance
Record Group 156 — 7th Cavalry
SUMMARY STATEMENTS OF ORD. AND ORD. STORES IN THE HANDS OF TROOPS

3rd Quarter – September 30, 1873

														Ammo			
		Spen. .50	Spring. .50	Rem. .50	Sharp's .50	Sharp's .50 M. 70	Ward Burton .50	Colt Per. .44	Rem. Per. .44	S/W .44	Rem. Single Brl.	Lt. Cav. Sabres	Cav. Equip. Sets Of	S/W .44	Rem. Single Brl. .50	Colt's Altered .44
A	Ft. Abe Lincoln, D.T.				76			3				76			1000	
B	Ft. Abe Lincoln, D.T.				82			78				89	77			
C	Ft. Rice, D.T.				81			65	12			82	78			
D	Camp Terry, D.T.	4			75			3	73			61				
E	Ft. Lincoln, D.T.				72			9				58				
F	Ft. Lincoln, D.T.		17	18	6	14	19	64			77	87			15740	
G	Ft. Lincoln, D.T.				74				69			80				
H	Camp near Ft. Rice, D.T.				67			1	70			75	78			
I	Camp Terry, D.T.				71					35		51	58	3385		
K	Ft. Rice, D.T.		14	9		24	11	40	1			75	83			
L	Ft. Lincoln, D.T.				42	12		46	21			45				
M	Ft. Rice, D.T.				40							60				
	Sin. C. (Adjt.), St. Paul, Minn.							4				2				

Chief of Ordnance
Record Group 156 — 7th Cavalry
SUMMARY STATEMENTS OF ORD. AND ORD. STORES IN THE HANDS OF TROOPS

4th Quarter – December 31, 1873

		Spen. .50	Spring. .50	Rem. .50	Sharp's .50	Sharp's .50 M. 70	Ward Burton .50	Colt Per. .44	Rem. Per. .44	S/W .44	Rem. Single Brl.	Lt. Cav. Sabres	Cav. Equip. Sets Of	Ammo S/W .44	Ammo Rem. Single Brl. .50	Ammo Colt's Altered .44
A	Ft. Lincoln, D.T.				76			3			76	76			1000	
B	Ft. Lincoln, D.T.				82				78			89				10676
C	Ft. Rice, D.T.				80				53	11		82				
D	Ft. Totten, D.T.	4			75						73	61				
E	Ft. Lincoln, D.T.				64			9				58				
F	Ft. Lincoln, D.T.		17	18	20	19		64			76	87		76	15340	
G	Ft. Lincoln, D.T.				74				66			80				
H	Ft. Rice, D.T.				65				53			75		73		
I	Ft. Totten, D.T.				71					36		51	58	1385		
K	Ft. Rice, D.T.		14	9		11	22	38	1			75	82			
L	Ft. Lincoln, D.T.				42			46	21			45				
M	Ft. Rice, D.T.				40							60				

Chief of Ordnance
Record Group 156 — 7th Cavalry
SUMMARY STATEMENTS OF ORD. AND ORD. STORES IN THE HANDS OF TROOPS

1st Quarter – March, 1874

		Spen. .50	Spring. .50	Rem. .50	Sharp's .50	Sharp's .50 M-1870	Ward Burton .50	Colt Per. .44	Rem. Per. .44	S/W .44	Rem. Singl. Brl.	Lt. Cav. Sabres	Cav. Equip. Sets Of	Ammo S/W .44	Ammo Rem. .50	Ammo Colt Revol. .45	Ammo Spring. Cal. 50 M-1868	Ammo Spring. Carb. .45	Ammo Colt for Metal. Ammo .44
A	Ft. Abe Lincoln				76			3			73	76			900				
B	Ft. Abe Lincoln				82				78			89							
C	Ft. Rice				79				53	11		82							
D	Ft. Totten	4			75			2			73	61							
E	Ft. Lincoln				64			9				58							
F	Ft. Lincoln		17	18	20	19		64			74	87			14530				
G	Ft. Lincoln				74				66			80							
H	Ft. Rice				58				52			75	73						
I	Ft. Totten				71					36		51	58	7200					
K	Ft. Rice		14	8		21	10	36	1			75	72						
L	Ft. Lincoln				37			37	21			45							
M	Ft. Rice				28							46							

Chief of Ordnance
Record Group 156 — 7th Cavalry
SUMMARY STATEMENTS OF ORD. AND ORD. STORES IN THE HANDS OF TROOPS

2nd Quarter – June, 1874

	Spen. .50	Spring. .50	Rem. .50	Sharp's .50	Sharp's .50 M-1870	Ward Burton .50	Colt Per. .44	Rem. Per. .44	S/W .44	Rem. Singl. Brl.	Lt. Cav. Sabres	Cav. Equip. Sets Of	Ammo S/W .44	Ammo Rem. .50	Ammo Colt Revol. .45	Ammo Spring. Cal. 50 M-1868	Ammo Spring. Carb. .45	Ammo Colt for Metal. Ammo .44
A Fort Lincoln				64						1	76				73			
B Fort Lincoln				75			73				84				63		83	
C Fort Rice		11		79			53	11			82				83			
D In the field — Mont. Terr.	4			63				70			61							2
E Ft. Lincoln				81			9				83			83				
F Camp near Ft. Lincoln		17	18	42	14	19	64			73	87			14000	73			
G Ft. Lincoln				74				65			95				70		83	
H Ft. Rice		11		81				81			84	73			82			
I In the field				62					33		36	58	6630			1		
K In the field		12	7		20	10	25	25			75				82	11		
L Ft. Lincoln				77	12			1			84				73		83	
M Ft. Rice				35							45				70	10		
Adjt. St. Paul, Minn.											2				3			

Chief of Ordnance
Record Group 156 — 7th Cavalry
SUMMARY STATEMENTS OF ORD. AND ORD. STORES IN THE HANDS OF TROOPS

3rd Quarter – September 30, 1874

	Spring. Cal. 50 Musket Mdl. 1868	Sharp's Cal. 50	Spring. Cal. 50	Spring. Cal. 45	Ward Burton Cal. 50	Colt Per. Cal. 44	Rem. Per. .44	S/W Cal. 44	Colt Met. Ammo Cal. 44	Rem. Sngl. Brl.	Colt Revol. .45	Lt. Cav. Sabres	Ammo S/W .44	Ammo Rem. Sngl. Brl. .50
A Livingston, Ala.		103		83							83	76		900
B Camp near Shreveport, La.		137		83		73					77	84	out of ammo	
C Ft. Rice		54	2	83							82	82		
D Ft. Totten		62					67		2		83	61		
E Greensboro, Ala.		119		83		7					83	75		
F Ft. Lincoln		36	5	83						3	75	87		
G Shreveport, La.		119		83							82	95		
H Ft. Rice	2	81		83			81				80	82		
I Ft. Totten	1	59						31			83	36	5358	
K nothing entered														
L Ft. Lincoln		89		83							83	84		
M Ft. Rice	10			83							68	44		
(Adjt.) St. Paul, Minn.				4							3	2		

U.S center fire cal. 50 had already been issued in abundance and — carbine ball cal. 45 — revolver ball cal. 45.

Chief of Ordnance
Record Group 156 — 7th Cavalry
SUMMARY STATEMENTS OF ORD. AND ORD. STORES IN THE HANDS OF TROOPS

4rd Quarter – December 31, 1874

														Ammo	
	Spring. Cal. 50 Musket Mdl. 1868	Sharp's Cal. 50	Spring. Cal. 50	Spring. Cal. 45	Ward Burton Cal. 50	Colt Per. Cal. 44	Rem. Per. .44	S/W Cal. 44	Colt Met. Ammo Cal. 44	Rem. Sngl. Brl.	Colt Revol. .45	Lt. Cav. Sabres	S/W .44	Rem. Sngl. Brl. .50
A Livingston, Ala.			4	83							81	76		
B Camp near Shreveport, La.		5		81							77	84		
C Ft. Rice, D.T.		40	2	83							81	82		
D Ft. Totten, D.T.		60					63		2		83	61		
E Opelika, Ala.				83							81	75		
F Ft. Lincoln, D.T.			5	83						3	75	87		
G Shreveport, La.		5		82							78	82		
H New Orleans, La.	2			79							74	80		
I Ft. Totten		58						29			83	36	4119	
K Ft. Wingate		83					55					29		
L Ft. Lincoln				83							83	83		
M Ft. Rice		1		79	1						64	52		
(Adjt.) Ft. Lincoln				4							3	2		

(vertical note between Rem. Sngl. Brl. and the ammo columns: "out of ammo.")

Chief of Ordnance
Record Group 156 — 7th Cavalry
SUMMARY STATEMENTS OF ORD. AND ORD. STORES IN THE HANDS OF TROOPS

1st Quarter – March, 1875

	Carbines									Muskets					
	Spring Cal. 50 Musket (M)1870	Spring. Cal. 50	Sharp's .50	Spring. .45 Cal.	Rem. Per. .44	Colt Met. Ammo Cal. 44	Rem. Sngl. Brl.	Colt .45	Lt. Cav. Sabres	Spring. .50 Cal. 1868 M	Spring. .45 Cal.	Cav. Equip. Sets Of	Saddles Leather Covered	Saddles Rawhide	Ammo S/W .44
A Livingston, Ala.		4		83				82	76						
B Shreveport, La.			5	78				75	68						
C Ft. Rice, D.T.		2	40	82				80	82						
D Ft. Totten, D.T.			55		64	2		83	59						
E Opelika, Ala.				81				81	75						
F Ft. Lincoln, D.T.		5		83			3	75	80						
G Shreveport, La.			5	80				77	70						
H New Orleans, La.	2			79				73	80						
I															
K															
L Ft. Lincoln, D.T.				83				83	84						
M Ft. Rice, D.T.				79				64	52						

Chief of Ordnance
Record Group 156 — 7th Cavalry
SUMMARY STATEMENTS OF ORD. AND ORD. STORES IN THE HANDS OF TROOPS

2nd Quarter – June 30, 1875

		Carbines						Muskets							
	Spring Cal. 50 Musket (M)1870	Spring. Cal. 50	Sharp's .50	Spring. .45 Cal.	Rem. Per. .44	Colt Met. Ammo Cal. 44	Rem. Sngl. Brl.	Colt .45	Lt. Cav. Sabres	Spring. .50 Cal. 1868 M	Spring. .45 Cal.	Cav. Equip. Sets Of	Saddles Leather Covered	Saddles Rawhide	Ammo S/W .44
A Ft. Randall, D.T.			4	82				82	61				71		
B Shreveport, La.			5	77				75	62				67		
C Ft. Rice, D.T.				79				79	82					68	
D Ft. Lincoln, D.T.			9	83	3			83	81				74		
E															
F Ft. Lincoln, D.T.		5		81			3	75	80				84		
G Shreveport, La.			5	79				74	68				56		
H Camp at Ft. Randall	2			79				73	79				73		
I Ft. Lincoln, D.T.			5	83				83	56			84		70	2700 Rnds.
K															
L															
M Ft. Rice, D.T.				79				64	52					62	
Adjt. Ft. Lincoln, D.T.				4				3	2						
Nov. 8th Band Ft. Lincoln								13		1	50			52	27

Chief of Ordnance
Record Group 156 — 7th Cavalry
SUMMARY STATEMENTS OF ORD. AND ORD. STORES IN THE HANDS OF TROOPS

3rd Quarter – September 30, 1875

	Muskets		Carbines				Pistols					
	Spring. Cal. 50 M-1868	Spring. Cal. 50 M-1870	Spring. Cal. 50	Sharp's .50	Spring. Cal. 45	Rem. Per. .44	Rem. Sngl. Brl.	Colt .45	Lt. Cav. Sabres	Saddles Leather Covered	Saddles Rawhide	Ammo S/W .44
A Ft. Lincoln, D.T.				4	82			82	61	71		
B Shreveport, La.				5	77			75	62	74		
C Ft. Rice, D.T.	2				79			79	82	68		
D Ft. Lincoln, D.T.				9	83	3		83	81	74		
E												
F Ft. Lincoln, D.T.			5		81		3	75	80	84		
G Shreveport, La.				5	79			74	68	56		
H Camp near Cheyenne Agency, D.T.		2			79			66	79	73		
I Ft. Lincoln, D.T.					83			83	56		70	2700 Rnds.
K												
L Ft. Totten, D.T.					83			82	84	84		
M Ft. Rice, D.T.					78			69	52		70	
Adjt. Ft. Lincoln, D. T.					4			3	2			

Chief of Ordnance
Record Group 156 — 7th Cavalry
SUMMARY STATEMENTS OF ORD. AND ORD. STORES IN THE HANDS OF TROOPS

4th Quarter – December 31, 1875

		Muskets			Carbines			Pistols						
		Spring. Cal. 50 M-1868	Spring. Cal. 50 M-1870	Spring. Cal. 45	Spring. Cal. 50	Sharp's .50	Spring. Cal. 45	Rem. Per. .44	Rem Sngl. Brl.	Colt .45	Lt. Cav. Sabres	Saddles Leather Covered	Saddles Rawhide	Ammo S/W .44
A	Ft. Lincoln, D.T.					4	82			82	55	60		
B	Shreveport, La.					5	77			75	61	74		
C	Ft. Lincoln, D.T. (assigned to Capt. Custer)	2		1			85			79	82	118		
D														
E														
F	Ft. Lincoln, D.T.				5		79		3	72	80	80		
G	Shreveport, La.					5	79			76	68	70		
H	Ft. Rice, D.T.						75			64	78	56		
I	Ft. Lincoln, D.T.						83			83	56		55	2700 Rnds.
K														
L	Ft. Totten, D.T.						82			82	84	86		
M	Ft. Rice, D.T.						74			69	52	69		
Adjt., Ft. Lincoln, D.T.							4			15	2	18		

Chief of Ordnance
Record Group 156 — 7th Cavalry
SUMMARY STATEMENTS OF ORD. AND ORD. STORES IN THE HANDS OF TROOPS

1st Quarter – March 31, 1876

		Muskets		Carbines			Pistol			
		Spring. Cal. 50 M-1868	Spring. Cal. 45	Spring. Cal. 50	Sharp's Cal. 50	Spring. Cal. 45	Colt .45	Lt. Cav. Sabres	Saddles Leather Covered	Ammo S/W .44
A	Ft. Lincoln, D.T.				4	81	82	55	60	
B	Shreveport, La.				5	71	70	60	66	
C	Ft. Lincoln	2	1			85	79	82	118	
D										
E	Ft. Seward, A.T.					77	80	73	59	
F	Ft. Lincoln, D.T.			2		78	72	72	68	
G	Shreveport, La.				5	78	76	68	70	
H										
I	Ft. Lincoln, D.T.					83	83	56	55	2700 Rnds.
K										
L	Ft. Seward, D.T.					82	82	84	80	
M										
Adjt. Ft. Lincoln, D.T.						4	15	2	22	

A UNIFORM CHANGEOVER

In 1872, new regulations for uniform and dress of the army were introduced. As compared to the old patterns, this was a desirable change of dress in nearly all particulars. The most serious objection to the new dress was its expensiveness. While the men did not believe, as some carping persons hinted, that it was an attempt to drive poor men, who had no means except their pay, out of the Army, yet it was true that junior officers who had families to support were gravely pondering how they might equip themselves. Nearly all had clothing and equipment which would take years to wear out; and replacements would be a hardship. Letters of protest against the injustices inflicted upon these men by the additional expense poured into the War Department. One would suppose that there had been no fault found with the present uniform, no call for a change, but that a state of blissful content with their clothes pervaded the whole service, while the facts were that the board was convened in consequence of dissatisfaction widely spread and clamorously expressed, in innumerable letters from all parts of the country, and the solid arguments advanced in favor of a change. There can be no doubt in the mind of any fair-minded soldier that there was an almost universal desire for change. The question arose: Has the change on the whole been judicious?

The question seemed to have had several aspects, including appearance and utility. The soldier did not put appearance first simply because he considered it more important, but because he considered the impression which an object makes upon the eye before discussing its fitness.

The only change in the chasseur (fatigue cap) was to make it more roomy and allow it to fit on top of the head comfortably, instead of being kept in place by an elastic. The change in the dress hat was radical, and here the board could not have made a change which would not be an improvement. The old hat was ugly, uncomfortable, and unsoldierly. The new patterns for the infantry were the shako, and for mounted troops, the helmet with horse-hair plume. Advantages of the shako were forcibly presented by comparing the handsome and soldierly shako used by the light artillery, crowned by its horse-tail plume, with the attempt to combine the ugly features of the steeple-crowned Puritan and the southern slouched hat made ridiculous with its draggled plume. The new shako had two advantages over that used by the light artillery. It was not so high and heavy, and it dispensed with the gold cord and trappings. In short, it

Courtesy Author's Collection

Fatigue hat, model 1872, also referred to as "Kepi." Took the place of the Forage cap. The government defined this Kepi as the "Chasseur Pattern" an almost direct copy from the French Army hat. Was issued to our troops with a slight modification in 1875, and worn late as 1898. Designed for fatigue duty, on post, stable or guard. Saber (or Sabre) is the light Cavalry model of 1860 with leather sword. Knot designed to keep around wrist so it could not be dropped.

Model 1872 Cavalry enlisted man's helmet.

Lieutenant Colonel George A. Custer's model 1872 Cavalry dress helmet, with 7th Regimental brass number.

Dress coat for enlisted men after 1872. Faced and trimmed in the color of the branch. Short standing collar with a 4 inch color patch on each side. The number of the Regiment or Corps badge in brass, as shown here.

was plain, comfortable and soldierly. The helmet, being of felt, was lighter than the artillery shako, fitting close to the head, being substantially a skull cap. It was admirably adapted to the requirements of the mounted service. The result was a hat in every way superior and probably no more expensive than the previous monstrosity.

In regard to the coat, the change was principally in the matter of appearance. One of the first requisites in the army was that feeling of pride and superiority which was well summed up in the French "esprit de corps." The new uniform would hopefully increase enlistments and attract a better class of men, who were certainly not likely to be fascinated by the previous uniform. The old coat was too plain for dress uniform and not sufficiently comfortable for fatigue. The blouse was too tight in the body, short in the sleeves, shabby, giving the wearer a slouchy appearance. The proposed coat was handsome and soldierly, the blouse was neat and comfortable and possessed this great advantage: it was so unlike the civilian sack-coat that it could be recognized at once as military.

Cutting loose from old traditions unsuited during that day and age showed the army's evident desire for reform, or was it that they were finally considering the soldiers' comfort, with a new change in uniform.

During the Civil War, the U.S. government system of clothing measurements had been made in four sizes. Number 1 was from size 30 to 32; Number 2, from 34 to 36; Number 3, from 38 to 40; and Number 4, 42 to 44. These numbers were usually stamped inside the sleeve of a jacket or dress coat, with or without arsenal markings.[1] During the postwar period, this number was increased to 5, as requisitions were constantly calling for larger sizes in order to permit soldiers to tailor their uniforms to their measurements.[2] This exhausted the supply of larger-sized garments, leaving an assortment of improper sizes at depots. In the Annual Report of the Quartermaster General, 1877, it is stated that the uniforms were so well cut to fit the proportions of a soldier that there was no need for company tailors to alter garments as they had done in the past. Army hats also came in four sizes, Number 3 being equivalent to a size 7½.[3]

As early as 1862, the Quartermaster General[4] had approved and purchased over 10,000 pairs of buffalo overshoes on an experimental basis and sent to isolated posts in the north. This was not a regular item of issue; however, frequent references of articles sent to northern garrisons are recorded

Courtesy Gordon Corbett, Jr.
Shoulder straps, the length of the shoulder, set in color of the branch coat sleeves had a vertical 3-button patch.

Courtesy Gordon Corbett, Jr.
Rear — Skirts were slashed and faced with color of branch, ornamented with 4-buttons.

1. The Guidon, Cavalry Collectors Association, July-September, 1969, p. 13. Also, Quartermaster Support of the Army, History of the Corps, by Erna Risch, Quartermaster Historian's Office, Office of the Quartermaster General, Washington, D. C. 1962 (U.S. Government Printing Office), p. 502.

2. Ibid.

3. The Troopers, S. E. Whitman, Hastings House, N. Y., 1962.

4. Brigadier General Montgomery C. Meigs was Quartermaster General from May 15, 1861 to February 6, 1882.

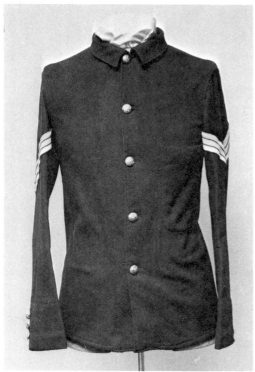

Courtesy Gordon Corbett, Jr.
The 1872 model enlisted man's fatigue coat. Regulations called for a "dark blue blouse of navy flannel," according to pattern. In 1874, piping "in the color of the arm" was sewn on the collar and cuffs. Some officers and troopers acquired 7th Cavalry embroidered patches and sewed these on fatigue coat collars and shirt collars.

Courtesy Gordon Corbett, Jr.
Side view of Sergeant's fatigue.

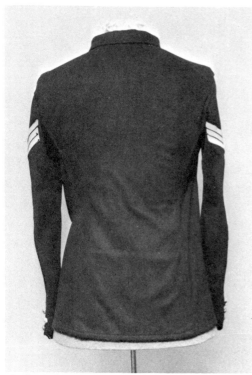

Courtesy Gordon Corbett, Jr.
Rear of fatigue coat.

with the Clothing Division up to 1867, particularly for the Department of the Dakota.[5] Winter clothing, out of necessity, was being experimented by the Clothing Bureau due to a series of complaints that soldiers had lost limbs during the severe winters. During the early 1870's, efforts were made to experiment with Arctic overcoats, caps with pull-down ear flaps, gauntlets and overshoes. Various types of animal skins were used, such as beaver, muskrat, seal, bear, sheepskin, and buffalo, not to mention condemned blankets as another source. Buffalo hide garments proved most effective, gaining a high acceptance at the remote posts. As far as the buffalo overcoat, its only drawback was, "Being too heavy, bulky in spots,

5. Uniforms of the Army Prior and Subsequent to 1872, Donald E. Kloster, Parts 1 and 2, Military Collector and Historian, Winter 1962.

Courtesy Dr. L. A. Frost Collection

Custer's 5 button blouse.

Courtesy Arizona Historical Society Library

A five button undress blouse for officers, with black braid scrolls on sleeves and breast, was introduced in 1872. It was worn in either field or garrison. All the braid was removed in 1875, according to G. O. 96, but many officers continued to wear this model long after this date. Coat was slashed at the hip on each side for sword slings. Sword belt was worn under the coat.

and not all easy to get around with.''[6] But it did keep a man from freezing.

It was advised by Quartermaster General M. C. Meigs that troops who equipped themselves with suitable winter garments such as fur mittens, caps, overshoes, and buffalo coats, purchase these out of company funds, as practiced in prewar years, the clothing being retained as company property and only drawn from stock when necessitated. Meigs promised that when funds became available the Department proposed to provide these items; however, mittens and overshoes would be charged to the soldier at government cost. Buffalo overcoats still remained the property of the government; they were only provided when the need was certified by the military department. While the great buffalo herds were being slowly reduced in number by

6. Letter in Author's Collection from Private William E. Smith, Fort Abraham Lincoln, December 19, 1875, to "Friend Herb." Smith was in Company D at the Little Big Horn.

Courtesy Arizona Historical Society Library

Model 1872 dress coat for officers. The two double stripes with buttons below the points (on each cuff) indicate, Captain, 1st Lieutenant, 2nd Lieutenant, and additional 2nd Lieutenant. Three stripes indicate a Colonel, Lieutenant Colonel and Major.

Museum curator at West Point, poses with buffalo coat buttoned-up to chin. After 1880, these coats became too expensive due to the dwindling buffalo herds. Blanket-lined canvas overcoats then replaced them.

Full length buffalo coat worn by a buffalo soldier of the 25th Infantry.

the white hunter, a scarcity of robes made overcoats prohibitive in price.[7] Soldiers would have to settle for blanket-lined canvas coats in substitute.

One soldier writes to the Army and Navy Journal an explanation of his views:

Sir:

The time in which "Uncle Sam" proposes to change the habiliments of the army will soon be here, and as a natural consequence all are more or less anxious to see whether the uniform is an improvement of the old. The old uniform manufactured during the last years of the war is certainly —

to use a mild expression, "a sham." Scarcely any two garments are the same color, especially the reference to uniform coats, pants and blouses. In a lot of a hundred pairs of pants there are often found all shades from a deep to a pale muddy blue, while the uniform coats and blouses range from gray-green to black.

As regard to shape all are uncouth as they come from the quartermaster's department, and are totally unfit to be worn until altered and refitted at an expense of from $8 to $10 for each suit; and herein lies the cause of nearly all the complaints about the insufficiency of the clothing allowance as established by General Orders Number 75, A.G.O. Series of 1871. There are comparatively few men in the service who actually draw all the articles of clothing allowed by that order, but I care not how economical men may be with their clothing they cannot save enough (the value of the articles not drawn) to pay more than one-half of the cost of altering and refitting the articles drawn, and of course the deficiency must be made good out of their monthly pay.

7. Tales of the Buffalo Hunters, E. L. Reedstrom; Guns Magazine, August 1973, p. 40.

Very generally company commanders compel the
men to have their clothing altered and refitted, and
even where they do not, a man's pride and comfort
compel him to do so.

It is to be hoped that the new uniform will be an
improvement of the old, as regards color and material, and that it will be in a condition to be worn when
issued, or that the Government will make the allowance sufficient to enable to have the soldier have it
refitted at a cost not exceeding the value of the articles not drawn.

The change of uniform is going to be a very considerable expense to all men who have been in the
service any length of time, as nearly all have at least
two suits of the old uniform on hand, which will be
almost a dead loss to them, as they cannot dispose of
it for more than a mere trifle, and it is scarcely probable that they will be permitted to wear it after the
new is issued. It would be nothing more than an act
of justice for the Government to issue the first suit of
the new uniform free of cost to the soldier, or allow
him a just and equitable amount of money for the
clothing now on hand and rendered worthless by the
change.

The officers are going to petition Congress for
indemnity for the loss incurred by the change, and I
think it would be advisable for the privates to do
likewise if it should be necessary to resort to such
measures to obtain justice.

Signed,
M. Murat[8]

---

8. Army and Navy Journal, October 19, 1872, p. 154.

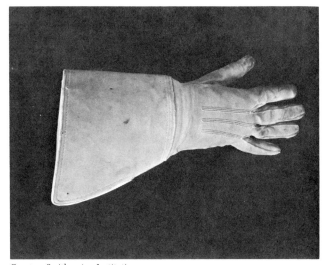

Courtesy Smithsonian Institution
Leather gauntlet owned by General George A. Custer.

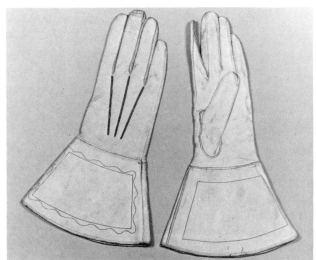

Courtesy Gordon Corbett, Jr.
Leather gauntlets were usually worn in the field. Gloves, often
called "Berlin" gloves were required to be worn in garrison,
dress parade and at ceremonies. The material was a kind of
worsted woven of merino wool. Army regulations provided that
General Officers and Staff Officers wear buff or white gloves,
and officers of Artillery, Infantry and Cavalry wear white only.
Photo shows a pair of "fawn-colored" gauntlets.

Courtesy Smithsonian Institution
Shirt, drawers and stockings, old pattern prior to 1872. From the
Quartermaster General, "uniforms of the Army prior and sub-
sequent to 1872."

To the Editor of the
Army and Navy Journal

Concerning the recent change in the army uniform, I would call attention to one or two important
considerations in connection therewith, much affecting the interests of all concerned, but which I am
sure have been overlooked by the department,
otherwise it is but fair to presume that a clause would
have been inserted to remedy the omissions referred
to. I allude to the fact that no provision has been
made to reimburse the soldier for the clothing or old
uniform now remaining on hand. The consequent
loss is much greater than many would conceive, for,
in addition to the loss of so many garments, as drawn
from the stores, many have gone to the expense of
altering, etc., owing to the fact that no Government
clothing issued heretofore was never known to fit
properly a man of natural or undeformed proportions.

Under these circumstances, would it not be just
that Government should furnish the first outfit of the
new uniform free of charge? Even then it is evident
that the soldier would be, in many cases, the loser, as
many have now on hand two or more outfits of the
old uniform, which, unless the suggestion I propose
to adopt or some other mode of reimbursement, will

be a dead loss. For instance; could not the heavy
woollen pants and flannel blouse be superceded by a
dark linen suit, which would have the advantage of
being comfortable and more easily kept clean than
the white linen in summer. It would certainly not be
more expensive than the heavy garments, and would
do away with the wonder we often hear visitors express to see the soldier sweltering in the sun during a
drill of two hours, or striving to cool himself off
while in the city on pass, by drinking that which only
makes him hotter.

"Bold Soldier"
Atlanta, Georgia
September 16, 1872[9]

Some communications from enlisted men
to the Army and Navy Journal indicate that
they did not fully understand the nature of
the soldiers' money allowance for clothing.
The money allowance for clothing for each
year of a soldier's enlistment was ascertained by adding together the established
cost in money value of all the articles of
clothing which he was entitled to receive
during the year. If a soldier did not draw all
the clothing to which he was entitled during
the year, he received the regulation value in
money of the articles not drawn. Therefore,
the greater the money price of any article
not drawn, the more money he received on
settlement of his money allowance for
clothing. The allowance of clothing was
seldom changed, the regulation price of
each article of that allowance changed almost yearly. After the stock left on hand at
the close of the war was exhausted, the
money value of every article of a soldier's
allowance was liable to change with changing tariffs, wages, and commercial values. It
was the custom to issue a general order once
a year, in which prices were stated, based
upon the contracts and purchases of the
clothing provided for the year's consumption.

The money price charged the soldier, of
the war stock, had been twice reduced —
33⅓% each time. The articles purchased to
replace those of the war stock exhausted,
probably in all cases cost more than the

Courtesy Smithsonian Institution
Shirt, drawers and stockings, new pattern subsequent to 1872.

9. Army and Navy Journal, September 28, 1872.

Courtesy U.S. Signal Corps (Brady Collection)

1st Sergeant John W. Comfort, wearing his new 1872 issue uniform. Buffalo robe at his right.

Courtesy Arizona Historical Society Library

Chapeau-De-Bras, pattern of 1872. Worn by Staff and General Saff Officers for full dress.

general orders was ample, and the soldiers generally, by care of their clothing, except upon exceptionally hard service, managed to avoid drawing some articles of the allowance. For these the paymaster paid them the

Courtesy National Archives

Private Comfort, Troop "A," 4th U.S. Cavalry, displaying his field uniform of the period (1877). Comfort was broken from 1st Sergeant to Private several years earlier. Note navy collar and piping of the Corps on cuffs, pocket and collar.

price charged for those in store at the close of the war, and the cost would be increased. The number of articles necessary to be purchased each year in consequence of the old stock becoming exhausted had increased. It was expected, that the money allowance for clothing would increase every year until the war stock was exhausted, and the new uniform would probably be more costly than the plainer uniform of the late war.

The standards for wool blankets, boots, and bootees had been improved. The year's supply of those articles were to be the best ever issued to the troops. But the increased cost of clothing and equipment fell as a burden not upon the soldier, but upon the treasury. The allowance established by

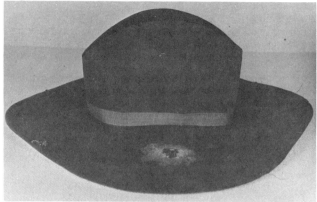

Courtesy North Dakota State Historical Society

Side view of the 1872 pattern hat which received complaints from the troopers. Worn in the field, exposed to the weather, the hat lost its shape and began to go to pieces. When soaked, the brim flopped around like elephant ears. It was . . . "the most useless, uncouth rag ever put on a man's head."

Courtesy North Dakota State Historical Society

This 1872 pattern campaign hat was found on the Custer battlefield. A bullet hole is seen on the left. The hat is black and has no ventilation. When the brim was hooked-up it afforded no protection. (See photograph of officers of the Black Hills Expedition, 1874, wearing hat hooked-up.)

Courtesy Author's Collection

Wide brim hats from the East were favorites with officers in light colors. Hats similar to this one with wide brims and sometimes a low crown were often worn in the field. (Not regulation.)

Courtesy National Archives

A recent arrival from Jefferson Barracks, Missouri. Most recruits posed for photographs at their permanent stations to send home to families and friends. Standing proud in his new uniform, with saber and white gloves, he also is sporting a cold sore above his lip.

government price as savings on the allowance. The greater their price the greater the soldier's profit.

In this period very large scales of surplus and damaged or inferior clothing were sold at auction, often at very low prices. Dealers who purchased these inferior goods sent them to post traders and settlers, who sold them to soldiers. The soldiers wore these condemned clothes, for which they paid a nominal price, and thus, not drawing the corresponding articles from the quartermaster, got credit for the savings at government prices, and thus made considerable gains. The money paid to the army since the war under the head of savings on the soldiers' allowance of clothing was a very large sum.

Probably some of the complaints of inferior quality of clothing in the army resulted from the quite extensive use of this cast-off and rejected material, condemned and sold by the quartermaster's depart-

1872-1881 full dress. Officers and enlisted men. Cavalry — Artillery — Infantry.

Rear side of Captain Ludlow's jacket.

Buckskin jackets were in style with the officers of the 7th Cavalry. Every outfit was different, generally designed by the individual himself and tailored by someone on post or back "stateside." Indian women, or wives of Indian Scouts were quite handy in quill work and design, embellishing these jackets with colorful symbols. Pictured here is a buckskin jacket worn by Captain William Ludlow, engineering officer during the Black Hills Expedition in 1874.

ment, but introduced into the army in consequence of the low price at which the auction purchasers were able to dispose of them.

Military Division of the South
Major General I. McDowell
Headquarters
Louisville, Kentucky

Civilian Clothing:

It appearing from the proceedings of general court martial held in this department that the soldiers have civilian clothing in their possession, and that they wear such clothing when on pass or furlough, thereby subjecting themselves to arrest as deserters, by department commander, the attention of post and battery or company commanders is called to Paragraph 115, Revised U.S. Army Regulations of 1863, which directs that, "Soldiers will wear the prescribed uniform in camp or in garrison, and will not be permitted to keep in their possession any other clothing."[10]

10. Army and Navy Journal, June 14, 1873, p. 696.

1872
UNIFORM AND DRESS OF THE ARMY
OF THE
UNITED STATES.

UNIFORM, DRESS, EQUIPMENTS, &c.

No officer or soldier of the Army shall wear any other than the prescribed uniform, when on duty.

COATS.
FULL DRESS FOR OFFICERS.

All officers shall wear a double-breasted frock coat of dark blue cloth, the skirt to extend from one-half to three-fourths the distance from the hip joint to the bend of the knee.

For a General: Two rows of buttons on the breast, twelve in each row; placed by fours; the distance between each row five and one-half inches at top and three and one-half inches at bottom; stand-up collar, not less than one nor more than two inches in height, to hook in front at the bottom and slope thence up and backward at an angle of thirty degrees on each side, corners rounded; cuffs three inches deep, to go around the sleeves parallel with the lower edge, and with three small buttons at the

Courtesy West Point Museum Collection

Beaded designs on this buckskin jacket show Indian handycraft. The owner, Captain William Ludlow, seemed to possess more than one buckskin outfit, and with good reason, they were hard to keep clean. When wet, they fell out of shape and "weighed a ton." However, during cold weather they were great wind-breakers.

under seam; pockets in the folds of the skirts, with two buttons at the hip and one at the lower end of each side-edge, making four buttons on the back and skirt of the coat; collar and cuffs to be of dark blue velvet; lining of the coat black.

For a Lieutenant General: The same as for a General, except that there will be ten buttons in each row, on the breast, the upper and lower groups by threes, and the middle groups by fours.

For a Major General: The same as for a General,

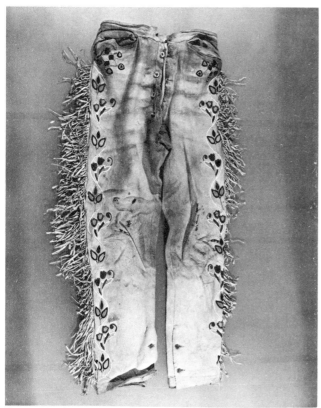

Courtesy West Point Museum Collection

Trousers to match with beaded designs. As buckskins were usually worn in the field or on expeditions, they were constantly in need of repairs after several months.

Courtesy West Point Museum Collection

Rear view of Captain Ludlow's beaded buckskin. As many jackets were trimmed with fringe it evidently had its purpose. During wet weather the fringe accumulated most of the droplets of water. During body movements, the drops of water ran off easily.

except that there will be nine buttons in each row, on the breast, placed by threes.

For a Brigadier General: The same as for a General, except that there will be eight buttons in each row, on the breast, placed by pairs.

For a Colonel, Lieutenant Colonel, and Major: The same as for a General, except that there will be nine buttons in each row, on the breast, placed at equal distances; collars and cuffs of the same color and material as the coat. The upper half of the cuffs to be ornamented with three double stripes of gold braid running the length of the cuff, pointed at their upper ends, and with a small button below the point of each stripe, according to pattern.

For a Captain, 1st Lieutenant, 2nd Lieutenant, and Additional 2d Lieutenant: The same as for a Colonel, except that there will be seven buttons in each row, on the breast, and two stripes on the cuffs.

For all Storekeepers: A single-breasted coat, as lately worn by Captains of the staff, with staff shoulder-straps to indicate rank.

This coat shall be worn on all dress occasions, such as reviews, inspections, dress parades, guards, and courts-martial. It will be habitually worn at battalion drills, except in hot weather, or when otherwise exceptionally directed by the commanding officer.

UNDRESS FOR OFFICERS.

For fatigues, marches, squad and company drills, and other drills when authorized by the commanding officer, and for ordinary wear: A sack coat of dark blue cloth or serge; falling collar; single breasted, with five buttons in front, same as those worn on the dress coat; with black braid, one-fourth of an inch wide, extending from each button and button-hole back six inches and terminating in "herring-bone" loops.

The skirt to extend from one-third to two-thirds the distance from the hip joint to the bend of the knee, and to be slashed at the hip on each side; a knot of

Courtesy Custer Battlefield Museum

Buckskins belonging to Custer on display at the Custer Battlefield Museum. Caption above reads: "For field service he wore this outfit. It helped make him more romantically conspicuous."

Courtesy Smithsonian Institution

Custer had several buckskin outfits in his wardrobe. The one he wore was similar to this coat which was left behind. Note large falling collar and U.S. brass buttons. Custer designed his own buckskin outfits, probably with some help from his wife Elizabeth.

An ordinary plain fringed buckskin jacket worn on expeditions by
Lt. Henry Martin Harrington (USMA 1872), killed at the Battle of
the Little Big Horn.

black braid, one-fourth of an inch wide, on the upper
part of the cuff, according to pattern.

The shoulder-straps will always be worn with it.
Black braid binding, one-half of an inch wide,
around edge of coat.

For Storekeepers: Of pattern above described, but
without braid.

For Chaplain: Plain black frock coat with standing
collar; one row of nine black buttons on the breast,

A good example of a scout in fringed buckskins holding a Winchester '66 model.

with "herring-bone" of black braid around the buttons and button-holes.

COATS.
FOR ENLISTED MEN.

For Infantry: Single-breasted, dark blue basque,
according to pattern deposited in Quartermaster
General's Office, piped with sky-blue; collar same
height as for officers' coat, faced with skyblue cloth
four inches back on each side, cut square to hook up
close in front; number of regiment or badge of corps
in yellow metal in middle of sky blue facing of collar
on each side; skirt of coat on each side of opening
behind to be faced with sky-blue cloth, ornamented
with four buttons, as per pattern. Two straps of dark
blue cloth, piped with the same color as the facings,
let into the waist-seam on each side the coat and
buttoning above the hip to sustain the waist-belt;
shoulder-straps of cloth the color of the facings let
into the shoulder-seam and to button over the
shoulder-belts at the collar-seam with one button;
shoulder-straps for Engineer soldiers to be scarlet,
piped with white.

*For Enlisted Men of Artillery, Engineers, and
Ordnance:* Same as for Infantry, except that the fac-

ings shall be scarlet for Artillery, scarlet and white for Engineers, and crimson for Ordnance.

For Cavalry and Light Artillery: Same as for Infantry, excepting that it is shorter in the skirt, and the facing upon the skirt put on differently, according to pattern in the Quartermaster General's Office; facings for Cavalry yellow, and for Light Artillery red.

Coats for Musicians: Ornamented on the breast with braid same color as the facings, running from the button as now worn, the outer extremities terminating in "herring-bones" and the braid returning back to the buttons.

Coats for Hospital Stewards: Same as for Infantry, except the facing to be of emerald green.

Coats for Ordnance Sergeants: Same as for enlisted men of Ordnance.

Whenever the dress coat is worn by enlisted men, it will invariably be buttoned up and hooked at the collar.

For fatigue purposes, for general wear, and on field service; A dark blue blouse of navy flannel, according to the pattern deposited in the Quartermaster General's Office.

Blouses for winter wear to be lined.

Courtesy Herb Peck, Jr.

Fringed jackets became such a fad that easterner's visiting the frontier, brought along their hunting dress made up of cloth with fringe simulating leather. With regulation dress not as strict in the field, troopers who could afford these outfits . . . wore them, probably not as elaborate as this trooper pictured here. Soldiers borrowed such outfits to have their pictures taken to show the folks back home.

Courtesy National Archives

A striking example of showmanship was "Buffalo" Bill Cody. His buckskins were elaborately adorned with beaded designs, and trimmed out with beaver, otter, mink, and muskrat. It is quite possible that famous scouts such as Cody may have had something to do with the buckskin fringed fashions.

BUTTONS.

The same as now worn for all Officers and enlisted men. *Storekeepers:* General Staff button.

TROWSERS.

For General Officers, Officers of the General Staff, and Staff Corps: Dark blue cloth, plain, without stripe, welt, or cord.

For all Regimental Officers of Cavalry, Artillery, and Infantry: Light blue cloth, same shade of color as prescribed for enlisted men, with stripe one and one-half inches wide, welted at the edges; color, that of facings of their respective arms, except infantry, which will be dark blue.

Storekeepers: Dark blue cloth, with black stripe one and one-half inches wide.

For Chaplains: Plain black.

For Enlisted Men of all Arms and of the Ordnance Department: Sky blue mixture, pattern now worn; waistband three and a half inches wide, to button with two buttons in front; pockets in front, opening at top.

Sergeants to wear a stripe one inch wide, color of facings; and Corporals to wear a stripe one-half inch

Courtesy Smithsonian Institution
U.S. Army Bootee of type adopted in 1873.

wide, color of facings, except Infantry, which will be dark blue.

For Engineers: According to pattern in Quartermaster General's Office.

For Ordnance Sergeants: Crimson stripe, one inch and one-quarter wide.

For Hospital Stewards: Emerald green stripe, one inch and one-quarter wide.

All stripes to be of cloth.

One-third of the trowsers of enlisted men issued on requisition shall be sent to posts cut out but not made up. The material of each pair of trowsers, with the buttons, thread, needles, and all necessary trimmings, shall be rolled up in a bundle, securely fastened and marked with the size of the trowsers.

Trowsers for all mounted men to be re-enforced.
There shall be a 5th size, larger than No. 4.

CRAVATS.
For all Officers: Black; the tie not to be visible at the opening of the collar. Neither cravats nor stocks will be worn by enlisted men when on duty.

BOOTS AND SHOES.
For all Officers: Shall be of black leather and come above the ankle.

For Enlisted Men of Cavalry and Light Artillery: Boots, to come above the swell of the calf of the leg; shoes, Jefferson rights and lefts, according to pattern.

For Enlisted Men of Artillery, Infantry, Engineers, and Ordnance, and all other Enlisted Men: Jefferson rights and lefts, according to pattern.

Top-boots may be worn by mounted men.

HAT OR CAP (FULL DRESS).
For General Officers, Officers of the General Staff, and Staff Corps: Chapeau, according to pattern.

For Officers of Light Artillery and Cavalry: Black felt helmet, with gold cords and tassels, and gilt trimmings, according to pattern.

For all Storekeepers: Forage Cap of dark blue cloth, without braid; badge same as for General Officers.

For all other Officers: Of dark blue cloth, ornamented with gold braid and trimmings, according to pattern.

For Enlisted Men of Light Artillery and Cavalry:

Black felt helmet, same pattern as for officers, with cords and tassels of mohair — red for Light Artillery and yellow for Cavalry. Helmet, ornamented with yellow metal trimmings, as per pattern.

For all other Enlisted Men: Of blue cloth, same pattern as for officers, ornamented with mohair braid of the same color as facings of the coat; trimmings of yellow metal, according to pattern.

FORAGE CAP.
For General Officers: Of dark blue cloth, chasseur pattern, with black velvet band and badge in front.

For all other Commissioned Officers: Of dark blue cloth, chasseur pattern, with badge of corps or regiment in front, top of badge to be even with top of cap, and according to pattern in Quartermaster General's Office.

For all Enlisted Men: Of plain blue cloth, same pattern as for officers, with badge of corps or letter of company of yellow metal worn in front as for officers.

FORAGE CAP BADGES.
For General Officers: A gold embroidered wreath on dark blue cloth ground, encircling the letters U.S. in silver, old English characters.

For Officers of the General Staff, and Staff Corps: Same as for General Officers, with the exception of those for Ordnance Officers, which will have a gold embroidered shell and flame on dark blue cloth ground.

For Officers of Engineers: A gold embroidered wreath of laurel and palm encircling a silver turretted castle on dark blue cloth ground.

For Officers of Cavalry: Two gold embroidered sabers, crossed, edges upward, on dark blue cloth ground, with the number of the regiment in silver in the upper angle.

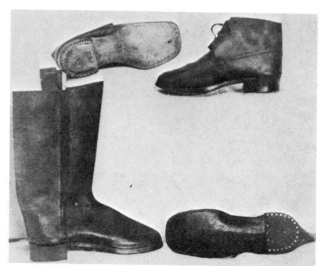

Courtesy Smithsonian Institution
New pattern shoes, brass screwed 1872. Old pattern boots, sewed prior to 1872.

For Officers of Artillery: Two gold embroidered cannons, crossed, on dark blue cloth ground, with the number of the regiment in silver at the intersection of the cross-cannon.

For Officers of Infantry: A gold embroidered bugle, on dark blue cloth ground, with the number of the regiment in silver within the bend.

FATIGUE HAT.

For Officers and Enlisted Men: Of black felt, to pattern, to be worn only on fatigue duty and on marches or campaigns.

PLUMES FOR OFFICERS.

For General-in-Chief: Three black ostrich feathers.

For other General Officers, for Officers of the General Staff, and Staff Corps: Two black ostrich feathers.

For Regimental Officers of Foot Artillery and Infantry: Of cocks' feathers, to rise five inches above the top of the cap, front feathers to reach the vizor, rear feathers to reach the top of the cap, with gilt ball and socket: color of plume to be red for Artillery and white for Infantry.

For Officers of Light Artillery and Cavalry: Horse-hair plume; gilt ball and socket, plume to be long enough to reach the front edge of the vizor of the helmet: color of the plume to be red for Light Artillery and yellow for Cavalry.

PLUMES AND POMPONS FOR ENLISTED MEN.

For Artillery: Red pompon, pattern shape; ball and socket of yellow metal.

For Infantry: White pompon, same shape and with same ball and socket as for Artillery.

For Ordnance: Crimson pompon, same ball and socket as for Artillery.

For Engineer Troops: Red pompon, with white top; same ball and socket as for Artillery.

For Light Artillery: Red; and for Cavalry, yellow horse-hair plume, same size and length as for officers; socket according to pattern.

SPURS.

For all Mounted Officers: Yellow metal or gilt.

For all Mounted Men: Of yellow metal, plain surface.

GLOVES.

For General Officers, Officers of the General Staff, and Staff Corps: Buff or white gauntlets or gloves.

For Field Officers of Artillery, Cavalry, and Infantry; for Officers of Light Artillery and Cavalry: White gauntlets or gloves. All other Officers, white gloves.

For all Enlisted Men: Of white Berlin, to be issued as clothing.

Courtesy Dr. L. A. Frost Collection

General Custer's boots (Civil War) and canvas covered trunk, stenciled with his name and regiment. Boots are of the later pattern.

SASH.

For General Officers: Buff silk net, with silk bullion fringe ends; sash to go twice around the waist and to tie behind the left hip, pendent part not to extend more than eighteen inches below the tie.

SWORD-BELT.

For all Officers: A waist-belt, not less than one and one-half nor more than two inches wide, with slings of the same material as the belt, with a hook attached to the belt on which to hang the sword.

The belt to be worn outside the full dress coat and underneath the undress sack.

For General Officers: Of red Russia leather, with three stripes of gold embroidery, as per pattern now worn.

For all Field Officers: One broad stripe of gold lace on black enameled leather, according to pattern.

For all Officers of the General Staff, and Staff Corps, below the rank of Field Officers: Four stripes of gold, interwoven with black silk, lined with black enameled leather, according to pattern.

For Company Officers of Cavalry, Artillery and Infantry: Four stripes of gold lace, interwoven with silk of the same color as the facings of their arms of service, and lined with black enameled leather.

For all Storekeepers: Of black enameled leather, of patterns lately worn.

On undress duty, marches, and campaigns, officers may wear a plain black leather belt.

For all Non-Commissioned Officers: Plain black leather.

SWORD-BELT PLATE.

For all Officers and Enlisted Men: Gilt, rectangular, two inches wide, with a raised bright rim; a silver wreath of laurel encircling the "Arms of the United States," eagle, shield, scroll, edge of cloud and rays bright. The motto "E pluribus unum" upon the scroll; stars also of silver, according to pattern.

SWORD AND SCABBARD.

General Officers: Straight sword, gilt hilt, silver grip; brass or steel scabbard, same as now worn.

For Officers of Light Artillery and Cavalry: Sabre and scabbard as now worn, and according to pattern in Ordnance Department.

For Officers of the Pay and Medical Departments: Small sword and scabbard, according to pattern in the Surgeon General's Office, as now worn.

For all other Officers: Same as the small, straight sword now worn by the officers of the General Staff, and according to pattern in the Ordnance Department.

The sword and sword-belt will be worn upon all occasions of duty except stable and fatigue.

When not on military duty, officers may wear swords of honor, or the prescribed sword, with a scabbard, gilt, or of leather with gilt mountings.

SWORD-KNOT.

For General Officers: Gold cord, with acorn end.

For all other Officers: Gold lace strap, with gold bullion tassel, as now worn.

EPAULETTES.

For the General of the Army: Of gold, with solid crescent; device — two silver embroidered stars, with five rays each, one and one-half inches in diameter, and the "Arms of the United States" embroidered in gold placed between them.

For a Lieutenant General: Three silver embroidered stars of five rays each, respectively, one and one-half, one and one-quarter, one and one-eighth inches in diameter. The largest placed in the centre of the crescent; the others, placed longitudinally on the strap and equidistant, ranging in order of size from the crescent.

For Major General: Same as for Lieutenant General, omitting smallest star, and the smaller of the two remaining stars placed in the centre of the strap.

For a Brigadier General: Same as for a Lieutenant General, omitting all but the largest star.

SHOULDER-KNOTS.

*For Officers of the Adjutant General's and Inspector General's Departments, and for Aides-de-Camp to General Officers:** Of gold cord, Russian pattern, on dark blue cloth ground; insignia of rank and letters of corps or designation of regiment embroidered on the cloth ground, according to pattern; an aiguillette of gold cord to be worn with the right shoulder-knot and permanently attached thereto, according to pattern.

For Officers of other Staff Corps: Same as above described, without the aiguillette.

For Officers of Cavalry, Artillery, and Infantry: Of the same pattern as for the Staff Corps, but on cloth of the same color as the facings of their arm, with insignia of rank and number of regiment embroidered on the cloth ground, according to pattern.

For Regimental Adjutants: Of the same pattern as for other officers of their arm, but with aiguillettes attached.

INSIGNIA OF RANK ON SHOULDER-KNOTS.

For a Colonel: A silver embroidered eagle at the centre of the pad.

For a Lieutenant Colonel: Two silver embroidered leaves, one at each end of pad.

For a Major: Two gold embroidered leaves, one at each end of pad.

For a Captain: Two silver embroidered bars at each end of pad.

For a 1st Lieutenant: One silver embroidered bar at each end of pad.

For a 2nd Lieutenant: Plain.

For an Additional 2d Lieutenant: Same as 2d Lieutenant.

The above insignia to be the *same* as prescribed for the shoulder-straps.

SHOULDER-STRAPS.

For the General of the Army: Dark blue cloth, one and three-eighths inches wide by four inches long, bordered with an embroidery of gold one-fourth of an inch wide; two silver embroidered stars of five rays each, and gold embroidered "Arms of the United States" between them.

For a Lieutenant General: The same as for the General, except that there will be three silver embroidered stars of five rays, one star on the centre of the strap, and one on each side, equidistant between the centre and outer edge of the strap, the centre star to be the largest.

For all Major Generals: The same as for the Lieutenant General, except that there will be two stars instead of three; the centre of each star to be one inch from the outer edge of the gold embroidery on the ends of the strap; both stars of the same size.

For a Brigadier General: The same as for a Major General, except that there will be one star instead of two; the centre of the star to be equidistant from the outer edge of the embroidery on the ends of the strap.

*See Miscellaneous.

Officer's saber, model 1872, with leather sword knot. Officer's shoulder straps. (Left to Right) Lieutenant-Colonel — silver embroidered leaves. Major has gold embroidered leaves. Colonel — silver embroidered eagle. Captain — 2 gold embroidered bars at each end. 1st Lieutenant (not pictured) has one gold bar at each end. 2nd Lieutenant — No bars (plain field).

For a Colonel: The same size as for a Major General, and bordered in like manner with an embroidery of gold; a silver embroidered spread eagle on the centre of the strap, two inches between the tips of the wings, having in the right talon an olive branch, and in the left a bundle of arrows; an escutcheon on the breast, as represented in the "Arms of the United States." Cloth of the straps as follows: for the General Staff and Staff Corps, dark blue; Artillery, scarlet; Infantry, sky blue; Cavalry, yellow.

For a Lieutenant Colonel: The same as for a Colonel, according to corps, omitting the eagle, and introducing a silver embroidered leaf at each end, each leaf extending seven-eighths of an inch from the end border of the strap.

For Major: The same as for a Colonel, according to corps, omitting the eagle, and introducing a gold embroidered leaf at each end, each leaf extending seven-eighths of an inch from the end border of the strap.

For a Captain: The same as for a Colonel, according to corps, omitting the eagle, and introducing at each end two silver embroidered bars of the same width as the border, placed parallel to the ends of the strap, at a distance between them and from the border equal to the width of the border.

For a 1st Lieutenant: The same as for a Colonel, according to corps, omitting the eagle, and introducing at each end one silver embroidered bar of the same width as the border, placed parallel to the ends of the strap, at a distance from the border equal to its width.

For a 2d Lieutenant: The same as for a Colonel, according to corps, omitting the eagle.

For an Additional 2nd Lieutenant: The same as for a 2d Lieutenant.

Officers serving in the field may dispense with the prescribed insignia of rank on their horse equipments, and may wear overcoats of the same color and shape as those of the enlisted men of their commands, and omit epaulettes, shoulder-knots, or other prominent marks likely to attract the fire of sharpshooters; but all officers must wear the prescribed buttons, stripes, and shoulder-straps, to indicate their corps and rank.

The shoulder-strap will be worn whenever the epaulette or shoulder-knot is not.

CHEVRONS.

The rank of non-commissioned officers will be marked by chevrons upon both sleeves of the uniform coat and overcoat, above the elbow; of cloth of the same color as the facings of the uniform coat, divided into bars a half inch wide by black silk stitching, except for Engineers, which will be white stitching and piped with white, points down, according to new patterns in Quartermaster General's Office, as follows:

For a Sergeant Major: Three bars and an arc.

For a Quartermaster Sergeant: Three bars and a tie of three bars.

For a Principal Musician: Three bars and a bugle.

For an Ordnance Sergeant: Three bars and a star.

For a Hospital Steward: A half chevron of emerald green cloth one and three-fourths inches wide, piped with yellow cloth, running obliquely downward from the outer to the inner seam of the sleeve, and at an angle of about thirty degrees with a horizontal, and in the centre a "caduceus" two inches long, the head toward the outer seam of the sleeve.

For a 1st Sergeant: Three bars and a lozenge.

For a Battalion or Company Quartermaster Sergeant: Three bars and a tie of one bar.

For a Sergeant: Three bars.

For a Corporal: Two bars.

For a Pioneer: Two crossed hatchets, of cloth, same color and material as the facings of the uniform coat, to be sewed on each sleeve, above the elbow, in the place indicated for a chevron (those of a corporal to be just above and resting on the chevron), the head of the hatchet upward, its edge outward, of the following dimensions, viz:

Handle, four and one-half inches long, one-fourth to one-third of an inch wide.

Hatchet, two inches long, one inch wide at the edge.

To indicate service: All non-commissioned officers, musicians and privates, who have served faithfully for one term of enlistment, will wear as a mark of distinction upon both sleeves of the uniform coat, below the elbow, a diagonal half chevron, one-half inch wide, extending from seam to seam, the front end nearest the cuff, and one-half inch above the point of the cuff, to be of the same color as the edging on the coat.

In like manner an additional half chevron, above and parallel to the first, for every subsequent term of enlistment and faithful service. Distance between each chevron one-fourth of an inch.

Service in war will be indicated by a white stripe

on each side of the chevron for Artillery, and a red stripe for all other corps, the stripe to be one-eighth of an inch wide.

OVERCOAT.

For General Officers: Of dark blue cloth, closing by means of four frog buttons of black silk and loops of black silk cord; cord down the breast, and at the throat by a long loop "à echelle," without tassel or plate, on the left side, and a black silk frog button on the right; cord for the loops fifteen hundredths of an inch in diameter; back, a single piece, slit up from the bottom from fifteen to seventeen inches, according to the height of the wearer, and closing at will by buttons, and button-holes cut in a concealed flap; collar of the same color and material as the coat, rounded at the edges, and to stand or fall; when standing to be about five inches high; sleeves loose, of a single piece and round at the bottom, without cuff or slit; lining woolen; around the front and lower borders, the edges of the pockets, the edges of the sleeves, collar, and slit in the back, a flat braid of black silk one-half an inch wide; and around each

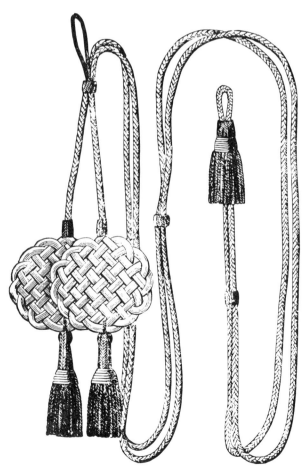

Cord with tassels for U.S. Helmet.

frog button on the breast a knot two and one-quarter inches in diameter, of black silk cord, seven hundredths of an inch in diameter, cape of the same color and material as the coat, removable at the pleasure of the wearer, and reaching to the cuff of the coat sleeve when the arm is extended; coat to extend down the leg from six to eight inches below the knee, according to height.

To indicate rank: There will be on both sleeves, near the lower edge, a knot of flat black silk braid, not exceeding one-eighth of an inch in width, and composed of five braids, double knot.

For all other Officers: Dark blue close fitting double-breasted surtout coat, with a cape, made to detach from the coat and fall to the tips of the fingers when the arm and hand are extended; the skirt of the coat for mounted officers to reach half way between the knee and the sole of the foot; for dismounted officers, three inches below the knee.

The coat to have seven buttons on each breast of the same pattern as those on the uniform coat. The insignia of rank on the sleeve, as follows, viz:

Colonel, five braids, single knot.
Lieutenant Colonel, four braids, single knot.
Major, three braids, single knot.
Captain, two braids, single knot.
1st Lieutenant, one braid, single knot.
2d Lieutenant and Additional 2d Lieutenant, without braid.
Military Storekeepers and Chaplains, without braid.

On the frontier and campaign, officers may wear the soldier's overcoat, with insignia of rank on the sleeve.

For Enlisted Men of all arms: Of sky blue cloth of the pattern now used in the mounted service.

OTHER ARTICLES OF CLOTHING AND EQUIPMENTS.

Flannel shirt, drawers, stockings, and stable-frock: The same as now furnished.

Stable-frocks for Mounted Men: Of white cotton, made loose and extending well down to the knee, without sleeve or body lining; to button in front.

Blanket: Woolen, gray, with letters U.S. in black, four inches long in the centre; to be seven feet long and five and a half feet wide, and to weigh at least five pounds; to be made of wool; the blanket now issued to troops in California to be the standard.

Canvass overall for Engineer Soldiers: Of white cotton; one garment to cover the whole of the body above the waist — the breast, the shoulders, and the arms; sleeves loose, to allow free play of the arms, with a narrow wristband buttoning with one button; overalls to fasten at the neck behind with two buttons, and at the waist behind with buckle and tongue.

For Cavalry and Light Artillery: White cotton overalls, to cover only the waist. These overalls are to be worn at all stable duties.

Sets of stencil plates of letters and numbers of two sizes (inch and half inch) for marking equipments, &c., shall be furnished by the Quartermaster's Department to each company commander and regimental adjutant.

SIGNAL SERVICE.

For the Chief Signal Officer: The same uniform as for the Adjutant General's Department, without the aiguillettes.

The uniform of the Enlisted Men of the Signal Service shall be as follows:

The Cavalry uniform, except that the trimmings and facings be orange instead of yellow, bearing a device on the sleeve of the coat, as follows: crossed signal flags, red and white, on dark blue cloth; size of flags three-fourths of an inch square; length of staff three inches, after the pattern in the office of the Chief Signal Officer of the Army. This device to be worn by the non-commissioned officers above the chevrons; by privates of the first class on both arms; and by privates of the second class on the left arm only, in the same position as the chevron of non-commissioned officers.

HORSE FURNITURE.
FOR GENERAL OFFICERS AND
THE GENERAL STAFF.

Housing for General Officers: To be worn over the saddle; of dark blue cloth, trimmed with two rows of gold lace, the outer row one inch and five eighths wide, the inner row two inches and one-fourth; to be made full, so as to cover the horse's haunches and forehands, and to bear on each flank corner the following ornaments, distinctive of rank, to wit:

For the General of the Army: A gold embroidered spread eagle with two stars and "Arms of the United States" between them.

For Lieutenant General: A gold embroidered spread eagle and three stars.

For Major Generals: A gold embroidered spread eagle and two stars.

For Brigadier Generals: A gold embroidered spread eagle and one star.

Saddle-cloth for General Staff Officers, and Officers of the Staff Corps: Dark blue cloth, of sufficient length to cover the saddle and holsters, and one foot ten inches in depth, with an edging of gold lace one inch wide.

For all other Officers: Dark blue felt, according to pattern; worn under the saddle and trimmed around the edges with cloth one and one-half inches wide, color as follows:

Infantry, sky blue.
Artillery, scarlet
Cavalry, yellow.

For Infantry, Cavalry, and horse equipments, knapsacks, haversacks, &c., and tools and materials for Cavalry, according to patterns in Ordnance Office. See Ordnance Memoranda No. 13, and General Orders No. 60, War Department, series of 1872.

MILITARY ACADEMY.

The uniform of the Professors and Sword Master at the West Point Military Academy shall be the same as now worn, excepting they will be permitted to wear the dark blue sack coat prescribed for Army officers, with the buttons of the General Staff to be worn on both coats.

FOR CADETS.

The same uniform as now worn.

MISCELLANEOUS.

Aides-de-Camp and the Military Secretary, who have *increased* rank, will wear the aiguillette with the uniform of the General Staff.

Aides-de-Camp to Major and Brigadier Generals will wear the aiguillete with the uniform of their Regiments and Corps.

Whenever the full dress coat is worn by officers on duty the prescribed epaulettes or shoulder-knots will be attached. Letters to be embroidered on shoulder-knots in old English:

Adjutant General's Department.
Inspector General's Department.
Bureau of Military Justice.
Signal Service.
Quartermaster's Department.
Subsistence Department.
Medical Department.
Pay Department.
Engineer Corps.
Ordnance Department.

Sashes will no longer be worn by officers below the grade of Brigadier General, or by non-commissioned officers.

Officers when not on duty are permitted to wear a buff, white, or blue vest, with the small button prescribed for them.

When the trowsers and flannel shirts now in store shall have been issued or otherwise disposed of, the troops serving in warm climates will, upon requisitions approved by commanding officers, be supplied with those articles of a lighter texture, but of the same material, cut, and color as those furnished the other troops of the Army.

Bands will wear the uniforms of their Regiments or Corps. Commanding officers may at the expense of the Corps, sanctioned by the Councils of Administration, make such additions of ornaments as they may judge proper.

Amendments made to the Regulations of 1872, since their promulgation to the Army.

* * * * * * * * * * * *

The new sword for staff and foot officers, prescribed by General Orders No. 92, Adjutant General's Office, 1872, will be supplied with two scabbards, one *nickel plated*, to be worn with the dress, and one *browned*, with the undress uniform.

(G.O.97.A.G.O. November 8—1872)

* * * * * * * * * * * *

The provisions of General Orders 92, War Department, Adjutant General's Office, are hereby so far modified as to substitute for the letters "A.D.," "E.C.," and "O.D.," upon the shoulder-knots for officers of the Adjutant General's Department, Corps of Engineers, and the Ordnance Department, a solid shield of silver, bearing thirteen stars, according to pattern, a silver turreted castle of metal, and a shell and flame in silver embroidery, respectively. Each of the designations to be one and four-tenths inches in width by nine-tenths of an inch in height.

On the forage-cap badge for officers of the Adjutant General's Department the designated shield will be substituted for the letters "U.S."

The only uniform required to be worn by Chaplains is that described under the heading of "Undress for Officers." The braid upon the Chaplain's coat to be of the same width and put on in the same manner as upon the undress coat for officers.

The pompons and braid upon the caps of Hospital Stewards to be of emerald green, same ball and socket as for artillery soldiers; the wreath in front of cap of brass, inclosing the letters "U.S." in Roman, of white metal. Other cap trimmings the same as for other enlisted men.

For enlisted men of Ordnance and Engineers the same wreath as for Hospital Stewards, inclosing the letters "O.D." and "C.E." in Roman, of white metal.

The sword-belt will be worn outside the overcoat by all officers below the grade of Brigadier General.

NOTE. — Swords of prescribed patterns will be distributed to Arsenals as soon as manufactured, for sale to officers.

A reasonable time after December 1 will be allowed to officers at remote stations to enable them to procure swords from the Ordnance Department.

The uniform for Chief Musicians will be prescribed by the commanders of the regiments in which they serve.

The uniform of the band at West Point will be as now worn.

(G.O.107—A.G.O. December 14, 1972)

* * * * * * * * * * * *

Uniform for Commissary Sergeants.

Same as for Ordnance Sergeants, except as follows:

Facings, stripes, pompon, and chevron, to be cadet gray instead of crimson.

Crescent (points front) of same color as chevron and above it, instead of a star.

Distinctive badge for coat collar, hat, and cap, to be a crescent of white metal, points in same vertical line.

(G.O.38—A.G.O.,—March 20—1873.)

* * * * * * * * * * * *

The provisions of General Orders Nos. 92 and 107, series of 1872, are hereby modified as follows:

I . . . Whenever the full dress coat is worn on armed duty, and not in the field, by officers below the grade of Brigadier General, the shoulder-knots, gilt sword-belts, and, by those officers for whom they are prescribed, the nickel-plated sword-scabbards, will be worn.

II . . . Whenever the sack coat is worn on armed duty the dark sword-scabbard and black sword-belt will be worn by those officers for whom they are prescribed.

III . . . The chapeau will be worn with the front peak turned slightly to the left, showing the gilt ornaments upon the right side.

IV . . . Enlisted men of the Engineer Corps, instead of a wreath with the letters "E.C.," will wear in front of their caps the castle with the letters of their companies; and enlisted men of the Ordnance Department, instead of a wreath with the letters "O.D.," will wear in front of their caps the shell and flame; both of the above to be according to patterns in the Quartermaster General's Office.

V . . . The aiguillette, instead of being permanently attached to the shoulder-knot, may be made separate, so as to be attached to the coat underneath the knot by means of a strap or tongue passing through the lower fastening of the knot.

VI . . . When not on armed duty, officers may wear the dress coat with the shoulder-straps attached.

VII . . . The helmet cords will be attached to the left side of the helmet and come down to the left shoulder, where they are held together by a slide; one cord then passes to the front and the other to the rear of the neck, crossing upon the right shoulder and passing separately around to the front and rear of the right arm, where they are again united and held together by a slide under the arm; the united cords then cross the breast and are looped up to the upper button on the left side of the coat.

VIII . . . Chief trumpeters and saddler sergeants will wear chevrons according to patterns in the Quartermaster General's Office.

IX . . . The fatigue hat will not be worn in garrison by officers or enlisted men except when on fatigue duty.

X . . . Until further orders, the single-breasted overcoat, with the additional cape, may be issued to, and worn by, enlisted men of all arms of the service, in lieu of the double-breasted overcoat.

XI . . . The badge of corps and letter of company will both be worn in front of the forage cap by enlisted men of Artillery, Infantry, Cavalry, and Engineers. Enlisted men of Ordnance will wear the badge of corps only.

XII . . . The dimensions of the shield for the officers of the Adjutant General's Department, authorized by War Department General Orders No. 107, of 1872, will be according to pattern in the Adjutant General's Office, instead of the dimensions fixed by the said order. For an Assistant Adjutant General with rank of Colonel it will be worn on the bullion of the knot, midway between the upper fastening and the pad.

(G.O.67—A.G.O.June 25—1873)

* * * * * * * * * *

The Service Chevrons prescribed in General Orders No. 92 of 1872, from this office, to be worn by enlisted men, will conform in color to the arms of service in which the soldier served. If he has served more than one enlistment, in different arms, the Service Chevron will be of different colors to correspond.

(G.O.92—A.G.O. September 15—1873.)

* * * * * * * * * *

The following changes in the uniform and dress of the Army having, in conformity with the 100th Article of War, been submitted by the Secretary of War to the President, and by him approved, are hereby adopted:

1st. Officers are permitted to wear a plain dark-blue body-coat with the button designating their respective corps, regiments, or departments, without any other mark or ornament upon it. This coat, however, is not to be considered as a dress for any military purpose.

2d. Cap badges for all officers of Infantry will be two gold-embroidered rifles without bayonets, barrels upward, on dark-blue cloth ground, with the number of the regiment in silver in the upper angle, according to pattern in Quartermaster General's Office.

Badge for all enlisted men of Infantry except Field and Band Musicians the same insignia, in brass, with the letter of the company, also in brass, above the number of the regiment.

Field and Band Musicians will continue to wear the bugle and letters as at present prescribed.

3d. This new regulation concerning insignia for Infantry officers will go into effect on or before the 1st June, 1876.

The new insignia for enlisted men of Infantry will be issued and worn as soon as it is received from the Quartermaster's Department, on which the necessary requisitions will be made.

4th. Undress sack-coats for officers will hereafter be of the same pattern and material as that now worn, without the black braid, and no slashes at the hips.

The sword and sword-belt will be worn outside the coat.

(G.O.96—A.G.O.November 19, 1875)

* * * * * * * * * *

I ... Hereafter the chevrons upon the overcoats of non-commissioned officers of Infantry will be of dark blue cloth, instead of light blue, as prescribed in General Orders No. 92, of 1872, from this office. Chevrons, similar to those prescribed for the uniform-coat, will be worn by non-commissioned officers upon the sleeves of their blouses.

II ... The letter of the company will be placed in the *lower* angle, and the number of the regiment in the *upper* angle, of the cap-badge for enlisted men of Infantry — prescribed in General Orders No. 96, of 1875, from this office.

(G.O.21—A.G.O. March 20, 1876)

* * * * * * * * * * * *

Hereafter the cap-badges, numbers of regiments, and letters of companies will be worn by enlisted men of the army in the following manner, viz:

For Light Artillery and Cavalry Soldiers — the numbers of their regiments in the upper, and the letters of their companies in the lower, angles of the badges of their respective arms upon the forage caps; the helmets and trimmings according to the patterns now worn.

For Ordnance Sergeants and soldiers — the "shell and flame" on dress and forage cap.

For Hospital Stewards — the letters "U.S." in white metal, inclosed by wreath, on dress and forage caps.

For Commissary Sergeants — crescent in white metal, the points in a vertical line, on dress and forage caps.

For Engineers — the castle, with letter of company above it, on dress and forage caps.

For Artillery — the crossed cannon, with number of the regiment in upper, and letter of company in lower, angles, on dress and forage caps.

For Infantry — the crossed rifles, with the numbers of regiment and the letters of the company placed as for Artillery, upon dress and forage caps.

For Field and Band Musicians — bugle, with numbers of regiment in the center, and the letters of the company above the bugle.

The cap trimmings for enlisted men of all arms and corps will be of yellow metal, unless otherwise specified.

(G.O.8—A.G.O. February 8, 1877)

* * * * * * * * * * *

Hereafter General Officers above the grade of Brigadier General will be allowed, at their option, to wear the sash across the body from the left shoulder to the right side.

The sash may be of buff silk and gold thread.

(G.O.11—A.G.O. February 12, 1877.)

* * * * * * * * * * *

Hereafter, Military Storekeepers in the Quartermaster's Department holding the rank of Captain will wear the uniform prescribed for Assistant Quartermasters with the rank of Captain.

(G.O.23—A.G.O. May 14, 1878.)

* * * * * * * * * * *

VIII ... "Meritorious non-commissioned officers of the Army recommended," under the provisions of law above quoted, will receive a certificate to that effect from the Adjutant General of the Army, and will be known in the service as "candidates for promotion," and will have the title of "candidate" prefixed to that of their rank on all rolls, returns, orders, and correspondence. They will be entitled to wear on each sleeve of their coat a single stripe of gilt lace, similar to that worn by commissioned officers, but will be entitled to this privilege so long only as they maintain the specially honorable position of "candidate."

(G.O.62—A.G.O. August 16, 1878)

* * * * * * * * * * * *

By direction of the Secretary of War, the uniform and dress of officers of the Signal Corps will be the same as that for the Chief Signal Officer, the usual distinction being made for the grades.

The distinctive insignia on the cap and shoulder-knot will be according to the pattern deposited in the office of the Chief Signal Officer.

(G.O.86—A.G.O. December 3, 1878.)

* * * * * * * * * * * *

5th. *Clothing and Uniform.* — No marked change in existing patterns will now be sanctioned. The distinctive colors of cloth and familiar ornaments to distinguish the arm of service and the rank of the wearer must not be altered. The linings and facings of the overcoats will be made to conform to the trimmings of the uniform. Helmets will be worn for all mounted troops and hats for foot troops. The Quartermaster's Department will provide a reasonable quantity of fur coats and overshoes, and of the canvas overcoat described by the Board, the pattern of which will be deposited with Quartermaster General, for issue to troops in actual service at the extreme northern latitudes; and in extreme southern latitudes in summer commanding officers are authorized to sanction, on duty, the blue flannel sack coat, white pants, and a straw hat; the two latter must be bought out of the pay of the soldier of the local merchant or trader. Whenever the enlisted men wear such summer clothing the officers must in like manner conform. The distinctive shoulder-strap must always be worn on duty. After January 1, 1880, the cuff ornaments prescribed in General Orders No. 92, of 1872, will be discontinued.

(G.O.76—A.G.O. July 23, 1879)

* * * * * * * * * * * *

Chaplains may wear on the uniform coat prescribed for them in General Orders No. 92, of 1872, a shoulder-strap of black velvet, with a shepherd's crook of frosted silver on the center of the strap. They may also wear a black cord on the outer seam of the trousers prescribed for Chaplains in the same order.

(G.O.10—A.G.O. February 18, 1880.)

* * * * * * * * * * * *

By direction of the Secretary of War the following modifications in the uniform of the Army are made:

I . . . the dress cap for regimental officers and men will be discontinued and in lieu thereof the following adopted:

Helmets for field officers. — According to the pattern on file in the office of the Quartermaster General. Body: of cork or other suitable material covered with black cloth, or of black felt at the option of the wearer. Trimmings: cords and tassels, top piece and plume-socket, chain chin-strap and hooks, eagle with motto, crossed cannon, rifles, or sabers, all gilt, with the number of the regiment on the shield in white; plume of buffalo-hair, white for infantry, yellow for cavalry, and red for artillery.

Helmets for other officers of mounted troops and of Signal Corps. — Same as above, except that color of plume shall be orange for Signal Corps.

Helmets for other officers of foot troops. — same as above, except that the trimmings are as follows: Top piece, spike, chain chin-strap with hooks and side buttons, eagle with motto, crossed rifles or cannon, all gilt, with the number of the regiment on the shield in white.

Officers' summer helmets. — Body: of cork as per pattern in the office of the Quartermaster General, covered with white facing-cloth; top piece, spike, chain chin-strap, and hooks, all gilt.

Helmets for all mounted troops. — Body: of black felt as per pattern in the office of the Quartermaster General, with leather chin-strap, large crossed cannon or sabers, letter of company and number of regiment, plain side buttons, top piece and plume-socket, all brass; horse-hair plumes and cords, and band with rings of the color of the arm of service.

Helmets for all foot troops. — Of same pattern and material as for mounted troops, with leather chin-strap; and plain side buttons, top piece and spike, of brass.

Trimmings. — Commissary sergeants, a crescent of white metal; hospital stewards, a wreath of brass, with letters U.S. in white metal; engineers, a castle, with letter of company; ordnance, a shell and flame; artillery, crossed cannon; infantry, crossed rifles, and letter of company and number of regiment, all in brass.

The allowance of helmets will be one in the first and one in the third year of enlistment.

Cork summer helmets will, in hot climates, be provided for enlisted men, as indicated in General Orders, No. 72, Adjutant General's Office, 1880.

II . . . The issue of gray flannel shirts will be discontinued as soon as the present stock on hand shall have been exhausted. A shirt of dark-blue flannel with pipings of the color of the arm of service will be substituted therefor which will be issued at the rate of three in the first year and two in each of the second, third, fourth, and fifth years of enlistment. They may be worn in summer without the blouse.

III . . . Only one blouse will hereafter be annually issued to each enlisted man. This will be lined.

IV . . . Suitable knit undershirts, at the rate of three per year, will be supplied in addition to the blue flannel shirts.

This order will go into effect, except for cavalry and light batteries, on the 1st of July next or as soon thereafter as the supplies can be procured by the Quartermaster's Department; for cavalry and light batteries whenever the present stock of helmets is exhausted by issues.

* * * * * * * * * * * *

Officers may use the new helmet immediately if they so desire.

(G.O.4—A.G.O. January 7, 1881)

* * * * * * * * * * * *

Judge advocates of the Army and professors of the Military Academy are authorized to wear the plain dark-blue body-coat prescribed in General Orders, No. 96, War Department, Adjutant General's Office, November 19, 1875; the buttons on the coat to be the same as for the general staff.

(G.O.20—A.G.O. February 15, 1881.)

THE RED MAN

"When we first beheld the red man, we beheld him in his home, the home of peace and plenty, the home of nature. Sorrow furrowed lines were unknown on his dauntless brow. His manly limbs were not weakened by being forced to sleep in dreary caves and deep morasses, fireless, comfortless and coverless, through fear of the hunter's deadly rifle. His heart did not quake with terror at every gust of wind that sighed through the trees, but on the contrary, they were the favored sons of nature, and she like a doting mother, had bestowed all her gifts on them. They stood in their native strength and beauty, stamped with the proud majesty of free born men, whose souls never knew fear, or whose eyes never quailed beneath the fierce glance of man. But what are they now, those monarchs of the west? They are like withered leaves of their own native forest, scattered in every direction by the fury of the tempest.

The red man is alone in his misery. The earth is one vast desert to him. Once it had its charms to lull his spirit to repose, but now the home of his youth, the familiar forests, under whose graceful shade, he and his ancestors stretched their weary limbs after the excitement of the chase, are swept away by the axe of the woodman; the hunting grounds have vanished from his sight and in every object he beholds the hand of desolation. We behold him now on the verge of extinction, standing on his last foothold, clutching his bloodstained rifle, resolved to die amidst the horrors of slaughter, and soon he will be talked of as a noble race who once existed but have now passed away."

Respectfully submitted,
G. A. Custer
Cadet U.S.M.A.

To Lieut. Childs,
    Inst. in Ethics[1]

To the Indian, the name of each tribe has a significance, which is represented by a sign that is well understood by them all. As examples: the Comanche, or "Snake", is indicated by making a waving motion with the hand, in imitation of a crawling reptile; the Cheyenne, or "Cut Arm", by drawing the hand across the arm to imitate cutting it with a knife; Arapahoes, or "Smellers", by seizing the nose with the thumb and forefinger; the Sioux, or "Cut Throats", by drawing the hand across the throat horizontally in one motion; the Pawnees, or "Wolves", by placing a hand on each side of the forehead, with two fingers pointing toward the front, to represent the narrow ears of the wolf; the Crow, by imitating the flapping of the bird's wings with the palms of the hands.

When approaching strangers, the plains Indians put their horses at full speed, racing head-on toward the party. Anyone unaccustomed to this peculiar habit might drop from their saddle and prepare for a battle with loaded weapons, thinking the onrushing horsemen were hostile. However, this was the custom with friends or enemies. How did one know whether they were peaceful or hostile? The question was usually answered by some experienced buckskinned plainsman. When a party is discovered approaching, and is near enough to distinguish signals, all that is necessary in order to ascertain their disposition is to raise the right hand, with the palm in front, and gradually push it forward and back several times. Indians understand this to be a command to halt, and, if they are not hostile, it will be obeyed immediately. On the other hand, if they continue to charge, the horse was considered to be the best target. Chances were that, in the fall, the Indian would break something or become dazed. Another shot would finish him off. It must be remembered that many westerners considered all Indians as savages. Killing an Indian was given no more regret than killing a wild animal in the hunt.

The aptness of the Indians in "tracking" was described by a contemporary writer:

---

1. This thesis was written May 5, 1858, and respectfully submitted to his instructor, Lieutenant Childs, at the United States Military Academy. It shows Custer's great admiration and respect for the American Indian. (Libby Custer microfilm, Custer Battlefield Museum, No. 5570.)

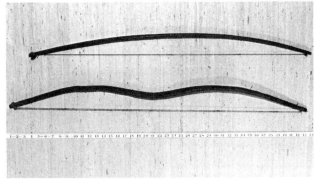

Courtesy J. J. Narus Collection

Northern plains Indian bow variations. Top: Straight bow. Bottom: Sinew-backed and wrapped bow.

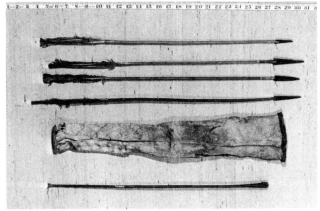

Courtesy J. J. Narus

Plains Indian arrows, various sizes for various tribes. Top four have trade metal war arrowheads (steel), used by hunter and warrior. Plain buckskin quiver . . . beaded at opening. Bottom: Wooden bird and small game point arrow (end feathers broken away).

"Almost all the Indians whom I have met with are proficient in this species of knowledge, the faculty of acquiring which appears to be innate with them. Exigencies of woodland and prairie life stimulate the savage from childhood to develop faculties important in the acts of war and in the chase. I have seen few white men who were good trailers, and practice did not seem very materially to improve the faculties in this regard. They have not the same acute perceptions of these things as the Indian or the Mexican. It is not apprehended that this difficult branch of woodcraft can be taught from books, as it pertains almost exclusively to the school of practice; yet I will give some facts relating to the habits of the Indians that will facilitate the acquirements: A party

Courtesy J. J. Narus Collection

Indian tools of war.

of Indians, for example, starting on a war excursion, leave their families behind, and never transport their lodges; whereas, when they move their families they carry their lodges and other effects. If, therefore, an Indian trail is discovered with the lodge poles upon it, it has certainly not been made by a war party; but if the track does not show the trace of the lodge poles, it will be equally certain that a war or hunting party has passed that way, and if it is not desired to come in conflict with them, their direction may be avoided. An Indian, on coming to a trail, will generally tell at a glance its age, by what particular tribe it was made, the number of the party, and many other things connected with it astounding to the uninitiated. I remember upon one occasion, as I was riding with a Delaware upon the prairies, we crossed the trail of a large party of Indians traveling with lodges. The track appeared to me to be quite fresh, and I remarked to the Indian that we must be near the party. 'Oh, no,' said he, 'the trail was made two days before, in the morning,' at the same time pointing with his finger to where the sun would be at about 8 o'clock. Then, seeing my curiosity was excited to know by what means he arrived at this conclusion, he called my attention to the fact that there had been no dew for the last two nights, but on the previous morning it had been heavy. He then pointed out to me some spears of grass that had been pressed down into the earth by the horses' hoofs, upon which the sand still adhered, having dried on, thus clearly showing that the grass was wet when the tracks were made."[2]

Firearms did not immediately eliminate use of the bow and arrow. By 1874, breech-

2. Army and Navy Journal, March 9, 1867, unsigned by writer.

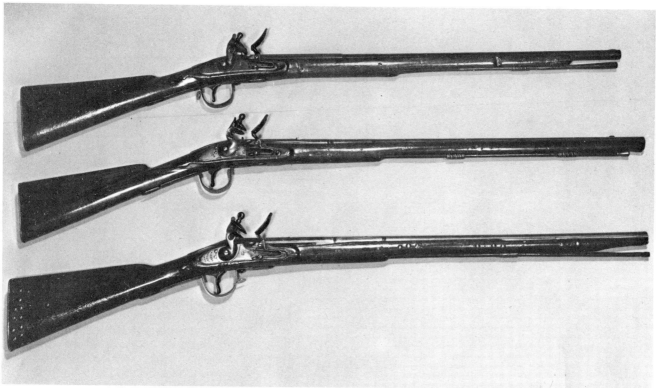

From the Arnold Marcus Chernoff Collection

From above: Northwest type flint lock trade musket barrel is partially round, partially octagonal. It has .60 cal. barrel markings, two British proof marks with the number 24 between them also what they call the tombstone fox marking with E. B. below it which is Hudson Bay marking on the top flat. Lock plate marking is "Parker Field & Company, 1863." Also with the tombstone fox under the pan. The musket has one brass ramrod pipe, it has the cast brass dragon sideplate and a brass buttplate fastened with 5 screws. The stock shows evidence of being shortened slightly with a crude pewter or lead cap on the fore-end. Trigger guard is of the large iron type. Evidence of a few missing tacks in the stock. Same general description as above. Lock plate marked "W. Chance & Son" Tombstone fox under the pan has the letters "I.A." below it. Stock has a seated fox facing left in a ½ inch circle. This weapon was made in England for the American Fur Co. Gun is the same as number 1 only difference is Parker Field & Co. *1868.* The stock has 2 rows of brass tacks parallel to the buttplate and a few tacks along the fore-arm.

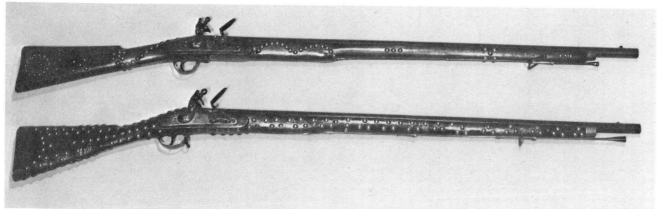

From the Arnold Marcus Chernoff Collection

From above: Flint lock musket, overall length 56 inches approx. 78 cal. full round barrel with 2 English view proofs. Lock plate is marked "TOWER" with GR under crown, CHG under edge of primer pan. Ramrod pipe, small trigger guard, buttplate and sideplate are of heavy cast brass. Profusely tack studded, also with a signaling mirror surrounded by brass tacks in the butt. Same as above except lock plate is marked "SARGENT FAIRFAX" and the stock does not have the signaling mirror.

From the Arnold Marcus Chernoff Collection

From above: Indian trade rifle, percussion cap. Heavy octagonal barrel 31½ inches long in .50 cal. Overall length 48 inches. Marked on top of the barrel is "LEMAN, LANCASTER, PA." and the word "Warranted." On the lock plate is the typical "LEMAN, LANCASTER, PA" markings with the sparce roll engraving on the plate and hammer. The buttplate, patch box trigger guard and ramrod pipes are all of brass. This weapon does not show signs of having been tack decorated but has a rawhide repair at the wrist of the stock. This weapon is pictured in the U.S. Cartridge Co. Catalog of 1905 page 87 item number 326. Also in the book "Firearms in the Custer Battle" by J. E. Parsons & J. S. Du Mont page 28, item number 5. Description same as above but rawhide repair on the fore-end 12 inches long. Pictured in "Firearms of the Custer Battle" page 28, item number 4. Description and measurements are the same as above two weapons but with rawhide repair on fore-end 6½ inches long and brass tacks on either side of the fore-end plus a row of brass tacks following the curve of the buttplate.

loading weapons had been obtained by most of the older warriors, through trade, gift, capture or theft. The poor warrior used the bow exclusively, but even the rich warrior who possessed one or more breech-loading weapons used bow and arrows occasionally.

The "tools of war" are made with care by all races in all countries. Indians were no different. Many hours went into selecting wood for their bows and arrows, and often perilous journeys were made to obtain it. The wood preferred for the bow was bois d' arc, also called Osage orange. Hickory, ironwood, ash, white elm and mulberry were also used. The wood selected was straight grain and free from knots, and usually worked to size and shape while still green. When worked to a proper finish, it was rubbed with fat or animal brains to make it pliable. After more seasoning, the stick was polished by hand rubbing. Glue was then applied and spread on evenly, and fresh or wet sinew from the back of a buffalo bull or deer was wrapped around the wood. Another coat of glue was applied and then rubbed to smoothness. The sinew, after drying, would shrink tightly to the wood and this and the glue made the bow strong.[3]

Highly prized bows were made by fitting together pieces of horn with glue, and wrapping them tightly with sinew or strips of deer gut. The disadvantage of this bow was that it might be useless during wet weather. Sinew-backed bows were carried among the Blackfeet, Sioux, Ute, Crow, Cree, Cheyenne and Hidatsa, but never among the southeast tribes. A person not accustomed to a bow of this kind would barely spring it two or more inches, but an

3. Twenty Years Among Our Hostile Indians, J. Lee Humfreville, Retired Captain, U.S. Cavalry, Hunter & Co., New York, 1899, p. 120.

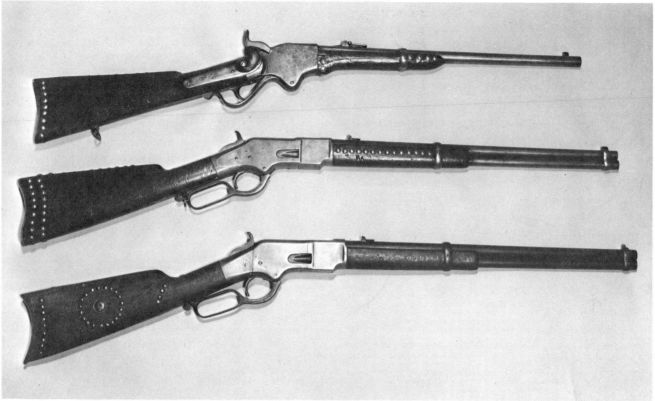

From above: Spencer Carbine .50 cal. Fore-arm shows slight pommel wear also decorated with brass tacks. Stock is also decorated with tacks on both sides and on the comb. Winchester Model 1866 Carbine .44 rimfire cal. There is a row of brass tacks on either side of the fore-arm. A row of tacks on the comb of the stock and two rows of tacks parallel to the butt of the stock. This weapon is pictured in "Firearms of the Custer Battle" on page 34, item number 3. Winchester Model 1866, .44 rimfire. This weapon has seen much use. On the right side of the stock is a circle of brass tacks with a large brass nail in the center, on the left side is a cross of 13 tacks. Also a row of tacks parallel to the buttplate and a few tacks on the small of the stock.

Indian would spring it a foot or more, giving the arrow a tremendous amount of velocity. An Indian with a strong bow could drive an arrow half its length into the body of a buffalo. The bowstring was made of twisted sinews, was very strong and generally lasted a long time. The sinews used were from buffalo and deer. Tendons were shredded into fine threads, soaked in glue and, while still damp, twisted into a round, even cord, ten times the strength of a cotton cord of equal size. Particularly that of the bears tendons, sometimes used in making bowstrings. Comanches contend that strands from horses' tails, when properly made, were the best material because they would not break easily and were not injured by moisture. Stretching during the wet season rendered the sinew string ineffective.

Similarly, water damage made the percussion caps carried by the pioneers for their muzzle loaders incapable of flashing. Both races were handicapped by wet weather and partly for this reason there were fewer fights during damp or rainy weather. The Indians, however, partly overcame the disadvantage by keeping the bowstring under the armpit to keep it dry.[4]

The shaft of the arrow varied in length among different tribes, and was usually made from dogwood, mature ash, or the straight, slender branches of the red willow, and generally cut in late winter when the sap was down. The selected sticks were free of knots and branches, smooth as pos-

4. Handbook of the American Indians, Frederick Webb Hodge, Part 2, p. 90; Smithsonian Institute, Bureau of American Ethnology, 1912, Bulletin 30.

sible, and almost as thick as the little finger. After the shafts were cut to proper lengths, they were placed in bundles of twenty, wrapped with a hide cover, and hung at the top of the tipi. Here they were seasoned for several weeks by the smoke of the lodge fire. If there were any insects within the shafts, they would be killed. After the shafts were well seasoned, bark was carefully peeled from each stick, then the shafts were scraped to proper size. To insure uniform thickness, two pieces of sandstone were used, with a semicircular groove in the center of each. The two stones were held together, and the shaft pushed through and worked back and forth until perfectly round. A notch to fit the bowstring was then cut at one end, "V" shaped for a fiber bowstring and "U" shaped for a sinew or rawhide string. The arrow maker then cut a thin slit, about three-quarters of an inch deep, at the head of the arrow shaft, to insert the arrowhead. The depth of these slits varied by individual preference, as well as by size and shape of the arrowhead being used.

The arrowhead was pushed into the slit and bound tight with glue and sinew.

Some Indians placed the arrowhead in the same plane with the notch for the string. It was believed that this allowed the arrow to penetrate deep into an animal, passing between the ribs, which are up and down. For the same reason, the blade of the war arrow was placed at a right angle with the notch, as the ribs of the human enemy are horizontal. As the arrow rotated in flight, it is doubtful the arrowhead hit precisely as planned. The point or head was ordinarily made of hoop iron, frying pan bottoms or stove parts, these materials being available after looting the prairie travelers' wagon trains.[5]

Feathering is an important feature of the arrow. Flight and accuracy depended greatly upon the feathers, differing in the species of birds, number of feathers, length and manner of setting. Feathers of the wild turkey were highly prized, as were those of

---

5. Ibid.

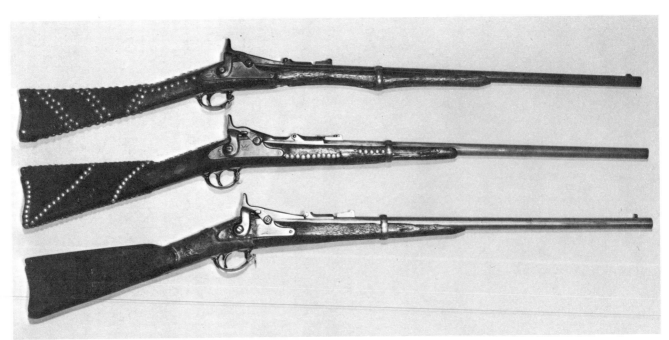

From the Arnold Marcus Chernoff Collection
These three rifles are all about the same. They are Springfield trap door rifles that have been cut down to carbine length, all are either tack decorated or repaired with rawhide. All the butt plates are missing and the fore-arms show much pommel wear.

the buzzard and owl. Only the feathers from the hawk and eagle were damaged by excess dampness and blood. Some hunting arrows used for small game, such as birds or fish, received no feathers; others received two or three. For larger game, along with war arrows, three feathers were fletched, equally set apart from one another around the shaft. The feathers were positioned either flat or radiating, the ends lashed with sinew, straight or doubled under, and the middles were either free or glued down. In length, they varied from the short feathering on Southwestern arrows, with long reed shafts and heavy foreshafts, to the long feathering on Plains arrows, with their short shafts of hard wood.[6]

_____
6. Ibid.

Arrows bore the owner's identifying bands of color. A combination of several colors was applied in bands toward the feathered end of the arrow. Some rubbed colors into lightning marks as the owner's personal crest. Arrows were prized possessions, and every effort was made to preserve and retrieve them. When crossing or swimming a stream, Indians shot their arrows into the air so they would fall in a marked area on the opposite side, and retrieved them after they had waded across. The extreme range of flight, the certainty of aim and the piercing power of Indian arrows are not known today, but stories about them have been greatly exaggerated. The warrior closed in as near as possible to his target, and, in shooting, he drew his right hand to

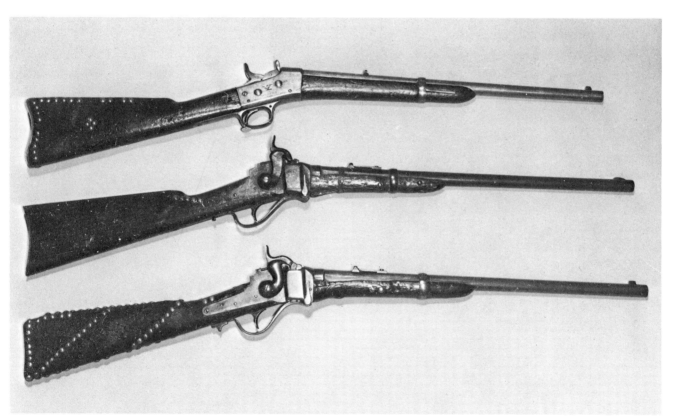

From the Arnold Marcus Chernoff Collection

From above: Remington rolling block carbine in .50-70 cal. The right side of the frame is marked with an eagle "US" below it and "SPRINGFIELD" and below that 1870. At one time there were many tack decorations on this weapon a few still remaining on both sides of the stock. The fore-arm shows signs of pommel wear. This weapon had to be taken from a Cavalry trooper because there was no way an Indian would be able to purchase this government issue weapon. Sharps carbine 1859. Cartridge model is .50 cal. Fore-arm has been cracked and has a rawhide repair also has brass tacks but most are missing. Sharps Carbine 1859, .52 cal. Stock of this weapon shows much signs of use, butt plate is missing, many brass tacks in stock, most of them lost in fore-arm. Gun is pictured on the back cover of "Firearms of the Custer Battle," item number 2.

Courtesy Old Army Press   *Painting by E. L. Reedstrom*

Cheyenne Warrior

glue or stretch the sinew bindings, loosening the head from the shaft, if not removed immediately. It is hardly worthwhile putting any stock into stories of soldiers walking around with arrowheads in their bodies. Extremely few such cases occurred. If the arrowhead were not extracted quickly, a victim would either bleed to death or suffer infection from the rust or dried matter on the points.[8]

The Plains Indians grooved their better arrows from the head to the feathers. Just why these grooves were made is uncertain. A popular theory was that the grooves allowed the blood from the victim to flow down the shaft, to weaken him. Another

8. Ibid.

Courtesy U.S. Signal Corps photo (Brady Collection)
1866 — Yankton Sioux

his ear, the pull of his bow scarcely exceeding 60 pounds, and let fly a silent, yet powerful and effective weapon. The military dreaded its reputed deadly aim and tremendous velocity.[7]

Arrowheads were shaped for particular uses. The hunting arrow had long, tapering blades, the rear shoulders sloping backward. The blade was fastened to the shaft firmly and could easily be withdrawn from the wound. The blade on the war arrow was usually short, with sharp edges, the rear shoulders sloping forward, forming barbs. Their attachment to the shaft was slight, and often glue was used instead of sinew wrappings. It was intended that the head would remain in the wound and kill eventually, if not immediately. The accumulation of blood in a short time would dissolve the

7. The Mystic Warriors of the Plains, T. E. Mails, Garden City, N. Y., Doubleday & Co., 1972, p. 415.

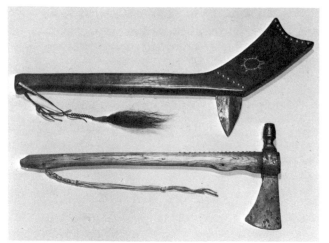

Gun stock war club, made of heavy wood (walnut?) dark in color. Inserted at the forward end at the point of percussion is a roughly made spear tip 3½ inches long. There are brass tack decorations at the end of the club and also where the blade is fitted, and a circle of brass tacks on one side and on the other side a turtle in small iron tacks. Early well forged pipe tomahawk 1750-1780. Used by the eastern and Canadian tribes. Oak haft brass tacks on the upper side near the head, with a buckskin wrist strap.

Extremely large Plains type pipe tomahawk, with a bleeding heart piercing and two round holes. The haft is of hickory almost completely round, brass tack decorated and also three bands of brass wire wrappings. Haft is also file branded. The haft terminates in a headed sleeve with a beaded flap attached. The fringes are 13 inches long, flap also has tin cone danglers. The haft is not pierced for smoking.

theory was that grooves made the game bleed more freely, leaving a trail to follow. These shallow grooves, unevenly wavy, with some patterns running straight or roughly zigzag, are generally called "blood grooves" or "lightning marks." It is also said that the grooves symbolized lightning striking, which the Indian believed would make

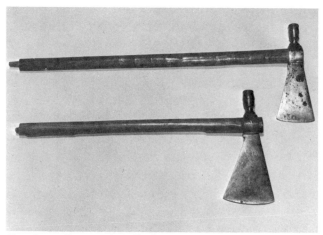

Plains type tomahawk (Sioux). Well made head with a sturdy simple hickory file branded haft. Same as above but with plain haft.

the arrows' flight true and deadly. The most practical explanation is that the grooves were made to keep the arrows from warping.

The great Western movement saw every imaginable type weapon come into Indian hands. Rifles were acquired through trade, gift, capture or theft. The Indian became adept with these weapons and used them in warfare against white expansion and to advantage in hunting. Firearms could bring down the largest buffalo in the herd with little or no effort.

The Indian was adept at killing buffalo from horseback. He copied the rapid-fire trick of the white hunter. With his gun already primed with powder, he could spit a musket ball down the barrel from a supply carried in his cheek. Riding horseback at break-neck speed with little care in seating the musket ball on the powder charge frequently resulted in bursting the fusils. Often, in loading and pointing, the ball would roll away from the powder charge and lodge somewhere in the barrel, far from its proper place. When the gun was fired under such circumstances, there was likelihood that the explosion would cause the light iron cylinder to rip open just below the ball. As a result of such an accident, it was not at all uncommon for the hunter to lose an eye or a hand. Not all trade guns were booby traps; even superior guns might blow up under careless handling by Indians.

Maintenance of his weapon was rarely considered by the Indian. The gun was neglected while exposed to rain, dust and hard wear. When the stock was badly cracked or broken, he mended the part with wet rawhide which, on drying, shrank to a strong and usually satisfactory repair. Brass tacks set in good-medicine designs decorated many guns, and sometimes mirrors were imbedded in the stock to "sun signal" from one to another.

How good a shot was the Indian? Most records indicate that he wasn't much of a marksman. During fighting with the white invader, it has been said that Indians often shot their own people by mistake.

The advent of the metallic cartridge confused many Indians. Accustomed to muzzle loading, Indians rammed metallic ammunition down the muzzles of breech loaders, often with disastrous results. It was also reported that U.S. Army recruits, after being issued the breech loader, complained that the government had neglected to issue a ramrod.[9]

When the government issued clothing to the noble red man, he commonly fashioned these articles of dress to suit himself. The Indian, upon receiving a pair of government trousers, would cut them up and use the legs for leggings. If he received a pair of

From the Arnold Marcus Chernoff Collection

Large basic Plains pipe tomahawk with intricate piercings. Haft is plain and simple except near the mouth piece there are four raised carved projections. Large Plains pipe tomahawk with crude engravings on both sides of the blade, on one side is four leaves with wavy lines extended from the tips, on the other side is an Indian in full headdress with a sabre in his right hand, attacking another Indian who has a knife in his right hand. Haft is very sturdy and file branded with a coarse rasp. Spontoon pipe tomahawk. It has a tall slender pipe bowl with top and bottom moldings. The blade is kite shaped and is stamped with a series of cresents and stars. Haft is oak with notches cut just below the head and has been file branded.

boots, he would cut the tops away to use the soles for moccasins. The brims from black campaign hats were cut off, and the crowns streaked with various colors and ornamented with feathers. Another use for the crown was in making an Indian war bonnet, the skull cap becoming a base on which to sew beaded decorations and feathers.[10] For some reason, the "Hardy hat" was much preferred by Indians, especially if it still retained the plume. It seemed to be worn as a badge of honor, and many Indians took great care in preserving it.[11]

Beaded work sewn to buckskin strips was used as shoulder decorations attached to army blouses. Stories are told of a large Indian trying on a small blouse, the sleeves two or three inches above his wrists, the front far from ever being buttoned over a

---

9. Army and Navy Journal, June 15, 1867, p. 684.

10. Ten Years with General Custer Among the Indians, Captain John Ryan; The Town Crier, Newton Centre, Mass., March 5, 1909.

11. Ibid.

well-protruding stomach. Indians often tried to imitate their soldier visitors. A soldier recalls one incident: "In 1868 the Indians tried to imitate our officers and especially the paymaster. The latter, in paying the troops at the different forts was in the habit of riding in the ambulance from one fort to another, under escort of either a commissioned or non-commissioned officer in charge of a few men. Satanta of the Kiowas and Little Raven of the Arapahoes, both chiefs, thought they would imitate the paymaster. They managed to get the running gear of two old style carryalls, and a set of horse harnesses, and hitch up a couple of their ponies. Satanta and Little Raven rode around in these carriages and had behind them as their guard an escort of mounted Indians, and wearing uniforms similar to that of our officers. After a short while it was a common thing to see them riding into the forts and camps and holding a pow-wow with the officers."[12]

Whenever the leaders of a hostile tribe wished to know the complete strength of any cavalry troop (or company) encamped, they would send scouts to that camp under false pretense to survey the company streets and count the troopers' saddles that were stacked before each tent. Anything else of unusual interest would be reported to the hostile camp as far as field pieces, number of horses, weighing the general strength of the over-all command.[13]

Captain John Ryan described customs of Indians on the warpath: "The only clothing worn by a Sioux warrior was a bonnet of eagle feathers, a piece of cloth about the hips, and mocassins, sometimes leggins. Usually the body was painted black with yellow strips and the hair unbraided. The horses' tails were dyed and their bodies decorated with paint. The supplies and extra equipage were packed on ponies and cared for by the squaws. The Indians always braided upon their heads a small lock of hair about three inches across, separated from the rest of the hair and called a scalp-lock. This was kept braided at all times, ready to be taken off by whoever killed them in battle. This was a custom among all the tribes, and, if an Indian did not have a braided scalp-lock, he was considered not a warrior and afraid to fight."[14]

"The Indians had different kinds of war implements. There (sic) tomahawks were of various styles, some having a blade eight or ten inches long and as keen as a razor. The poles were used as the bowls for pipes, and attached to them were handles some two and a half feet in length. Thus they had both tomahawk and pipe in one. Then there were several kinds of battle axes, and the most of them I saw had a curved handle of wood, shaped like that of a plow, about three feet long, into the ends of which had been set fully six small butcher knives.[15] These blades were seven or eight inches wide (he probably means seven or eight inches long), sharpened on both edges, and placed probably one and half or two inches from each other. These were considered a terrible weapon in an engagement as an Indian could ride up to an enemy, and taking the axe in both hands, strike with all six blades."[16]

Quivers made of rawhide and filled with arrows were hung over one shoulder, and it was surprising how rapidly Indians could reach over the shoulder, take arrows from quivers, place them in the bows and shoot.[17]

"They had several methods of scalping, one tribe would cut a diamond-shaped

---

12. Ibid.

13. The Town Crier, Newton Centre, Mass., Feb. 19, 1909; also see E. B. Custer Microfilm, Custer Battlefield Museum, Reel 6, No. 6406.

14. The Town Crier, Newton Centre, Mass., Feb. 19, 1909; also see E. B. Custer Microfilm, Custer Battlefield Museum, Reel 6, No. 6406.

15. The Town Crier, Newton Centre, Mass., Feb. 19, 1909, Captain John Ryan.

16. E. B. Custer Microfilm, Custer Battlefield Museum, Reel 6, No. 6408.

17. Town Crier, Newton Centre, Mass., Feb. 26, 1909, Ryan's story.

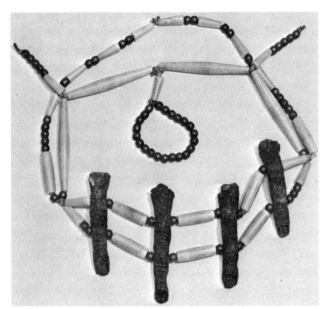

Courtesy Arnold Marcus Chernoff Collection   *Photo by Mariam E. Vrtik*
Cheyenne Finger Necklace

piece from the scalp-lock, another tribe a square patch, others a round patch. If we found the body of one of our men lying scalped on the ground, we could not tell which tribe did it unless some of the scouts were with us. They knew immediately by the shape of the piece cut from the scalp."[18]

A victim of Indian vengeance gives the following account of being scalped by a warrior that had left him for dead: "I was in the Infantry. Custer had command of the troops. There was quite a force of cavalry with us, but these were about a mile in the rear when we first discovered the reds. Some of the troops had been sent around so as to attack from the other side. The reds were encamped in a sort of a valley, and we were within eighty rods of them for half an hour before daybreak. Just in the gray of the morning the firing commenced on both sides, and we had it all our own way for a few minutes, the cursed snakes being much confused and not knowing what was up. At length they rallied, and we could hear Black Kettle shouting and ordering. The vermin got into holes and behind rocks — any-

where they could find a place, and began to fight back with a will. We fired wherever we could see a top-knot, and shot squaws — there were lots of them — just as quick as Indians. When it was fully daylight we all gave a big yell, and charged right down into camp. The lodges were all standing yet, and lots of Indians in them. As we ran through the alleys, a big red jumped out at me from behind a tent, and before I could shorten up enough to run him through with my bayonet, a squaw grabbed me around the legs and twisted me down. The camp was full of men fighting, and everybody seemed yelling as loud as he could. When I fell, I went over backward, dropping my gun, and I had just got part way up again, the squaw yanking me by the hair, when the Indian clubbed my gun and struck me across the neck. The blow stunned me; the squaws kept screeching and pulling my hair out in handfuls. I heard some of our boys shouting close by, and the squaw started and ran, one of the boys killing her not three rods off.

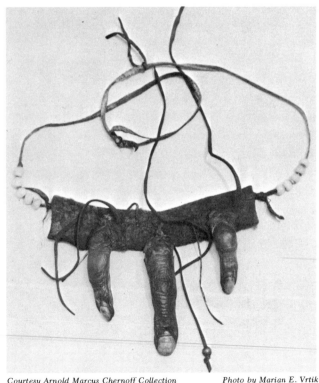

Courtesy Arnold Marcus Chernoff Collection   *Photo by Marian E. Vrtik*
A Cheyenne Finger Necklace

———
18. Ibid.

The Indian stepped one foot on my chest, and with his hand gathered up the hair near the crown of my head. He wasn't very tender about it, but jerked my head this way and that, like Satan. My eyes were partially open, and I could see the bead-work and trimming on his leggings. Suddenly I felt the awfullest biting, cutting flash go round my head, and then it seemed to me just as if my whole head had been jerked clean off. I never felt such pain in all my life; it was like pulling your brains right out; I didn't know any more for two days or three days, and when I came to I had the sorest head of any human being that ever lived. If the boys killed that viper they didn't get back my scalp; perhaps it got lost in the snow. I was shipped down to Laramie after a bit, and all the nursing I got hain't made the hair grow out on this spot yet."[19]

19. Army and Navy Journal, June 26, 1869, p. 710 (unsigned).

Courtesy Herb Peck, Jr.

Tintype of Good Buffalo, one of Red Cloud's chiefs. Late 1860's. (Scratched into plate — up the left leg is "Good Buffalo.") Right side. Indian on left — unknown.

Courtesy Herb Peck, Jr.   Photo by C. Winkler

Commanche braves.

Few people have escaped death at the hands of the Indians and returned to a normal civil life minus their scalps. These few who were great sufferers were plagued with headaches, earaches, nervous prostration and constant colds. The tops of their heads, lacking hair and skin, were subject to suffering with every seasonal change.[20]

Indian mutilations of their enemies were beyond description. Their belief was that the body in the next life appeared the same in form as it was when the earthly life departed it; whole or mutilated, it so remained in the spirit land through eternity. By mutilating their victims, they endeavored to make his existence in the next life as miserable as possible.[21]

Positive evidence that a scalp taken was actually that of an Indian was said to be that the hairs would be covered with nits.[22] At times, warriors would produce a scalp claimed to be that of an enemy, but actually from a dog, or a coarse tuft of a horse's tail. These substitutes were passed off on thrill-seeking eastern dudes accompanied

20. Twenty Years Among Our Hostile Indians, J. L. Humfreville, Hunter & Co., N. Y., 1899.

21. Hand Book of the American Indians, Vol. II.

22. A nit is the egg of a louse or other parasite insect; also the insect itself when young.

by a gruesome story to back it up. The presence of nits on the hair was considered proof that the scalp was taken from an Indian.

Plains Indians had a peculiar custom called counting coup. The first to strike an enemy claimed the highest honor. The coup could be counted with the warrior's hand, his bow, his lance, a rifle, or a coup stick, carried especially for touching an enemy. The first to touch an enemy was allowed to wear an eagle feather upright at the rear of his head. The second to touch could wear the feather tilted to the left; the third won the right to wear an eagle feather horizontally, while the fourth could wear a buzzard feather hanging vertically. Coups were awarded for touching and not killing. Among some tribes, the taking of a scalp was of minor importance compared to the counting of coups.[23]

War shields were important in defensive equipment used by the warrior in open country, and were believed to be indispensible against enemies' weapons. The shield could stop an arrow or turn the stroke of a lance, but afforded little protection against a bullet.

The war shield of the equestrian warrior of the plains was round, varying from 13 to 28 inches in diameter, averaging about 18 inches. The covering was thick buffalo hide taken from the animal's hump and shoulder. The shield was usually carried on the left arm by means of a belt passing over the shoulder in such a way as to permit the free use of the left hand to grasp the bow or steady a rifle. By dextrous movements of the body, without the use of the hands, the shield could be passed from side to side or slung around the back in retreat.

The owner rarely made his own shield. He received it from a dreamer, usually an

23. The Comanches, Wallace & Hoebel, University of Oklahoma; The Sioux, Hassrick, University of Oklahoma; Twenty Years Among the Hostile Indians, Humfreville, Hunter & Co., N. Y.

Courtesy Herb Peck, Jr.   *Photo by L. C. Kelley*

Big Elk, Cheyenne chief.

Courtesy Herb Peck, Jr.

Big Horse — Cheyenne chief. Squaw and pappoose.

Courtesy Herb Peck, Jr.

Commanche brave and squaw. Note straw hat on man.

Courtesy Herb Peck, Jr.   *Photo by G. D. Francis*

White Ghost, Sioux.

older man or medicine man, who made it on request as instructed for a trade in blankets, horses or other valuable properties. Every shield originated in a dream, in which the dreamer was told by a spirit how many shields he might make, how they were to be painted and decorated, what symbols must be painted on his body and on his pony. There were sacred obligations which he was to observe through life to obtain the protection of the shield spirit, which could be a bird, a being of the tribal pantheon, or one of the many personified powers of nature. The war shield constituted a sacred possession from the time it was fabricated for him until it was laid beneath his head in the grave. All designs were applied in ceremonies prescribed by tribal customs. A

violation of the sacred obligations would destroy the shield's power.

The shield not only protected the Indian in battles, but also vibrated with spiritual powers. By holding it toward the sun, he could draw powers from the heavens that would last him an indefinite period of time. It was placed next to him with all his worldly goods when he died, to protect him on his final journey into the land of death.

There are instances where Indians had used bits of metal, pebbles and nails for shot when they lacked lead balls for their muzzle loaders. Indians owning metallic-cartridge guns sometimes maintained their ammunition supply with considerable ingenuity. The use of rimfire shells primed with phosphorus soaked from match heads and center-fire primers made from percus-

Thunder Hawk — Crow Indian.

Cotton Man — Dakota Indian.

sion caps carried the warrior over until supplies could be traded or stolen.

Survivors of the Reno command at the Little Big Horn reported accurate sharpshooting of one Indian using a "buffalo rifle," either wounding a trooper or "blowing his head off," as the troopers bobbed up and about in their cramped, semi-entrenched positions. Forked sticks found on the battlefield indicated that Indians used the old buffalo hunters' method of steadying their aims.

After the Reno court testimony, officials in Washington ordered the Ordnance Department to assemble captured Indian weapons for testing to see whether they were superior to the government issue. Tests were made of Sharps carbines, Sharps buffalo rifles, Spencer carbines, Henry and Winchester rifles, Hawkens, Lemons and an assortment of Kentucky rifles, Parker trade muskets, double-barrel shotguns, and a few assorted revolver and percussion pistols.

In testing these weapons at Springfield Armory, Ordnance experts were amazed at the poor condition of the assorted guns; some could not be made to fire at all. After the Little Big Horn, efforts were made to deprive Indians of ammunition for the guns taken from the field. General Alfred Terry issued orders that all arms of caliber .45 in the hands of guides, Indian scouts, interpreters and Indian allies be turned in and replaced by arms and ammunition of .50 caliber. It seems apparent that this was an attempt to make government ammunition unserviceable in the captured weapons.

After firearms came into the hands of the Indian, the tomahawk became less important as a war weapon. Although it was commonly carried by the warrior, it was generally used as a pipe; the metal, hollow head formed the tobacco bowl, and the handle, sometimes studded with brass tacks, was made as a stem. Ax heads were usually made of iron or steel procured from white traders.

Courtesy Herb Peck, Jr.
Kiowa Chief: Name unknown. From the collection of Thom. Nast.

Courtesy National Park Service, Department of Interior, Custer Battlefield Museum
White Swan — one of Custer's scouts.

Peculiar-looking assortments of clubs, painted in gaudy colors, studded with brass-headed nails, with formidable knife blades protruding from them, were carried for ceremonial purposes or special occasions. Indians enjoyed seeing themselves portrayed as fierce warriors because of carrying these ugly-looking and useless weapons. Nothing would tickle his vanity more than to have his picture taken with his favorite club in hand. If Indians met in hand-to-hand combat, the weapon commonly used was the knife. Some duels with knives were of the bloodiest kind, involving stabbing and slashing with much fury until both warriors died, locked in each other's arms.

The plains Indian warrior, preparing for battle, stripped himself of all clothing, with the exception of a loin cloth, cartridge belt and moccasins. Leggings were sometimes used if an area being traveled was heavy with brush.

If an Indian warrior was fortunate enough to have a variety of colors, he painted his face and body with stripes and spots to please his individual but spirit-guided ideas. War paint was not adopted particularly to frighten the enemy. Not at all. It was usually a symbol with a meaning behind it, showing the intentions of the warrior. As an example: Two yellow bands across the nose would mean, "I have two sisters captured as hostages, I intend to free them." Another, showing a slash from the cheek to the chin on each side of the face,

Photo by E. L. Reedstrom
Typical Indian style blanket wrap around . . . Plains Indian.

"We are after the Indians hot blast, and I tell you the man who picks these fellows up finds himself woefully deceived. A part of our troop have been on the trail of a small band of Sioux, and they had dodged us, and beat us, until we determined to have them, and it appeared, so suddenly, too, that there was no chance for them to escape. Each man seated himself squarely in his saddle and, with revolver in hand, we dashed on. There squat each identical Sioux on his pony, just as though we were miles away, and as stoically indifferent as though they didn't care a continental. As we, at full gallop, drew near, the officer in command felt that we were riding into some trap, but it was too late to sound retreat, and on we went. I think the distance between us and the Sioux and their ponies was just twelve feet, before a single redskin had moved a muscle; from the shoulders of each identical Sioux came the firey red blanket he wore, and up and down it was shaken vigorously in the very face of our horses. We had boasted a great deal over those horses, and they would do anything we wanted them to — that is to say, they would drive through a prairie fire, alongside a buffalo bull through a prairie dog village, and over dead Indians, but I tell you, you ought to have seen them, to a horse, turn tail and run from these

meant, "My dearest relatives have been killed, I shall avenge them." A red chin meant, "I am out to destroy the despoilers of my land." Face painting was not always intended for battle, as, for example, an Indian who painted teardrops running down his cheek signaled, "I am appealing to the Great Spirit for rain." Painting the face or body was a way of mental conditioning; warriors painted themselves with personal protective designs. Some designs designated membership in warrior societies, and this helped the war chiefs to identify them.[24]

Indians often displayed a show of courage in the face of the enemy. In one instance, a group of Sioux warriors went further than that; they coaxed a small cavalry troop into disorganized bafflement. As one trooper writes of the spectacle:

Courtesy Author's Collection
A posed photo of White Eagle and trooper Narus discussing Indian moccasin tracks made by various tribes. White Eagle, a scholar on the subject, travels around the country touring schools and benefits by appointment, still finds time to work with the author and the 2nd Re-activated Cavalry.

---

24. Bureau of Ethnology, 27th Report, pp. 358-62.

blankets. We were getting along so nicely and each trooper was so eager to make a dead sure thing of his redskin, that we let the horses have much their own way, and we repented of it. Just as frightened as they could be, they paid no attention to curb, and away they went in every direction. Troopers were sprawling on the ground, and others were hanging to horses' manes, with both feet not only out of the stirrups, but pointing up in the air. It was the worst stampede I ever saw, and I have looked at "some" in my day. If the Sioux had followed up, they might have made a few scalps, but they were so well pleased with the result of the trick, that those who were unhorsed near them say they disappeared as if they had gone down through the earth. When our troop assembled, we one and all declared that the thing was the best of the kind ever heard of, but determined that we would pay them back for it one of these days, and we will."[25]

Horse painting was common to the plains Indian. Colorful symbols told the Indians' war experiences. A warrior would sometimes paint his horse with the same pattern and colors he would use on his own face and body. When he prepared himself for journeys into enemy country, he painted himself and his horse at the same time. The painted horse carried a symbolic description of his rider's heroism on past raids, although the horse may not have participated in that particular event. As an example, the Sioux warrior placed a red left- or right-hand print on the horse's front shoulder or rear rump, often called a blood mark; this denoted a specific war achievement.[26] A red circle painted around the horse's eye gave him alert vision; around the nose, gave him a sharp sense of smell. Thunder stripes on the horse's front legs pleased the Great Spirit; arrowheads on all four hoofs was a symbol of swiftness and nimblefootedness. Scars or marks from a previous battle were encircled with red paint, as symbols of honor. If a scar was not circled, it was painted over to show where the animal had been wounded. Feathers braided into the tail or the mane meant that the horse had

Art by E. L. Reedstrom

Typical Plains Indian rawhide shield, possibly Sioux. Decorated with owl and prarie chicken feathers; bear claws for courage, turtle tails show spiritual powers. Also buffalo or cow tails.

done a brave deed during battle, by rushing on the enemy or knocking him down and stamping on him. Tying a medicine bag on the bridle was to protect the horse from injuries so the warrior could ride his mount through a battle and return in safety. An upsidedown hand print was the symbol for warriors going out on a do-or-die mission; only then was this special mark used. A rectangle showed that the warrior had led a war party; a cluster of large dots indicated that a dream had revealed that hail would fall at a propitious place and time while pursuing the enemy. Three or four short horizontal stripes on the horse's front legs meant the coup marks struck by the warrior. A rounded or square hoof mark meant a successful horse raid; blotchy or several unusual, heavy-shaped imprints were painted as an expression of mourning on the death

25. Army Navy Journal, June 11, 1870.
26. This red hand print was the highest honor; in some tribes it meant that the warrior had knocked down the enemy or an adversary had been killed in a hand-to-hand conflict.

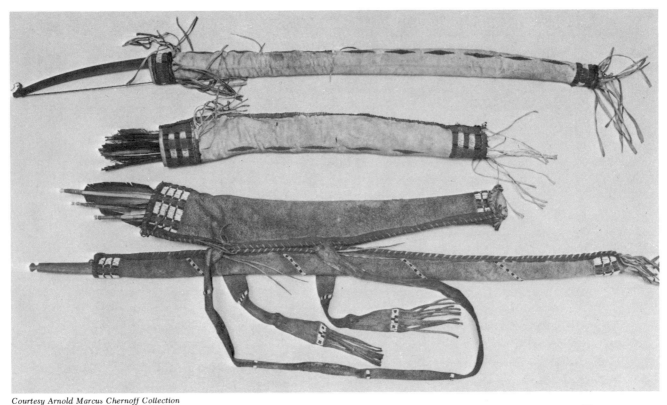

Bows and quiver cases of buckskin filled with arrows. Top set — Sioux. Used at Little Big Horn. Bottom — Cheyenne.

of his owner. Lightning streaks in a zig-zag symbol, running from the rump to the rear leg and from head down to the front foreleg, meant speed and power. Circles, widely painted on the rear rump and the front shoulder, with another color in the center, often meant a breast work where enemies were slaughtered. Warrior Society markings usually took up about one-third of the horse's rump or the full portions of the head, breast and front forelegs. These markings were often stripes or spots applied over large painted areas.

It was believed that knotting the horse's tail prevented an enemy from seizing it during battle and unseating the warrior. Another idea was to get the horse's tail out of the way by binding it into a bunch with leather thongs or strips of colorful cloth so that, in close combat, the loose tail would not be distracting or become entangled in hanging ropes or other battle gear. Fringes,

feathers and red strips of blanket were favorite adornments. The mane was sometimes braided and bedecked with a number of eagle feathers.

It was often surprising to see with what skill a warrior managed a vicious or untrained horse, with nothing on the animal but a rope around the lower jaw and looped about the animal's neck. He was perfect master of his horse, twisting and turning him within his own length, and in every direction, without apparent injury to the animal. Indian saddles were rarely used in hunting or in battle. The hunter knew that saddle trappings could be caught in a buffalo's horns, unseating the rider or dragging him to his death. In battle, he was free to direct his pony by knee or body movements, utilizing the horse's body to shield himself from his enemies' bullets. With this free movement, he could swing from one side to another, firing his weapon beneath the horse's neck by thrusting his arm through a rope loop suspending him with freedom of both arms to discharge an arrow or fire a rifle. Soldiers who witnessed this technique often mentioned the superb horsemanship of the Indian as he seemed to disappear from his mount, then reappear again.

Signaling

When a small pile of wood had been burned down to charcoal, no larger than a dinner plate, it was fanned to a red-hot mass of coals. Leaves, grass or vegetable matter was placed over the top of the coals and a blanket was laid over this for a moment or two; the warrior grasped the center of the blanket with his thumb and forefinger, pulling up the center in three successive jerking motions, each higher than the other, forming something similar to a foot-high miniature teepee. After the Indian thought he had enough smoke accumulated beneath the blanket, two men, one at each end of the blanket, would flip it, and up would go a puff of smoke. By throwing the blanket back over the coals, the signal could be repeated, over and over again. There was no danger of burning the blanket because of the green leaves or grass. Puffs of smoke rising in a single column or in separate columns could convey messages in similar fashion to Morse code, by using sequences planned earlier.

Waving the blanket overhead could be for the purpose of attracting attention. By code agreed upon, three times overhead in a rotating fashion indicated attack. Arm signals, holding a rifle a certain way, or waving a lance could be used as prearranged signals. Whistles made of turkey-leg bone produced a shrill noise, easily heard above the confusion of battle. Mirrors, reflecting the sun's rays, could be seen for miles across the prairie. This system was used in similar fashion to smoke signaling. One long pause of light, followed by two short flashes,

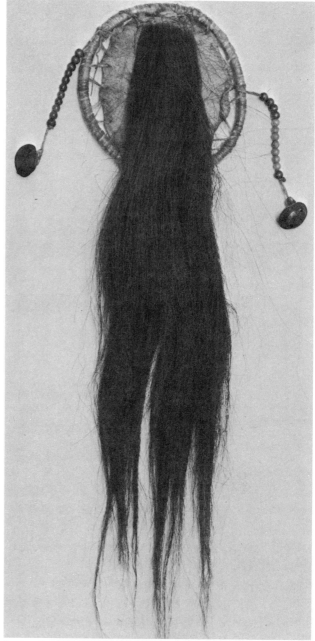

Courtesy Arnold Marcus Chernoff Collection
Human scalp mounted on hoop with trade bead decoration. 1860-1885 period.

might mean, "the soldiers are coming." On horseback, the Indian signaled by riding in a circle, zig-zagging, or racing from one point to another several times. Robes and arm signals helped to convey a complicated message. These maneuvers could be seen at a considerable distance, and were not repeated more than twice. Some messages could mean, "Who are you?", a signal for alarm, a call to halt, discovering buffalo, the war party's success in an attack, surrender, a request to come on, or a suitable camp site.[27]

The Indian blanket had many uses in warfare and signaling, and also potential meaning in the manner in which it was worn about the body. As a blanket was worn differently, it gave the wearer's disposition. When a man walked through a village, he was recognized as a bachelor or a married man, whether a visitor or a young warrior. In meetings with white men or other tribes, the blanket could be carried in such a way as to indicate peace or friendship.

The elderly man wrapped the blanket loosely about the waist, bunched or tucked into a fold, leaving the remainder of the blanket hanging freely, barely touching the ground.

27. Thirty-three Years Among Our Wild Indians, Dodge, pp. 425-34.

Bachelors would completely cover the shoulder on the right side, but the blanket would slide down the back, over the left hip and up the front, where the two parts would be held in the middle between forefinger and thumb, leaving his left side open over his heart.

The married man draped the blanket over both shoulders and held it together at the middle of the stomach or at chest level. He was also seen wearing it about the waist, in a loose manner, but higher than the elderly men.

The hunter or warrior wrapped the blanket about his waist, knotting it in front of his right hip, in a tuck or fold, a corner of the blanket about 10 inches from the ground. The way the blanket was wrapped about the waist made it easier to mount a horse and ride with some freedom.

In meetings, councils and on greeting friends, the blanket was partially folded and wrapped below the rib cage, a portion

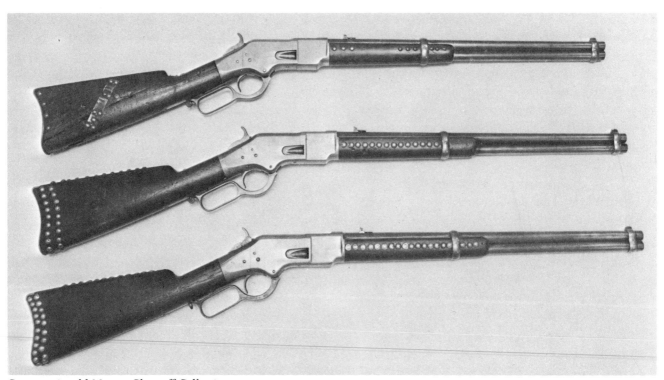

Courtesy Arnold Marcus Chernoff Collection
1866 Winchester Rifles — decorated with brass tacks by Sioux Indians. These weapons were used at the Little Big Horn. Top gun belonged to Sitting Bull and is well documented.

thrown over the left forearm, in the manner of a businessman carrying his raincoat. This means, "I come in peace," or friendship, and was used by head tribesmen in visiting the white man.

There were many other ways of wearing the blanket. These seemed to be the most important:[28]

When an Indian addresses an audience, the blanket is drawn about the chest, directly beneath the armpits, one end held loosely with the left hand, the entire left arm hidden, the blanket somewhat draped over the left forearm, hanging loosely.

The blanket is drawn about the chest, directly beneath the armpits, carried around the back and draped over the left shoulder, in the manner of a cape, hiding the left arm completely, to indicate a change of attitude.

In meditating, the Indian wears his blanket thrown over the head, exposing his nose and eyes, grasping the blanket together at the stomach.

When the blanket is thrown over the head, hanging loosely about the body, it denotes anger.

As a foot-note to the discovery of chloroform, someone tells the following story of the use of that drug:

Soon after its peculiar properties became known, a quantity of it came into the possession of Colonel May, commanding a fort in the Indian country. One day he assured his redskin visitors that he could kill a man and restore him to life at pleasure, and proposed to experiment on one of their number. To this they grunted serious objections, but consented to let him try his skill on a small dog that accompanied them. Taking it into an adjoining tent, he soon returned with it, apparently dead; and, to convince them that there was no trick about it, he cut off a piece of the dog's tail, and

then another and another, until the whole appendage was gone. As the dog showed no signs of life under this severe treatment, the test was pronounced satisfactory, and the colonel retired a second time to work the miracle of restoration.

Pretty soon he returned where the Indians were sitting and threw down among them the tailless but now particularly lively cur, which darted out of the tent in a twinkling. The redskins sprang to their feet and followed at full speed, too much frightened to speak, or venture their persons again about the diabolical premises. Three years after, the colonel and a few others were crossing the plains and encountered a small party of Indians. Each company ran to a little eminence and began scrutinizing the other to see whether they were friends or enemies. At length, the leader of the savages began gesticulating and brandishing something over his head to indicate that he knew the white officer was a friend. The token of recognition and friendship thus brandished turned out to be a section of the dog's tail which the colonel had cut off years before. The Indians ever afterward entertained a most profound respect for an officer who could restore the dead to life, and they evidently regarded any attack upon his command as a waste of ammunition.[29]

Indian Burial Grounds

To the Editor of the Army and Navy Journal:

SIR: It is well known that the Indians of the Plains generally have their cemeteries high up among the trees in some grove bordering upon one of the many rivers that run through their hunting grounds. When one of their number dies — warrior, squaw or papoose — the body, after due solemnities, is placed upon a kind of stage or platform,

28. These examples derive from photographs and from the assistance of Basil White Eagle, star of radio, movies and, now, TV; also from Fred Hackett of Chicago, who helped to compile this material. Mr. Hackett worked at the Pine Ridge Agency for a number of years in the early 1900's.

29. Army and Navy Journal, Oct. 29, 1870, p. 171.

Two Indian war shields and a lance. Left shield is Cheyenne — with horse hair lock and feather decoration. At right — a Crow shield, painted cover over heavy hide. Sioux lance with tin cone danglers.

already built among the branches of one of their grove trees, where the body is laid out without a coffin or shroud, other than, perhaps, a buffalo skin or blanket, with all the dead one's worldly possessions placed by its side. If it be the remains of a warrior, his weapons — hatchet, bow and arrow — as also his tobacco pipe and pouch, are placed beside him, so that he may go all equipped to the happy hunting grounds, already prepared for him by the Great Spirit, where in company with his ancestors who have gone before, he expects to roam and hunt to his heart's content, there to remain forever, unmolested by the intrusive white man. Oftentimes several bodies, probably all of one family, are placed among the branches of the same tree.

Here, on the Laramie River, can be seen the remains of such an Indian cemetery, established by one of the Sioux tribes many years ago, where there stood, undoubtedly,

in all its primitive grandeur, a large and beautiful cottonwood grove, until it was, for the most part, cut down and hacked up, as usual, by the white man, who must have his firewood and building material. Few only of the old trees are left standing, and up among the branches of one or two of them may be seen the remains of the platform where an Indian body once lay, together with the remnants of skins, cooking utensils, etc., scattered about and half buried in the ground below. But even these few *graves* have been desecrated, ruthlessly torn down by the ever-curious and intrusive white man, who, not satisfied to drive the red men from their hunting grounds, must even break up, like the iconoclasts of old, their idol burying grounds so dear and sacred to them. What wonder, then, that the Indian looks upon the advance of the white man with increasing aversion and hate.

A few years ago, one of the Sioux chiefs,

Spotted Tail, was permitted to bury the remains of his daughter, most dearly beloved by him, in our post cemetery, and the necessary material was furnished for the purpose. A large box covered with red flannel and containing the remains of the chieftain's daughter, was placed upon four posts set firmly into the ground, where it may still be seen, a most singular spectacle in a cemetery — a huge box covered with red flannel and placed upon stilts, some ten feet in the air.

The Indians seem to have good reasons for adopting this method of burying their dead. It is observed that any kind of flesh hung up in the air, which in this region is very dry, will speedily give up its moisture, shrink and wither up, so as to prevent decay and all disagreeable odors, and becomes thereby well preserved. So, in this manner, the Indians wishing to preserve the remains of their departed friends, hang them up in the air, where they gradually mummify, and become greatly reduced in size and weight, though their identity is, in some manner, preserved, and the form, if left undisturbed, is said to remain for years unchanged.

Language Without Words

When two Indians met on horseback, each unable to understand the other's language, communications were established by the use of "hand talk." Most signs that were used were easily understood and universal throughout the plains. The "greeting" sign was arm extended, palm forward, right hand opened. By leaving the hand in this greeting position, and closing the fist, leaving the index and middle fingers standing together, the speaker could say, "Hello, friend." Moving the two extended fingers and touching the lips indicated, "Hello, brother."

The next gesture is the sign for "good." The right fist is closed over the heart then swept forward and to the right. All questions generally start with the query sign; the palm forward, the fingers spread, fluttering the hand sideways. This has several meanings: "Who," "what," "why," "how," "where," depending on what signs followed. After the greeting, the next sign was, "What tribe are you?" The Indian sign for redman was made by rubbing the fingertips of the right hand over the back of the left hand in a circular motion, then pointing to the warrior or friend before him. Each tribe had its sign of identification as previously explained.

To ask a name in sign language, the query sign was given, then the speaker pointed to the person he was questioning with the left hand held in front of his face, then gave the "talk" or "called" sign by putting his right fist in front of his mouth, and opening the fingers as he snapped his hand forward several inches. A Sioux would not tell his name, but would travel for half a day to find someone to tell it. He believed that if he should speak his own name it would be bad luck.[30]

Among all the people in the world speaking different languages, no general means of communications is readily understood. Yet, through the medium of sign language, the Indian possesses a means of communication which is a great deal shorter than by word of mouth. The Indians cannot throw any light on its origin, only to say it has been handed down from their ancestors, from a remote period. Nothing has been more useful. Through the silent means of communication, a member of any tribe from the southern portion of American to the boundaries of Canada can communicate easily with any other, even among tribes that were unconscious of the existence of the other.[31]

Indian Sign Language

Abandon — Both hands closed, held to left side near breast; then dropped downwards and to the

30. The Newton Circuit, March 12, 1909; also, see E. B. Custer Microfilm, Custer Battlefield Museum, No. 6412.

31. Twenty Years Among Our Hostile Indians, J. Lee Humfreville, Hunter & Co., N. Y., 1899.

rear, opening them as if throwing away some object.

Aboard — Left hand flat, about ten inches from body, palm up. Right fist on left palm, thumb at top.

Above — Right hand rests on left hand, in flattened position; then right hand raises above left hand.

Absent — Right hand closed, held a little below front of right shoulder; then moved down slightly. Or, right hand held flat, back up, in front of body, fingers pointing front and left; then swing hand to right front, turning hand with thumb up and back down, then return to first position.

Abuse — Index and second finger of right hand brought near mouth, moving hand quickly toward person indicated; repeat.

Accompany — Left hand flat, back to left, in front of body; bring extended right index finger, pointing to front, to the center of left palm.

Ache — Right index finger pushed in motion parallel to part hurting, then hold spread fingers of both hands in front of body, waving them to indicate throbbing.

Across — Left hand flat, back up, about foot away from body; pass part-clenched right hand, in curve, over left.

Add — Right hand flat on left palm in front of body, lift upwards a few inches several times, indicating making a pile.

Advance — Right hand pointed forward, palm down, about a foot from body. Left hand in same position, immediately behind right hand. Both hands then moved forward in short jerks.

Advance Guard — Left hand about foot from center of body, held flat, palm down. Right hand in front of left, index finger pointing up, then change to left hand, indicating "looking."

Afraid — Both hands extended in front, then brought back and down slightly, while curving index fingers. Right hand only may be used for this sign.

After (or Future) — Right and left index fingers extended together toward left, then right hand pulled backward to right a few inches, then right hand is passed beyond left hand.

Afternoon — Incomplete circle formed with thumb and right index finger. Raise directly overhead and sweep down toward horizon.

Agent — Right hand, back up, held to left face even with eyes, pointing index finger left, then draw index finger above eyes, bringing hand to right side; right index finger at side of body, pointing upwards; hand raised in gradual circle to top of head, arching front and down; right hand held flat, back to right, point front and up, shoulder height, then hand moved out and down; almost fisted, pass tips of right fingers downward in curve several times, passing mouth, using wrist movement.

Agreement — Hands clasped in front; holding left hand down, back to front, in front of body, fingers pointing right, then pantomime writing on left palm.

Ahead — Both index fingers pointed together toward left, then bring right hand to right and rear.

Aid — Hands on ledge, flat, in front of body, slightly apart, with right hand above and to the rear of the left slightly, then wrist-action movement up and down to indicate work; left hand held flat, in front, with back to left; right index finger extended against center of left palm, pointing forward.

Aim — For rifle, aim imaginary weapon; for bow and arrow, hands motion as if drawing bowstring.

All — Right hand flat, breast high, moves in horizontal circle from right to left.

All — Both extended hands point at each other in front of chest, loosely wiping ends of right-hand fingers across palm and fingers of left, and vice-versa.

All Right — Same as "All," followed by "Good."

Alone — Right index finger held upwards in front of neck, then moved outwards in waving motion.

Among — Left fingers spread about foot from breast, then weave right index fingers through extended left fingers.

And — Left hand held flat in front, with back to left; right index finger, pointing to front, brought to center of left palm.

Angry — Fist of right hand, touching back of thumb close to forehead; with wrist, give twisting motion.

Annihilate — Left hand flat in front of body, then wipe right hand flat across left hand.

Antelope — Palms forward, place both hands beside head, with four fingers on each side pointed upward.

Arapahoe — Sign for "Indian," followed with partially curved right hand, tapping several times at left breast.

Arise — Palm up on right hand, index finger pointed forward, bring palm to upright position.

Arrive here — Left palm flat against left breast; bring index finger of right hand briskly against back of left hand.

Arrow — Cup left hand, hold near left breast, then with right hand indicate drawing arrow from cup.

Artilleryman — Sign for "White Man," "Soldier," "And," "Large" and "Gun."

Astride — Spread first and second fingers of right hand, setting them astraddle the flattened upright left hand.

Attack — Same as "Charge."

Autumn — Left hand held open, back out, thumb and fingers spread, in front of shoulder, moving upward slightly; then right hand in front of shoulder, index and thumb about an inch apart, other fingers closed, lower edge of hand pointing up and forward, with waving motion indicating leaf on tree.

Barracks — At eye level, right hand held to left face, back up, with index pointing left, then drawing index finger across eyes to right side of face; then "Soldier" sign; then, with fingertips interlaced horizontally, hands in front of body.

Battle — Loose fists, palms facing, in front, shoulder high, slightly apart; move one hand toward, other away from body several times; then "Shoot," both hands pointing toward each other.

Bear — (1) Partly closed hands along head. (2) Clawing motion, with hands clawing downward.

Bed — Left palm up, fingers extended right front, near left breast; right palm up, close to left, then move right hand ahead and to right; then lower extended flat hands, sweeping left hand in front of right chest, next to right hand in similar position, pointing right, then incline head to right.

Behind — "Time" sign, then bring right hand right and rear, indicating length of time by space between hands.

Below — Backs up, in front of body, rest left hand on right; then drop right below left to indicate distance.

Belt — Pantomime as if clasping on a belt.

Beyond — Extended left hand, back up, brought a foot in front of body, fingers pointing right; extended right hand, back up, brought between left hand and body, fingers pointing left; right hand swings out and up in curve beyond left, turning right palm back up as it moves.

Big — Fingers together and slightly cupped, bring palms close together, then apart, indicating size.

Blanket — Hands near neck, close to shoulders, moving right hand to left, and left to right.

Blood — First two fingers of right hand against nostrils, with right hand in front of mouth, move down like trembling.

Bow (to shoot) — Closed left hand extended front, right hand in fist, as if pulling bowstring.

Brave — Left fist slightly to left of center body, right fist above and in front; elbow moves right fist downwards, passing finger joints near left knuckles.

Break (as, a stick) — Hands in loose fist, close together, backs up, twisting them right and left.

Breakfast — Same as "Eat."

Brother — First two fingers of right hand together, back up, touch lips, hand brought straight out from mouth; then raise right index finger, back out, in front of face.

Buffalo — Palms inward, partly closed hands brought near sides of head, raising hands until wrists are on head, and carry forward.

Buffalo Robe — "Buffalo" and "Blanket" signs.

Burn — "Shoot" sign, indicating damage done by fire.

Bury — "Blanket" sign; then slightly compress hands, backs out, resting right fingers against left palm, horizontally, rotating fingers around each other; then, with both hands, indicate pawing, moving hands from right down to left rear, in curve; repeat.

Buy — Back of right hand to right, well away from body, index and thumb almost touching, other fingers closed; then sign for "Exchange."

Cannon (large gun) — Signs for "Gun" and "Large."

Cartridge — Right index finger extends horizontally and points forward, thumb pressing second joint; also can use "Gun" and "Shoot."

Carry — Thumb of right fist against right shoulder; left fist against right, stopping forward, indicating heavy load.

Cattle (buffalo) — "Buffalo" sign; then extend flat left hand and arm to right front, with right fingers separated above left wrist; then brush ends of fingers on left forearm every few inches towards elbow.

Cavalryman — Signs for "White Man," "Soldier" and "Ride."

Charge — (against others) Closed hands, backs up, near right shoulder, moving hands sharply front and left while snapping them open.

Cheyenne — "Indian" sign, then left and right index fingers extended, right index finger giving slashing motion to left index finger.

Chief — Right index finger at side, pointing up; hand raised slowly in circle to top of head, then arched forward and down.

Coffee — Back down, extend left hand in front of body, bringing right hand, closed, slightly over left, moving in small circle, as if grinding.

Comanche — "Indian" sign; then hold right index finger waist high on right, moving in waving motion slightly forward.

Cook — "Work" and "Eat" signs.

Council (in circle) — Hands in loose fist, little fingers touching, extended in front of body, moving in circle, meeting with backs to body; then "Talk" to right and left.

Coward — Pointing to person, make "Afraid" sign.

Crazy — Compressed right hand brought up close to forehead, turning hand to make small circle toward left.

Cross (a stream) — Same as "Across."

Crow — Hands flat at shoulders, indicate wing motion; then "Indian."

Dakota — See "Sioux."

Dangerous — (1) person — "Heart" followed by holding right fist near chest, throwing opening hand out and downward to the right. (2) place — indicate what makes it dangerous.

Daybreak — Backs out, extend hands horizontally, little finger of right hand touching index finger of left, raising the right hand slightly.

Deer — Horns indicated with fingers of both hands spread, held above sides of head.

Destroy — Left hand flat in front of body; then right hand flat wipes across left hand.

Dismount — "Horse" sign; raise and lower right hand, pointing to ground with fingers.

Distant — Partly closed and near body, with back facing right, place right hand in front of right breast, slightly below shoulder height; raise and push hand forward; greater distance indicated by more extended forward thrust.

Do not — "Work" and "No" signs.

Dollar — "Money" sign, raising right index finger to indicate "one."

Drink — Form cup shape with right hand, bring from above toward mouth, indicating drinking.

Early — morning — "Daybreak" and "Little" signs; evening — "Sunset" and "Little" signs.

Eat — Loosely compress right hand, mass finger tips in downward curve past mouth several times.

Enemy — "Friend" and No" signs.

Enter — Fingertips interlaced, horizontally, hands in front of body at right angles; compressed left hand held extended in front of body, and loosely compressed right hand brought down and out, under left.

Escape — Cross wrists, both hands lightly compressed; separate hands quickly to right and left; then "Go" sign.

Evening — "Sun" sign, sinking in west, then "Night" and "Little."

Exchange (or Trade) — Index fingers pointed upward; then swing them past each other in an arc.

Far — Same as "Distant."

Fast — Left hand, back to left, held in front of body; then with flattened right hand, hold back to right, somewhat to rear of left. Right hand quickly passes left in a slight downward, then upward curve.

Fear — Same as "Afraid."

Flag — Right hand flattened held in front of right shoulders, with left fingers on right wrist; then wave right hand several times.

Follow — Left hand in front of right, palms facing, both hands in forward zigzag pattern.

Forest — Open hands about foot in front of shoulders, backs out, fingers spread; slow upward movement, then right hand to right and front; then sign for "Plenty."

Fort — "White," "Soldier" and "House" signs.

Freeze — Both loosely fisted hands near front of body, shoulder high, body bent slightly forward, tremble hands and arms as if shivering; "Water" sign; then again at shoulder height, left palm flat, thumb up, strike left palm with loosely fisted right hand several times.

Friend — Palm out, extend first two fingers of right hand upwards in front of neck; raise until fingertips are head high.

Gallop — First, sign for "Ride," then hands held edgewise are moved vertically, in arcs, near the left side of the body.

Give me — Back of hand down and left, thumb flat on top side, pointing up, about neck high and extended; slightly lower hand as it is brought toward body.

Go ahead — Both fists near breast, arms rigid, then move slightly forward as if a forced push.

Good — Pointing left, right hand, back up and palm flattened, is placed close to left breast; then hand is rapidly moved horizontally front and right.

Grass — Palms up, fingers separated, slightly cupped and pointing upward, hold arms fully down in front of body, then swing hands apart.

Gun — Pantomime shooting a gun, followed by "Fire" sign.

Half Breed — Right hand flat, palm up, in center of chest, with little finger closest to chest, move hand about a foot to left then to right.

Halt — Palm out, in front of body, right hand flat at shoulder height; quickly move hand forward and down, abruptly stopping movement.

Hat — With index finger and thumb spread horizontally and other fingers folded, place hand high on forehead, thumb on right side; lower to about eye level.

Hatchet — Left hand holding right elbow, arm extended with hand flat, making movements as if chopping; then loosely compressed hands, palms facing, lower edges forwards, several inches apart, right heel even with left index finger, then move right hand directly over left.

Hear — Cup hand behind right ear.

Heart — Compress right hand over heart with all four fingers close together, pointing downward.

Help — "Work" and "With" signs.

Hide — Flat left hand angling downward to right; right hand in opposite position; pass right hand under left.

Horse — Left hand on edge, back to outside, outward from left breast. Also can use illustration of right first two fingers straddling edge of left hand.

Hungry — Palm up, little finger nearest body, hold right hand flat and move to and fro as if sawing.

Hunt — First two fingers of right hand, palm down, brought forward and upward to eye level and moved so fingers point upward.

Indian — Left hand, back up, extended slightly in front; rub with right hand from wrist down to knuckles and back twice.

Keep — Grab left index finger with right hand, right hand above left, and move slightly left and right.

Knife — Right flat hand close to face, lower edge barely over mouth; hand moves upward and left several times, indicating cutting.

Lake — "Water" sign; then make circle shape with both thumbs and index fingers, swing wrists together and separating tips of index fingers.

Large — "Big" sign.

Listen — Right fingers cupped near right ear; wrist turns hand back and forth as if listening.

Little — Right hand shoulder high, back toward right, thumb tip against inside tip of index finger.

Lost — See "Hide."

Many — Curve fingers, pointing forward, holding the hands well out in front of body; move hands toward each other, curving downward vertically, then move them upwards slightly, holding hands opposite and slightly apart.

Me — Right thumb pointed at breast.

Meat — Left hand, palm down, held flat in front of left breast; right hand flat, palm up, pantomime slicing left palm.

Meet — Both index fingers pointing up, other fingers loosely clenched, bring hands together until index fingertips meet.

Midnight — "Night" sign; then left index extended, back to left, hold left hand extended in front of left chest; repeat with right hand on right side, raising it up and over in an arc so right index tip rests on middle joint of left index finger.

Moccasin — Spread thumbs and index fingers pass upward from toes to ankles, palms close to feet, right hand running over right foot and left hand running over left foot.

Mountain — Loosely closed hand brought upward; then hold left palm straight up and strike with right fist several times.

Much — See "Many."

Mule — Palms forward, extend both hands alongside ears, fingers upward; use wrists to move hands forward and backward.

Name — Right thumb touches index finger; index finger snapped out but extended.

Negro — Sign for "White Man"; then point to something black.

Night — Hands extended, palms down, front of body, right hand slightly elevated, about a foot apart; pass right hand to left and left to right, slightly turning hands.

No — Palm down, right hand extended flat in front of body, fingers pointing left and forward; swing to right front while turning thumb, placing thumb up and down, returning to first position.

Officer — Same as "Chief."

Old — Right hand pantomimes holding onto walking stick; hand moves up, forward, down, and back in curve; repeat.

Over — Same as "Across."

Pack — Cup left hand in front of body, palm toward body; pat back of left hand with cupped right hand; then pat right hand with left.

Peace — Hands clasped in front of body, palm of left hand up.

People — With index fingers pointed upwards, hands clenched loosely, little fingers below, hold both hands on either side of chest and move slightly toward shoulders.

Pistol — "Gun" sign; then hold up separated digits of right hand and left index finger to indicate "six."

Plenty — Extend both hands well out on either side; then cup and bring together as if gathering.

Pony — "Horse" and "Little" signs.

Poor — Back out, hold left index finger pointed up; then scrape downward with right index finger.

Powder — Left hand, back down, in front of body; rub digits of right hand together just above left hand.

Prairie — Both hands extended, touching, at face level, with palms up and fingers pointed forward; separate hands to left and right on even plane.

Private Talk — Left hand extended, back up, near left breast; use "Little Talk" sign beneath but near left palm.

Railway — "Wagon" and "Fire" signs, then "Fast" sign.

Rain — Loosely clenched hands, backs up, held close at front of head; hands lowered slightly by wrists, at the same time opening the hands. Repeat.

Retreat — "Charge" sign, then use wrists to turn hand, making fingers point to the rear.

Ride — (animal) — "Horse" sign, then hands move forward in small arcs. (vehicle) — "Horse" sign, then closed right hand slightly below right shoulder is brought to left palm.

River — "Water" sign; then right hand moves to lower left face, index finger pointing left; then move hand to right with index finger horizontal, swinging to position in front of right shoulder.

Road — Palms up, hand flat, alternate pushing hands back and forth.

Run — Signs for "Walk" and "Fast."

Saddle — Insides of both wrists touch in front of chest, hands closed; keep position and push hands back as far as possible.

Salt — Tongue touched with tip of right index, other digits compressed; then "Bad" sign.

Sergeant — "Whites" and "Soldier" sign, then mark stripes on arm with right index finger.

Scout — (person) — Right hand, palm out, near right shoulder, first two fingers in "V" pointing up; hand moves several inches forward and upward; (to scout) — Add bringing right first two fingers opposite eyes, then point fingers in direction person is looking.

Seize — Open hands in front of body; close rapidly and bring toward body, as if grasping something.

Shoot — Back up, place loosely clenched right hand in front of chest, with first three fingertips pressed against ball of thumb; snap fingers out from thumb as hand moves out, down and left.

Sick — Extended fingers of both hands, hold in front of stomach; wave them in and out several times, as if throbbing.

Sign Language — Left hand flat, palm down, extended, touch back of left fingers with middle fingers of right hand, reverse, then "Talk" sign.

Silent — Tips of right fingers over lips, and nod head forward.

Sioux — Flattened right hand drawn from left to right in front of neck, as if cutting off the head.

Smoke — "Fire" sign, then continue bringing hand higher than head.

Snow — All fingers spread, fingers down, place hands in front of face, lowering in circles to represent whirling snow.

Soldier — Closed fists, thumbs touching, in front of chest; then separate evenly to left and right.

Speak — See "Talk."

Start — Right hand flat in front of body, pointing right and down; move hand forward and use wrist to raise fingers forward and upward.

Stay — Loosely clenched right hand forward and slightly below right shoulder; move hand downward a short distance.

Steal — Extended left hand, palm down, in front of left chest; right hand loosely clenched, pass right curled index finger under and near left hand until right wrist is near left palm, then draw back right hand.

Steamboat — Hollowed hands held together, cupped in shape of boat, pushed forward to indicate direction; then "Fire" sign with hand held slightly above head height.

Strike — Left hand, back down, in front of left breast; right hand strikes palm of left as if chopping with hatchet.

Strong — "Brave" sign; or, right fist held above left fist, striking over and down, twisting as if breaking stick.

Summer — "Grass" sign, holding hands high.

Sun — Allow one inch between tips of index finger and thumb on right hand; hold toward east, then arc toward left.

Sunset — Right thumb and index finger form partial circle, extending right hand to right about a foot upward, then lower to horizontal position.

Surround — Both thumbs and index fingers form spaced semi-circle; bring together to complete flat circle.

Talk — Right index fingernail pressed against thumb, moving hand slightly forward, snapping index finger straight forward. Repeat.

Tell Me — Right hand, palm up, flat in front of mouth slightly; draw toward lips quickly.

Talk to Me — Same as "Tell Me."

There — Same as "Stay."

Tired — Backs up, index fingers together, hold extended, then lower slightly and draw closer to body a few inches.

Together — Same as "With."

Tomorrow — "Night" sign; then hands level and flat, palms down, in front of face, slightly separated; hands up and out in curve, ending near shoulders with palms up; then, with left hand, pantomime sun rising in East.

Track — "Walk" sign, then point downward.

Trail — "Track" sign; then bring two first fingers of right hand to in front of eyes, then point in direction desired.

Trap : (metal) — Point to something metal; then hold closed hands together, knuckles touching, index fingers curved to touch; bring sides of index fingers together.

Treaty — (between tribes) — "Work," "Smoke" signs; then clasp hands in front of body; (with whites) — clasp hands in front of body, then "Write" sign.

Understand — Right hand, back up, near left chest; hand sweeps out and slightly up, turning until palm almost up; extend thumb and index horizontally, pointing finger left and thumb forward, with other fingers closed.

Up — Point upward with right index finger.

Us — "Me" or "All" sign.

Village — Index fingers crossed at first joints, followed by "Many" sign.

Wagon — Palms up, hold hands about four inches apart in front of body, with index fingers curved upwards; make circular motion with index fingers.

Wagon-road — "Wagon" and "Road" signs.

Walk — (person) — hands flat in front of body, extended side by side; move right forwards, up and down, forming oval circle; repeat with left; as left comes down, bring right to rear, and repeat first position. (animal) — close hands and form oval circle as before.

Want — Right hand close to chin, forming open circle between thumb and index finger; move hand down in small arc, then out and up; by wrist action, turn hand so little finger is level with index finger.

War — Same as "Fight."

War-Club — Indicate size of stone on war-club; show rawhide by grasping left index finger with right hand; then strike forward and downward with right hand.

War-Dance — "Fight" sign; then spread fingers, pointing up, side by side but apart a few inches; move up and down several times to indicate a hopping action.

Watch — Form a horizontal circle with left thumb and index finger; then, with tip of right index finger, move around over circle; then bring first two right fingers in front of eyes and point at circle; then place right hand, palm down, near left breast; arc hand out and up, turning so palm is nearly up, other fingers closed, thumb and index finger extended horizontally, index pointing left, thumb pointing forward; then "Sun" sign.

Water — Right hand cupped, palm up, fingers pointing left and up; place slightly above and in front of mouth and tip as if drinking.

We — Same as "All."

Whiskey — "Fire" and "Water" signs.

White Man — Right hand, palm down, to left face level with eyes, index finger pointing left, then draw hand to right with index finger passing over brow; then raise right index finger, back out, in front of face.

Wickiup — With indexes extended, first joints lapping, hold hands slightly in front of body; change so backs of hands are up, edges forward, fingers separated and very slightly cupped, then arc hands downward.

Wind — At height of shoulders, hold hands with palms down near body, and wave hands like wind blowing.

Winter — Hands closed, forearms vertical, slightly apart; then tremble hands to indicate cold.

Wiped Out — Left hand flat, placed in front of body, then wiped across with flattened right hand.

Wood — Left hand, fingers spread, about foot in front of shoulder, palm inward, moving upwards slightly; then flat right hand near right chest, striking down to left; then reverse with left hand chopping to right.

Work — Hands flat, on end, in front of body, slightly separated, with right hand above and behind left; then raise and lower with wrists.

Wound — Right index finger in front of body, move quickly toward body, turning finger left or right, grazing body.

Write — Left hand flat, palm up, fingers pointing right; then pantomime pencil between right thumb and index finger and simulate writing on left palm.

Yes — Right hand, palm to left, shoulder high near right chest, index finger pointing up, other fingers loosely closed, with thumb resting on second finger; move hand left and down slightly, while closing index finger over thumb.

You — Index finger of right hand pointed at person indicated.

You or Yours — Point to person; then hold closed right fist in front of neck, palm left; swing hand downward and twist with wrist so thumb points forward.

SITTING BULL'S DESCRIPTION OF THE BATTLE

An interesting contribution to the literature of our Indian war is contained in the report of two interviews with Sitting Bull, one by the correspondent of the New York World and one by the correspondent of the New York Herald, who accompanied the Sitting Bull Commission to the Headquarters of the Sioux leader, who disclaims the title of "chief." Major Walsh, of the Canadian police, explained to the Herald reporter that Sitting Bull's position was anomalous. Major Walsh said: "His own tribes, the Hunkpapas, are not all in fealty to him. Parts of nearly twenty different tribes of Sioux, besides a remnant of the Hunkpapas, abide with him. So far as I have learned he rules over these fragments of tribes, which compose his camp of 2,500, including between 800 and 900 warriors, by sheer compelling force of intellect and will. I believe that he understands nothing particularly of war or military tactics, at least not enough to give him the skill or the right to command warriors in battle. He is supposed to have guided the fortunes of several battles, including the fight in which Custer fell. That supposition, as you will presently find, is partially erroneous. His word was always potent in the camp or in the field, but he usually left to the war chiefs the duties appertaining to engagements. When the crisis came he gave his opinion, which was accepted as law."

The World correspondent, who seems from his letter to be a Frenchman, talked French with Sitting Bull. He gives part of his interview with the chief in that language. Sitting Bull talks very good French, with a poetry of expression that is remarkable. The important part of both interviews is the account given by Sitting Bull of Custer's last fight. The interview with the World man took place in Sitting Bull's lodge, in presence of two Indians, "Little Current" and "Marmot." The account of it is as follows, omitting only some rambling poetical remarks with which it is interspersed:

"There was a pause here, and the Marmot rose, and howling to us again, threw himself by the door. I then asked Sitting Bull what he had to propose respecting the future of the Indians in the United States. He said:

'I will tell you in a few words. I know that my people cannot become part of the white people—cannot mix with them as the slave black people mix. We are people by ourselves. The Great Spirit made us as we are. It is not our fault that we are Indians. We know that we are dying out. I remember when I was a boy the old men of our race telling how they had heard the old men, their fathers, tell of the days when the Indians were indeed a great people. But that is past. We are dying out. We shall soon disappear. The white man is taking our place.

Now, we cannot prevent that. It is the will of the Great Spirit. Let the white man succeed us. It is God's will. But still it must be God's will, for he is a just and kind father, that the white man should treat us kindly. He is now stronger than we. Let the strong be kind. God is strong. He is kind. The Great Spirit, I am sure, has not ordered that we, the weaker people, should be put to death like dogs. Now what I say is just this: Let the Great Father give our people a tract of land somewhere, a tract of land on which they can hunt a little, fish a little, and cultivate the ground a little. Let him put the Sioux here, the Crows there, the Blackfeet in this spot, the Nez Perces in that and so on, giving each nation its own dominion (puissance). Let him not think that we will fight one another. We are dying, we cannot fight one another. Then let him appoint good servants, not cheats, to keep watch over us and see that our old men and the sick are not left to die like dogs. If sometimes we cannot live by the chase or by the land, why then let him give us food. Then we shall be quiet and die off quietly. But let not the Great Father put bad men over us. Let him not give bad agents power over us. Let him not leave us a prey to wicked men who fill our young warriors with whiskey and teach them to rob and murder. My people, the Sioux nation, want a Catholic missionary. They are good men. They are the best servants of the Great Spirit. They know our people well. Let them be the agents of the Great Father. They will serve him as well as they serve the Great Spirit. I think that is all. Bad agents make the good Indian bad. The good priest will make the good Indian still a better one. He is the great friend of the children of the prairies (des enfants des prairies).'

"Little Current spoke on this subject at some length, re-echoing the words of his chief. He added, however, that before the red men died out they would have a big fight, and several times repeated what Sitting Bull said just before. 'They are going to kill us in some way, and it will become us to die fighting.' He said the agents stole what the Great Father gave the Indians in the States, and on this Sitting Bull nodded his head, and said:

'Les Americains ont d'abord donne aux Indiens de gros sacs de farine, du sucre et des couvertures; l'annee suivante ils n'olt donne que la meitle; les annees d'apres ils allerent en diminnant, et aujourd'hui ils ne donnent plus qu'une poignee de farine.'

"He asked me to be sure and make that public, viz:

'At first the Americans gave the Indians big sacks of flour, sugar and blankets; the year following they only gave them half. In subsequent years they kept on diminishing it, and to-day they do not give them more than a handful of flour.'

"His idea seemed to be that the bad agents were responsible for this reduction.

"In conclusion I asked Sitting Bull to tell me about the Custer fight. I told him the Americans accused him of massacring Custer's command. He said:

'I know they do. If Custer had killed all my people the Americans would have said he had won a great fight. I did not massacre Custer. He was a brave man, but he had no caution. The Marmot is brave, but he is cautious and cunning too. Custer was brave, but he was careless. He rushed upon us. We were strong. I had five times as many warriors as he. We were posted well. If he had had as many soldiers as I had braves, and I had had only as many braves as he had soldiers, I could have beaten him all the same. I was posted well. I had the ground. He rushed upon us. He came with a loud shout into the ravine. I expected it. I knew what he would do. I had heard of him. Little Current there knew him well. We were ready for him. As soon as he rushed in we closed up the ravine. We shut him in. What can you do when you are shut in all round? He rode very fast all over, shouting. He wanted to ride through us. At last one of my braves, Maneekolikonuah (the Grass-Eater) shot him. The Marmot would have taken him. When he fell the soldiers kept on fighting, but they could not see their way out. It was Custer's fault. Why did he take them into such a place! He was too brave. It is better to be afraid than too brave, like Custer. I did not murder them. We thought Reno was with Custer at first; and when Reno came along after, we thought it was the chief (Terry), and made away because we were tired. Reno stopped. Then we went off. My braves did not touch the dead soldiers. We went away and left them. Miles is like Custer. I think he is his brother. I mean that he has no caution. It is not just to say we murdered Custer. He murdered himself. That is all.'

"Little Current added that Custer was a fool. He thought he could do anything. A brave man is very good, but a chief ought to be cunning too. Custer was a good fighter but a bad chief. Howard was a good chief. He was very careful. He did not throw away soldiers. He was careful. He did not try to do too much.

"It was now 8 o'clock. A police picket of a sergeant and five troopers stationed in a block-house just outside the camp had business with Sitting Bull at half past, and we closed our talk and crossed the gorge and up the steep brae in the driving storm. My quarters for the night were in the block house, and Sitting Bull talked with us there for another hour on the Red Deer country, his future home, and other matters. On leaving he accepted some tobacco, and according to Indian etiquette I accompanied him back to his tepee. He enjoined me to remember him to Stamixotoken on my return next day to this post, and bade me be sure and make it known that he did not murder Custer. He sent the faithful Marmot back with me to the blockhouse, and I left the famous warrior with a hearty 'good night' and a warm handshake. On the 9th he comes here to see Colonel McLeod on camp matters. His people have plenty of fuel and want for nothing in the way of food. They are comfortable and seem happy enough, trusting implicitly to Sitting Bull, who is a very able and polished intercessor between them and the police officers."

Sitting Bull seems to have been much more affable with the World man than with the Herald man, probably on account of his being French. It has frequently been said that he loves the French on account of French missionaries who taught him their language. Not understanding French the Herald reporter was obliged to converse through an interpreter. After the usual manner he dilutes it as much as possible so as to spread it over the greatest possible space. He says:

"Sitting Bull is about five feet ten inches high. He was clad in a black and white calico shirt, black cloth leggings, and moccasins, magnificently embroidered with beads and porcupine quills. He held in his hand a foxskin cap, its brush dropping to his feet; with the dignity and grace of a natural gentleman he had removed it from his head at the threshold. His long black hair hung far down his back athwart his cheeks and in front of his shoulders. His eyes gleamed like black diamonds. His visage, devoid of paint, was noble and commanding; nay, it was something more. Besides the Indian character given to it by high cheek bones, a broad, retreating forehead, a prominent aquiline nose and a jaw like a bulldog's, there was about the mouth something of beauty, but more of an expression of exquisite, cruel irony. Two interpreters brought chairs and seated themselves, and at a neighboring desk the stenographer took his place. I afterward learned that two Sioux chiefs stood on guard outside the door and that all the Indians had arms ready to spring in case of a suspected treachery. On the previous night two of the Indians had been taken suddenly ill and their sickness had

been ascribed by some warriors to poison. So restless and anxious were all the savages that nothing but the influence and tact of Major Walsh could have procured for me the following colloquy with the Sphinx of the Northwest:

"You are a great chief," said I to Sitting Bull, "but you live behind a cloud. Your face is dark; my people do not see it. Tell me, do you hate the Americans very much?" A gleam as of fire shot across his face. 'I am no chief.' "What are you?" 'I am,' said he, crossing both hands upon his chest, slightly nodding and smiling satirically, 'a man.' "You say you are no chief?" 'No!' (with considerable hauteur) "Are you a head soldier?" 'I am nothing — neither a chief nor a soldier.' "What? Nothing?" "Nothing." "What, then, makes the warriors of your camp, the great chiefs who are here along with you, look up to you so? Why do they think so much of you?" 'Oh, I used to be a kind of a chief; but the Americans made me go away from my father's hunting ground.' "You do not love the Americans?" You should have seen the savages lips. "I saw today that all the warriors around you clapped their hand and cried out when you spoke. What you said appeared to please them. They liked you. They seemed to think that what you said was right for them to say. If you are not a great chief, why do these men think so much of you?"

"At this Sitting Bull, who had in the meantime been leaning back against the wall, assumed a posture of mingled toleration and disdain. 'You people look up to men because they are rich; because they have much land, many lodges, many squaws?' "Yes." 'Well, I suppose my people look up to me because I am poor. That is the difference.' In this answer was concentrated all the evasiveness natural to an Indian. "What is your feeling toward the Americans now?" He did not even deign an answer. He touched his hip, where his knife was. I asked the interpreter to insist on an answer. 'Listen,' said Sitting Bull, not changing his posture, but putting his right hand out upon my knee. 'I told them to-day what my notions were — that I did not want to go back there. Everytime that I had any difficulty with them they struck me first. I want to live in peace.' "Have you an implacable enmity to the Americans: Would you live with them in peace if they allowed you to do so; or do you think that you can only obtain peace here?" 'The White Mother is good.' "Better than the Great Father?" 'Howgh.'

(We pass over the less important parts of the interview to come to Sitting Bull's account of the Custer massacre, condensing it by omitting some of the reporter's questions):

'Many of the chiefs knew the Long Haired Chief, but I never saw him. He was a great warrior. He was a mighty chief. We thought we were whipped. Not at first, but by and bye, yes. Afterwards no. Our camp was attacked some two hours past the time when the sun is in the centre of the sky. The Long Hair commanded. The chiefs saw him — not here but there (Pointing on a map to where Custer was repulsed, on the north bank of the Little Big Horn). I was lying in my lodge. Some young men ran into me and said, "The Long Hair is in the camp. Get up. They are firing into the camp." I said all right. I jumped up and stepped out of my lodge; here (pointing to the group of Hunkpapa lodges designated as "abandoned lodges" on the map). The first attack was made here, and the old men, squaws and children were hurried away toward the other end of the camp. Some of the Minneconjou women and children also left their lodges when the attack began.'

'We fell back, but it was not what warriors call a retreat; it was to gain time. It was the Long Hair who retreated. My people fought him here in the brush (designating the timber behind which the Indians pressed Reno) and he fell back across here'

(placing his finger on the line of Reno's retreat to the northern bluffs). "So you think that was the Long Hair whom you people fought in that timber and who fell back afterward to those heights?" 'Of course.' "What afterward occurred? Was there any heavy fighting after the retreat of the soldiers to the bluffs?" 'Not then; not there.' "Where, then?" 'Why, down here;' and Sitting Bull indicated with his finger the piece where Custer approached and touched the river. 'That,' said he, 'was where the big fight was fought, a little later. After the Long Hair was driven back to the bluffs he took this road (tracing with his finger the line of Custer's march on the map), and went down to see if he could not beat us there.'

(Here the reader should pause to discern the extent of Sitting Bull's error and to anticipate what will appear to be Reno's misconception or mistake. Sitting Bull, not identifying Reno in the whole of this engagement, makes it seem that it was Custer who attacked, when Reno attacked in the first place, and afterward moved down to resume the assault from a new position.)

"When the fight commenced here," I asked, pointing to the spot where Custer advanced beyond the Little Big Horn "What happened?" 'Hell!' "You mean, I suppose, a fierce battle?" 'I mean a thousand devils.' "The village was by this time thoroughly aroused?" 'The squaws were like flying birds; the bullets were like humming bees.' "You say that when the first attack was made off here on the right of the map, the old men and squaws and children ran down the valley toward the left. What did they do when this second attack came from up here toward the left?" 'They ran to the fight — the big fight.' "So that, in the afternoon, after the first fight, on the right hand side of the map was over, and after the big fight toward the left hand side began, you say that the squaws and children all returned to the right hand side, and that the warriors, the fighting men of the Indian camps, ran to the place where the big fight was going on?" 'Yes' "Why was that? Were not some of the warriors left in front of these intrenchments on the bluffs, near the right side of the map? Did not you think it necessary — did not your war chiefs think it necessary — to keep some of your young men there to fight the troops who had retreated to these intrenchments?" 'No' "Why?" 'You have forgotten' "How?" 'You forget that only a few soldiers were left by the Long Hair on those bluffs. He took the main body of his soldiers with him to make the big fight down here on the left.' "So there were no soldiers to make a fight left in the intrenchments on the right hand bluffs?" 'I have spoken. It is enough. The squaws could deal with them. There were none but squaws and pappooses in front of them that afternoon.' "Well then," I inquired of Sitting Bull. "did the cavalry, who came down and made the big fight, fight?" Again Sitting Bull smiled. 'They fought. Many young men are missing from our lodges. But is there an American squaw who has her husband left? Were there any Americans left to tell the story of that day? No.' "How did they come on to the attack?" 'I have heard that there are trees which tremble.' "Do you mean the trees with trembling leaves?" 'Yes' "They call them in some parts of the Western country Quaking Asps; in the Eastern part of the country they call them silver Aspens." 'Hah! A great white chief, whom I met once, spoke these words: Silver Aspens, trees that shake: those were the Long Hair's soldiers.' "You do not mean that they trembled before your people because they were afraid!" 'They were brave men. They were tired. They were too tired.' "How did they act? How did they behave themselves?" At this Sitting Bull again arose. I also arose from my seat, as did the other persons in the room, except the stenographer.

"When the great crowds of your young men crossed the river in front of Long Hair what did they do? Did they attempt to assault him directly in his front?" 'At first they did, but afterward they found it better to try and get around him. They formed themselves on all sides of him except just at his back.' "How long did it take them to put themselves around his flanks?" 'As long as it takes the sun to travel from here to here.' (Indicating some marks upon his arm with which apparently he is used to gauge the progress of the shadow of his lodge across his arm, and probably meaning half an hour. An Indian has no more definite way than this to express the lapse of time). 'The trouble was with the soldiers,' he continued; 'they were so exhausted and their horses bothered them so much that they could not take good aim. Some of their horses broke away from them and left them to stand and drop and die. Then the Long Hair, the General, found that he was so outnumbered and threatened on his flanks, he took the best course he could have taken. The bugle blew. It was an order to fall back. All the men fell back fighting and dropping. They could not fire fast enough, though. But from our side it was so,' said Sitting Bull, and here he clapped his hands rapidly twice a second to express with what quickness and continuance the balls flew from the Henry and Winchester rifles wielded by the Indians. 'They could not stand up under such a fire,' he added. "Were any military tactics shown? Did the Longed Haired Chief make any disposition of his soldiers, or did it seem as though they retreated all together, helter skelter, fighting for their lives?" 'They kept in pretty good order. Some great chief must have commanded them all the while. They would fall back across a coulie and make a fresh stand beyond on higher ground. The map is pretty nearly right. It shows where the white men stopped and fought before they were all killed. I think that is right-down there to the left, just above the Little Big Horn. There was one party driven out there, away from the rest, and there a great many men were killed. The places marked on the map are pretty nearly the places where all were killed.' "Did the whole command keep on fighting until the last?" 'Every man, so far as my people could see. There were no cowards on either side.' "This big fight, then, extended through three hours?" 'Through most of the going forward of the sun.' "Where was the Long Hair the most of the time?" 'I have talked with my people; I cannot find one who saw the Long Hair until just before he died. He did not wear his long as he used to wear it. His hair was like yours,' said Sitting Bull playfully touching my forehead with his taper fingers. 'It was short, but it was of the color of the grass when the frost comes.' "Did you hear from your people how he died? Did he die on horseback." "All were dismounted?" 'Yes.' "And Custer, the Long Hair?" 'Well, I have understood that there were a great many brave men in that fight, and that from time to time, while it was going on, they were shot down like pigs. They could not help themselves. One by one the officers fell. I believe the Long Hair rode across once from this place down here' (meaning the place where Tom Custer's and Smith's companies were killed) 'to this place up here' (indicating the spot on the map where Custer fell), 'but I am not sure about this. Any way it was said that up there where the last fight took place, where the last stand was made, the Long Hair stood like a sheaf of corn with all the ears fallen around him.' "Not wounded?" 'No.' "How many stood by him?" 'A few.' "When did he fall?" 'He killed a man when he fell. He laughed.' "You meaned he cried out?" 'No, he laughed; he had fired his last shot.' "From a carbine?" 'No, a pistol.' "Did he stand up after he first fell?" 'He rose up on his hands and fired another shot, but his pistol would not go off.' "Was anyone else standing up when he fell down?" 'One man was kneeling; that was all. But he died before the Long Hair. All

this was far up on the bluffs, far away from the Sioux encampments. I did not see it. It is told to me. But it is true.' "The Long Hair was not scalped?" 'No. My people did not want his scalp.' "Why?" 'I have said; he was great chief.' "Did you at any time," I persisted, "during the progress of the fight believe that your people would get the worst of it?" 'At one time, as I have told you, I started to tell the squaws to strike the lodges. I was then on my way up to the right end of the camp, where the first attack was made on us. But before I reached that end of the camp where the Minneconjou and Hunkpapas squaws and children were and where some of the other squaws — Cheyennes and Ogallallas — had gone I was overtaken by one of the young warriors, who had just come down from the fight. He called out to me. He said: 'No use to leave camp; every white man is killed'. So I stopped and went no further. I turned back, and by and by I met the warriors returning.' "But in the mean time," I asked, "were there no warriors occupied up here at the right end of the camp? Was nobody left, except the squaws and the children and the old men, to take care of that end of the camp? Was nobody ready to defend it against the soldiers in those intrenchments up there?" 'Oh,' replied Sitting Bull again, 'there was no need to waste warriors in that direction. There were only a few soldiers there in those intrenchments, and we knew they wouldn't dare to come out.' "While the big fight was going on," I asked Sitting Bull, "could the sound of the firing be heard as far as those intrenchments on the right?" 'These squaws who were gathered down in the valley of the river heard them. The guns could have been heard three miles or more.'

As Sitting Bull arose to go I asked him whether he had the stomach for any more battles with the Americans. He answered: 'I do not want any fight.' "You mean not now?" He laughed quite heartily. 'No; not this winter.' "Are your young braves willing to fight?" 'You will see.' "When?" 'I cannot say.' "I have not seen your people. Would I be welcome at your camp?"

After gazing at the ceiling for a few moments Sitting Bull responded: 'I will not be pleased. The young men would not be pleased. You came with this party (alluding to the United States Commissioners) and you can go back with them. I have said enough.' "With this Sitting Bull wrapped his blanket around him and after gracefully shaking hands, strode to the door. Then he placed his fox-skin cap upon his head and I bade him adieu."*

---

*... Army and Navy Journal, November 24, 1877; pages 245-246.

BIBLIOGRAPHY

A list of books and articles containing excellent general information about the history and people on the 1860-70 frontier would include the following:

Campbell, Walter Stanley (Stanley Vestal), *Warpath and Council Fire; the Plains Indians' Struggle for Survival in War and in Diplomacy*, Random House, Inc., New York, 1948.

Custer, Elizabeth; *Boots and Saddles*, Harper and Brothers, New York, 1885; *Following the Guidon*, Harper and Brothers, 1890.

Custer, General G. A., *My Life on the Plains*, Sheldon and Co., New York, 1874.

Danker, D. F., editor, *The Journal of an Indian Fighter; the 1869 Diary of Major Frank J. North*, Nebraska History, June 1958.

Downey, Fairfax David, *Indian-Fighting Army*, Charles Scribner's Sons, New York, 1941.

Forsyth, George A., *The Story of the Soldier*, Appleton-Century-Crofts, Inc., New York, 1900.

Grinnell, George Bird, *Fighting Cheyennes*, University of Oklahoma Press, Norman, Oklahoma, 1956.

Herr, John K., and Edward S. Wallace, *Story of the U.S. Cavalry*, Little, Brown and Co., Boston, 1953.

Hull, Myra, editor, *Soldiering on the High Plains: The Diary of Lewis Bryan Hull, 1864-1866*, Kansas Historical Quarterly, February 1938.

Mattison, Ray H., *The Army Post on the Northern Plains, 1865-1885*, Nebraska History, March 1954.

Ostrander, Alson Bowles, *Army Boy of the Sixties; a Story of the Plains*, World Book Co., Yonkers-on-the-Hudson, 1924.

Rickey, Don, *War in the West – the Indian Campaigns*, Custer Battlefield Historical and Museum Association, Crown Agency, Montana, 1956.

Wellman, Paul Iselin, *Death on Horseback; Seventy Years of War for the American West*, Garden City Publishing Co., New York, 1950.

Welty, R. L., *The Army Post on the Frontier*, North Dakota Historical Quarterly, April 1928; *The Frontier Army on the Missouri River, 1860-1870*, North Dakota Historical Quarterly, January 1928.

Much of the technical information appearing in this book came from the following sources:

Carter, Captain W. H., *Horses, Saddles and Bridles*, Leavenworth, Kansas, 1895.

Hutchins, Cavalry Campaign Outfit at the Little Big Horn, *Military Collector and Historian*, Winter 1956.

Ordnance Manual for the Use of Officers of the U.S. Army, Lippincott and Co., New York, 1862.

Outline Description of U.S. Military Post and Stations in Year 1871, U.S. Quartermaster Department.

Parsons, John E., and John S. DuMont, *Firearms in the Custer Battle*, Stackpole Co., Harrisburg, 1954.

Regulations for Uniforms and Dress of Army of the U.S., July 1872, Adjutant General's Office.

Childs, *Revised Regulations for the Army of the U.S., 1863*.

Safranek, V. F., *Complete Instructive Manual for the Bugle, Trumpet, Drum*, Carl Fischer, Inc., New York.

Uniforms of the U.S. from 1774 to 1889, Quartermaster General.

U.S. Ordnance Department, Ordnance Memoranda No.'s 8, 13, 15, 18.

ORIGINAL DOCUMENTS

Congress, Library of, Manuscript Division; W. J. Ghent collection, Box 2, Correspondence file; also, Record Group 11700.

Craig, Report of Sgt. Robert, 1st Squad, Company "E," Second Re-activated Cavalry, author's collection.

Custer Battlefield Museum, Elizabeth Custer Collection on microfilm, Rolls 1-8, 9-14, 15-19.

Narus, Report of Cpl. J. J., 1st Squad, Company "E," 2nd Re-activated Cavalry, author's collection.

Swieca, Report of Mitchell, Cpl., 1st Squad, Company "E," 2nd Re-activated Cavalry, author's collection.

MANUSCRIPTS

Court Martial of General G. A. Custer, Judge Advocate General's Office, 1867.

PERIODICALS

Army and Navy Journal, 1869-1870; *Army and Navy Journal*, a weekly national military trade newspaper, New York; 1st publication, August 1863.

Black Hills Engineer, November, 1929; January, 1930; November, 1931; April, 1941.

Braden, Charles, "An Incident of the Yellowstone Expedition of 1873," *Journal of the U.S. Cavalry Association*, October, 1904.

Bradley, James H., "Journal of James H. Bradley. The Sioux Campaign of 1876 Under the Command of General John Gibbon . . . ," *Contributions to the Historical Society of Montana*, Vol. II, 1896. (Also contains Matthew Carroll's Diary.)

Brigham, Earl K., "Custer's Meeting with Secretary of War Belknap At Fort Abraham Lincoln," *North Dakota History*, April, 1952.

Brininstool, E. A., "Derudio's Thrilling Escape," *Hunter-Trader-Trapper*, March 1933; "Custer Battle War Party," *Hunter-Trader-Trapper*, August, 1933; "Col. Varnum at the Little Big Horn," *Hunter-Trader-Trapper*, June, 1927.

Bull, Joseph White, "The Battle of the Little Big Horn," *Blue Book*, September, 1932.

Cavalry Journal, The, published monthly by the U.S. Cavalry Association.

Cody, William F., "Famous Hunting Parties of the Plains," *The Cosmopolitan*, June, 1894.

"Custer Battle Number," *The Teepee Book*, Vol. II, No. VI, June, 1916. (Reprinted in 1926 by the National Custer Memorial Association.)

Custer, G(eorge) A(rmstrong), "Battling with the Sioux on the Yellowstone," *The Galaxy*, Vol. XXII, No. 1, July, 1876.

Daly, Henry W., "The War Path," *American Legion Monthly*, April, 1927.

Davis, Theodore R., "A Summer on the Plains," *Harpers Monthly*, February, 1868.

DeLand, Charles Edmund, "Basil Clement (Claymore), the Mountain Trappers," *South Dakota Historical Collections*, Vol. XI, 1922; "The Sioux Wars," *South Dakota Historical Collections*, Vols. XV and XVII, 1930 and 1934.

Dixon, James W., "Across the Plains with General Hancock," *Journal, Military Service Institution*, June, 1886.

Dugard, W. T., "The True Story of Custer's Last Stand," *Frontier Stories*, Vol. 14, No. 1.

Dustin, Fred, "George Armstrong Custer," *Michigan History Magazine*, April-June, 1946.

Eastman, Charles A., "Rain-In-The-Face," *The Outlook*, October 27, 1906; Eastman, Charles A., "Rain in the Face . . . ," *The Outlook*, Vol. 84, No. 9, October 27, 1906.

Fiske, Frank B., "The Taming of the Sioux," *Bismarck* (North Dakota) *Tribune*, 1917.

Frink, Maurice M., "And Battles Long Ago," *Outing Magazine*, October, 1915.

Frost, L. A., "Custer Favored a Remington," *Gun Report*, October, 1968.

Frost, Lawrence, "Courtmartial Sentences General Custer," *Great Guns*, December, 1952.

Fry, James B., "Custer's Last Battle," *Century Magazine*, January, 1892.

Galaxy Magazine, March-June and September-November, 1876.

Garland, Hamlin, "General Custer's Last Fight as Seen by Two Moons," *McClure's*, September, 1898.

Gibbon, John, "Last Summer's Expedition Against the Sioux and Its Great Catastrophe," *American Catholic Quarterly Review*, April, 1877; "Hunting Sitting Bull," *American Catholic Quarterly*, October, 1877.

Godfrey, Edward S., Major, "Cavalry Fire Discipline," *Journal of the Military Service Institution*, Vol. XIX, No. 83, September, 1896. (The author cites examples from his wealth of combat experiences against Indians, 1868 through the Battle of Wounded Knee in 1890. Brigadier General, United States Army Retired, "Battle of Wounded Knee," *Winners of the West*, Vol. XII, No. 2, January, 1935.) "Custer's Last Battle," *The Century Illustrated*, Vol. XLIII, No. 3, January, 1892; "Some Reminiscences, Including the Washita Battle, November 27, 1868," *The Cavalry Journal*, October, 1928.

Goplen, A. O., "The Historical Significance of Fort Lincoln State Park," *North Dakota History* (reprinted), Vol. 13, No. 4, 1946.

Graham, William A., " 'Come on! Be Quick! Bring Packs!' Custer's Battle Plan, the Story of His Last Message, as Told by the Man who Carried It," *The Cavalry Journal*, Vol. XXXII, No. 132, July, 1923; "Custer's Battle Flags," *The Westerners Brand Book, 1950*, Los Angeles, 1951 (available as a separate reprint); "The Lost is Found," *Cavalry*, July-August, 1942.

Gray, John S., "The Reno Petition," *The Westerners (Chicago) Brand Book*, Vol. XXIV, No. 6, August, 1967; "Captain Clifford's Story of the Sioux Wars of 1876 . . . ," *The Westerners (Chicago) Brand Book*, Vol. XXVI, Nos. 10 and 11, December, 1969 and January, 1970.

Hammer, Kenneth M., "Marcus Albert Reno," *The Westerners New York Posse Brand Book*, Vol. 8, No. 3, 1961; "Men with Custer," The Old Army Press, Fort Collins, Colorado, 1972.

Harper's Weekly, 1861-1869, 1877, 1910.

Hawley, Paul R., "Did Cholera Defeat Custer?" *Journal, Surgery, Gynecology and Obstetrics*, May, 1947.

Hills, Louis E., "With General George A. Custer on the Northern Pacific Surveying Expedition in 1873," *Journal of History*, Vol. 8, No. 2, April, 1915. (Published by the Reorganized Church of Jesus Christ of Latter Day Saints at Lamoni, Iowa.)

Hixon, John C., "Custer's 'Mysterious' Mr. Kellogg: Mark Kellogg's Diary," *North Dakota History*, Vol. 17, No. 3, July, 1950. (Available as a separate reprint.)

Hudnutt, Dean, editor, "New Light on the Little Big Horn, Hitherto Unpublished Letters of a Soldier Describing the Stricken Field of the Little Big Horn," *The Field Artillery Journal*, Vol. XXVI, No. 4, July-August, 1936.

Hughes, Robert P., "The Campaign Against the Sioux in 1876," *Journal, Military Service Institution*, January, 1896.

Hunt, Fred A., "A Purposeful Picnic," *The Pacific Monthly*, Vol. XIX, Nos. 3 and 4, March and April, 1908.

Hunt, Frazier, "The Romantic Soldier," *Redbook Magazine*, August-September-October, 1928.

Hutchins, James S., "The Seventh Cavalry Campaign Outfit at the Little Bighorn," *The Military Collector and Historian*, Vol. VII, No. 4, Winter, 1956.

Jacker, E., "Who is to Blame for the Little Big Horn Disaster?" *American Catholic Quarterly Review*, October, 1876.

Johnson, Barry C., notes and introduction, "With Gibbon Against the Sioux in 1876. The Field Diary of Lt. William L. English," *The English Westerners' Brand Book*, Vol. 8, No. 4, July, 1966, and Vol. 9, No. 1, October, 1966; notes and introduction, "Dr. Paulding and His Remarkable Diary. A Jaundiced Look at Gibbon's Montana Column of 1876," *The English Westerners Society Sidelights of the Sioux Wars*, 1967.

Kanipe, Donald A., "A New Story of Custer's Last Battle," *Contributions to the Historical Society of Montana*, Vol. IV, 1903.

Kansas Historical Quarterly, Vol. XIV; *Kansas Historical Quarterly*, Vol. XXII, 1956; Vol. XXIV, 1958.

Kellogg, Mark, "Mark Kellogg's Diary," *North Dakota History*, Vol. XVII, No. 3, July, 1950; also, *The Westerners Brand Book (Chicago Corral)*, 1945-46.

King, Charles, "Custer's Last Battle," *Harpers New Monthly Magazine*, Vol. LXXXI, No. CCCLXXXIII, August, 1890.

Libby, O. G., editor, "The Arikara Narrative of the Campaign against the Hostile Dakotas, June, 1876," *North Dakota Historical Collections*, Vol. 6, 1920.

Lovell, Frank, 5th Cavalry, 1872-77, "Indian Fighter Recalls Eventful Days of the Frontier," *Winners of the West*, Vol. XVI, No. 7, August, 1937.

Luce, Edward S., editor, "The Diary and Letters of Dr. James DeWolf . . . His Record of the Sioux Expedition of 1876 as Kept Until His Death," *North Dakota History*, Vol. 25, Nos. 2 and 3, April-July, 1958. (Available as a separate reprint.)

MacLaine, Bob, "Rosters, Muster Rolls and Survivors," *Little Big Horn Associates Newsletter*, Vol. I, No. 6, June, 1967.

Mattison, Ray H., "Fort Rice — North Dakota's First Missouri River Military Post," *North Dakota History*, April, 1953; editor, "The Diary of Surgeon Washington Matthews, Fort Rice, D.T.," *North Dakota History*, Vol. XXI, Nos. 1 and 2, January and April, 1954.

McBlain, John F., "With Gibbon on the Sioux Campaign of 1876," *Cavalry Journal*, Vol. IX, June, 1896. (Author was a Second Cavalry enlisted man in the middle 1870's.)

McClernand, Brigadier General Edward J., "With the Indians and the Buffalo in Montana," *Cavalry Journal*, Vol. XXXV, No. 145, October, 1926.

McCormack, George R., "Man Who Fought with Custer," *National Republic*, Vol. XXI, No. 11, March, 1934.

Montana, The Magazine of Western History, Vol. XVI, No. 2, Spring, 1966. Special Custer edition.

Montgomery, Mrs. Frank C., "Fort Wallace and Its Relation to the Frontier," *Collections of the Kansas State Historical Society, 1926-1928*, Vol. XVII, 1928.

Murray, Robert A., "The Custer Court Martial," *Annals of Wyoming*, Vol. 36, No. 2, October, 1964. (Available as a reprint from the Wyoming State Historical Society.)

Nixon, John R., 7th Cavalry, 1890, "Memoirs," *Winners of the West*, Vol. XV, No. 7, July, 1938.

North Dakota History, "Jacob Horner of the 7th Cavalry," Vol. XVI, No. 2, April, 1949.

Nugent, William D., "Thrilling Experiences of William D. Nugent, A Troop, 7th Cavalry, Near Custer Battlefield (1876)," *Winners of the West*, Vol. III, No. 2, February, 1926.

O'Harra, Cleophas Co., "Custer Expedition Number," *The Black Hills Engineer*, Vol. XVII, No. 4, November, 1929. (A quarterly published by the South Dakota State School of Mines.)

Portland (Maine) *Sunday Times*, "Sergeant James A. Richardson," June 29, 1909.

Reedstrom, Ernest L.

Little Big Horn Associates Newsletter:
"A Follow-Up on Harrison's 'Another Eye Witness' Account on D. H. Ridgeley, Trapper in the Sioux Country," Vol. III, No. 3, p. 6, Fall, 1969.
"Accoutrements in 1876," Vol. III, No. 4, pp. 4-7, Winter, 1969.
"Hancock Expedition (1867): with Record of 'Indian War' Proclamation," pp. 3-4, official record owned by author, authorizing the burning of a Cheyenne Village by General Hancock. (Custer refers to this order as the one that set the Indians in war with the whites, pp. 5-8.)
"The Red Cravat," Vol. III, No. 3, pp. 17-18, Fall, 1969.

Research Review, Little Big Horn Associates:
"The 7th's Prairie Dandies," Vol. IV, No. 3, pp. 14-16, Fall, 1970.
"The War Horse," Vol. IV, No. 4, pp. 2-4, Winter, 1970. (Also see "Reedstrom's 'To the Last Man'" by George Wenzel Schneider, pp. 7-8.)
"California Joe," Vol. IV, No. 2, pp. 1-7, Summer, 1970.

Guns Magazine:
"Hawken Rifles, Part 1," May, 1970, p. 26.
"Hawken Rifles, Part 2," June, 1970, p. 22.
"California Joe — True Frontier," April, 1972, p. 15.
"Comeback for the Cavalry — Western Horseman," August, 1972, p. 64.
"Fort Ben Harrison," May, 1972, p. 34.
"Tales of Buffalo & The Frontier," August, 1973, p. 40.
"Military Accoutrements, Part 1," October, 1971, p. 42.
"Military Accoutrements, Part 2," December, 1971, p. 30.
"The 17 Day Hero," February, 1971, p. 30.
"Blackpowder — Guns & Ammo," 1974: (1) 'Hawken Rifle — King of the Mountain,' p. 22; (2) 'The Log Cabin Sport Shop,' p. 56; (3) 'Shoot Those Civil War Carbines,' p. 114; (4) 'Shoot Original Black Powder Arms,' p. 168.
(Also: Color photo of Custer Equipment, September, 1974, p. 38.)

Reid, Russel, "Fort Abraham Lincoln," *North Dakota History*, October, 1946.

Russell, Don, "Veteran Madsen," *Winners of the West*, Vol. XXI, No. 2, February, 1944; "Some Thoughts on Brevet Commissions — and Custer," *The Westerners (Chicago) Brand Book*, Vol. XVI, No. 7, Chicago, September, 1959.

Russell, Don and Millbrook, Minnie Dobbs, "Custer on the Defensive," *The Westerners (Chicago) Brand Book*, Vol. XXV, No. 6, August, 1968.

Ryan, Sergeant John, Seventh Cavalry, 1866-76, "Custer's Last Fight," *Billings* (Montana) *Times*, July 5, 1923.

Sandoz, Mari, "There were Two Sitting Bulls," *Bluebook Magazine*, November, 1949.

South Dakota Historical Collections, Vol. VII, 1914. (Contains A. B. Donaldson's "The Black Hills Expedition" and a reprint of Custer's report from Executive Document No. 32, 43rd Congress, 2nd session.)

Stewart, Edgar I., "The Reno Court of Inquiry," *The Montana Magazine of History*, Vol. II, No. 3, July, 1952; "I Rode with Custer," *Montana Magazine of History*, Vol. 4, No. 3, Summer, 1954; "The Literature of the Custer Fight," *The Pacific Northwesterner*, Vol. I, No. 1, Winter, 1956-57; "Which Indian Killed Custer?" *Montana, the Magazine of Western History*, Vol. 8, No. 3, July, 1958.

Taft, Robert, "The Pictorial Record of the Old West, [Part] IV, Custer's Last Stand," *The Kansas Historical Quarterly*, Vol. XIV, No. 4, November, 1946.

Taunton, Francis B., and Barry C. Johnson, "Custer's Trial; the Aftermath. Review by Judge Advocate General Holt; and Final Action by General Grant," *The English Westerners Brand Book*, Vol. 10, No. 4, July, 1968.

Utley, Robert M., "The Celebrated Peace Policy of General Grant," *North Dakota History*, July, 1953.

Vestal, Stanley, "Sitting Bull and Custer's Last Stand," *Adventure*, February 1, 1932; "The Man Who Killed Custer," *American Heritage*, Vol. VIII, No. 2, February, 1957.

Watson, Elmo Scott, "The 'Custer Campaign Diary' of Mark Kellogg," *The Westerners Brand Book 1945-46*, Chicago, 1947.

Weir, Lieutenant W. B., "Infantry Equipments, Ordnance Notes No. LXVII," *Ordnance Notes, Nos. 4-67*, 1877. A discussion of suggested modifications in uniforms and equipments used in western campaigning.

Westerners Brand Book 1944, Chicago, The, 1946.

Wilson, James G., "Two Modern Knights Errant," *Cosmopolitan*, July, 1891.

Winners of the West, 1922-1944. The official publications of the National Indian War Veterans, from the organization's National Headquarters, St. Joseph, Missouri.

NEWSPAPERS

Bismarck Tribune, August, 1874; July 6, 1876.

Chicago Interocean, August 27, 1874.

Daily Grafic, New York, July 10, 1876.

Iowa State Register, March 21, 1877.

Leavenworth Daily Conservative, p. 1, col. 4, July 10, 1867.

Newton Circuit, The, Newton Centre, Massachusetts, various dates; July 9, 1909, July 16, 1909, September 3, 1909.

New York Herald, February 10, 1876; July 6, 1876.

New York Times, February 14, 1869; April 13, 1874.

Winners of the West, St. Joseph, Missouri.

BOOKS & PAMPHLETS

Amaral, Anthony A., *Comanche, the Horse that Survived the Custer Massacre*, Westernlore Press, Los Angeles, 1961.

Annual Report on Indian Affairs from 1867 to 1878.

Army of the United States – 1861, Revised Regulations for the (uniform, dress and horse equipment), by Authority of the War Department, G. W. Childs, Philadelphia, 1862. (Also in reprint by the Smithsonian Institute, Washington, D. C., 1961.)

Army of the United States – July 1872, Regulations for the Uniform and Dress of the, by Authority of the War Department, Washington, Government Printing Office, 1872. (Also in reprint by Jacques Noel Jacobsen, Jr., Manor Publishing, Staten Island, New York.)

Army, The Ordnance Manual for the Use of the Officers of the United States – 3rd Edition, J. B. Lippincott & Co., 1861. Recent edition printed in 1970 by Ordnance Park Corporation with limited copies up to 2,000.

Army Register for January 1871, Official, published by Order of the Secretary of War, Adjutant General's Office, Washington, January 1, 1871.

Army Register from 1861 to 1878.

Bates, Charles Francis, *Custer's Indian Battles,* published by the editor, Bronxville, New York, 1936; *Fifty Years after the Little Big Horn* [cover title], (1926?).

Blish, Helen H., text, and Amos Bad Heart Bull, drawings, *A Pictographic History of the Oglala Sioux,* University of Nebraska Press, Lincoln, 1967.

Bonney, Orrin H. & Lorraine, *Battle Drums and Geysers,* Sage Books, The Swallow Press, Inc., Chicago.

Bourke, John G., *On the Border with Crook,* Charles Scribner's Sons, New York, 1891.

Bowers, Claude G., *The Tragic Era,* Houghton Mifflin Co., Cambridge, Massachusetts, 1929.

Boynton, Edward C., *History of West Point,* New York, 1863.

Brady, Cyrus T., *Indian Fights and Fighters . . . ,* McClure, Phillips & Co., New York, 1904; Doubleday, Page & Co., Garden City, New York, 1904.

Brill, Charles J., *Conquest of the Southern Plains . . . ,* Golden Saga Publishers, Oklahoma City, 1938.

Brininstool, E. A., *Troopers with Custer . . . ,* The Stackpole Company, Harrisburg, 1952 (Originally: "The Trooper Series. A Trooper with Custer . . . ," The Hunter-Trader-Trapper Co., Columbus, Ohio, 1925); *Fighting Red Cloud's Warriors,* Hunter-Trader-Trapper Co., Columbus, Ohio, 1926.

Brown, Barron, *Comanche, the Sole Survivor of All the Forces in Custer's Last Stand, the Battle of the Little Big Horn,* Burton Publishing Company, Kansas City, 1935.

Brown, G. H., *Record of Service of Michigan Volunteers in The Civil War,* Ihling Bros. & Everard, Kalamazoo, Michigan, 1903: Vol. 31, First Michigan Cavalry; Vol. 35. Fifth Michigan Cavalry; Vol. 36, Sixth Michigan Cavalry; Vol. 37, Seventh Michigan Cavalry.

Brown, Jesse, and A. M. Willard, edited by John T. Milek, *The Black Hills Trails . . . ,* Rapid City Journal Company, Rapid City, South Dakota, 1924.

Brown, Mark H., and W. R. Felton, *The Frontier Years, L. A. Huffman, Photographer of the Plains,* Henry Holt and Company, New York, 1955.

Bruce, Robert, editor, *Custer's Last Battle . . . ,* published by the editor, New York, 1927; *The Fighting Norths,* Brooklyn Eagle Press, 1932.

Bulkley, John M., *History of Monroe County,* 2 vols., Lewis Publishing Co., Chicago, 1913.

Burdick, Usher L., *The Last Battle of the Sioux Nation,* Worzalla Publishing Co., Stevens Point, Wisconsin, 1929; editor, *David F. Barry's Notes on "The Custer Battle,"* Wirth Brothers, Baltimore, 1949 (First Edition: The Proof Press, Baltimore, 1937).

Bureau of Ethnology; (Annual Report of) J. W. Powell, 1888-89 (Government Printing Office).

Burgum, Jessamine Slaughter, *Zezula, or Pioneer Days in the Smoky Water Country . . . ,* Getchell & Nielsen, Valley City, North Dakota, 1937.

Burt, Mary E., *The Boy General,* Charles Scribner's Sons, New York, 1901.

Byrne, P. E., *Soldiers of the Plains,* Minton, Balch & Company, New York, 1926.

Carrington, Henry G., *Ab-Sa-Ra-Ka . . . ,* J. B. Lippincott, Philadelphia, 1878.

Carroll, John M., *Custer in Periodicals;* a bibliographic checklist; Old Army Press, 1975.

Catton, Bruce, *A Stillness at Appomattox,* Doubleday & Co., Inc., Garden City, N. Y., 1954; *Glory Road,* Doubleday & Co., Inc., 1952; *Mr. Lincoln's Army,* Doubleday & Co., Inc., 1951.

Cavalry Tactics, D. Appleton & Company, New York, 1874.

Chandler, Melbourne C., *Of Garry Owen in Glory, the History of the Seventh United States Cavalry Regiment,* published by the author, 1960.

Chronological List of Actions with Indians: 1866 to 1891, Adjutant General's Office.

Coburn, Wallace David, *The Battle of the Little Big Horn,* The Overland-Outwest Publications, 1934. (Also in *Montana, the Magazine of Western History,* Vol. 6, No. 3, July 1956.)

Connelley, William E., *Wild Bill and His Era,* Press of the Pioneers, New York, 1933.

Court-Martial Orders, Index of General, Adjutant General's Office, 1878, Washington Government Printing Office, 1879. (G.C.M. Orders No. 41, charging Major M. A. Reno, 7th Cavalry, unbecoming of an officer.)

Crawford, Lewis F., *Rekindling Camp Fires . . . ,* Capitol Book Co., Bismarck, North Dakota, 1926.

Crawford, Samuel J., *Kansas in The Sixties,* A. G. McClurg & Co., Chicago, 1911.

Custer Battlefield Historical and Museum Association, *Entrenchment Trail,* Billings, Montana, no date.

Custer, Elizabeth B., *Boots and Saddles, or Life in Dakota with General Custer,* Harper & Brothers, New York, 1885; *Tenting on the Plains or General Custer in Kansas and Texas,* Charles L. Webster & Company, New York, 1887; *Following the Guidon,* Harper & Brothers, New York, 1890.

Custer, George A., *My Life On the Plains. Or, Personal Experiences with Indians,* Sheldon and Company, New York, 1874; *Reports on the Black Hills Expedition, August 2, 1874 to August 15, 1874.*

Custer, Milo, Custer Geneology, Bloomington, Illinois, 1944.

Daly, L. H., *Alexander Cheves Haskell,* Plimpton Press, Norwood, Massachusetts, 1934.

Davies, Henry E., *General Sheridan,* Appleton & Co., New York, 1899.

De Barthe, Joe, *The Life and Adventures of Frank Grouard,* Combe Printing Co., St. Joseph, Mifsouri, 1894.

De Forest, J. W., *A Volunteer's Adventures,* Yale University Press, New Haven, Connecticut, 1946.

Dellenbaugh, Frederick S., *George Armstrong Custer,* The Macmillan Co., New York, 1917.

De Trobriand, Phillippe, *Military Life in Dakota,* Alvord Memorial Commission, St. Paul, Minnesota, 1951.

Dictionary of American Biography.

Dixon, Joseph K., *The Vanishing Race . . . and the Indians' Story of the Custer Fight,* Doubleday, Page & Company, Garden City, New York, 1913.

Dodge, Richard I., *The Plains of the Great West . . . ,* G. P. Putnam's Sons, New York, 1877; *Our Wild Indians . . . ,* A. D. Worthington and Company, Hartford, 1882.

Dodge, T. A., *A Bird's-Eye View of Our Civil War,* Houghton, Mifflin & Co., New York, 1883.

Donald, David, *Divided We Fought,* The Macmillan Co., New York, 1953.

Downey, Fairfax, *Indian-Fighting Army,* Charles Scribner's Sons, New York, 1951 (reprinted, The Old Army Press, 1972).

DuBois, Charles, *Kick the Dead Lion . . . ,* published by the author, Billings, Montana, 1961 (first edition, 1954).

Dunn, J. P., *Massacres of the Mountains . . .* , Harper and Brothers, New York, 1886.

Dustin, Fred, *The Custer Fight, Some Criticisms of Gen. E. S. Godfrey's "Custer's Last Battle"* . . . , privately printed, Hollywood, California, 1936; *The Custer Tragedy* . . . , Edward Brothers, Inc., Ann Arbor, Michigan, 1939.

Eastman, Charles A., *Indian Heroes and Great Chieftains*, Little, Brown and Company, Boston, 1918.

Ege, Robert J., *"Settling the Dust," a Brief for a Much-maligned Cavalryman,* published by the author, Great Falls, Montana, 1968.

Farley, J. P., *West Point in the Early Sixties*, Parfracts Book Co., Troy, New York, 1902.

Farnsworth, F. E., and L. S. Trowbridge, *Michigan at Gettysburg,* Winn & Hammond, Detroit, 1889.

Finerty, John F., *War-path and Bivouac, or the Conquest of the Sioux* . . . , Donohue & Henneberry, Chicago, 1890.

Foner, Jack D., *(The United States Soldier) Between Two Wars (1865-1898): Army Life & Reforms,* Humanities Press, New York, 1970.

Forsyth, George A., *The Story of the Soldier,* D. Appleton and Company, New York, 1900.

Fougera, Katherine Gibson, *With Custer's Cavalry,* The Caxton Printers, Ltd., Caldwell, Idaho, 1940.

Frackelton, Will (as told to Herman Gastrell Seely), *Sagebrush Dentist,* A. C. McClurg & Co., Chicago, 1941.

Frazer, Robert W., *Forts of the West,* University of Oklahoma Press, Norman, Oklahoma, 1965.

Frost, Lawrence A., *The Custer Album, a Pictorial Biography of,* Superior Publishing Company, Seattle, 1964; *The Court-Martial of General George Armstrong Custer,* University of Oklahoma Press, Norman, Oklahoma, 1968.

Frost, Lawrence A., *General Custer's Libbie,* Superior Publishing Company, 1976.

Fry, James B., *Military Miscellanies,* Brentano's, New York, 1889.

Gibbon, John, *Gibbon on the Sioux Campaign of 1876,* The Old Army Press, Fort Collins, Colorado, 1969 (originally: "Last Summer's Expeditions against the Sioux," *American Catholic Quarterly Review,* Vol. II, April and October, 1877).

Graham, W. A., *The Story of the Little Big Horn,* Military Service Publishing Company, Harrisburg, 1941 (first edition: The Century Company, New York, 1926; editor, compiler, *The Official Record of a Court of Inquiry . . . upon the Request of Major Marcus A. Reno, 7th U. S. Cavalry, to Investigate His Conduct at the Battle of the Little Big Horn . . . ,* published by the editor, Pacific Palisades, California, 1951; *The Custer Myth, a Source Book of Custeriana,* The Stackpole Company, Harrisburg, 120Grant, Jesse R., *In the Days of My Father General Grant,* Harper & Brothers, Publishers, New York, 1925.

Green, Horace, *General Grant's Last Stand,* Charles Scribner's Sons, New York, 1936.

Grinnell, George Bird, *The Fighting Cheyennes,* Charles Scribner's Sons, New York, 1915; *The Cheyenne Indians,* 2 vols., Yale University Press, New Haven, Connecticut, 1923.

Gurowski, Adam, *Diary from March 4, 1861 to November 12, 1862,* Lee and Shepard, Boston, 1862; *Diary from November 18, 1862 to October 18, 1863,* Carleton, New York, 1864; *Diary: 1863-'64-'65,* W. H. & O. Morrison, Washington, 1866.

Hancock, Mrs. W. S., *Reminiscences of Winfield Scott Hancock,* Charles L. Webster & Co., New York, 1887.

Hanson, Joseph Mills, *The Conquest of the Missouri,* A. C. McClurg & Co., Chicago, 1909; Murray Hill Books, Inc., New York, 1946.

Harrison, Joseph T., *The Story of the Dining Fork,* C. J. Krehbiel Co., Cincinnati, 1927.

Hazen, W. B., *Our Barren Lands . . . ,* Robert Clarke & Company, Printers, Cincinnati, 1875; *Some Corrections of Life on the Plains,* Ramaley & Cunningham, St. Paul, Minnesota, 1875.

Hebard, Grace Raymond, *Washakie . . . ,* The Arthur H. Clark Company, Cleveland, Ohio, 1930.

Hein, O. L., *Memories of Long Ago,* G. P. Putnam's Sons, New York, 1925.

Heitman, Francis B., *Historical Register & Dictionary of the United States Army, from Its Organization, September 29, 1789, to March 2, 1903;* Vols. 1 and 2, Government Printing Office, Washington, 1903; University of Illinois Press, Urbana, Illinois, 1965.

Herr, John K., and Edward S. Wallace, *The Story of the U.S. Cavalry,* 1775-1942, Little, Brown and Company, Boston, 1953.

Hesseltine, William B., *Ulysses S. Grant: Politician,* Dodd, Mead & Co., New York, 1935.

Historical Register and Dictionary of the United States Army, 1789-1903 (2 vol.), Government Printing Office, Washington, D.C. (1903); Reprint, University of Illinois Press, Urbana, 1965.

Holley, Frances Chamberlain, *Once Their Home or Our Legacy from the Dahkotahs . . . ,* Donohue & Henneberry, Chicago, 1890.

Horses, Diseases of the, U.S. Department of Agriculture, Government Printing Office, Washington, D.C., 1907.

Howard, James H., editor, *The Warrior Who Killed Custer. A Personal Narrative of Chief Joseph White Bull,* University of Nebraska Press, Lincoln, 1968.

Humfreville, V. Lee, *Twenty Years Among our Hostile Indians,* Hunter and Co., New York, 1899.

Hunt, Frazier, *Custer, The Last of the Cavaliers,* Cosmopolitan, New York, 1928.

Hunt, Frazier and Robert, *I Fought with Custer, the Story of Sergeant Windolph, Last Survivor of the Battle of the Little Big Horn,* Charles Scribner's Sons, New York, 1947.

Hyde, George, *Red Cloud's Folk, a History of the Oglala Sioux Indians,* University of Oklahoma Press, Norman, Oklahoma, 1937.

Hyde, George E., *The Life of George Bent,* University of Oklahoma Press, Norman, Oklahoma, 1968.

Indians vs The United States, Court of Claims of The United States; The Sioux Tribe of, 2 vols., 1937.

Innis, Benn, *Blood Knife!,* The Old Army Press, 1973.

Jackson, Donald, *Custer's Gold, the United States Cavalry Expedition of 1874,* Yale University Press, New Haven, 1966.

Jackson, Helen, *A Century of Dishonor,* Roberts Brothers, Boston, 1886.

Jenney, W. P., *Report of a Reconnaisance of the Black Hills of Dakota,* Washington, 1876.

Johnson, Barry C., *Case of Marcus A. Reno,* The English Westerners' Society, London, 1969.

Johnson, Virginia Weisch, *The Unregimented General, a Biography of Nelson A. Miles,* Houghton Mifflin Company, Boston, 1962.

Kansas Historical Collections, Vols. X, XI, XV, XVI, XVII.

Keim, De B. Randolph, *Sheridan's Troopers on the Border: a Winter Campaign on the Plains,* Claxton, Remsen & Haffelfinger, Philadelphia, 1870; David McKay, Philadelphia, 1891.

Kidd, J. H., *Personal Recollections of a Cavalryman,* Sentinel Printing Co., Ionia, Michigan, 1908.

Kimball, Maria Brace, *A Soldier-Doctor of Our Army, James P. Kimball . . . ,* Houghton Mifflin Company, Boston, 1917.

King, Charles, *Campaigning with Crook and Stories of Army Life,* Harper & Brothers, New York, 1890.

Knight, Oliver, *Following the Indian Wars . . . ,* University of Oklahoma Press, Norman, Oklahoma, 1960.

Koury, Michael J., *Diaries of the Little Big Horn*, The Old Army Press, 1968.

Kuhlman, Charles, *Gen. George A. Custer, or Lost Trail and the Gall Saga . . .* , published by author, Billings, Montana, 1940; *Legend into History*, The Stackpole Company, Harrisburg, 1951; *Did Custer Disobey Orders at the Battle of the Little Big Horn?*, The Stackpole Company, Harrisburg, 1957.

Lanman, Charles, *The Red Book of Michigan*, E. B. Smith & Co., Detroit, 1871.

Leckie, William H., *The Buffalo Soldiers*, University of Oklahoma Press, Norman, Oklahoma, 1963.

Lewis, Berkeley, R., *Small Arms & Ammunition in The United States Service – 1776-1865;* Smithsonian Institution Press, Washington, D. C. (1st print, 1960).

Linderman, Frank Bird, *Red Mother*, The John Day Company, New York, 1932.

Little Big Horn, (The); 1876, Documents and Rosters; compiled and annotated by Loyd J. Overfield, II; Arthur H. Clark Company, Glendale, California, 1971.

Longstreet, James, *From Manassas to Appomattox*, J. B. Lippincott Co., New York, 1896.

Lord, F. A., *They Fought for the Union*, Bonanza Books, New York; *Civil War Collector's Encyclopedia*, The Stackpole Company, Harrisburg, Pennsylvania, 1963.

Lord, F. A., and Arthur Wise, *Uniforms of the Civil War*, Thomas Yoseloff, New Jersey, 1970.

Lothrop, Charles H., *A History of the First Regiment Iowa Cavalry Veteran Volunteers . . .* , First Iowa Cavalry Association, Lyons, Iowa, 1890.

Lounsberry, Clement A., *Early History of North Dakota . . .* , Liberty Press, Washington, D. C., 1919.

Luce, Edward S., *Keogh, Comanche and Custer*, Dedham, Massachusetts, 1939.

Ludlow, William, *Report of a Reconnaissance from Carrol, Montana Territory, on the Upper Missouri to the Yellowstone National Park and Return in 1876*, Washington Government Printing Office, 1876; *Report of a Reconnaissance of the Black Hills of Dakota*, Washington, 1875.

Luther, Tal, *Custer High Spots*, The Old Army Press, 1972.

Macartney, C. E., *Grant and His Generals*, McBride Co., New York, 1953.

Maine, Floyd Shuster, *Lone Eagle, the White Sioux*, The University of New Mexico Press, Albuquerque, 1956.

Mallery, Garrick, "Picture-Writing of the American Indians, Charles E. McChesney's Account of the Battle of the Little Big Horn," *Tenth Annual Report of the Bureau of American Ethnology*, Washington, D.C., 1893.

Manypenny, George W., *Our Indian Wards*, Robert Clarke & Co., Cincinnati, 1880.

Marquis, Thomas B., *Memoirs of a White Crow Indian*, The Century Co., New York, 1928; *A Warrior Who Fought Custer*, The Midwest Company, Minneapolis, 1931; *Sketch of the Custer Battle*, privately printed, Hardin, Montana, 1933; *She Watched Custer's Last Battle*, privately printed, Hardin, Montana, 1933; *Which Indian Killed Custer*, privately printed, Hardin, Montana, 1933; *Two Days After the Custer Battle . . .* , privately printed, Hardin, Montana, 1935.

Masters, Joseph G., *Shadows Fall Across the Little Horn*, "*Custer's Last Stand*," University of Wyoming Library, Laramie, Wyoming, 1951.

McAuliffe, Eugene, *When Can Their Glory Fade? . . .* , published by the author, Omaha, Nebraska, 1952.

McClellan, George B., *McClellan's Own Story*, Charles L. Webster & Co., New York, 1887.

McClemand, Edward J., *With the Indian and the Buffalo in Montana, 1870-1878 . . .* , The Arthur H. Clark Company, Glendale, California, 1969 (originally: *The Cavalry Journal*, October, 1926, and succeeding two issues).

McCreight, M. I., *Chief Flying Hawk's Tales*, Alliance Press, New York, 1936.

McLaughlin, James, *My Friend the Indian*, Houghton Mifflin Company, New York, 1910.

McVey, Everett E., *The Crow Scout Who Killed Custer*, published by the author, Billings, Montana, 1952.

Medals of Honor, Government Printing Office, Washington, 1897.

Meredith, Roy, *Mr. Lincoln's Contemporaries*, Charles Scribner's Sons, New York, 1951.

Merington, Marguerite, editor, *The Custer Story, the Life and Intimate Letters of General George A. Custer and His Wife Elizabeth*, The Devin-Adair Company, New York, 1950.

Merril, Edward, *Auld Lang Syne*, no date, no publisher.

Michigan Historical Collections, Vols. 39 and 40.

Miles, Nelson A., *Personal Recollections of General Nelson A. Miles*, The Werner Co., Chicago, 1897; *Serving the Republic*, Harper & Brothers, New York, 1911.

Miller, David Humphreys, *Custer's Fall, the Indian Side of the Story*, Duell, Sloan and Pearce, New York, 1957.

Mills, Anson, edited by C. H. Claudy, *My Story*, privately published, Washington, D. C., 1918.

Milner, Joe E., and Earle R. Forrest, *California Joe . . .* , The Caxton Printers, Ltd., Caldwell, Idaho, 1935.

Mokler, Alfred James, *Transitions of the West . . .* , R. R. Donnelly & Sons Company, Chicago, 1927.

Mole, H. H., and R. D. Miller, *A Photographic History of General George A. Custer's Expedition to the Black Hills of South Dakota in 1874*, Pierre, South Dakota, 1940.

Monaghan, Jay, *Custer, The Life of General George Armstrong Custer*, Little Brown and Company, Boston, 1959.

Montana Historical Contributions, Vols. I, II, IV, IX.

Moore, James, *Kilpatrick and Our Cavalry*, W. J. Widdleton, New York, 1865.

Mulford, Ami F., *Fighting Indians in the 7th United States Cavalry*, Corning, New York, 1878.

Neihardt, John G., *Black Elk Speaks, Being the Life Story of a Holy Man of the Oglala Sioux*, William Morrow & Company, New York, 1932.

Nevins, Allan, *Hamilton Fish: The Inner Story of the Grant Administration*, Dodd, Mead & Co., New York, 1937.

Newhall, F. C., *With General Sheridan in Lee's Last Campaign*, J. B. Lippincott & Co., Philadelphia, 1866.

North Dakota, Collections of the State Historical Society of, Vol. I, 1906.

North Dakota Historical Collections, Vols. I, VI, VII.

Noyes, Al. J., *In the Land of Chinook, or the Story of Blaine County*, State Publishing Co., Helena, Montana, 1917.

Nye, Elwood L., *Marching with Custer, a Day-by-day Evaluation of the Uses, Abuses, and Conditions of the Animals of the Ill-fated Expedition of 1876 with Introduction and Photo Research on the Equestrian Custer by Carroll Friswold*, The Arthur H. Clark Company, Glendale, California, 1964.

Official Register of Officers and Cadets of the United States Military Academy, 1857-1873.

Ohio Archaelogical and Historical Publications, Vol. XV.

Overfield, Loyd J., II, compiler, *The Little Big Horn – The Official Documents with Rosters of Officers and Troops*, The Arthur H. Clark Company, 1971.

Paine, Bayard H., *Pioneers, Indians and Buffaloes*, The Curtis Enterprise, Curtis, Nebraska, 1935.

Parsons, John E., and John S. duMont, *Firearms in the Custer Battle*, The Stackpole Company, Harrisburg, 1953.

Paxson, Frederic L., *History of the American Frontier*, Houghton Mifflin Co., New York, 1924.

Perkins, J. R., *Trails, Rails and War*, Bobbs-Merrill Co., Indianapolis, 1929.

Poinsett, J. R., *U.S. Cavalry Tactics – 1841*, in three parts.

Praus, Alexis A., *A New Pictographic Autobiography of Sitting Bull*, Smithsonian Institution, Washington, 1955.

Pride, W. F., *The History of Fort Riley*, no publisher, Fort Riley, 1926.

Rebellion Records, War of the — otherwise known as *Official Records of the Union and Confederate Armies*.

Reece, Richard, *Reece's Medical Guide*, Albert Colby & Sons, Baltimore, 1873.

Remsburg, John E. and George J., *Charley Reynolds . . .*, H. M. Sender, Kansas City, 1931.

The Reno Court of Inquiry, Abstract of the Original Record of Proceedings; with Preface by Colonel W. A. Graham, Stackpole Company, (1954).

Reno Court of Inquiry, The Chicago Times Account, The Old Army Press, 1972.

Reusswig, William, *A Picture Report of the Custer Fight*, Hastings House, New York, 1967.

Rickey, Don, Jr., *History of Custer Battlefield*, Custer Battlefield Historical and Museum Association, Billings, Montana, 1967.

Risch, Erna, *Quartermaster Support of the Army – A History of the Corps, 1775-1939*, Quartermaster Historians Office, Office of the Quartermaster General, Washington, D.C., 1962.

Rister, C. C., *Border Command*, University of Oklahoma Press, Norman, Oklahoma, 1944.

Robertson, J., *Michigan in the War*, W. S. George & Co., Lansing, 1882.

Rodenbaugh, T. F., *From Everglade to Canon with the Second Dragoons*, D. Van Nostrand, New York, 1875.

Roe, Charles F., *Custer's Last Battle*, New York, 1927.

Roenigk, Adolph, *Pioneer History of Kansas*, published by the author, 1933.

Ronshelm, Milton, *The Life of General Custer*, Cadiz Republican, Cadiz, Ohio, 1929.

Russell, Don, *Custer's Last, or, the Battle of the Little Big Horn . . .*, Amon Carter Museum of Western Art, Fort Worth, 1968; *Custer's List. A Checklist of Pictures Relating to the Battle of the Little Big Horn*, Amon Carter Museum of Western Art, Fort Worth, 1969.

Salisbury, Albert and Jane, *Here Rolled the Covered Wagons*, Superior, Seattle, 1948.

Sandoz, Mari, *Crazy Horse, the Strange Man of the Oglalas*, Alfred A. Knopf, New York, 1942.

Schaff, Morris, *The Spirit of West Point*, New York, 1907.

Schmitt, Martin F., editor, *General George Crook*, an autobiography, University of Oklahoma Press, Norman, Oklahoma, 1946.

Schmitt, Martin F., and Dee Brown, *Fighting Indians of the West*, Charles Scribner's Sons, New York, 1948.

Schultz, James Willard, *William Jackson, Indian Scout . . .*, Houghton Mifflin Company, Boston, 1926.

Scott, Hugh L., *Some Memoirs of a Soldier*, The Century Co., New York, 1928.

Scudder, Ralph E., *Custer Country*, Binford & Mort, Publishers, Portland, Oregon, 1963.

Seitz, Don C., *The Dreadful Decade*, The Bobbs-Merrill Co., Indianapolis, 1926.

Sheridan, Philip H., *Outline Description of the Posts in the Military Division of the Missouri*, Jameson & Morse, Chicago, 1876; *Records of Engagements with Hostile Indians*, Chicago, 1882; *Personal Memoirs of Philip H.*

Sheridan, 2 vols., Charles L. Webster & Co., New York, 1888.

Sherman, W. T., *Memoirs of Gen. W. T. Sherman*, 2 vols., Charles L. Webster & Co., New York, 1891.

Sherwood, Isaac R., *Memories of the War*, H. J. Chittenden Co., Toledo, 1923.

Shields, G. O., *The Blanket Indian of the Northwest*, Vechten Waring Company, New York, 1921.

Smithsonian Report – 1879.

South Dakota Historical Collections, Vols. II, III, VI, VII, XI, XV, XVII.

Spotts, David L., edited by E. A. Brininstool, *Campaigning with Custer and the Nineteenth Kansas Volunteer Cavalry . . .*, Wetzel Publishing Company, Los Angeles, 1928.

Spotts, D. L., *Battles and Leaders of the Civil War*, 4 vols., The Century Co., New York, 1888.

Standing Bear, Luther, edited by E. A. Brininstool, *My People the Sioux*, Houghton Mifflin Company, Boston, 1928.

Stands in Timber, John, and Margot Liberty, *Cheyenne Memories*, Yale University Press, New Haven, 1967.

Stanley, D. S., *Report of the Yellowstone Expedition of 1873*, Government Printing Office, Washington, 1874.

Stanley, Henry M., *My Early Travels and Adventures in America and Asia*, Vol. I, Charles Scribner's Sons, New York, 1895; 2 Vols., Sampson, Low, Marston & Co., London, 1895.

Steckmesser, Kent Ladd, *The Western Hero in History and Legend*, University of Oklahoma Press, Norman, Oklahoma, 1965.

Steffan, Randy, *United States Military Saddles, 1812-1943*, with illustrations by the author, University of Oklahoma Press, 1973.

Stewart, Edgar I., *Custer's Luck*, University of Oklahoma Press, Norman, Oklahoma, 1955; *Penny-an-Acre Empire in the West*, University of Oklahoma Press, Norman, 1968.

Stewart, Edgar I. and Jane R., editors, *The Field Diary of Lt. Edward Settle Godfrey . . .*, The Champoeg Press, Portland, Oregon, 1957.

Sturgis, Thomas, *Common Sense View of the Sioux War*, Sentinel Office Print, Waltham, Massachusetts, 1877.

Tallent, Annie D., *The Black Hills . . .*, Nelson-Jones Printing Co., St. Louis, 1889.

Taylor, Joseph H(enry), *Sketches of Frontier and Indian Life . . .*, published by the author, Pottstown, Pennsylvania, 1889; *Kaleidoscopic Lives . . .*, published by the author, 1902 (first edition: 1896).

Tepee Book, The, 1916 and 1926.

Terrell, John Upton, and George Walton, *Faint the Trumpet Sounds . . .*, David McKay Company, Inc., New York, 1966.

Terry, Alfred H., *The Field Diary of General Alfred H. Terry, the Yellowstone Expedition – 1876*, The Old Army Press, Bellevue, Nebraska, no date (1969).

Tily, James C., *Uniforms of the U.S. Navy*, Thomas Yoseloff, 1964.

Topping, E. S., *The Chronicles of the Yellowstone . . .*, Pioneer Press Company, St. Paul, 1883.

Tremain, H. E., *Last Hours of Sheridan's Cavalry*, Bonnell, Silver & Bowers, New York, 1904.

Tucker, W. W., *The Grand Duke Alexis in the United States*, Riverside Press, Cambridge, Massachusetts, 1872.

Upton, Emory, *Infantry Tactics – Double & Single Rank, Revised*, D. Appleton & Co., New York, 1875.

Utley, Robert M., *Custer's Last Stand . . .*, published by the author, Dayton, Indiana, 1949; *Custer and the Great Controversy, the Origin and Development of a Legend*, Westernlore Press, Los Angeles, 1962; *Frontiersmen in Blue 1848-1865*, Macmillan Publishing Co., Inc., New York, 1967; introduction, *The Reno Court of Inquiry, The*

Chicago Times Account, The Old Army Press, Fort Collins, Colorado, 1972; *Frontier Regulars – 1866-1890*, Macmillan Publishing Co., Inc., New York, 1973.

Van de Water, Frederic F., *Glory-Hunter, A Life of General Custer*, The Bobbs-Merrill Company, Indianapolis, 1930.

Vaughn, J. W., *With Crook at the Rosebud*, The Stackpole Company, Harrisburg, 1956; *The Reynolds Campaign on Powder River*, University of Oklahoma Press, Norman, Oklahoma, 1961; *Indian Fights, New Facts on Seven Encounters*, University of Oklahoma Press, Norman, Oklahoma, 1966.

Vaughn, Robert, *Then and Now; or Thirty-Six Years in the Rockies . . .*, Tribune Printing Company, Minneapolis, 1900.

Vestal, Stanley, *Sitting Bull, Champion of the Sioux, A Biography*, Houghton Mifflin Company, Boston, 1934; *War Path, the True Story of the Fighting Sioux . . .*, Houghton Mifflin Company, Boston, 1934; *Warpath and Council Fire . . .*, Random House, New York, 1948.

Victor, Frances F., *Eleven Years in the Rocky Mountains . . .*, Columbian Book Company, Hartford, 1877.

Wagner, Glendolin Damon, *Old Neutriment*, Ruth Hill, Publisher, Boston, 1934.

Waldo, Edna La Moore, *Dakota . . .*, Capital Publishing Co., Bismarck, North Dakota, 1932.

Walker, Judson Elliott, *Campaigns of General Custer in the Northwest, and the Final Surrender of Sitting Bull*, published by the author, New York, 1881.

Westerners, Potomac Corral of the, Great Western Indian Fights, Doubleday & Company, Inc., New York, 1960.

Wheeler, H. W., *Buffalo Days*, The Bobbs-Merrill Co., Indianapolis, 1925.

Whittaker, Frederick, *A Complete Life of Gen. George A. Custer*, Sheldon & Company, New York, 1876.

Williamson James J., *Mosby's Rangers*, Sturgis & Walton Co., New York, 1909.

Wing, Talcott E., *History of Monroe County, Michigan*, Munsell and Co., New York, 1890.

Winstock, Lewis, *Songs & Music of the Red Coats, 1642-1902*, The Stackpole Company, Harrisburg, 1970.

PRINTED DOCUMENTS

Army, Reports of the General of the, 1876.

Army, Office of the Adjutant General, United States, *Decorations of the United States Army, 1862-1926*, Government Printing Office, Washington, 1926.

Army, Military Division of the Missouri, United States, *Outline Description of the Posts in the Military Division of the Missouri, Commanded by Lt. General P. H. Sheridan*, Chicago, Illinois, 1876.

Army, Surgeon General's Office, United States, Assistant Surgeon George A. Otis (compiler), *A Report of Surgical Cases in the United States Army, 1865-1871, Circular No. 3.*

Army, Returns from the Regular (Cavalry Ret.), September 1866-December 1873, National Archives, Roll 71.

Congress, 39th; *Miscellaneous Document No. 41*, 1867.

Courts Martial Orders, 1869, General, Headquarters, Department of the Missouri, United States Army, Government Printing Office, St. Louis, Missouri, 1870.

Court Martial Orders, 1870, General, Headquarters, Department of the Missouri, United States Army, Government Printing Office, St. Louis, Missouri, 1871.

Engineers, Appendixes to the Report of the Chief of, House of Representatives Executive Document I, Part 2, Vol. II, Part III, 44th Congress, 2nd Session, Washington, D.C., 1876. (Appendix 00 contains Maguire's report and map.)

Engineers, Appendixes to the Report of the Chief of, House of Representatives Executive Document I, Part 2, Vol. II, 45th Congress, 2nd Session, Washington, D.C., 1877. (Appendix PP contains the reports of Maguire, McClernand, Wallace and Wilson.)

Executive Document No. 184, House of Representatives, 44th Congress, 1st Session, *Military Expedition Against the Sioux Indians*, Washington, D.C., 1876.

Executive Document No. 240, House of Representatives, 41st Congress, 2nd Session, *Difficulty with Indian Tribes*, Washington, D.C., 1870.

Hancock, W. S., *Reports of Major General W. S. Hancock upon Indian Affairs, with Accompanying Exhibits*, Washington, D.C., no publisher, no date (1868?).

Heitman, Francis B., *Historical Register and Dictionary of the United States Army, 1789 to 1903*, Vol. I, Government Printing Office, Washington, 1903.

Hershler, N., *The Soldier's Handbook*, Government Printing Office, Washington, 1884.

Howard, Diary of George S., Co. E, 2nd C., Winners of the West, No. 3, February 1937.

Indian Tribes, Report on the Condition of the, Washington, 1867.

Indian Agency . . . , Report of the Special Commission Appointed to Investigate the Red Cloud, Government Printing Office, Washington, D.C., 1875.

Ludington, Col. M. T., *Uniforms of the Army of the United States, from 1774 to 1889*, Quartermaster General's Department, 1889.

Ludlow, William, *Report of a Reconnaisance of the Black Hills of Dakota, Made in the Summer of 1874*, Government Printing Office, Washington, D.C., 1875.

Meigs, Brevet Major General M. C., *Annual Report of the Quartermaster General, 1866*.

Reconstruction, Report of the Joint Committee on, 39th Congress, 1st Session, Washington, 1866.

War . . . , Report of the Secretary of, Vol. 1, House of Representatives Executive Document I, Part 2, 44th Congress, 2nd Session, Washington, D.C., 1876. (Contains the reports of Sherman, Sheridan, Terry, Gibbon, Reno and Benteen.)

War, Reports of the Secretary of, 1867 to 1877.

War, Report of the Secretary of, Sheridan's Report, Vol. 1, 1869.

War, Report of the Secretary of, Vol. 1, 1876.

War, Letter of the Secretary of, . . . Information in Relation to the Late Indian Battle on the Washita River, Senate Executive Document No. 18, 40th Congress, 3rd Session, Washington, D.C., 1869.

War, Report to the Secretary of, *Annual Report of the Chief of Engineers (1876)*, 1877.

War, *Report to the Secretary of*, Chief of Engineers, Vol. II, Part III, Appendix 00, p. 700, 1876.

War Department, *Revised United States Army Regulations of 1861, and . . . Articles of War, to . . . June 25, 1863*, Government Printing Office, Washington, 1863. (The regulations embodied in the 1863 edition remained standard until the extensive revisions undertaken in the 1880's.)

War Department, *Annual Report of the Secretary of War, for the Year 1876*, Vol. I, Government Printing Office, Washington, 1876.

Weir, Lt. W. B., "Infantry Equipments, Ordnance Notes No. LXVII," *Ordnance Notes Nos. 4-67*, 1877. (A discussion of suggested modifications in uniforms and equipments used in western campaigning.)

INDEX

— A —

Alburger. Pvt., 37
Alcatraz Island, 189
Alexis, Grand Duke of Russia, 74-76
Allen (zoologist), 78
Amaral, Anthony A., 229
American Express Company, 32
American Rifleman, 262
Andruss, Elias Van Arsdale, 189
Appeles, leader of Academy band, 189
Arkansas River, 11, 23, 43-45
Arlington National Cemetery, 241
Armaments, *see* weapons
Army-Navy Journal, XVII-XVIII, XX; 77, 107, 155, 157-58, 188, 201, 242, 251-52, 291-92, 333
Army Starr, 261
Artillery, 162
Artist's Life, 88
Asch, Dr. Morris J., 56
Austrian tunic, 157

— B —

Bailey House, 178
Baker, Bvt. Lt. Col. John P., 202
Baliran, Augustus, 80, 99-100
Ball, Capt., 138
Ball, Pvt. John, 80, 138
Baltimore Gazette, 32
Bannerman, Francis, catalog, 248
Barnes, Surgeon Gen. J. K., 160
Barnitz, Bvt. Col. Albert, 56
Barnitz, Capt., 61
Barrows, Samuel J., 86
Baseball in Black Hills, 92
Bear Butte, 87, 94
Beaver Creek, 49, 116
Belknap Case, 272
Belknap, Gen. William W., secretary of war, 76, 101, 103-06, 199
Bell, Lt. James M., 53-54, 56-57
Bell, William A., 34
Belle Fourche River, 87, 96
Belle Pierre Hills, 86
Benet, Gen. Stephen Vincent, 255, 263, 273
Bennett (general ass't., scientific party), 78
Bennett, James Gordon, 103
Benteen, Capt. Frederick W., 54, 56, 65, 67, 96, 110-11, 123-24, 128-30, 132-33, 135-46, 184, 230
Benton, Lt. Col. J. G., 258
Berdan priming, 257
Big Creek, or Timber, 180
Big Horn Mountains, 138
Big Horn River, 80, 120, 122, 133, 230
Bismark, D. T., 82, 84, 99-100, 105, 230, 272
Bismark Tribune, 86, 94
Bitters, John, 179
Black Hills, 86, 88, 92, 94, 97-98, 112-14, 152, 184, 214
Black Hills Expedition, 1874, 84-98, 262-63, 266
Blakeslee Quickloader, 12
Blinn, Mrs. Clara, 67
Blinn, Willie, 67

Blucher (Custer dog), 184
Blue Danube, The, 88
Board of Officers (Army), 156-57, 237, 249, 251-52
Board of Revision, 201-02
Bouyer, Mitch, 121
Boxer priming, 257
Bozeman Trail (Road), 23, 43
Braden, Lt. Charles, 80-81
Bradley, Capt. E. M., 30
Bradley, Lt. Col. L. P., 78
Brewster, Daniel A., 73
Brisbin, Maj. James S., 119, 121
Brown, Lt. Micah Ryder, 23
Brunswick, Hotel, 104
Brush, Lt. Daniel, 78
"Buckskin Joe" (Cody's horse), 75
Buffalo hunters, 326
Buffalo, N.Y., 15
Bull Bear, 28
Burkman, John, 111

— C —

"Cadet gray", 160
Cairo, Illinois, 77
Calhoun, Lt. James, 76, 123, 133, 138, 141-42, 144
"California Joe" (Scout), 47-50, 53, 55, 61-63
Cameron, Sec. of War, Simon, 198
"Camp Center", Kansas, 15
Canadian River, 49, 69
Canadian Trappers, 152
Cannon Ball Creek, 110, 272
Cannonball River, 86
Carbine, .45, 200, 207, 227-28
Carland, Lt., 99
Carr, Gen. Eugene A., 49, 69
Carrick, Cpl. William, 64
Castle Creek and Valley, 91-92
Cavalry, 162, 186-87; *and*: bureau, 211-12; drill regulations, 201; organization of, 21-22, 77, 79. *see also*, Seventh Cavalry, weapons, uniforms, forts, etc.
Cavalry tactics, XX, 186, 197-208; *also*: Carbine, 207; Cooke tactics, 198-201; four elements in manuals, 203; manual of instruction, 204-08; saber exercises, 204-07; Upton's tactics, 199-201.
Cave Hills, 96
Chasseurs, 197
Cheyenne Agency, 96
Cheyenne Dog Soldiers, 46, 69, 74
Cheyenne River, 94
Chicago Inter-Ocean, 86
Chicago World's Fair, 1893, 231
Childs, Lt., 311
Chilton, Capt. Robert Hall, 15
Chivington, Col. John M., 24, 28
Cholera, 40-41
chloroform legend, 333
Christer, Pvt. Thomas, 64
Cimarron Crossing, 32
Cimarron River, 45, 229
Cincinnati Gazette, 175

Civil War, XIX-XX, 1, 3, 5, 13, 123, 129, 131, 173, 189, 197, 200, 202, 209, 237, 239-41, 247-49, 251, 258, 260-61, 263
Clark, Ben, 65
Clover, Pvt. Eugene, 65
Clymer, Heister, 104-107
Coates, (Army Surgeon), 37-38
Cody, "Buffalo Bill," William S., XIX-XX, 75, 162
Colorado Volunteers, 24
Colt revolver, 12, 197, 207-08, 261-66; *see also* weapons
Comanche, (horse survivor, L.B.H.), 46, 229-31
Commissioner of Indian Affairs, 16
Comstock, William (Wild Bill), 38
Conrad, Charles Magill, Sec. of War, 15
Cooke, Philip St. George, XX, 198
Cooke, Lt. Adj. Col. W. W., 35, 37, 54, 69, 123, 133, 135, 138-40
Cooke tactic system, 198, 200-01
Corbin, Jack, 62-63
Council Grove, 183
Crawford, Col. Sam, 69
Crawford, Gov. Samuel J., 50
Crimean War, 197
Crittenden, Lt. J. J., 133, 138
Croften, Maj. Robert E. A., 78
Crook, Gen. George, 214-15, 274
Crooked Creek battle, 45-46
Crystal Springs, 105
Curtis, William Eleroy, 86-87
Custer, Boston, 76-77, 123, 133, 138
Custer, Elizabeth (Libbie), 2, 3, 35, 42-43, 47, 74, 76-78, 82-83, 97, 100, 103-105, 110, 123, 130, 183-84, 186, 189
Custer, Gen. George Armstrong, XIII, XIX-XX, 2-5, 23, 28, 33, 63, 74, 76-78, 82, 100, 103-04, 106-154, 173, 175, 180, 183-85, 188-89, 214, 229-30, 237, 247-49, 261-63, 266-67, 269, 272-73; *and also:* angered at supply refusal, 121; arrest, 107; arrest-charges-trial, 42-43; assembles officers, 127; assigned Kentucky post, 74; at Fort Leavenworth, 43; at Monroe, Mich., 43, 46; battle of Washita, 55-62; battle plans, 124; Benteen objects, 124; Black Hills expedition, 84-98; Civil War record, 131; command annihilated, 130; conflict with Benteen, 65; deals with Cheyenne over white girls, 72-73; decides on night move, 126; describes "California Joe," 47; expedition from Ft. Rice, 78; fails to locate Indians (LBH), 128; favorite maneuver, 129; "Grant's revenge," 108-09; Gen. Sherman message, 46; hosts Grand Duke Alexis, 74; hunts Cheyennes, 69; in New York, 104; in politics, 104; last campaign, 111-54; last message, 140, 143; LBH battle report, Terry, 131-34; leaves command, 115; letter from Storrs, 104-05; Maneekolikonuah shoots Custer (LBH), 343; news slow (LBH), 149; note to Pres. Grant, 106; nothing heard, 138; observations on Indians, 311; officer reports village smoke, 127; prepares for summer campaign, 103; protests irregularities, 103; receives Terry's orders, 122-23; regiment marches out, 123-24; Reno report, 134-39; reprimanded by Sheridan, 107; Sitting Bull describes LBH, 342-43; smokes peace pipe, 69-70; snowbound, 105; snubs Sec. Belknap, 101; strange mirage, 110; studies Wellington, Napoleon, 43; testifies before committee, 105-06; tracking Pawnee-Killer, 36-40; view of Reno, 117; winter campaign, 50; Yellowstone expedition, 78-81.
Custer Gulch, 91, 94
Custer Hill, 140-41, 143, 229
Custer, Margaret Emma, 76, 77-78, 110
Custer, Lt. Thomas Ward, 4, 37, 42, 51, 56, 93, 99-100, 105, 123, 133, 138-39, 141, 144, 185, 347
"Custer's Butcher," newspaper account, 149
"Custer's Last Stand," 146, 149
"Custer's Luck," 107, 146

— D —

Dakota Column, 106
Dakota Territory, 77
"Dandy" (Custer horse), 86, 110, 184

Davis Creek, 115
Davis, Jefferson, 221
Davidson, John W., 1
Deadwood City, 180
Democratic Party, 104
Denver, Colo., 11
Departments of the Army: Dakota, 82, 123-24, 273-74; Missouri, 23, 49, 80-81, 273-74; Platte, 273-74; South, 74; Texas, 273-74
Department of the Interior, 100
DeRudio, 1st Lt. Chas. C., 136
DeWolf, acting surgeon, J. M., 133, 135
du Mont, John S., 262-63
Dickey, Sr. Capt. C. A., 78
Dodge, Col., 175
Dooney, Pvt. Thomas, 65
Double-barrel shotguns, 326
Double rank deployment, 197
Douglas, Maj. H., 16, 18
Downer's Station, 42
Dragoons, 197
Dyche Museum, 231
Dyche, Prof. Lewis, 231
Dyer, Bvt. Maj. Gen., A. B., 263, 269
Dysentery, 181-82

— E —

Edgerly, 2nd Lt. Winfield S., 136
Eliza (Custer's black servant), 43
Elizabethtown, Ky., 74, 76
Elliott, Maj. Joel, 37, 45, 52-53, 56-57, 59-60, 64-66
Ellis, Edward S., XIX
English soldiers, 202
Equipment (military), 159, 186-87
Evans, Col. Andrew W., 49, 68

— F —

Far West, 117-122, 133, 230
Fauntleroy, Col. T. T., 15
Fencing, 201-02
Fighting tactics (Indian), LBH, 139
Firearms in the Custer Battle, 262-63
First Dragoons, 15, 197-98
Fitzpatrick, Thomas, 65
Floral Valley, 88
Forsyth, Brev. Gen. G. A., 86
Forts: Abercrombie, 152; Arbuckle, 65; Bascom, 49, 68; Buford, 101; Cobb, 67-68; Dodge, 11, 16-18, 30, 32, 45-6, 49, 67, 229; Ellis, 132; Harker, 5, 11, 23, 39-40, 42, 67, 181, 183; Hays, 32, 35, 40, 73, 180-81; Hooper, 32; Laramie, 84, 92-94; Larned, 23-25, 32, 40, 44; Leavenworth, 15, 23, 32, 42-43, 74; Lincoln, Abraham, 81-85, 94, 97, 99-101, 103, 105, 109-10, 152, 183, 253, 272; Lyon, 10, 32, 49; Mason, 218; McKeen, 82; McPherson, 34, 74-75; Meade, 231; Peck, 80; Randall, 268; Rice, 78, 84, 96, 268; Riley, 1-2, 5, 10, 14-15, 23, 40, 42, 157, 231, 261; Sedgwick, 36, 42, 175; Sturgis, (Camp), 180; Sully, 268; Totten, 78, 231, 261; Union, 273-74; Wadsworth, 78; Wallace, 34-35, 38-40.
Fort Union Arsenal, 273-74
Frankford Arsenal, 265
French, Capt. Thos. B., 136
French Creek, 92
French shako, 157
Frontier life, military, 173, 178, 190-96; *also:* animal feed, 192; "buffalo chips," 192; dangers of attack, 191; escort, 192; flood dangers, 192; glossary of army slang, 195-96; grass fires, 194; horse care, 191-93; Indian tactics, 191; inspection of arms, 192; Knowledge of country, 192; marching-encampment, 190-95; parlay with Indians, 193; pursuit by Indians, 193; pursuit of Indians, 194-95; sentinal duty, 193; supplies, equipment, 190-91; treatment of wounds, dis-

eases, 193-94; wagon formation, 192-93; warning on Indian stealth, 194.
Frost photograph, 262-63

— G —

Garlington, 1st Lt.-Adjutant Ernest A., 231
Garrison duty, 99
GarryOwen, march, 55, 63, 86, 88, 97, 110, 140, 188-89; lyrics, 190
Gatling guns, 85, 133, 266-74, *also*: advantages, 268-69; arsenals, 273; artillery category, 269; attitude of Custer, 266-67; Benét dispatches, 273; Custer refuses Gatlings, 266; delays for LBH use, 273; destroys scouts, 266; guns cumbersome, 266; improvements, 268-70; inventor, 268; LBH terrain, 266; Low battery organized, 272; Low's orders, 273; manual, 270; manufacturers, 269; mobility, 270; "novel engine of war," 268; Reilly replies, 273-74; supply of, 273; training gun crews, 267; value in Texas Indian fight, 266.
Gatling, Dr. Richard Jordan, 268
German soldiers, 202
Gettysburg, 247-49
Gibbon, Gen. (or Col.) John, 116-117, 119-123, 126, 130, 133, 145, 229, 266
Gibbs, Maj. Alfred, 2
Gibson, 1st. Lt. Frank M., 136
Girard, 230
Girl I Left Behind Me, 86
Godfrey, Lt. Edward Settle, 56-58, 60-61, 111, 136, 189, 229
Gold discovered, Black Hills, 90-92, 94, 97-98
Grand River, 86
Grant, Brev. Lt. Col. Fred, 86, 92
Grant, Orvil, 103, 105-106
Grant, Pres. Ulysses S., XX, 86, 103-104, 106
"Grant's Revenge," 108-109
Grey, Zane, XIX
Grinnell, George Bird, 85
Guerrier, Edmund, 27-28
"Gum Blanket" (poncho), 187-88
Guns, *see* weapons

— H —

Hale, Lt. Owen, 56, 58
Hamilton, Capt. Louis McLane, 35, 42, 45, 53, 55-56
Hancock expedition, 270
Hancock, Maj.-Gen. Winfield S., 23, 26-33, 35, 42-43
Hare, 2nd Lt. Luther R., 136
Harney, Gen. William S., 161
Harney's Peak, 89, 92, 94
Harper's Magazine, 23
Harrington, Lt. Henry M., 133
Hart, Col., 89
Harvey, W. S., 51
Hayes City, 178-81
Hazen, Col. William B., 67, 101, 107
Heart River, 86
Henry Carbine, 246, 251
Henry rifles, 346
Hickok, James Butler (Wild Bill), 23, 27, 178-80
Hiddenwood Creek, 86
Hodgson, Lt. Benjamin H., 133, 135
Honsinger, Dr. John, 80, 99-100
Horses, cavalry, 211-18; *also*: ailments, 217-20; bags, 233-34; bit, 232; blooded horses, 213; "boots and saddles," 216; branding, 211; bridle, 232; brief history of, 213; campaign system, 216-17; carbine, 227-29; Comanche story (LBH), 229-31; costs, 211-13; curb-ring, 232; equipment, 212, 231-36; gear, list of, 231; grooming, 215; halter, 232; head gear, 232; head stall, 232; horsemanship, 223-25; miscellaneous, 233-34; modifications, 234-36; mustang, 213; pistols, 226-27; saber use, 225; saddles, 220-23, 232-33 (*see also*, types); stirrups, 233; stock farms, 209-10; training schools, 225-26; veterinarians, 213-14; water bridle, 232; wild horses, 213.

House of Representatives, 104
Howard, Gen. George S., 343
Hughes, Capt., 118
Hussar saddle, 197
Hussars, 197
Huston, Lt.-Col. Daniel, Jr., 82

— I —

Illingsworth, W. H., 85, 95
Indian battle tactics, 186
Indian Bureau, 100, 102-03
Indian Wars, 237, 260
Indians, *see Native Americans*
Infantry, 162
Ingraham, Prentiss, XIX
Interior Department, U. S., 16
Inyan Kara Creek, 88

— J —

Jackson, Lt. Henry, 37-38
Jessup, Gen. T. S., 15
Johnson, Pvt. Charles, 37, 42
Junction City, 11

— K —

Kansas Expedition, 26-32
Kansas Museum of Natural History, University of, (Dyche Museum), 231
Kansas Pacific Railroad, 1, 11, 34, 42, 178, 181
Kansas River, 15
Kansas Volunteer Cavalry, 50, 64, 69, 73
Kellogg, Mark, 111, 115, 138, 149
Kempitski (artist), 78
Kennedy, Sgt. Maj. Walter, 64
Keno, "Honest John," 84
Keogh, Capt. Myles Walter, 46, 117, 123, 133, 139, 141-42, 144, 189, 229-30; *see also*, Comanche
Kentucky rifles, 326
Ketchum, Adjutant, 80
Kidder, 2nd Lt. Lyman S., 35-36, 38-39, 42
Kile, Pvt. John, 180
Kilpatrick, Maj. Gen. Judson, 249
King, Charles, XIX
Kinzie, 2nd Lt. Frank X., 272
Knappen, Nathan H., 86
Korn, Farrier Gustav, 231
Kuhlman, Dr., 144
Ku Klux Klan, 74
King, Pvt. James, 95

— L —

Lacey & Philipps, 221
Lancers, 197
Lanigan, Pvt. Jeremiah, 180
Lautz, Lt., 175
Lazelle, Maj. Henry, 78
Leavenworth, Col., 17
Leavenworth Daily Conservative, 34
Lee, Gen. Robert E., 249
Liberty & Mischief (Custer dogs), 183-84
Lincoln, President Abraham, 214
Lippncott, Capt. (Dr.) Henry, 56, 64
Little Big Horn Associates, XIII
Little Big Horn Battle (LBH), XIX-XX, 55, 109, 118, 120, 122, 125-29, 132-35, 138, 140, 143, 146, 148, 150, 189, 229-31, 237, 248-49, 262-63, 266-67, 273, 326, 341, 343, 345, *and also*: Battle Reports, 132-39; Casualties, 133-38; Eyewitness account, 149-54; Interpretation of, 140-49; Last Campaign, 110-30. See also, Custer, Seventh Cavalry, Comanche, Native Americans, individuals, etc.

Little Heart River, 110-111
Little Missouri River, 96, 103, 114-115
"Long Hair" (*see* G. A. Custer)
Lord, G. W., acting surgeon, 133
Low, 2nd Lt. W. H., 121, 266, 268, 272-73
Ludlow, Capt. William, 85, 97, 109

— M —

Machin, Vice Chancellor, 74
Maida (Custer favorite dog), 185
Mackenzie, Col., 257
Maclay, Lt., 268
Marsh, Prof. Othniel N., 85
Mathey, Lt. E. G., 53, 136
Martini, John, 124, 140
McAdam, Lt. John, 78
McCleave, Hall, 152
McClellan, Capt. George B., 197
McClellan saddle, 199-200, 220-23
McDougall, Capt. Thomas M., 135
McDowell, Maj. Gen. I., 296
McIntosh, 1st Lt. Donald, 133, 135
McKay, William T., 86, 90-91, 94
McLeod, Col., 344
McWilliams, Pvt., 116
Medical treatment, 176-78
Medicine Lodge Peace Treaty, 43-44
Mercer, Cpl. Harry, 64
Mexican War, 3
Meyers, Capt. Edward, 54
Michigan Cavalry Brigade, 247, 249
Miles, Bvt. Maj. Gen. Nelson A., 266, 343
Milligan, Pvt. William, 65
Mills, Gen. Anson, 243
Minneapolis Tribune, 149
Missouri River, 77, 98, 103, 272
Mitchell, Capt. W. G., 30
Mizpah Creek, 117
Mocking Bird, The, 88
Monroe, Mich., 43, 46, 76, 78
Monument Creek, 49, 68
Monument Station, 32
Moore, Lt. Col. Horace L., 69
Moylan, Capt. Myles, 80
Mulberry Creek, Texas, fight, 266
Murphy, John, 58
Mustang, 213
Myers, Pvt. John, 65

— N —

National Union Party, 104
Native Americans
        Customs and Battle Techniques
                arrowheads, 318; bow-arrow, 312-19; bow-types,
                314-15; blanket trickery, 328-29; blanket uses,
                328-29, 331-33; burial grounds, 333-35; clothing,
                320-21; "counting coup," 324; deprived of ammuni-
                tion, 326; feathering, 316-17; firearms, 312, 319-20;
                forked sticks used, 326; Great Spirit, 342; horse
                painting, 329-30; other mount adornments, 330-31;
                imitate soldiers, 321; LBH sharpshooting, 326;
                makeshift shot, 325-26; mutilation, 323; on war path,
                321, 328; pipes, 321; Plains Indian custom, 311;
                quivers, 321; scalping, 321-23; shaft, 315-16; shields,
                324-25; sign language, 335-41; Sitting Bull LBH bat-
                tle described, 341-48; smoke signals, 331-32; sur-
                vivor of scalping, 322-23; tomahawks, 321, 326;
                tracking ability, 311-12; war clubs, 326; war excur-
                sion habits, 312; war paint, 327-28
        Tribes
                Apaches, 18, 24, 43, 68
                Arapahoes, 15-16, 24, 43-44, 69, 321

Arikara, 85
Blackfeet, 314
Cheyennes, 15, 18, 23-30, 43-44, 63, 68-73, 189, 311,
        314
Comanches, 44, 46, 67-68, 73, 229, 266
Cree, 314
Crow, 314
Delawares, 24, 38, 312
Hunkpapas, 341, 347
Kaws, 183
Kiowas, 15, 18, 25, 43-44, 46, 67-68, 73, 266, 321
Lipans, 15
Marmot, 342-43
Minneconjou, 345, 347
Omahas, 183
Pawnee-Killer, 36
Rees, 78
Sioux, 17-18, 23, 30, 43, 73, 84, 89, 92-93, 98-100, 105,
        107, 109, 119-120, 124, 133-34, 137, 149, 314,
        328, 341, 347
Snakes, 311
Utes, 44, 314
Chiefs/leaders
        Big Bear, 17
        Big Head, 73
        Black Kettle (Mah-wis-sa), 59-60, 62-64, 67-68, 189
        Bob-tailed Bull, 138
        Bull Bear, 28
        Crazy Horse, 98, 103
        Dull Knife, 73
        Fat Bear, 73
        Hard Rope, 50
        Hidatsa, 314
        Kicking Bird, 17-18
        Lame White Man, 141
        Little Beaver (Chief), 50, 54
        Little Current, 342-43
        Little Raven, 17, 69, 321
        Little Robe, 69
        Little Rock, 64
        Lone Wolf, 67-68
        Medicine Arrow, 69-70, 73
        One Stab, 89, 138
        Rain-in-the-Face, 99-100
        Red Cloud, 23
        Roman Nose, 28, 34-35
        Santanta (White Bear), 18, 67-68, 321
        Sitting Bull, 80, 96, 98, 100, 103, 109, 134, 149-50,
                152, 341-48; *and also*: description of, 344; tells
                of LBH Battle, 342-48; opinion of Americans,
                345; "Sphinx of the Northwest," 344
        Spotted Tail, 75, 89
        Stone Forehead, 69
        Tall Bull, 27, 73
        Yellow Bear, 69
Others
        Bloody Knife (Custer scout), 79, 85, 89, 92-93, 138
        Crow scouts, 126, 133, 138
        Osage (scouts), 50, 54-55, 63
        Ree scouts, 135
        "Romeo" (scout), 57, 59, 71
        Sioux scouts, 89
New York Grafic, 152
New York Herald, 63, 103, 105, 138, 341, 344
New York Times, 65-66, 175
New York Tribune, 86, 175
New York World, 341-42, 344
Nitschke, Paul, veterinary surgeon, 218
Northern Pacific Railroad, 77, 82

— O —

"Obscure" books, XIX
O'Fallon's Creek (s. fork), 116
Ogden, H. A., XX

Ord, Gen., 274
Ordnance Department, 237, 240, 242, 248, 251-53, 263, 268, 273, 326
Ordnance summaries, supplies of weapons, 1867-76, 275-85
Ordnance Testing Board, 261, 263
Oregon incident, 202
Overland Stage Lines, 11, 39
Owl River, 86

— P —

Parker trade muskets, 326
Parsons, Capt. Charles Carroll, 23, 42
Parsons, John E., 262-63
Pawnee Fork, 27-28
Payment, Union Army, 4
Pennsylvania Railroad, 74
Penrose, Capt. William H., 49
Pioneer Press & Tribune, 154
Pistols, 226-27, 259-66
Plains, Life on the, 4-5, 16-20
Platte River, 15, 98
Poinsett, Sec. of War, J. R., 197
"Poinsett Tactics," see Cavalry Tactics
Pompey's Pillar, 81
Pond Creek Station, 34
Pope, Lt. James W., 266
Pope, Gen., 274
Porter, James E., acting ass't. surgeon, 133, 136, 138
Potomac Supply depot, 209
Powder River, 89, 102, 116-118
Powell (photographer), 78
Proctor, Sec. of War, Redfield, 201
Pumpkin Creek, 117
Punishment in army, 173-76; also: barrel, 173; bound-gagged, 173; branded for desertion, 175-76; Custer, 175; drill, 174; flogging, 175; knapsack drill, 174; offenses, 173; "wooden overcoat," 173-74

— Q —

Quartermaster Department, 155, 162, 164-72, 209, 212

— R —

Rath, Charley, 16
Rations, 188
Red Deer Country, 343
Red River, 15, 49, 68-69
Red River Carts, 152
Red Water Valley, 87
Reed, Henry Armstrong, 133, 138
Reedstrom, Lisle, XIII, XIX-XX
Regimental commander, 217
Reilly, Capt. J. W., 257-58, 273-74
Reilly, Lt. W. V., 133, 138
Remington, Frederic, XX
Remington guns, 12, 95, 123
Remington revolver, 49, 245-46, 261
Reno Court of Inquiry, 1879, 143, 230
Reno Hill, 145
Reno, Maj. Marcus, 109-11, 117-19, 123-24, 128-39, 140, 145, 151, 254-56, 326, 343, 345; and LBH battle report, 134-39
Republican River, 73
Retter, Dr. (geologist), 78
Returns of Regular Army Regiments, Reports & Records of Events, 217
Revolution, The, XX
Reynolds, Gen., 190
Reynolds, "Lonesome Charley," 85, 93-94, 99, 112-113, 115, 138
Rheuben, Rush, 84
Richards, Charles B., 261
Ridgeley, D. H., battle witness, LBH, 149-154
Rifles furnished Indians, 44

Riley, Bvt. Maj. Gen. Bennett, 15
Rio Grande River, 74
Robbins, Lt. L. M., 35
Rock Island Arsenal, 273-74
Rocky Mountains, 11, 15
Roller, Pvt. William, 87
Rosebud River, 116, 118-20, 122, 124, 126-27, 132-35, 150
Ross, Horatio Nelson, 86, 90-91, 94
Royal Artillery dress, 157
Ryan, Capt. John, 53, 321
Russian government, customs, 74

— S —

Saber, or Sabre, 225-26, 258-59; and exercises, 201
Saddles, cavalry, 220-24; also: Campbell, 220; Cogent, 221; Grimsley, 220; Hope, 220; Hungarian, 221, Jones, 220; McClellan, 220-23
St. Louis, Mo., 83
St. Louis Democrat, 65-66
St. Paul, 105, 109
St. Paul Pioneer Press, 149
Saline Valley, 43, 63
San Antonio Arsenal, 273-74
Sand Creek attack, 24, 32
Santa Fe, W. M., 11, 44
Scalping by Indians, 322-23
School of soldier, dismounted, 225; other "schools" also listed
Schools of troops, platoon, squadron, 197
Scientific party with army, 78
Scotts 1834 Tactics, 197
Second Dragoons, 197
Sempker, Sgt. Charles, 96
Seventh Cavalry, XIX-XX, 1-2, 5, 11, 23, 33-34, 43, 45, 50-51, 63, 66, 73-74, 76-77, 78, 82, 84, 109-11, 124, 126-31, 134, 143-44, 149, 157, 175, 178, 180, 183-84, 186-87, 229-31, 237-38, 240, 247, 253-55, 261, 270; and also: Composition, 111, 15-day Little Big Horn Expedition, 121-22; forces at Little Big Horn, 120; List of Troops, 10; Reno, 134-39; Terry report, 132-34; wills made out, 121. see also: Custer, Little Big Horn, Native Americans, Cavalry (general), forts, officers, enlisted men, individuals, etc.
Seventh Cavalry Regimental Band, 188
Seward (civilian), 175
Sharpe, Pvt. Cal., 65
Sharps carbine, 80, 240, 245, 249-51
Shenandoah Valley, 202
Sheridan, 202
Sheridan, Gen. Phil (Little Phil), XX, 43, 46, 49, 59, 61, 63-64, 67-69, 73-74, 81, 103-104, 107, 266
Sherman, Lt.-Gen. W. T., XX, 35-36, 46, 104, 106-107, 109
Short Pine Hills, 96
Sign language, 311
Slang expressions, army, glossary, 195-96
Slang names for guns, 264
Slim Buttes, 87
Smith, Lt. Algernon E., (LBH), 141, 144, 347
Smith, Bvt. Maj. Gen. Andrew Johnson, 3, 23, 29-30, 42
Smith, Capt. E. W., 123, 133-34
Smith & Wesson, 247, 263, 265
Smokey Hill route, 270
Smokey Hill River, stage route, 11, 27, 39-40
Soldiering, discussion of, 6-10
Solomon River raid, 45
Solomon Valley, 43, 63
Southern Plains, 73
Spencer Carbine, 12, 55, 123, 240, 246-49
Spring Creek, 88
Springfield Armory, 242, 247
Springfield rifle, 44, 49, 75, 84-85, 242, 251-58
Standing Rock Agency, 99
Stamixo token, 343
Stanley bridge, 116
Stanley, Col. D. S., 78

Stanley, Gen. David, 80
Stein (veterinarian), 230
Stewart attachment for pistols and sabers, 240-41
Stock farms (military), 209-11
Storrs, S. J., 104-105
Strawhorn shooting, 179
Stuart, Jeb, 248-49
Sturgis, Lt. J. G., 133, 138
Sturgis, Bvt. Maj. Gen. Samuel D., 230
Sully, Bvt. Brig. Gen. Alfred, XX, 45-46, 49-51, 229
Supply depots, 209

— T —

Taft, Alphonso, sec. of war, 106
Talbot, Jones & Company, 269
Tarifa, Spain, 189
Taylor, "Muggins," 132
Tefault incident, 179
Tennyson, Alfred Lord, 181
Terry, Gen. Alfred H., XX, 78, 86, 103, 105, 109, 111-12, 115-117,
    138, 145, 251-53, 266, 274, 326, 343; and also: calls confer-
    ence on Far West, 119; decides Custer to attack, 120; first
    report of LBH battle, 132-34; orders Custer ahead, 117;
    written orders to Custer, 122-23
Texas, 68, 74
Texas service, 188, 190
Third cavalry, 182
Thomas Drum Saloon, 180
Thompson, Capt. William, 54
Tilford, Col. Joseph G., 92, 95-96
Tolliver, Barney, 37
Tongue River, 79, 96, 117, 119
Tullock's Creek, 122, 133
Turner, Pvt. George, 87

— U —

Uniforms (military), 2, 11-14, 27; and also: Badges of rank,
    epaulettes, chevrons, etc., 169-70; blankets, miscellaneous,
    171-72; boots, 168; borrow from Europeans, 157; buttons,
    166-67; "cadet gray," opposition to, 160; changes de-
    manded, 161; cost, 158-59; criticism, 155-56; dress, 164-66;
    frontier problems, 156; Harney hat, 161; hats, caps, 167-68;
    ill-fitting, 158; medical report, 160-61; mildew in storage,
    157; new code, 156-57; overcoats, 170-71; regulation, offi-
    cial, descriptions of, officers & enlisted men, 164-72; shirts,
    171; shoes-boots, discussion of, 161-64; soldiers com-
    plaints, 163; Southwest variation, 159; sword, belt, 168-69;
    trimmings, 167-68; trousers, 167; weather considerations,
    158-59.
Uniform & Dress & Undress Regulations, 1872, U. S. Army,
    297-310; and also: Academy attire, 306; boots-shoes, 301;
    buttons, 300; caps-badges, 308; chevrons, 304-05; coats,
    enlisted men, 299-300; coats, officers, 297-98; cravats, 301;
    directive, 308; epaulettes, 303; fatigue hat, 302; forage
    badges, 301-02; forage cap, 301; gloves, 302; hat-cap, 301;
    helmets, officers-troops, 309; horse furniture, 306; insignia,
    303; miscellaneous clothing, 305-06; miscellaneous regula-
    tions, 306-08; overcoat, 305; plumes (officers), 302;
    plumes-pompons (enlisted) 302; sash, 302; shirts, 309-10;
    shoulder-knots, 303; shoulder straps, 303-04; spurs, 302;
    sword-belt and plate, 302-03; sword-knot, 303; sword-
    scabbard, 303; trousers, 300-01; undress officers, 298-99.
Uniform changes, 286-310; also: allowance for clothing, 293-94;
    buffalo overcoat, 289; buffalo overshoes, 288; chasseur or
    "kepi" fatigue cap, 286; coat, 287-88; complaints, 295-96;
    helmet, 287, 309; prices, 293-95; Puritan hat, 286; shako,
    286-87; sizes, 288; soldiers views, 291-93; "southern
    slouch," 286; surplus, 295-96; tradition broken, 288; winter
    clothing, 288-91
Union Metallic Cartridge Company, 257
United States Cartridge Company, 257

United States Commission, 341, 348
Upton, Lt.-Col. Emory, 200-01
Upton's Tactics, 199-202

— V —

Varnum, Lt. Charles A., 80, 127, 133, 136
Vic (Custer horse), 184

— W —

Wallace, Lt. George D., 88, 97, 123, 125-28, 136
Walnut Creek raid, 45
Walsh, Maj. (Canadian police), 341
War Department, 103-104, 197-98, 212, 220, 259, 263, 286
Ward, T. A., 154
Washington, D.C., 105, 272
Washita, battle of the, 48, 55-62, 63, 77, 247; also: newspaper
    account, 65-67
Washita River, 63-64, 67, 189
Watson, Camp, 202
Weapons, 237-285; also: accouterments, 238-39; Allin conversa-
    tion, 251; American Rifleman on Colt, 262; ammunition
    expended, 256; army revolver, 263; ballistics, 257; Benét
    cup primers, 250; black powder, 251; Blakeslee carbine
    boxes, 238, 248; breech-loaders, 242, 250; cap pouch,
    237-38; carbines, 245; care of weapon, 264; cartridge boxes
    obsolete, 242; cartridges, 248; cavalry gear memorandum,
    242-45; cavalry and other models, 262; cavalry saber belt,
    240; Colt, 261-66; Dyer carbine pouch, 238-39; Frost
    photograph, 262-63; Gatling gun, 266-74 (see also sep
    item); gilding metal, 265; infantry cartridge pouch, 237,
    241; initial Colt order, 262; "king of pistols," 263; McK-
    eever pattern, 241; makes listed, 326; Martin bar-anvil, 250;
    memorandum on small arms, 251; metallic cartridge, 249;
    Mills patent, 241; performance at LBH, 254; pistols, 241,
    259-66; problems with Springfield, 254; Remington Sys-
    tem, 252-53; Reno views, 254-56; report on Colt, 262; saber,
    241, 258-59; Sharps, 249-51; Sharps cartridge box, 240;
    shoulder slings, 239-40; slang names for Colt, 264; small
    arms board, 263; Smith-Wesson, 247; Smith-Wesson model
    "rival", 263; Spencer, 246-49; Spencer carbine cartridge
    boxes, 237-38; Spencer discontinued, 249; Springfield,
    251-58; statistics; drawbacks, of Colt, 264-66; study by
    Ordnance Board, 251; summary report, 253-54; testing
    board, 263; weapons at LBH, 262-63; whet-grind stones,
    259; see also individual listings
Weir Hill (Point), 141, 143-44
West, Capt. Robert M., 42, 54, 60, 129, 136
West Point Academy, 189
West Virginia Cavalry (1st), 249
Williams, Capt. (Dr.) J. W., 85, 87, 116
Williams, Cpl. James F., 65
Williams, Sgt. Frederick, 34
Winchell, Prof. N. H., 85, 92
Winchester company, 257
Winchester rifles, 257, 346
Witness; Little Big Horn battle, see Ridgeley, D. H.
Wister, Owen, XIX
Wolf Creek, 49-52
Wood, W. H., 86
Woodhull, Bvt. Lt. Alfred A., 161
Wounded Knee, S. D., 231
Wright, Gen., 34
Wynkoop, Edward W., 29-30, 44

— Y —

Yankton, D. T., 77
Yates, Capt. George W., 99, 133, 138
Yellowstone Expedition, 85, 99, 262-63, 266
Yellowstone River, 79-80, 85, 117-118, 120, 124, 133, 135, 225, 266